Handbook of
Organization Theory
and Management

PUBLIC ADMINISTRATION AND PUBLIC POLICY

A Comprehensive Publication Program

Executive Editor

JACK RABIN
Professor of Public Administration and Public Policy
School of Public Affairs
The Capital College
The Pennsylvania State University—Harrisburg
Middletown, Pennsylvania

56. *Handbook of Public Sector Labor Relations*, edited by Jack Rabin, Thomas Vocino, W. Bartley Hildreth, and Gerald J. Miller
57. *Practical Public Management*, Robert T. Golembiewski
58. *Handbook of Public Personnel Administration*, edited by Jack Rabin, Thomas Vocino, W. Bartley Hildreth, and Gerald J. Miller
59. *Public Administration: A Comparative Perspective, Fifth Edition*, Ferrel Heady
60. *Handbook of Debt Management*, edited by Gerald J. Miller
61. *Public Administration and Law: Second Edition*, David H. Rosenbloom and Rosemary O'Leary
62. *Handbook of Local Government Administration*, edited by John J. Gargan
63. *Handbook of Administrative Communication*, edited by James L. Garnett and Alexander Kouzmin
64. *Public Budgeting and Finance: Fourth Edition, Revised and Expanded*, edited by Robert T. Golembiewski and Jack Rabin
65. *Handbook of Public Administration: Second Edition*, edited by Jack Rabin, W. Bartley Hildreth, and Gerald J. Miller
66. *Handbook of Organization Theory and Management: The Philosophical Approach*, edited by Thomas D. Lynch and Todd J. Dicker

Additional Volumes in Preparation

Handbook of Public Finance, edited by Fred Thompson and Mark T. Green

Organizational Behavior and Public Management: Third Edition, Revised and Expanded, Michael L. Vasu, Debra W. Stewart, and G. David Garson

ANNALS OF PUBLIC ADMINISTRATION

1. *Public Administration: History and Theory in Contemporary Perspective*, edited by Joseph A. Uveges, Jr.
2. *Public Administration Education in Transition*, edited by Thomas Vocino and Richard Heimovics
3. *Centenary Issues of the Pendleton Act of 1883*, edited by David H. Rosenbloom with the assistance of Mark A. Emmert
4. *Intergovernmental Relations in the 1980s*, edited by Richard H. Leach
5. *Criminal Justice Administration: Linking Practice and Research*, edited by William A. Jones, Jr.

Handbook of Organization Theory and Management

The Philosophical Approach

edited by

Thomas D. Lynch

Public Administration Institute
Louisiana State University
Baton Rouge, Louisiana

Todd J. Dicker

School of Public Affairs and Administration
Western Michigan University
Kalamazoo, Michigan

MARCEL DEKKER, INC.   NEW YORK · BASEL · HONG KONG

ISBN: 0-8247-0113-5

The publisher offers discounts on this book when ordered in bulk quantities. For more information, write to Special Sales/Professional Marketing at the address below.

This book is printed on acid-free paper.

MARCEL DEKKER, INC.
270 Madison Avenue, New York, New York 10016
http://www.dekker.com

Current printing (last digit):
10 9 8 7 6 5 4 3 2 1

PRINTED IN THE UNITED STATES OF AMERICA

PREFACE

This book is addressed to uniting philosophy and public administration. Few subjects are more influenced by philosophy than the form of governance a public selects to guide and administer its public affairs. Yet, the literature has been strangely silent about the relationship between the two—until now. It is our hope that this book will inspire many more efforts to explore this most important of relationships, especially because the real work has only just begun. At the dawn of a new millennium, it is particularly appropriate to build such bridges from the past to the future and to rediscover our roots while contemplating our intellectual progress.

The history of this project began while Thomas D. Lynch, the senior editor, was teaching a graduate seminar at Florida Atlantic University. The course required students to examine the philosphical and epistemological foundations of modern organizational and political theory. Students loved the seminar as it opened their eyes to a much larger world than traditional courses in organization theory typically covered. The understanding that public administration's current tasks and ideas are relevant to the most sophisticated work in intellectual history is always a remarkable discovery, and to integrate those ideas with modern approaches to organizational management is an enlightening process. However, Dr. Lynch was frustrated by the lack of integrated literature on this subject. Todd J. Dicker, one of Dr. Lynch's brightest Ph.D. students in this seminar, was kind enough to join this massive project, which took over three years to complete.

The process of recruiting chapter contributors began by carefully scanning the body of literature to identify potential authors. A great deal of effort was devoted to identifying potential authors who had already made significant contributions to the literature on their topics and had established reputations as thinkers and scholars. The editors are extremely proud of the caliber of those authors who have contributed to this volume and the extraordinary quality of their contributions.

A very pleasant adidtion to this project was Lia Pelosi at Marcel Dekker, Inc. Under her gentle and positive prodding, the project kept moving along on schedule. Thanks are necessary to Ms. Pelosi, who also had the challenge of copyediting the manuscript. In addition, Mrs. Shirley DeJean, Secretary of the Public Administration Institute at LSU, deserves thanks. A special thank you must go to Richard Omdal, Dr. Lynch's voluntary graduate assistant, who deserves to be singled out. Mr. Omdal, now a Ph.D. student, worked for Dr. Lynch without compensation. His tireless management of a large number of manuscripts and a mountain of correspondence, especially during the summer months while Dr. Lynch was traveling, eased the lengthy process of completing this project. His useful observations and comments greatly improved the overall quality of the manuscript.

Finally, Todd would like to thank Tom Lynch for originally igniting his interest in philosophy and epistemology, and for adding tinder to the fire by inviting him to participate in this project. The experience of combining so many individuals' efforts into a cohesive work has left a deep and lasting impression on his thoughts and vision of how our epistemology has evolved through history into its current form.

Thomas D. Lynch
Todd J. Dicker

Contents

CONTRIBUTORS

Ralph Clark Chandler, Ph.D. Professor, School of Public Affairs and Administration, Western Michigan University, Kalamazoo, Michigan

Brian J. Cook, Ph.D. Associate Professor and Chair, Department of Government and International Relations, Clark University, Worcester, Massachusetts

Peter L. Cruise, Ph.D. Assistant Professor, School of Liberal Studies and Public Affairs, Golden Gate University, San Francisco, California

Lance deHaven-Smith, Ph.D. Professor and Director, Reubin O'D. Askew School of Public Administration and Policy, Florida State University, Tallahassee, Florida

Todd J. Dicker, Ph.D. Assistant Professor, School of Public Affairs and Administration, Western Michigan University, Kalamazoo, Michigan

Laurent Dobuzinskis, Ph.D. Associate Professor, Department of Political Science, Simon Fraser University, Burnaby, British Columbia, Canada

Larkin Sims Dudley, Ph.D. Assistant Professor, Center for Public Administration and Policy, Virginia Polytechnic Institute and State University, Blacksburg, Virginia

Stephen L. Esquith, Ph.D. Professor, Department of Philosophy, Michigan State University, East Lansing, Michigan

David John Farmer, Ph.D. Professor, Department of Political Science and Public Administration, Virginia Commonwealth University, Richmond, Virginia

Charles J. Fox, Ph.D. Professor, Department of Political Science, Texas Tech University, Lubbock, Texas

Mark F. Griffith, Ph.D. Associate Professor, Department of History and Social Sciences, The University of West Alabama, Livingston, Alabama

Akhlaque U. Haque, Ph.D.   Assistant Professor, Department of Government and Public Service, University of Alabama at Birmingham, Birmingham, Alabama

Cynthia E. Lynch, M.P.A.   President, Scott Balsdon, Inc., Baton Rouge, Louisiana

Thomas D. Lynch, Ph.D.   Professor, Public Administration Institute, E. J. Ourso College of Business Administration, Louisiana State University, Baton Rouge, Louisiana

Lawrence L. Martin, Ph.D.   Associate Professor, School of Social Work, Columbia University, New York, New York

Alan C. Melchior, Ph..D.   Assistant Professor, Department of Political Science, Towson University, Towson, Maryland

Hugh T. Miller, Ph.D.   Associate Professor, Department of Public Administration, Florida Atlantic University, Palm Beach Gardens, Florida

Paul Rich, Ph.D.   The University of the Americas, Puebla, Mexico and The Hoover Institution, Stanford University, Stanford, California

Michael W. Spicer, Ph.D.   Professor, Department of Urban Studies, Maxine Goodman Levin College of Urban Affairs, Cleveland State University, Cleveland, Ohio

James A. Stever, Ph.D.   Professor, Department of Political Science, University of Cincinnati, Cincinnati, Ohio

Camilla Stivers, Ph.D.   Professor, Levin College of Urban Affairs, Cleveland State University, Cleveland, Ohio

John W. Swain, Ph.D.   Assistant Professor, Department of Political Science, The University of Alabama, Tuscaloosa, Alabama

Robert P. Watson, Ph.D.   Assistant Professor, Department of Political Science, University of Hawaii at Hilo, Hilo, Hawaii

William L. Waugh, Jr., Ph.D.   Professor, Department of Public Administration and Urban Studies, Georgia State University, Atlanta, Georgia

1

THE LENS OF UNDERSTANDING

Thomas D. Lynch
Public Administration Institute, E. J. Ourso College of Business Administration, Louisiana State University, Baton Rouge, Louisiana

Todd J. Dicker
Western Michigan University, Kalamazoo, Michigan

I. INTRODUCTION

There are infinite ways to see the realities of the world encompassing a complex subject like Public Administration.* This book examines the remarkable patterns of ideas that we call philosophy and how those patterns become our lens of understanding on what we think of as reality. This examination is far from exhaustive as to achieve such a goal is not humanly possible.

Indeed, our original outline for this book listed eighty-six potential chapters, a list that even at that size we considered far from complete. However, an attempt is made to identify and discuss some of the most important philosophies and movements that have influenced contemporary Public Administration. We start with the classics and end with the postmoderns. Along the way, we mention many, but not all, of the greatest, and a few of the less famous thinkers that have crafted the lenses we use to define and understand what we call Public Administration.

This is a collection of chapters contributed by various scholars. Authors who wrote about philosophers and thinkers were asked to place the thought and work of the person being discussed within the context of the endemic influences of their time. Specific world events, historical trends, transitions in power or authority, or changes in thought that have influenced these people are also discussed in each chapter. Personal experiences of the subject that may have had profound effects upon their thought are important to give the reader insight into the motivation and psyche of the subject and in explaining how those experiences shaped their work. Authors were also asked to examine the theoretical influences upon each subjects work. The educational background, including who the subject may have studied with and where they studied, is linked to later thought. Specific individuals, schools of thought, and personal relationships are explored along with the influences such experiences had on the subjects thinking. The major and minor works of the subject are developed and linked to mod-

---

*The convention of capitalization shall be used to denote a self conscious study and discipline.

ern Public Administration theory. Direct comparisons are made between differing schools of thought and conflict between various scholars on the importance and application of each subjects work. Finally, the authors own assessment of the importance of each individuals work is a thread that ties these various components throughout each chapter.

Chapter authors who focused upon a school of thought or social movements were asked to describe the development of Public Administration thought and theory in light of these powerful elements of our history. Theoretical antecedents of each movement are described, incorporated, and linked to other important movements and individuals. Similarities and differences between movements are explored, and influences of one movement upon another are highlighted. Special emphasis is given to discussing the linkages between movements and modern Public Administration thought, including the most important personalities that contributed or opposed each movement.

The organization of the following chapters is fairly simple. In most cases, thinkers and movements are addressed in chronological order. While we also might have organized our chapters along other themes, we believe that a chronological treatment allows the reader to place ideas and movements in historical perspective. A full integration of the development of ideas is achieved when one observes those foundations and ideas that serve as precursors to a concept, and also understand the linkages between that same concept and subsequent ideas that are built upon it.

This combination of presentations provides a unique and remarkable "picture" of the various lenses that we continually view through, understand, debate, and argue over the continuous flow of discussions on proper public management and policy. Once understood, the lens helps explain our myopic corrections that are sometimes more limiting than our natural vision, however limited it might be.

A.   Modernism and Public Administration Theory

Contemporary Public Administration can be thought of in terms of what is called modernist thinking and to a much lesser degree various counter perspectives.

There are twenty-two chapters in addition to this introductory one organized into seven parts. Less directly but nevertheless significant are the premoderns, represented in this book by Plato and Jesus. Few would argue whether or not Plato has influenced Western thought, but with our tradition of secularization we rarely speak of Christianity except within the walls of churches. Nevertheless, it radically changed Western thought and particularly influenced the views of the non modernists.

In defining modernist, Rene Descartes, Francis Bacon, and many others could be cited, but the modernist perspective is represented in chapters concerning Niccolo Machiavelli, Jeremy Bentham, John Locke, and Adam Smith. These philosophers were secular thinkers that focused on the good of the people as defined by rigorous rational thought associated with the scientific method. Many defined nineteenth century liberalism with its distrust of government as a social instrument, but had great faith in the rational thinking capacity of mankind to discover, articulate, and apply knowledge. In contemporary language, liberal has shifted in meaning, primarily due to progressives as explained by Professor Larkin, to embrace and envision government as a social instrument. In both the nineteenth and twentieth centuries, the hallmark of modernists is their faith in human reason to discover truth and use it improve the human condition. Modern science is a product of that faith.

One could easily stop with the modernist as their influence is so significant on Western thought, but there are other views that are becoming increasingly heard and influential. Two philosophers, David Hume and Edmund Burke, questioned the capability of human reason to seek out and find knowledge that should particularly be used to guide our civilization. Later modernist opponents cited in this book are Marshall Dimock, Jean-Paul Sartre, John Rawls, and the school of thought known as Phenomenology. Each builds on earlier philosophers and challenges the fundamental core of modernist thought.

However, returning to the modernist for a moment, how did their thinking influence the creation and later evolution of American Public Administration? This question is answered in the chapters on Woodrow Wilson, Progressivism, the Bureau Movement, and Herbert Simon. Wilson played the unusual triple roles of academic, practitioner, and progressive reformer. These intellectuals and political reformers literally changed the direction of modernism and made it the dominant agenda for America. Herbert Simon took the epistemological view of Bentham, that was developed to its logical rigorous extent by Ludwig Wittgenstein, and applied it via Herbert Simon to the new field of Public Administration.

Possibly because of later modernist opposition, the discontent with American government policy, information technology, and increasingly hostile reaction to intellectual thought, there was a direct challenge to modernist thinking. Postmodernism arose first with Friedrich Nietzsche but gained much of its current direction from Ludwig Wittgenstein who had abandoned his earlier version of modernism called logical positivism. Three chapters were devoted to explaining this powerful and influential lens that is just beginning to influence Public Administration.

Where does that leave us as we try to understand Public Administration? Clearly, the modernist lens remain powerful. Students and practitioners go to school and learn subjects like Total Quality Management, risk management, benefit cost analysis, public choice theory, and many other approaches grounded in modernism. Nevertheless, there are alternative lenses that are acceptable to the intellectual community such as organization behavior and stressing the importance of writing in plain English. One emerging contemporary perspective is public entrepreneurialism and a chapter is devoted to this lens. The final chapter is an attempt to look at contemporary developments by transcending the historically used lens and offering yet another perspective to view Public Administration as it emerges into the twenty-first century.

II. PREMODERN

A. Plato and the Invention of Political Science

Professor Ralph Clark Chandler begins our discussion by going to the very roots of political philosophy, Plato. In astounding depth and lucidity, Chandler shows how Plato moved beyond the endemic semi-religious speculation of the day to a much tougher, more precise form of criticism and discussion that explored moral philosophy and logical and metaphysical theory. We learn how Plato understood and taught that conceptual understanding was different from understanding of the natural world and that Plato concentrated on the form and purpose of a thing rather than its material constitution or the cause for something's behavior. Translating much of the material and commentary from the original Greek, Professor Chandler provides us with extraordinary insight into the teachings of Plato and their myriad applications to modern Public Administration theory.

B. Jesus and Public Administration

Professor Lance deHaven-Smith explains how Jesus transformed the Roman Empire and Western civilization from a culture centered on valor into a culture centered on love and mercy. To deHaven-Smith, Jesus was a theo-political revolutionary in his teachings that focused on ending oppression. Jesus sought to undermine Greek and Roman culture by replacing mercy for justice, forgiveness for judgment, and love for law. Jesus wanted people to accept personal responsibility and not mindlessly follow collective condemnation. We are not to merely bow to and accept status and authority. As administrators, we are to decode the language and peer pressures. We are to look to the moral context of our situation. From this perspective, professional martyrdom does have value. DeHaven-Smith calls upon us to face the moral challenges as individuals and as a profession and not hide from our consciences by thinking in terms of the common structure but be responsible for the moral judgments that are a part of what we do in life. Ultimately, we must realize there is a higher purpose to be served.

III. MODERNIST DEFINED

A.   Niccolo Machiavelli and Modern Public Administration

Professor John W. Swain explains the contributions of Niccolo Machiavelli to modern Public Administration by detailing his life, times, and writings. Swain then explains the contributions of Machiavelli to modern philosophy, modern science, and Public Administration. The secularization of Public Administration began with Machiavelli who saw life as a human enterprise with humanity serving its own needs in politics, science, and other activities rather than humanity serving God or at least being God centered. To Machiavelli, human beings are alone in the universe exercising their capacities to serve themselves as best they can. Machiavelli, who is both blamed and praised for his thinking, is nevertheless influential as he created the concept of modern Public Administration.

In the modern view, Public Administration is primarily a means with values led largely for others to decide how to rule the society for the larger public good. With Machiavelli, effectiveness becomes central and moral neutrality is essential. With remarkable insight, Swain shows the relationship between the modern executive and Machiavellian concepts by tracing those views through Hobbes, Locke, Montesquieu, the American founders, and "classical" Public Administration writers such as Luther Gulick and Frederick Winslow Taylor. Machiavelli's Prince has been constitutionalized in the American political order and can be seen today as hired guns called lawyers, public management analysts, pollsters, and public policy analysts. Machiavelli taught us to focus on the public as the primary basis for the political stability. Public needs or wants become the rationale for the state. Thus, polls and building relations with the public via proper media relations becomes important in establishing the all important "appearances." The focus on technique and its use of technical neutrality are directly traceable to Machiavelli.

B.   Mercantilism

The origins of Mercantilism lie somewhere around the lifetime of Machiavelli, and are explored with great mastery by Professor Paul Rich. Rich describes the extraordinary degree of influence Mercantilism had on the structure and form of political governance. Its weaknesses and strengths were debated by a wide range of thinkers, including Jeremy Bentham, Edmund Burke, John Stuart Mill, and Adam Smith, among others. Rich also develops the assumptions and implications of Mercantilism to their logical conclusions, and applies them to current theories of public organization.

C.   Jeremy Bentham: Utilitarianism, Public Policy, and the Administrative State

Professor Lawrence L. Martin explains Jeremy Bentham and his influence on modern thought. Martin introduces us to Bentham as an activist, explains his life, summarizes the major works of Bentham, and explains his influence. Bentham was the leader of reformers that were called philosophical radicals and included John Mill and his more famous son John Stuart Mill. Bentham was an empiricist who advocated the use of quantitative methods in social observation and the development of a value free language devoid of emotional and ambiguous terms in the tradition of the early Ludwig Wittgenstein. This influential modernist founder of utilitarianism advocated the "greatest good for the greatest number" and with it shaped the modern notions of democracy, analytical techniques such as benefit cost analysis, and the role of policy analysis in public policy making. To Bentham, utilitarianism was the "public interest" and the welfare state was a series of rewards and punishments designed to regulate human behavior. Bentham was a social activist with the interests of the public central to his values but always mindful of how policies were implemented including their procedures.

D.   John Locke's Influence on American Government and Public Administration

Professor Mark F. Griffith explains the influence of John Locke on American government and the version of Public Administration that evolved in America. Griffith notes that Locke profoundly influenced powers and the idea that property was the basis for prosperity. Locke, the modernist, was the bridge between Thomas Hobbes and Niccolo Machiavelli and Jean-Jacques Rousseau. John Locke was the ultimate spin doctor of words who carefully masked his radicalism with great caution and complex arguments that challenged the then existing order. Locke embraced constitutionalism that was later also embraced by Edmund Burke and Woodrow Wilson. Locke's vision of ethics with its faith, prudence, and self-control combined with this hedonism greatly influenced the modernist view that stressed the importance of individual pursuit of happiness. To Locke, government was meant to protect private property and business. His views are reflected in such common practices as planning, zoning, and the importance of creating private and public wealth for society. Griffith notes the critical role of government is to maintain order and the instrument of accomplishing that end is the political structure of the administrative state. Nevertheless, Locke must be understood not as a twentieth century liberal who supports growth of the administrative state but in terms of a nineteenth century liberalism that saw government as potentially destructive. He distrusted government power and explained how it should be curbed.

E.   Adam Smith's Legacy

Professor David John Farmer explains the modernism of Adam Smith that reflected neither Hume's skepticism about the power of human reasoning nor the later extreme skepticism that emerged with postmodernism period. Smith was a nineteenth century liberal as was his championing of liberal capitalism. Farmer argues that we commonly misread Adam Smith as he did recognize the limitations of his argument. Farmer applies some post modernism of his own by arguing economics is rhetoric and the limits of Smith's reasoning for our times. In particular, Farmer argues against public choice economics (citing Vincent Ostrom and others) that he considers is the spiritual descendant of the critical referent of efficiency to this school of thought and its contemporary influence on the field. Farmer explains the contemporary post modernists believe such an underlying referent is impossible as is any underlying referent. Smith, a modernist of his times, influenced society by seeing through a lens that described problems and prescribed solutions. Farmer notes that because Adam Smith's lens shaped Public Administration, he deserves attention. Smith was a writer so strong that he changed the lens for many and influenced the way we look and act in the world.

IV. EARLY LOYAL OPPOSITION TO THE MODERNIST

A. David Hume and Public Administration: Empiricism, Scepticism, and Constitutionalism

Professor Michael W. Spicer explains David Hume in terms of his life, times, and contributions to Public Administration. Hume believed that all knowledge derives from our experience rather than reason and stressed the significance of scepticism in questioning the reality of our knowledge. Spicer addresses Hume's empiricism, scepticism, and his political writings on constitutionalism. Although logical positivism and linguistic analysts reject Hume's atomistic approach to knowledge, they nevertheless use Hume's empiricism in which ideas can only be derived from impressions. Thus, Hume influenced Public Administration writers such as Herbert Simon as explained later in Professor Cruise's chapter. Hume's scepticism ran counter to any objective claims to knowledge and thus challenges a core belief of the modernist. Hume's scepticism appears to have influenced Edmund Husserl's phenomenology discussed later in Professor Waugh's chapter and affirmed the radical subjectivity of human experience. Meaning is defined by the human mind through its experience in the world.

For Spicer, Hume's notion that political power must be constitutionally checked is particularly important and can be seen reflected in Madison's *Federalist Number 10*. As defined by Hume, constitutionalism means the use of different institutional mechanism to check the government officials abuse of discretionary power. Hume said, "separate interest be not checked, and be directed to the public, we ought to look for nothing but faction, disorder, and tyranny from such a government." (1) Thus, Hume is at the heart of American government and the world of American Public Administration.

B. Edmund Burke: The Role of Public Administration in a Constitutional Order

Professor Akhlaque U. Haque explains that Edmund Burke, who was the voice of dissent of modernism, laid the foundation for a broader role for Public Administration in the constitutional order. Burke especially contributed to legitimacy of administrative discretion because public administrators are representatives that are guided by the laws made by elected representatives. His views can be seen in John Rawls and public entrepreneurialism discussed in a latter chapter. He also contributed to our understanding for the need to be aware of human fallibility and self-interest. He felt the potential for abuse of discretionary power must be checked through forming a unified administration and adhering to the laws of the land. To Burke we must recruit and retain people of good conduct as a necessary practice of government. Edmund Burke was a critic of human reason and his nineteenth century conservative solution was applying a constitutional order much like David Hume.

As ethics continue to grow in importance in Public Administration, Edmund Burke becomes more important to us. According to Edmund Burke, broader knowledge and constitutional ethics need to be stressed more than technical knowledge. To Burke, trust built upon administrative values is critical to preserve the integrity of public institutions. Public Administration must develop systems that allow and encourage ethical values to be developed through our institutions based on constitutional principles. Edmund Burke's contribution to us was his exemplary effort to establish a just, orderly, free society under constitutional principles and moral ideals. His efforts provide us with vital insights into the applications in the art of governance.

V. AMERICAN MODERNIST INFLUENCE

A. Making Democracy Safe for the World: Public Administration in the Political Thought of Woodrow Wilson

Professor Brian J. Cook explains that Woodrow Wilson, a late convert to modernism, was influenced by Edmund Burke's stress on societal order and the controlling force of law. He stressed the critical role and influence of the views of the mass citizens and the importance of subordinating administration to public opinion. For Wilson the people needed to maintain control over the president as the nation's leader and interpreter of national policy. Unity, institutional cooperation, and presidential leadership of party and Congress as opposed to administration were the centerpiece of governance.

Wilson laid importance conceptual and practical building blocks for modernist Public Administration. Wilson helped establish social science and political science as important academic disciplines. Within them, Public Administration grew. Certainly, his own research contributed to the academic importance of Public Administration at its beginning including at some point the famous and often misunderstood politics-administration dichotomy.

Unfortunately, his more subtle and complex understanding of administration did not have the influence that would be expected from a former President of the United States that also was one of the first three Americans that wrote academically on Public Administration. For example, his own practical ideas of grants-in-aid and regulatory programs became central to common practice in American Public Administration. Professor Cook makes the case that the writings of Wilson need actually to be studied more and not less for a proper understanding of Public Administration.

B. Progressivism: Critiques and Contradictions

Professor Larkin Sims Dudley does not address a philosopher but rather a political reform era that largely defined contemporary America and significantly influenced the world. From approximately 1880 to 1914, the progressive reform era changed the political landscape of America and set the reform direction in the nation that would continue until the 1970s. One of its accomplishments was the creation of Public Administration as a professional field and academic subject. Although remarkably influential, there was no perfect consensus among the reforms. However, they did have a buoyant faith in the progress of mankind born out of the modernist belief in rational thought and scientific protocol to discover and define truth. They sought reform through science and the scientific management based on a Baconian idea of science.

Before 1900, American public life was largely shaped by classical nineteenth century liberalism that was wed to laissez faire economics. It was a country that valued nationalism, was committed to representative and weak government, supported personal freedom, and assumed that natural laws governed society. Social reformers, including labor unions, sought and achieved their first reform measure for the whole nation that was a direct reaction to the worst consequences of industrialism. They sought not to dismantle the economic and political institutions but only to reform them based on their faith in humanity's ability, through purposeful action, to improve their society. They embraced secularization, a rationality of instrumentalism, separation and specialization in life, bureaucratization, and the key role of science to advance humanity. Progressives believed the good society was efficient, organized, and cohesive. Progressive intellectuals and reformers transformed the dominant nineteenth century liberalism, broadening their allegiance to include the bourgeois and working class, and embracing ideals of equality along with their older values of individual freedom. Significantly, they dropped their close association with laissez faire economics and saw government as the best tool for social change especially to control the power of business.

C.   The Bureau Movement: Seedbed of Modern Public Administration

Professor Camilla Stivers explains the importance of the bureau movement in shaping "classical" Public Administration, and on the importance of the bureau movement in the larger progressive era. The bureaus were privately sponsored agencies of municipal research created by progressives to systematically investigate government practices and lessen the hold of the machine bosses on urban politics and policy making. Stivers traces the history, philosophy, and influence of the bureau movement on modern Public Administration. She argues the impact is worthy of deeper reflection and more equivocal than the relatively basic and mostly sanguine accounts in the contemporary literature. She stresses that we can learn from their remarkable efforts and raise our sights to encompass more fully the substantive dimensions of Public Administration for the public good.

D.   Of Proverbs and Positivism: The Logical Herbert Simon

Professor Peter L. Cruise explains how Herbert A. Simon brought logical positivism to Public Administration. In the late 1940s and 1950s, as a young University of Chicago doctoral student, Herbert Simon challenged the pioneering work of classical Public Administration writers like Frank Goodnow, Leonard White, W. F. Willoughby, Luther Gulick, and Lyndall Urwick. Although he built on the works of Chester I. Barnard, Simon fundamentally shifted the locus and focus of the study to the point that the new field of

Public Administration almost disappeared from the academic and professional landscape. His critique was a bomb that called into the question the academic legitimacy of the field and its approach to study. Simon brought logical positivism to Public Administration and Cruise explains the evolution of that important epistemological and philosophical bomb shell. Its antecedents included empiricism, modern science, the scientific method, and logical atomism. Influences include Alfred North Whitehead, Bertrand Russell, and especially Ludwig Wittgenstein and the other writers of the Vienna Circle. Cruise details the effects of logical positivism on Public Administration and places it in perspective by citing counterattacks on it such as phenomenology and the questions raised about qualitative research methodology. Simon forced the field into a period of introspection and eventually lead to a counter trend that embraced the importance of value based issues for the profession.

VI. LATER MODERNIST OPPOSITION

A. Marshall Dimock's Deflective Organizational Theory

Professor James A. Stever explains the large and sprawling landscape of concepts, approaches, and arguments that constitute the contributions of Marshall Dimock to Public Administration. Stever argues that Dimock challenged conventional wisdom with a gradual deflection away from conventional organization and administrative theories and toward the embrace of premises that were not shared by the milieu in which he operated. In the process of explaining Dimock, Stever lays out the evolution of Public Administration itself in the United States. Dimock linked Public Administration back to classical thought and he was the first to renounce modernist presuppositions. This can be seen in Dimock's theory of organizational leaders and his rejection of the modern idea of progress and growth/decay explanations for organization development.

B. Phenomenology

Professor William L. Waugh, Jr. explains phenomenology and its contribution to Public Administration. One of the strongest opponents of logical positivism is the phenomenologists who argued that the research methods of the physical sciences are ill-suited to the study of human behavior and the human "world." For them, to understand human behavior one must recognize that perceptions differ and how one perceives the world defines how one acts in the world. Thus, "reality" is merely a social construct. Phenomenology is a philosophical perspective achieved by eliminating one's assumptions and biases concerning everything except the perceived reality. This philosophical approach underlies the world of existentialist Jean-Paul Sartre and Albert Camus and psychologist Viktor Frankl. Mostly associated with Edmund Husserl, phenomenology is essentially an analytical method or framework for describing and explaining social relationships and psychological orientations. Phenomenologists attempt to account for the subjective qualities that either are assumed by logical positivism and empiricist to be unreal or are treated as objective, observable phenomena when they are not. Briefly, they focus on meaning and not reality. Professor Waugh notes that phenomenology has been absorbed into the literature and language of the field especially in terms of how people do and do not relate to bureaucratic organizations and government programs.

C.   Jean-Paul Sartre

Professor William L. Waugh, Jr. goes on to explain Jean-Paul Sartre and existentialism. Waugh notes that Sartre tells us that individuals have a responsibility to exercise their freedom to act to preserve individual and societal options for the future. By existension, public administrators have a responsibility to themselves and society to understand the true essence of the world around them and to initiate action to alleviate conditions that constrain freedom of action. Interestingly, Sartre borrowed from the German idealists of the 1920s and he made existentialism a subject of literary commentary and social debate. The debate later influenced the American 1960s and 1970s; fueling the political discussions, and encouraging political activism among students and scholars. Today, existentialism and transcendentalist phenomenology are alternatives to empirical social sciences. They find their greatest influence in determining and applying ethical standards, as well as encouraging proactive public administrators.

D.   John Rawls and Public Administration

Professor Stephen L. Esquith explains the influence of the contemporary philosopher John Rawls on contemporary Public Administration. Although Rawls ideal democratic society says nothing directly about the practice of governing complex organizations such as government, he does influence a whole school of Public Administration thinking called the "New Public Administration." Like Edmund Burke, Rawls argues that once a just constitution and related laws have been made then higher rules can be applied with full knowledge by judges and administrators. Rawls like Edmund Burke is not a fan of classical utilitarian principles. He rejects the idea that the institutions that form the basic structure of a well-ordered society should be designed to manage society's social resources as efficiently as possible. Rawls does not favor efficient administration for its own sake. Rawls's views constitute an attack on the first fifty years of Public Administration theory that was modernist and stressed the central value of efficiency.

Rawls's theory of justice was influential in the Public Administration of the 1960s and the 1970s, but only implicitly, as his works do not address the field directly. His key influence was the notion of social equity that was embraced by New Public Administration of the 1970s. Like the pre-modernist Jesus, he argues social equity should supersede efficiency and economy as the rationale or justification for policy positions. Thus, to him, ethics, honesty, and responsibility in government become central to the field. New Public Administration argues that public administrators are not mere implementors of fixed policy decisions of elected leaders but those public administrators also have a public trust. They have to provide the best possible public service with the costs and benefits being fairly distributed among the people. With New Public Administration, effective public administration is redefined into the context of active and participative citizenry. Through supporters like H. George Frederickson, Rawls introduced distributive justice, administrative ethics, and participation back into the field. For example, Frederickson argues that administrators must rise above the rules and routines of organizations to always assert first the self-respect and dignity of the individual citizen.

VII. RISE OF POSTMODERNISM

A. From Positivism to Post-Positivism: An Unfinished Journey

The contemporary world of philosophy is called post-positivism. Professor Laurent Dobuzinskis defines this nebulous concept as all societal trends that pose a challenge to the set of institutions and cultural patterns we have inherited from industrial society as it existed prior to the emergence of the information revolution in the 1960s. He explains to us the segment of modernism called positivism and its impact on Public Administration at the beginning of the twentieth century. He traces the origins of Public Administration to the time when its political and cultural climate was receptive to the idea that science could provide answers to the society's problems. This later debunked view was that Public Administration organizations were like machines that could be designed and controlled by experts. Dobuzinskis continues his chapter by raising the more contemporary question that public choice theory is a return to the debunked influence of positivism on the field. His chapter notes the post-modernism character of New Public Administration and finishes by saying that Public Administration can develop a "more adequate science" by using a post-positivism perspective.

B. On the Language of Bureaucracy: Postmodernism, Plain English, and Wittgenstein

Professor Robert P. Watson explains the contribution of Wittgenstein to contemporary Public Administration. Ludwig Wittgenstein is unique in philosophy in that his contributions were two fold in two significantly different ways. Earlier in the book, Professor Cruise explains the influence of Wittgenstein on logical positivism and subsequently public administration. Watson explains the later influence of Wittgenstein when he completely disagreed with his earlier work and focused our minds on the profound influence of language on the nature of understanding itself. His later work refocused the very course of modern philosophic thought away from a theory of knowledge based on logic and shifted it to linguistic analysis. Wittgenstein's influence can be seen in postmodernism that is discussed later by Fox and Miller. Watson presents a potentially practical and positive contribution of Wittgenstein in his discussion of "bureaucratese."

C. Postmodern Philosophy, Postmodernity, and Public Organizational Theory

Professors Charles J. Fox and Hugh T. Miller explain not one philosopher but a set of philosophers called the postmodernist. If one had to cite the leading postmodern thinners, clearly Friedrich Nietzsche must be mentioned as the first postmodern philosopher and Ludwig Wittgenstein must be mentioned as the most influential in the group. If one had to cite an area that developed the philosophy the most, clearly France is where this philosophy has found the most fertile ground to grow. Fox and Miller define the major themes of postmodern philosophy, sketch the contributions of the major postmodern thinkers, define the postmodern condition, and speculate about the effects of postmodernism on governance.

Fox and Miller introduce us to the vocabulary and concepts of postmodern thought. For example, postmodern thought is defined as the rejection of universalism, essentialism, ontological realism, and meta narratives. In other words, postmodern thought rejects any absolute historical and universal truth such as God or a universal knowledge based on science. They even reject the quest for such truths. Postmodernism's lens sees multiple paradigms in which one paradigm believer cannot logically dispute the correctness of another paradigm believer. However, within a paradigm or localized logic we can use language games to at least rule out some nonsensical reasoning. For postmoderns, the self is not subjectively determined but largely influenced by the inherited language games of the time and culture. There is no centered unified self but rather we are split between our conscious and unconscious. Knowledge is merely institutional rules that guide us and our discourse. Truth is merely vocabulary that arbitrarily defines itself as definition especially to fundamental concepts such as "being." Words are only replacements for things and nothing more.

Fox and Miller pose the question, "What does postmodern thought do to help us in Public Administration?" It teaches us the foolishness of most so-called policy decisions. We also learn the organization structure is in itself a system of power. Lastly, we learn that reality is not important but rather what is important is the measure that is used to indicate the condition of reality. Fox and Miller end with a call for a common ground to improve public conversation.

VIII.   POSTMODERN ALTERNATIVE

A.   Public Entrepreneurism: A New Paradigm for Public Administration?

Professor Alan C. Melchior addresses the contemporary and emerging public entrepreneurialism that is alerting Public Administration to the most recent technological and social paradigm shift influencing society. He argues that public entrepreneurial advocates like David Osborne and Ted Gaebler are inadequate, but that they do highlight the importance of competitiveness as a value for public administration that can supplement or replace efficiency. However, neutral competence and "justice as fairness" remain a moral imperative. Although entrepreneurial theory does not provide a basis to understand the administrative state, it is significantly challenging the older lens of understanding. Propelled by the rapid advances in information technology, technical revolutions permit managerial and even political and social revolution rather than marginal modifications. The ability of society to cope with popular demands for both moderate taxes and high quality public service may well depend upon the ability to utilize fully the possibilities made available by advancing information technology. Certainly, public entrepreneurialism is one of the new possibilities that is emerging as American society moves into the twenty-first century.

B.   Twenty-first Century Philosophy and Public Administration

In our final chapter, Thomas D. Lynch and Cynthia E. Lynch bring together many of the ideas and perspectives contributed to the discussion and address the question of where we go from here. In this chapter they provide a critique of both modernist and post modernist philosophy in an attempt to rethink the role of philosophy in understanding Public

Administration theory. The authors suggest that a primary goal of an epistemologist examining Public Administration thought is to have the ability to "think outside the box" created by traditional forms of understanding. By doing this, one identifies those ideas that transcend traditional borders of our limited knowledge, and expand our boundaries in the process.

IX. CONCLUSION

Although there are infinite ways lenses can examine a complex subject like Public Administration, there does appear to be a pattern to the one examined in this book. The pattern is predicated upon the value perspective taken on by the philosopher as they assumed the answer to three questions:

- In making judgments for society, are most of us essentially either altruistic or materialistic and driven by our egos?
- In making decisions and defining knowledge, is it possible for mankind to be successful using rational analysis based on empirical inquiry?
- Is government potentially an appropriate instrument in shaping society?

By applying these assumptions to the authors examined, we can learn a great deal about philosophy and its influence on Public Administration. Let us scale each question from high to low. Thus, for the first question, that addresses the altruistic/materialistic dimension, a rating of "high" means the philosopher strongly agrees that people use essentially an altruistic vision of how individuals make judgments for society. For example, Jean Rousseau and Thomas Jefferson would rank a "high." In contrast, Hobbes would ranks as a "low."

For the second question, that addresses the rational dimension, a rating of high means a strong behavior in the capability of rational or scientific thought as the proper tool to address and resolve important decisions. For example, modernists like Locke and Bentham would rank as "high." In contrast, Edmund Burke and Rawls would rank "low." For the third question, that addresses the government capability dimension, a rating of high means a strong believer that government is a positive instrument to address and resolve society's problems. For example, Woodrow Wilson would rank as "high." In contrast, modern twentieth century conservatives would rank as "low."

This comparative scheme is a three dimensional box with the length, width, and breadth reflecting a low to high scale. Thus, one can catalog each philosopher or school of thought that creates the lens which we use to view Public Administration. The following table presents a simple matrix that summarizes the three dimensions in terms of contemporary ideology. Of note is that twentieth century liberal and conservative are at polar opposites of in this table. This helps explain how various groups in political contests can look at the same facts and reach totally different answers. Their respective lenses are sufficiently different that they come to different conclusions.

Although the answer to all three questions are answered in a co-determinant manner, that need not be necessary. Philosophers or reformers can say the answers are really a mix of high and low depending on the circumstances of the time and place. A good example in American history of a person who answered the questions as a "mix" is James Madison, the father of the U.S. Constitution. Philosophers or reformers could also refuse to

Table I   Assumptions and Philosophy Matrix

Dimensions			Contemporary Ideologies
Altruistic/ Materialistic	Rational	Government Capability	School
High	High	High	Twentieth Century Liberal
High	High	Low	Nineteenth Century Liberal
High	Low	High	
High	Low	Low	
Low	High	High	
Low	High	Low	
Low	Low	High	Nineteenth Century Conservative
Low	Low	Low	Twentieth Century Conservative

answer and say the question is really not that significant as they understand the larger questions of mankind. A good example of the latter is Jesus. He argued that each person should give to Caesar what is Caesar's but render unto God was is God's. For example, the question of government efficacy per se was not central to His perspective. In other words, we can think outside the box used to describe the three dimensions.

NOTES

1. D. Hume, *Essays, Moral, Political, and Literary*, Indianapolis, Indiana: Liberty Press, 1987, p. 42.

Part I
Premodern

PLATO

Until philosophers are kings, or the kings and princes of this world have the spirit and power of philosophy, and political greatness and wisdom meet in one, and those commoner natures who pursue either to the exclusion of the other are compelled to stand aside, cities will never rest from their evils—no, not the human race, as I believe—and then only will this our state have a possibility of life and behold the light of day (*The Laws*, Book V, section 493).

JESUS

Blessed are the eyes that see the things which ye see: For I tell you, that many prophets and kings have desired to see those things which ye see, and have not seen them; and to hear those things which ye hear, and have not heard them (Luke 10:23).

2

PLATO AND THE INVENTION OF POLITICAL SCIENCE

Ralph Clark Chandler
Western Michigan University, Kalamazoo, Michigan

"The safest general characterization of the European philosophical tradition is that it consists of a series of footnotes to Plato."

> Alfred North Whitehead
> *Process and Reality*, II, I, I (1929)

"And this which you deem of no moment is the very highest of all: that is whether you have a right idea of the gods, whereby you may live your life well or ill."

> Plato
> *Laws*, 888 (348 BCE)

The resurgence of interest in Plato among contemporary scholars may be attributed to at least three factors: the decline in civility leading one to reflect on Plato's solution to incivility in one of the most uncivil ages of all, his own; the increasing interest in soul (*psyche* (1)) as a category in understanding human behavior, including behavior in organizations (2), and the renewed attention to things historical in the theory and practice of public administration (3).

The deeper reason behind the Plato revival is man's abiding interest in what Plato called forms. In our day we tend to call forms principles, and they include such things as justice, beauty, honesty, goodness, and courage. Many people feel these principles are more real than anything we can see, hear, or touch. Despite the flux, change, impermanence, and chaos (4) astride the world, there are certain principles which are fixed and do not change. A modern Platonist might say, for example, that justice continues to exist no matter how muddleheaded we may be about its precise nature and no matter how baffled we are in complex situations where equally just principles seem to be in conflict. To support his view of the nature of reality Plato brought to bear impressive quantities of reasonable and emotional evidence, so that even those who disagree with him are forced to take him seriously. His chapter in the history of human thought is well footnoted indeed.

Plato has not been universally admired. Following Thomas Jefferson's denunciation of Plato in the early nineteenth century (see footnote 83) scholars in the mid-twentieth century also found reason to renounce Plato. In 1940, for example, Carl J. Friedrich called on the world to stop idolizing Greek political experience (5). "So deeply rooted in the state-polis was Greek culture," he wrote, "that any glorification of this particular cul-ture-pattern carries with it an exaltation of the state." Friedrich warned that the effective secular organization of the community is not the highest value of humankind, closing his analysis with the words: "Let us beware of the heritage of the Greek polis: it is a veritable Trojan horse, smuggled into our Christian civilization."

The most seething critique of Plato's political philosophy in modern times was de-livered by Karl L. Popper in 1950. Popper viewed Plato's proposal to reconstruct the nat-ural harmony of society with grave suspicion.

> The more we try to return to the heroic age of tribalism, the more surely do we arrive at the Inquisition, at the Secret Police, and at a romanticized gangsterism. Beginning with the suppression of reason and truth, we must end with the most brutal and vio-lent destruction of all that is human. *There is no return to a harmonious state of nature. If we turn back, then we must go the whole way—we must return to the beasts* (6).

The charge that Plato's social conservatism amounted to totalitarianism stands alongside the claim by others that since Plato was the first champion of the division of sovereign power, he was the first Whig. Only one thing is certain: Plato's description of life in a democratic society remains to this day the most incisive critique of democracy. The buoyant diversity and creative pluralism of the democratic society are its glory, but they are often the path to dissolution and disintegration when its members forget that they are not merely individuals with rights and liberties but also social beings with duties and obligations.

I. THE LIFE OF PLATO

Let us try to fix Plato's place in the development of Greek culture. He was born in Athens in 427 BCE (7) and given the name Aristocles, which he later changed. Plato's father was Ariston, a direct descendant of Codrus, the last king of Athens. His mother was Peric-tione, a direct descendant of Solon, the lawgiver who laid the foundations for the stable society of classical Athens. Ariston died in Plato's childhood, and his mother then married her uncle, Pyrilampes, an intimate of Pericles as well as a prominent supporter of Peri-clean policies. Besides Plato, Ariston and Perictione had at least three other children. There were two older sons, Adimantus and Glaucon, who appear as young men in Plato's *Republic*, and a daughter, Potone, about whom we know nothing. Pyrilampes and Peric-tione also had a son, Antiphon, who appears in Plato's *Parmenides*. Plato tells us regretfully that Antiphon gave up philosophy for horses (8).

Plato was born four years after the beginning of the Peloponnesian War, which ended in the crushing defeat of Athens at the hands of Sparta. Around him was a brilliant cultural environment. In letters, the arts, religion, and philosophy the age is unparalleled in the history of the world. The tradition included the *Iliad* and the *Odyssey*, the first liter-ary monuments of the life and spirit of the Greeks. Then came the lyric poets, followed towards the end of the sixth century and throughout the fifth by the emergence of both tragedy and comedy.

Contemporary with these literary phenomena, philosophy appeared. A number of speculative thinkers were preoccupied with the problem of the constitution of the exter-nal universe. What is its underlying first principle, and what is the nature of being? Their orientation was towards the without, the outer, the outside. Chief among them was Parmenides, who insisted that only being is, and that the world of our senses and the phe-nomena of motion are illusory. Heracleitus held that the characteristic factors of the exter-nal world are flux and change. Nothing is fixed.

Next to the work of the poets and philosophers we find the sculpture of Pheidias and his associates, the brilliant architecture illustrated in the buildings on the Acropolis. We see the beginnings of history with Herodotus. A standing mystery is why all of this should have happened in the same fifty years. Heracleitus, Pheidias, Herodotus, Aeschy-lus, Sophocles, Euripides, and Aristophanes were all contemporaries (9).

And then there was Socrates. His dates, 470–399, are not without significance. He was born ten years after the conclusion of the Persian Wars. He lived through the years of Athens' breathtaking rise to the peak of its intellectual and artistic supremacy. He wit-nessed the operation of Athenian democracy at its best and saw it slowly succumb to the blandishments of imperialism. Finally, he lived through the last horrible days of the Athenian defeat by Sparta and then suffered execution at the hands of a corrupt and deca-dent caricature of the great Athenian democracy of his youth.

Plato met Socrates in the year 407 when Plato was twenty years old. It was the deci-sive event in Plato's life. He spent considerable time with the master until Socrates' death in 399. What Plato found was a philosopher who cut radically across the conventional mode of philosophizing and turned its orientation from without to within. Socrates added to the enterprise of philosophy the whole domain heretofore preempted by the epic and lyric poets and dramatists. Since Socrates, philosophy in the West has been concerned not only with the constitution of the external world and the nature of being, but also with ethics, the nature of knowledge, and the relation of the inner man to the outer world. This shift in the orientation of philosophy constitutes one of the most significant events in the development of Western civilization and culture (10).

As late as 403, four years before Socrates' death, Plato was still looking forward to a political career. It was the standing conviction of his family, rich in the tradition of Solon, that it was the imperative duty of the philosopher to devote the best of his manhood to the service of his fellow citizens as a statesman and legislator. It was the age of Pericles and the close association of Plato's stepfather with Pericles, elected general every year from 443 until his death in 429, meant that affairs of state were commonly discussed in Plato's hearing. Plato's subsequent dislike of democracy was not the dislike of ignorance but that of a man who knew too much.

It was in September, 403, that democracy was restored in Athens after a seventeen month rule by a group of oligarchs called the Thirty Tyrants. Upon Athens' defeat in the Peloponnesian War in April, 404, the Spartan leader, Lysander, chose thirty men to run the Athenian government and write new laws following the "ancestral constitution" (pa-trios politeria) of Athens. Plato's mother was the niece of the leader of the thirty, Critias. In a systematic purge of their democratic opponents, the thirty executed some 1,500 promi-nent Athenians and alienated the people by stationing a Spartan garrison on the Acropo-lis. When democrats finally overcame the garrison and killed Critias, amnesty was extended to all who had cooperated with Lysander except the thirty (11).

Plato was horrified to see that the amnesty excluded the now elderly Socrates, whose circle included not only Critias but Plato's uncle (Perictione's brother), Charmides, who had fallen with Critias in battle. As one of the presidents of the assembly (ekklesia), Socrates was understood by the democrats to be an accomplice in the illegal arrest and ex-ecution of a fellow citizen whose property the oligarchs had wanted to confiscate. The fact was that Socrates openly ignored an order by the thirty to arrest the citizen. He was nevertheless charged with impiety, specifically with introducing new gods and corrupting young men. His subsequent condemnation and execution put an end to Plato's political aspirations. In politics nothing could be achieved without a party, said Plato, and the treatment of Socrates by both oligarchs and democrats proved that there was no party in Athens with whom an honorable man could associate. Socrates was seventy-one and Plato twenty-eight (12).

The friends of Socrates felt themselves in danger after his death, and a number of them, including Plato, withdrew for a while to the neighboring city of Megara. They lived there under the protection of Euclides, a philosopher who was among the foreign friends of Socrates present at his death. Plato then visited Italy and Sicily, where he was repelled by the sensual luxury of the life lived there by the well-to-do. He finally returned to Athens, watching the public conduct of the city and drawing the conclusion that good government can only be expected when "either true and genuine philosophers find their way to political authority or powerful politicians by the favor of providence take to true philosophy." At about the age of forty Plato founded the Academy, at last discovering his true work in life. For another forty years he would be the first president of a permanent institution designed to pursue a science that would later be called political science.

Plato's contemporary, Isocrates, presided over a similar and older institution, but Isocrates agreed with the man-in-the-street about the uselessness of science. He boasted that the education he had to offer produced expertise in opinions that would provide the ambitious aspirant to public office with points of view that could be expressed with a maximum of polish and persuasiveness. So far was Plato's Academy from such an interest in rhetoric that the backbone of his curriculum was pure mathematics. The two types of men who would be successfully turned out at the Academy over the next three centuries were original mathematicians on the one hand and skilled legislators and administrators on the other. The Academy was the direct progenitor of the state university in its classical manifestation. It was an institution which aimed to supply the state with legislators and administrators whose intellects had been developed in the first instance by the disinterested pursuit of truth for its own sake. The immediate and perceptible outward sign of the new order of learning in the Greek world was that, whereas in the age of Plato's birth aspiring young Athenians had to depend on the lectures of peripatetic foreign sophists for their higher education, they could now learn from Plato and his faculty at a university with a fixed domicile and a constitution (13).

During the twenty year period from 387 to 367 Plato was mainly occupied with the work of organizing and maintaining his school. Lecturing was part of his work, and we know from his pupil Aristotle that he lectured without a manuscript. Plato's firmest pedagogical conviction was that nothing really worth knowing could be learned by merely listening to instruction. Learning happened in dialogue as mind interacted with mind, as words spontaneously forced other words, and as the partners in learning discovered things they did not know until they spoke. As long as reason guided their discourse, they would discuss what they had always known but did not know that they knew until they rescued it from their minds and the common store of the race.

The best minds of the Mediterranean world joined Plato. The first mathematician of the time, Eudoxus of Cnidus, moved from Cyzicus to Athens to make common cause with Plato. The academic movement went outward as well. As new Greek settlements were established all over the Mediterranean Basin, representatives of the Academy were called upon to help establish constitutions in the colonies. Aristotle was such a consultant and gathered a collection of one hundred and fifty-eight of these constitutions (14).

Most of Plato's dialogues had been composed by his fortieth year. Between the ages of forty and sixty he labored to stabilize the curriculum of the Academy and establish there a comprehensive inquiry about the nature of political things. Then, in his sixtieth year, Plato went off on an adventure. In his earlier travels in Sicily he had won the whole-hearted devotion of a young man of ability and promise, Dion, son-in-law of the reigning tyrant of Syracuse, Dionysius I.

Dionysius I died in 367, leaving as his successor Dionysius II, a young man of thirty whose education had been neglected, leaving him totally unfit to take up his father's task of checking the eastward expansion of the Carthaginians. This trading empire was threatening the very existence of Greek civilization in Sicily. The strong man of Syracuse at the moment was Dion, brother-in-law of the new tyrant, the same man who had been so powerfully attached to Plato twenty years before. Dion thoroughly believed in Plato's views about the union of political power with science and conceived the idea of bringing Plato to Syracuse to educate his brother-in-law. Plato did not feel the chances of success were promising, but the Carthaginian danger was very real if the new ruler of Syracuse should prove unequal to his task. It would be dishonorable to the Academy if no attempt were made to put its theory into practice at this critical juncture in Greek history. Accordingly, Plato agreed to accept Dion's invitation (15).

On arrival, Plato at once offered Dionysius a serious course on geometry. For a while things went well. Dionysius liked Plato, and geometry became the fashion at his court. But the educational scheme wrecked on a double obstacle. Dionysius had limited intellectual capacity on the one hand, and he developed strong personal jealousies of Dion on the other. Dion was therefore banished, and Plato was told to return to Athens. Dionysius kept up a personal correspondence with Plato, however, and Plato did everything in his power to reconcile Dionysius and Dion. His efforts failed. Not only did Dionysius confiscate Dion's property, but he also forced his wife, Dionysius' sister, to marry another man. Stubbornly Plato made another voyage to Syracuse and spent nearly a year there (361–360) trying to remedy the situation. Still a diplomatic failure, Plato eventually went back to Athens to spend the rest of his long life lecturing to his associates in the Academy and composing his longest and most practical contribution to the literature of moral and political philosophy, the *Laws* (16).

II. THE SOCIETAL CIRCUMSTANCES OF PLATO'S THOUGHT

It is important to understand the context of Plato's personal life. It is equally important to understand the societal circumstances in which Plato invented political science. His ideas about organization theory and management will follow in Part III, with the reader hopefully bearing in mind that Plato's ideas about these subjects were often contrary to actual Athenian practices. By understanding the practices in the first place we will be able to appreciate more fully Plato's objections to them and why the debate he instigated continues in our own day.

In the pre-Greek world, advanced peoples had learned to live with nature by wresting secrets from her through patient observation and then applying them to gainful purposes. But such practical knowledge never lost its close association with demons and myths, fears and hopes, and punishments and rewards. The pre-Greek conception of nature viewed physical phenomena as essentially individual, unique, and incalculable rather than general, universal, and predictable. The Greeks were not the first to think about the recurrent regularities in the natural world, but they were the first to develop—going beyond observation and knowledge—the *scientific attitude*, a new approach to the world that constitutes to this day one of the distinctive elements of western life. Classical Greek thought tried to tame man and nature through reason.

Greek inventiveness and originality lay not in this or that political theory but in the invention of the scientific study of politics. Pre-Greek political thought had been a mixture of legend, myth, theology, and allegory (17). If there were an element of independent reasoning, it served as a means to a higher end, usually to be found in the tenets of a supernatural religious system. The contribution of Jewish thought to the political heritage of the world has been the idea of the brotherhood of man, a concept deeply rooted in monotheism. By contrast, polytheism made it difficult for the Greeks to see the basic oneness of mankind, and their religious pluralism reflected their inability to transcend, intellectually and institutionally, the confines of the city-state.

From a social point of view, the Judeo-Christian tradition was opposed to slavery on principle, a unique position in antiquity. It established a weekly day of rest, still unknown in many parts of the world, and it contained a host of protective rules in favor of workers, debtors, women, children, and the poor. The concept of *covenant*, first appearing in the agreement between God and Abraham, is a frequent theme in the Bible whenever momentous decisions were to be made. It was revived centuries later in the Puritan attempt to build a new religious and civil society, when President Woodrow Wilson, a devout Presbyterian, named the constitution of the League of Nations a covenant, and when President Bill Clinton baptized his legislative program in 1992 "a new covenant" between his administration and the American people.

However significant Judaic contributions to western civilization may be, they never were, nor were they meant to be, political science. They were political and social *ethics* rather than science, and as such constitute one of the three chief tributaries to the mainstream of western civilization, the other two being the Christian principle of *love* and the Greek principle of *rationalism*.

The first work that deserves to be called political science in that it applies systematic reasoning to political ideas and institutions is Plato's *Republic* (18). After almost twenty-four hundred years it is still matchless as an introduction to the basic issues that confront human beings as citizens. In order fully to understand the concerns of the *Republic*, however, it is first necessary to recount the immediate constitutional history of at least two Greek city-states, Sparta and Athens. The city-state, the *polis*, was a territory and a set of institutions of great variety in size, shape, and social and political organization. It was a community of citizens (adult males), citizens without political rights (women and children), and non-citizens (resident foreigners and slaves). The community lived under a written constitution, and it was independent of any outside authority. It occupied a defined area, often much larger than the city itself. Athens, for example, controlled the entire peninsula of Attica. Although the land at large may have been virtually empty of residents or occupied only intermittently by farmhouses, villages, or small towns, there was a single focal point around which religious, political, and administrative authority gathered. That was the city, the *polis* proper. It was usually fortified, and it always offered a market (an *agora*), a place of assembly, and a seat of justice and government, both executive and deliberative. The early city-state government tended to be either monarchic or aristocratic; the latter was usually oligarchic or democratic.

The sense of community was everything. By the classical period of the fifth and fourth centuries there were hundreds of federations of Greeks living around the shores of the Mediterranean "like frogs around a pond," as Plato put it. From the central sea of the Aegean with its island communities, and the coastal towns of Turkey and eastern and southern Greece, the colonies had spread to northern Greece, the Black Sea coast and southern Russia, to Sicily and southern Italy, and as far west as Provence, Spain, and North Africa (19). The Greeks said that living in a *polis* was the only form of civilized life.

Aspects of the social and economic life of the cities varied greatly from region to region. Some had large agricultural territories and serf populations. Others were heavily engaged in trade in raw materials such as corn, olive oil, dried fish, wine, metals, timber, slaves, or manufactured goods, either made on the spot or imported from other cultures. There was a huge outflow of Greek goods from such cities as Corinth and Thebes, and of skilled labor such as doctors, stonemasons, and professional mercenaries from Athens and Sparta. The functions of the cities varied greatly as well. Some were essentially fortresses. Others were founded on a religious shrine. Most had ports, and all had interior land and an administrative center. Plato in the *Laws* and Aristotle in the last two books of the *Politics* insisted that it was possible to discover an ideal city behind the multifariousness of the real Greek cities.

In his dialogues Plato portrays Athens in vivid detail as a world of young and godlike intellectuals meeting in private houses for conversation and social drinking, strolling in suburban parks or walking down to the Piraeus for a festival, listening to famous visitors skilled in rhetoric or philosophy (20). But when Plato was writing, Athens was fighting a long and bloody war in which at least half her population died, many of them from a particularly horrible plague which scarred even those who survived it. The plague was partly the consequence of the unsanitary conditions in which vast numbers of Athenian citizens were camped on every available yard of open land within the city walls. The way down to the Piraeus must have been as filthy, stinking, and crowded as the slums of Calcutta.

The *polis* was essentially a male association. Male citizens joined together in making and carrying out all decisions affecting the community. The origin of this phenomenon lay in military campaigns and the right of warriors to approve or reject the decisions of their leaders. The development of the *polis* was the extension of this practice of approval to all aspects of social life, with the partial exception of religion (21). Direct participation in making rational choices after discussion was the central political commitment of all Greek cities.

The organization theory behind the *polis* was related to natural and earlier forms of association. Anthropologists often call these associations kinship groups. Most Greek cities divided their citizens into hereditary tribes. Dorian cities traditionally possessed three tribes and Ionian cities four (22). The divisions were for military and political purposes, sanctioned by tradition and reinforced by specially organized state religious cults. A closer look at organization theory in Athens will illustrate.

In about 507, Cleisthenes, head of the great noble house that had supported Solon, the Alcmeonidae, took advantage of recently successful Spartan arms and political intrigue to offer a new socio-political structure to Attica that would serve it well for two hundred years. Cleisthenes changed the number of tribes from four to ten. The essence of the new system was the recognition that small local units, i.e., country villages, towns, and territorial wards of the city should control their own affairs independent of local aristocrats such as himself. For state purposes, these *demes*, as they were called, were grouped into larger coherent geographical blocks (with some gerrymandering), and it was from these blocks that the ten new tribes were constructed. Each tribe would have one block from the geographical regions called the Plain, the Coast, and the City. The army and all other parts of the administrative system, above all the Solonian Council, were based on the tribes. The Solonian council, the primary governing conclave, was composed of fifty representatives from each tribe, each tribal contingent serving as a standing committee of the whole council for one-tenth of the year.

Thus an Athenian *in his village* could make good use of whatever self-confidence he may have had. He could simultaneously develop a sense of nationality as the citizen of a city-state. Did Cleisthenes promote a change of attitude with his reforms or did he merely reorganize a change that had already occurred? Whatever the answer, he was wise enough not to tamper with existing social groups and their cherished cults. Instead he created a new organizational structure. The village or deme became an administrative unit (23), and the principle of *isnomia* was established. *Isnomia* was the condition in which final political authority was vested in the citizenry, and the city's fate was determined by majority vote.

Even more important to the ordinary Athenian citizen than local or central governmental organization was the phratry (*phratria*). This is the sole context in Greek of the important linguistic root common to most Indo-European languages found, for example, in the Celtic *brathir*, German *Bruder*, English *brother*, Latin *frater*, and French *frère*. In Greek it designates the non-familial type of brotherhood that originally was an aristocratic warrior band but became the larger social organization that dominated a citizen's life. The community, the *polis*, was a brotherhood. Each phratry worshipped a male and a female god. In Athens it was Zeus Phratrios and Athena Phratria. Annual festivals were held in honor of these gods and various rites of passage were observed in what the Greeks called the seasons of the soul. At an early age, for example, the young male Athenian was presented to the phratry by his father and relatives at the altar of Zeus Phratrios. Later, the acceptance of his first sacrifice signified his acceptance into the community. In adolescence he was again presented and dedicated his shorn hair to the god. The phratry then voted to admit him as a member and inscribed his name on the list of the brotherhood. It was also the phratry who witnessed the solemn betrothal ceremony that was the central public act of an Athenian marriage, and who celebrated the final consummation of the marriage with a feast paid for by the bridegroom. Thus the phratry was involved in all the main stages of a man's life and was the focal point of his daily activity. When in difficulty, when a man needed witnesses at law, for example, he turned first to his phratry.

Sparta had a similar theory of brotherhood but worked it out quite differently. The male citizen body was divided into *syssitia*, or mess groups, on which the entire social and military organization of the state rested. From the age of seven, boys were given a state-organized upbringing and brigaded into age groups. They lived communally from the age of twelve and were taught multiple skills useful to self-reliance and survival. The boys were provided with inadequate food and clothing to toughen them. At twenty they were officially inducted into their *syssitia*, where they had to live until the age of thirty. Even thereafter they were required to eat daily common meals in their mess groups, to which they contributed food from the land allotted to them and farmed under their supervision by state-owned slaves. The slaves were descendants of the original inhabitants of the Spartan territory, and they required constant suppression. The theoretical elegance of the Spartan social system and the way it built on traditional Greek customs much impressed ancient political thinkers and offered a counter-ideal to Athenian democracy (24).

Unlike Sparta, who froze her institutions, the other Greek cities were networks of associations in transition. There were aristocratic religious groups called *gennetai* who claimed descent from a common ancestor and monopolized the priesthoods of the more important city cults. There were drinking groups occasionally mobilized for political ends. There were groups associated with the various sporting complexes or *gymnasia* of the city. There were benefit clubs, burial clubs, and clubs associated with individual trades and activities. There were mystical sects and intellectual organizations such as Plato's Academy. The range of such associations is shown by the Athenian law relating to them: "If a deme or *phrateres* or worshippers of heroes or *gennetai* or drinking groups or funerary clubs or religious guilds or pirates or traders make rules amongst themselves, these shall be valid unless they are in conflict with public law."

The associations helped to create the sense of community and belonging that was the essential feature of the *polis*. The ties of kinship by blood were matched by multiple forms of political, religious, and social groupings, and of companionship for a purpose, whether it was voyaging, drinking, or burial. This conception of citizenship made civil war an even more poignant experience. When the democrats and oligarchs of Athens battled in 404 friend fought friend to the death.

In such a world it might be argued that multiple ties limited the freedom of the individual, and there is certainly a sense in which the conception of the autonomy of the individual apart from the community is absent from Greek thought. The freedom of the Greeks was public freedom, externalized in speech and action. It derived from the fact that the same man belonged to a deme, a phratry, a family, a group of relatives, and a religious association. Living in this complex world of conflicting groups and social duties, he nevertheless had the freedom to choose between their demands and so to escape any particular dominant form of social patterning. This explains the coexistence of the group mentality with the amazing creativity and freedom of thought in classical Athens. The freedom that results from belonging in many places is no less a freedom than that which results from belonging nowhere (25).

In many ways the Greek family is the key to Greek organization theory. It was monogamous and nuclear, being composed of a husband and wife with their children. But Greek writers tend to define the household as an economic unit and to regard other dependent relatives and slaves as part of it. The family fulfilled a number of social functions apart from economic ones. It was the source of new citizens. In the classical period the state established increasingly stringent rules for citizenship and thus for legitimacy. In Athens a citizen had to be the offspring of a legally recognized marriage between two Athenian citizens whose parents were also citizens. It became impossible for an Athenian to marry a foreigner and very difficult to obtain recognition for the children of any foreign liaison. This was a democratic ideal, the imposition of the social norms of the peasant majority on an aristocracy that had previously behaved very differently. The aristocracy had frequently married outside the community and determined its own criteria for legitimacy. Even the great Pericles, the author of the first citizenship laws, was forced to seek permission from the Assembly to legitimate his son by his Milesian mistress, Aspasia. Pericles had divorced his Athenian wife in 445, and his two sons by her had died of the plague during the Peloponnesian War. The Athenians granted legitimacy to Aspasia's son, but not without considerable debate.

Intimately connected with citizenship was the inheritance of property. Greek society in general did not practice primogeniture, the right of the eldest son to inherit. Rather, the property was divided equally by lot between all surviving sons, so that the traditional word for an inheritance was a man's *kleros* or lot. The Athenian family tended to be unstable for this reason, because each family survived only as long as its head. Athenian government was unstable for the same reason. Leaders were replaced virtually every year as new ones were selected by lot. The ideal was to keep government in the hands of amateurs and out of the hands of professional administrators. Government agencies would thus be more responsive to citizen demands. The lot could fall on any citizen, who, having served as Commissioner of Grains for one year, for example, was not subject to reelection to the same position.

Marriage was endogamous, within a close circle of relatives, in order to preserve family property from fragmentation. The Athenian family clearly served as a means of protecting and enclosing women (26). Women were citizens, with certain cults reserved to them and not available to foreign women, but women were citizens only for the purpose of marriage and procreation. Otherwise they lacked all independent status. They could not enter into any transaction worth more than one *medimnos* of barley, and they could not own any property with the exception of their clothes, jewelry, and personal slaves. At all times they had to be under the protction of a *kyrios*, or guardian. If they were unmarried the *kyrios* was their father or closest male relative; if married it was their husband; if widowed it was their son or other male relative by marriage or birth.

The two types of occasion when a woman could be involved in property transactions illustrate the nature of her protection. The first concerns the dowry. It was the duty of the *kyrios* to provide a dowry for all women in his family. The lack of a dowry demonstrated extreme poverty and might lead people to expect that no legal marriage had taken place. The formula in the betrothal ceremony was:

> I give this woman for the procreation of legitimate children.
> I accept.
> And (*e.g.*) three talents dowry.
> I am content.

Marriage was deemed to have taken place on receipt of the dowry. Although the dowry accompanied the woman, it did not belong to her. It was in the complete control of her husband. In the case of divorce or the death of the husband, however, it could be reclaimed along with the woman.

A woman could also be the carrier of property in the absence of a will and of male heirs. In this case the woman became an *epikleros*, or heiress. Her name was publicly proclaimed in the Assembly, and she and the property were adjudged to the closest male relative of the deceased who was prepared to marry her. It was often her paternal uncle.

A system of law and private property reflects the prejudices of the society that creates it. The Athenian attitude toward women was an effect of democracy (27). Aristocratic women had been freer in earlier times, but the coming of democracy meant the imposition of the social norms of the majority. Many peasant societies combine a high value placed on women with mistrust of them. Semonides of Amorgos in the sixth century described the appalling varieties of women that the gods had made to be a burden on men. Only one type is any good, and she is like the bee.

> She causes his property to grow and increase, and she grows old with a husband whom she loves and who loves her, the mother of a handsome and reputable family. She stands out among all women, and a godlike beauty plays around her. She takes no pleasure in sitting among women in places where they tell stories about love (28).

Such attitudes compound fear of the irrational and passionate nature of women with an exaggerated belief in their value and the importance of protecting them from the public eye. In agrarian societies these attitudes are held in check by the need for women's labor in the fields. With the advent of urban life women were confined to the house, and increased wealth brought with it aspirations to liberate them even from domestic duties. In a dialogue of Xenophon, Socrates confronts the problem of a friend who finds himself with fourteen female relatives living in his house. All of them were well brought up and therefore unused to any form of work. Socrates persuades his friend that he should nevertheless provide them with suitable work such as spinning. Their tempers will be much improved, says Socrates, although they will now complain of the idleness of their protector. But, concludes Socrates, his duty is to protect "as a sheepdog cares for the sheep" (29).

With the honorable exception of Plato, as we shall see, classical Greek philosophers agreed that women were less endowed with reason than men. Even Plato's celebrated student, Aristotle, could say, "the deliberative faculty is not present at all in the slaves, in the female it is inoperative, in the child undeveloped." The family is a natural relationship involving ruler and ruled and "as regards male and female this relationship of superior and inferior is permanent." It was left to the tragedians, however, to portray truly the predicament of women in Athenian society as repeatedly they made them the most powerful figures in Greek tragedy. Sophocles wrote for everywoman in classical Greece:

> But now outside my father's house I am nothing; yes, often I have looked on the nature of women thus, that we are nothing. Young girls, in my opinion, have the sweetest existence known to mortals in their fathers' homes, for innocence keeps children safe and happy always. But when we reach puberty and understanding, we are thrust out and sold away from our ancestral gods and from our parents. Some go to strangers' homes, others to foreigners', some to joyless houses, some to hostile. And all this, once the first night has yoked us to our husband, we are forced to praise and say that all is well (30).

It is not easy to come to terms with such attitudes toward women in Athenian society, if only because we idealize the Greeks as the originators of western civilization. We might remember, however, that the position of Athenian women was in most important respects similar to that of the two-hundred million women living today under Islam. The systematic mutilation of millions of young women in Africa through so-called female circumcision is another standing reminder of male fear of the feminine.

The consequences of these attitudes in Athens, combined with the importance placed on male social groupings, was to establish public life as the center of the *polis*. The balance in ancient Athens was shifted away from the family and towards the community, hence the magnificent festivals and displays and the great public buildings constructed both for religious and political purposes. The Athenian male spent his time in the *agora* surrounded by these buildings (31). In contrast, his home was mean and unimpressive. It was not safe in a democracy to exhibit a lifestyle different from that of other citizens. A man's life was lived in public not in private. Here lies the fundamental reason for the achievement of Athens in exemplifying the ideal type of the ancient city. The erosion of the family was the price paid for her success in escaping from the ties of tribalism and kinship to create a new type of social and political organization.

III. CONTEMPORARY GOVERNMENT IN THE GREEK WORLD

We have seen something of Plato's personal history and something of the societal norms in the midst of which he invented political science. Now we must pay closer attention to contemporary government in the Greek world. From the *Iliad* and the *Odyssey* an outline of governmental practice in early Greek city-states can be derived (32). There was a king and a series of sub-kings or nobles and a system of classes. The king consulted his leading subjects in council, and decisions were announced to the people assembled in the *agora*. Administration at the summit was still largely household administration carried out by a group of domestic servants with specific functions. These were supplemented by *therapontes*, a class of higher servants recruited from the noble families and arranged in ranks. Those at the top assisted the king in his religious duties, or as heralds representing him at public functions, carrying his scepter or insignia of power. The *therapontes* served at the royal feasts, acted as messengers endowed with royal power, convoked the council, made proclamations to the people, carried the royal orders in battle, and bore the royal authority on missions abroad. Junior *therapontes* were assigned lesser responsibilities such as control of the stables or armory. Thus the Homeric king had a group of ministers, not quite an administrative class, in his household based upon the tribe to which the individual minister belonged. Recruitment of the army and the provision of ships and supplies to meet public needs were all allocated according to tribe. Each tribe made its contribution as commanded by the king through tribal leaders who held their hereditary titles from the king (33).

By the beginning of the sixth century the Homeric kingship had declined in power. It survived only in Sparta where a curious system of two kings was devised, the kings representing the two royal houses out of which the state had emerged. The Spartan kings acted jointly and exercised a check upon each other. They wielded simultaneously the authority of high priest and army commander, though they lost most of their judicial power to the *gerousia*. An interesting exception was the kings' plenary judgment on all matters concerning public roads (34).

The *gerousia* was a council of elders consisting of the two kings and twenty-eight members of noble families over sixty years of age. Their selection was acclaimed in the *apella* (assembly) as the "prize of virtue." Every Spartan citizen over thirty years of age sat in the *apella* as a duty rather than a right. Day-to-day public administration was carried out by *ephors* (35).

The ephorate consisted of five citizens chose by lot, a process Aristotle called "excessively childish." The senior *ephor* gave his name to the Spartan year. As an administrative class *ephors* began as special assistants to relieve the kings of troublesome responsibilities beyond their personal control. Over the years they became guardians of the rights of the people, watching jealously over the conduct of the kings. They accompanied the kings on all official occasions and had the power to call them to account. Each month the *ephors* exchanged oaths with the kings, the king swearing to rule according to the city's established laws, the *ephors* swearing on behalf of the city to keep the king's position unshaken as long as he abided by his oath. The balance of obligation was clear. The *ephors* had general control over the kings' conduct, could prosecute the kings before the Spartan supreme court, and settled disputes between them. The *ephors* could enforce the kings' appearance before their board at their third summons. Two of them accompanied the kings on all military campaigns (36).

It would be wrong to interpret Spartan organization theory as a straightforward contest between kings on the one hand and *ephors* on the other. Though the latter combined executive, judicial, and disciplinary powers, and, unconstrained by written laws, dominated the everyday administration of affairs, every Spartan citizen knew that their office was held for one year only and that it was not renewable. The eligibility of all Spartans for the office meant a wide range of possible support for the monarch despite the popular, anti-aristocratic nature of the position. Finally, much of the time of the ephorate was spent on dealing with the indigenous and often rebellious *helot* serf population, over whom the ephorate exercised the arbitrary power of life and death (37).

The development of public administration in Athens took a different form. The important names in Athens on this subject are Draco, Solon, and Pisistratus. By about 630 the kings of the city-state of Attica were being replaced by tyrants, fringe members of the aristocracy who usurped power with the support of discontented members of the community, often democrats. Their popularity depended upon their ability to curb the power of other aristocrats and to build public works. Tyranny was not a special form of constitution, nor was it necessarily a reign of terror. The tyrant might rule directly, or he might retain existing political institutions but exercise a preponderant influence over how they worked. His rule could be benevolent or malevolent. Tyranny was given a bad name by Plato and especially by Aristotle, for whom it was the worst possible form of government (38).

Doing good by arbitrary methods never satisfied the Greeks. As early as 620 Draco put Athenian laws into writing. He established a constitution based on the franchise of hoplites, the citizens who made up the Greek heavy infantry in times of war. Draco's laws are known for the severity of their penalties. When asked why he specified death as the penalty for most offenses, he replied that small offenses deserved death and he knew of no severer penalty for great ones. The fourth century orator Demades said that Draco wrote his laws in blood instead of ink.

After just twenty-five years Draco's law code was drastically revised by Solon, elected chief magistrate of Athens in 594. Solon was a poet as well as a politician, and he did not like killing people. He could have made himself tyrant, but, as he wrote, "Tyranny is a very pretty position. The trouble is that there's no way out of it." Solon served as *archon*, the highest of three magisterial positions that had replaced the Athenian king while simultaneously he kept the idea of tyrant at bay. The other two positions were *basileus* or religious leader and judge in religious cases, and *polemarch*, judge in all cases involving non-citizens and commander-in-chief of the army. The *archon* was supreme judge in all civil cases and defender of the property rights of citizens (39). All three magistrates were elected annually. The selections were controlled by the Council of the Areopagus, or elders, in whose hands all governing power ultimately rested.

Solon laid the foundations of Athenian democracy. In his reforms citizens were to meet in the *ekklesia*, or general assembly, and henceforth participate in the election of the magistrates. All citizens were eligible to sit in a new popular court, the *heliaea*, which gradually took over all the judicial functions of the city. The Council of the Areopagus was deprived of its deliberative function and ceased to participate directly in both administration and legislation. It assumed the new role of protector of the constitution, with supervisory powers over the magistrates and censorial authority over citizens.

In the middle of the sixth century Attica was divided between those who lived along the coast, land that might be generating new wealth in the form of olive oil, for example, and the great outback. The interior was rich enough but geographically and culturally was far from the center of commerce. Its leader was Pisistratus, a blue-blood who understood economic development and who parlayed produce from the plain of Marathon and silver deposits from Attica's southeast corner into what can only be called a golden age of tyranny. From his consolidation of power in 546 until his death in 527 Pisistratus did more to encourage Athenians toward national unity, local pride, and individual dignity than any previous leader. He directed attention to the city of Athens as the population center of Attica, and there he built public works, temples, fountain-houses, and drains. Most important of all, he fostered the cult of the goddess Athena, patroness of Athens and of Pisistratus himself. He created national festivals and games, the Panathenaea, at which prizes were jars of Attic olive oil, and the Dionysia, where began one of Athens' greatest creations, the drama (40).

Pisistratus lent money to poor farmers and established a panel of itinerant judges to settle local disputes, previously in the hands of the local aristocrat. It is a paradox that an autocrat, a tyrant, could in fact promote individual freedom and dignity as much as Pisistratus did. Solon had opened government to new men but had done nothing to diminish the power of the aristocrat at the local level beyond robbing him of legalized mastery over the poor around him. Now the aristocrat had either died in the last battle against Pisistratus or thought it prudent to go into exile. Even if the aristocrat stayed, he knew he had to acknowledge the existence of someone more powerful than himself. The average citizen either lost his master or realized that the masters who were left did not matter as much as before. Such a realization was the first step towards being one's own master and towards citizenship in Plato's *Republic* as well as St. Augustine's *City of God*.

Following the defeat of the Persians at the great sea battle of Salamis in 480, the Greeks for a time achieved a high degree of unity (41). The unity was based on two factors directly related to organization theory:

1.   The Greeks learned that what they called barbarians, i.e., those who spoke a language other than Greek, were militarily inferior to Greek hoplites. The hoplite phalanx, later to be fully exploited by Alexander the Great, proved at Marathon that it could win against cavalry, archery, and any infantry formation thrown against it, however armed or brigaded. Hoplites formed a line eight men deep, helmeted, corsleted, and greaved, presenting a solid front of round shields. The shields were clamped on to the left arm of the hoplites by two grips while each hoplite thrust his spear forward. The phalanx won by cooperative weight and cohesion, victory lying with men who kept their order, did not break, and advanced in practiced unison. As the mid-seventh-century Spartan poet, Tyrtaeus, put it: "Stand near and take the enemy, strike with long spear or sword, set foot by foot, lean shield on shield, crest upon crest, helmet on helmet."

2.   Revised Athenian political institutions had created a population that fought willingly as free men, "fearing the laws more than Xerxes," as Demartus put it. A new political confidence inspired the Athenians as the old aristocratic control waned in an increasingly powerful Assembly. Aristotle illustrates the matter in his discussion of the curious institution of ostracism first used by the Athenians in the decade after Marathon (42). Ostracism was Cleisthenes' idea. The Assembly could decide every year to send one of the city's political figures into temporary ten-year exile without loss of property. The explicit reason for the first three ostracisms was suspicion of treachery in connection with the Persian invasion. Aristotle shrewdly observed that the courage to exercise such power is as significant as the occasion to exercise it. Appeasement was understood to be treason in unified Athens.

Mainland unity led to the Confederacy of Delos and hence to the Athenian Empire. The victory at Salamis taught the Athenians that supremacy at sea was the key to Greek security. Over two hundred cities thereafter joined a sea defense league. Some contributed ships, others money to build ships. The money was collected by ten *hellenotamiae* or "Treasurers of the Greeks," who were all citizens of Athens. The money was paid into the treasury at Delos where the council of the confederacy met to decide general policy. Each member state had one representative on the council, regardless of size, but Athens, by virtue of her wealth, influenced the votes of the smaller cities and dominated the confederacy. What began as a naval union developed into an empire. Gradually the other city-states were absorbed, leaving only the ship-contributing cities of Lesbos, Chios, and Samos with any real autonomy. In 454 the treasury of the confederacy was transferred to Athens, and Athenian overlordship became an accepted fact. The very idea of empire was anathema to the spirit of the Greeks, however, and within fifty years the Athenian Empire had ceased to be.

It was in the rejection of empire that Athens achieved her greatest glory. The period corresponded roughly with the life span of a single politician, the great orator Pericles (495–429). Plato lived in the generation immediately following Pericles and spent much of his intellectual energy contesting the influence of this charismatic figure and the administrative forms democracy took under his leadership of the Assembly in the years 443–429. Pericles was elected general every year during this fifteen year period, and Plutarch described him as "Athens' unchallenged leader." We must rely on Aristotle (384–322) for a description of Greek public administration during the Periclean Age (43).

The *Constitution of Athens* divided the most important public offices into two levels. In the top level were:

1.   the magistrates who were concerned with general control of the whole range of public life and responsible for convening and introducing matters to the Assembly;

2.   the generals who were charged with the defense of the city, including superintendence of the city gates and walls and the inspection and drill of citizens (44); and

3.   the financial officers, known variously as auditors, accountants, examiners, and advocates of the fisc (45), who received and audited the accounts of other officers.

At the second level of public office, described by Aristotle as "absolutely indispensable" were:

1.   the *agoranomos* who was charged with the care of the market place as well as the supervision of contracts and the maintenance of public order;

2.   the *astynomos*, or city manager, who was responsible for oversight of both public and private property in the center of the city plus the maintenance and care of buildings and roads;

3.   the *agronomoi* who were to protect the forests, superintend the city-state's boundaries, and prevent boundary disputes;

4.   the receivers of accounts, or treasurers, who received and held public revenues and disbursed moneys to the several departments of government;

5.   the public recorders who were concerned with the registration of private contracts and court decisions and the issuance of indictments; and

6.   the executors of sentences, the officials who served court decisions on citizens, took custody of prisoners, and recovered debts.

These magistrates constituted the executive management department of the city-state (46). At issue throughout the last half of the fifth century was whether these and other officers of the state should be elected or chosen by lot. Selection was usually by lot on the theory that the gods were more likely to make a wise selection than citizens. Great store was placed in the fact that the Greek magistrate was not a specialist, and that rotation in office every year insured responsiveness to citizen concerns. It gradually became customary, however, for certain offices with responsibilities of a high order to be elected. These were Treasurer of the Military Chest, Disburser of the Theatrical Dole, Curator of Fountains, and the *strategoi* or military commanders. Citizens chosen for diplomatic missions were also elected for the obvious reason that personality was an important factor in the mission's success.

There was a special class of officers who served the cult of civic deities. They went by various titles in different city-states, e.g., priest, superintendent of sacrifice, guardian of the shrine, and steward of religious property. Where it was the custom to conduct public sacrifice on the city's common hearth, the duty was assigned to an archon, or, where a king remained, to him as his chief remaining function under a mixed constitution.

As Plato was to lament, the system had serious flaws (47). One was that the magistrate's activities were subject to microscopic review at all times. It began with inquiry about his character and reputation at the time of his selection. At the examination, the *dokimasia*, he had to produce witnesses to attest to his character as well as present documents proving his adequate military service, payment of taxes, family conduct, and fulfillment of religious obligations. Any citizen could show cause before the court why the magistrate-elect should not be confirmed in his office. On relinquishing office the magistrate's conduct while in office and his accounts were subject to careful scrutiny by a special board whose report had to go to the courts either for specific charges to be laid or for discharge to be approved. Even if the magistrate were given a clean bill by the board, it was still possible for a citizen to bring charges in the Assembly and show why the discharge should not be granted. Given this continuous system of public inquest, it is hardly surprising that Plato characterized Greek public administration as unenterprizing (48).

Plato had other criticisms such as the payment of magistrates whom he thought should serve gratis as an act of civic obligation, and especially the payment of citizen-judges in the *heliaea*. He reserved his most stinging commentary on Athenian democracy for the expert speech writers and orators—sophists he called them—who were able to sway untutored judges and make justice a sometime thing. Plato was scandalized by the fact that slaves could be forced to give evidence before Athenian courts under torture. Such assessments drove him to write his two masterworks on political science, the *Republic* and the *Laws*.

IV. PLATO'S GREAT WORKS ON ORGANIZATION THEORY AND ADMINISTRATIVE PRACTICE

Not only Plato but other writers such as Aristotle, Thucydides, and Xenophon advanced a science of politics based on Greek organization theory and administrative practice. Plato alone set out to do nothing less than design an ideal society that would assure the good life for all its citizens. The *Republic* and the *Laws* are successive versions of his utopia.

The *Republic* was composed when Plato was about forty, the *Laws* in the last thirteen years of his life. He had not finished revising and editing the *Laws* when he died at age 81. So we have his views on statecraft at two very different stages of his life. The *Republic* was much influenced by the Spartan system. Leadership was to rest in the hands of philosopher-kings, citizenship was to be divided into classes resting securely on the inherent abilities of the individual, and children were to be educated—perhaps indoctrinated is a better word—so as to develop effectively within the sphere to which they had been called. In the *Laws* the realities of life overtook Plato, and his ideal state was then closer to earth. His philosopher-kings, originally conceived in the plural, were changed into a philosopher-king in the singular. Plato was deeply affected by the failure of his personal missions to Syracuse to persuade the tyrant Dionysius to adopt the principles of the *Republic*. His new scheme attempted to combine the virtues of monarchy and democracy in a mixed polity (49).

A.   The Republic

The *Republic* comes down to us with a double title: *The State*, or, in Latin, *respublica*, whence the name by which it is generally known, and *Or Concerning Justice*. While it is obviously a treatise on political science and jurisprudence, it is considerably more than that. It is an attempt at a complete philosophy of man. It is concerned with man in action, and it is therefore occupied with the problems of moral and political life. But man as a whole cannot be understood apart from his thinking, says Plato, so the *Republic* is also a philosophy of man in thought and of the laws of his thinking. The *Republic* forms a single and organic whole (50). The question which Plato set himself to answer was simply this: what is a good man, and how is a good man made? Such a question might belong only to moral philosophy, but to the Greek a good man must be the citizen of a state. Upon the first question, therefore, a second naturally followed: what is a good state, and how is a good state made? Moral philosophy thus ascended into political science. The quest does not end there, however. To a follower of Socrates it was plain that a good man must be possessed of knowledge. A third question therefore arose: what is the ultimate knowledge of which a good man must be possessed in order to be good? That is for metaphysics to answer. When metaphysics has given its answer, still a forth question emerged. By what methods will the good state lead its citizens towards the ultimate knowledge which is the condition of virtue? To answer this question a theory of education is necessary. Plato thought that if his scheme of education were to work satisfactorily, a reconstruction of social life must also be attempted, and a new economics must reinforce the pedagogy (51).

The *Republic* is written in the imperative mood, not to analyze but to warn and counsel. It is in many respects a polemic directed against current teachers and the practices of contemporary politics. The teachers against whom it is directed are the younger generation of sophists, of the type Plato had already portrayed in the *Gorgias*. They and not Socrates, in Plato's view, were the true corrupters of the youth of Athens by the lectures they gave and the training in politics they professed to give. They had preached a new ethics, or "justice," of self-satisfaction. They had revolutionized politics by making the authority of the state a means to the self-satisfaction of its rulers.

Plato made a strong case against democracy in the *Republic*. Interestingly enough, the origins of Plato's disenchantment with democracy went back to the funeral orations of Pericles, who died the same year Plato was born in 429. By the time of Athen's prolonged war against Sparta in the middle of the fifth century (the Peloponnesian War), democratic institutions had been nearly perfected. An Assembly of the people deliberated, with all Athenians who were citizens participating. The selected leader who ruled over and governed the Assembly was first among equals. His position was not a permanent leasehold but a temporary obligation and honor. All citizens could speak freely in the Assembly as part of the law-making process (52).

Pericles used the occasion of the burial of Athenian war dead to offer paeans to Athenian democracy. Later democrats embraced his efforts as the most splendid examples of epideictic oratory on record (53). In ancient democracy words reigned supreme, particularly those spoken before one's fellow citizens. Classics scholar Nicole Loraux goes so far as to say that Athenian democracy was "invented" through rhetoric, particularly the funeral oration, a practice peculiar to Athens. "In and through the funeral oration," she writes, "democracy becomes a name to describe a model city" (54).

Pericles used the solemn ritual of burying the war dead in the struggle against Sparta to do more than honor those who "shall not have died in vain," in the words of Abraham

Lincoln's *Gettysburg Address*. He used his orations to define and refine Athenian democracy and to explain why sacrifice in her name was a noble and worthy thing Pericles emphasized the uniqueness of Athens, not just its constitution and laws but also the qualities of mind and the habits of thought that defined what it meant to be an Athenian. Unlike the Spartans, the Athenians were not forced by painful discipline to conform. Rather, they were self-conscious citizens and patriots who chose the city over their own lives. One can imagine mothers and fathers gathered to bury their beloved sons hearing Pericles proclaim:

> Our constitution is called a democracy because power is in the hands not of a minority but of the whole people. When it is a question of settling private disputes, everyone is equal before the law; when it is a question of putting one person before another in positions of public responsibility, what counts is not membership of a particular class, but the actual ability which the man possesses (55).

These democratic sentiments ran counter to the traditional Greek outlook which from Homer onward had divided men into high and low, good and bad, worthy and unworthy. Tradition held that it is through the acceptance of such distinctions, the recognition that all men are *not* equal, that peace and harmony in the community are to be maintained. The conventions had weakened during the last decades of the fifth century, and Plato wanted to restore them. To this extent his political thinking can be called reactionary, but in a more profound sense it was revolutionary. Although of high birth and wealthy family himself, Plato rejected birth or property as the ground for discrimination. He followed Socrates in seeking a new basis for political power in the inner character and mentality of men themselves. Socrates had held that true wisdom, the right use of reason, was the hallmark of quality among human beings, not possessions or noble blood or the pretended knowledge of those usually regarded as wise. Plato carried this view further by molding it into a coherent picture of human society based not on tradition or convention but on nature and reality as a whole.

Several strands of thought were interwoven in the formation of the patterns of human society as Plato saw it. One was the idea of differences in natural aptitude, easily recognizable since many skills were obviously handed down from father to son. In the *Republic* natural aptitude is the foundation for the division of labor and the creation of a professional army from those innately fitted for soldiering. The distinction between philosophers, men of true wisdom, and the rest of the community is justified by their inborn aptitude for reason and thought.

A second feature of Plato's approach to social patterns and organization theory is his view of individual psychology. He says the *psyche* is made up of three elements: appetite, spirit, and reason. Men fall into natural divisions according to the predominance of one or the other of these elements in their make-up (56).

The most important feature of all, however, is the relation which Plato sees between human groupings and their metaphysical thought. Just as there is a great gulf between the forms known to the mind and the appearances perceived by the senses, between the dark cave of illusion where we live and the bright realm of knowledge to which a few may escape, there is a deep division between "those who can appreciate the eternally immutable and those who lose their way amidst multiplicity and change" (57).

With an innate fitness for the task of *knowing*, guided by the reasoning element within him, and lifted above ordinary humanity by his vision of the highest truth, Plato's wise man is thus *by nature* distinct from all others. He is made of gold. Lesser men are made of silver, and still lesser ones of iron and brass. Thus the ideal state is divided into three classes: the rulers, the fighters, and the working population, e.g., farmers, merchants, craftsmen, and laborers. Each of these has its appointed function, and each concentrates entirely upon the discharge of its function. Government, defense, and sustenance—the three necessary functions of the state—are made into professions and assigned to professional classes. It is only with the governing and fighting classes that Plato is really concerned. He shares the bias against labor and business that seems to be characteristic of aristocrats in all ages. The regulation of the economic order in the *Republic* illustrates the contempt of the nobleman for the prosaic existence of those who must work for a living. They are only interested in appetite, the desire to fulfill material wants.

The rulers (called guardians) and fighters (called auxiliaries) must be trained for their work by every means available to the state (58). The social system surrounding these privileged classes must include material as well as spiritual things. Plato suggests a system of communism so ordered that it will set the time and the minds of the guardians and auxiliaries free from material cares. He deprives both the administration and the army of private property, thus consecrating them to their public duties.

One of the two points at which the *Republic* is most suggestive for modern public administration is in the threefold class division that distinguishes the functions of ruling and administering the state from all other crafts. The main difference between the philosopher-rulers and the producers in the *Republic* is that between *political wisdom* and *technical knowledge*. Only the philosophers have insight into human problems, and that insight is more than specialized learning. The craftsman, by contrast, including perhaps the quantitative analyst, the statistician, the computer information specialist, and the media relations expert in our own day, may have no comprehensive understanding of the purpose of the state or its administrative agencies. He has limited knowledge of a technical nature. Technical, procedural, and instrumental knowledge is advisory knowledge, says Plato, and not policy making knowledge (59).

The other point of direct applicability to modern public administration, indeed to all political life in the United States, is Plato's excoriation of rhetoricians. His political argument against democracy is stark and simple. It deteriorates into license as people do whatever they want, whenever something much lower in Plato's ranking of human possibilities than "the spirit" moves them. All sorts of unchecked dispositions are given free rein, and they are encouraged by those who manipulate through rhetorical speech. They take over the souls of the young, at whatever chronological age the young reside. Ideologues confuse the simple minded and call forth the basest motives and fears of their fellow citizens. Of the rhetoricians—he would have included the political advertising consultants and campaign managers of our day—Plato said:

> Once they have emptied and purged [the good] from the soul of the man whom they are seizing . . . they proceed to return insolence, anarchy, wastefulness, and shamelessness from exile, in a blaze of light, crowned and accompanied by a numerous chorus, extolling and flattering them by calling insolence good education; anarchy, freedom; wastefulness, magnificence; and shamelessness, courage (60).

Plato sharply divides rhetoric from dialectic and opinion from knowledge. The high-minded search for truth looks nothing like the forensic feats of Thrasymachus in the Athenian Assembly (61). Plato's dialectic of knowledge is set up in opposition to a democratic rhetoric of persuasion. He calls sophists, who plied rhetoric professionally, panderers. In the Platonic dialogue that bears the name of the rhetorician Gorgias, Socrates maneuvers Gorgias into declaiming that speech making is not concerned with helping the "sick"—the vast multitude to whom Plato's physician would bring philosophic and political health—learn how to live in order to be well. Rather, it involves only freedom for oneself, the power of ruling by convincing others to concur in one's argument. Gorgias is trapped by Socrates into admitting that oratory is not about right or wrong but mere persuasion, a "spurious counterfeit of a branch of the art of government"—the branch known as democracy (62).

In Plato's scheme of things democracy contains no authentic or meaningful speech, only the babble of the ignorant. The ignorant are stuck in mere opinion and frequently give in to base instinct. Hope lies with what Plato called "the more decent few" who can master desire. The more decent few—the guardians—must forbid speeches about the gods and expunge all tall tales of ancient heroes, for poetry inflames the many. Plato found Homer, Hesiod, and other masters of Greek literature opprobrious and corrupting. Toward the end of the *Republic* he presents the conclusion that "all poetry, from Homer onwards, consists in representing a semblance of its subject, whatever it may be, including any kind of human excellence, with no grasp of reality." In fact, the artist is assigned a place below the shoemaker or smith, because these craftsmen have at least a limited *direct* knowledge of reality, whereas the artist "knows nothing worth mentioning about the subjects he represents." Art, therefore, "is a form of play, not to be taken seriously." Because the poet, by appealing to sentiment rather than reason, "sets up a vicious form of government" in the individual soul, "we shall be justified in not admitting him into a well-ordered commonwealth (63).

The ruler must occasionally lie for the benefit of the city. Plato often compares rulers to doctors, and the ruled to patients, and he says that "for a private person to mislead the rulers we shall declare to be a worse offense than for a patient to mislead his doctor." He attacks such crimes as "fatal" and "subversive" in a state. Though the ruled are under no circumstances permitted to deviate from the truth, particularly in their relations with the rulers, the latter may lie "in the way of a medicine." Just as a medicine may be handled only by a doctor, "if anyone, then, is to practice deception, whether on the country's enemies or on its citizens, it must be the rulers of the commonwealth, acting for its benefit; no one else may meddle with this privilege." (64)

The achievement of a just state, a perfect anti-democracy, requires the creation of such a powerful, all-encompassing bond between individuals and the state that all social and political conflict disappears, discord melts away, and the state comes to resemble a single person, a fused, organic entity.

Private marriage, family life, and child rearing, at least for the guardian class, must be put away. The guardians must have no competing loyalties other than their wise devotion to, and rule over, the city. A systematic meritocracy must prevail in which children are organized and characterized as raw material to be turned to the good of the unified city. A child from the lower orders of society, those stuck in the mire of ignorance, may perchance show discernible sparks of future wisdom. If so, that child must be removed from his or her parents, "without the smallest pity," and trained to be one of the brightest and best. Plato's explicit purpose with this social engineering is to prevent the emergence of hereditary oligarchies and to ensure the continuation of rule by a natural elite. A system of eugenics is devised among his guardians to match up males and females with the most likely mates to produce vigorous, healthy offspring. Immediately after birth, a baby is removed from the biological mother and sent to a central nursery where its rearing is entrusted to experts (65).

In the *Republic* we find the prototypical anti-democratic fear, that things will easily fall apart if a city is anything but organically united. Scattered throughout the treatise are words that evoke a sense of chaos and disintegration: asunder, destroy, dissolves, overwhelms, splits, evil. Other terms are designed to prevent the anarchy that democracy leads to: dominate, censor, expunge, conform, bind, make one. For Plato every conflict is a potential cataclysm. Every discussion in which differences are stated is a threat portending disintegration. Every sally is an embryonic struggle unto death. Every distinction is a possible blemish on the canvas of harmonious and unsullied order (66).

Plato seeks "a rest from trouble." In perhaps the most famous passage of the *Republic* he says that unless either philosophers become kings or kings become philosophers trouble will continue.

> Until philosophers are kings, or the kings and princes of this world have the spirit and power of philosophy, and political greatness and wisdom meet in one, and those commoner natures who pursue either to the exclusion of the other are compelled to stand aside, cities will never have rest from their evils,—no, nor the human race, as I believe,—and then only will this our state have a possibility of life and behold the light of day (67).

The harmony that results from joining politics with philosophy produces a unique kind of pleasure for him or her who does the joining. The knowledge of the real that wisdom embraces is finally an aesthetic experience that is infinitely more rewarding than power. Beauty is stronger than power, and they who attain it will never make trouble again (68).

B.   The Laws

The *Laws* is not only the longest of Plato's writings, but it also contains his latest and most mature thought on the subjects that he held most dear to his heart all his life—ethics, education, and jurisprudence. The purpose of the *Laws* is severely practical and does not appeal to readers who care more for metaphysics and science than for morals and politics. More than any other work of Plato, the *Laws* stands in direct relationship to the political life of the age in which it was composed. It is meant to satisfy a pressing felt need.

In the last twenty years of Plato's life it was becoming more and more obvious that the old city-states which had been the centers of Hellenic spiritual life had had their day. Athens herself had become a second-rate power. Sparta had been crushed by the brilliant successes of Epaminondas, who established Thebes as the predominant power in Greece for a generation (69). Meanwhile the very existence of Hellenic civilization continued to be threatened by the encroachment of Persia in the east and Carthage in the west. We know now that the historical solution to the problem was to be provided by the rise of the Macedonian monarchy and the achievements of kings Philip and Alexander. But the work of Philip was only beginning in Plato's last years.

The occasion of the *Laws* was the founding of new Greek cities in the Mediterranean basin and the refounding of old ones. Epaminondas, for example, built Megalopolis as the new center for Arcadia and restored Messene. According to Greek tradition the first thing to be done in such a situation was to provide the new or revised community with a complete constitution and fundamental law. The accepted practice was to summon experts in politics as advisers in the task. In the fifth century Pericles had employed Protagoras in this way, to give advice on the laws to be made for Thurii, for example. In the fourth century Plato's Academy was constantly being asked for consultants to do the same sort of work (70). The Academy was recognized as the society of experts in jurisprudence. Hence it was desirable that men anticipating being called upon to legislate should be provided with an example of the way in which the work should be done. The *Laws* is Plato's example.

The marks of old age are written obvious throughout the *Laws*. Like Prospero in *The Tempest*, the last of Shakespeare's plays, Plato has come to feel that the men who play their part in the "unsubstantial pageant" of life are

> such stuff
> As dreams are made of.

Plato says that "man in his fashion is a sort of plaything of God, and this, in truth, is the best of him." (71) He has come to feel that God is everything and that man is very little. There is forgetfulness in the *Laws*, and there is less artistic power than in the rest of Plato's work. He virtually abandons the dialogue and makes the *Laws* a monologue by an Athenian stranger in the presence of two patient, and generally polite, listeners—a Cretan and a Spartan. In reading the *Laws* one has to remember that Plato believed discourse should wander with the argument (72).

The first two books of the *Laws* deal with song and dance and wine and their place in education. Plato writes with great psychological insight about the moral influence of music on character and the victory over self that is involved in the proper use of wine. He rejects the Spartan view that wine should be avoided. The seductions of pleasure must be faced in the convivial use of wine, says Plato, just as the Spartans taught valor by exposing the young to pain and peril. The better half of valor is mastery over one's desires, and the true way to master temptation is to stand up to it, not to make its occurrence artificially impossible.

The third book treats the historical development of states. Plato reconstructs prehistory, having man move from the nomad to the agricultural state, and from the life of the family group to that of the city. He has a vivid sense of the enormous lapses of time and the numerous changes that must have gone to the making of society before historical records began. Alone among the Greeks, he has a genuine sense of how recent the historical period of human life is. For the theory of politics, Book III enunciates the principle of the division of sovereign power. Sovereignty must combine the "popular" element with "something of personal authority," and it must unite "monarchy" and "freedom." There must be a seat of authority somewhere, wrote Plato, but authority must not degenerate into regimentation. The individual must be free, but his or her freedom must not be anarchial (73).

Book IV is the prolegomena of politics. The first lesson in practical constitution-making is to be well informed about the topography, climate, and economic resources of the state for which we are to legislate, as well as the character of its inhabitants. Plato wants his territory to be varied, containing arable, pasture, and woodland, but the land should not be extremely fertile. If it is too fertile, production for the foreign market would be encouraged. The city should be some miles from the sea, though there should be a place in its territory that would make a good harbor. The city-state must be self-supporting and independent of imports. It should not have easy access to the sea, the great highway of commerce. The spirit of the community must not be commercialized. This is the first principle of a good constitution (74).

The next four books are concerned with the construction of a constitution, including a system of education and social relations to be based on law and to come next in order of excellence to that outlined in the *Republic*. Book V establishes the first rule of the constitution, that of self-reverence. The soul is more than the body, and the body is more that its possessions. A man must prize his soul more than his body and his body more than his goods. The second rule is that we cannot expect men regularly to choose the noble life unless they are persuaded that it is also the most pleasant. Plato contends that even by the rules of Hedonic calculus, if one only states the rules correctly and works the sum right, and morally best life will be found to be also the most pleasant (75).

Book V argues that the size of the community, the number of households, must be kept permanent. If the population grows beyond the number the territory can support, it will begin to expand at the cost of wrong to its neighbors. If the population falls below a certain number, it will not be adequate for its own defense. The actual number of households will depend on the size of the territory, but Plato imagines it fixed at 5,040, a number divisible by all integers up to 10. This number is practical, says Plato, because it facilitates the division of inhabitants into administrative groups (76).

Once the idea of administration is thus introduced in Book V Plato then devotes Book VI to the appointment of various magistrates and administrative boards. The most important magistracy is that of the guardians of the constitution, a body of thirty-seven men of approved character and intelligence who must be at least fifty years old at the time of appointment and who must retire at the age of seventy. Their functions are to watch over the interests of the laws in general and in particular to take charge of the register of properties and penalize any citizen guilty of fraudulent concealment of income. They also preside at the trial of grave offenses. They are elected by votes given in writing and signed with the voter's name. The election has several stages by which three hundred names are first selected and finally reduced to thirty-seven, three for each tribe with an odd man to prevent an equal division of opinions.

The most important administrative board is the Board of Education, followed closely in prestige by the Board of Family Life. The latter assures that marriage is regarded as a solemn duty to society. It is the duty of married couples, for example, to present the city with worthy offspring. There is a third board, the Board of Ladies, charged with supervising the behavior of married couples and advising them about conception. The board will have general control over married people for ten years after marriage, and it will treat its responsibilities from both a eugenic and moral point of view. If a marriage remains childless after ten years the Board of Ladies will arrange for dissolution on equitable terms. It will also act as conciliator in conjugal disputes (77).

The seventh book of the *Laws* contains Plato's most important and detailed scheme for universal education. The level of educational demands has risen from the *Republic*. The task of education must begin before a child is born. An expectant mother must take whatever exercise is required in the interest of her unborn child (78). A baby should be sung to in order to keep it from being frightened. It is a bad moral beginning for the child to be allowed to become fitful or passionate. Children should be left to invent their own games, but from the age of three they should be brought together daily in the various temples to play under the supervision of women appointed by the Board of Ladies. These women will have the opportunity to see if the nurses are bringing up their charges in the way the state expects (79). At the age of six lessons will begin in earnest, and with them the segregation of girls from boys. Both genders, however, are to be taught to ride and use the bow, sling, and dart. Care should be taken to train the children to be ambidextrous. It is of great practical importance, says Plato, to have two right hands.

Then Plato launches into a long discussion of the importance of music in one's education. It produces both mood and character, he says, and each type of musical form permitted in the state must be consecrated "as to the culture of a god." It is one of the most important functions of the Board of Education to see that "wailing" is not permitted and that blasphemy in music is punished. Musicians must feel that their work is prayer.

For the first time in western education Plato conceives of secondary schools with proper buildings and grounds. The teachers in these schools will have to receive salaries, and therefore they must be foreigners. The Minister of Education must be especially careful to select sound prose works for reading on morals and law. The main curriculum was to be made up of what Plato termed "the three branches of knowledge," i.e., arithmetic, geometry, and astronomy. We must remember that until Plato's dialogues and Aristotle's treatises were written most of the prose literature in the fourth century consisted of scientific discourses by the Ionians, particularly technical writing on medicine.

Book VIII provides for the culture of the state. Every month of the year and every day of the month is given its appropriate worship. The object of Book VIII is to place the whole of daily life in the community under a religious sanction. There will be gymnastic and musical contests as part of the state's regular worship. Plato lays down regulations for monthly exercises of the citizen militia as well as for special festivals. The militia training will include strength and endurance contests with "real military value." Mimic warfare must reflect actual warfare as closely as possible, with the spice of real danger about it. Girls and women must share in the drills, "so far as their physique permits" (80).

Books IX through XII are the heart of the *Laws* and represent the finest writing in the Platonic corpus. The ninth book contains the criminal code of the ideal constitution, the tenth is "the book of the law of religion," in which Plato discusses the principles of true religious belief and fixes the penalties for the crime of heresy, the eleventh deals with legislation for the security of private property and trade, and the twelfth returns to public and civil law in ways reminiscent of the idealism of the *Republic*.

The crimes in the criminal code of Book IX, in order of their gravity, are sacrilege, treason, and parricide. Plato says that perpetrators of these capital crimes must die. The laying down of a capital sentence must not penalize the criminal's innocent family by the confiscation of its property, however, and the family's honor must not be tainted by the criminal's offense. The code distinguishes violation of rights from the causation of damage, and in the case of the former, it distinguishes between violence and craft. Plato lists regulations and penalties for the cases of homicide, suicide, maiming, wounding with intent to kill, and minor assaults. The penalties depend both on the main distinctions laid down for each case, and the status of the parties, whether citizen, alien, or slave (81).

In Book X we see the theology of Platonism. Without it the theology of the early Christian church would be unintelligible, the neo-Platonist creedal statements of early Christianity would be the curious professions of a mystery religion, and the administrative practices of the medieval papacy might be understood only as the baptized procedures of the Roman imperium (82). Plato was at once the creator of natural theology and the first thinker to propose that false theological belief should be treated as a crime against the state and repressed by the civil magistrate (83). Plato was convinced that there are certain truths about God that can be strictly demonstrated, and that the denial of these truths leads to bad living. The three heresies Plato regards as morally pernicious are, in order of their moral turpitude: (a) atheism, the belief that there are no gods at all, the least offensive of the three, (b) Epicureanism, the doctrine that God is indifferent to human conduct, and (c) worst of all, the doctrine that an impenitent offender can escape God's judgment by gifts and offerings. It is morally less harmful to believe that there is no God than to believe in a careless God, and it is better to believe in a careless God than a venal one. Against these three heresies Plato holds that he can prove the existence of God, the reality of the providential and moral government of the world and man, and the impossibility of bribing the divine justice. In pursuing his proofs Plato attains a height of argument not far removed from the greatest of the Hebrew prophets (84).

Book XI establishes regulations to prevent dishonesty in buying and selling, as well as procedures for writing and executing wills, caring for orphans, disinheriting a son, and enforcing the proper supervision of the insane and mentally deficient. Rules are laid down about the admission of evidence in courts of law and the penalties for perjury. Litigiousness, a common Athenian failing, should be checked by penalizing the vexatious prosecutor. If his motive was gain, the penalty should be death (85). What the Romans called the commercial law of the first part of Book XI had a considerable influence on the development of Roman commercial law.

With the twelfth and final book of the *Laws* we return to the sphere of public law and the law of the constitution. Embezzlement of public funds, an offense regularly charged against every Attic politician by his enemies, is unpardonable in Book XII and in a citizen must be punished by death, regardless of the magnitude of defalcation (86). To ensure that magistrates do their duty, Plato adopts the ancient Attic practice of requiring every public administrator at the end of his term of office to submit to an audit, giving special care to the appointment of the board charged with conducting the audit.

Plato concludes that it is not enough to have made a good constitution for the virtuous society. There is a need for constant vigilance to preserve governmental institutions from degeneration. This vigilance will be exercised by the "nocturnal council," so called from the stipulation that its daily sessions are to be held before daybreak. Officially called the Committee of Public Safety, these twenty to thirty men are the brain of the constitutional system (87). To discharge its functions the council must have a thorough understanding of the end to which all social life is directed. Its members will require much more in the way of education than anyone else in the community. Really to understand what goodness is, they must be able to see "the one in the many" and to appreciate and realize the great truth of the unity of all virtues (88). They must have genuine knowledge of God and the ways of God.

Finally, the men who are the intellect of the state must thoroughly understand the natural theology laid down in Book X. Scientific astronomy with its doctrine of the regularity and order of celestial motions is the chief foundation of the whole Platonic *apologia* for ethical theism. A complete knowledge of astronomy is indispensable for any member of the nocturnal council. When astronomical knowledge is combined with insight into the true nature of the soul as the one source of movement, it leads directly to piety. Then the guardian grasps the principle of the causal priority of soul in the scheme of things. This mention of the guardian brings us back full circle to the *Republic* (89).

As a younger man Plato had believed in the free rule of a personal intelligence duly trained for its work. He had hoped to train such intelligence himself along the lines propounded in the *Republic* and pursued in the practical curriculum of the Academy. At Syracuse he had seemed to find his opportunity. He could show the value of philosophy by turning a young tyrant into a philosopher-king and pointing the way for the salvation of Greece. He failed. Casting about for another way, he concluded that if he could not train a philosophic ruler who could rule without law, then he would make law itself philosophic. He would still be turning philosophy to practical account, which was always the thought dearest to his heart. Thus the law-state, combined with a mixed constitution, came to be the dominant political idea of Plato's later years. In the end he returned to the traditional

Greek idea of the rule of law, an idea against which he had forcefully rebelled most of his life. In the most splendid irony of classical antiquity, its most brilliant mind finally had to give up the project of substituting mind itself for the laws it makes. Man is indeed the plaything of the gods.

V. THE SOUL IN GREEK POLITICAL THEORY

Greek political theory is distinctive in its focus on the soul. All the major Greek thinkers, led by Plato, held that one cannot reflect well upon political institutions without first reflecting, about human flourishing and the psychological structures that facilitate or impede it (90). Their ideas about virtue, education, and passion are integral to their political theory, since they hold that a just city can only be achieved by emotionally balanced and virtuous individuals. Institutions in turn also shape the souls of individuals and their possibilities for flourishing.

Ideas about the soul and political theory have re-entered modern literature in a powerful way (91). Many organization theorists are fascinated by the fact that the Greek word for soul, *psyche*, also means *butterfly*. The soul can take flight. In the *Odyssey* Homer speaks of the soul "flitting out like a dream and flying away." Depth psychologists such as Sigmund Freud and Carl Jung tell us, however, that the individual soul can only flourish, and organizations can only flourish, when the soul occasionally flies to the underworld to see where the deeper part of the self resides. We do not like to do that. Jung writes: "The dread and resistance which every natural human being experiences, when it comes to delving too deeply into himself, is, at bottom, the fear of the journey to Hades" (92).

Yet Hades is where our collective past and our multiple selves still live during much of the year before, with Persephone, we rise to the spring. We are obliged to confront the shadows there and perhaps suffer the kind of defeat that Plato suffered at Syracuse. The cost of refusing to go to Hades or Syracuse can be severe. The idea of utopia may have to suffer disillusionment before we can construct the laws that give us comfort in the natural rhythms of life. Plato himself endured such a disillusionment, but then his butterfly flew to Olympus.

NOTES

1. Greek words as commonly translated in English will occasionally be referenced so that the reader might associate the other contexts in which the same Greek idea has entered modern discourse. In Jungian psychology, for example, *psyche* has its own particular meaning, i.e., the totality of all psychological processes, both conscious and unconscious. Likewise the Latin translation of soul or *psyche*, i.e., *anima*, has itself become a metaphor in analytic psychology meaning the inner feminine side of a man, or, with its masculine ending, *animus*, the inner masculine side of a woman. Together *anima* and *animus* become what Jung calls the soul-image, or the representation, in dreams and other products of the unconscious, of the inner personality, usually contrasexual. The Hebrew version of soul, *psyche*, and *anima* is *nephesh*, literally translated "hot blood coursing through one's veins," with the suggestion that understanding historical activity, both by God and man, is the key to the meaning of life.
2. In current leadership writing one finds such book titles as *Leading With Soul* (Bolman and

Deal, 1995); *Gods of Management*, (Handy, 1995); and *Synchronicity: The Inner Path of Leadership* (Jaworski, 1996).

3. One of the results of the Waldo Symposium held at the Maxwell School of Citizenship and Public Affairs, at Syracuse University, June 27–30, 1996, was the observation by several of the eighty-two scholars present that history should be taken more seriously by American public administrationists. This essay is one effort in that direction.

4. Platonists have found allies they did not expect among modern chaos theorists, who insist that order always underlies chaos. There are "strange attractors," argues Margaret Wheatley, for example, which draw random movements into unseen regularities. The computer modeling of assembled strange attractors, first demonstrated in weather systems, can create images of great beauty, thus illustrating Plato's identification of the rational and the beautiful. See Margaret J. Wheatley, *Leadership and the New Science* (San Francisco: Berett-Koehler, 1992); James Gleick, *Chaos, Making a New Science* (New York: Penguin, 1987); John Briggs and F. David Peat. *Turbulent Mirror* (New York: Harper and Row, 1989). And remember Alexander Pope's signal lines from *Windsor Forest* (1713):

    > Not chaos-like, together crushed and bruised
    > But, as the world harmoniously confused:
    > Where order in variety we see,
    > And where, though all things differ, all agree.

5. Carl J. Friedrich, "Greek Political Heritage and Totalitarianism," *Review of Politics*, II, April, 1940, pp. 218–225.

6. Karl R. Popper, *The Open Society and Its Enemies*, Princeton, New Jersey: Princeton University Press, 1950, p. 195.

7. All subsequent dates unless otherwise noted will be BCE, Before the Common Era.

8. Plato never married. He remained devoted to his mother as long as she lived. She was still alive as late as 366 when Plato was 62 and returning to Athens from his latest adventure in Syracuse. Since Socrates became the leading character in Plato's philosophical dramas, the Dialogues, and given the fact that Socrates never wrote anything, there has been a good deal of debate about how much in Plato's writings is his own and how much is a record of the actual thought of the historical Socrates. The argument is futile. There can be no doubt that Plato's insight was profoundly conditioned by Socrates, but, given the creative genius and imagination of Plato, it is likely that Plato himself would not be able to say where Socrates left off and Plato began. The Socrates of Plato and the Socrates of history are a double star which I believe not even the spectrum analysis of the latest philology can ever resolve.

9. For these and other observations about Plato and his thought, the author is indebted to the work of F. M. Cornford, Benjamin Jowett, Whitney J. Oates, A. E. Taylor, and especially his teacher at Columbia University, John Herman Randall.

10. Despite the cultural genius of the age, there was an incredible amount of political contentiousness that mirrors our own time. Pheidias, for example, was prosecuted and ostracized in 438, charged with impiety. He fled to Olympia, where the Eleans killed him after he made the Zeus, often called the most outstanding statuary of the ancient world. It was made of gold and ivory over a wooden core, with embellishments in jewels, silver, copper, enamel, glass, and paint. Despite his ignominious end, Pheidias's pupils, particularly Agoracritus, Alcamenes, and Paeonius, dominated Athenian sculpture for a generation. Roman neo-classical sculpture looked chiefly to Pheidias for its inspiration and techniques.

11. Most of the thirty escaped to Eleusis but were tracked down and killed within two years. The idea of rule by "the best people" died with them. The idea of rule by "the best person," i.e., the chief or king, would now compete historically with the democratic ideal.

12. Of the twenty-three dialogues Plato would later write, four dealt directly with the trial and

death of Socrates. In the first, the *Euthyphro*, Socrates stands outside the courthouse in which he himself will soon be put on trial for his life and engages in a discussion on the nature of piety. The dialogue has its roots in the fact that Euthyphro is about to prosecute his own father on a charge of murder. Socrates says that a man who would bring such a charge based only on ritual observance must either know the true meaning of religion or have a touch of madness in his make-up.

In the second, the *Apology*, Socrates presents his own case to the jury. He reminded the jury that he had served the state as a foot soldier in the battles of Potidaea, Amphipolis, and Delium, where he acquired a reputation for courage. He had served with distinction as an officer of the Assembly. But he said unequivocally that disaster awaited his country if the policies which now prevailed were not modified and if the quality of thought which Athens was now applying to her problems was not improved.

In the third, the *Crito*, Socrates is in prison awaiting execution. A wealthy friend, after whom the dialogue is named, visits him to attempt to persuade him to escape. Socrates explains why he cannot. It would be false to everything he had thought or done in his seventy years if, in this personal crisis, he ran away to save his life. He must follow the course that reason dictates. He is not concerned with what the many think, nor is he fearful of their power. He is concerned only with the man who has understanding. As for the power of the many to destroy him, he does not think the purpose of life is merely to remain alive, but to live the good life. This requires him to affirm that the good man will not do wrong because others have done wrong. He has been a lifelong citizen of Athens, he has accepted her laws, and he has been so devoted to her that he has never had any inclination to travel. He cannot now live abroad as an object of ridicule and a sycophant. If he subverts the laws of Athens, although they may have dealt unjustly with him personally, he will be held in suspicion wherever he flees as a corrupter of law and order.

In the fourth dialogue, the *Phaedo*, Socrates' friend, Phaedo, relates to another friend, Echecrates, the story of Socrates' final hours. He is kind, humorous, detached, and not apprehensive, explaining with animation why he believes the soul persists after death. Socrates then drinks the cup of hemlock as prescribed by law and addresses Crito: "Crito, I owe a cock to Asclepius; will you remember to pay the debt?" Asclepius, son of Apollo, was the Greek and later Roman god of healing, so there is bitter irony in this pledge of a sacrificial offering by a patient who is past healing. "Such was the end, Echecrates, of our friend; concerning whom I may truly say, that of all the men of his time whom I have known, he was the wisest and justest and best."

13. Plato's house was situated just to the northwest of the Dipylon gate in Athens. The gymnasium was nearby, sacred to the hero Academus, who eventually gave his name to the Academy. The gymnasium was originally a place of exercise for citizens serving as hoplites, or heavy infantry, in he Athenian army. It was no more than an open space with a water supply and a shrine. Shade and shelter were provided by groves of trees. In the fourth century the gymnasium at Athens was frequented more and more by citizens interested in philosophy and became the intellectual center for all Greece. More specialized architecture was then required, and the gymnasium became an enclosed area, its buildings arranged on the courtyard principle. Plato was buried somewhere on the grounds of the Academy, but the exact location is unknown.

14. More than two hundred fragments from this collection have been preserved in quotations by later Greek authors, eighty-six of which are taken from the *Constitution of Athens*. Both aristotle and Xenophon wrote commentaries on the *Constitution of Athens*, the Spartan sympathizer Xenophon conceding that democracy, though repellent, was rational in Athenian circumstances. Xenophon was one of the most brilliant and courageous cavalry commanders of the ancient world and fought for the Spartan cause at Coronea against, among others, his fellow Athenians. The battle at Coronea in 394 was described by him as "like no other in my time." It

rid central Greece of Athenian control and established the superiority of the Spartan phalanx as an infantry tactic.

15. It has been argued that Plato's object was to set up in the most luxurious of Greek cities an imitation of the imaginary city of the *Republic*. In his *Epistles* Plato says explicitly that his object was the practical one of equipping the young Dionysius for the immediate duty of containing the Carthaginians, and, if possible, expelling them from Sicily. He wanted to make Syracuse the center of a strong constitutional monarchy to embrace the whole body of Greek communities on the island.

16. The quarrel between Dionysius and Dion went on long after Plato withdrew from Sicilian politics. Dion made up his mind to recover his rights by force. With enlistments of fighting men from the Peloponnese and the active concurrence of many of the younger members of the Academy, Dion made a dash across the water in the summer of 357, captured Syracuse, and proclaimed its freedom. Plato wrote him a letter of congratulations. Like Plato himself, Dion believed in strong, though law-abiding, personal rule and disappointed the Syracusan mob by not establishing a democracy. Neither did he manage his associates well. He dismissed his admiral, Heraclides, which set the stage for Dion's assassination by another of his entourage, Callippus. Plato continued to believe strongly in the fundamental honesty and appropriateness of Dion's political aims, however, and wrote two letters to the remnants of his party calling on them to be faithful to Dion's idealism.

17. The most obvious examples of such a pre-historical mixture of legend, myth, theology, and allegory are Homer's *Iliad* and *Odyssey*. These are narrative poems of impressive length—several hundreds of pages of long lines which would take about twenty-four hours to read at conversation speed. Epic poets do not write history, as Aristotle observed in his *Poetics*. They are large-scale artists who write about life and death, victory and defeat, glory and ignominy, war and peace, as well as courage, pride, and honor. They are also honest enough to write about the mean and the vengeful. The archetypal beauty of man's struggle with duty in every age is caught, for example, in Agamemnon's speech as he looks at the walls of Troy after nine years of siege.

> And now nine years of mighty Zeus have gone by,
> and the timbers of our ships have rotted away and the
> cables are broken and far away our wives and our
> young children are sitting within our halls and
> wait for us, while still our work here
> stays forever unfinished. . . .
>
> —The *Iliad*
> (2. 134–8)

18. The *Republic* belongs in the middle group of the Platonic dialogues completed before Plato was forty. He spent the last half of his eighty-one years building the Academy and writing the late group of dialogues, closing with the *Laws*, still unedited at the time of his death. The early dialogues are the *Apology* (actually a monologue), *Crito*, *Euthyphro*, *Ion*, *Lesser Hippias*, *Greater Hippias*, *Laches*, *Lysis*, *Menexenus*, *Protagoras*, *Euthydemus*, *Charmides*, *Lovers*, *Hipparchus*, and *First Alcibiades*. The middle dialogues are the *Gorgias*, *Meno*, *Phaedo*, *Symposium*, *Republic*, *Phaedrus*, and *Cratylus*. The late dialogues include the *Theaetetus*, *Parmenides*, *Sophist*, *Statesman*, *Phileus*, *Timaeus*, *Critias*, and *Laws*.

The above lists are placed chronologically by the prominence of certain stylistic features such as the avoidance of hiatus, but this is fragile aid and in the case of a conscious literary artist always revising his work. We do not yet possess an adequate statistical analysis of Plato's style. A rough grouping is possible, however, because the middle and late dialogues are radically different from the early ones. They are much longer, mostly undramatic, especially in their use of Socrates, and above all they are didactic. The stylistic changes reflect a shift away from the personal urgency of Socratic inquiry toward Plato's own views which the figure of Socrates serves merely to present. This is particularly true in Plato's theory of the good society in the *Republic* and his cosmology in the *Timaeus*.

19.   Calling these dispersed settlements colonies is something of a misnomer. A colony was a state-organized enterprise, often sent in a direction that would further the state's interest, but these "colonies," while originally state organized, quickly became independent units. Typically they kept no more than sentimental and religious ties with their mother city, and often, as in the case of Syracuse and Corinth, the daughter far surpassed the mother in wealth and prestige. The settlers remembered more vividly and with more gratitude the man who led them out. Over-population, an occasional famine, and political trouble, for example, could easily persuade a government to unload some of its marginal citizens and send them off into the unknown with a religious blessing. Just as mixed were the motives for going: compulsion, desperation, ambition, to farm, to trade, to take a chance. This is precisely how the American colony of Georgia was founded in the 1730s, mostly by the debtors and social outcasts of England. Australia had similar origins.

20.   The coup de grace of these idyllic descriptions is when Socrates is in prison under sentence of death. The authorities allow groups of his friends to visit and discuss such questions as whether he should escape and the nature of life after death. Finally, Socrates drinks the hemlock, and his limbs slowly lose sensation as he converses peacefully and rationally. In fact Athenian prison conditions were not as clean and humane as Plato suggests, and the medical effects of hemlock are not mere numbness of the limbs.

21.   The exception is partial because Greek religion is primarily a public religion rather than a religion of the individual. The Greek *poleis* had scores of gods with anthropomorphic characteristics peculiar to the cult practices of each city. Despite local variations, however, the Twelve Gods of Olympus presented a recognizable picture throughout the Greek world. They are Aphrodite, Apollo, Ares, Artemis, Athena, Demeter, Dionysus, Hephaestus, Hera, Hermes, Poseidon, and Zeus. The personalities of these gods, first explored in the poems of Homer and Hesiod, are given archetypal interpretation in the work of Jungian analyst Jean Shinoda Bolen. See *Goddesses in Everywoman* (New York: Harper and Row, 1984) and *Gods in Everyman* (New York: Harper and Row, 1989).

22.   Dorian refers to the powerful ethnic group that invaded Greece in about 1200 and occupied Achaea and especially the Peloponnese about eight years after Troy fell. The Greeks had a romantic story about their arrival called *The Return of the Heraclidae*. Ionian refers to the other main linguistic and religious subgroup in ancient Greece, the ethnic group that settled the central west coast of Asia minor and the offshore islands. They were refugees from the Greek mainland. The precociousness of the Ionians was celebrated throughout the ancient world. See, for example, the brilliant picture in the *Hymn to Delian Apollo*.

23.   One of the most important functions of the deme was to maintain the citizen lists. There was a complex procedure ensuring enrollment on the citizen list and an equally complex legal machinery for appeal in case of exclusion. Because of the connection with citizensh, membershp in the deme remained hereditary, regardless of actual domicile. Every Athenian citizen was required to state his deme in any official transactions. Thus Socrates' official designation was "Socrates son of Sophroniscus of the deme of Alopeke." However great population movements may have been, the deme remained the geographical focus for Athenians not just because they may have lived there at one time but because that was the place of their authenticated existence.

24.   From the early seventh century on, the rules for the Spartan system of military training laid down by her great lawgiver, Lycurgus, turned Sparta into the most efficient military power in Greece. It held ruthless mastery over the southern half of the Peloponnese and by stages acquired subtle control over the rest of the peninsula. Paradoxically, the Spartans also produced a constitution which guaranteed some form of political equality to all citizens. The constitution was unusual in that Sparta retained its hereditary kingship while all other Greek city-

states were in process of losing theirs. More oddly still, there were two kings, drawn from two great houses, who by their friendship or rivalries could only emphasize the basic aristocratic principle of dependence of the small upon the great. The kings were the military commanders. With the council of aristocrats, the *gerousia*, they initiated most political decisions and handed down most judicial opinions. But there was also an assembly of all Spartan citizens which met at fixed times and passed final judgment on most things that mattered. We are speaking of all Spartan citizens who had survived their training and the Spartan wars and who had been allotted state land in the conquered territories with helots (slaves) to work it. They called themselves *homoioi*, equals. The question remains: what kind of man is produced when a child is completely robbed of home and family between the ages of five and thirty and even thereafter is compelled to devote his days to military training and his evenings to the company of his messmates. One answer is the story of Leonidas, king of Sparta from 490 to 480, who marched to the Battle of Thermopylae with three hundred men to aid the Athenian cause against a vastly superior Persian army. The three hundred were all "men who had sons living." They repelled Persian assaults for two days, counter-attacking fiercely. They all died.

25. The society in which the individual belongs nowhere tends to be united only in its neuroses. American society, easily as pluralized as Athenian society, has increasingly succumbed to Alexis de Tocqueville's worst case scenario penned in the 1830s. He feared that narrowly self-interested individualists, disarticulated from the saving constraints and nature of the overlapping associations of social life, would require more and more controls from above to mute the disintegrative effects of individualism. American democracy did free individuals from the constraints of older, undemocratic structures and obligations, but it also unleashed an individualism of a peculiarly cramped sort. An acquisitive commercial republic engenders new forms of social and political domination that Tocqueville called egoism to distinguish it from the notions of human dignity and self-responsibility central to a flourishing democratic way of life. All social webs that once held persons intact having disintegrated, the individual finds himself or herself isolated and impotent, exposed and unprotected. He and she then hunker down in defensive lifestyle enclaves, forbidding the entry of others. As political theorist Michael Walzer has written:

> We are perhaps the most individualistic society that ever existed in human history. Compared certainly to earlier, and the Old World societies, we are radically liberated, all of us. Free to plot our own course. To plan our own lives. To choose a career. To choose a partner or a succession of partners. To choose a religion or no religion. To choose a politics or an anti-politics. To choose a lifestyle—any style. Free to do our own thing, and this freedom, energizing and exciting as it is, is also profoundly disintegrative, making it very difficult for individuals to find any stable communal support, very difficult for any community to count on the responsible participation of its individual members. It opens solitary men and women to the impact of a lowest common denominator, commercial culture. It works against commitment to the larger democratic union and also against the solidarity of all cultural groups that constitute our multiculturalism. (*Citizenship and Civil Society*, Rutgers, NJ: New Jersey Committee for the Humanities Series on the Culture of Community, October 13, 1992, part 1, pp. 11–12).

26. The position of women in classical Greece changed considerably with the rise of Macedonia under Philip II, 382–336. The great Macedonian princesses of the two generations after Philip's son, Alexander the Great, 356–323, were, in W. W. Tarn's words, the most competent group of women the world had yet seen. "They played a large part in affairs, received envoys and obtained concessions for them from their husbands, built temples, founded cities, engaged mercenaries, commanded armies, held fortresses, and acted on occasion as regents or even co-rulers. The influence of a woman like Arsinoe Philadelphus, beautiful, able, master-

ful, on the men who served her was evidently enormous." (W. W. Tarn, *Hellenistic Civilization*, New York: Meridian Books, 1952, p. 98).

From the Macedonian courts relative freedom broadened down to the Greek homeland. Those women who desired emancipation, probably a minority, were able to obtain it in considerable measure. Although magistrates called *gynaeconomi*—supervisors of women—appeared in some cities, the only thing they are known to have sueprvised was the education of girls. Stoicism, which subsequently inspired a better definition of marriage in the Roman jurists, also helped to raise women's status.

27. In Sparta, never a bastion of democracy, the freedom of women was notorious and much disapproved of by philosophers who idealized Sparta otherwise. Spartan women, for example, could inherit land in their own right, so that by the third century two-fifths of the land was in their hands.

28. Quoted in John Boardman, Jasper Griffin, and Oswyn Murray, *The Oxford History of the Classical World*, New York: Oxford University Press, 1986, pp. 213–14.

29. Xenophon, *Memorabilia* 2.7.

30. Sophocles, *The Tragedies*, 583.

31. *Agora* is simply the Greek term for an area where people gathered together for the political functions of the *polis*. The area was sacred and subject to rules of purity. There was often a sanctuary there containing an altar to the city's chief god, in the case of Athens to the goddess Athena. The shape of the *agora* depended on the nature of the available site. It was irregular at Athens but strictly rectangular in newer cities. Architecturally the *agora* needed to be no more than space defined by marker stones rather than buildings, as was originally the case at Athens. When buildings were constructed for the various functions of the *agora*, they were placed along the boundary, which they helped to define, rather than in the *agora* space itself. The buildings came to include lawcourts, offices, and meeting places for public officials. Extended porticoes—called stoas—came to dominate the architecture of the *agora*, often with long lines of rooms behind them.

32. It should be noted that not all Mediterranean city-states were Greek, and that whether they were Greek, Phoenician, Mycenaen, Minoan, or Etruscan, they differed markedly in public administration theory and practice from that of Egypt. For two millennia prior to the establishment of the earliest Mediterranean city-state—Carthage, established in 814 by the Phoenician Dido, sister of the king of Tyre—Egypt had a stable and long enduring system of public administration based on professionalism and large scale organization. Egyptian organization remained personal rather than objective or bureaucratic, contrasting sharply with the small-scale and decidedly amateur public administration of the rest of the Mediterranean basin. Egyptian administration was personal in that civil servants were agents of the pharaoh and partook of his grandeur.

33. This system survives in striking detail in the modern kingdom of Saudi Arabia. The great families, tribes, of the kingdom are assessed whatever amounts the king finds necessary to remain "protector of the two holy mosques." The king in turn allocates portions of the state's oil revenues to the tribes in his favor. Preference is still given to the descendants of those who fought most valiantly with Abdul Aziz al-Saud when he established the kingdom in 1932. Each tribe is also allocated a carefully derived number of ministers to serve in what amounts to a household civil service. When the author traveled to Saudi Arabia sveral years ago to be made an honorary member of the largest family in Saudi Arabia, the Otabis, he expected to see the family exceptionally well represented in King Faud's service. No so. "The family of Abdul Aziz is one of the smallest in the kingdom," the author was told. "We must keep the larger families in check by the kinds of offices they are allowed to hold."

34. See J. B. Bury, *A History of Greece*, 2nd ed. London: Macmillan, 1913, p. 122. After eighty-five years of scholarship, Bury remains one of the most dependable sources of information about governmental infrastructure in ancient Greece.

35. *Ephors* governed in Thera, Cyrene, Euesperides, and Heraclea in Lucania, as well as Sparta.

Since these were all Dorian city-states, it is probable that the ephorate predates the Dorain invasion of Greece. The word *ephor* is derived from the Dorian Greek *ouros* meaning guardian or overseer.

36. Alexander Hamilton was taken by the Spartan system and argued for aspects of it at the Constitutional Convention of 1787. He particularly liked the idea of appointing senators for life, after the Spartan *gerousia*. He lost the lifetime appointment idea for the United States Senate but won it for the Supreme Court. Not quite a monarchist, Hamilton nevertheless believed in strong executive power so that in his official conduct as the first Secretary of the Treasury he behaved much like an *ephor*.

37. One cannot consider the relationship between the *ephors* and the kings of Sparta without recalling the circumstances of Magna Carta. The "great charter" of English liberties forced upon King John by his barons at Runnymeade on June 15, 1215, made England a limited monarchy, as was Sparta. Just as the great Spartan lawgiver, Lycurgus, gathered, adapted, and condified the common law of the Spartan tribes, so did Henry II (1154–1189) send representatives from he king's bench to the countryside to gather, adapt, and codify the common law of England. The king himself, Henry's son, John, and every subseequent king and queen of England has been held accountable to the law agreed to at Runnymeade. While the Homeric kingship corresponds to modern Saudi Arabia, the Spartan kingship corresponds to modern England.

38. Tyranny hardly ever lasted more than two generations. Tyrants typically ruled in periods of growing confidence and prosperity. They encouraged national cults, sponsored public works, acted as patrons to writers and artists, and glorified both their cities and themselves. But they themselves often became the cause for new discontent.

39. Solon's success lay in his ability to handle property rights issues. Power in Athens at the turn of the sixth century lay with those who controlled a wide-spread share-cropping system. A large number of Athenians, i.e., "the people," paid one-sixth of their produce to a land owner, not to the state, in return for freedom to work his land. The land owners held a monopoly of the important magistracies and of the membersh of the Council of the Areopagus. The Council was in fact recruited largely from ex-magistrates. A citizen assembly did exist, but it was allowed only to show preference for the candidates of one noble faction or another when magistrates were elected. The Council of the Areopagus and the magistrates, indistinguishable in class or interest, ran Athens.

   Solon's task as he perceived it was to find a way for those who had power to keep it, along with their property and their heads, while giving the people "the dignity that was their due." He accomplished his purpose by focusing on the fact that all debts were secured upon the person of the borrower, so that a defaulting share-cropper became a defaulting debtor. He canceled existing debts and forbade personal security. Share-cropping ceased to exist. "I freed the soil of Attica that had once been enslaved," said Solon. No Athenian could henceforth suffer the indignity of enslavement for debt. To the property owners the shrewd Solon gave a radical new law. Access to major political and military office, including the archonsh, previously restricted by convention to a limited group of families, the *eupatridae* (the "well born"), was now to be determined by wealth in land. All Athenians were divided into four classes. To the top class or classes went the top offices, to the lowest, the *thetes*, only membership in the Assembly. The potential number of "those with power" was doubled. Solon was a practicing politician. He was a good and brave man who gave Athenians a chance at peaceful change. They did not immediately take it. After a half-century of intermittent tyranny a young supporter of Solon, worse still a relative, put himself in charge in 546. His name was Pisistratus.

40. Although Greek contests, *agones*, were most often athletic contests, music, poetry, and equestrian competitions were also popular. The Dionysia and Panathenaea added tragedies, comedies, and dithyrambs (choral songs) to the competitive agenda. They also honored professional reciters of Homer called rhapsodes and professional charioteers who would often race nearly nine miles to earn laurel or olive wreaths. Athens was especially generous to victors. By the middle of the fourth century victors at the Great Panathenea were awarded gold

crowns and bulls as well as the traditional amphorea of olive oil. To lose in a contest was shameful, and the incidence of failure-induced depression and mental illness was high.

41. The Persian Wars are a long and complex chapter of Greek history. By 546 the expanding Persian Empire, having absorbed the greater part of the Middle East and Asia Minor, appeared among the Greeks of the Aegean's eastern coastline. The Ionians had previously enjoyed a comparatively unoppressive dependence on the non-Greek powers of the hinterland, especially Lydia under its amiable King Croesus (560–546). Now the Persians installed or supported compliant tyrants in the Ionian cities and moved south to take over Egypt in 525. The Persians then moved along the coast of North Africa and in 514 crossed over into Europe. To the immediate northwest of the Persian homeland they established a presence in Thrace and influence as far west as Macedon. Thus the Greek mainland and offshore islands were beset to north, south, and east, while another alien power, Carthage, was pressing from the west. The stage was set for a Persian invasion, and the Greek states were divided in their response to that possibility. Some wanted to collaborate, including the most powerful family in northern Thessaly, the Aleuadae. One of the two Spartan kings, Demaratus, found refuge in the Persian court after a quarrel with the other king, Cleomenes. As Athens was freeing herself of her tyrants and coming to appreciate the democratic constitution that Cleisthenes had advanced, the rejected tyrants were going over to the Persians, including the exiled son of Pisistratus. Finally the Athenians decided to fight. They supported the Ionian cities in a revolt against the Persians in 499 and thus ushered in what the historian Herodotus called "the beginning of trouble."

    The Persians resolved to punish the Athenians in 490. They sent a fleet with a huge army across the Aegean to land on Attic soil at Marathon. Outnumbered more than four to one, the Athenians won the battle, losing some two-hundred men to the Persians' 6,000. Ten years later the Persian king, Xerxes, renewed the war, hurling 200,000 men against the Greeks at the narrow coastal pass of Thermopylae. By now the Spartans had joined the Athenians and sent King Leonidas with a small Peloponnesian force of three hundred Spartan "equals" to defend the pass. They held out magnificently for two days against the best that Xerxes could send against them. Every Spartan died. Their Theban allies surrendered. The Greeks evacuated Attica and teased the Persians into a great sea battle in the narrow strait between the island of Salamis and the mainland. The Greek navy under Themistocles won a resounding victory, breaking Xerxes' fleet and his nerve. On the very same day the Greeks of Syracuse, in Sicily, crushed the Carthaginians at Himera.

42. When an Athenian citizen wished to banish another citizen whom he considered dangerous to the state, all he had to do was pick up one of the many pieces of pottery, known as an *ostracon*, that lay about in the market place, write on it the name of the citizen he wished to have banished, and put it in the voting urn placed there especially for that purpose. To be effective at least six thousand citizens had to cast such a vote.

43. It is useful to remember that both Aristotle and Plato wrote after the defeat of Athens in the Peloponnesian War, and that both philosophers were concerned about the decline of the city and how to eliminate the ills that beset the body politic. The material in this section is taken from *The Politics of Aristotle*, Oxford: Oxford University Press, 1946, Book VI, Chapter VIII.

44. One of Plato's criticisms of Pericles was that his losing strategy as general during the Peloponnesian War was to stay inside the city walls and rely on Athens' sea power and superior financial resources to outlast the Spartans. Pericles did not count on a plague which decimated the Athenian population and killed first his two sons and then himself.

45. The fisc or *fiscus*, originally meaning basket or money-bag, was the public treasury. By Hadrian's time, in Roman administration, the post of *advocatus fisci* was such a major position that it commanded its own sphere of administrative law, separate from both public and private law.

46. There were still lesser offices, and it is not discernible from Aristotle whether they were common only in the richer city-states or were universal in the 158 constitutions he surveyed. The

responsibilities of these lower offices included the supervision of women, supervision of children, enforcement of obedience to the law, control of physical training, superintendence of athletic contests, and superintendence of dramatic competitions. Aristotle argued forcefully that supervision of women and children were out of place in a democracy.

47. See a complete discussion of these flaws in R. J. Bonner, *Aspects of Athenian Democracy*, The University of California Press: Berkeley, California, 1933.

48. A common practice in Greek public administration about which little is known is the assistance given to magistrates by public and personal slaves who supplied both scribal ability and administrative expertise to short-timers. The widespread use of boards made up of a representative from each of the ten tribes also added an element of collective responsibility to the use of the power that was available to magistrates if they chose to use it.

49. Only one theme remains constant in the *Republic* and the *Laws*, and indeed in all of Plato's writings. Foreign trade is such a despised occupation that it must be left to the aliens who always formed a non-citizen class in Greek cities. One of the worst societies Plato can think of is Carthage, built almost entirely on foreign trade.

50. Despite its organic wholeness the *Republic* can be seen as a number of treatises. There is a treatise on metaphysics exhibiting the unity of all things in the idea of the good. There is one on moral philosophy investigating the virtues of the human soul and showing their union and perfection in justice. There is a treatise on education inspiring Rousseau to say of the *Republic*, "It is not a work upon politics, but the finest treatise on education that ever was written." There is a treatise on political science which sketches the polity and the social institutions, especially those of property and marriage, which should regulate the ideal state. And there is a treatise on the philosophy of history which explains the process of historical change and the gradual decline of the ideal state into tyranny. Such differentiation of knowledge into separate studies had not yet publicly appeared, however, as it would with Aristotle. In the *Republic* the philosophy of man stood as one subject against the other great subject of Greek speculation, the philosophy of nature.

51. In his brilliant *Greek Political Theory*, London: Methuen and Company, Ltd. Sir Ernest Barker describes the *Republic* as a "philosophy of mind" in all its manifestations. He compares it to Hegel's sketch of philosophy entitled the "philosophy of mind" in which Hegel discusses the inner operations of mind as consciousness and as conscience. Its external manifestations are in law and social morality (the sphere of the state), and its "absolute" activity is in art, religion, and philosophy. The similarities between Platonic and Hegelian thought are striking."

52. See Jean Bethke Elshtain, *Democracy On Trial*, New York: Basic Books, 1995, especially Chapter 4, Democracy's contentious past.

53. Epideictic oratory is memorial public oratory imbued with an explicit political content. Lincoln's *Gettysburg Address* is the best American example of this kind of speech making.

54. Nicole Loraux, *Inventing Athens: The Funeral Oration in the Classical City*, Cambridge, Massachussetts: Harvard University Press, 1986, p. 202.

55. Thucydides, *History of the Peloponnesian War*, (Rex Warner trans.), New York: Penguin Books, p. 143.

56. In drawing these conclusions Plato was greatly influenced by Pythagoreans who looked upon themselves as a small, select community of wisdom in a world of folly. They divided humanity into three types comparable with the three kinds of people who came to the Olympic games: those who came to buy and sell, those who came to compete, and those—the best of all—who came to look on.

57. The *Republic*, p. 484 b.

58. By the time of the *Laws*, written almost forty years after the *Republic*, Plato had concluded that the overseer of education should be the best and most illustrious man in the community. In Book VI at 765 d he writes that the "President of the Board of Education must be a man over fifty, with children of his own, and elected for a period of five years." He was to be the premier in Plato's commonwealth.

The training of the guardians and auxiliaries begins before they are born. The pairing of the parents is arranged by a preconceived plan that is to insure the highest physical and mental qualities of the offspring. Nothing is left to personal whim or accident from infancy on, and the process of education, both theoretical and practical, continues until the age of fifty. Literature, music, physical and military insutruction, elementary and advanced mathematics, philosophy and metaphysics, and subordinate military and civil service assignments (a succession of internships with increasing responsibility followed each time by further study), are the stages of the planned program for training philosopher-rulers. Even after the age of fifty most of the time of the philosopher-rulers will be spent in study, though they all will take their turn at the troublesome duties of public life.

59. See William Ebenstein, *Great Political Thinkers, Plato to the Present*, 4th Ed., New York: Holt, Rinehart, and Winston, Inc., 1969, pp. 7–9.

60. The *Republic*, VI, 493.

61. The celebrated sophist Thrasymachus argued simply that justice is the interest of the stronger party. He played an important part in the development of Greek oratory by his elaboration of the appeal to the emotions by means of elocution and delivery. He invented a prose style that paid particular attention to rhythm. See "prose-rhythm, Greek," in Simon Hornblower and Antony Spawforth, Editors, *The Oxford Classical Dictionary*, Third Ed., New York: Oxford University Press, 1996, pp. 1260–1261.

62. Plato, *Gorgias*, (Walter Hamilton trans.), New York: Penguin Books, 1971, p. 44.

63. The *Republic*, X, p. 602. Modern authoritarian rulers are as well aware as Plato that poetry, fiction, and other kinds of imaginative literature can be more dangerous than factual historical, political, or economic analysis. In this century three of the most influential books against totalitarian government have been novels: Arthur Koestler's *Darkness at Noon*, George Orwell's *1984*, and Boris Pasternak's *Dr. Zhivago*.

64. The *Republic*, Ill, p. 408. An illustration of a medicinal lie is the fable of the origins of the class system, according to which God put gold into those who are fit to rule, silver into the auxiliaries, and iron and brass into the farmers and craftsmen. "I shall try to convince," Socrates says, "first the rulers and the soldiers, and then the whole community," and if they accept this fable, all three classes will think of each other as "brothers born of the same soil" and will be ready to defend their land, which they will eventually think of as "mother and nurse." It is significant that Plato's example of a medicinal lie relates, not to a matter of subordinate expediency and convenience, but to the root of his ideal political community, namely, the inequality of the threefold class system.

65. Guardian women who have given birth may nurse infants but not their *own*. Each mother nurses the anonymous baby presented to her when she enters the segregated children's quarter of the city. Should a mother get to know her own infant, she would have a private loyalty at odds with her unitary bond to the city. Should the infant be inferior it would be sent down to the lower orders, and a mother bonded to her baby might object to such a necessary move. Plato wanted no unpleasantries in his guardian encampment.

66. J. B. Elshtain takes Plato fully to task at this point in her *Public Man, Private Woman: Women in Social and Political Thought*, Second Ed., Princeton, New Jersey: Princeton University Press, 1993.

67. The passage, from Book V, section 493.

68. See E. B. Portis, *Reconstructing the Classics: Political Theory From Plato to Marx* Chatham, NJ: Chatham House Publishers, Inc., 1994, particularly Chapter 2, "Plato and the Politics of Beauty."

69. Epaminondas' invasion of the Peloponnese in 367 finally put an end to Sparta's three-hundred-year-old Peloponnesian League and liberated Messenia. Plato began work on the *Laws* shortly after that, probably on his return from Syracuse in the year 360 at the age of sixty-eight. Thus Plato spent the last thirteen years of his life on the *Laws*, dying before he could revise, edit, and polish the work. It was put in circulation by his friends within a year of his death in 347.

70. Plato himself was asked to legislate for Megalopolis, and, though he declined, Plutarch tells us he sent Aristonymus to do the job. At other times he sent Phormio to Elis, Menedemus to Pyrrha, Eudoxus to Cnidus, and Aristotle to Staginus.

71. The *Laws*, p. 803 c.

72. There is a palpable difference between the *Republic* and the *Laws* in this respect. In the former, the argument may wander from the road, but it stays fairly close at hand and can be readily brought back. In the latter the argument wanders farther afield until Plato awakens to the fact and seeks to recall it by devious ways. "The argument ought to be pulled up from time to time, and not be allowed to run away, but held with bit and bridle." The *Laws*, p. 701 c.

73. The *Laws*, p. 694 a–701 d.

74. At this point one can only ponder Madison's statement about the American constitution: "We are founding a great commercial republic in which interest will play the role of virtue."

75. The *Laws*, p. 732 e–734 e.

76. Even a cursory reading of Plato reveals his fascination with numbers. Mathematics was by no means the only science he cultivated at the Academy, but it was the one which exercised the most thoroughgoing influence on later intellectual developments. All the chief writers of geometrical textbooks known to us between the founding of the Academy and the rise of the scientific schools of Alexandria were scholars Plato brought to Athens to work with him. Theaetetus completed the edifice of solid geometry at the Academy, for example, and Eudoxus invented the ancient equivalent of integral calculus.

77. Among the many other duties of the Board of Family Life and the Board of Ladies, perhaps the most interesting is Plato's insistence on enforcing the law that men must marry between thirty and thirty-five and women between sixteen (or eighteen) and twenty. One of the reasons we know Plato did not live to edit the *Laws* is that at paragraph 785 he says age sixteen for women and at paragraph 833 he says eighteen. He was too fastidious a writer to let such an inconsistency go uncorrected. The man who published the *Laws* within a year of Plato's death, his pupil and amanuensis, Philip of Opus, chose to let this and other discrepancies stand.

78. The *Laws*, p. 789 d.

    The Athenian. Well, then, when a body is subjected to vast augmentation of bulk without a counterbalancing abundance of appropriate forms of exercise, the consequences are disastrous in all sorts of ways. That, I think is a known fact?

    > *Clinias.* Indeed it is.
    > *The Athenian.* And so the period when the body is receiving its principal increment from nutrition is also the period when it demands the maximum of exercise.
    > *Clinias.* What sir? Are we actually to impose the maximum of exercise on infants and new-born babies?
    > *The Athenian.* Not precisely that; we must impose it at a still earlier stage while the child is being nursed in its mother's womb.
    > *Clinias.* What, my dear sir! On the embryo? You cannot mean that!
    > *The Athenian.* Indeed I do . . .

79. The *Laws*, p. 793 d–794 c.

80. The *Laws*, p. 829–835 d.

81. The modern reader is impressed by the special severity with which injuries committed by a slave on free persons is treated. Plato and his contemporaries considered such crimes mutiny and the most fundamental threat to the sacred order.

82. Thomas Jefferson in volume XIV of his collected works strongly disagrees with any credit given to Plato for a positive influence on Christianity. In a letter to John Adams on July 5, 1814 Jefferson says, "In truth Plato is one of the race of genuine sophists, who has escaped the oblivion of his brethren, first, by the elegance of his diction, but chiefly, by the adoption and

incorporation of his whimsies into the body of artificial Christianity. His foggy mind is forever presenting the semblances of objects which, half seen through a mist, can be defined neither in form nor dimensions. Yet this, which should have consigned him to early oblivion, really procured him immortality of fame and reverence. The Christian priesthood, finding the doctrines of Christ leveled to every understanding, and too plain to need explanation, saw in the mysticism of Plato materials with which they might build up an artificial system, which might, from its indistinctness, admit everlasting controversy, give employment for their order, and introduce it to profit, power, and preeminence" (pp. 148–149).

83. There are striking similarities between Book X of the *Laws* and the beliefs and practices of the theocracy of Puritan Massachusetts. The Puritan divines constantly called upon the civil magistrates to suppress heresy.

84. The Protestant Reformation is based on the worst of Plato's heresies. The selling of indulgences by the papacy, the buyer to escape God's judgment by such a gift of money, was the last straw for Martin Luther and other Augustinian monks who, like St. Augustine, had drunk deeply of Platonic philosophy.

85. The prosecutor in Athens was very similar in the role he played to the prosecutor in modern American courts. The severe penalty of death for motives of personal gain in the *Laws* is because of the heinousness of the attempt to make the court of justice itself accessory to the infliction of a wrong.

86. The *Laws*, p. 942 a.

87. The number of men on the council varies because it must include all ex-ministers of education, as many as are living, as well as the current minister. The other members are ten judges and ten younger men between the ages of thirty and forty.

88. The Laws p. 965 c,d,e.

89. A close reading of the *Laws* reveals many echoes of the *Republic*. Plato's vision of philosopher-kings recurs at p. 709 e–712 a, for example. At p. 739 b–e, and again at p. 807 b, he again affirms that the communism of the *Republic* is the true ideal.

90. See *The Oxford Classical Dictionary*, Political theory, pp. 1206–1207.

91. See for example, Alan Briskin, *The Stirring of Soul in the Workplace*, San Francisco: Josey-Bass Publishers, 1996, especially The dance of souls in organizations, pp. 29–31.

92. C.G. Jung, *Psychology and Alchemy*, (R. F. C. Hull trans.), Princeton, New Jersey: Princeton University Press, 1953, p. 336.

BIBLIOGRAPHY

Agard W. R. *What Democracy Meant to the Greeks*, Chapel Hill, NC: University of North Carolina Press, 1942.

Aristotle. *The Politics*, (Ernest Barker trans.), Oxford: Oxford University Press, 1946.

Aristotle. *The Constitution of Athens*, (Kurt von Fritz and Ernst Kapp trans.), New York: Hafner Publishing Company, 1966.

Baldry H. C. *The Unity of Mankind in Greek Thought*, Cambridge, MA: The Cambridge University Press, 1965.

Barker E. *Greek Political Theory*, London: Methuen and Company, 1918.

Boardman J., Griffin J., and Murray O. (eds.). *The Oxford History of the Classical World*, Oxford: The Oxford University Press, 1986.

Bolen J. S. *Goddesses in Everywoman*, New York: Harper and Row, 1984.

Bolen J. S. *Gods in Everyman*, New York: Harper and Row, 1989.

Bonner R. J. *Aspects of Athenian Democracy*, Berkeley, CA: University of California Press, 1933.

Briggs J. and Peat F. D.: *Turbulent Mirror*, New York: Harper and Row, 1989.

Brishim A. *The Stirring of Soul in the Workplace*, San Francisco: Josey-Bass Publishers, 1996.

Bury J. B. *A History of Greece*, London: Macmillan, 1913.

Crombie I. M. *An Examination of Plato's Doctrine*, London: Methuen, 1962.

Durant W. *The Life of Greece*, New York: Simon and Schuster, 1939.

Ebenstein W. *Greek Political Thinkers, Plato to the Present*, (4th ed.), New York: Holt, Rinehart, and Winston, Inc., 1969.

Elshtain J. B. *Public Man, Private Woman: Women in Social and Political Thought*, Princeton, NJ: Princeton University Press, 1993.

Elshtain J. B. *Democracy on Trial*, New York: Basic Books, 1995.

Encyclopaedia Britannica, (15th ed., Vol. 8), Chicago: Encyclopaedia Britannica, Inc., 1974.

Freeman E. A. *History of Federal Government in Greece and Italy*, London: Macmillan, 1893.

Friedrich C. J. Greek Political Heritage and Totalitarianism, *Review of Politics*, II (April, 1940), pp. 218–225.

Gladden E. N. *A History of Public Administration*, Vol. 1, London: Frank Cass, 1972.

Gleick J. *Chaos, Making a New Science*, New York: Penguin, 1987.

Gwatkin H. M. and Whitney, J. P. (eds.). *The Cambridge Medieval History*, Vol. 1, Cambridge, MA: Cambridge University Press, 1911.

Herodotus. *The Histories*, (Harry Carter trans.), New York: The Heritage Press, 1958.

Homer. *The Iliad*, (Robert Fitzgerald trans.), Franklin Center, PA: The Franklin Library, 1976.

Homer. *The Odyssey*, (Robert Fitzgerald trans.), Franklin Center PA: The Franklin Library, 1976.

Hopper L. J. *The Early Greeks*, New York: Barnes and Noble, 1976.

Hornblower S. and Spawforth A. (eds.): *The Oxford Classical Dictionary*, (3rd ed.), Oxford: Oxford University Press, 1996.

Jefferson T. *Writings*, Vol. XIV, Washington: The Library of Congress, 1903.

Jones A. H. H. *The Greek City*, Oxford: Oxford University Press, 1940.

Jung C. G. *Psychology and Alchemy*, (R F C. Hull trans.), Princeton, NJ: Princeton University Press, 1953.

Larsen J. A. O. *Representative Government in Greek and Roman History*, Berkeley, CA: University of California Press, 1966.

Levinson R. B. The Republic Revisited, *Yale Review*: XXIX, (Autumn, 1939), pp. 153–166.

Loraux N. *Inventing Athens: The Funeral Oration in the Classical City*, Cambridge, MA: Harvard University Press, 1986.

Plato. *The Republic*, (Benjamin Jowett trans.), New York: Random House, 1958.

Plato. *The Laws*, (A. E. Taylor trans.), New York: Everyman's Library, 1960.

Plato. *The Trial and Death of Socrates*, (Benjamin Jowett trans.), New York: The Heritage Press, 1963.

Plato. *Lysis; Or Friendship; The Symposium; and Phaedrus*, (Benjamin Jowett trans.), New York: The Heritage Press, 1968.

Plato. *Gorgias*, (Walter Hamilton trans.), New York: Penguin Books, 1971.

Plutarch. *Twelve Illustrious Lines*, (John Dryden trans.), Franklin Center, PA: The Franklin Library, 1981.

Popper, K. R. *The Open Society and Its Enemies*, Princeton, NJ: Princeton University Press, 1950.

Portis E. B. *Reconstructing the Classics: Political Theory from Plato to Marx*, Chatham, NJ: Chatham House Publishers, Inc., 1994.

Sealey R. *A History of the Greek City-State, 700–338 B.C.*, Berkeley, CA: University of California Press, 1976.

Sophocles: *The Tragedies*, (Alan E. Cober trans.), Franklin Center, PA: The Franklin Library, 1981.

Tarn W. W. *Hellenistic Civilization*, New York: Meridian Books, 1961.

Taylor A. E. *Plato: The Man and His Work*, Norwalk, CT: The Easton Press, 1991.

Thucydides. *The History of the Peloponnesian War*, (Richard Crawley trans.), Franklin Center, PA: The Franklin Library, 1980.

Walzer M. *Citizenship and Civil Society*, New Jersey Committee for the Humanities Series on the Culture of Community, Rutgers, NJ, 1992.

Warner R. *The Stories of the Greeks*, New York: Farrar, Straus, and Giroux, 1967.

Webster T. B. Z. *From Mycenae to Homer*, London: Methuen, 1958.

Whealey M. J. *Leadership and the New Science*, San Francisco: Berrett-Koehler, 1992.

Xenophon. *Memorabilia*, (H. Tredennick trans.), New York: Loeb, 1977.

3

JESUS AND PUBLIC ADMINISTRATION

Lance deHaven-Smith
Florida State University, Tallahassee, Florida

Public administration has normative aims: it seeks to promote among other things, democracy, compassion, and justice. To be sure, the discipline is also committed to the rule of law, but no responsible public administration scholar or practitioner would advocate blind adherence to a legal system, as the literature of New Public Administration notes. Public administration is not just a subfield of administration in general, or of the study of bureaucratic organizations. Public administration includes the study of ethics, politics, political theory, and public policy. It is more than mere managerial effectiveness, it is also a search, in theory and practice, for good government in the broadest sense of the term.

The normative goals of public administration inevitably require that public administration professors and practitioners take a critical, perhaps even oppositional, stance toward established political systems. Public administrators must judge the institutions they study and manage, otherwise, they cannot know whether these institutions are good. Therefore, the profession of public administration carries an ethos into the heart of public organizations; it is, so to speak, a conscience within the chain of command.

The teachings of Jesus are pertinent to public administration, because Jesus took this same stance toward government. He was not merely, or even primarily, a sage of ethics and morality. He had aims for political organizations. He lived under a lawful state whose laws were oppressive. In opposition to this state, he wanted to establish a truly excellent government, a "Kingdom of God." His strategy for achieving this kingdom involved a subtle confrontation with power, and in many respects it as successful. As Machiavelli, Nietzsche, Strauss, and others have demonstrated (and lamented), the teachings of Jesus transformed the Roman Empire, and western civilization in general, from a culture of valor into a culture of love and mercy.

Modern public administration can learn something from Jesus' strategy of political change. Public administration, like Jesus, has no power, either within itself or over elected officials, beyond the force of conscience. If he was nothing else, Jesus was a master at mobilizing the spiritual within the political.

I. JESUS THE MESSIAH

To understand Jesus' ideas about government and public administration, some Christian misconceptions must be shed. The teachings of Jesus contain obvious references to political objects; Jesus spoke of kingdoms, laws, commandments, judgment, kings, governors, punishment, obedience, defiance, mercy, and other elements of political systems. The founders of Christianity gave these words a meaning that Jesus never intended. Christianity came to see Jesus as a God, and the Kingdom of God as a supernatural domain in the sky or in the distant future.

Although recent research on the historical Jesus has tried to avoid conflating the teachings of Jesus with Christianity, even modern scholarship has not completely escaped the influence of Christian dogma. In particular, modern scholarship has never taken quite seriously Jesus' most important assertion: his claim about being the messiah foretold by the prophets. If Jesus was using the term as it was understood in his day, he meant by this that he was going to overthrow the Roman Empire. The messiah would, in the words of a Davidic Psalm cited by Jesus himself, "make thine enemies thy footstool," "fill places with dead bodies," and "wound the heads over many countries" (Psalm 110; Matthew 22:41–45). Understandably, modern scholars have found it difficult to accept that Jesus had such seemingly unrealistic ambitions. How could Jesus have believed he had any chance against what was then the most powerful military state the world had seen? Hence, much research on Jesus in this century has been devoted to explaining away Jesus' messianic claim.

Three lines of retreat from the revolutionary Jesus have been taken. The most extreme route, which was paved by Bultmann, has been to argue that Jesus never assumed the messianic title at all. According to this view, the messianic tradition associated with Jesus was a post-crucifixion addition to the Jesus legend. This theory has been countered by Hengel and others, who have pointed out that the disciples would never have believed and proclaimed Jesus to have been the Messiah if Jesus had not taught them this while he lived (1).

The two other paths taken in order to escape Jesus' political messianism have been to conclude that Jesus simply redefined the messianic role. Analysts coming from a more or less traditional Christian perspective have maintained that Jesus saw himself as a messenger of divine salvation rather than of political liberation (2). Although those who are more historical-critical than traditional in orientation doubt that Jesus made claims to divinity, they do not turn back to the messianic image current in Jesus' day. Rather, they argue that Jesus must have seen himself as a messiah of love, wisdom, or healing (3).

We should take Jesus at his word: He said he was the Messiah, and hence he must have had a plan for overthrowing, subverting, or in some other way transforming the Roman Empire. The evidence that Jesus hoped to undo the Empire is extensive. The first time Jesus preached, he indicated that he was not a healer or a teacher, but a political savior. He read a passage from Isaiah about a person who would be anointed by the Spirit of the Lord, and he announced that he was this person (Luke 4:18–20) (4). Although Jesus did not read this passage in its entirety—to do so might have provoked Roman reprisals because it was so blatantly anti-Roman—the passage described, as his audience would have known, a deliverer who would declare "the day of vengeance of our God" and force Israel's enemies to "repair the waste cities" and "the desolations of many generations" (Isaiah 61).

Jesus was constantly called the "son of David" (Matthew 1:1; 2:27; 12:23; 15:22;

20:30–31; 21:9, 15; 22:42; Mark 10:47–48; Luke 18:38–39). He never objected to this appellation. David was a prophet, a liberator, and a king. If Jesus believed that he was a savior in David's image, then who was Jesus' Goliath if not the Roman Empire?

The Gospels also show that Jesus aimed to be some sort of king (Buchanan 1984): Jesus was called a king by others (Matthew 2:2, 21:4, 27:29, 27:42; Luke 19:38, 23:36; John 1:49, 19:14); he referred to himself as a king (Matthew 25:34, 40); he appears to have been known to the multitudes as a king (Matthew 15:9, 12, 18; Mark 15:31–32; John 12:13, 15, 18:39, 19:3); the central element of his message was about establishing a "kingdom" (Matthew 4:17, 4:23, 9:35, 13:11, 24:14; Mark 1:14–15, 4:11; Luke 4:43, 8:1, 10–11, 9:2, 16:16); he was called "the son of David," who was a king (5); he was said to have been born in Bethlehem (Matthew 2:1; Luke 2:4; John 7:42), which was also the birthplace of King David (1 Samuel 17:15, 20:6). The main question at Jesus' Roman trial was whether he *declared* himself to be a king (Luke 23:2; John 18:33–37); at this trial, he did not deny his kingship (Matthew 27:11; Mark 15:2; Luke 23:3; John 18:36–37); and, at the instruction of the Roman Governor, a sign was placed on Jesus' cross saying "THIS IS JESUS THE KING OF THE JEWS" (Matthew 27:37; Mark 15:26; Luke 23:37; John 19:19).

Another reason for suspecting that Jesus was a theo-political revolutionary is that his teachings have had profound effects on *political* life. *Did not Jesus himself tell us to know a prophet by his fruit* (Matthew 7:16, 20)? With the possible exception of Socrates, Jesus is the thinker who has most influenced the politics of Western civilization. He fostered the idea of government as "public service" (Matthew 20:27), from which grows the modern belief that leaders are accountable to those whom they govern. He taught us to temper law with mercy (Matthew 7:1; Luke 6:37); to put more emphasis on intentions than on actions and consequences (Matthew 15:20; John 13:10); to give everyone a fair hearing, and to avoid judging hastily (John 8:7). Indeed, we do not yet know when or how Jesus' influence on our politics will culminate, for it continues to unfold even today, in new evangelical movements, in the rise of the Christian Right, and through the many religious organizations formed in his name which affect modern politics both directly through their own political activities and indirectly by molding the political attitudes of large segments of the population.

II. THE POLITICS OF JUDAISM

Recent research on the Gospels has suggested that something other than the religion of Christianity lurks behind Jesus' teachings, but analysts have nevertheless been unwilling to let go of Christian images altogether. While abandoning the Christian doctrine that Jesus was God-made-flesh, many in the field seem to want to hold onto the Christian picture of Jesus as a leader who accepted a border between faith and politics. The main finding of recent scholarship on the historical Jesus is that Christianity emerged from an earlier "Jesus movement," which embraced many ideas later declared heretical by Church organizers (6). Scholars note that the New Testament, around which Christianity was formed, represents a mere subset of the writings circulating in the Jesus movement when the New Testament was codified by Augustine and others in the fourth century; the so-called "gnostic gospels" by Thomas, Philip, and Mary Magdalene, were excluded (7). Many biblical scholars have also concluded that the canon Gospels themselves reveal a break between Christianity and the larger, more diverse Jesus movement preceding it (8).

The canon Gospels are now believed to be Christian constructions based on a lost document called "Q" (short for the German *Quelle*, meaning "source") containing only a series of sayings and not a story about Jesus' death and purported resurrection (9).

However, while scholars have been willing to say that the religion that arose in Jesus's name was not the religion Jesus espoused, they have not taken the next step, which is to consider whether Jesus was exclusively or even primarily a religious figure at all. As much as researchers may believe that they have shed their Christian biases, they are looking at the historical Jesus through an anachronistic Christian lens simply by virtue of the fact that they continue to interpret Jesus in a-political terms. The distinction between faith and politics underlying the classification of Jesus as a spiritual leader but not a political revolutionary was foreign to Jesus and to Judaism. The messiah anticipated by the prophets was to be both a prophet and a king. Seeing himself in these terms, Jesus not only healed, preached, and taught, he also delivered new laws and advocated a new kingdom.

Issues of politics and government were central to the entire Judaic culture out of which Jesus arose, because Judaism developed (or God revealed himself to the Jews), in reaction to a series of political encounters and conflicts. At the risk of oversimplification, this process of development/revelation can be reconstructed as a dialectic between faith and oppression. The first crisis was idolatry. In the midst of nations that legitimated their rule through idol worship, Abraham realized (or it was revealed to Abraham) that he could secure independence for himself and his children only by worshiping a single, invisible god, as opposed to "graven images." Apparently, this simple theology maintained the Jews throughout a long nomadic period and even kept them free in Egypt for four centuries. But when Jews began to outnumber Egyptians, they encountered another political threat. The Egyptians began to fear the Jews and to explore ways of decimating their population (Exodus 1). They sought to crush them through forced labor, and when this failed they tried to absorb them biologically by killing all Jewish male infants, an effort which, if it had been successful, would have required the Jewish women to marry Egyptians in order to reproduce. In reaction to this genocidal plot, Moses became inspired by the idea of (or God spoke to Moses about) a promised land, which allowed Moses to lead the Jews to safety. This new idea or revelation was sufficient to sustain the Jews through forty years of wandering in the desert. However, it proved inadequate once they had settled in Israel, because their new neighbors were both hostile and barbaric. Therefore David, along with Samuel and Saul, added clear geographical borders to the nation and established a military power to protect themselves.

The teachings of Jesus can be seen as another step in Judaism's development, in this instance in reaction to Roman imperialism. Rome necessitated a cultural advance within Judaism because it presented a new form of tyranny. In earlier eras of oppression, the Jews had been tyrannized or held captive in other lands, threatened by invasion, and pressured to assimilate. In this context, Moses and David had sought liberty for their people by calling on them to remain true to Jehovah, find a land of their own, and protect it with military force.

Roman imperialism brought a more subtle tyranny that was neither direct nor geographically bounded. In a primitive form of what we now call "federalism," the Romans allowed subject nations to practice their "local" religions and maintain their local governments so long as the people obeyed secular (Roman) law governing property rights, the rights of various categories of individuals, and the limits of subjugated states. In other words, the Romans instituted a separation of church and state. The border between Jewish faith and Roman law was clearly visible at the trial of Jesus. The priests had to take Jesus to Pilate because, while they had considerable leeway to impose penalties for crimes against Jewish law/religion, they could not impose the death penalty. This power was reserved to the Roman Governor, and Pilate had to be convinced that the crimes of Jesus were against the laws of Rome and not Israel.

Roman law, and the separation of church and state on which it rested, was legitimated on the basis of Greek philosophy. The Greeks were confronted, as we are today, by many different cultures, each claiming to be the highest culture or the one true faith. Greek philosophy sought to make sense of this multiculturalism by drawing a distinction between convention and nature. The detailed laws and gods of individual cities were seen as largely conventional or accidental, but above these local laws the Greek philosophers described abstract principles by which human beings were thought to have to live if they were to fulfill their potential as reasoning creatures. Plato (but not Aristotle) said that these abstract principles or ideals (*logoi*) existed in heaven. One of the highest principles was believed to be justice, which was defined as giving to each person what he deserves. From this philosophical root grew property rights, different civil rights for different social classes, limits on the powers of subjugated states, limits on the powers of the Roman state (vis a vis local governments, creeds, and citizens), and other principles of Roman law so important to western civilization.

This new form of imperialism undermined the cultural efficacy of Judaism as a defense against subjugation, because, rather than attacking the nation, land, and faith of the Jews, it placed them in a secular cage. The priests rabble-roused to prevent "graven images" of Roman eagles from being displayed near the temple, and the Pharisees advocated a withdrawal into strict Jewish customs so as not to become tainted by Roman influences. But these strategies were ineffective against Roman rule, and in some ways even bolstered it, because they acceded to the overarching prison of Roman law.

III.   THE POLITICS OF JESUS

The teachings of Jesus can be viewed as redirecting Judaism toward the Empire's foundations. This is essentially the conclusion reached by Spinoza in *A Theologico-Political Treatise*. Jesus announced a new means of deliverance, one based not on *separating* from oppression geographically and spiritually—such a separation was no longer effective—but on *ending* oppression, everywhere and forever. The "promised *land*" was replaced by a promised "*kingdom of God*." In line with the Judaic tradition of Moses and David, Jesus meant by this kingdom, not a future world order of disembodied souls or resurrected bodies, but an earthly government founded on new, anti-Roman principles. Justice was to be replaced by mercy, judgement by forgiveness, and law by love.

Jesus believed that the Roman Empire could be overturned by undermining Greek and Roman culture. This is not to say he expected no violence, only that the violence would come late in the revolution's development. He warned at least two cities of the destruction they would face if they did not heed his call. However, if violence was used too soon; if the Empire was not first hollowed out culturally, the movement would fail. As Jesus told Peter at his arrest, "those who live by the sword die by the sword." The Jesus movement could only live by initially being a cultural movement, or by concealing its political implications.

The Roman Empire was very stable, and was enthusiastically embraced by most of its subject nations, because, despite being incredibly brutal and exploitative, it claimed to represent the highest laws, the laws of nature and of heaven. Against this legitimation, Jesus advocated another kind of kingdom, a kingdom of God in which the rulers would be servants, the last would be first, the captives would be released, and the brokenhearted would be comforted. He believed that if he could just fill the old bottle of Roman authority with his new wine of love and mercy, the bottle would break and the wine would spill across the earth.

IV. JESUS' MANNER OF SPEAKING

How was Jesus to communicate his inspiring message to others? His only option was to use religious metaphors, at least if he planned to speak publicly, for this was the only realm of mass communication that the Romans did not censor. Jesus knew well the risks of speaking too freely in his captive kingdom. He had been a disciple of John the Baptist, whom Herod beheaded. Moreover, the Gospels contain numerous stories about plots against Jesus. Because of his popularity as a healer, the Pharisees "held a council against him, how they might destroy him" (Matthew 12:14–15). The priests, scribes, and elders plotted to kill him (Matthew 26:3–4). The Pharisees sought out the Herodians, the Jewish supporters of Herod and Rome, and tried to find "how they might destroy him" (Mark 3:6; see also Mark 11:8). The chief priests and the scribes "sought how they might take him by craft, and put him to death" (Mark 14:1; see also Luke 6:7, 19:47, 22:2; John 5:18, 7:1). Clearly, Jesus was a marked man, and he knew it.

Additionally, he was not indifferent to the danger. When he learned that the Pharisees were plotting against him, "he withdrew himself from thence" (Matthew 12:15). When he was urged by his disciples to go to the feast of the tabernacle in Judea, he initially declined, saying that he would be persecuted, but later he did attend, "not openly, but as it were in secret" (John 7:2–10). On the day that he sent his two disciples to prepare the room for what would prove to be his last supper, he had made prior arrangements to have them be met discretely, like secret agents, by "a man bearing a pitcher of water" (Mark 14:13). On the night when he was arrested, he had withdrawn into a garden and had posted Peter, James, and John to watch over him (Mark 14:33). Peter, if not the others, was armed (John 18:11). Obviously, Jesus wanted to avoid being apprehended.

So Jesus offered two teachings. To his students he taught methods for confronting and subverting power and glory, but to the "multitudes," as he called them (Matthew 15:32; Mark 8:2), he told parables seemingly about a heavenly kingdom that would eventually descend to earth, righting all wrongs and rewarding the meek, the loving, and the faithful. This would explain why he was such a popular speaker. In the heart of occupied Jerusalem, at the center of the temple, watched carefully by the Roman troops, spied on by Herod's agents, surrounded by the puppet priesthood, he could tell the crowds his stories. Many could understand his hidden meanings, but the authorities could never, without deceit, convict him of sedition.

That Jesus had an esoteric teaching for his disciples was well known in the ancient world. We catch glimpses of this in the Gospels. After Jesus preached to the crowds from a boat by the shore where they gathered, his disciples asked him why he spoke to the multitudes in parables rather than directly, as he did with the disciples. Jesus explained that he had to speak in code: "Unto you it is given to know the mystery of the kingdom of God: but unto them that are without, all these things are done in parables, that seeing they may see, and not perceive, and hearing they may hear, and not understand" (Mark 4:11–12; see also Matthew 13:11). Outsiders were given parables because if the true message of Jesus, the *political* message, had been understood, Jesus would have been executed immediately, as eventually he was. The Gospels also say that Jesus took care *never* to speak straightforwardly to the multitudes. "But without a parable spake he not unto them: and when they were alone, he expounded all things to his disciples" (Mark 4:34; Matthew 13:34). That Jesus spoke so often in parables is an indication in itself of the fact he was delivering an encoded message.

The gnostic gospels say this directly. According to the Gospel of Thomas, Jesus explained that "it is to those who are worthy of my mysteries that I tell my mysteries. Do not let your left hand know what your right hand is doing." (10) Similarly, the Gospel of Philip includes a parable about a sensible householder. "He served the children bread. He served the slaves meal. And he threw barley and chaff and grass to the cattle. He threw bones to the dogs and to the pigs he threw acorns and slop" (Philip, para. 80). This parable recalls Jesus' injunction in the Gospel of Matthew not to give what is holy to dogs, and not to cast pearls before swine, "lest they trample them under their feet, and turn again and rend you" (Matthew 7:6). Jesus knew that the Romans and their puppet government and priesthood (the "dogs" and "swine") would try to stamp out his ideas and kill him if they understood him, so Jesus concealed his political gems in a religious treasure-chest that the authorities and even some of the disciples could not open.

Some of Jesus' disciples believed they had found the key to Jesus' hidden message once Jesus was crucified (11). They thought it was the prophecy of Isaiah, who had said that a lamb would die for the sins of humankind. They began to interpret the idea of the messiah in a new way, as a divinity rather than an inspired revolutionary. Although many modern scholars have rejected the belief that Jesus was truly of divine origin, they have perpetuated this mistaken conception of the messiah as an other-worldly savior by assuming that it was the conception held by Jesus.

V.   JESUS' VIEW OF HISTORY

The main evidence, both then and now, for thinking that Jesus saw himself as having supernatural connections was his assertion that he would "destroy this temple that is made with hands, and within three days . . . build another made without hands." (12) Out of the numerous parables and aphorisms that Jesus offered during his brief ministry, this was the only statement brought forward at his trial before the Sanhedrin (Matthew 26:61–62; Mark 14:58). By then, the comment had become so notorious that, not only did witnesses report it to the high priests, those who watched him be crucified quoted it as well and mocked Jesus for having said it (Matthew 27:39–40; Mark 15:29–30).

The meaning of this statement was, and still is, the central question surrounding the mission, nature, and destiny of the movement Jesus initiated. Although modern Christians and others may wish to assume that the meaning is obvious, the people who lived during the beginning of the Christian era were deeply divided over the message Jesus intended. The people to whom Jesus made the remark took him literally; they thought he was saying that he could *physically* replace the temple in three days. They asked in astonishment, "Forty and six years was this temple in building, and wilt thou rear it up in three days?" (John 2:20). In contrast, at the trial when the remark was reported by witnesses, the high priest did not understand it, and he asked Jesus to explain it (Matthew 26:61;

Mark 14:60). Later, the people who wrote the canon Gospels interpreted the statement as a veiled reference to Jesus' bodily resurrection; in John's words, Jesus "spake of the temple of his body" (John 2:21). However, Stephen, the first martyr after Jesus, preached something else entirely; Stephen taught that, when Jesus said "he shall destroy this place," Jesus meant he would "change the customs which Moses delivered us" (Acts 6:14). In short, some of Jesus' listeners thought he was speaking of the temple literally as a building, others concluded that he was speaking figuratively about his own body, and still others decided that he intended the temple as a symbol for the Judaic laws.

Assuming that Jesus was using religious metaphors to subvert the legitimacy of the Roman Empire, his statement about destroying and remaking the temple probably referred to the historical process by which the Roman system of power and glory would be overturned. On this view, when Jesus said the "temple made without hands" would come in three *days*, he meant that it would come in three *stages*, three alternating periods of darkness and light. As we have seen, this had been the experience of the Jews throughout their history. The darkness of idolatry had been followed by the light of Abraham, the darkness of Egypt by the light of Moses, and the darkness of the Canaanites by the light of David. The future, or "the world to come," unfolds in fits and starts, as long nights are ended unexpectedly by sudden dawns.

Many of Jesus' parables and aphorisms related in some way to this vision of history. He compared the staggered coming of the kingdom to a landowner returning home unannounced (Mark 13:35); a wedding to which some guests are invited at the last minute (Matthew 22:14); a sudden storm presaged only by a red morning-sky (Matthew 16:2); a dinner party suddenly opened up to the poor (Luke 14:16–24); and a thief in the night who surprises a watchman (Luke 12:37–40). Jesus also spoke of several temptations that would sidetrack humanity from its spiritual growth (Luke 4:1–12; Matthew 4:1–10). Clearly, Jesus saw the coming of the kingdom of God, not as a gradual humanization or spiritualization, but as a process with many sudden stops and starts.

Jesus seems to have thought that he and his followers, and those who would continue their efforts in the future, would function as revolutionary catalysts causing the kingdom of God to materialize, in a series of conflicts or nights and days, as people began to question the legitimacy of the Roman Empire. Jesus did not envision his movement as a large organized religion withdrawn from political life, but, rather, as an army of cultural subversives who, like Jesus, would confront political and religious leaders intellectually in public, protest decadence and hypocrisy through symbolic actions (such as overturning the tables of the money changes), and, if necessary, give their lives for their beliefs. Jesus compared the carriers of his ideas to ingredients, such as yeast (Matthew 13:33, 16:6, 11–12; Mark 8:15; Luke 12:1, 13:21) and salt (Matthew 5:13; Mark 9:49–50; Luke 14:34–35), which are used in very small amounts in cooking to produce large changes in texture and flavor. He expected his followers to be "the salt of the earth" (Matthew 5:15).

Unfortunately, although this was the path taken by Philip, it was not followed by Peter, and the rest, as they say, is history. The parables and concepts Jesus had used to at once both convey and conceal his political messages were taken literally by the Church founders. At first these teachings retained some of their explosive potential in the Roman Empire simply because they spoke of a higher kingdom, but Rome eventually neutralized them by gradually pushing Christians away from doctrines threatening to the Empire's legitimacy. An example of the lines along which this conflict took place, as well as of the tactics used by Rome, is the torture of Christians who would not pledge allegiance to the emperor. Needless to say, such persecution placed considerable pressure on Church leaders to formulate interpretations of Jesus consistent with Roman imperialism—no easy task, given that Jesus was crucified under this very system. The solution was to define Jesus as a deity, push the kingdom of God into the distant future, and expect it to come through divine intervention rather than inspired political activism. The decisive moment in this process of co-option occurred when Constantine called the Council of Nicene, which adopted the Nicene Creed and declared Jesus to be "of one substance" with God.

VI.   A "JESUSIAN" PUBLIC ADMINISTRATION

A public administration modeled along the lines of the teachings of Jesus would try to be the salt of the earth. During his interrogation by the high priest the night before he was taken to Pilate, Jesus presented a model for doing this. Basically, Jesus sought to make people take responsibility for their actions even though they were acting as agents in a larger system of power. At one point, Jesus was asked by the high priest to explain his doctrine, and Jesus refused, telling the priest that he had spoken "openly to the world" and that if the priest wanted to know his views he should "ask them which heard me" (John 18:20–21). Jesus knew that he had spoken obliquely, and that only those with "ears to hear" could have understood his teachings about the kingdom of God. He demanded that the Priest take responsibility for showing that Jesus had been blasphemous, which would have required the priest to interpret Jesus' teachings and thereby render a personal judgement as to their meaning and acceptability. But as soon as Jesus had spoken, he was slapped by one of the officers of the court, who said, "Answerest thou the high priest so?" (John 18:22). The officer was demanding that Jesus acknowledge the power and glory of the high priest by being less assertive in his answers. Significantly, at this point Jesus did not turn the other cheek. Instead, he argued back, telling the guard, "If I have spoken evil, bear witness of the evil: but if well, why smitest thou me?" (John 18:23). Again, Jesus insisted that those who persecuted him should show why they believed he was guilty, not just mindlessly join the collective condemnation, and he refused to bow to their status and authority.

The idea that Jesus advocated passive obedience to authority because he said that people should turn the other cheek when they are struck, is a complete misinterpretation of his teachings. His remark about turning the other cheek was simply an example given in his sermon on the mount to stress the importance of becoming as perfect as possible so that law and power will not be needed to maintain order (Matthew 5:39; Luke 6:29). The remark was a call for love, not for mindless obedience to the law or to abuse. Jesus' real attitude toward authority was revealed in his reaction to the guard and to the high priest; he stood up to them and demanded that they be accountable for their actions.

Jesus did the same thing directly to Pontius Pilate when Pilate asked him whether he claimed to be the king of the Jews. Jesus responded, "Sayest thou this thing of thyself, or did others tell thee of it?" (John 18:34). Jesus was not seeking to understand the basis of Pilate's accusation; he knew that he was being accused of attempting to organize the Jews in rebellion. Rather, he was trying to force Pilate to take, or at least to assign, responsibility for the charges. Once again, Jesus was pushing the issue of accountability. He wanted Pilate to be specific as to who was making the charges, because he knew well that the Sanhedrin and the Roman authorities, like all worldly power, operated in exactly the opposite fashion, that is, to detach actions from individuals and thereby create larger "forces" that move along as if they were beyond any single individual's control.

Today, the skill of forcing responsibility to be acknowledged is recognized in government, but it is not studied and taught. Anyone who has ever participated in an administrative staff meeting or a meeting of a political body knows that many of the undercurrents in such settings center precisely around issues of responsibility and morality. People talk like Jesus did at his trial; they are seldom frontal. They ask questions: "What happened to this or that?" "What do you think?" "When was that due?" Further, they ask such questions not only or even primarily to gather information but to link actions and consequences with individuals. The language used in the hallways of power to describe this maneuvering testifies to this. We speak of "sandbagging," "smoking him out," "deflecting the blame," etc.

A Jesusian public administration would consciously decode this language in relation to the moral context of the administrator. Currently, the discipline ignores the very important phenomenon of administrative maneuvering, because public administration is not as morally self-conscious as it should be. If the discipline and the profession were to consciously embrace a political ideal and an awareness of the power of morality in history, they would be able to hear the language of administration clearly. They would learn and teach the art of the parable, the subtle question, the statement with hidden meanings.

At the same time, public administration would begin to think in a more sophisticated way about its audiences. Public administration professors and practitioners do not speak to a single set of listeners, a monolithic group of "policy makers." The potential targets for our words include business, labor, legislators, elected executives, many kinds of special interests, racial and ethnic minorities, students, housewives, the military . . . the list could continue indefinitely. Who among these audiences can be expected to attend to our messages? Who will merely use our reports and statements as ammunition in partisan battles, twisting our ideas to fit their propagandistic needs? Who, in other words—or in Jesus' words—are the children, the parents, the swine, and the dogs? Now, here is a good topic for public administration research.

A Jesusian public administration would also place value on what might be called "professional martyrdom," and the profession would organize itself accordingly. Jesus understood his crucifixion correctly to be a potentially explosive event in the evil system of power surrounding him. He wanted those responsible to be identified with their actions. By not physically fighting back or verbally mocking his accusers, he denied his captors the opportunity of blaming him for their decision. Through his life and death, Jesus showed the world the human face of those who were then, and are still now, allowing themselves to be swept along by the dark forces of power and glory.

Today, most public administration scholars and practitioners are well aware that the professional public administrator is frequently caught in deep conflicts between his or her conscience and the requirements of law, custom, or political expediency. Often, public administrators find themselves faced with professional crucifixion if they stand up to elected officials or to administrative superiors. For a while, artful administrators can choose their words carefully and maneuver with skill to put responsibility where it belongs, but, eventually, if they truly follow the voice of the spirit within them, they will find themselves before the equivalent of the Sanhedrin.

The discipline of public administration should prepare its students to face these challenges, and the profession should organize itself to provide support. Jesus warned his followers that they would be brought before "governors and kings," and he instructed them on how to behave. He also taught them to take time to strengthen their relationships with another. They broke bread together. They washed one another's feet. They sang and they danced.

Today, the greatest threat to public administration is that it will go the way of Pontius Pilate, who tried to hide from his conscience by appealing to the command structure of which he was a part. At the trial of Jesus, Pilate literally washed his hands of responsibility. Public administration, as a profession and a discipline, does this same thing whenever it focuses too narrowly on management and becomes blind to the aims and consequences of the kingdom it administers. Certainly, the push to become scientific, to assess policies on the basis of their "impacts," and to value efficiency above fairness and mercy, are retreats from the demands of the spirit. The lesson of Jesus is that, if we truly want good government, we must keep the largest questions before us. We must always be clear that we serve a king, or an ideal, higher than any worldly government.

NOTES

1. M. Hengel, *Studies in Early Christology*, Edinburg, 1995, and Preface 1996, in *The Charismatic Leader and His Followers*, Edinburg: T & T Clark, 1996.

2. For a literature review, see the excellent defense of this position by L. T. Johnson, The search for the (wrong) Jesus, *Bible Review*, December, 1995.

3. Examples here abound. A few are: P. Berger, Charisma, religious innovation, and the Israelite prophecy, *American Sociological Review*, December, 1963. M. Casey, *From Jewish Prophet to Gentile God: The Origins of New Testament Christology*, Louisville, Kentucky: Westminster/John Knox Press, 1991. R. A. Horsley, *Jesus and the Spiral of Violence: Popular Jewish Resistance in Roman Palestine*, San Francisco: Harper & Row, Publishers, 1987. G. Santayana, *The Idea of Christ in the Gospels, or God in Man: A Critical Essay*, New York: Scribner, 1946. T. Sheehan, *The First Coming: How the Kingdom of God Became Christianity*, New York: Random House, 1986. G. Tinder, *The Political Meaning of Christianity: An Interpretation*, Baton Rouge: Louisiana State University Press, 1989.

4. See Luke 4:18. The words Luke says that Jesus read are from Isaiah 61:1, but Luke misquotes them slightly, perhaps to conceal Jesus's political agenda. The quote from Isaiah is, "The Spirit of the Lord GOD is upon me; because the LORD hath anointed me to preach good tidings unto the meek; he hath sent me to bind up the brokenhearted, to proclaim liberty to the captives, and the opening of the prison to them that are bound." Luke has Jesus speaking of the "deliverance" of the captives rather than their "liberty," and he omits the last phrase about opening the prison. However, the careful reader would have known to look up the verse in Isaiah, and there the reader would have seen that this whole section in Isaiah is about a faith-inspired revolution against oppression. This way of concealing politically sensitive messages in public statements is consistent with what Strauss describes in *Presecution and the Art Writing*, Chicago: The University of Chicago Press, 1952.

5. For connections between Jesus and various leaders within the Jewish tradition, see D. C. Allison, Jr., *The New Moses: A Matthean Typology*, Minneapolis: Fortress Press, 1993.

6. See Sheehan, op cit., and Casey, Maurice. *From Jewish Prophet to Gentile God: The Origins of New Testament Christology*, Louisville, Kentucky: Westminster/John Knox Press, 1991.

7. E. Pagels, *The Gnostic Gospels*, New York: Vintage Books, 1979, 1989.

8. For a summary of this literature in relation to biblical exegesis, see S. D. Moore, *Post Structuralism and the New Testament: Derrida and Foucault at the Foot of the Cross* (Minneapolis: Fortress Press, 1994).

9. B. Mack, *Q—The Lost Gospel*, San Francisco: Harper San Francisco, 1993. A. Jacobsen, *The First Gospel*, Missoula: Polebridge, 1992. J. Kloppenborg, *The Formation of Q*, Philadelphia: Fortress Press, 1987. H. Koester, *Ancient Christian Gospels: Their History and Development*, Philadelphia: Trinity Press International, 1990. For criticism of the 'Q' thesis, see E. Linnemann, Is there a gospel of Q?, *Bible Review*, August, 1995.

10. The Gospel of Thomas, paragraph 62. Throughout this chapter, when I cite the gnostic gospels, the source is Robinson (1978).

11. I say "some" of the first disciples rather than all, because I believe Philip, Thomas, and Mary Magdalene may have understood the political message. Their gospels contain a number of indications to suggest they did, but we cannot be certain, because they wrote, like Jesus spoke, to conceal. I also think Judas understood it, and that that is why he could betry Jesus to the authorities.

12. John 2:18–19 quotes Jesus as saying, "Destroy this temple, and in three days I will raise it up." I am using the quote by Jesus' accuser at his trial, as reported in Mark 14:58. There are at least two reasons for thinking that the latter is the more accurate quote. First, the quote in John suggests that Jesus challenged his listeners to tear down the temple themselves, but Jesus clearly saw himself as tearing down the temple or, more precisely, the temple law. Second, Stephen was tried for saying that Jesus would "destroy this place" and "change the customs which Moses delivered us" (Acts 6:14). For political reasons, the Book of John may have played down the fact that Jesus was wanting to eliminate the authority of institutionalized religion.

Part II
Modernist Defined

MACHIAVELLI

But we now come to the case where a citizen becomes prince not through crime or intolerable violence, but by the favor of his fellow citizens, which may be called a civic principality. To attain this position depends not entirely on worth or entirely on fortune, but rather on cunning assisted by fortune. One attains it by popular favor or by the favor of the aristocracy. For in every city these two opposite parties are to be found, arising from the desire of the populace to avoid the oppression of the great, and the desire of the great to command and oppress the people (*The Prince*, Chapter IX).

MERCANTILISM

Although mercantilist doctrine is at a sharp discount among economists, mercantilist sentiment endures both among unions and businessmen whose immediate interests are threatened by foreign competition, and among public officials responsive to the complaints of their constituents (R. Leckachman, in *The Fontana Dictionary of Modern Thought*, London: Fontana/Collins, 1977).

BENTHAM

It is the greatest happiness of the greatest number that is the measure of right and wrong (*A Fragment on Government*, 1776).

LOCKE

Every one as he is bound to preserve himself, and not to quit his Station willfully; so by like reason when his own Preservation comes not in competition, ought he, as much as he can, to preserve the rest of Mankind, and may not unless it be to do Justice on an Offender, take away, or impair the life, or what tends to the preservation of the Life, liberty, Health, Limb or Goods of Another (*Two Treaties on Government*, 1690).

SMITH

By pursuing his own interest he frequently promotes that of society more effectively than when he really intends to promote it. I have never known much good done by those who affected to trade for the publick good (*An Inquiry into the Nature and the Causes of the Wealth of Nations*, 1776).

4

NICCOLO MACHIAVELLI AND MODERN PUBLIC ADMINISTRATION

John W. Swain
The University of Alabama, Tuscaloosa, Alabama

I. INTRODUCTION

We live today in a profoundly Machiavellian world. Niccolo Machiavelli, a practicing public administrator in Florence, became an author and founded modernity, the modern human enterprise. Public administration is an integral part of that enterprise, which is characterized by humanity serving its own needs in politics, science, and other activities. After Machiavelli, humanity generally has found itself no longer serving God or gods, or conforming to what is said about the order of nature. Alone in the universe, human beings exercise their capacities to serve themselves as best they can. Public administration as it is known today has emerged as a part of the modern enterprise.

For hundreds of years, people have blamed, praised, and puzzled over Machiavelli's writings. Blame for Machiavelli focuses on the vulgar, crude, and shocking advice he gives that suggests deceit, fraud, cruelty, and murder. Blame for Machiavellian vulgarities has been widespread since shortly after his death and the dissemination of *The Prince*, the basis for most opinions about him. Criticisms appear to be most pronounced among Catholic thinkers and in the English-speaking world, particularly in Elizabethan times in both political writings and popular fiction. English plays of the period frequently relied on a stock character who schemed and was generically called "Machiavel."

Praise for Machiavelli comes from appreciation of his Florentine and Italian patriotism, his steadfast commitment to principles, his service as a Florentine public administrator, and his new perspective on the world. Puzzlement over his writings arises from difficulties in reconciling the apparently blameworthy and praiseworthy aspects of his work as well as from the problems inherent in deciphering his sometimes contradictory arguments. His obvious mistakes and contradictions stoke this puzzlement because he says different things in different places about the same thing; he misreports his sources; and he differs in his accounts with other accounts on contemporary actions and words (1).

Notwithstanding these difficulties, no question exists regarding Machiavelli's influence on the modern world. Less well appreciated is his influence, mostly indirect, on modern public administration. His influence on the modern world can best be comprehended by examining the world about which Machiavelli thought. Against that backdrop, his influence on philosophy and science, political philosophy, political science, and public administration can be discerned.

A.   Machiavelli's Life and Times

Machiavelli's life and his time entangle. Biographies on him read like general histories of renaissance Florence and Italy, and general historical accounts of the time and place usually mention him and major events related to his life.

Niccolo Machiavelli was born on May 3, 1469, in Florence, Italy, in the midst of the Renaissance, a period marked by tremendous changes in both the cultural and the political spheres in Italy and the rest of Europe. The Renaissance, a French word meaning "rebirth," was so named by those who saw the Middle Ages, the period from the fall of Rome until the renewed interest in classical achievements, as a dark time from which human beings had just awakened. Those naming the Renaissance were a new group of intellectuals—members of the social elite who were literate and acutely aware of the achievements of classical antiquity.

According to these intellectuals, human beings could now resume civilization, which was defined as taking the positive ideas and ideals of the ancient Greeks and Romans and combining them with the newly revived human spirit. The core of the Renaissance celebrated the human spirit that energized and motivated individuals to achieve great results once they became aware that the human spirit existed. Although they still paid lip service to the spiritual world, the leaders of the Renaissance ushered in a new secularism. For these intellectuals, reality now could be found in the tangible, the role of human beings on earth, and the celebration of beauty, not salvation in the hereafter. Florence became a leading center in the age. Contemporary works of art and literature reflected the new ideas. Leonardo da Vinci's paintings of religious figures show their human characteristics, and Michelangelo's sculptures reflect human attributes in heaven itself. The writings of Petrarch and Boccaccio contain reflections on the role of human beings in society and how they can find rewards in society.

The change in the political structures within and among the various Italian city-states and European nations was also enormous. In the fifteenth century, the five major Italian states displayed diverse forms. Florence and Venice were republics, Naples was a kingdom, the Papal States constituted an elective monarchy, and Milan was a despotism. In addition, despite formally being a republic with a tradition of self-rule, Florence had basically been indirectly ruled by the Medici, the rich banking family, since 1434. The Medici had widespread support, but as trade and communication increased and rigid class structures began to ease, other influential citizens began to demand a share of political decision making. In Florence as elsewhere in Italy, the threatened oligarchy used their main weapon, money, and hired mercenaries to protect their interests, both internally and externally. The focus was on political maneuver and diplomacy, not actual combat, however. Thus, a premium was placed on tricking one another to gain advantages. Diplomats skilled at discerning intentions were highly valued.

Each of the five leading city-states jockeyed for position with one another, forming alternating power balances to keep Venice and the Papal States in check. A crucial event occurred in 1494 when Milan invited the French into Italy as an ally, which opened the way for other foreign invaders. This lead to later interventions by the French, Spanish, English, Germans, and Swiss. Florence generally sided with the French, whereas the Papal States, especially under Julius II, attempted to play France and Spain against each other.

France became formally allied with Florence in return for monetary payments necessary to fund mercenary troops and commanders. The alliance was not a stable one, though, as Florence did not always pay its debts promptly. The French threatened the Florentines about the payments and allowed Pisa, their most important subordinate territory, to revolt against Florence.

Much of the change experienced by Italy and the other European states was the result of problems within the Christian Church. The Church had been the authority on religious life in most of Europe as the single official religion and dominated intellectual life as the source of learning and education. Nevertheless, it engaged in ongoing internal doctrinal disputes that consumed much of its attention and energy as it strove to provide correct doctrine. Those persons with a scholastic bent favored adherence to official church doctrines that showed all human knowledge in relation to divine revelation. Human knowledge was subordinate, derivative, and certainly less important than divine revelation, and secular rulers were subordinate to the pope. The new intellectuals of the Renaissance challenged conventional belief by positing the importance of classical antiquity and suggesting an independence or autonomy of human activities. As a result, the Christian Church no longer had a monopoly of learned opinion, even though most people were pious. The challenge diminished the dominance of Church doctrine and offered alternative views of politics.

Orientations of the Church created other conflicts. The Church had become rich and powerful because of its religious control of the people and ownership of property. Its top positions became politically determined and open to persons who had not dedicated their lives to Christianity and who in many cases did not seem to be believers in any serious sense of the word. In Italy, unlike the rest of Europe, the Church existed as a separate political power. The pope headed the territorial entity called the Papal States and typically paid more attention to temporal rather than spiritual matters. Italy was the canvas upon which popes' temporal ambitions were depicted.

Political relations within and among Italian city-states divided into pro- and anti-papal factions. These factions changed depending on circumstances, particularly on who was pope and who appeared ascendent at any particular point in time. In contrast, although top church positions in other countries went to worldly oriented individuals, and leaders in those countries formally acknowledged the pope's spiritual ascendancy, those other countries were not riven by papally driven or focused territorial ambitions. In short, politics in Italy in the fifteenth century were in a state of chaotic flux, accentuated by the relatively rapid turnover in popes, whose average tenure was less than ten years. As Machiavelli later noted, the papacy was too weak to unite Italy and too strong to allow anyone else to do so (*The Prince*, Chapter XII).

In the 1490s, a backlash against the new secularism occurred in Florence. Many were troubled by the focus on worldliness and turned to Savonarola, a friar who urged that the state be dedicated to the service of religion. He was believed by many to have predicted several unexpected events, including the French incursion into Italy. Savonarola's words were made even more appealing by the actions of the current Florentine leader, Lorenzo de' Medici (Lorenzo the Magnificent), whose rule over Florence had gradually become tighter and tighter and whose greed had led him to engage in more and more corruption.

In addition, the corruption of the Church in Rome had worsened. The pope, Alexander VI, provided numerous positions and advantages to his relatives, had cardinals and others killed so that he could take their property, and created church positions so that he could sell them. These actions added to the corruption already prevalent (e.g., layper-sons purchasing power and favors through the papacy and the church hierarchy and priests and monks vigorously violating their oaths of poverty and chastity). In 1494, Savonarola instigated the exile of the Medici; he then helped create a republican govern-ment and declared Christ the ruler of Florence.

Fortune soon changed, however. Savonarola's popularity proved to be short-lived as the idea of sacrifice quickly lost its appeal. Former Medici supporters, who had been in conflict with one another, started to focus on issues on which they found agreement, not differences. In addition, Savonarola was excommunicated by the pope because of his out-spoken criticism of papal corruption. On May 23, 1498, Savonarola was hanged and then burned at a stake, and a new government was created. Many powerful Florentines ap-proved of the idea of a republican form of government and began looking for like-minded people to fill government positions. They soon enlisted the services of a young man named Niccolo Machiavelli.

Little is known of Machiavelli's early years. He was born into a middle-class family that had been among the lesser nobility. His father was a doctor of law. According to one biographer, Machiavelli's father did not work very hard at his profession, and most of the family income was derived from inherited land (2). His father read books avidly and spent most of his money buying volumes on various subjects, especially law. Machiavelli began learning Latin at the age of seven and was taught arithmetic when he was eleven. Apparently, he never learned Greek and was not trained to become a "learned man." In-stead, his father provided him with an education suitable for a position in the civil ser-vice. He was apparently well regarded by his family because they chose him to write a letter arguing a legal matter, despite the fact that his father was a lawyer. His education, which consisted primarily of reading and observation, served him well in his new posi-tion in the government.

Machiavelli was elected to the position of secretary of the Second Chancery, a gov-ernmental organization concerned with administering domestic and foreign affairs, by a Florentine governing body just five days after Savonarola was burned at the stake. The position was the top one in the Second Chancery, which was slightly less prominent and less prestigious than the First Chancery. The precise reasons for his selection for this posi-tion have always remained unclear; he did not seem to be extremely well-known and was probably elected because someone prominent pushed his nomination (3).

Whatever the cause, Machiavelli accepted the position and began immediately to fulfill his duties. In general, his job as secretary was to gather information, provide advice, process paperwork, pass on orders, and ensure that orders were carried out. Specifically, he wrote thousands of letters, reported on the war situation with Pisa, served in a diplo-matic role for Florence in dealing with other powers, oversaw the prosecution of unsuc-cessful and successful efforts directed at recapturing Pisa militarily, and managed the implementation of a newly formed citizen militia.

As secretary, he traveled and observed situations firsthand, and many of these expe-riences provided the bases for his later ideas. In studying the war situation in regard to Pisa, for example, Machiavelli went to France and saw how the French viewed the Italian city-states in general, and Florence in particular: without respect, always counting costs, and full of irresoluteness. He also saw the weakness of Italy in which a variety of rival fac-tions were constantly fighting, using allies and hired mercenaries who did not feel alle-giance to anyone. Most important, he saw that alliances were kept only by threats backed by arms and that mere friendship did not guarantee peace because one could not trust that such a relationship would last.

Machiavelli also observed the mostly successful military career of Cesare Borgia. Borgia, the son of Pope Alexander VI, conquered much of central Italy by acting quickly when circumstances changed and deciding matters immediately. In addition to the good fortune of support from the pope, Borgia was prepared for war, took risks, and was not hesitant to turn on friends and allies as he deemed necessary. Borgia's good fortune came to an end when Alexander VI died in 1503 and papal support ended. Indeed, Machiavelli's war stories really were about wars.

Machiavelli's experiences with mercenaries led him to propose repeatedly the creation of a citizen militia in Florence, but the well-off, mostly merchants and landowners, opposed the idea because they were concerned that a trained militia could turn against those in power. Machiavelli's efforts bore fruit when he convinced Soderini, the leading political figure in Florence, of the advantages of a citizen militia. Machiavelli worked tirelessly in the administrative effort to create the militia and by 1506 was able to report that the endeavor was successful.

Although Machiavelli's work was very well regarded, other factors suspended his administrative career. Various factions in Florence were becoming dissatisfied with Soderini, to whom Machiavelli was tied, at least in spirit. It does not seem that Machiavelli owed his job to Soderini, but he supported many of Soderini's actions and the idea of republican government. Soderini had developed a strong relationship with France, a country then out of favor with Pope Julius II. Soderini tried to keep Florence neutral between the French and the pope, but the effort led to great strains domestically in Florence. Supporters of the Medici began to receive support from Julius. Julius made Cardinal Giovanni de' Medici, son of Lorenzo the Magnificent, his legate at Bologna in an effort to encourage Soderini's rivals to see the Medici as the alternative to the current government. Dislike of the Medici had diminished over the years; current family members seemed much more moderate than the former rulers. Soderini resigned in 1512 after months of his rule being weakened by internal and external strife, especially that caused by the pope and the Spaniards, whose army was threatening Florence when he resigned. Ridolfi was selected as the new leader, and the Medici were welcomed back into the city as private citizens.

The Medici's status as private citizens did not last long, however. Ridolfi, under pressure from Medici supporters, resigned, and the Medici began to run Florence again. Machiavelli's position as secretary was now at stake. Machiavelli tried to convince the Medici that, as a public servant, he owed his allegiance to the state, not a faction, and that he could serve the Medici as well as he had served the previous government. The Medici, however, did not see Machiavelli as a neutral figure in their struggle with Soderini and his supporters. On November 7, 1512, Machiavelli was dismissed from his position.

Although depressed by his dismissal, Machiavelli sought a philosophical perspective. In a letter to Soderini, he noted how circumstances change and how one must accommodate oneself to those changes. In effect, he said, fate rules (4).

Fate took an even more negative turn for Machiavelli in February 1513 when he was arrested because his name appeared on a list of potential supporters of a conspiracy against the Medici. He was tortured and imprisoned, but then fate changed again in March. Cardinal de' Medici became Pope Leo X and granted general amnesty to those still imprisoned for the conspiracy. Machiavelli remained in Florence in an effort to obtain employment with the new regime, but no one wanted him or his services. He finally gave up and retired to his country home at Sant' Andrea, seven miles from Florence.

Unhappy with the turn of events, Machiavelli resolved to stop thinking about politics at one point. His abiding interest continued, however, and he discoursed on current events with his friends, including some who were in favor with the Medici regime and some who were republicans.

During his period in Sant' Andrea, Machiavelli wrote most of his significant works while seeking another post in Florentine government. In 1513, Machiavelli produced *The Prince*. It appears that he was working on the longer *Discourses on the First Ten Books of Titus Livius* when he conceived of writing the shorter work. *The Prince* was written for the sake of dedicating it to a Medici. Machiavelli, ever the pragmatist, planned to dedicate the book to Giuliano de' Medici in an obvious attempt at ingratiation, but Giuliano died, and Machiavelli eventually dedicated the book to Lorenzo de' Medici, Giuliano's nephew. Machiavelli had hoped that the book would not only be useful but also assist him in getting a job with the government. The Medici distrust of him ran deep however, and no immediate offer of employment developed.

The Medici apparently expressed no interest in Machiavelli until 1520 when they commissioned him to write a history of Florence, which he did. Following that, he was in communication with various Medici officials in Florence and Rome and undertook some other minor commissions for them.

The Medici did not benefit from Machiavelli's advice and efforts; they were forced from power in Florence in 1527 in favor of a republic. Once again, though, Machiavelli was seen as being positioned on the wrong side. He was now viewed as someone who worked with the Medici and thus could not be trusted in the new government, which had a Savonarolan character (5).

This ironic twist of fate, together with ill health, proved too much for Machiavelli. On June 21, 1527, he died, just days after being rejected by the new government.

B.   Machiavelli's Writings

Machiavelli's writings are vast in number, diverse in character, and excellent in their style and expressiveness. He wrote numerous official letters and reports on foreign countries, rulers, and particular situations. He corresponded for pleasure and on business matters. His four principal works discuss politics, military affairs, and Florentine history. His other literary efforts include two plays, a short story, a variety of poetry, and an essay on the Italian language. In all, Machiavelli returns repeatedly to certain themes and issues that focus on the human condition, particularly as it manifested itself in Italy during his time.

His four principal works are *The Prince*, *Discourses on the First Ten Books of Titus Livius* (*Discourses* hereafter), *The Art of War*, and *The History of Florence*. His literary efforts include the plays *Mandragola* and *Clizia*, the short story *Belfagor*, and the essay *Dialogue on Our Language*.

The Prince was dedicated to a Medici, and the *History of Florence* was commissioned by a Medici. The *Discourses* were dedicated to two republicans who "should be" princes, and the leading characters in *The Art of War* are republicans. Both *The Prince* and the *Discourses* indicate that they contain all the author knows from reading ancient authors and observing contemporary events (6). Of varying lengths, they are essentially operating manuals for acquiring and maintaining governments.

The Prince, his most famous work, serves as the source of most Machiavellian quotations and as the primary basis for his reputation. He modeled it ostensibly on the "mirror of princes" genre, which is exemplified by Xenophon's *Cyropaiedeia* (literally "The Education of Cyrus"). *The Prince* purports to explain what a new ruler needs to know to rule successfully. The *Discourses* parallels the text of *The Prince* in many ways and serves the same purpose for republicans.

Aside from his political works, Machiavelli's other writings place him at least in the front ranks of his time as a historian, military theorist, playwright, and Italian literary stylist. Machiavelli's *The History of Florence* covers the city's history primarily in terms of political events that focused on political divisions, the effects of the papacy, the folly of relying on mercenaries, and the downfall of regimes because of the development of civic factions. It cleverly directs attention away from particular events during the period when Machiavelli served Medici opponents. Machiavelli's historical writings, which also include poems, accord him recognition as one of the two leading historians of the sixteenth century (7).

The Art of War, formally a dialogue, provides a technical description of how to prepare for and conduct war using examples of ancient practice. That work, "the first classic of modern military science," earned Machiavelli recognition as being in the first rank by later military theorists such as Clausewitz (8). Machiavelli's literary efforts earned him recognition as one of the most outstanding Italian literary stylists (9). His play *Mandragola* is considered the best Italian comedy ever written (10).

II. CONTRIBUTIONS

Machiavelli's contribution to public administration is much the same as to modernity in general, but public administration as it is known today should be understood as required by the modern enterprise, human beings self-consciously serving their own needs. With public administration, governments serve human needs. Machiavelli founded or created modernity by successfully teaching that human beings are on their own and should strive to serve their own needs as they see them (11). Public administration is in the business of serving collective needs. The lineage from Machiavelli to public administration is historically long and from diverse sources but fairly easy to discern once attention is directed to it. Machiavelli created the modern perspective in philosophy, science, political philosophy, and political science. Through that modern perspective public administration derives its own perspective and its reason for being.

Modern science enables human beings to manipulate nature and produce many desired outcomes because it is oriented from human needs toward understanding things; things are understood not simply as they are but as means to satisfying human wants. Modern philosophy separates human beings from transcendent realities and keeps their feet firmly planted in secular reality. Modern political philosophy starts from the same place as modern philosophy and science; it understands the political enterprise as establishing stable governance to facilitate fulfilling human needs conceived first of all as the basic material needs. Modern political philosophy creates the viewpoint that people have no other recourse than manipulating reality for human needs.

Modern political philosophy as it developed along one line affected public administration the most through Hobbes, Locke, Montesquieu, and the American founders. That line of development focuses on understanding and managing reality, particularly correctly arranging political power rather than the ends of human existence. After Hobbes, these modern thinkers express themselves more moderately and add other elements to the Machiavellian project but remain true to its basic features.

Modern political science refines Machiavelli's techniques by providing additional doctrines for legitimacy and additional mechanisms for molding people into stable political orders. It has created modern forms of government that serve as the context for public administration. Of particular interest is an invention of Machiavelli's that can be found in all modern government: the executive. Public administration is mostly execution in executive organizations.

Modern governing requires ministering to the public because they are generally the most important and reliable source of political support. The progressive movement, starting in the latter part of the nineteenth century and continuing until the middle of this century, succeeded in broadening the relatively modest scope of government services in the United States. Modern public administration developed out of the progressive movement in the effort to provide more services, in contrast to the less formalized American approaches to public administration chronicled by Leonard D. White. Although progressives might have seen themselves as practical persons working to deal with real problems, they were the agents of a Florentine public administrator turned political philosopher. They advocated broadening the scope of government and brought us the administrative state (12).

Machiavelli created the world within which modern public administration exists. He created modernity, which particularly impacts modern public administration in respect to its perspective, the modern states in which it is found, and the mission of serving people's needs. The Machiavellian modern perspective can be seen in philosophy and science generally, in public administration's technical and neutral orientation, and in the palpable compatibility of Machiavelli's administrative and management views with twentieth-century authors. The modern state is characterized by executives and an emphasis on providing for human needs through public administration. Machiavelli's contributions are discussed below.

A.   Modern Philosophy and Modern Science

Machiavelli is not often noted as a philosopher or scientist. However, his general perspective, which may be taken as an exaggeration of the Renaissance perspective, is synonymous with that of modern philosophy and modern science. In Machiavelli's time, philosophy and science were two overlapping terms with philosophy considered broader.

Machiavelli's philosophic perspective, which he displays rather than argues, is skeptical, empirical, rational, and humanistic. Machiavelli is skeptical in the common sense of the word rather than in the philosophic tradition of Skepticism. He shows that he is not inclined to accept or believe things and that he requires that points be proven. In various places in his writings, he indicates that he does not believe an author was correct (e.g., *Discourses*, Book II, Chapter 5). Machiavelli is empirical in relying on sensory evidence and disbelieving imaginary things. He observes actual events. He is rational in believing that there are reasons for things being the ways they are and that understanding the ways of things is possible from logical reasoning. He writes, "It is well to reason about all things" (13). Machiavelli is humanistic in the sense of placing human beings at the center of things.

His humanistic perspective is interesting both for what it rejects and for what it affirms. Machiavelli's humanistic perspective is most important for rejecting both Christianity and classical philosophy. Christianity and other religions teach about supernatural things, and Machiavelli indicates his lack of agreement with Christianity in a number of places in his writing. In Chapter VI of *The Prince* he discusses Moses as one of four greatest examples of private individuals "who have become princes through their own virtue and not by fortune" (14). Machiavelli writes that one should not speak of Moses in that way because he merely carried out God's orders, but thereafter Machiavelli treats Moses as acting on his own account and not as God's agent. He treats Moses similarly in the *Discourses*, (Book II, Chapter VIII). Machiavelli proceeds similarly in *The Prince* (Chapter XI) by discussing ecclesiastical principalities in secular terms, after saying they were beyond human understanding and maintained by God. Similarly, he indicates that religions are supplanted by other religions due to human actions (*Discourses*, Book II, Chapter V), which pointedly ignores the teaching of Christianity that God sent his son Jesus to earth. Explicit argumentation against Christianity was impolitic during Machiavelli's time, but he adequately indicates his disbelief in Christianity without being unnecessarily offensive or imprudent.

Machiavelli also rejects classical philosophy, which, in contrast to religion, deals with things in terms of "nature." Reality is spoken of as nature, which has a particular order or arrangement of things. Also, particular things are discussed as having their own natures, which order or guide them. Machiavelli does not deny the existence of nature in the sense of reality but does deny the existence of an transcendent order to reality and that particular things have invariable natures. The order of nature in classical philosophy provides the basis for understanding the universe.

For Plato, nature is ordered by the forms, the eidos. Visible reality is a pale reflection of the pure forms of things. In the famous allegory of the cave in *The Republic*, visible reality relates to the forms in the same way as do shadows of crudely formed clay representations of things seen in flickering candlelight relate to the real things. For Aristotle, nature is ordered by teleological causality; of the four kinds of causes, "teleos" causes by providing the end toward which things naturally incline.

Machiavelli's rejection of an orderly nature can be found in his emphasis on the role of chance and fortune in the world. In many places, he essentially states that chance or fortune rules (*The Prince*, Chapter VI, and *Discourses*, Book I, Chapter II), although in many other places he discusses being prepared for fortune, chance events. The world is chancy; therefore, one should be as prepared as possible for whatever occurs as were the exemplary princes cited in Chapter VI of *The Prince*.

In Chapter XV of *The Prince*, he rejects consideration of "imaginary principalities," which would include Plato's *Republic* where Socrates creates a city in speech and explains how the eidos relate to visible reality. His view of causality does not involve "teleos." Also, Machiavelli suggests that at least human nature is somewhat malleable and not invariant.

In this view, neither a revealed religion nor an orderly nature provides clues for human beings to understand the world: no gods pronounce themselves, priests have no special legitimacy, and nature fails to offer a shape of things within which humanity has a special place. Instead, people find themselves in a chancy, chaotic world.

Machiavelli turns his and others' attention to understanding the world based on a human perspective: one looks within rather than up (to God, gods, or earthly agents) or around (the order of nature) to get one's bearings. Such is the modern philosophic viewpoint, which is particularly evident in philosophy from Descartes onward: "I think, therefore I am."

Machiavelli's perspective contributes to the development of modern science by freeing modern human beings from the authority of God, his minions on earth, and the ancients. Machiavelli exemplifies an inductive method of discovery of knowledge that contrasts with the deductive character of most scholastic and ancient knowledge. Although precursors of modern science are found prior to Machiavelli and much development of modern science was of a different character than his work, Machiavelli's perspective and influence can be seen in the development of modern science.

Earlier figures, such as Nicholas of Cusa and Roger Bacon, had emphasized systematic observation, and Leonardo da Vinci contemporaneously and independently developed an accurate understanding of human anatomy and conceived of several science principles unknown before his time. Another contemporary, Copernicus, and his assistant, Kepler, are generally credited with beginning the revolution of modern science by Copernicus placing the sun at the center of the solar system and by Kepler doing the mathematical calculations to show that the planets' orbits are elliptical.

Machiavelli's perspective and influence can be found in the work of Francis Bacon, Hobbes, and Descartes. Francis Bacon, an early exponent of inductive reasoning and empirical science, unequivocally endorses Machiavelli's perspective when he says, "We are much beholden to Machiavelli and others that write what men do, and not what they ought to do" (15). Hobbes used Machiavelli's perspective to investigate the world. Like the Florentine, he rejected the authority of the ancients and the scholastics; unlike him, he wrote extensively on scientific subjects in a modern manner (e.g., human perception). Descartes admired Hobbes and wrote him a letter in his youth, derived much of his orientation to methods from Bacon, and in private letters said "he accepted 'the principal precept' of Machiavelli" (16). Francis Bacon and Descartes followed Machiavelli's perspective and greatly developed the idea of inductive observation into the rudiments of the modern scientific method, including the application of mathematics (17).

B.   Modern Political Philosophy

Machiavelli is generally accorded credit for establishing modern political philosophy. Socrates was said to have called philosophy down into the polis, the city-state political entity of the ancient Greeks, from above. Socrates applied philosophy to politics. In contrast, Machiavelli decided that political philosophy did not require traditional philosophy or theology when he detached it from them. Modern political philosophy is humanistic in perspective. It starts from existing conditions, either actual or hypothetical, to theorize about what should be done politically, the political ought. For Machiavelli, the existing conditions are tripartite: the current political chaos of Italy that was described earlier, the origins of political communities, and the examples of antiquity.

First, contemporary Italian political chaos was brought about, he argued, because of the weaknesses of the teaching of the Christian Church (to them life in this world is but a pale reflection of the rewards of an afterlife), the obvious disbelief by much of the leadership of the Church toward that teaching, and the paucity of capable political leaders. The resulting political chaos required solution. Machiavelli hoped his teaching would be applied in Italy, and he insisted in the concluding chapter of *The Prince* that a united Italy could be created.

Second, Machiavelli theorized about the human condition in the beginnings, both the beginnings that brought people together into political communities and the beginnings of political orders or regimes that shape people into particular political communities. Machiavelli took his bearings not from any human end, such as a teleos to politics or an afterlife, but from the efficient causes of human behaviors. In doing so, he examined situations that were extreme cases, especially those that involved innovations, the creation of new things.

The condition of human beings initially was few in number and dispersed like the beasts. When their numbers increased, human beings came together in groups and built cities to unite in defense from one another. Machiavelli, shortly after rejecting another well-known Aristotlean position (the division of regimes into just and unjust), denies both the political nature of human beings asserted by Aristotle and the biblical story of the Garden of Eden (*Discourses*, Book I, Chapter II).

Later modern political philosophers follow Machiavelli in using a state of nature formulation, most notably Hobbes, Locke, and Rousseau who dwell explicitly on the logical consequences of humanity's original condition. What human beings are most needful of in this state of nature is security. Interestingly, human beings need security from one another because nature does not provide enough bounty, as Machiavelli said about why the Gauls invaded Rome, or they are not satisfied with the bounty provided by nature (*Discourses*, Book II, Chapter VIII). Human beings are so acquisitive that their appetites are not limited (*Discourses*, Book I, Chapter V; *The Prince*, Chapter III).

Machiavelli discussed the origins of cities by advancing his own version of a cycle of government theory that had been originated by the Greek Polybius (*Discourses*, Book I, Chapter II) (18). When human beings come together they choose a leader, establish laws that constitute justice, and thus begin a political community. A leader is elected because of positive qualities, and polities generally maintain themselves as long as the leader maintains those qualities.

A polity degenerates when the sovereign becomes a hereditary and nonelective ruler. This results in tyranny because rulers indulge their own pleasures, become hated by the populace, become fearful because of popular hatred, and act to protect themselves against the people. Eventually, a tyrant is overthrown by the public under the leadership of a few outstanding individuals, who become the new leaders.

The new aristocratic rulers govern well, but their children allow the government to become oligarchic, the rule of a few in their own interest. The oligarchic government is overthrown in turn, and a popular government is instituted. Popular government degenerates after a generation into licentious or anarchy, whereupon rule is given to a single individual again.

Cities will inevitability go through this cycle if they can manage to continue to exist independently. However, historical examples prove that it is possible, at least to some extent, to overcome the inevitability of the cycle by combining into one government the elements of the rule of the one, a few, and the many, as was done intentionally by the Spartan legislator Lycurgus and as occurred by chance in Rome. Machiavelli's solution to the problem of the instability of government is a very conventional one, even though the problem is not.

In advocating a compound republic, Machiavelli shows why he chose the Roman path over the Spartan one. The Roman path enables a republic to defend itself against outside forces more easily and surely whereas the Spartans were lucky that they were not conquered by a larger power. The question eliciting the choice of Sparta or Rome is the question of whether to place the greater political power in the hands of the few, who sometimes are called the great and who are or pretend to be superior to most people, or the many. Machiavelli preferred greater power in the hands of the many; he advocated popular government in the sense of the many participating because, on balance, it gives a polity greater capacity to act and, therefore, to survive. The relevant power here is the power to win militarily against other polities. Because of their hand in the government and their desire to continue to secure its benefits, most people support compound governments.

Third, Machiavelli used the existing conditions of antiquity by relying on ancient examples, especially from Rome, that contrast greatly with the Italian political chaos created by the defects of the Church in Rome. He indicated that modern peoples had been weakened by Christianity. He asserted that people can learn what they need to do by carefully studying the superior examples of ancients, which partially involves not being Christian. Machiavelli indicated a preference for ancient practice over ancient theory. His modern theory is based on ancient practice. Ancient examples shield some of his teaching from the less educated or less interested because his examples prove the opposite of what he says explicitly.

As is the case generally with people claiming to be realistic rather that idealistic, Machiavelli coped with the problem of his own ideals. Some historians portray Machiavelli as a somewhat impractical theoretician who was comparatively naive, in contrast to his friend Francesco Guicciardini, a Medici supporter and the greatest historian of the sixteenth century (19). In realist-idealist debates, the meaningful focus is on the appropriate standards (e.g., what are the real ideals?). Realists typically deny the meaningfulness of idealists' ideals in the sense of them being appropriate, whether the ideals are called imaginary, unattainable, or detrimental; idealists argue the contrary.

Realists must either accept a lack of ideals or find a source or basis for ideals. Machiavelli found his standards, his source for oughts, in existing conditions, particularly human nature and the beginnings of things. Human beings find themselves in a situation involving an improvident nature and often a lot of other less than helpful people. People need to satisfy their material wants for food and shelter and the corollary requirement for security in their possessions. Needs guide human beings. The new standard or ideal for collectivities of human beings is fulfilling needs. Human nature, particularly needs, becomes the source of the ends to pursue. In addition, the ends do not involve what is considered the highest in human nature but the lowest, the ever-present needs. This view involves a radical transformation or reformulation of the meaning of good and bad and the ends of political communities.

Machiavelli portrays human nature primarily in terms of needs and emotions. Human beings possess various needs that include the following: the need to acquire material requirements, which cannot be satisfied because of an unlimited appetite and an uncertain future; the need of a few people to dominate, which is associated with a desire for attention or glory; the need of most people to avoid being dominated, which can be called liberty or freedom; the need to innovate; the need to observe innovations; and the need to be secure. Emotions of note include hope, fear, love, and hate. Machiavelli derives his ends from needs and suggests using needs and emotions to attain his ends. Necessity rather than choice produces better results (*Discourses*, Book I, Chapter I).

The ends of Machiavelli's political community are fulfilling needs, which requires security more than anything else. Security is achieved through enabling people to pursue material well-being and their other needs in such a way that they balance one another in a stable regime. Security is also achieved by being prepared for avoiding conquest, which ultimately leads to conquering other political communities first. "Good arms," which Machiavelli uses to include military means, exist especially for the sake of external relations but also can be used internally for maintenance of regimes.

Only within this context of the ends of political community coming from needs and those ends being served by manipulating emotions does the meaning of Machiavellianism as being cunning and using brutality make sense. In Chapter XVIII of *The Prince*, he suggests that a successful prince must be cunning like the fox and brutal like the lion. Machiavelli does not suggest being cunning or brutal as art forms or as intrinsically good. Brutality in the sense of killing people or otherwise causing them harm and cunningness in the sense of engaging in deception are means to ends. The ends are a secure and stable political order within which people can fulfill their needs. The ends justify the means for Machiavelli because there are no other acceptable standards to be concerned with meeting: "and in the actions of all men, and especially of princes, where there is no court to appeal to, one looks to the end. So let a prince win and maintain his state: the means will always be judged honorable, and will be praised by everyone" (20). Machiavelli rejects all other standards for justifying means.

Machiavelli's writings frequently have a paradoxical or ironic quality as he transforms terms in respect to their meaning relative to good and bad, including, particularly, good, bad, and virtue. For example, Machiavelli talks about a conspirator who was unable to commit a murder in church and failed in the conspiracy on that account (*Discourses*, Book III, Chapter 6). Machiavelli suggests that the ends of political stability require "well-committed cruelties" (*The Prince*, chapters IX and XIII). The unreal expectations of previous teachings impelled human beings to fail to do what is necessary, particularly in Italy, and thereby caused great harm without producing great benefits.

Machiavelli emphasizes fraud and force as means because they are the most efficacious in manipulating people to do what he believes they should do. He discusses appearances and emotions in chapters XV–XIX of *The Prince*. He begins by dismissing "imaginary republic and principalities" and "how one should live." In effect, he suggests that propaganda become an official policy because people react to appearances. The appearances that he most recommends are ones that engender fear and love. Both should be relied upon but fear more than love where both are not possible. Appearances that generate hate and contempt should be avoided to the extent possible (e.g., if a situation is such that someone is going to hate a ruler, it is better that the persons doing the hating are less powerful and as far away from the ruler as possible). Fear is to be relied on the most because it generally appears to be the best motivator and the one most easily manipulated by a ruler. People love at their own choice while they fear at the ruler's choice (*The Prince*, Chapter XVII).

The greatest founders of governments that Machiavelli cites as examples to follow are shown to have committed serious crimes (e.g., Romulus killed his own brother for the sake of founding Roman, a well-committed cruelty apparently). Founding and crime are not different in character except that successfully founding serves more persons' needs. Founders are public-spirited criminals. Machiavelli takes his bearings from foundings but also suggests refounding and readjusting political orders. Not only are the greatest founders in effect excused for their crimes because of the consequences of their foundings, but Machiavelli appears to suggest also that criminal activities may be appropriate in the ordinary operations of political orders if justified by the requirements for stability.

Although much more could be written about Machiavelli's political philosophy, the essential aspects are covered here for the present audience. Modern political philosophy has developed in many different respects. Machiavelli disengaged political philosophy from the standards of religion and a transcendent nature. Subsequent modern political philosophers have pursued political philosophy in terms of rights, history, and an essentially subjective human existence. Our own American experiment in self-government proceeds from Machiavelli's development of modern political philosophy.

C.   Modern Political Science

Machiavelli separated modern political science, the study of politics, from political philosophy by separating the study of the means from the ends of politics (21). Modern political science after Machiavelli generally follows the modern scientific method. Modern political science is especially about the means of politics, how things are done, rather the ends of politics. Modern political science is essentially behaviorally oriented in the sense of determining what means of acting politically cause particular behavioral results. In modern political science, much attention is focused on the causes of behavior, which often involve needs and emotions in some fashion, and regular patterns of behavior, which are often called institutions.

In ancient political science, politics was studied in terms of making the right decisions; modern politics is studied in terms of what means produce what results. Also, the study of international relations occurs in modern political science in contrast to its treatment by ancient historians. Modern political science, as it stretches from the time of Machiavelli, can be divided primarily between that undertaken inside and outside academic environs. Prior to this century, few who wrote about the science of politics were in academic life, and most were somehow connected to the practice of politics. Currently, for the most part, those who write about the science of politics are members of political science departments. The earlier writers tend to be more institutionally oriented and the later group more behaviorally oriented.

The earlier modern writers on the science of politics include the founders of the United States. Their goals and solutions to pursuing governmental stability are Machiavellian in the more generous sense. Alexander Hamilton, John Jay, and James Madison, writing as Publius, provide an example in essays written in support of ratifying the U.S. Constitution. The essays, published as *The Federalist*, exhibit a self-conscious understanding of modern politics involving different things than ancient politics. They include particularly modern institutional inventions in the science of politics:

> The efficacy of various principles is now well understood, which were either not known at all, or imperfectly known to the ancients. The regular distribution of power into distinct departments; the introduction of legislative balances and checks; the institution of courts composed of judges holding their offices during good behavior; the representation of the people in the legislatures by deputies of their own election; these are wholly new discoveries, or have made their principal progress towards perfection in modern times (22).

Two of the most frequently recognized aspects of our constitutional system, separation of powers and multiplicity of interests, are excellent examples of modern institutional solutions that the ancients probably would not have considered. The separation of powers, which is the division of governing powers between the three branches of government, is supplemented by federalism. Federalism is the division of governing powers between the federal and state governments. It is also supplemented by bicameralism, the division of legislative powers between two houses. Publius argues in *Federalist* 51 that these divisions of governing power are appropriate because human beings are not angels and need to be set to watching each others' actions carefully.

The pattern of the separation of powers recalls Machiavelli's recommendation to divide power between the one, the few, and the many. The multiplicity of interests (based on the different actual ways people have of acquiring) contributes to stability by making a single oppressive majority unlikely because it would be difficult to constitute a majority so as to take extreme advantage of one part of the political community. In *Federalist* 10, Publius advocates the utility of the multiplicity of interests approach after explicitly rejecting as unworkable the traditional classic teachings about how to attain stability.

Academic political science work tends to be behaviorally oriented and scientific in the sense of being empirically based and quantitatively analyzed insofar as possible. Examples include voting behavior, public opinion, legislative behavior, causes of war and nonwar, and political similarities and dissimilarities between countries.

One aspect of modern political science studied by earlier writers and academics is the modern institution referred to as the executive. Because of the importance of that institution to understanding Machiavelli's relationship to public administration, it will be discussed within that topic.

D.   Influences on Public Administration

Public administration, which, as described by Leonard D. White, "consists of all those operations having for their purpose the fulfillment or enforcement of public policy," derives much of its contemporary being from Machiavelli (23). It can be called Machiavellian because Machiavelli created the modern enterprise that has become centered on public administration; the modern executive, under whose auspices most public administration takes place as execution of policy; and the modern perspective, within which public administration operates.

1.   The Modern Enterprise

Public administration is concerned with administering to public needs and is at the heart of the modern enterprise begun by Machiavelli. The modern enterprise transformed politics and government from improving people to meet higher standards to improving the standards of services for people. In Chapter XIV of the first part of his *Leviathan*, Hobbes continued that enterprise by making human needs into "rights" and political communities into social contracts for securing rights that formerly were unlimited but ineffectually secured. Locke sustained it by making Hobbes's views appear moderate and reasonable by making the state of nature and government appear less harsh. The American founders advanced it by creating governments to secure rights. Progressives, who heard other modern voices speaking about advances in human history and who wanted governments to serve a wider range of needs than the founders, fostered the creation of the administrative state. The modern project continues and is carried out in large part by public administrationists who serve people's needs.

2.   The Modern Executive

Public administration is primarily the execution of policies. Executing policies means taking actions to put general decisions into particular effect. Those executing are implementing general decisions made by someone else. In modern governments, public administration mostly operates under the auspices and authority of executives who are charged with the responsibility of overseeing execution of policies. Public administration is executive in character and hence Machiavellian in that sense. The oft-commented on technical and neutral character of public administration may be partially traced to its executive underpinning originated by Machiavelli.

Machiavelli invented the modern executive (24). Machiavelli's Prince is the prototype of the modern executive, who is simultaneously superordinate and subordinate. His Prince is awe-inspiring and active in doing needful things, executing. Today, those in public administration focus on the activity of the executive, especially as extended into administrative agencies, and mostly do not notice the awe-inspiring character of the executive because Machiavelli's conception has been refined through the efforts of Hobbes, Locke, Montesquieu, and the American founders (25).

Machiavelli's Prince is designed especially to inspire awe and the fear of losing what people hold dear: life, loved ones, and possessions. The Prince does so by boldly executing plans and a few people. The Prince is a device to strike fear in the hearts of the public because they tend to forget the fear they have at the time of foundings that make them behave in a public-spirited fashion. The guilt or innocence of particular individuals executed does not seem at all important for Machiavelli. The Prince enables political communities to overcome the cyclical revolution of political orders or regimes by regularly reenacting an initial founding that reveals to individuals the brute necessity of submitting their wills to another's will. Machiavelli emphasizes the superordinate aspect of the Prince, but even in that light the Prince serves the public.

The Prince is not a scaled-back divine-right monarch or like any another ruler previously proposed. All previous accounts of rulers discussed their right or entitlement to rule (i.e., why these particular people should be in charge). For ancient authors, the best rulers were entitled to rule; for Christians, the Pope and divine-right monarchs had an inherited divine grant of authority. For Machiavelli, the role of the Prince is not a matter of right or legitimacy but a function that needs to be carried out to maintain political stability. He seems to prefer that one person acting as the Prince be killed by another as that is awe-inspiring.

Aristotle and Machiavelli start off in the same place in conceiving of governing. Both assert the requirement that someone interpret laws for specific situations, which is also the fundamental basis of the public administration question of discretion. Then, they diverge. Aristotle argues for rulers applying laws to situations with justice as the end. He reserves a few low political offices, which might be called executive in character, for carrying out decisions that are necessary if law is to be followed (26). Machiavelli generally recommends executions to maintain stability and focuses his teaching on promoting his original version of the executive: the Prince.

Machiavelli's Prince has been constitutionalized in the American political order, thanks especially to Locke. The American executive appears much more subordinated than his Prince. Our presidency is constitutionally limited in legal powers, subject to laws, checked by the other two branches' powers, potentially subject to impeachment and conviction by Congress, and dependent on popular support. Still, when our presidents see a need to act, they have been willing to do what they think necessary in the absence of law or contrary to law while invoking the name of the people. Abraham Lincoln is the most outstanding example of a president acting from necessity, and he is revered as one of our greatest leaders. Some aspects of Machiavelli's Prince are evident in the discussion of the presidency in *The Federalist*.

Public administrationists follow the less prominent teaching concerning the Prince's doing needful things, the subordinate part of the modern executive. In doing so, they execute law in the positive sense of providing services but also have to exercise discretion.

Like other executive officials, public administrators are formally subordinate to others but, in reality, are primarily in control of carrying out their responsibilities.

Machiavelli shows relatively little in the way of substantive positive government programs. He does indicate that the Prince should deal with the basic problem of political stability by preventing others from dominating the people, maintaining fear, not taking advantage of the people by taking their property, and providing for the common defense. An exception is a series of suggestions in the last paragraph of Chapter XXI of *The Prince*. They include a rudimentary economic development policy of low taxes and incentives for economic activity and a public relations program of entertainment and personal appearances.

Machiavelli's Prince and modern executives do not seem very similar at first glance. They have different titles and different levels of authority. Mansfield, however, finds seven elements of the modern executive in Machiavelli, some of which are also characteristic of or exhibited by public administration practice. Those elements include: using punishment for political purposes, elevating war and foreign affairs above peace and domestic affairs, using indirect government, portraying execution as a universal technique, emphasizing decisiveness, valuing secrecy, and making one person the chief executive (27).

Punishment carried out by executives serves political purposes by encouraging others to undertake actions considered good and to avoid actions considered bad. The legality and justice of actual punishments are far less important in Machiavelli's doctrine than the fact that other people are impressed by the punishments. Contemporary, albeit milder, administrative examples of similar use of punishments might include the U.S. Internal Revenue Service planning its criminal prosecutions with the intent of having convictions occur during the personal income tax filing season to promote tax compliance and police departments publicizing the names of persons arrested for soliciting prostitutes. Executive punishment also prevents many people from attempting to punish those whom they perceive as having wronged them. Those who perceive wrongs can hope for executive punishment and will fear punishment for themselves if they disturb public tranquility. Discretionary use of authority by executive officials is often used as punishment. A separate and independent judiciary, emphasized by Montesquieu, diminishes the political authority of chief executives but has less influence at lower administrative levels where discretion is exercised. Publius speaks of the presidency being useful "where the terror of an example was necessary" (28).

War and foreign affairs assume primacy for Machiavelli's executive because he sees the same situation internally and externally for a political community. In both cases, the rule is conquer or be conquered. The two causes of the demise of political orders are internal instability arising from the people forgetting their fear and an inability to prevent external forces from conquering them (*The Prince*, Chapter XIX). The one art that the Prince needs to know is war (*The Prince*, Chapter IX). The internal and external situations go hand in hand; internal order contributes to the exercise of power externally, and the use of power externally justifies internal order. The executive conquers internally and externally. The language and imagery of war appears particularly attractive to recent American presidents (e.g., President Johnson's War on Poverty).

Indirect government means that executives do not rule in their own name. They claim to act as an agent for someone else by formally using the authority of those for whom they act (i.e., the people). Indirect government allows an executive to rule in effect while claiming to carry out responsibilities. Indirect government makes people see themselves as subjecting themselves to self-rule and thereby helps overcome the public's desire to avoid being ruled. The people's dissatisfaction with submitting to an executive is mitigated by the idea that they are really imposing requirements on the executive to carry out for them. Public administrators display this notion in that they, too, get their authority from the people ultimately by way of delegation from the executive. Involving people in the actions of and responsibility for government increases the people's governability.

Machiavelli suggests that executive actions are a universally applicable technique in the sense of not being bound to any form of government. For Machiavelli, the form of a political order in respect to the distribution of offices is not important as it was for the ancient authors. They devoted much attention to discussing the best regime, whereas Machiavelli seems relatively indifferent to whether a government is a republic or a principality. What matters is the effective use of techniques. Executives, whether royal or republican, should maintain order using Machiavelli's techniques regardless of form of government. Publius also expresses this view to a qualified degree in *Federalist* 68:

> Though we cannot acquiesce in the political heresy of the poet who says:
>> 'For forms of government let fools contest—
>> That which is best administered is best,'—
> yet we may safely pronounce, that the true test of a good government is its aptitude and tendency to produce a good administration (29).

One early public administration author, Woodrow Wilson, wrote about learning the technique of how to sharpen a knife from a villain without necessarily acquiring anything more than knife-sharpening skills (30). His words suggest that techniques are neutral between forms of government and can be transplanted from one to another easily. Also, Wilson advocated more power for the president in *Congressional Government*.

Decisiveness, in the sense of acting suddenly and unequivocally, changes situations and brings attention to the executive. Undertaking initiatives and being energetic are synonymous with decisiveness. For Machiavelli, after an act has been performed, one can find the words to explain it. Deeds come before words. Working through decisions so that deeds fit words is overly deliberative; exactly what course is chosen matters less than that action is vigorously pursued. In *Federalist* 70 to 77, Publius also expresses this view when he recommends a vigorous executive: "Energy in the executive is a leading character in the definition of good government" (31). Progressives and contemporary advocates of an administrative state support an energetic executive sector (32).

Executives, and also conspirators, value secrecy to prevent others who may not agree with executives' intentions from learning about them. In many cases, successful executions of intentions, especially illegal ones, may be aided by secrecy. Secrecy may require deception or fraud. In public administration, secrecy allows persons with knowledge to surprise other people and to avoid being surprised in turn. Public administrators are lesser executives carrying out their responsibilities to achieve effectiveness.

Machiavelli emphasizes the utility of having one person be responsible for executing designs because it is better to have one opinion and because one person can be motivated by the ambition of being the executive and being glorified for successes. Publius follows this view in *Federalist'* 70 and 72. Unity supports energy and also "Decision, activity, secrecy, and dispatch" (33). In administrative theory, Weber and Gulick suggest that having one person heading an organization increases its effectiveness.

Machiavelli's Prince appears extreme because of later developments that have toned down, softened the rough edges, and hidden from view the brutality, immorality or amorality, and cunning of the executive. Machiavelli's prototype executive has been more refined than changed. Public administration follows in the executive tradition started by Machiavelli by displaying many of the same elements that are incorporated in his executive, the Prince.

3.   The Modern Perspective

With the modern enterprise, Machiavelli created the modern perspective within which public administration operates. That perspective is peculiarly characterized by a political concern for the effectiveness of executive organizations. In that vein, Machiavelli's writings display many concepts incorporated into modern public administration. Unlike any other author up to his time, Machiavelli has many of the qualities of a public management analyst or a public policy analyst. The affinity of Machiavelli's perspective with modern public administration can be shown by looking at that perspective generally and by comparing some of his statements with two major well-known twentieth-century doctrines of major influence in public administration: Luther Gulick's functions of the executive (POSDCORB) and Frederick Winslow Taylor's four principles of scientific management.

a.   MACHIAVELLI AND POLICY.   That Machiavelli displays many of the concerns of a public management analyst or public policy analyst is understandable because of his concern about pursuing security and well-being for the public. Unlike earlier thinkers who viewed the public more as a backdrop or a means than a central concern or an end, Machiavelli focuses on the public as the primary basis for political stability and public needs as the rationale for the state. On that basis, relations with the public (public relations in its fullest sense) matter, which makes appearances (public relations as currently understood) important because for Machiavelli, as discussed earlier, the public mostly consumes appearances.

Machiavelli examines many policy questions and reaches many conclusions. For example, in situations where two neighboring entities are about to engage in warfare, it is better to pick a side than to try to remain neutral (*The Prince*, Chapter XXI). Machiavelli's concern in analyzing policy options involves the idea of effectiveness; he suggests doing what will achieve success, that is, achieving objectives. The term "policy" as used by Elizabethans was associated with Machiavelli and with the idea of a set of self-conscious choices for public actions oriented toward success. Critics suggested that the use of this Machiavellian policy perspective was defective because it abstracted from moral concerns in the sense of doing the proper thing (34).

Today, few think that an alternative to policy in the Machiavellian sense exists. Policies are techniques, ways of doing things, that are intended to accomplish ends. In that sense, policies are technical, as was sharpening a knife for Woodrow Wilson. Also, policies are neutral in that they abstract from other concerns (e.g, do not deal with normative standards). Some contemporary public administration authors seem to view policy as ethical (e.g., they express a preference for situational ethics) (35).

Machiavelli's emphasis on using proper techniques for achieving ends is neutral in respect to who actually uses the techniques. He believes his techniques will lead to success. His neutrality is evident from his apparent indifference to whoever uses his techniques because he provides advice freely to many people: Italians and those invading Italy, royalty and republicans, and those conspiring and those conspired against (*The Prince*, Chapter XIX and *Discourses*, Book III, Chapter 6) (36). The technical neutrality of modern public administration thus traces to Machiavelli.

In analyzing options, Machiavelli expresses himself in the "on the one hand and on the other hand" manner of public administrationists. He writes, "And thus it is seen in all human affairs, upon careful examination, that you cannot avoid one inconvenience without incurring another" (37). He continues a few sentences later, "And therefore in all our decisions we must consider well what presents the least inconveniences, and then choose the best, for we shall never find any course entirely free from objection" (38).

b. MACHIAVELLI AND POSDCORB.   In "Notes on the Theory of Organization," Luther Gulick declares that "POSDCORB" indicates the functional work elements of organizations' chief executives. POSDCORB stands for planning, organizing, staffing, directing, coordinating, reporting, and budgeting (39). Machiavelli indicates in his writings why and how such functions need to be performed by his Prince. Once again, Machiavelli contributes the modern perspective to public administration, especially the political perspective of an executive serving the needs of the public.

In respect to planning, which for Gulick involves outlining objectives and methods, Machiavelli preaches preparedness in the sense of constantly planning ahead to see what situations may arise and how they might be handled. He writes in Chapter III of *The Prince*: "What all wise princes should do: they not only have to have regard for present troubles but also for future ones, and they have to avoid these with all their industry because, when one foresees from afar, one can easily find a remedy for them but when you wait until they come close to you, the medicine is not in time because the disease has become incurable."

In Chapter VI, he indicates that the greatest founders were prepared to act when fortune gave them an opportunity. In Chapter XIV, he suggests that princes always be industrious in preparing themselves for war by practicing with deeds and with the mind to be able to cope with any unforeseen events. In Chapter XXIV, he says that previous princes came to ruin in adverse times because they did not foresee and act on future storms during calm times. Machiavelli suggests planning for the sake of maintaining political stability, which also requires military capabilities.

In respect to organizing, which for Gulick entails establishing a formal authority structure, Machiavelli speaks more to the issue of authority than to specific hierarchical divisions of authority and more generally to ordering people. Machiavelli expresses a concern for his Prince maintaining authority and position. The most important thing is to gain and hold popular support. The most likely threat is from the few who are or consider themselves great and who think themselves equal to the Prince. Some of the few are obligated or dependent on the Prince's good fortune whereas others are more concerned with themselves.

The Prince should fear those more concerned for themselves and use his power to make and unmake persons considered great to obviate the danger they pose during times of adversity (*The Prince*, Chapter IX). More generally, Machiavelli suggests that people are matter that can be shaped into various forms (e.g., republics and principalities). He writes about the greatest founders in Chapter VI of *The Prince*: "And as one examines their actions and lives, one does not see that they had anything else from fortune than the opportunity, which gave them the matter enabling them to introduce any form they pleased" (40). In respect to formal authority structures, per se, Machiavelli uses terms denoting a military hierarchy of officers and responsibilities in *The Art of War* without a great deal of discussion.

In respect to staffing, which for Gulick is the whole personnel function, Machiavelli treats that function in *The Art of War* in great detail. He explicitly addresses the selection of soldiers and their training, supervision, motivation, and discipline. Machiavelli describes an interesting merit pay system from ancient practice: a portion of every soldier's pay during campaigns was held by the flag bearer to encourage the soldiers to protect their flags (41).

In respect to directing, which for Gulick means deciding matters and issuing orders, Machiavelli indicates that the Prince is well-advised to maintain command of his state absolutely in terms of being in control of decision making, to supervise the work of his ministers by praising good actions and correcting bad ones, and to make his own decisions. In chapters IX, XXII, and XXIII of *The Prince* Machiavelli suggests that the Prince oversee the operations of government, which appears reasonably close to how Gulick describes executive directing, "serving as the leader of the enterprise" (42). On the other hand, Machiavelli shows little concern with the difficulties of decision making or communications beyond making sure that soldiers get their orders from their leadership (43).

In respect to coordinating, which for Gulick involves interrelating the various parts of the work, Machiavelli offers little in the way of insight beyond arguing for keeping one's army in "good order." By doing so, Machiavelli insists that a numerically inferior army that is superior in discipline can be relied on to defeat a numerically superior army (44).

In respect to reporting, which for Gulick means the executive keeping himself and his subordinates informed of what is going on and informing those to whom he is responsible, Machiavelli emphasizes the latter and indicates that his Prince "informs" others by appearances, which are often deceptive, and decisive actions, which may be forceful. He suggests that the Prince select wise advisors, maintain their faithfulness, and encourage them to speak the complete truth, but only on matters about which he asks and nothing else. He suggests that this policy also guards against flattery (*The Prince*, chapters XXII and XXIII). Machiavelli does not envision the same kind of reporting system as Gulick because the public is easily fooled. Machiavelli's reporting system is hierarchically up to the Prince, and the Prince serves the public by reporting to them what he thinks appropriate.

In respect to budgeting, which Gulick understands as fiscal planning, accounting, and control, Machiavelli displays an understanding of economy in the use of resources as well as brutality and efficiency in the use of tax resources. Machiavelli is a fiscal conservative. He displays this clearly when he suggests that although a reputation for liberality in the sense of lavish displays or special treatment for a few involving large expenditures is good, the effects of such large expenditures are extremely bad for a state and a prince. Therefore, having a reputation for meanness in the sense of not making unnecessary expenditures is better.

Fiscally this means avoiding needless expenditures and needless taxation, avoiding taking subjects' property, and holding onto resources for the sake of military defense. Needless expenditures by princes lead either to poverty or to levying new, additional, or extraordinary taxes on people and taking their property. These actions tend to agitate the people and cause them to hate the Prince and hold him in contempt, both of which are not recommended. In addition, a Prince requires tax revenues to engage in military defense without unduly burdening the people, from whom he generally should draw support in his governance. However, liberality is recommended when dealing with the booty of conquest (*The Prince*, chapters III, XVI, and XVII).

In summary, Gulick, writing more than 400 years after Machiavelli, displays a remarkably similar viewpoint on executive functions. This does not mean that Gulick got his ideas from Machiavelli, but it does support the view that Machiavelli initiated the perspective within which Gulick worked.

c. MACHIAVELLI AND SCIENTIFIC MANAGEMENT.   Various management-oriented authors have given Machiavelli a reputation as providing advice for managers. They see his suggestions in *The Prince* as counsel applicable to management, even though the advice cited is primarily suitable for chief executives, those who would be chief executives, and perhaps heads of organizations who would dominate situations to maintain order—killing people has long since been frowned on as a management technique.

Machiavelli's advice in regard to management may be more easily found in *The Art of War* where he details how to undertake large-scale enterprises. One way of approaching his advice on management is to compare his account with more recent work. Here, Machiavelli's statements are compared with Frederick Winslow Taylor's principles of scientific management that have had a impact on the development of the theory and practice of public administration. Again, the object is not to show that a writer important to modern public administration derived his particular ideas from Machiavelli, but instead to show that the perspective initiated by Machiavelli establishes a framework within which management theorizing as known today occurs. That this view is true can be shown by establishing a fundamental similarity between Taylor's and Machiavelli's discussions of management.

Taylor's four principles of scientific management are relatively simple to state: managers of enterprises develop a science of work, select workers suitable for doing that work, bring the science of work together with the workers, and, finally, do whatever else is necessary to facilitate work being performed effectively and efficiently (45). Machiavelli generally fosters a favorable view of rational, empirical inquiry directed toward practical ends by denigrating religion, received authority, and accounts of beneficent nature.

In *The Art of War*, Machiavelli expresses favorable views on human efforts to improve their situation. He says "the defects of nature may be supplied by art and industry—which in this case is more effective than nature" (46). Also, he favors learning the principles of practical arts when he says that "every art has its general rules and principles upon which it is founded" (47). That work symbolizes his effort to learn about conducting war, which can be seen as equivalent with internal political governance or as a necessary adjunct (*The Prince*, chapters IX and XIX). He discusses all aspects of military affairs based on ancient authors, contemporary examples, and his own reasoning on the subject matter. For example, he recommends the use of particular weapons, particular formations, methods of fortification, and even obliquely angled wheel spokes. Although some of his views have proved to be historically wrong, his study of conducting war was seriously undertaken and has been well regarded by other leading figures on war (48).

Although Machiavelli seems to disagree with the view that there is one best way in politics (because events depend on chance), he clearly favors routine operating procedures. In *The Art of War*, for example, he argues that armies should always encamp in the exact same way for the sake of defense (49). Machiavelli and Taylor do not concern themselves with abstract matters but instead with discovering the best possible techniques for the sake of creating better results. Machiavelli does not use time and motion studies or modern engineering techniques, but, as Taylor does later, Machiavelli presents what he suggests is knowledge of how real things work and not just traditional rules of thumb, opinions, or guesswork.

The second and third principles, selecting workers and bringing them and the science of the work together, generally encompasses what is called personnel management, how to deal with people in respect to productive enterprises. Both Taylor and Machiavelli explicitly discuss selection, training, remuneration, motivation, supervision, and discipline. Taylor was often criticized as being less than affable when relating to working people, and Machiavelli expresses a generally harsher management style befitting military affairs; nevertheless both stressed communicating to subordinates the appropriateness of collective cooperation based on collective self-interest.

Taylor's fourth principle essentially involves managers providing for the availability of the appropriate workers, information, tools, and material along with their proper ordering so as to make it possible for workers to do their work as efficiently and effectively as possible. Taylor contrasts the newer active management style of scientific management with the older one of managers simply directing that workers accomplish some result. For Machiavelli, officers serve as managers in gathering intelligence, creating stratagems, supplying provisions, and deciding how armies should act and react in particular situations (50).

Thus, despite writing approximately four centuries earlier, Machiavelli discusses the conduct of war in a manner similar to Taylor's principles of scientific management. Both Machiavelli and Taylor are concerned with managing enterprises, and both have a technique-oriented, means-ends rationality, empirical, and material view.

III. CONCLUSION

Like Bacon, we are much beholden to Machiavelli. His origination of the modern enterprise of serving human needs created the need for modern public administration, the modern perspective that emphasizes effectiveness (and hence techniques that are morally neutral), and the executive. Modern public administration helps to fulfill Machiavelli's vision of the future. Critics of the Machiavellian project point to the neutrality of techniques (i.e., moral abstraction) that they claim has lead to a modern spiritual crisis of meaning and large-scale oppression of people in totalitarian regimes (51). Modern public administration, like techniques, is instrumental in the sense of being in the service of something or someone. Although modern science and public administration serve brilliantly, ultimately they must be judged by the standards or ends that they serve.

ACKNOWLEDGMENTS

I would like to acknowledge some of the intellectual debt owed to others in preparing this chapter. My original understanding of Machiavelli derives from the work of Leo Strauss in *Thoughts on Machiavelli* and my undergraduate teacher, John R. Kayser, who introduced me to Machiavelli and Strauss. More recently, I have benefitted greatly from the work of Harvey Mansfield, Jr. I would also like to acknowledge the gracious help of my thoughtful wife in preparing this manuscript.

REFERENCES

1.   E. Cassirer, *The Myth of the State*, Yale University Press, New Haven, Connecticut, 1971, pp. 116–128; F. Raab, *The English Face of Machiavelli: A Changing Interpretation 1500–1700*, Routledge and Kegan Paul, London, England, 1965, pp. 1–3, 69, and 77–80; L. Strauss, *Thoughts on Machiavelli*, University of Washington Press, Seattle, Washington, 1969, pp. 35–37; and H.

C. Mansfield, Jr., *Machiavelli's New Modes and Orders: A Study of the Discourse on Livy*, Cornell University Press, Ithaca, New York, 1979, pp. 436–438.

2.   R. Ridolfi, *The Life of Niccolo Machiavelli*, University of Chicago Press, Chicago, Illinois, 1963, p. 2.

3.   R. Ridolfi, p. 18.

4.   J. R. Hale, *Machiavelli and Renaissance Italy*, Collier Books, New York, 1960, p. 121.

5.   J. R. Hale, p. 38.

6.   L. Strauss, p. 17; and C. Mansfield, p. 9.

7.   G. C. Sellery, *The Renaissance: Its Nature and Origins*, University of Wisconsin Press, Madison, Wisconsin, 1950, p. 155.

8.   N. Wood, Introduction, in Niccolo Machiavelli, *The Art of War* (Ellis Franeworth, trans.), Bobbs-Merrill Co., Indianapolis, Indiana, 1965, p. xxxiii; see also pp. xxv–xlvii.

9.   J. R. Hale, p. 30.

10. H. Paolucci, Translator's Introduction, in Niccolo Machiavelli, *Mandragola*, (Anne and Henry Paolucci, trans.), Bobbs-Merrill Co., Indianapolis, Indiana, 1957, p. vii; and O. Evans, Introduction, Niccolo Machiavelli, *Clizia*, (Oliver Evans, trans.), Barron's Educational Series, Great Neck, New York, 1962, p. 1.

11. L. Strauss, *Natural Right and History*, University of Chicago Press, Chicago, Illinois, 1965, p. 177; L. Strauss, Marsilius of Padua, in *History of Political Philosophy*, L. Strauss and J. Cropsey (eds.), Rand McNally & Co., Chicago, Illinois, 1969, p. 245; W. Winiarski, Niccolo Machiavelli, in *History of Political Philosophy*, p. 247; H. C. Mansfield, Jr., *Machiavelli's Virtue*, University of Chicago Press, Chicago Illinois, 1996, p. 109; and Cassirer, p. 128 and p. 140.

12. R. J. Stillman, *Preface to Public Administration: A Search for Themes and Direction*, St. Martin's Press, New York, New York, pp. 13–16 and 53–72; and J. A. Rohr, *To Run a Constitution: The Legitimacy of the Administrative State*, University Press of Kansas, Lawrence, Kansas, 1986, pp. 59–170.

13. N. Machiavelli, *The Prince and The Discourses*, Random House, New York, New York, 1950, p. 168; see also p. 261.

14. N. Machiavelli, *The Prince*, (H. C. Mansfield, Jr., trans.), University of Chicago Press, Chicago, Illinois, 1985, p. 22.

15. W. Winiarski, p. 247; and Cassirer, p. 119

16. R. Kennington, Rene Descartes, in *History of Political Philosophy*, p. 380.

17. R. R. Palmer and J. Colton, *A History of the Modern World to 1815*, (4th ed.), Alfred A. Knopf, New York, New York, 1971, pp. 295–305.

18. H. C. Mansfield, *Machiavelli's New Modes and Orders*, pp. 35–40; and Strauss, *Thoughts on Machiavelli*, pp. 290–291.

19. G. C. Sellery, p. 48 and p. 155; R. Ridolfi, p. 188 and p. 241; and Raab, p. 3.

20. N. Machiavelli, *The Prince*, p. 71.

21. L. Strauss, *Thoughts on Machiavelli*, p. 259; and H. C. Mansfield, *Machiavelli's Virtue*, pp. 279–280.

22. A. Hamilton, J. Jay, and J. Madison, *The Federalist*, Random House, New York, New York, n.d., p. 48.

23. L. D. White, *Introduction to the Study of Public Administration*, (4th ed.), Macmillan Co., New York, New York, 1955, p. 1.

24. H. C. Mansfield, Jr., *Taming the Prince: The Ambivalence of Modern Executive Power*, Free Press, New York, New York 1989, pp. 121–149; and D. K. Nichols, *The Myth of the Modern Presidency*, Pennsylvania State University Press, University Park, Pennsylvania, 1994, pp. 139–152.

25. H. C. Mansfield, *Taming the Prince*, pp. 181–278; and D. K. Nichols, pp. 152–168.

26. H. C. Mansfield, *Taming the Prince*, pp. 38–44.

27. H. C. Mansfield, *Taming the Prince*, pp. 130–149.

28. A. Hamilton, J. Jay, and J. Madison, p. 483.

29. A. Hamilton, J. Jay, and J. Madison, p. 444.

30. W. Wilson, The Study of Administration, in *Classics of Public Administration*, (3rd ed.), J. M. Shafritz and A. C. Hyde (eds.), Brooks/Cole Publishing Co., Pacific Grove, California, 1992, p. 23.

31. A. Hamilton, J. Jay, and J. Madison, p. 455.

32. R. J. Stillman, pp. 61–63; and J. A. Rohr, pp. 135–153.

33. A. Hamilton, J. Jay, and J. Madison, p. 455.

34. Raab, pp. 78ff.

35. C. J. Fox, The use of philosophy in administrative ethics, in *Handbook of Administrative Ethics*, T. L. Cooper (ed.), Marcel Dekker, New York, 1994, pp. 83–105; R. C. Chandler, Deontological dimensions of administrative ethics, in *Handbook of Administrative Ethics*, pp. 147–156; and G. M. Pops, A teleological approach to administrative ethics, in *Handbook of Administrative Ethics*, pp. 157–166.

36. H. C. Mansfield, *Machiavelli's New Modes and Orders*, pp. 317–343; and Strauss, *Thoughts on Machiavelli*, p. 27.

37. N. Machiavelli, *The Prince and The Discourses*, p. 127.

38. N. Machiavelli, *The Prince and The Discourses*, p. 127.

39. L. Gulick, Notes on the Theory of Organization, in *Papers on the Science of Administration* L. Gulick and L. Urwick (eds.), Institute of Public Administration, Columbia University, New York, New York, 1937, p. 13.

40. N. Machiavelli, *The Prince*, p. 23.

41. N. Machiavelli, *The Art of War*, pp. 141–142.

42. L. Gulick, p. 13.

43. N. Machiavelli, *The Art of War*, pp. 107–109.

44. N. Machiavelli, *The Art of War*, pp. 168–169.

45. F. W. Taylor, *The Principles of Scientific Management*, Harper & Brothers Pub., New York, 1942, p. 85

46. N. Machiavelli, *The Art of War*, p. 25; see also p. 151.

47. N. Machiavelli, *The Art of War*, p. 102.

48. N. Wood p. xxxiii–xlvii.

49. N. Machiavelli, *The Art of War*, pp. 150–159

50. N. Machiavelli, *The Art of War*, pp. 161, 171, 191, 195, and 205–206.

51. L. Strauss, *Thoughts on Machiavelli*, pp. 9–14 and pp. 298–299; and W. Winiarski, pp. 273–275.

5

MERCANTILISM
The Great Temptation

Paul Rich
The University of the Americas, Puebla, Mexico and
The Hoover Institution, Stanford University, Stanford, California

Mercantilism, which transcends party loyalties, is ironically a philosophy about which Alexander Hamilton and the latter American progressives would have been in agreement (1). At its simplest, it is the conviction that economic and parallel social goals can be helped along by selective bureaucratic intervention—that Public Administration is capable of positive contributions to the market (2). More pretentiously, it often has offered a philosophic justification for activist administration (3).

In an era where delayering, devolution, relimiting, reinventing, and, more ominously, *downsizing*, have become winning phrases, mercantilism seems old fashioned (4). The Mont Pelerin Society, Milton Friedman, Friedrich Hayek, and the so-called Chicago School of Economics appear to be in semi-permanent ascendancy from Canada to Chile, with great consequences for bureaucracy and Public Administration (5). Well out of favor is the notion that the state is "Savior in Residence" and that administrators are its necessary acolytes (6).

Mercantilism has been given a formal but premature burial on numerous occasions. Typical is this internment by one dictionary-maker

> mercantilism. Commercial policy pursued by England, Holland and other European nations in the 16th and 17th centuries, as nations expanded the commercial sectors of their economies and a shift of emphasis towards trade and away from domestic agriculture occurred. The policy was aimed at securing an inflow of precious metals and raw materials in return for an outflow of finished goods. It went hand-in-hand with aggressive nationalism and the search for overseas colonies . . . The final demise of the system came in the 19th century with the triumph of FREE TRADE (7).

However, another lexiconographer at least has had the common sense to remark that, "Although mercantilist doctrine is at a sharp discount among economists, mercantilist sentiment endures both among unions and businessmen whose immediate interests are threatened by foreign competition, and among public officials responsive to the complaints of their constituents." (8)

Whenever free trade and unbridled entrepreneurship has seemed at its zenith, mercantilism and the demands of Public Administration that it makes has nevertheless persisted (9). Even Adam Smith, who expended considerable energy in *The Wealth of Nations* to attacking mercantilism (10), had his own ideas as to what the bureaucracy should do.

This surprisingly included reviving the spirit of courage (11)! (One recalls that Smith was a Commissioner of Customs for Scotland.)

Interventionism and the army of administrators necessary to make it work is always around the corner (12). The consequences of such intervention have been sharply criticized not only in the present era (13) but for centuries. William Pitt surveyed his age and laconically commented, "commerce had been made to flourish by war" (14). While government intervention in the economic order, ostensibly in the case of mercantilism interests of promoting a successful trade balance, has not always been so extreme as a war, critics claim that the results generally have been anything but an unqualified advertisement for the policy. Yet, despite the inflationary pressures and low levels of consumptions which are associated with such interventionism, administrators find it a perennial popular panacea. Mercantilism is a great temptation (15).

In that respect, many administrators are not as far from their Elizabethan Age counterparts as they might think (16). Nevertheless, many definitions of mercantilism emphasize its *past* glories rather than suggesting any contemporary relevance, as if it was almost entirely a topic for historians (17). It is mentioned more in romantic accounts of Britain's Virgin Queen (Elizabeth I) and the great trading companies, and in connection with beaver pelts and the indigo trade, than with the prospects of the European Union (18). Its influence on the careers of men like Francis Drake and Walter Raleigh is discussed and not its influence on the fortunes and misfortunes of Ross Perot or Carlos Salinas. There is little suggestion in this historically-oriented literature that the concept lights fires in the hearts of modern bureaucrats. But it does.

I.   MERCANTILISM AND PUBLIC ADMINISTRATION

Discussion of the theoretical underpinnings of Public Administration necessarily involves an appraisal of the legacy of mercantilism. From the time of the European cultivation of colonies prior to the American Revolution, to the era of negotiations resulting in the North American Free Trade Agreement, mercantilism has had a profound and not always salutatory effect on Public Administration. Mercantilism's somewhat unremarked status is partly because of its glib description as a spent historical force and a museum item rather than a living ideology (19). Fairly typical of some prevailing current attitudes are Douglas Greenwald's dismissive remarks: "Mercantilism was an economic policy pursued by almost all of the trading nations in the late sixteenth, seventeenth, and early eighteenth centuries, which aimed at increasing a nation's wealth and power by encouraging the export of goods in return for gold." (20)

Mercantilism is one of those ideologies which everyone *believes* that they understand, but which few do. Therefore, it needs far more attention and explanation from Public Administration scholars than it is receiving: "As a category which embraces the economic thought of several nations during an epoch of social transformation, mercantilism is a term which threatens to lose all specificity in its drive for comprehensiveness." (21) In short, the word as now employed is often a catchall phrase for big government intervention, rather than for the selective interventionism which was its intellectual hallmark and still makes it an attractive defense of activist public administration.

In actual fact, few movements have had more lasting influence on the development of Public Administration or roused more controversy (22). To understand the significance of mercantilism, one must recall that the theoretical progeny (and predecessors) of modern state interventionism in economic affairs are mercantilism and neomercantilism (23). As suggested, these are much misunderstood terms, still useful but often employed too loosely: "The historian who is concerned with the doings of governments, however, needs to use the concept with a care amounting to suspicion . . ." (24). Mercantilists (unlike merchants) are almost invariably associated with statist views. Thus, the perennial waves of distrust of government centers for it disapprobation. In a free wheeling Marco Polo or latter-day F. W. Woolworth sense, such merchants never existed. For good or ill, they are the lobbyists for increased administrative intervention in the economic process.

To understand mercantilism, a reading of the classic Chapter 23 of Maynard Keynes' *General Theory* is essential. Although mercantilists for shadowed Keynesian economics, Keynes possibly provided it with the theoretical basis it had lacked. "Mercantilism" Keynes writes, "is a continually developing doctrine of the role of the national state in economic and social affairs, and the term *neo-mercantilism* is merely a means of distinguishing between the absolutist or oligarchical form and that of a more democratic society" (25). *Pace* Keynes, the renaming of mercantilism as "neomercantilism" goes in the face of the remarkable continuity of the doctrine over the years. In aspect of that continuity is its hand-in-glove relationship to nationalism (26).

Like the medical practice of blood-letting, mercantilism is a doctrine and practice which its opponents suspect is sometimes worse than what it sets out to cure. With the triumph of the free marketers, who appear everywhere triumphant in the aftermath of the Soviet Union's collapse, statism replaced communism as a muck racking epithet to fling at an opponent. Even a Democratic President, Bill Clinton, talked about less government control in order to win re-election.

Nevertheless, despite recurring opposition to mercantilism as a philosophy, it has proved to be self-renewing on more than one occasion. To the convinced free marketer this is news of an unwelcome suitor's embrace, because mercantilism presupposes the value of guidance and direction from Public Administrators. Its instruments in the past were monopolies and chartered companies with their official sponsorship and bureaucratic control (27). Jacob Viner remarks about the early mercantilists and administration: "In the regulation of foreign trade, the mercantilist countries used a variety of administrative devices. In a number of countries, state trading-monopolies were established with respect to particular commodities, and especially minerals where the country in question was an important source of world-supply." (28)

Arguably mercantilism was one of the causes of the American Revolution because colonists opposed the British Parliament's economic meddling. It was part of the conflict between the North and South leading to the Civil War. Today free traders claim the tools of mercantilist skulduggery are increased administrative machinery, lengthy statutes, constantly growing tax codes and bad faith in trade agreements. According to the free traders, all of this, along with the detested administrators with their red tape who are considered to be the instigators, should be swept away to insure prosperity. But whether or not the free market and less government controls are capable of bringing the promised land, there always lurks in the background policy debates and management reform during "downsizing" and the fight against bureaucracy the possibility of the resurrection of the ancient foe.

Mercantilism is regarded as a crafty old protagonist, as is its presumed ally, the bureaucracy. The more positive side of Public Administration's involvement in economic affairs gets little attention in accounts of the current trade dilemmas. The bad press is partly because mercantilism started as an élitist philosophy, in the service of royalty. It was a helpmate of absolution, borrowed from Descartes the atomic theory of matter, and held almost as a moral principle that the state had a duty to impose its discipline on the atomic chaos of society. A foundation stone is Antoyne de Montchrétien's *Tachté de l'oéconomic politique dédié en 1615 au roy et la reyne mère du roy*, which is directly concerned with Public Administration's effect on national economy. It sees such administration as an extension of the administration of the royal household and thus deriving its authority from the religiously sanctified prerogatives of the monarch (29).

As an ideology, it long ago lost such lofty connotations and can just as easily be embraced by populists. As a rationalization it is not the exclusive property of liberals. Mercantilism is ecumenical. By no means has the conservative wing of American politics, despite rhetoric about reducing the size of the bureaucracy, been anti-mercantilist. Theodore Roosevelt for example attacked Woodrow Wilson's New Freedom platform, and replied to charges that he was too interventionist with a celebrated defense:

> The key to Mr. Wilson's position is found in the statement . . . that "The history of liberty is a history of the limitation of governmental power, not the increase of it." This is a bit of outworn academic doctrine which was kept in the schoolroom and the professional study for a generation after it had been abandoned by all who had experience of actual life. It is simply the laissez-faire doctrine of the English political economists three-quarters of a century ago . . . To apply it now in the United States, at the beginning of the twentieth century, with its highly organized industries, with its railways, telegraphs and telephones, means literally and absolutely to refuse to make a single effort to better any one of our social or industrial conditions. Moreover, Mr. Wilson is absolutely in error in his statement, from the historical standpoint so long as governmental power existed exclusively for the king and not at all for the people, then the history of liberty was a history of the limitation of government. But now the governmental power rests in the people, and the kings who enjoy privilege are the kings of the financial and industrial world; and what they clamor for is the limitation of governmental power, and what the people sorely need is the extension of governmental power (30).

The long history of mercantilism raises doubts about whether it's enemies really defeated it, no matter how out of fashion it now appears to be. It continues, somewhat out of context, to draw considerable strength from respect for the work of classical economists and philosophers (*e.g.*, David Hume). They contributed to its democratization, seeing it as beneficial to the *hoipolli* as well as to patricians (31). The nation-state in their view would benefit everyone by its interventionist commercial policies, but this was a proposition which like phlogistism was never to be proved.

What did happen was that Public Administrators acquired a lasting ally and a philosophical *raison d'etre*—or an intellectually respectable excuse to mettle, depending on one's viewpoint. Moreover, by no means has the conservative wing of American politics, despite considerable rhetoric about reducing the size of the bureaucracy, been consistently and uniformly anti-mercantilist. This can be attributed partly to mercantilism's and neomercantilism's nationalistic character.

Mercantilism's acceptance by the American founding fathers is ironic considering their objections to British mercantilism. The mercantilist spirit was present at the Constitutional Convention (32). Alexander Hamilton, then and in his subsequent career, was eloquently opposed to Thomas Jefferson's agrarianism partly because he thought it would keep America perennially poor. Success was to come through export and government intervention to achieve that was completely justified. Hamilton's economics were nationalist economics. He therefore favored protective tariffs, subsidies, and prizes.

Given the nationalistic appeal of mercantilism, it attracts the sort of rhetoric that characterized Ross Perot's anti-NAFTA speeches. In Mexico much of the opposition to NAFTA could have been used by Perot with a simple inversion of country names. That fact is that, "Of itself, neomercantilism unfortunately offers many temptations to the evil that accompanies the good there is in nationalism. Examples include the belligerent statements of Theodore Roosevelt, the invasion of Vera Cruz ordered by the internationalist Wilson, Franklin Roosevelt's love for naval construction (fortunate, as it happened), and Secretary Ickes' allocation of public works funds to the building of warships until stopped by Congress (unfortunately, as it turned out)." (33)

Americans of all political persuasions, including those in the conservative wing of the Republican Party, have been quick to demand government intervention when it served economic aspirations: consular appointments, an isthmian canal, undersea cables, and farflung military forces. The Monroe Doctrine put an economic as well as a political wall around the Western hemisphere. In his celebrated *Influence of Sea Power on History* (1890) Admiral Alfred T. Mahan (1840–1914) argued for a strong navy to protect commercial expansion. Hawaii was acquired in what amounted to a businessmen's coup. Theodore Roosevelt's policies were called "Dollar Diplomacy."

At the same time that twentieth-century American conservatives wanted government reduced as much as possible, they also advocated government intervention for nationalist goals. An Elizabethan mercantilist would agree with Newt Gingrich and his Congressional allies. To them priority must be given to advancing one's national economic interests rather than those of the world at large. The government is a proper vehicle to accomplish such ends.

Instead of bullion, which their sixteenth and seventeenth-century predecessors worshipped, modern mercantilists perform *puja* to export figures and a positive balance sheet. From this, there follow important implications for those trying to understand the possible influence on Public Administration of mercantilist philosophy in a free trade era (34).

Early mercantilists believed in a static cake over which contending parties fought for the largest piece. This belief in a finite wealth can be seen in much of the doubt today about free trade and less government controls. Issues vary by century. The antiquarian one is about how to enforce policies that would aid bullion accumulation, while the modern one is about how to administer with an eye to create favorable export figures. Mercantilists generally favor policies which (sometimes inadvertently) not only increase the bureaucracy but encourage competition among states including a competition which degenerates easily into conflict (35).

Heckscher claims that mercantilism and laissez-faire, although apparently each other's contending opposites, produce similar behavioral results: amorality, ruthlessness, and a lack of humanitarianism (36). This was evident during the NAFTA negotiations, when blatant jockeying for position and cynical justification by avarice were underlying themes, rather than an overwhelming desire to help Mexican campesinos or peasant farmers (37). At times during the fight for ratifying NAFTA in the United States, the Elizabethan mercantilist Thomas Mun could have been one of the speech writers. His treatise *England's Treasure by Forraign Trade, or the Ballance of our Forraign Trade in the Rule of our Treasure* (1628) with its views of the sterility of domestic economic activity in comparison and the rewards of exporting seemed to be the bedside reading of both George Bush and Bill Clinton.

An appreciation of just how deeply rooted mercantilism is in American economic history and in the psyche of administrators proves an essential step to understanding the tensions of current international and domestic political scene. The apparent triumph of free market economics does not afford permanent protection against economic nationalism. As free trade increasingly creates hardship on certain parts of a country's population, a return to mercantilism becomes more likely. However, this contemporary variety is a narrow mercantilism which favors lobbies and pressure groups (38). Anatole France told the story of a boy who was taken by a relative to see the Chamber of Deputies in Paris. He could not follow the debate and asked what it was about when they emerged on the street. His relative said, "They were discussing the cost of the First World War." "And what did they decide?" the boy asked. "They decided that the cost was 23 trillion francs." "And what about the men and women who were killed?" "Oh, they were included." (39)

II.   THE OLD WORD IS ADEQUATE

As already mentioned, those who have noticed that mercantilism is not as antiquarian a subject as some believe have resorted to the term *neo-mercantilism*. Apparently, the "New" explains the doctrine's annoying resilience. Others have employed such terms as *cameralism, imperial mercantilism, pseudo-mercantilism*, and such counter-concepts such as *anti-mercantilism, fiscalism*, and *semi-fiscalism* (40). In actual fact, rehabilitation of the term is scarcely necessary. "Mercantalism is a *continually developing* doctrine of the role of the national state in economic and social affairs, and the term *neo-mercantilism* is merely a means of distinguishing between the absolutist or oligarchical form and that of a more democratic society." (41)

Mercantilism is not an extinct ancient cult like drudism. If comparisons are to be made and a religious analogy pressed, mercantilism can be seen to resemble Catholicism. It was wounded by reformations but it has tremendous resilience. The acolytes are therefore still needed. To be unaware of mercantilism's ideological staying power is to neglect a major *mea culpa* of Public Administration. While the fortunes of political parties wax and wane, there are ideological forces that continually impact Administration and have enormous residual power. Mercantilism has enjoyed remarkable recoveries from what seemed to be the last convulsions of its final demise. For example, to twentieth-century social visionaries it seemed irrelevant to a triumphant socialism (42). Socialism waned, capitalism scored impressive victories, and mercantilism remained on the scene—albeit chastened.

The decline of mercantilism might be interpreted as a barometer reading. It points to, at least, the temporary decline of statism and the yielding to an internationally minded class. Mercantilism is a principal contributor to the ethos of state-building. Its purported decline introduces a conundrum, which is that nationalism is strong at the same time that globalism is growing.

Globalism has not defeated nationalism. This fact should be a warning to those who talk so confidently about free markets and downsizing. Certainly the nation-state is under considerable attack and hence mercantilism could be assumed to be on the defensive (43). However, a less nationalistic stance is not dominating the world political agenda. Indeed, strong mercantilism sentiment has accompanied increasing American concern over trade imbalances. Sometimes this was perversely done by masquerading as free trade enthusiasm. The debate over NAFTA is a strong case in point. Adam Smith's accusation, that mercantilists were unable to differentiate between wealth and treasure, seeing gold bars as the end when the real end was consumable and usable goods, still holds true in a sense. (His invocation as the patron saint of selective interventionism therefore is remarkable.) Statism and avarice to continue.

Mercantilism is not necessarily bad. George Lodge writes,

> Government policies—those that promote and those that constrain industry—are critical to competitive success. To the extent that the policies affect all the players in an industry, collective action is required in order to encourage and assist government decision makers to make a clear and consistent definition of community need in a timely way (44).

There are degrees and kinds of mercantilism and they call forth different varieties of Public Administration. A descriptive phrase commonly used for what is considered a benign modern version is *moderate statist*:

> The moderate statist ideology of neomercantilism, however, has forebears as old as the medieval parliaments that grew into our institutions of representative government. If age lends interest and dignity, therefore neomercantilism must approached in a spirit of respectful inquiry (45).

The temptation to which those who espouse "modern moderate mercantilism" succumb is to use government as the "hair of the dog," believing that corrective administration of some sort is a means to economic prosperity.

This "one more for the road" is sometimes as enticing to conservatives as it is to their liberal foes, although differences between the traditional political camps remain:

> In the days of Ronald Reagan and George Bush, the trade debate was split between two camps: laissez-faire vs. interventionists. Republicans, by and large, didn't want to interfere with the normal course of 'free markets.' They argued that well run companies would make their own trade alliances and that the U.S. Government had a role to play mainly as multinational referee (46).

Washington does not vote Democratic accidentally. Nevertheless the temptation to resort to mercantilism is always there, no matter who wins.

In fact, as far as American politics are concerned, the celebrated mercantilist position of Mun and other seventeenth-century writers returned, if indeed it ever went away. The imbalance of trade issue now is high on every party's and every candidate's worry list. The objections to mercantilism—the alleged narrowness of its focus, the way it narrows policy concerns, its failure to contribute to the construction of an adequate general economic theory—are seemingly forgotten (47).

III.   THE EVER-ATTRACTIVE OPTION

The fight between mercantilism and genuine free trade is an ancient one. Proponents of free trade have discerned its origins in the dimmest past, long before the Elizabethan mercantilists. F.A. Hayek made the case for trade as "an indispensable institution." He cited archaeological evidence of its existence in the Palaeolithic age of more than 30,000 years ago, and of obsidian shipments from the island of Melos to Greece in the seventeenth millennium B.C. (48) Hayek observed that trade was older than the state, and that,

> The more one learns about economic history, the more misleading then seems the be-
> lief that the achievement of a highly organised state constituted the culmination of the
> early development of civilisation. The role played by governments is greatly exagger-
> ated in historical accounts because we necessarily know so much more about what or-
> ganised government did than about what the spontaneous coordination of individual
> efforts accomplished (49).

He argued convincingly that,

> Governments have more often hindered than initiated the development of long-dis-
> tance trade. Those that gave greater independence and security to individuals engaged
> in trading benefited from the increased information and larger population that re-
> sulted, yet, when governments became aware how dependent their people had be-
> come on the importation of certain essential foodstuffs and materials, they themselves
> often endeavored to secure these supplies in one way or another (50).

He concluded that government intervention often damaged economic improvement and
brought desirable cultural evolution to an end. "What led the greatly advanced civilisation
of China to fall behind Europe was its governments' clamping down so tightly as to leave
no room for new developments, while, as remarked . . . Europe probably owes its extraordinary expansion in the Middle Ages to its political anarchy." (51)

Mercantilism remains part of the ethos of state-building and this bolsters it as an
ever attractive policy option. A rationale will be found for its continuance regardless of
whether the right or the left is politically in ascendancy. Its demise seemingly threatens la
patrie on the grounds that when mercantilism is out of favor, the exclusive loyalty to the
nation state thought so desirable allegedly gives way to an internationally minded class.
Quite apart from distaste of any hint of incipient world federalism, there is no notion of
give-and-take in trade in some politicians' approach to economics. Mercantilism, albeit
presented in a Madison Avenue wrapping, is thus appealing as a part of a winning domestic platform no matter who is running.

With the collapse of the Soviet Union, economic models have far outstripped war
games as a think tank pursuit. The next war is seen as an economic one and the voters' re-
venge would be swift for that rash politician who would subordinate growth and employment to grand strategy. "Economic growth is the most important social policy objective a
country can have other than keeping its people physically safe," writes Newt Gingrich.
Adding, "America's future depends on economic growth. Economic growth depends on
our ability to compete in the world market." (52)

So interventionism often makes political campaign sense. However, Japan is not today's Venice, Germany is not an enlarged Hanseatic League, and Microsoft is not the East
India Company (53). Mercantilism faces a vastly more complex world than that of pirate
adventurers. The perils of confrontation are much enhanced since Penn made his celebrated remark about commerce and war. Therein is a danger to world community (54),
for every nation-state has an itchy finger on the trigger of covert protectionism. Every nation's politicians have a thinly disguised belief in the efficacy of interference. How much
good faith is there to free trade agreements?

With the apparent renewal of American conservatism, achieving an understanding of the true nature of mercantilism becomes tremendously important. More realism
about the pain that is going to accompany a genuine shift to free trade and the unregulated society is needed. This is demonstrated by the fact that often jejeune arguments for
winning the trade wars via government intervention are being made at the same time

and by the same people who advocate staunch individualism and demand independence from the tentacles of government organization (55). This was illustrated by the chorus of presidential candidates in the 1995–1996 primary sweepstakes who frequently made up in passion what they lacked in administrative and economic sophistication. Much of their rhetoric was blanketly against interventionism (56). Those in favor of government programs and their administrators, no matter how benign, were castigated (57).

Yet for all the prominence of arguments against bureaucracy in American political life, the most prominent example of free trade legislation, NAFTA, had its secret interventionists on both sides (58). Those in favor and against the treaty each had a private agenda. There was no one during the adoption debate who was completely candid. While NAFTA put the seal of approval on the re-ascendancy of the notion that health and prosperity come from a favorable balance of trade, each participant of course went into the treaty with the idea that it would be the winner. They were rather like jockeys in a horse race as they all were convinced that they would cross the finish line first. The considerable control mechanisms of NAFTA and its complementary and growing bureaucracy should be regarded with considerable pessimism (59).

Paul Krugman and others charged that an obsession with trade competitiveness diverted policy makers from what should be the real focus, domestic productivity. In the case of the United States where only about ten percent of the U.S. output goes in exports, that argument has merit. Administrators in such a situation would appear to get their priorities wrong when they concentrate on trade wars as opposed to domestic issues. In more heavily export-oriented countries, the concern about other countries as rivals would still seem valid.

Lester C. Thurow, Professor of Management at the Alfred Sloan School of Massachusetts Institute of Technology, pleaded for changing the focus of the discussion:

> In the traditional theory of comparative advantage, Boskin and Krugman are correct. [Michael J. Boskin, Chairman of President Bush's Council of Economic Advisers and Senior Fellow, Hoover Institution.] Natural resource endowments and factor proportions (capital-labor ratios) determine what countries should reproduce. Governments can and should do little when it comes to international competitiveness. With a world capital market, however, all now essentially borrow in London, New York or Tokyo regardless of where they live. There is no such thing as a capital-rich or capital-poor country. Modern technology has also pushed natural resources out of the competitive equation. Japan, with no coal or iron ore deposits, can have the best steel industry in the world (60).

He adds,

> A passion for building a world-class economy that is second to none in generating a high living standard for every citizen is exactly what the United States and every other country should seek to achieve. Achieving that goal in any one country is no way stops any other country from doing likewise (61).

Beggar-thy-neighbor policies are not the road to economic well being. For example, devaluation may earn a temporary competitive advantage, but in the case of poor countries there is a high longterm price to be paid in encouraging capital formation. On the other hand, real free trade, that is free trade in which countries do not seek in mercantilist-fashion to grab an unfair temporary advantage, may well be the catalyst of development for a world whose future political stability depends on economic growth (62).

For politicians to genuinely repudiate mercantilism, sincerely renouncing bureaucratic interference in the market and thus letting the chips fall where they may, would be to witness one of the greatest acts of collective *bari-kari* in organizational history. Keynes remarked, ". . . the ideas which civil servants and politicians and even agitators apply to current events are not likely to be the newest." (63) Like the proverbial cat, mercantilism has many lives, and has provided Public Administration both with organizational theory *and* organizational justification for centuries (64).

NOTES

1. Sometimes the term is merely hurled as an epithet without any clear understanding of its ramifications. *E.g.* E. Groseclose, *Money and Man*, New York: Frederick Ungar, 1961, pp. 90–91.

2. The opponents of this thesis often rely on the argument that a government bureaucracy cannot cope with the complexity of the modern market, no matter how large a force is put to the task. R. B. McKenzie, *Bound to Be Free*, Stanford, California: Hoover Institution Press, 1982, p. 61.

3. "The paradox of capitalism lay in its principled opposition to bureaucratic management being accompanied by a process of economic development and rationalization which sought state support *where it was advantageous* and which led both to the bureaucratization of capitalist enterprises as they in size and scope and to the extension of the ideology of rational planning and calculation in social life." E. Kamenka, *Bureaucracy*, Oxford: Basil Blackwell, 1989, p. 133. (Emphasis added.)

4. Recent scholarship suggests that Bernard Mandeville, of *The Fable of the Bees* (1714) fame was a convinced mercantilist rather than exponent of laissez-faire individualism, although this is disputed. D. A. Irwin, Introduction Jacob Viner, *Essays on the Intellectual History of Economics*, D. A. Irwin (ed.), Princeton, New Jersey: Princeton University Press, 1991, pp. 21–22. Viner provides outstanding commentary on the history of mercantilism.

5. See A. Toffler, *Powershift: Knowledge, Wealth, and Violence at the Edge of the 21st Century*, New York: Bantam Books, 1990, p. 165 *ff*, pp. 258–259.

6. G. J. Stigler, *Memoirs of an Unregulated Economist*, New York: Basic Books, 1988, p. 114.

7. C. Cook, *Dictionary of Historical Terms*, (2nd ed.), New York: Peter Bedrick Books, 1991, pp. 224–225.

8. R. Lekachman, entry for "mercantilism" in A. Bullock and O. Stallybrass (eds.), *The Fontana Dictionary of Modern Thought*, London: Fontana/Collins, 1997, p. 384.

9. S. P. Hays, *The Response to Industrialism: 1885–1914*, Chicago, Illinois: The Chicago History of American Civilization Series, University of Chicago Press, 1957, p. 164.

10. See J. Z. Muller, *Adam Smith: In His Time and Ours*, Princeton, New Jersey: Princeton University Press, 1993, pp. 79–80.

11. Stigler, *Memoirs*, p. 114.

12. "According to a convention widely honored by politicians, pundits, and the few historians still interested in presidents, liberal administrations produce liberal legislation, and conservative administrations produce conservative legislation. The reality is always more complicated . . .". L. P. Ribufflo. Why is There So Much Conservatism in the United States, *American Historical Review*: 99, p. 443, 1994.

13. M. Friedman writes about government programs, "Find out what the well-meaning, public-interested persons who advocated its adoption expected it to accomplish. Then reverse those expectations. You will have an accurate prediction of actual results." M. Friedman, Laws That Do Harm, K. R. Leube (ed.), *The Essence of Friedman*, Stanford, California: Hoover Institution Press, 1987, p. 127.

14. qtd. W. L. Dorn, *Competition for Empire*, Harper & Row, New York, 1940, p. 70. See also

R. Rosecrance, *The Rise of the Trading State: Commerce and Conquest in the Modern World*, New York: Basic Books, 1986, p. 7.

15. Use of mercantilist ideology is a temptation both for liberals and conservatives: ". . . much American conservatism in the twentieth century has rested on a philosophical foundation not readily distinguishable from the liberal tradition, to which it is, in theory, opposed." A. Brinkley, The Problem of American Conservatism, *American Historical Review*: 99, p. 415, 1994.

16. There are longstanding *national* differences regarding mercantilism related to what could be called different management styles—which in turn arise out of ideology: "British administrative pioneers took a macro-view of administration, seeing industry and government within the context of national society and not as worlds in themselves. They hoped that industry and government would be concerned with the broad implications of progress in modern society, such as the effects of mechanisation, specialisation and division of labor. Contributors to the British philosophy of Administration had reservations, therefore, not only about American scientific management but about the whole trend of scientific progress. Indeed, their ethical ideal confirms the move in Britain this century away from an individual laissez-faire approach to societal problems to an acceptance of the need for industry and government to assume joint responsibility for the type of society being created." R. M. Thomas, *The British Philosophy of Administration: A Comparison of British and American Ideas, 1900–1939*, London and New York: Longman, 1978, 155. See Viner, *Essays*, p. 52.

17. See Rosecrance, p. 139.

18. Viner attempts, ". . . to limit the application of the term to the special and dominant aspects of thought and practice with respect to international economic relations during the fifteenth to eighteenth centuries." Viner, *Essays*, p. 262.

19. Of course, clearly the nature of interventionism is profoundly changing: ". . . in times of rapid change, requiring instant or imaginative responses, cutting ministries or departments out of the loop comes to be seen as the only way to get anything done, which accounts for the proliferation of ad hoc and informal units that increasingly honeycomb governments, competing with and sapping the formal bureaucracy." Toffler, *Powershift*, p. 264.

20. D. Greenwald, Mercantilism, Douglas Greenwald (ed.), *Encyclopedia of Economics*, McGraw-Hill, New York, 1982, p. 647.

21. D. McNally, *Political Economy and the Rise of Capitalism: A Reinterpretation*, University of California Press, Berkeley, 1988, p. 23.

22. "In Britain in particular, although there was general approval in principle of mercantilism, there was almost equally general dislike of the administrative institutions and practices essential to its effective execution. The British public was jealous of the exercise of power by the executive branch of the national government . . ." Viner, *Essays*, p. 271.

23. Dr. Johnson defined a merchant as "One who trafficks to remote countries," E. L. McAdam Jr. and G. Milne, *Johnson's Dictionary: A Modern Selection*, Victor Gollancz, 1982, p. 248.

24. D. C. Coleman, Editor's Introduction, D. C. Coleman (ed.), *Revisions in Mercantilism*, Methuen, London, 1969,

25. *Ibid.*, p. 4.

26. "Mercantilism was a body of economic and political doctrine formulated to serve an essentially new type of community organization, the nation-state, with precise boundaries, and with objectives, loyalties, and recognized moral obligations largely confined to these boundaries . . . The mercantilists sought for their nations, as ultimate ends, both power and plenty, and believe that each was a prerequisite for the attainment of the other. They developed, on Machiavellian boundaries, a nationalistic ethic, where, as against other peoples outside the national boundaries, 'raison d'état', or the national interest, would be the predominant criterion for policy . . .". Viner, *Essays*, p. 45.

27. R. Rosecrance, *The Rise of the Trading State: Commerce and Conquest in the Modern World*, Basic Books, New York, 1986, p. 27.

28. Viner, *Essays*, p. 51.

29. See *ibid.*, p. 69.

30. E. O. Golob, *The "ISMS": A History and Evaluation*, Harper & Brothers, New York, 1954, p. 114–115.

31. However, Viner asserts that the classical school of economists saw trade as mutually beneficial rather than a win-lose situation, and that, "The classical school also rejected the mercantilist stress on the balance of trade and on the national supply of the precious metals." Viner, *Essays*, p. 273.

32. *Ibid.*, p. 100–101.

33. *Ibid.*, p. 168–169.

34. ". . . historians are now shifting the whole debate about mercantilism into new ground by insisting on relating economic ideas to policy in its immediate executive context of particular problems of markets, costs, interest groups, fiscal necessities, and the like. This salutary exercise, to say the least, is throwing up more diversity than homogeneity compared with the older academic pursuit of placing ideas in logical sequence with their precursors and successors to form a smooth evolutionary sequence uncomplicated by the problem of trying to relate them to their 'external' context. Peter Mathias, Preface, Coleman (ed.), *Mercantilism*, p. viii.

35. E. P. Heckscher, Mercantilism, Coleman (ed.), *Mercantilism*, p. 25.

36. *Ibid.*, p. 33.

37. See C. E. Black, *The Dynamics of Modernization: A Study in Comparative History*, New York: Harper & Row, 1966, p. 290.

38. Speaking about the assumptions which underlie modern mercantilism, and which characterized socialism: ". . . behind each of these elements we find a single obsolete assumption about knowledge: the arrogant belief that those in command—whether of the party or of the state—know what others should know . . . This constipated approach to knowledge blocked economic development even in low-level smokestack economies; it is diametrically opposed to the principles needed for economic advance in the age of the computer." Toffler, *Powershift*, p. 415–416.

39. J. L. Adams, *The Prophethood of All Believers*, G. K. Beach (ed.), Boston: Beacon Press, 1986, p. 253.

40. Coleman, "Editor's Introduction," Coleman (ed.), p. 3.

41. Golob, p. 94.

42. A. J. P. Taylor with a rashness unbecoming a leading historian told BBC listeners in 1945 that the proponents of private enterprise were "a defeated party which seems to have no more future than the Jacobites in England after 1688." D. Marquand, Big ends or little ends, Alan Ryan (ed.), *After the End of History*, London: Collins & Brown, 1992, p. 107.

43. "Corporations and government are separated by a turbulent sea, stirred by currents of power and influence, rippled with suspicion, and swept occasionally with gales of corruption . . .". George C. Lodge, *Perestroika for America: Restructuring U.S. Business-Government Relations for Competitiveness in the World Economy*, Boston: Harvard Business School Press, 1990, p. 153.

44. Lodge, *Perestrokia*, p. 146.

45. Golob, p. 69.

46. M. Zielenziger, Why debate over trade is political quagmire, *San Jose Mercury News*, August 18, 1995, p. 1E.

47. J. Schumpter and J. Viner conducted a spirited exchange over recurring mercantilism. Schumpter thought that Viner had missed desirable aspects of the doctrine, to which Viner replied that ". . . the events of recent decades have only strengthened rather than weakened my conviction of the faults, analytical, practical, utilitarian, of the mercantilist approach to international economical problems." Viner, *Essays*, p. 338.

48. F. A. Hauyek, *The Fatal Conceit: The Errors of Socialism*, W. W. Bartley III (ed.), University of Chicago Press, 1988, p. 39. *Cf.* S. K. Sanderson, *Social Transformations: A General Theory of Historical Development*, Oxford: Blackwell, 1995, pp. 174–175.

49. *Ibid.*, p. 44.

50. *Ibid.*

51. *Ibid.*, p. 45.

52. N. Gingrich, *To Renew America*, New York: HarperCollins, 1995, p. 68.

53. "Japan is a kind of Venice, and the Federal Republic of Germany a lineal descendant of the Hanseatic League." Rosecrance, p. 227.

54. See R. W. Tucker and D. C. Hendrickson, *The Imperial Temptation: The New World Order and America's Purpose*, New York: Council on Foreign Relations Press, 1992, p. 201.

55. "The state, as a rhetorical construct, is logically opposed to individual agency. In Kapferer's felicitous terms, the legends of people undermine the myths of state." M. Herzfeld, *The Social Production of Indifference*, Chicago and London: University of Chicago Press, 1992, p. 21.

56. Lamar Alexander, erstwhile Republican candidate for the White House and former governor of Tennessee was emotive: "That the main engine by which the American dream can be realized is not government at any level but opportunity, initiative, and personal responsibility. The surest path to the promise of American life leads through ourselves, our families, and our communities. It does not pass through distant bureaucracies, experts, or policymakers. . . . a revival of our spirit, character, and sense of responsibility will go hand in hand with diminished reliance on government." L. Alexander and C. E. Finn Jr., *The New Promise of American Life*, Hudson Institute, 1995, p. 10–11.

57. "[Gore favors] . . . a more aggressive, vigorous, and enveloping federal government whose savings from efficiencies in one domain would pay for expansion into another and whose heightened credibility would induce the citizenry to want it to do more and more." C. E. Finn Jr., Herbert Croly and the Cult of Governmentalism, Alexander and Finn, *The New Promise*, p. 29.

58. "So pervasive is the cult of governmentalism in contemporary society that it has also begun to draw followers from conservative precincts." Finn, Herbert Croly, p. 36.

59. Keynes remarked about an earlier but similar time, "The mercantilists were under no illusions as to the antinationalistic character of their policies and their tendency to promote war. It was national advantage and relative strength at which they were admittedly aiming." J. M. Keynes, *The General Theory of Employment, Interest, and Money*, San Diego: Harcourt Brace & Company, 1964, p. 348.

60. L. C. Thurow, Microchips, not potato chips, *Foreign Affairs*: 73, p. 189, 1994.

61. *Ibid.*, p. 192.

62. While there is no question but that developing countries are bearing considerable pain in anticipation of ever increasing access to American markets, the past offers only limited assurance that domestic politics in the United States will support the true spirit of free trade. The danger then is that having given up so much and sacrificed so much in the name of free trade and downsizing government, countries that have embraced the rebounding free market ideology will be denied its benefits, and mercantilism or worse might resurge on their part.

63. J. M. Keynes, p. 384.

64. But, the more one learns about economic history, the more misleading then seems the belief that the achievement of a highly organised state constituted the culmination of the early development of civilization. The role played by governments is greatly exaggerated in historical accounts because we necessarily know so much more about what organized government did than about what the spontaneous coordination of individual efforts accomplished." F. A. Hayek, *The Fatal Conceit: The Errors of Socialism*, W. W. Bartley III (ed.), *The Collected Works of F. A. Hayek*, Vol. I, Chicago, Illinois: University of Chicago Press, p. 44.

6

JEREMY BENTHAM
Utilitarianism, Public Policy, and the Administrative State

Lawrence L. Martin
Columbia University, New York, New York

I. INTRODUCTION

Jeremy Bentham (1748–1832) was an eccentric eighteenth century English genius of many interests. He was also the acknowledged leader of a group of social and political reformers known as the philosophical radicals that included among its numbers John Mill and his more famous son John Stuart Mill (1). Bentham's studies, writings, and advocacy touch on a variety of disciplines including: criminal justice, economics, law, philosophy, political science, public administration, public policy, social welfare, and sociology (2). Bentham possessed a passion for writing, religiously compiling fifteen folio pages a day for most of his life. Bentham could put forth a veritable torrent of words on just about any topic of the day. For example, in 1790 when inflation significantly increased the number of paupers in England, Bentham produced over 2000 pages dealing with the social problem and proposed changes to the Elizabethan Poor Laws (3). Bentham was also a wordsmith adding such items to the popular lexicon as: "minimize," "maximize," "rational," "codify," and "demoralize." Bentham was also the first person to use the term "international" (4).

Despite his prodigious output, Bentham cared little for what might be called formal publishing. Many of his writings were published anonymously, or under assumed names, or not at all. He frequently worked on several projects at once and often set manuscripts aside "temporarily," never completing them. His two most famous works, *Introduction to The Principles of Morals and Legislation* and *A Fragment on Government* were both published in incomplete forms (5).

What is known today about Jeremy Bentham—or more correctly what is *believed* to be known—is based largely on his collected works arranged and published in 1843, a decade after his death, by the executor of his estate John Bowering. Bowering took considerable liberties in his role as Bentham's editor. For example, Bowering consistently deleted anything he thought offensive to the English establishment of the time. The end result of Bowering's efforts is a work that has been called "defective in content as well as discouraging in form" (6).

To a great extent, contemporary opinion concerning Jeremy Bentham has been colored by Bowering's incomplete and censored work. An effort to correct this flawed picture has only recently begun. Since the 1960s, a small group of English scholars calling themselves the "Bentham project" has been busily engaged in arranging, cataloguing, and publishing Bentham's collected papers which are held in trust by University College London. While it is too early to speculate how much the contemporary view of Jeremy Bentham may eventually be altered by the work of the Bentham project, the picture that we have of Jeremy Bentham today is certainly more complete than the one we had in the past.

While Bentham was many things, first and foremost he has been described as: a social scientist, a reformer, and what today we might call a public administrator (7).

A.   Bentham as Social Scientist

As a social scientist, Bentham was an empiricist who advocated the use of quantitative methods in social observation and the development of a value free language devoid of emotional and ambiguous terms. Bentham was fascinated by what he believed was the ability of language to obfuscate and mystify the common place. He was particularly critical of the law in this regard. Bentham sought to demystify language. His concern with language and its interpretation sets him apart from other thinkers of the European Enlightenment (7). Bentham believed that the key to demystifying language was in making sentences, rather than words, the unit of analysis. This focus on sentences presages the work of both Ludwig Wittgenstein and Bertrand Russell (7).

More than anything else, Bentham wanted to develop a science of human behavior based on first principles. In this regard, he fancied himself as the Isaac Newton of the social sciences (8). Utilitarianism—sometimes referred to as the "greatest good for the greatest number" or the "greatest happiness" principle—was Bentham's guiding light (3). In public policy terms, utilitarianism was Bentham's conceptualization of the "public interest" (9). In particular, Bentham sought to develop a quantitative approach to the application of the utilitarian rule. Bentham was perhaps overly concerned with quantification and measurement, causing John Stuart Mill to comment that the value of Bentham's accomplishments lie "not in his opinions but in his method" (7). While Mill's comment may overstate the case, Bentham was nevertheless dedicated to what can be called an "exhaustive analytical method," which he believed formed the basis of political and moral science (7). John Stuart Mill would eventually break with his mentor, Bentham, over this quantitative perspective—choosing instead a more qualitative interpretation of the utilitarian rule. The quantitative/qualitative disagreement between Bentham and John Stuart Mill is not unlike the quantitative/qualitative debate that rages in the social sciences today—the more things change, the more they stay the same.

B.   Bentham as Reformer

The central focus of Bentham's work was on political, legal, and social reform. The central question for Bentham and the utilitarians was: "Who are the savages and how can they be civilized?" The utilitarian answer was the creation of the welfare state that would set up a series of rewards and punishments to regulate human behavior (11). Utilitarianism is viewed today as a conservative doctrine due in large measure to its social control aspects. In the socially stratified England of the eighteenth century, however, the utilitarian principle, "the greatest good for the greatest number," was a radical, if not revolutionary, concept. The utilitarian principle was devoid of any social class distinction in that it treated each individual the same. In the utilitarian calculus, each individual was given a value of "one," regardless of his or her social class. The individualistic elements of Bentham's philosophy were stressed by his followers until the middle 1860s at which point the "socialism lurking in the 'greatest happiness of the greatest number' turned individualism into collective responsibility through the use of government to ameliorate social problems" (11).

Bentham became a social reformer not by storming barricades, but by attempting—through his writings, correspondence, and face-to-face discussions—to convince people in positions of power and influence to implement his ideas. His voluminous writings essentially became legislative source books for his followers (12). Bentham was hardly the type of individual one might conceive of as a social reformer in 18th Century England. He was, after all, a Tory. Bentham became a radical reformer only after it became obvious to him that the extreme social and economic inequality that existed in the England of his day would not be altered through words alone. Social reform and political reform, Bentham believed, were bound together. Among the social reforms advocated by Bentham and the philosophical radicals were: a national system of public education, a national health service, the nationalization of welfare, the abolition of capital punishment, a national census, and the restructuring of the London police. Among the political reforms advocated were: annual elections, equal size electoral districts, a broad suffrage, and the secret ballot (13).

C.   Bentham as Public Administrator

Although he never held any public office or government position of trust, Bentham thought like a public administrator. He had what might be called a "practitioner's perspective." Bentham was concerned as much with *doing* and he was with *knowing*; he was fond of saying that "knowing without doing is worthless" (12). Bentham was concerned with making better public policies (or what today might be called policy analysis), but he was even more concerned with how policies get implemented (what today might be called implementation theory). Consequently, Bentham not only prescribed policies, but he also went to great lengths to prescribe procedures for how the policies should be implemented.

An example of Bentham's "top-down" approach to policy implementation is drawn from his ideas and writings about the administration of justice as expressed in *The Constitutional Code*. Bentham believed that justice should be swiftly administered. In order to ensure that it was, he advocated holding court sessions during evenings and on weekends. Moving from policy to procedure, Bentham prescribed that judges could sleep when they were not otherwise occupied. However, a judge ". . . is to sleep in a bed with his feet towards the entrance. On each side and at the foot of the bed rise boards across which may be slid another board equipped with paper and others materials. 'To exercise his function, the Judge has but to sit up in bed' " (14).

Bentham's attention—or perhaps over attention—to detailed procedures for implementing his policies sets him apart from most other eighteenth century thinkers on government. Bentham's empiricism probably caused him to be so concerned with procedures; he wanted to demonstrate that his alternative policies were in fact realistic and feasible (15). Bentham's goal, as outlined in *The Constitutional Code*, was no less than a "blueprint for a complete administrative state" (16).

II. BIOGRAPHICAL PROFILE

A. Younger Years (1748–1770)

Jeremy Bentham was born in 1748. His father was an attorney and an expectation existed that the young Jeremy would follow in the father's footsteps. He was a precocious child who reportedly knew the alphabet before he could talk and had read Paul de Rapin's eight volume *History of England* at the age of three (2,11). He received his primary education at Westminster School where he excelled in both Greek and Latin (2).

In 1760, at age 12, he entered Queen's College, Oxford, graduating in 1764 (6). He then proceeded to study law at Lincoln's Inn and was called to the bar in 1767 (17). Although he had a compelling interest in law and would write voluminously on the subject, he never practiced.

B. Middle Years (1771–1800)

During this period Bentham came into his family inheritance which provided him with an independent income and thus plenty of time and freedom for reflection and writing. In 1770, he made a brief trip to Paris. In 1774, he anonymously published an English language translation of Voltaire's *Le Taureau Blanc.*

In 1776, shortly after the American Declaration of Independence, John Lind, together with Jeremy Bentham as an anonymous co-author, published a pamphlet entitled *Answers to the Declaration of Independence of the American Congress* (18). Lind and Bentham attacked the declaration for asserting, among other things, that men have "unalienable rights" among which are life, liberty, and the pursuit of happiness. Lind and Bentham pointed out the logical problems associated with the assertion of unalienable rights, i.e., that governments must, from time-to-time, necessarily take life, limit liberty, and constrain the individual pursuit of happiness (18). Despite Bentham's aversion to the doctrine of "unalienable rights," or any doctrine based on the concept of natural rights, he nevertheless was eventually to declare that American democracy was "the best government that is or ever has been" (18).

Bentham published his first major work, *A Fragment on Government,* in 1776. The work was released anonymously in England and created considerable interest over both its content as well as its authorship (19). The book came to the attention of a certain Lord Shelburn, who became interested in Bentham's ideas. Through Lord Shelburn, Bentham was introduced to the French expatriate community living in England. These connections were later to assist in the circulation of Bentham's ideas inside France itself (2). Lord Shelburn was to subsequently serve a brief term as Prime Minister from 1782–1783.

From 1785 to 1788, Bentham visited his brother who was living in Russia. While in Russia, Bentham wrote much of the manuscript that was to eventually be published as the *Defense of Usury.* This book was to firmly establish Bentham as an advocate of laissez-faire in economics (6). In 1789, Bentham published the second of his major works, *An Introduction to the Principles of Morals and Legislation,* in which he introduced utilitarianism to a broader audience. The work was eventually translated into French and received widespread acclaim (2). The French believed they had found a kindred spirit in Bentham, an Englishman who understood the concepts of liberty, equality, and fraternity. In a show of solidarity with his ideas, France made Jeremy Bentham a French citizen in 1792 (11).

C. Later Years (1801–1836)

In 1809, Bentham became involved with prison reform. For several years, he lobbied diligently for his concept of a model prison, called the "panopticon." His efforts eventually came to naught. Bentham's public policy failures, such as the panopticon, led to his conversion by John Mill to radicalism in 1810. In 1811, a collection of Bentham's works entitled *Theorie des Peins and des Recompenses* were published in France by his admirer Etienne Dumont (2).

In 1818, Bentham drafted a series of parliamentary reform bills that were introduced in the House of Commons, but failed to pass (2). Bentham converted to democracy in his later years and became involved with liberal revolutionary movements in Spain, Portugal, Greece, and South America. He wrote *The Constitutional Code* at the invitation of Portuguese Cortes (15). He also corresponded with, and sent copies of various drafts of *The Constitutional Code,* to: the leaders of Greece in 1823–1825; Bernadino Rivadavia, President of Argentina in 1826–1827; Francisco de Paula Santander, President of Columbia from 1832–37; and Simon Bolivar, President of Columbia from 1821–1830. In 1823, Bentham helped found the Westminster *Review* a journal designed to help spread the word about utilitarianism (2).

Jeremy Bentham died at the age of 84. Shortly after his death, surrounded by his philosophical radicals, Jeremy Bentham's body was dissected (16). Ever the utilitarian, Bentham knew that medical schools were having difficulty acquiring bodies for anatomical study because of 18th Century superstitions. He concluded that more happiness would result for his body being studied than simply buried (12). After the dissection, Bentham's body was embalmed and placed in an upright position just inside the church at University College London where it can be seen to this day.

III. MAJOR INFLUENCES

The major influences on Bentham's thinking were: Bacon, Hobbes, Hume, Locke, Beccaria, Priestley, Helvetius, and D'Alembert (20). Bentham borrowed his empiricism from Bacon, his epistemology from Locke's *Essay Concerning Human Understanding*, and his methodology—including his concern for definition, clarification, and language—partly from Locke and partly from D'Alembert (20).

Bentham got his notions about sovereignty from Hobbes (17). He was a firm disbeliever in the concept of "natural rights." Bentham believed that people have only those rights that governments give them. Because of his strong stand against "natural rights," or any other rights based on what Bentham called an appeal to emotion rather than reason, Bentham's utilitarianism is generally considered to be "ill-liberal" (21).

Bentham developed his view on utilitarianism principally from Beccaria, Priestley, Hume, and Helvetius. Bentham read Beccaria's *Trattato Dei Delitti e Delle Pene*, or *Crimes and Punishments,* (1764), and Priestley's *Essay on the First Principles of Government* (1768) both of which contained the utilitarian principle. Bentham himself was never sure from which source he first learned about the "great truth" of the utilitarian principle. Bentham eventually came to accept Hume's identification of value with utility "as a practical philosophical base on which to found a simple but thorough program for the rationalization of law and morality" (22). Hume also taught Bentham how to apply the principle of utility to individual behavior. It was Priestly, however, from whom Bentham learned how to apply the principle to the ends of government (23). From Helvetius, and in particular *de l'E-sprit* (1769), Bentham came to accept the notion that "legislation arched high above all that men did" and thus provided the guidance in uniting the thoughts of Hume and Priestly (23).

IV. MAJOR WORKS

The extent that Jeremy Bentham is known today is generally through two of his works, *A Fragment on Government* (1776) and *Introduction to the Principles of Morals and Legislation* (1789). The third work discussed, *The Constitutional Code*, is hardly ever read today, an unfortunate situation because it contains many of Bentham ideas about public administration, public policy, and the administrative state.

A. A Fragment on Government (1776)

A Fragment on Government, referred to hereafter as the *Fragment*, is essentially a book on sovereignty (18). The discussion of sovereignty, however, is almost secondary to Bentham's real objectives of attacking the deplorable state of English jurisprudence and applying his utilitarian principle to the actions of government and specifically to legistation.

1.   English Jurisprudence

The full title of the *Fragment* is actually, "A Fragment on Government; Being An Examination of What is Delivered, On the Subject of Government in General In the Introduction to Sir William Blackstone's Commentaries: With A Preface, In Which is Given A Critique on the Work At Large." Blackston, the first Vinerian Professor of Law at Oxford, was the foremost English legal authority of the time. Blackstone's influence on English, as well as American legal education and thought is considerable. His *Commentaries*, for example, have gone through some twenty American editions (6). To Bentham, however, Blackstone represented a symbol and a target.

Upon beginning the study of law, Bentham found the various rights and duties of the various classes of mankind, jumbled together in one immense and unsorted heap: "men ruined for not knowing what they are neither enabled nor permitted to learn: and the whole fabric of jurisprudence a labyrinth without a clew" [sic] (24). Bentham is said to have viewed the English constitution as, ". . . a patchwork and antiquated product of casual contingencies, contradictory compromises, hasty amendments, and passing inspiration, bound with no logic and rooted in no principle" (25). Rather than contribute to what Bentham called the existing "heap," he chose to reform the law rather than practice it. In this task, according to John Stuart Mill, Bentham found the "battering ram more powerful than the trowel" (26).

Bentham was one of the first people to distinguish what the law is from what it ought to be (4). In the preface to the *Fragment*, Bentham drew a distinction between expositors and censors. An expositor is someone who explains the law as it is; a censor is someone who explains the law as it should be. Using this classification system, Blackston was an expositor and Bentham was a censor.

In the text of the *Fragment*, Bentham takes Blackstone to task in a number of areas, not the least of which is Blackstone's justification of the English Crown on the basis of a contract between the people and the sovereign. Bentham notes that only lawyers would attempt to justify the existence of the state on the basis of contract. Bentham then goes on to argue that the doctrine of contract can not be used to justify the existence of the state because governments enforce contracts, ergo: the state must already exist for a contract to be enforceable. Bentham suggests that citizens may have a moral obligation to obey the state, but they have no contractual obligation (24).

Another example of Bentham' attack on Blackstone and English jurisprudence comes from Chapter 3 of the *Fragment*, entitled "British Constitution" for what he considered yet another failure of logic. Blackstone went to great lengths to demonstrate that the English Constitution was all perfect. Somewhat humorously, Bentham demonstrates—using Blackstone's own logic—that one could likewise "prove" the British Constitution all perfect, all weak, or all foolish (27).

Aside from promoting utilitarianism at the expense of English jurisprudence, what exactly was Bentham attempting to accomplish with the *Fragment*? J. H. Burns and H. L. A. Hart, two prominent members of the "Bentham project," suggest Bentham was simply trying to demonstrate to students of the law how to emancipate their judgment from the shackles of authority (27). In other words, Bentham was a self-appointed instrument of the European Enlightenment who chose—using the *Fragment*—to focus on English jurisprudence.

2.   The Utilitarian Principle

On the first page of the preface to the *Fragment*, Bentham introduces the utilitarian principle: "it is the greatest happiness of the greatest number that is the measure of right and wrong" (28). Bentham's critique of Blackstone—including for example the doctrine of contract mentioned above—is essentially a way of showing that utilitarianism is a superior principle on which to base the law than are "particular local traditions of authority" (28). Bentham affirms in the *Fragment* that the guiding light of legislators must not be the will of the superior (the sovereign), or abstract appeals to such notions as contract, but rather the principle of utility. The principle of "utility" applied to legislation, according to Bentham, requires that the "greatest happiness" principle be the guiding light and the proper test of any proposed law is its utility to that end (25).

B.   An Introduction to the Principles of Morals and Legislation (1789)

Bentham begins his *Introduction to the Principles of Morals & Legislation*, referred to hereafter as the *Principles*, thusly:

> Nature has placed mankind under the governance of two sovereign masters, pain and pleasure. It is for them alone to point out what we ought to do, as well as to determine what we shall do (29).

Following this metaphorical introduction, Bentham then launches into a complete presentation and defense of utility as the first principle of morals and legislation. Juxtaposing the *Fragment*, and the *Principles*, the former represents Bentham's initial attempt to apply the principle of utility to government in general and legislation in specific. In the latter, Bentham is presenting the principle of utility as a full blown moral philosophy.

The *Principles* were intended as an introduction to a much larger work, but in true Bentham fashion, he never completed the manuscript. The *Principles* received considerable attention, albeit of a different nature, in both England and in France (25). In England, the Tories attacked the work as being "unpatriotic, un-Christian and materialistic" (25). Nevertheless, the work brought utilitarianism to the forefront in England and caused it to be taken as one side of many public policy debates (16). In France, the work was well received and recognized as being in the spirit of Voltaire and the European Enlightenment.

Although Bentham calls his guiding light the "principle of utility" in both the *Fragment* and the *Principles*, he later abandons it in favor of the "greatest happiness" principle. The reason for the change was Bentham's belief that the word "utility" simply caused too much confusion (30). Today, the term "utilitarianism" really has no precise meaning. However, the basic philosophical or moral tenet of utilitarianism, as the concept is generally understood, is simply that the merits of actions must be judged by their consequences (31). Today, utilitarianism is considered to be a teleological, or consequential, ethical theory. Teleological ethical theories hold that the moral worth of actions are determined solely by their consequences. This moral calculus supposedly allows the calculator to arrive at a measure of the utility involved in a given action or the various utilities involved in alternative actions.

Philosophers usually distinguish between act utilitarianism and rule utilitarianism (31).

1.   Act Utilitarianism

Act utilitarianism holds that each individual act should be evaluated by its consequences. Using the modern language of cost-benefit analysis—one of the more famous applications of the concept of utilitarianism—any action (or public policy) should involve a computation of both its costs and benefits (i.e., consequences). The benefits of any action (or public policy) must exceed it costs or the action should not be undertaken (32).

2.   Rule Utilitarianism

Rule utilitarianism, holds that it is the application of rules of law to individual cases that must be considered, rather than the application of an individual perception or personal calculus to an individual action. Laws in this case refer not to legislation, but to ". . . ordinary moral principles such as, truthfulness, honesty, and the like" (33). John Stuart Mill referred to these laws as secondary principles. The application of rule Utilitarianism follows the logic that: in the case of X situation, Y is justified if experience shows that in the overwhelming number of cases, Y "tends to promote the best consequences" (33). John Stuart Mill argued for rule utilitarianism by—naturally enough—appealing to the utilitarian principle: a rule is preferred if its consequences are better than having no rule (33). Talcott Parsons classifies Bentham as a rule utilitarian (33). Others make the more subtle argument that Bentham was actually an act utilitarian in his thinking and a rule utilitarian in his policies and procedures (34).

3.   Major Criticisms of Utilitarianism

The major criticism of utilitarianism in contemporary literature is that it does not provide an "adequate account of individual rights and entitlements and therefore fails to accord due respect to persons" (21). In the final analysis, utilitarianism is concerned only with maximizing utility, not with its distribution (21). Perhaps the most important of the recent critiques of utilitarianism can be found in John Rawls's *Theory of Justice* (35). Rawls argues that a calculus based simply on total utility is inherently unfair to the least advantaged groups in a society.

On a less philosophical and more mundane level, the problems associated with operationalizing utilitarianism in actual decision making have been known for some time. For example, William Whewell, in his *Lectures on the History of Moral Philosophy* (Cambridge, 1862), points out that: "determining the morality of actions by the amount of happiness (utility) which they produce, is incapable of being executed . . . (because) we can not calculate all the pleasure and pain resulting from any one action (parenthesis added) (36).

C.   The Constitutional Code (1830)

The Constitutional Code, hereafter referred to a as the *Code*, was yet another of Bentham's works published in an incomplete state. This almost unreadable work was published later in his life, just two years before his death. The tortious text undoubtedly explains why the work is seldom consulted today. Readability problems notwithstanding, the *Code* represents the culmination of Bentham's thinking which had evolved considerably over the years (37). The *Code* was designed as a model constitution, not a constitution for a specific country, but rather an "ideal code for an ideal republic" (38). The closest modern American equivalent to the *Code* might well be the model city and county charters developed by the National Municipal League. Bentham's *Code*, however, was designed for a considerably more complex unit of government, a nation state.

Unlike most other constitution makers, Bentham was concerned with more than simply enumerating the powers, functions, and structure of government. He was also concerned with explicating how the various institutions of government were to actually work and with the qualifications, duties, and responsibilities of the individuals who were to staff those institutions. Nearly eighty percent of the *Code* is actually devoted to what might be called bureaucratic concerns and personnel administration issues (14). Consequently, the *Code* can also be viewed as a treatise on public administration. Seen from this perspective, the *Code* has been called a "coherent and fully developed theory of administration" (38). A particularly interesting aspect of the *Code* is that it presents organizational theories and management concepts that are generally believed to have only been formulated in the early twentieth Century (37). In his detailed prescriptions about how the institutions of government are to actually perform, one can again see Bentham's concern with the "doing,"—or the practical side, of government—what today would be called public administration.

The *Code* is said to rest on three pillars: [1] a superordinate legislature, [2] the administrative structure, and [3] the administrative personnel (14).

1.   The Superordinate Legislature

The first of the three "pillars," the superordinate legislature, can be dispensed with quickly. Bentham did not believe in the separation of powers doctrine. Quite the contrary, he believed in an all powerful national legislature. If Bentham were to draw an organizational chart of his ideal republic, the executive and judicial branches of government would be shown as "reporting" to the legislative, the way English government has evolved. An understanding of the exalted position in which Bentham held the legislative function is necessary for a detailed appreciation of the *Code*, but not essential for an understanding of its administrative nature.

2.   The Administrative Structure

Chapter VIII of the *Code*, deals with the office of the Prime Minster, the executive branch head of Bentham's ideal republic (39). In this chapter, Bentham identifies what he believes to be the functions of the executive branch of government, or what today might be called the various domains of public administration. Some seventeen separately identifiable administrative functions are identified in the *Code* (40). Some of the more prominent administrative functions are: planning and directing; controlling; the personnel function; oversight (inspection, monitoring, and evaluation); procurement; archive maintenance; and the collection, reporting, and publication of national statistics and reports. In reviewing Bentham's administrative functions, little doubt exists that he is dealing with "administrative science" (37). L. J. Hume, in his *Bentham and Bureaucracy*, juxtaposes Bentham's list of administration functions with those of Henri Fayol and Luther Gulick. Hume concludes that all of Fayol's fourteen principles of management can be found in Bentham as well as all of Gulick's POSDCORB activities, with the exception of coordinating (37).

In Chapter IX of the *Code*, the organizational structure of Bentham's ideal republic is set forth (39). In addition to the usual ministries of government that one might anticipate in the 18th Century (i. e., Army, Navy, Foreign Affairs, Trade, and Finance), Bentham also proposed such unusual additions as: Education, Health, Indigence Relief (Welfare), Interior Communications, Domain, and Preventive Services. The Preventive Service Ministry duties were to be "the prevention of delinquency and calamity." In suggesting the creation of national ministries dealing with health, education, and welfare, Bentham was anticipating developments in the growth of government in 1830 that would not occur in the United States for another century.

Each ministry was to be headed by a single individual; Bentham believed in the unity of command. Bentham also had the audacity to suggest that ministers should be qualified for their jobs. The Minister of Health was to be trained in health. The Minister of Interior Communications was to be an engineer. The Minister of Indigent Relief was to be trained in political economy. And the Minister of Finance was to know what those "damned dots" mean (14).

Bentham did not choose to call the various units of his administrative structure "ministries" by chance. The choice of the term "ministry" was consciously chosen by Bentham because it is derived from Latin and means servant. Bentham was making a point, government officials are "servants" of the people (40).

3. Administrative Personnel

Bentham believed that a legal-rational approach to government administration could only be achieved by the creation of a "bureaucratic administrative staff" (41). Bentham also believed that government could only function to serve the utilitarian principle when the twin negatives of "self-preference" and "patronage" were constrained (41). Given these concerns, Bentham devotes considerable thought to the recruitment and selection of government personnel.

The major requirements for public service, according to Bentham, were moral, intellectual, and active aptitude (14). Bentham specifies policies and procedures governing personnel recruitment, selection, training, promotion, transfer, demotion, and dismissal. Selection, for example, is to be based on an open competitive examination in order to attract and secure the most able talent. Without actually using the modern term, Bentham is essentially describing a merit system. The objective of Bentham's merit system is captured by his phrase "aptitude maximized, expense minimized." Here, Bentham is clearly talking about the doctrine of efficiency and the search for efficiency in government.

V. BENTHAM'S INFLUENCE

In attempting to assess the influence of Jeremy Bentham, it is useful to divide the discussion into three parts; [1] public policy, [2] social reform, and [3] administrative reform.

A. Public Policy

The influence of Jeremy Bentham, and in particular the doctrine of utilitarianism, has had a profound and long lasting effect on public policy. It has been said of utilitarianism that of "all the philosophies that have had the most influence on public administrators in terms of intellectual rigor and social appropriateness, utilitarianism holds first place in theory, if not in actual practice" (42). Public choice theory, rational choice theory, game theory, cost-benefit analysis, and the decision sciences in general have their roots in utilitarianism.

B. Social Reform

An assessment of Jeremy Bentham as a social reformer is somewhat more complicated in that the discussion is inexorably tied to the history of British Socialism. Jeremy Bentham and the doctrine of utilitarianism significantly influenced the English Fabian Society and in particular Beatrice and Sidney Webb. The Webbs, in turn, influenced the British Labor Party and through the party, ultimately both the style and substance of the British welfare state. Thus, a direct link stretches from Jeremy Bentham and utilitarianism in the eighteenth Century to the creation of the modern welfare state in the twentieth Century.

Not all members of the Fabian Society were Benthamites—or even utilitarians—but certainly Sidney and Beatrice Webb were. And they were quite influential! Sidney Webb served on the executive committee of the Fabian Society for some fifty years and wrote some of its most influential publications (43). According to Beatrice, his wife and colleague, "Bentham was certainly Sidney's intellectual godfather" (44). Beatrice was also a utilitarian being directly influenced by her father—who had been in the employ of John Stuart Mill—as well as by Herbert Spenser, a family friend and a utilitarian (42). Sidney Webb served on the London County Council and was the author, almost verbatim, of the *Educational Acts of 1902 and 1903* (43). Beatrice Webb served on the Royal Commission on the Poor Laws from 1905 to 1909; her minority report, ". . . anticipated most of the social legislation brought finally into effect by the Labor government of 1945" (45). No less an authority than Talcott Parsons has said of Bentham that he ". . . is the intellectual father of British socialism (and) the proponent of the use of public authority as an instrumentality of social reform" (46).

C. Administrative Reform

In *The Constitutional Code*, Bentham laid the foundation for what he believed was an "efficient and benevolent" government. When Bentham published the *Code* in 1830, the British government was neither efficient nor benevolent (47). Within twenty years of the *Code's* publication, however, Bentham's recommendations can be seen in the creation of national ministries for education, welfare, and health. They had come into existence with passage by Parliament of respectively: the Education Act of 1833, the Poor Law Act of 1834, and the Health Act of 1848 (47). These acts and others—including the Factory Act of 1833, the Municipal Reform Act of 1834, and the Railway Act of 1840—were drafted by, lobbied for, and in some instances passed into law by Bentham's followers. In particular, *The Constitutional Code* is said to have been a major influence on both The Poor Law Act of 1833 and the Municipal Reform Act of 1835 (12).

The successful translation of Bentham ideas into law was due to his followers, sometimes called "Benthamites" and sometimes the "philosophical radicals." Included among Bentham's followers were the parliamentarians John Romilly, Edward Romilly, George Grote, Charles Buller, Arthur Roebuck, and Sir William Molesworth, as well as, important members of the English bureaucracy including Southwood Smith, Sir James Kay Shuttleworth, and Edwin Chadwick. The latter is looked upon today as the father of British sanitation (47).

VI. CONCLUSION

In considering the influence of Jeremy Bentham and his ideas specifically on government, public policy and the practice of public administration, Mary Peter Mack offers the following conclusion, "Seldom if ever in the history of ideas has a man's thought been so directly and widely translated into action" (48). Hanna Fenichel Pitlin provides a summation of the overall influence of Jeremy Bentham:

> Were Jeremy Bentham to return today, he would surely be pleased at the extent of his triumphs, the influence of his inventions, reforms, and vocabulary, the prestige of contemporary utilitarianism and its derivatives . . . Indeed, some of Bentham's ideas have become our commonplace assumptions, to the point where one might say that Bentham has triumphed in each of us (49).

REFERENCES

1. B. Russell, *A History of Western Philosophy*, Simon & Shuster, New York, 1945, p. 774.
2. M. Mack, Jeremy Bentham, *International Encyclopedia of the Social Sciences—Volume 2*, The MacMillan Company & The Free Press, New York, 1968, pp. 55–57 and Jeremy Bentham in *The New Encyclopaedia Britannica—Volume 2*, Chicago, 1984, pp. 837–838.
3. M. Mack, *Jeremy Bentham—An Odyssey of Ideas*, Columbia University Press, New York, 1963, p. 16.
4. H. Pitkin, Slippery Bentham—Some neglected cracks in the foundation of utilitarianism, *Pol. Theory* Vol.: 18, pp. 104–131, 1990.
5. M. Mack, *Jeremy Bentham—An Odyssey of Ideas*, Columbia University Press, New York, 1963, p. 20.
6. J. Burns and H. Hart, *An Introduction to the Principles of Morals and Legislation*, Oxford University Press, New York, 1970, pp. i–xxv.
7. H. Hart, *Essays on Bentham—Studies in Jurisprudence and Political Theory*, Clarendon Press, Oxford, 1982, pp. 1–11.
8. W. Mitchell, Bentham's felicity calculus, *Jeremy Bentham—Ten Critical Essays*, B. Parekh (ed.), Frank Cass, London, 1974, pp. 169–170.
9. L. Hume, *Bentham & Bureaucracy*, Cambridge University Press, New York, 1981, p. 240.
10. M. Mack, 1963, p. 207.
11. W. Durant and A. Durant, *The Age of Napoleon*, Simon and Schuster, New York, 1975, p. 407.
12. C. Everett, *The Education of Jeremy Bentham*, Columbia University Press, New York, 1931, pp. i–xviii.
13. *Encyclopaedia Britannica* in 2 above, p. 838.
14. T. Peardon, Bentham's ideal republic, *Can. J. of Econ. & Pol. Sci.* 17, pp. 184–203, 1951, quote appears on p. 134.

15. F. Rosen, Jeremy Bentham: Recent interpretations, *Pol. Studies*: 30, pp. 575–581, 1982.

16. R. Harrison, *Bentham*, Routledge and Kegal Paul, London, 1983, p. 1–4.

17. D. Monro, Jeremy Bentham, *The Encyclopedia of Philosophy-Volume 1*, The MacMillian Company & The Free Press, New York, 1967, pp. 280–285.

18. H. Hart, 1982, p. 62–70; quote on page 70.

19. T. Sprigge (ed.), *The Correspondence of Jeremy Bentham, Volume 1—1752–76*, The Athlone Press, University of London, 1968, p. xxvi.

20. M. Mack, 1963, pp. 13, 29, 109, 120; H. Hart, 1982, pp. 40–41.

21. P. Kelly, *Utilitarianism and Distributive Justice*, Clarendon Press, Oxford, 1990, pp. 1–2.

22. M. Walsh, *A History of Philosophy*, Geoffrey Chapman, London, 1985, p. 372.

23. M. Mack, 1963, p. 100–105.

24. J. Burns and H. Heart, *Jeremy Bentham—A Fragment on Government*, Cambridge University Press, New York, 1988, p. v–xxiii, quote on p. vi.

25. W. Durant and A. Durant, 1975, in 11 above, pp. 404–407.

26. G. Postema, Bentham's early reflections on law, justice and adjudication, *Revue Internationale de Philosophie*: 141, pp. 219–241, quote on p. 220.

27. J. Burns and H. Heart, pp. 84, and 114.

28. J. Burns and H. Heart, pp. xiv and 3.

29. J. Burns and H. Heart, p. 11.

30. M. Mack, p. 225.

31. T. Parsons, Utilitarianism, *International Encyclopedia of the Social Sciences—Volume 16*, The MacMillian Company & The Free Press, New York, 1968, pp. 224–236.

32. J. LaPlante and T. Durham, *An Introduction to Benefit-Cost Analysis for Evaluating Public Expenditure Alternatives*, Policies Studies Associates, Croton-on-Hudson, 1990.

33. T. Parsons in 31 above, p. 226.

34. R. Harrison in 16 above, p. 241.

35. J. Rawls, *A Theory of Justice*, Belknap Press of Harvard University Press, Cambridge, 1971.

36. W. Whewell, Bentham, *Jeremy Bentham—Ten Critical Essays*, B. Parekh (ed.) Frank Class, London, 1974, pp. 41–61, quote p. 45.

37. L. Hume, p. 1–8.

38. A. Dunshire, *Administration—The Word And The Science*, John Wiley & Sons, New York, 1973, pp. 58–60.

39. F. Rosen and J. Burns, *The Constitutional Code—Volume 1*, Clarendon Press, Oxford, 1983, Chapter VIII pp. 147–171, Chapter IX, pp. 170–457.

40. J. Steintrager, *Bentham*, Cornell University Press, Ithaca, 1977, p. 98.

41. L. Hume, pp. 216 and 257.

42. N. Henry, *Public Administration & Public Affairs*, Prentice-Hall, Englewood Cliffs, 1992, p. 394.

43. M. Cole, S. and B. Webb, *International Encyclopedia of the Social Sciences—Volume 16*, MacMillian & Company & The Free Press, New York, 1968, pp. 487–491.

44. A. McBriar, *Fabian Socialism and English Politics 1884–1918*, Cambridge University Press, Cambridge, 1962, p. 150.

45. M. Cole, p. 489.

46. T. Parsons, p. 233.

47. D. Roberts, *Jeremy Bentham and the Victorian Administrative State*, B. Parekh (ed.), Frank Class, London, 1974, pp. 187–204.

48. M. Mack, p. 57.

49. H. Pitkin, p. 105.

7

John Locke's Influence on American Government and Public Administration

Mark F. Griffith
The University of West Alabama, Livingston, Alabama

John Locke (1632–1704) was a British political philosopher who profoundly influenced the founders of the United States and the principles upon which the country was established, including the American system of public administration. He is most noted for his concept of separation of powers and for his ideas about property as the basis for prosperity.

Locke was the key figure in modern political philosophy who moderated the more radical teachings of Thomas Hobbes and Niccolo Machiavelli to make their ideas acceptable to democratic government. Locke's theories generally fall between those of Hobbes and Jean-Jacques Rousseau—with all three philosophers formulating theories of politics from the concept of "a state of nature." And Locke owes much to his predecessors Niccolo Machiavelli, Michel de Montaigne, Francis Bacon, and Rene Descartes for his theories. In addition, Locke reacts most often to Richard Hooker and Sir Robert Filmer, often using their writings to shield his own more controversial ideas from the casual reader. For public administration, especially organizational theory, Locke wrote about such diverse topics as education, money, democracy, and liberalism.

Locke wanted to appear less radical than he was. His writings, if read superficially, appear to contain many contradictory references. However, when read carefully, these contradictions can be reconciled. Locke used great caution and complex arguments, because his view of the philosophic origins of politics differed radically from the politics and culture of his times. His politics, emerging from what he and others called a state of nature, involved the underlying radical, modern premises about religion, virtue, morality, and the idea of what is good, all beliefs that challenged the established order. He was careful to write about these topics in couched language because such ideas could get him killed for the appearance of atheism, and in fact his beliefs eventually led to a period when Locke was exiled from England.

I. LOCKE'S BACKGROUND AND WRITINGS

John Locke was the son of a lawyer who was part of the minor gentry, which provided Locke with all the advantages of life. Locke had a standard British public education at

Westminster School, which is to say he was educated at one of the best private schools in the world. Later he attended Christ Church College at Oxford, studying such diverse topics as philosophy, botany, and medicine. He became an Oxford Don (college professor) in 1656. In 1666, because of his college medical teaching, he became the personal physician to Anthony Ashley Cooper who would later become the first Earl of Shaftesbury and who was a prominent Whig politician. This is the relationship that made Locke a player in the politics of his time because through Cooper he obtained numerous official positions and was introduced to the political, medical, and social circles of London. In 1668 Locke became a Fellow of Royal Society and interacted with many of the important scientists of his day, including Sir Isaac Newton (1).

From 1675 to 1689 Locke spent much of his time overseas. These travels resulted from both poor health, which would plague him for the rest of his life, and complications with his own political position. Locke was in France from 1675 until 1679 and then returned to England. In 1683 Shaftesbury died and Locke, believing himself to be in danger, fled to Holland. There he became embroiled in the most important controversy of his time, involving the power of the King and the English Glorious Revolution of 1688 (2).

In 1685 James II ascended to the throne with the support of a Tory majority in Parliament. The opposition Whig party, which was overwhelmingly Protestant, feared James because of his Catholicism. In 1688 it appeared that after James's death the throne would pass to his Catholic son, not to one of his Protestant daughters. These circumstances set the stage for the English Revolution, when the Whigs—using the political system to interrupt the divine line of kingly succession—helped give the throne to James's daughter Mary and her husband William of Orange. In return for the loyalty of the Whigs (including Locke), William and Mary accepted a bill of rights that gave Parliament sovereign powers, including power over taxes and the military, and so began the modern basis for executive and legislative power.

Locke's writings of the *Second Treatise* in 1689 was regarded as a defense of what had happened in 1688—the fundamental change from a monarchy to a rationally planned system of republican government—and is one of the reasons it was published anonymously. Locke's relationship with William and Mary led to his return to England in 1689 at the age of 58, his re-entry into English political life, and an expansion of his writing. Locke ended his public life, successfully, as a Commissioner for Trade in 1696 and retired to write and read until his death in 1704 (2).

Locke's major and minor works include a wide range of writings, all of which continue to have an influence to this day. His major works include: *A Letter Concerning Toleration* (1689), *Two Treatises of Government* (1690), *An Essay Concerning Human Understanding* (1690), *Some Considerations of the Consequences of the Lowering of Interest and Raising the Value of Money* (1692), *Some Thoughts Concerning Education* (1693), *Further Considerations Concerning Raising the Value of Money, wherein Mr. Lowndes's Arguments for it in his late Report concerning 'An Essay In the Amendment of the Silver Coins' are particularly examined* (1695), and *The Reasonableness of Christianity, as Delivered in the Scriptures* (1695).

Locke's minor works include: *Observations on the Growth and Culture of Vines and Olives* (written in 1679, published in 1766), and *A Letter to the Right Reverend Edward Ld. Bishop of Worcester Concerning some Passages Relating to Mr. Locke's Essay Concerning Human Understanding in a late discourse of his Lordships in Vindication of the Trinity* (1697).

Several more of Locke's minor works were published posthumously. Many of these works were commentaries on the Bible including: *A Paraphrase and Notes on the Epistle of*

St. Paul to the Galatians (1705), *A Paraphrase and Notes on the First Epistle of St. Paul to the Corinthians* (1706), *A Paraphrase and Notes on the Second Epistle of St. Paul to the Corinthians* (1706), *A Paraphrase and Notes on the Epistle of St. Paul to the Romans* (1707), *A Paraphrase and Notes on the Epistle of St. Paul to the Ephesians* (1707), and *A Paraphrase and Notes on the Epistle of St. Paul to the Galatians, I & II Corinthians, Romans, Ephesians, To which is Prefix'd an Essay for the Understanding of St. Paul's Epistles, by consulting St. Paul Himself* (1707). All of Locke's religious writings had a considerable influence on how the Bible was read in America; urging a more tolerant, moderate, government-friendly Christianity.

Finally, several volumes of Locke's complete work were published beginning with *The Posthumous Works of Mr. John Locke* (1706).

II. HUMAN UNDERSTANDING AND THE BACKGROUND TO POLITICS AND PUBLIC ADMINISTRATION

Locke is the founder of British empiricism, which is the theory that all knowledge is based on experience. To understand Locke's writings on politics and public administration we must begin with his ideas about human understanding, which provide the key to interpreting all of them. Locke's writings in *An Essay Concerning Human Understanding* were an attack on innate ideas—the belief that human beings began life with some preconceived ideas about first principles (3).

Locke believed that human beings begin life with minds that are a blank slate. For him the origin of ideas are experience, sensation, and reflection; therefore, morality has a rational basis. All ideas that people develop involve the formation and growth during their life or during the history of ideas. This separates Locke's ideas from Christian and natural law traditions, which were based on the belief in some kind of underlying basis for human understanding—in first principles, such as God or natural order—beyond human history and experience. Locke's *Essay* avoids making clear the ramifications for social and political change that he was espousing—ramifications that would become more evident in Locke's discussion of politics, which he wisely published anonymously (4).

Locke presents a uniquely psychological bent to his theory of human understanding. Thomas Pangle states that "Locke presents most clearly the underlying psychological basis for his doctrine of human nature and the moral law deduced from the nature in the *Essay Concerning Human Understanding*" (5). Locke's psychology involves the idea that human beings are driven by pain and the pursuit of happiness. Locke is turned away from a psychology of passion and toward reason. Locke's psychology established the groundwork for his teaching on property and his argument for what Rousseau would derisively call the bourgeoisie.

Locke's emphasis on development and experience are also considerations in educational theory. His most complete presentation on education is contained in his book entitled *Some Thoughts Concerning Education*, which was the first book-length work on education by a philosopher (5).

Locke's thoughts on education were based on his own view that young men should be taught to be gentlemen. (For Locke, women were relegated to the private world of the home, and he included no public role for women.) Locke in The Epistle Dedicatory to *Some Thoughts Concerning Education* wrote,

> The well Educating of their Children is so much the Duty and Concern of Parents, and the Welfare and Prosperity of the Nation so much depends on it, that I would have every one lay it seriously to Heart; and after having well examined and distinguished what Fancy, Custom or Reason advises in the Case, set his helping hand to promote every where that Way of training up Youth, with regard to their several Conditions, which is the easiest, shortest, and likeliest to produce virtuous, useful and able Men in their distinct Callings: Though that most to be taken Care of, is the Gentleman's Calling. For if those of that Rank are by their Education once set right they will quickly bring all the rest into Order (6).

Locke's standards involved a classical education combined with tolerant Christian principles, a mix of standards that would have been recognizable to Aristotle and Edmund Burke. This is a moral education, emphasizing social skills and self-control, which students learn by imitating experienced teachers.

Locke believed that certain good traits would bring pleasure and certain bad traits would bring pain. The good traits included; civility, generosity, humanity, artistic grace, honor, humility, industry, kindness, faith, scholarliness, modesty, politeness, prudence, reverence, self-control, self-denial, and self-restraint. The bad traits included captiousness, censoriousness, clownish behavior, contempt, craving, cruelty, domineering conduct, hypocrisy, indolence, lying, malice, negligence, rashness, sheepishness, bashfulness, stubbornness, and timidity (7).

Locke's lengthy list of good and bad traits reveals the breadth of thought Locke gave to the education of the young male aristocracy. This list of traits included most but not all of the necessary components to produce a well-rounded individual in the different facets of life: political, moral, spiritual, and emotional.

One striking omission, which is obvious from a comparison between Locke and such ancient writers on education as Plato, is Locke's lack of physical teaching. Locke de-emphasizes physical education and military training. For Plato physical education was essential for young men who were not ready for the challenges of deep thinking and who needed an outlet for their aggression. Locke limits his consideration of physical fitness to peaceful dancing. For Plato physical education is tied to military bravery, because physical education led to confidence in physical activities like war. Locke clearly is lacking in a teaching that involves war and education.

Locke's educational theory is associated with his view of ethics. His ethics involve two contradictory ideas; a form of hedonism, and the belief that ethics can be demonstrated in human actions. Locke's hedonism relates to his belief that most human actions are linked either to pleasure or pain. All humans react to one or the other; yet pain is clearly the more important motivating factor and the one factor that for Hobbes and Locke, leads to the need for government (8).

Locke's hedonism must be viewed in light of his own perspective on elitist education and would not be recognizable to a classical hedonist, because so much of his theory of education involves limiting passion. For classical hedonists, passion was part of the pleasure of hedonism.

When Locke discusses ethics, he delineates the ways in which passion must be limited. According to Locke, ethics is learned by example; specifically, from the examples of teachers who themselves had extensive life experience. Some examples can be drawn from the Bible or other sources of conduct, but these sources are less important than real human experience.

While it would be logical for Locke to use examples from politics to explain ethics, he compartmentalizes his thoughts and seldom crosses examples from politics with his ethical teaching. Nevertheless, Locke does use examples in education (learning by example), which reveal an underlying basis for an ethical society. Locke's ethical society is based on hedonism (pleasure and pain) combined with learning by example (which limits passion). This combination forms a moderate basis for politics based on work but discouraging the problems that can result from unrestrained passion.

The most often overlooked point of Locke's writings is that he believed that something akin to an educational precondition to good government exists, in addition to what we would today call political socialization. For Locke an educated elite was necessary to promote government by consent (5). Locke most obviously differs from other writers by separating his educational theory, which seems conventional, from his political theory, which is actually quite radical.

III. POLITICS

Locke's most political book, *Two Treatises of Government*, presents his case for what we would call modern liberal democracy. In this work Locke's ideas about politics are more extensive and complete than in any of his other writings, which typically had titles that intentionally limited the scope of Locke's thought, such as "some thoughts" or simply "a letter." In the preface to the book he claims to be telling the complete story of politics. Yet, he realized that during his lifetime his teaching would be controversial—even punishable by death; therefore, he did not reveal his authorship until he was near death. Nevertheless, during his lifetime many people knew he was the author.

In any comparison between the two treatises the *First Treatise* is clearly less dramatic and contains fewer obvious insights. Yet, the *First Treatise* is about religion and politics and is an attack on Sir Robert Filmer's *Patriarcha* (1680), which argued that the foundation for political power is religion and paternal power. Locke thought Filmer was wrong and believed that Filmer's ideas stood for tradition and in opposition to the changes that Locke advocated.

For Locke, the *First Treatise* provides the precondition, which is independent thinking and is necessary for his teaching in the *Second Treatise*. The *First Treatise* illustrates the problem of merely accepting paternal power or religious authority as the basis of knowledge (9). Furthermore, the *First Treatise* establishes the distinction between paternal power and political power, and advocates independent political thought, rather than following simple paternal or religious traditions in government.

The *Second Treatise* is the center of Locke's teaching about government and is subtitled *An Essay Concerning the True Original, Extent, and End of Civil Government*, which illustrates how complete he viewed his coverage of the topic.

Locke begins the *Second Treatise* with a discussion of political power.

> Political Power then I take to be a Right of making Laws with Penalties of Death, and consequently all less Penalties, for the Regulating and Preserving of Property, and of employing the force of the Community, in the Execution of such Laws, and in the defence of the Common-wealth from Foreign Injury, and all this only for the Public Good (10).

For Locke, political power is coercive and is tied to law and the preservation of private property, which are the general topics of the book. Topics such as the coercive nature of popular government do not seem radical to us today but were very radical ideas for his generation. Locke believed that to understand political power one must comprehend that politics emerges from natural law and the state of nature.

Locke must next reinvent natural law away from its historic base of Christian or Greek natural philosophy to a basis of human reason. Locke made this change because his theory of human understanding involved the denial of anything outside of human reason. Locke radically reoriented the basis of natural law to humans themselves in two ways; first, by making it natural for individuals to indulge in their primary desire to comfortably preserve themselves, and second, by making it natural for individuals to care about others.

> Every one as he is bound to preserve himself, and not to quit his Station wilfully; so by like reason when his own Preservation comes not in competition, ought he, as much as he can, to preserve the rest of Mankind, and may not unless it be to do Justice on an Offender, take away, or impair the life, or what tends to the Preservation of the Life, the Liberty, Health, Limb or Goods of Another (11).

Locke's natural law dictates that individuals take care of others, a situation that can only be enforced by government; so Locke turns to the creation of government. By emphasizing that natural law applies to all humans, Locke deviated from the belief in the kinds of governments created in antiquity—which were more concerned with the few than with everyone—and moved toward the modern idea that governments must consider all peoples.

To understand Locke's writings in the *Second Treatise* we must understand the concept of the state of nature. The state of nature involves a philosophical thought experiment, an experiment that reveals how human beings made the move from the prepolitical state of nature to a system of politics. The state of nature must be viewed in light of Locke's theory on human understanding because this philosophical experiment revealed human rational thought as the real basis for understanding politics.

Locke followed in the tradition of Hobbes, who was one of the first to use the state of nature of investigate the origin of politics. Hobbes's state of nature was a violent place where people were naturally barbarous and warlike, and so it became necessary to create a government that would preserve their lives. Locke accepted Hobbes's view that the first right government must preserve was the right to life. Yet, Locke masked this similarity because the idea that human beings were naturally warlike was an unacceptable, and even immoral thought, to people of that day. He meant to change the common understanding of the state of nature, making it more complicated—more benign and moral—because only a more benign moral state of nature was acceptable as the origin of government. Similarly, both Hobbes and Locke viewed the state of nature as a state that knew no common superior, where there was no one to enforce laws. Furthermore, for Hobbes and Locke no objective good or evil existed in nature (12).

Locke's view proceeded beyond Hobbes' thought when he developed his ideas of property and rights. For Locke the need for people to develop a system of property for self-preservation leads to the development of politics. For him human beings in the state of nature are equal and have rights. Human beings in the state of nature have the right to all things, the right to do as they want. Therefore, the state of nature is a state of war, because at all times there is the threat of the use of force. This threat can occur either in the state of nature or under government, but only through government can the threat of force be regulated (12).

Locke's view, that the primary basis for the state of nature is self-preservation, is the same as Hobbes's. In this sense, Locke makes Hobbes's standard of self-preservation one of the keys to modern society. For public administration the realization that American society is founded on the principle that the first rule of society is the preservation of order, for the purpose of protecting people, is a reminder of that police power is essential. Locke's thoughts greatly influenced the American regime; however, because of the many competing demands in public administration, police and order are often lower on the agenda. For regimes that are more greatly influenced by Locke, police and order are higher on the agenda.

Locke makes it clear that each individual in the state of nature has his own executive power, and each person is expected to carry out a fair standard of law and punishment. This executive power in the individual means that people are expected to act far more responsibly and morally than Hobbes believed they were capable (13).

Locke's discussion of executive power in government is somewhat dependent on our accepting that individuals have the power to punish crimes in the state of nature—real punishment in a Machiavellian sense. People who harmed others would incur all the wrath that a person who exhibited their animal-like behavior could muster. This includes capital punishment if the crime is so extreme that it warrants an ultimate punishment (13).

For Locke, peace can only be achieved through a government. Furthermore, government is the only vehicle to true liberty, because freedom only occurs when government creates a state of peace. Government is necessary to end the state of war in the state of nature and is meant to correct problems of nature. For Locke, the state of nature was practically illustrated by international relations, where countries act without the benefit of one overarching government. His argument that international relations represents a state of nature exemplifies Locke's similarity to Hobbes in terms of self-preservation. This view of international relations eventually led Locke to make a clear distinction between domestic politics and international politics (14).

Locke viewed the creation of government as the only method to protect rights. These rights include the right to life, liberty, and property. The right to life emerges from the necessity of self-protection, first in the state of nature and later under government. The right to liberty is related to the idea that governments are created and end only by common agreement. Locke's emphasis on property is his unique contribution to the history of political theory. But these rights according to Locke can only be protected by government (15).

For public administration, Locke's emphasis on rights gives administration its reason for existence. John Rohr discussing the administrative state writes,

> By protecting individual rights on a mass scale—and despite the paradox, that's what the administrative state does—the administrative state would seem to be a faithful servant of the original covenant by which we do the bidding of Hobbes and Locke and enter civil society to secure the protection of our individual rights (16).

Locke's teaching about rights provides the justification for revolution, which would have been his most threatening and controversial idea to the leaders of his time. Locke's argument has been viewed as a justification for the Revolution of 1688, but it is much more than that. More accurately, Locke's view of revolution is more conservative than the other modern revolutions, which shocked the world with their violence, because it includes equality, rights, and private property (17).

Locke's teaching is the basis for the American revolution, which was the most successful revolution in history. The difference between America and other countries has to do with the fact that the American's were influenced by Hobbes and Locke. This influence stands in counter-distinction to much of Europe, which was more influenced by the French Philosophis and Rousseau than by Hobbes and Locke. The conservative nature of Locke's teaching led the Americans to a successful revolution, without the horrible mob violence of the French Revolution. Nevertheless, Locke avoided the difficult question about how a government creates equality. This lack of equality at the founding of the United States eventually led to the Civil War in America.

Locke's most obvious influence was on Thomas Jefferson's conception that government's purpose was to protect "life, liberty, and the pursuit of happiness," which comes directly from Locke's "Life, Liberty and Estate" (15). The emphasis on the pursuit of happiness is derived from Locke's *An Essay Concerning Human Understanding* (18). In like manner, Jefferson's idea that government is based on the consent of the governed comes from Locke. Locke was also popular with James Madison and other influential members of the founding generation. The founders frequently referred to Locke's ideas during the constitutional convention of 1789 (19). Everything Locke wrote, from his religious writings to his political writings, was part of the American landscape at the creation of America. Yet, we must note that Locke was not always accurately understood, and in many ways Locke's writings were used on both sides of many an argument.

More generally, Locke is one of the founders of eighteenth-century liberalism. That form of liberalism was concerned with rights and was distrustful of government, because government was powerful, and such power endangered individual rights. Eighteenth-century liberalism stands in counter-distinction to the liberalism of today because today's liberals look toward a powerful government to protect individual and group rights. It is clear that for Locke and Hobbes government would inevitably become strong, resulting in the possibility that the very government that was established to protect rights might ultimately endanger them.

For public administration Locke's theory of revolution provides two challenges. First, no administrative state can encourage revolution; so the state must provide the services that prevent revolution. More problematic, bureaucracy must provide the means for change when the system moves away from maintaining a basis for society, such as the protection of rights. This is a serious challenge for public administration because the bureaucracy must then be proactive not reactive. A proactive bureaucracy must protect the people and realign the system within the original principles. It must then convince the rest of the political system, usually through the legislature, of the correctness and need for the realignment. A proactive bureaucracy is unusual, but Locke's theories demand such action under some conditions.

Locke must confront one of the basic problems that his teaching implies: How do we balance political power and individual freedom in governments that are created by consent? This question arises because while we lose some rights when we enter society, part of its duty is to protect other rights.

Locke's ideas on balancing power and freedom begin with his understanding of what we call modern executive power. A modern executive is a common superior, rather than an individual, that acts to provide the stability necessary for economic success. Although the executive should not have absolute power, he or she must have prerogative power: At times of stress the executive might need to assume the powers of a dictator. For Locke, the executive's powers must be particularly strong internationally, to deal with war and diplomacy, and limited nationally, so that the executive does not threaten the constitutional form of government. The constitutional structure limits the power of the executive, but at times, particularly during war, the executive must dominate (20).

Locke's conception of the executive problem highlights the dilemma of executive power, which is the kind of problem the United States is experiencing in modern times. How can our government be effective with weakened executive powers? Locke seems to indicate that a president must have the power to deal with a civil war, the way Abraham Lincoln dealt with the American Civil War. The American system provides the president with several provisions for extraordinary powers in times of crisis, including the oath of office, the take-care clause, and the authority as commander-in-chief of the armed forces. These provisions give the president extra power, but power short of prerogative (20).

Locke did not believe that the executive should have total authority. Instead, to limit executive power, he developed the idea of separation of powers. He envisioned a division of power between the executive branch of government and the legislative branch (21). This separation of powers has special significance for public administration as practiced in America: It creates a bureaucracy with two bosses, the executive and the legislative branches of government. Related to the problem is what can be called "mom and pop" leadership. When children want something they first go to one parent; and if they are unsuccessful, they go to the other, playing the parents against one another. For bureaucracies with two bosses, the mom and pop scenario demonstrates that the bureaucrats can play the executive branch against the legislative branch and vice versa. Locke's theory of the separation of powers, again, harkens back to the revolution of 1688, when William and Mary accepted the limitations imposed by Parliament in order to gain the throne during the revolution.

Government is created to assure the public good, an idea that runs through the *Second Treatise*. The public good involves settled laws. These laws are not natural but conventional because they are part of the consent upon which government is founded. Natural or religious laws are alien to Locke's concept of human understanding; so he moved toward a consensual basis for law, severing the classic philosophical and religious foundations for law, similar to the way he severed those foundations for government.

Locke also realized the need for independent judges. These judges while powerful were not part of the separation of power between the executive and the legislature. The judges functioned as mediators who settled disputes to avoid using force.

Locke was also necessarily concerned with legislative power. After 1688 Parliament became a legislative body with power, a monumental event; for before this time no such powerful legislature existed in the world. The previous Parliaments were dominated by the royalty. For Locke, the separation of powers and protection of rights required a legislative branch that had power to balance out the strong executive. The legislature is the only check on executive power to prevent the executive from becoming a dictator.

Locke's government is based on consent, and consent is always government by majority rule. Unfortunately, governments created by consent have the problems commonly associated with community and majority rule: In the state of nature, not everyone will consent to give up their rights to form a government that will guarantee some rights but limit others. For Locke it is enough that a majority wants to enter into government and the rest of the people grant what he calls tacit consent. The great bulk of people consent to government through simple participation. But this leaves the problem of minority rights in a majority government (22).

Locke's solution to the problem of minority rights involves government's role in preserving equality. Locke states that human beings in the state of nature are inherently equal. Therefore to protect minority interests government must sustain the equality inherent in the state of nature, a somewhat vague solution but the only one Locke provides. He implies that if government sustains equality, minority protection becomes less important because minorities will receive equal treatment under law. Furthermore, minorities will also be protected because the laws must be fair; so Locke has a kind of primitive notion of both procedural and substantive due process.

Locke was also concerned with limiting the power of religion, probably because of the religious strife he witnessed surrounding the events of 1688. Locke advocated religious toleration among different Christian sects and a gentler Christianity. He also believed that human reason should be used for interpreting the Bible. This rational basis for tempering religious fervor was important for Locke, because passionate belief caused political systems to become violent and fail. Locke believed that rational political systems based on his principles were the best hope for humanity to avoid religious strife (23).

In the *Second Treatise* Locke's discussion of family is most strongly related to his discussion of paternal power in the *First Treatise*. For him the apparent origins of society involve the nuclear family—mother, father, and children. Yet, he begins with the individual and not the group, because similar to his other teachings, the family is dependent on the reasoned construction of individuals. The importance of the individual is most evident in the limits to paternal power that Locke seeks to de-emphasize. His constitutional teaching suggests that a compact exists between the people and their government, just as a compact exists between a father and the family.

Locke writes about the need for husband and wife to stay together. This union is not based on love but on a contract (like a commercial contract) to raise children. A social contract is essential because of the long gestation period for human beings. Without a contract men would not be responsible for their children. This thought, while quite familiar today, is the origin of modern constitutionalism, which emerges out of the social contract (24).

Locke believed that children are the future and are their parents' legacy to the world. Yet, the whole of the *First Treatise* is an attack on paternal power as the basis for the family's relationships. What ties the children to the family? According to Locke, children have very limited rights. While they are growing, children are bound to the family through force and need. Later, they are bound by a natural law of inheritance. The father binds the family together, not through his power, but by dictating who will receive his inheritance. The family is based on the individual because it is the father's wealth through the power of his inheritance that dictates the politics in the family unit (24).

The *Second Treatise* is Locke's most famous but not his most comprehensive writing on the origins of money and property. It is Locke's teaching on property that sets him apart from Hobbes and Rousseau, the two other famous writers who begin with the state of nature. More generally, Locke's writings on property make him unique, separating him from his peers and the ancient religious and philosophic traditions. More than any other teaching, Locke's understanding of property links him uniquely to America.

Locke was most concerned in the *Second Treatise* with private property and the needs that go with it. Because of this emphasis on property, Locke influenced Adam Smith and all the subsequent writers on capitalism who came after him. Private property, money, and the resulting complications are at the heart of what Locke saw as the basis for politics, which is a far cry from the idea of political virtue that drove so many other political philosophers. The dominance of economic issues is a reduction in the end goals of society from the idealistic ends of the ancients; however, in many ways it made the end goals of society accessible. By making the end goals accessible, Locke stands as one of the founders of modern political economy. Locke joined politics to economy because economic success is tied to the social contract. For Locke, private property was the way to stabilize human existence, because individuals who had private sources of wealth were capable of taking care of themselves. For any system to work it had to provide individuals with a method to protect the private acquisition of property and hence some degree of wealth (25).

In the state of nature each person is his own judge according to Locke. Nevertheless, individual judgment will not work for private property claims or for business contracts because commercial contracts cannot be enforced without a fair way of judging claims, a way that is not based on self-interest. Governments begin to remedy the problem of self-interested judgment by providing the rules under which cases may be heard by courts, including whether individuals have the standing to sue when their rights are in danger, and ways to enforce contracts. In addition, Locke believed that for people to acquire and protect private property, government must establish settled laws. These settled laws are the conventional laws created by society. To establish private property, consistency of the law is the critical factor. In addition, impartial judges provide the necessary fairness to decide between competing claims. Impartial judges are particularly necessary for Locke, because land disputes are the kind of problem that could bring out the animal behavior in human beings (25).

For Locke, the idea of private property is related to the idea of labor. It is work that distinguishes what is held in common from what the individual owns. When people work the land they are building something, but their work is personally, self-interestedly significant only if people have title to their land, and only government can provide the means to make titles legal and permanent. These legal titles make the ownership of land and the protection of that land a government interest. If government supports the individuals, those individuals must no longer protect their land with brutal force as they would need to employ in the state of nature. Labor mixed with the land brings a kind of consistency to existence that the state of nature did not provide, because government secures and defends property claims (25).

For Locke, money changes everything and is conventional, not natural. When economy functioned on an agricultural barter system, there was no chance of a person trying to accumulate more than they could use, because of spoilage. But money allows people to accumulate all they need and much more. Accumulation of wealth is the reason Locke believed that people moved from a state of nature to government, so that government could regulate the unbridled nature of the accumulation of money (25).

Locke is not in favor of greed—the unlimited acquisition of wealth—because it could lead to a society that does not leave wealth for the common good. Acquisition has three limitations for Locke: First, people are limited to the accumulation of property that they can work with their own labor. This limit would dramatically reduce the amount of accumulated wealth, but modern investing techniques make work one of the least profitable ways to earn money. The industrial revolution and money made unlimited accumulation possible, and so Locke's first limit is no longer relevant (26).

The next limit is the concept of spoilage, which Locke developed from an agricultural economy. In agriculture, if someone tries to accumulate too much produce it will rot, so there is a natural limit to how much a person can use without waste. Locke uses the concept of spoilage as a limit to accumulation, even when money is introduced, and he implies that individuals should still accumulate only what they need. Locke's first two limits, accumulating only as much property as people can work themselves and spoilage, no longer limit acquisition in modern times. Nevertheless, Locke's concepts of limits emphasize his conclusion that it is necessary to have limits on wealth (26).

Locke's third limit to the acquisition of wealth is his idea that after the accumulation of individual wealth there must be at least as much left for the common good. This limit is in most ways no longer possible in a world that is increasingly privately owned. The implication for public administration is that common spaces, parks, and other open spaces must be preserved for the public good. Furthermore, zoning and building restrictions are clearly in line with Locke's limit to accumulated wealth (26).

Locke's discussion of the limits of accumulated wealth fit well with his conception of equality, but Locke never thought that incomes must be equalized. His concept of limits to accumulated wealth made Locke a favorite of the American founding generation, but he would not have been as popular if the founders fully understood his ideas. The founders apparently did not comprehend that his limits on accumulated wealth did not work well in a money economy. Later in history the character of the United States changed toward a government that favored the unlimited accumulation of wealth that Locke would have found problematic.

Locke is one of the writers who believed in optimism, and he believed that the general welfare of the country is increased when private wealth is enlarged. While he was concerned about the private accumulation of wealth, Locke recognized that productive individuals promote the general good for all people. Locke wrote that "he who appropriates land to himself by his labour, does not lessen but increase the common stock of mankind" (27). Locke's writing on the common benefits of private wealth make his limits on private wealth less meaningful, because Locke did not want private business hindered. He believed that if private business was hindered the common good would be hurt as well.

All of Locke's writings on private property provide the natural philosophical answer to the challenge that Marx and socialism posed to capitalism. Marx and others taught that individuals become selfish and greedy if they are allowed to own private property, and they theorized that private property led to the unlimited accumulation of wealth. Locke clearly has the answer to the Marxist attack on capitalism.

For Locke, capitalism and private property are related to work: If society discourages or prohibits private property it destroys the incentive to work, a view proven by the events in the former Soviet Union. Socialism destroyed the work ethic in the old Soviet Union, and the Lockean-influenced capitalism of the West now dominates. Yet, Locke goes beyond the simple idea of the good of private property, to a kind of ethic of responsible capitalism. Locke's entire discussion about the limits to accumulated wealth is an argument for limiting the impact that private property has on the public. Locke believed that nations that merged capitalism with some kind of common good would be successful, in contrast to Marx's belief that capitalism was a heartless system (which the early industrial revolution represented) and had corrupted society for the benefit of the few who had the wealth. While Locke himself had no teaching about the poor or about welfare, his liberal successors have had a profound influence on the creation of the modern welfare state. These Lockean regimes, more than any governments in history, have evidenced obvious concern for social issues and the environment.

Locke's other writings focus on different aspects of money, such as interest and prosperity. Once again Locke was the first philosopher to write major book-length works on economy, just as he was the first to write a book on education (28). As Patrick Kelly states, "Not only were Locke and his contemporaries forced to concern themselves with broader issues than interest rates and coinage standards in terms of balance of trade problems, the supply of money, and disruption to trade and finance brought about by war, but they were also led to consider the fundamental problems of stagnation and the means of stimulating economic growth" (29).

Some of his other writings involve the preconditions to economic success, which relate to democratic governments and capitalism. Like his earlier discussion of the need for good laws and fair judges in the *Second Treatise*, the success of democratic government and the existence of private property are dependent on peace. Settled times in foreign affairs results in the end of the state of war. Similarly, the state of war ends when humans enter government. Peace makes it possible for the existence of regular functions of government, including the regulation of property. Without peace, governments need more money and must raise taxes, which interrupts the regular operation of business. For Locke, war creates similar problems to the state of nature; it produces a situation in which prosperity is based on fortune not work.

Locke, being a British philosopher who was also concerned with politics, was naturally interested in the problems of balance of trade; and historically Britain had many problems with its balance of trade. Interruptions in the balance of trade were created by two problems, war and protectionism. Typically, when Great Britain played the critical role in the balance of power in Europe, Britain's own currency fluctuated wildly. War leads to inflation because the high costs of fighting a war forces governments to spend money faster and often run deficits. Money flooding the market creates inflation. Inflation drives the price of goods up and drives the value of currency down. Wartime spending creates either debts or new taxes to pay for the war. In either case war rearranges priorities and diminishes domestic priorities. Finally, war creates uncertainty and instability, which is problematic for business.

The history of Great Britain shows many changes between protectionism and free trade and provides important lessons for public administration. Administrative states are expected to enforce any kind of protectionism the political system enacts. Free trade is the natural road to prosperity and helps create a strong middle class. Free trade is detrimental only to people employed in industries that must compete with imports.

The problem of job competition, however, makes protection an attractive political option even at the expense of the common good. Industries affected by foreign competition want protection, and politicians want to get elected, so protectionism is an attractive choice for politicians. Nevertheless, it is clear that protection does not work in the long term, because protected industries have no incentive to fix what made them noncompetitive in the first place. In the short term, however, it does save some jobs and so remains a tempting political option.

IV. LOCKE AND PUBLIC ADMINISTRATION

Locke's influence on public administration relates to his extensive and wide-ranging influence on the founders of the United States and the principles upon which the county was established. Public administration is essentially an American idea that has influenced other countries and spread worldwide. Locke created the modern emphasis on constitutionalism that defines, in part, the relationship between the political system and the bureaucracy. Locke was also one of the creators of the idea of separation of powers, which makes public bureaucracy unique, because it must balance the often-conflicting demands of the executive and legislative branches. He was an important link in the development of modern executive and legislative power. John Rohr writes that the origin of public administration can be traced to Frank Goodnow, who stated that the "inclusion of judicial authority as part of executive power finds explicit support in John Locke" (30).

Locke also influenced modern educational theory, although not to the extent of someone like Jean-Jacques Rousseau. Locke's ethics and concept of hedonism have greatly influenced modernity: so many of the values evidenced in America are an amalgam of Locke's values. Ironically, both American popular culture and the critics of American popular culture are influenced by Locke. American popular culture has adopted a confusing blend of Lockean hedonism; the critics of American popular culture have adopted ethics from Locke's list of good traits, such as faith, prudence, and self-control. Both American popular culture and its critics have been influenced by Locke and Jefferson, especially by Locke and Jefferson's concepts of individual rights and the "pursuit of happiness."

Locke's influence on public administration is especially strong when it comes to property, money, scarcity, and prosperity. Locke makes it clear that government must protect private property and business. This protection is what administration does through planning and zoning. Much of the other regulatory functions of the administrative state involve the regulation of wealth—if not a Lockean limit on acquisition—at least some regulation of wealth.

The administrative state also regulates welfare, which is a natural extension of Locke's idea's about the common good. The prosperity of a broad-based middle class is directly related to Locke's ideas about private property. Locke's writings shed some light on the conflict between those who believe that economy is a zero-sum game and those who believe that the economy is able to grow its way out of problems. Clearly Locke believes in growth. For Locke, the increase in individual wealth is something akin to the recent belief in trickle-down economics, the belief that the general increase in wealth leads to a general increase for the common good.

Locke's concept of economic prosperity include thoughts on war and peace. Clearly peace is needed for prosperity. By ending the state of nature, governments create peace, which leads to prosperity. Within government, the administrative state is vital to successfully maintaining peace and to the outcome of war. Security issues in public administration are important for prosperity.

Domestically Hobbes and Locke both realized it was important to maintain order. Following Locke's teachings for public administration, maintaining order using police power, especially because of the many competing demands in society, must be the first item on the government's agenda.

The political structure that underlies the administrative state is clearly Lockean. Woodrow Wilson's classic false distinction between administration and politics is clearly an error that Locke would have seen, because the administrative state provides the support the political structure needs to ensure rights, property, and equality (31).

Finally, Locke's liberalism influenced liberalism at the founding of America; yet it is different than the modern version of liberalism, because Locke's version viewed government as a potentially destructive power, while modern liberalism views government as the solution. Therefore, modern liberalism has more influence over public administration and supports growth of the administrative state. Clearly, Locke distrusted government power, so he would not identify with today's liberals.

John Locke, one of the most influential writers in history, profoundly affected the principles upon which the government of the United States was founded. He leaves a legacy of thoughts on human understanding, religion, economics, and politics that still influence the structure, environment, and operation of public administration.

NOTES

1. The best general biography of Locke now available is M. Cranston, *John Locke: A Biography*, London: Longmans, Green and Co., 1966.
2. See, for instance, P. Laslett's introduction, in J. Locke, *Two Treatises of Government*, P. Laslett (ed.) Cambridge: Cambridge University Press, 1960; reprint, 1990, pp. 25–66.
3. J. Locke, *An Essay Concerning Human Understanding*, (abridged and edited with an introduction by A. D. Woozley), New York: New American Library, 1974, pp. 63–83.
4. J. Locke, *An Essay*, pp. 89–90.
5. Thomas L. Pangle, The philosophic understanding of human nature informing the Constitution, in *Confronting the Constitution: The Challenge to Locke, Montesquieu, Jefferson, and The Federalists From Utilitarianism, Historicism, Marxism, Freudianism, Pragmatism, Existentialism . . .*, (Allan Bloom ed., with Steven J. Kautz), Washington: AEI Press, 1990, p. 56.
6. J. Locke, *Some Thoughts Concerning Education*, (ed. with introduction, notes, and critical apparatus by John W. Yolton and Jean S. Yolton), Oxford: Clarendon Press, 1989, p. 80.
7. J. Locke, *Some Thoughts*, pp. 22–23.
8. J. Locke, *An Essay*, pp. 442–443.
9. H. C. Mansfield, Jr., *Taming The Prince: The Ambivalence of Modern Executive Power*, New York: The Free Press, 1989, p. 195.
10. J. Locke, *Two Treatises*, p. 268.
11. J. Locke, *Two Treatises*, p. 271.
12. J. Locke, *Two Treatises*, p. 67–92.
13. J. Locke, *Two Treatises*, p. 347, pp. 364–374.
14. J. Locke, *Two Treatises*, p. 276.
15. J. Locke, *Two Treatises*, p. 323.
16. J. A. Rohr, *To Run a Constitution: The Legitimacy of The Administrative State* Lawrence, Kansas: University Press of Kansas, 1986, p. 161.
17. See the discussion on revolution, in J. Locke, *Two Treatises*, p. 414–417.
18. J. Locke, *An Essay*, p. 173–174.
19. F. McDonald, *Novus Ordo Seclorum: The Intellectual Origins of the Constitution*, Lawrence, Kansas: University Press of Kansas, 1985, p. 7.
20. J. Locke, *Two Treatises*, pp. 374–380.
21. J. Locke, *Two Treatises*, pp. 117–121.
22. J. Locke, *Two Treatises*, pp. 111–112.
23. See, for example, Locke's discussion of religion in J. Locke, *A Letter Concerning Toleration*, J. H. Tully (ed.), Indianapolis: Hackett Publishing Company, 1983.
24. J. Locke, *Two Treatises*, pp. 303–318.
25. J. Locke, *Two Treatises*, pp. 285–302.
26. J. Locke, *Two Treatises*, pp. 299–301.
27. J. Locke, *Two Treatises*, p. 294.
28. M. F. Plattner, Capitalism, in *Confronting the Constitution: The Challenge to Locke, Montesquieu, Jefferson, and The Federalists From Utilitarianism, Historicism, Marxism, Freudianism, Pragma-*

tism, Existentialism . . ., A. Bloom (ed.), with of Steven J. Kautz, Washington, D.C.: AEI Press, 1990, p. 322.

29.   J. Locke, *Locke on Money*, (ed. with ancillary manuscripts, an introduction, critical apparatus, and notes by P. H. Kelly, 2 vols.), Oxford: Clarendon Press, 1991, pp. 39–40.

30.   Rohr, *To Run a Constitution*, p. 88.

31.   J. M. Shafritz and A. C. Hyde, (eds.), *Classics of Public Administration* (2d ed.), Chicago: Dorsey Press, 1987, pp. 1–28.

BIBLIOGRAPHY

Bloom, A., (ed.). *Confronting the Constitution: The Challenge to Locke, Montesquieu, Jefferson, and The Federalists From Utilitarianism, Historicism, Marxism, Freudianism, Pragmatism, Existentialism. . . .* With the assistance of Steven J. Kautz. Washington, D.C.: AEI Press, 1990.

Cranston, M. *John Locke: A Biography.* London: Longmans, Green and Co., 1966.

Horwitz, R. "John Locke and the Preservation of Liberty: A Perennial Problem of Civic Education." *The Political Science Reviewer* 6 (Fall 1976), pp. 325–53.

Locke, J. *Locke on Money.* Edited, with ancillary manuscripts, an introduction, critical apparatus, and notes by Patrick Hyde Kelly. 2 vols. Oxford: Clarendon Press, 1991.

Locke, J. *A Letter Concerning Toleration.* Edited by James H. Tully. Indianapolis: Hackett Publishing Company, 1983.

Locke, J. *An Essay Concerning Human Understanding.* Abridged and Edited with an introduction by A. D. Woozley. New York: New American Library, 1974.

Locke, J. *Some Thoughts Concerning Education.* Edited with introduction, notes, and critical apparatus by John W. Yolton and Jean S. Yolton. Oxford: Clarendon Press, 1989.

Locke, J. *Two Treatises of Government.* Edited with introduction and notes by Peter Laslett. 1960. Reprint, Cambridge: Cambridge University Press, 1990.

McDonald, F. *The American Presidency: An Intellectual History.* Lawrence, Kans.: University Press of Kansas, 1994.

McDonald, F. *Novus Ordo Seclorum: The Intellectual Origins of the Constitution.* Lawrence, Kans.: University Press of Kansas, 1985.

Macpherson, C. B. *The Political Theory of Possessive Individualism.* 1962. Reprint, London: Oxford University Press, 1972.

Mansfield, H. C. *Taming The Prince: The Ambivalence of Modern Executive Power.* New York: The Free Press, 1989.

Pangle, T. L. *The Spirit of Modern Republicanism.* Chicago: University of Chicago Press, 1988.

Rahe, P. A. *Republics Ancient and Modern: Classical Republicanism and the American Revolution.* Chapel Hill: University of North Carolina Press, 1992.

Rohr, J. *To Run a Constitution: The Legitimacy of The Administrative State.* Lawrence, Kans.: University Press of Kansas, 1986.

Shafritz, J. M., and A. C. Hyde, eds. *Classics of Public Administration,* 2d ed. Chicago: Dorsey Press, 1987.

Strauss, L. *Natural Right and History.* Chicago: University of Chicago Press, 1953.

Strauss, L. and J. Cropsey, (eds.) *History of Political Philosophy.* Chicago: University of Chicago Press, 1981.

Tarcov, N. *Locke's Education for Liberty.* Chicago: University of Chicago Press, 1984.

8

ADAM SMITH'S LEGACY

David John Farmer
Virginia Commonwealth University, Richmond, Virginia

Reading Adam Smith provides central insights about public organization and management; proceeding beyond Smith is also necessary. Adam Smith stimulates insights about the relationship between the economy and government, and between economic and political concerns. Smith sees economics and politics as dimensions of a larger philosophy of society, for example, and he regards the economy as providing the basic framework within which governmental issues must be considered. Adam Smith's legacy provides the conceptual space in which government and public administration are now viewed and understood. The conceptual space constitutes part of the basic assumptions, the conceptual foundation, of public administration thinking and practice. It is more than a mere set of limitations for such thinking; it is the conditioning force that helps to mold contemporary thinking about public administration and government. Proceeding beyond Adam Smith is essential in two respects. First, Adam Smith did not recognize the socially constituted character and the limitations of the conceptual space that his writings, and his legacy, have provided contemporary society. It is socially constituted because alternative understandings of this space can be developed; contrary to what he supposed, it is not an immutable given, not simply a recognition of the facts of nature. Second, Smith's specification of the space is questionable. Later in this chapter, it will be argued that subsequent thinking offers some better understandings of the conceptual space. These understandings show that the economic component is not as beneficent as Adam Smith suggests, undermining the naive faith of many of our contemporaries in the moral and providential guiding power of the market. Going beyond Adam Smith in these two respects provides public administration thinkers and practitioners with greater control over their own conceptual space.

The central thesis of this chapter is that, by exploring Adam Smith and his legacy, public administrationists can do what they should do—examine their latent assumptions. A first challenge in such an exploration is to get Smith right.

Adam Smith's ideas have been both read and misread, and the misreadings have become part of the excess baggage of Smith's legacy. Smith's claims about the character of the economic forces that surround and impact public sector activity are described in the chapter section entitled "Selected Smithian Contributions." From among his views, the description focuses on his doctrines of the invisible hand, the division of labor, and the stages of economic growth; parts of his political economy now abandoned, like the distinction between productive and unproductive labor, are also noted. The description also makes clear that Smith recognizes the limitations of the invisible hand and fears the propensity of capitalists to subvert government. A second challenge is to question the account he gives of the conceptual space, constituted by his view of economics, that underlies public administration and organizational theory. The section entitled "Importance of the Smithian Legacy" discusses the claim that the importance of Smith's views is in effect that he sets what he thinks are the parameters for modern government. This includes reflecting on the triumph of liberal democracy, the triumph of liberal capitalism, and the centrality of economic relations. In order to clarify the meaning of claiming that Smith is wrong not to recognize that the economic sphere is socially constituted, the section includes considering the notions of "economics as rhetoric" and of "new economics." It also explains the tension in Smith's view that the economic sphere is not only harmonious but also exploitative. A third challenge is to explore in specific terms the potential for public administration of an understanding of Adam Smith and his legacy. The section on "Incorporating Smith in the Field of Public Administration" analyzes three ways in which the Smithian legacy is of particular significance for public administration theory and practice. The results of the Public Choice approach are discussed, explaining what it means to speak of necessary waste in government; the potential is also noted for greater use of the deductive approach. The centrality of efficiency in public administration and in the Smithian legacy is explored. The limits of Adam Smith are also emphasized, especially in terms of current discussions of postmodernism and the third wave. But first, in the next section, we should explore the historical context of Adam Smith's thinking.

I.   HISTORICAL CONTEXT

Adam Smith was born in 1723 and died in 1790, spending most of his life in Scotland. Reared by his mother (his father died six months before his birth) in a small and declining Scottish seaport, Smith attended the Kirkcaldy burgh school until he went to the University of Glasgow at the age of 14. He began attending Oxford University at the age of 17 where he was a student for six years. At Oxford he read widely in ancient and modern foreign languages, and he became interested in a range of subjects including aesthetics. He pursued an intellectual life, and is described as having been always somewhat absent-minded and having acquired early on a habit of talking to himself when he was alone. Following two years of further study (while he lived with his mother in Kirkcaldy), he became a freelance lecturer in rhetoric and belles-lettres in Edinburgh—a job that he supposedly performed very well because he spoke without a Scottish brogue. He also gave private lessons in civil law. In 1751 he was appointed a professor at Glasgow University; until 1752 he was Professor of Logic, and from 1752 to 1764 of Moral Philosophy. He played a part in university administration, and later in 1787 he was elected the University's Lord Rector. For two years after 1764, he was tutor to the 3rd Duke of Buccleuch, a post that included travel to France and Switzerland and an opportunity to meet a wider circle of intellectuals. With periods in London, Smith then returned to Scotland. In 1778 he was appointed Commissioner of Customs for Scotland, and he lived in Edinburgh until his death.

To understand the historical context of Smith's life, we should comment on the Scottish enlightenment, capitalism, the industrial revolution, the eighteenth century, and on the fact that later readers interpret Smith from the perspective of their own centuries.

Adam Smith lived and died in a remarkable time: the period of the Scottish Enlightenment. Smith was a leading figure of this Enlightenment, an outburst of critical intellectual and other activity that included the work of such philosophers as Smith's friend David Hume and Frances Hutcheson. Hume (1711–1776), an important philosopher of empiricism, was the more celebrated; Hutcheson (1694–1746) was influential with his doctrine of moral sense. Adam Smith was also familiar with Enlightenment figures from other countries. He had a special reverence for Voltaire, Rousseau, and Montesquieu. The latter was a model for his social philosophy as was Sir Isaac Newton. Newtonian physics had had a great influence on Montesquieu (1689–1755), and Montesquieu was influential for almost a century on intellectuals interested in sociological issues. The Scottish Enlightenment was also an outburst that influenced the parallel American Enlightenment of Thomas Jefferson and the other founding fathers.

Smith's name is ineluctably associated with capitalism. Capitalism has been characterized by Max Weber as the rationalistic pursuit of wealth—and of the rational use of profit to acquire even more profit (1). Capitalistic enterprise requires the existence of a rationalistic economic system supportive of "buying and selling" which has the objective of ever increasing wealth. Because it rationally strives for more and more wealth, capitalism must value economic efficiency. As Baechler explains, the "specific feature that belongs only to the capitalist system is the privileged position accorded the search for economic efficiency" (2). Capitalism had long been a feature in Western Europe; capitalist relations of production are described as having gradually emerged in England in the fifteenth century (3). Scotland had only begun to develop economically in recent years. Long before Adam Smith's time, capitalism had been dominated by mercantilist economic policies. Such policies, discussed in another chapter in this book, were thoroughly rejected by Adam Smith. It fell to Adam Smith to propose a better account of how to increase and develop the wealth of nations.

Adam Smith—who died in 1790—never lived to see more than the beginning of the Industrial Revolution. The Industrial Revolution can be described narrowly as the development on a massive scale of the factory system of production; more appropriately, it can be described as the economic, social, and other changes that occurred when productive processes were mechanized to the extent that there was a gigantic shift from home production to factory production. The changes were both positive and negative. On the positive side, there were the accumulation of great wealth and the development of newer and better products. On the negative side, there was the development of much squalor in the rapidly developing towns and there was a severance between the new factory workers and their natural rural roots. Whether the workers had been better off in their cottages working from dawn to dusk or whether they were better off in the new factories is an example of a classic dispute. Dating the precise beginning of the Industrial Revolution is necessarily imprecise. Arnold Toynbee dates the beginning of the Industrial Revolution at 1760; but rapid growth in national output did not start until 1790. Important beginnings were made during the eighteenth century, in inventions, in changes in the textile industry, and in the agricultural revolution which had made possible a more productive use of acreage. But it is widely accepted that Adam Smith did not anticipate the Industrial Revolution. Blaug explains that, when *The Wealth of Nations* appeared, "the typical water-driven factory held 300–400 workers, and that there were only twenty or thirty such establishments in the whole of the British Isles. This helps to account for Smith's neglect of fixed capital and for the conviction, which he never really abandoned, that agriculture and not manufacture was the principal source of Britain's wealth" (4).

This serves to bring home the fact that Adam Smith's writings should be acknowledged as what they are—writings and ideas shaped within, and for, the eighteenth century context. But the issues discussed are so hot-button, and the underlying principles are of such broad scope, that Smith cannot be confined to his own century. As such, the following centuries were required to come to grips with Smith, to address him from their own perspective. Consider the American Revolution; Smith's *Wealth of Nations*, published in 1776 (the same year as *The Declaration of Independence*), proposes a solution to the North America problem. Smith proposes a set of alternative solutions. Either there should be voluntary separation, or there should be a common imperial parliament for North America and Great Britain, with the location of the parliament being determined by amount of taxes contributed. As he contemplated that North America would surpass Britain economically, Smith's second alternative contemplates the transfer of Parliament from London to New York. Clearly, this can be seen as an eighteenth century issue—a bold local move. But the longer term meaning of the parable is the injunction that political arrangements should reflect economic realities. The example of European countries and European union is a contemporary example: Smith could be expected to say that, within moral limits, national political aspirations should be subordinated to the economic forces making larger and super-national associations necessary.

As a writer whose influence has extended over more than two centuries, the Adam Smith legacy has been developed by later additions and later perceptions. As noted earlier, the misreadings have been as important as the readings. Adam Smith's ideas have been misread by commentators on both the left and the right. Smith's ideas have been misread, for example, by thinkers and by practitioners and by politicians and pundits wishing to gain support for their own agendas and ideas. Adam Smith, the father of economics and philosopher of the free market, was widely seen as a sort of icon of capitalism during the Reagan and Thatcher years. Nowadays he is similarly highly regarded by others like the New Right. Adam Smith, if resurrected, would reject the exaggeration of his views in the Smith legacy. Certainly Smith wanted a minimal role for government. However, a resurrected Smith would protest that it is going too far to suppose that he was simply a supporter of laissez-faire economics, holding that the one and only guide in human affairs (the new divinity) is the direction provided by the interaction of impersonal market forces.

II. SELECTED SMITHIAN CONTRIBUTIONS

Adam Smith has significant ideas to offer on political economy, on ethics, and on government; all have significance for the student of public administration. The character of the economic forces that surround and impact public sector activity can be described by selecting among Adam Smith's major contributions. This description focuses on his doctrines of the invisible hand, the division of labor, the stages of economic growth, and his distinction (which died essentially with the passage of the classical economists) between productive and unproductive labor. It also insists that Smith recognizes the limitations of his invisible hand and fears the propensity of capitalists to subvert government. No attempt is made here to cover all of Smith's economic (or other) ideas. Such an attempt would have to describe items like his analyses of value, wages, capital, rents, and circular flow.

Adam Smith's major works are his *Wealth of Nations* and *A Theory of Moral Sentiments*, and the best known and most influential is certainly *Wealth of Nations*. In this chapter, the *Wealth of Nations* is designated as *WN* and the *Theory of Moral Sentiments* as *TMS*. He worked on the ideas for these books—and on revising them—for much of his adult life. *WN* was published in 1776, the year of the Declaration of Independence. Dugald Stewart, one of Smith's students, reports that Smith gave lectures from 1750 onwards that included leading principles of Smithian political economy (5). *TMS* had been published first in 1759. It had been developed over eight years (as Raphael and Macfie describe it) from the final form of Smith's 1752 lecture notes on moral philosophy.

Smith's two major works are supplemented by lesser, but important, works like the student notes on his *Lectures on Jurisprudence* and Smith's *History of Astronomy*, a philosophical history. Smith's moral philosophy course at the University of Glasgow is described as having been delivered in four parts; natural theology, ethics, justice, and political arrangements based on expediency (6). Student notes on Smith's lectures are available on the last two of these parts for 1762–63 and 1763–64. Unfortunately, Smith insisted that his unpublished papers should be burnt on his death, and this serves to limit understanding of his intellectual development. Also unfortunate, Smith did not write a projected book (still promised in 1790) on his theory and history of law and government, which probably would have served to complete the project which he had of developing a full social physics. This is described as a social physics, because Smith saw himself in the role of an Isaac Newton in terms of developing (although not completing) a scientifically based study of man and society.

Adam Smith's most important contribution is to the development of a science of political economy. Popularly, he is often considered to be the father of economics; however, this claim has been disputed. Adam Smith's *Wealth of Nations* was not the first publication on political economy or economics. Economic analysis has been traced throughout the history of western Europe (7), for example, and political economy had emerged as a separate discipline of inquiry in the seventeenth century. But Smith's book *The Wealth of Nations* is the first major work on economics and his work served as an inspiration at least for the classical economists—like David Ricardo—that were to follow in the nineteenth century.

Smith's main purpose in writing *WN* is to examine the fundamental forces that underlie economic development. His main prescription was the system of natural liberty. This can be understood in one sense as an opposition to the mercantilist ideas which were already petering out in influence before Smith's time. Smith was opposed to the protectionism and economic management that mercantilism implied. Mercantilism embraced such views as the ideas that a favorable balance of trade is necessary to economic development, that "wealth consists in money," that exports and cheap labor are required, and that infant industries and manufacturers should be protected. In Smith's opinion, these were all fallacies. The character of the system of natural liberty can be seen by examining a central and influential idea of *WN*, the invisible hand doctrine.

The invisible hand doctrine claims that the pursuit of individual self-interest leads to a socially optimal result. One way of looking at this invisible hand doctrine is to understand it as claiming that, when each person attempts to maximize their own individual satisfaction (to get all they can for themselves, to gouge their neighbors), it is as if there is an "invisible hand" which arranges that society thereby achieves better outcomes than if each person had tried to act for the public interest. As he put it, "It is not from the benevolence of the butcher, the brewer, or the baker, that we expect our dinner, but from their regard to their own interest. We address ourselves, not to their humanity but to their self-love, and never talk to them of our own necessities but of their advantages" (8). If everyone in society tries to work for the public good, the view is that society will be worse off than if everyone worked for her own selfish interests. Another way, complementing the way just described, is to see the invisible hand as an equilibrating force. Adam Smith's version of the invisible hand can be described as "a poetic expression of the most fundamental economic balance of relations, the equalization of rates of return, as enforced by the tendency of factors to move from low to high returns" (9). It is the automatic pricing system that tends toward a final state of balance. In other words, Smith explains economic phenomena as parts of an interrelated system. Viner long ago noted that Smith is original in his "detailed and elaborate application to the wilderness of economic phenomena of the unifying concept of a co-ordinated and mutually dependent system of cause and effect relationships which philosophers and theologians had already applied to the world in general" (10).

Book 4 of *WN* presents a simplistic and invalid argument for the invisible hand doctrine. If each person is left alone and if she follows her own self-interest, she will maximize her own wealth; the sum of the wealth of the community is the sum of the wealth of individuals; and, therefore, an aggregate of people in a society will maximize aggregate wealth. Smith also presents a more sophisticated argument, which amounts to saying that perfect competition will match self-interest and optimal utility. On this latter argument, the invisible hand turns out (as noted above) to be the self-operating pricing mechanism, i.e., the powerful system of interaction of the forces of supply and demand that—under certain conditions—yields the best outcome. The "certain conditions" we would now recognize as perfect competition, a set of conditions that is found only rarely in the real world. Smith himself recognizes that certain institutional arrangements are necessary if the invisible hand is to work effectively. For example, Smith recognizes that the invisible hand will fail whenever there is a conflict of self-interest, and where self-interest leads to socially undesirable outcomes. Smith is right in his reservations. On the last point, for instance, consider a society which includes people and firms like an Al Capone, an airline company that wants to save money by short-circuiting good safety practices, a food company that wants to make invalid claims for the "beneficial" contents of its products; it defies imagination to suppose that the invisible hand will work perfectly in that society. In the same chapter where he is arguing for free trade, Smith recognizes that complete freedom of trade is a utopian idea; he approves of protecting infant industries and the navigation laws. Later in the same book, he recognizes that one duty of government is to provide for the supply of what are now called public goods, goods (like light houses) which possess external economies and which the entrepreneur will not suppy because she cannot expect to recover her costs.

If the invisible hand doctrine is true, it is a powerful endorsement for selfishness. If the doctrine is true, it is a powerful criticism of the public interest motivation for public sector employees. West points out that, as the nineteenth century advanced, the classical economists Nassau Senior and John Stuart Mill were among those who did not appreciate that Adam Smith recognized two invisible hands (11). The first hand affects the consequences of the actions of the self-seeking individual in the market place; the invisible hand ensures that an individual, seeking their own interest, actually achieves the public interest. "By pursuing his own interest he frequently promotes that of society more effectively that when he really intends to promote it. I have never known much good done by those who affected to trade for the publick (sic) good" (12). The second hand affects the consequences of actions of individuals seeking only the public interest through government intervention; unintentionally, they promote private interests.

In developing his ideas of a system of natural liberty, Adam Smith emphasized the importance of the maximum division of labor. For him, it was a key to economic development. He did not emphasize, as we should now, factors like mechanization, automation, labor force size, or labor quality. His best known example of the division of labor within a factory is that of the manufacture of pins, which he described as "a very trifling manufacture" (13). He explains that there are about eighteen distinct operations in pin manufacture, such as drawing the wire, straightening it, cutting it, grinding it, and whitening it. Doing all the tasks oneself, a single person could make perhaps one or twenty pins per day. With the labor divided, each person could make the equivalent of 4,800 pins per day. "Each person . . . might be considered as making four thousand eight hundred pins in a day. But if they had all wrought separately and independently, and without any of them having been educated to this peculiar business, they certainly could not each of them have made twenty, perhaps not more than one pin in a day . . ." (14). Division of labor also means, for Smith, the social division of labor. This is a system of interrelationships where each producer is specialized. Smith invites the reader to consider how a day-laborer's woollen coat is "the produce of the joint labor of a great multitude of workmen"; his examples are the "the shepherd, the sorter of the wool, the wool-comber, or carder, the dyer, the spinner, the weaver, the fuller, (and) the dresser. . ." (15). Smith emphasizes that, "It is the great multiplication of all the different arts, in consequence of the division of labor, which occasions, in a well governed society, that universal opulence which extends itself to the lowest ranks of the people. Every workman has a great quantity of his own work to dispose of beyond what he himself has occasion for . . ." (16).

Important parts of Adam Smith's economic perspective are abandoned in contemporary mainstream economic theory. An example is the distinction, common among all the classical economists, between productive and unproductive labor. For contemporary economists, no labor is unproductive, even if it has negligible social value (like producing a pet rock) or even if it has negative social value (like manufacturing contaminated street drugs). Smith distinguished between productive and unproductive labor. Examples of the latter include entertainers, professional people, civil servants, and menial servants; unproductive labor includes occupations that limit the potential for the division of labor. The ratio between productive and unproductive labor set these limits because, in Smith's view, it affects the size of the market. Thus, Smith considered the ratio to be a determinant of a nation's wealth. Buchanan (a founder of Public Choice Economics) argues that it is the neoclassical economists—not Smith and the classical economists—who are in error. He has attempted to show that, under certain conditions, the revealed preferences of people may be more fully satisfied where personal services are not purchased through the mechanism of employing menial servants (17).

The economic perspective in *WN* has clearly "evolved" in subsequent years. Ideas in *WN* have been developed, improved, and "added." The poetic formulation of the invisible hand doctrine in Adam Smith is an example of a developing economic idea, a point in the development of such an idea that began before Adam Smith and that finds expression in the mathematicization of the general economic equilibrium theory. The list is long of economists who have contributed to general equilibrium theory, beginning from Adam Smith contemporaries through Leon Walras to the present day. Ingrao and Israel argue that, throughout this history, general economic equilibrium theory has had an invariant paradigmatic core relating to the equilibrium's existence, uniqueness, and stability (18). Existence means that a state of compatibility can exist between all agents; uniqueness indicates that only one state is possible; and stability means that market forces will lead to this state. There have been various approaches. For example, Ingrao and Israel distinguish between the mechanistic approach of Leon Walras and Vilfredo Pareto, the model theory of John von Neumann and Paul Samuelson, and the axiomatic treatment of Gerard Debreu (19). Monetary theory is another example of an area that has been improved. Some have argued, for example, that monetary theory owes little to WN (20). There is progression in economic thinking—whether from development, improvement or additions—throughout the classical period, (the period which ran roughly from Adam Smith through Thomas Malthus, David Ricardo, Nassau Senior and John Stuart Mill); Ricardo and Mill, for instance, specifically tried to improve on Smith. Significant changes, like of marginal analysis (consideration of the forces acting on the unit at the margin of, say, production or consumption), came with the advent of neo-classical economists; and this phase, reaching a culmination with Alfred Marshall, can be dated very roughly from the middle of the nineteenth century. The Keynesian Revolution, inaugurated by the publication in 1936 of John Maynard Keynes' *General Theory of Employment, Interest, and Money*, clearly added important macro-economic chapters. Myriads of examples could be added.

The "Adam Smith problem" is the clash that has been noted between human benevolent motivation in *TMS* and human self-interest motivation that dominates *WM*. In fact, the problem is a non-problem. Raphael and Macfie, for example, write, "The so-called 'Adam Smith problem' was a pseudo-problem based on ignorance and misunderstanding" (21). They point out that comparing an earlier edition of *TMS* with edition 6 of the same book makes it clear that Smith did not change his view about the nature of human conduct. Adam Smith saw *WN* as a logical continuation of *TMS*. It is incorrect to think that *TMS* ascribes human actions to sympathy and *WN* ascribes them to selfishness. As Raphael and Macfie explain, sympathy is at the heart of Adam Smith's explanation of moral judgment. Motive is a different matter, and there are a range of these. *WN* simply chooses to focus on self-love or self-interest. *WN* and *TMS* are dealing with different aspects of humans. Sympathy operates especially well at close quarters. But the normal relationships in a commercial situation are too distant to permit the same scope to the operation of sympathy. It makes sense, consistent with *TMS*, for *WN* to focus on regard for self, a proper part of virtue in Smith's view.

The bulk of *TMS* is concerned with moral psychology; the last seventh of the book deals with moral philosophy. *TMS* can be seen as a discussion of how human beings, self-serving as they are, are able to create natural impediments against the inclinations of their own passions. Sympathy, a fellow feeling for the feelings of the other person "at the thought of his situation," is at the heart of Smith's moral psychology. Sympathy is the basis of our judgments about the propriety and merit of the conduct of others. Looking at one's own behavior as if one were another person allows one to evaluate one's own conduct. We can identify the general rules which govern conduct that gives rise to our sympathy. Smith's moral philosophy discussed the nature and basis of virtue. For Smith, there is no single criterion of virtue; it gives scope to propriety, prudence, and benevolence. Neither prudence (seeking self-interest) nor benevolence (seeking others' interests) is enough by itself. In this circumstance, the standard of what is appropriate behavior is given in considering the sympathetic feelings of the impartial spectator. Sympathy is the test of morality, the sympathy of the impartial and well-informed spectator. In commercial society, especially worthy are prudence and justice.

For the eighteenth century and for Adam Smith, jurisprudence concerned justice, police, revenue, and arms—with police used in its eighteenth century sense which Smith understood as including the cheapness of commodities, public security, cleanliness, and the opulence of the state. In *Lectures on Jurisprudence*, Smith first considers themes that include justice, the foundation of government and obedience, and his stages of development. Smith held that justice is the principal and chief objective of every system of government. Justice, for him, is a matter of abstaining from doing harm to another's person, property, or reputation. The objective of justice is to secure people from injury; it is not a question of allocation. Smith rejects the contractual notion of the origin of government and obedience. People constitute societies for the purposes of survival and reproduction, and they gradually form habits of obedience. He discusses obedience in terms of utility and authority, with the latter dependent on personal qualifications, age, wealth, and family status. The amount of obedience, which is strengthened by interest, depends on the stage of historical development. Smith identifies (also see *WN*) four stages of societal development—the hunter, the shepherd, the agricultural (containing three substages), and the present commercial stages. The stages do depend on the method of subsistence and the latter does shape understandings of justice, property, and government. However, Smith's system need not be read as contemplating economic determinism, with the stages developing automatically.

Reading *WN* by itself does tend to lead to misreading of Adam Smith. It is correct that Smith wants government to ensure individual freedom and, within the market mechanism, to facilitate the working of the economic system. It is correct that Smith wants governmental institutions to be continually and systematically adjusted to society's commercial demands. In his day, it will be recalled that he wanted the economic realities to be appreciated when considering the political arrangements with the American colonies.

It is correct that Smith wants the market to operate freely; he opposes the restrictions of the mercantilists, for example. He applauds "the progress of opulence," and sees the free market as the means to "universal opulence" (22). It is correct that Smith endorses commercial values. This is in spite of the fact that he considers the interests of capitalists opposed to the interests of the whole of society, because the rate of profit declines (in his view) as society's wealth increases. He holds that inequality stabilizes sentiments of justice, even though he holds that admiring the rich and despising the poor is "the great and most universal cause of corruption of our moral sentiments" (23). He holds that, even with inequality, the poor have the necessities for life. He claims that wealth increases the capacity for benevolence, even though commercial people can lead a life of propriety but not of complete virtue. It is correct that Smith would limit the functions of government, and that he would exclude any redistributive measures. He does hold that governmental bureaucracy is unproductive.

Smith does not understand economics to be an autonomous moral entity, however. In terms of study, Smith is a philosopher of society rather than an economist. He sees moral philosophy as encompassing morality, justice and police, the latter term being used in the sense noted earlier. The founder of political economy sees politics and economics as dimensions of a larger philosophy. For Smith, a value-free economics is only part of the story; he wanted to write a trilogy that would include his works on ethics, economics (or police), and government (or justice). As Winch comments, Smith would not have considered it worthwhile to have written a *WN* confined entirely to positivist propositions (24).

In terms of practice, Adam Smith wants a government that is capable of coping with the capitalists' ability to subvert government to private interests. He recognizes the necessity of government. Smith makes suggestions for the administration of justice; for example, he supports the separation of powers and he approves of fees for court services. He recognizes that the commercial stage of development made a standing army desirable. He favors the governmental provision of public goods, like bridges and canals. He favors governmental action not only in situations of market failure but also for specific policy purposes. Smith wants tax measures to reduce the number of alehouses, for example; he wants universal military training in order to encourage laborers (disenfranchised in that society) to play a part in the country's life. He wants other governmental intrusions in the public provision of elementary education and in ensuring that army officers are competent. Smith wants government to encourage membership in religious sects in order to offset the deterioration in morals that the poor experience in commercial society; it will be recalled that Smith had noted that "the poor person, coming from his village to the obscurity and darkness of the larger towns, would tend to abandon himself to every sort of low profligacy and vice" (25). He wants government institutions that are accountable to society, and not merely to special commercial interests. Viner does agree that there is a presumption against government throughout *WN*; nevertheless, he claims that Smith "saw a wide and elastic range of activity for government" (26).

Adam Smith does hold an invisible hand doctrine; but he is conscious of the limited functioning of the hand. Notice the qualifiers in Adam Smith's discussion in *WN* of the operation of the invisible hand. "Nor is it always the worse for society that it was no part of (his intention). By pursuing his own interest he frequently promotes that of the society more effectually than when he really intends to promote it" (27). Adam Smith recognizes that the invisible hand does not always work. Similarly he recognizes in *TMS* that sympathy does not always work, especially where relationships occur at a distance. He recognizes that neither the invisible hand nor sympathy work perfectly well. To a large extent, Smith did expect welfare to be maximized and harm to be minimized automatically. However, he certainly recognized the potential for the pursuit of self-interest—insufficiently controlled—to inflict unacceptable harm on others. Natural justice was not enough; government, though government is limited, is needed.

The ancestry of Adam Smith in creating the conceptual space for thinking about social issues (like public administration) is undeniable. He is a symbol of the free market, of the unfettered "propensity to truck, barter, exchange" (28). This is in spite of the fact that Adam Smith recognized that there are institutional limitations to the working out of the beneficial effects of the invisible hand. There is a division of opinion as to whether neoclassical perfect competition can be found in Smith's economics (29). As West puts it in summarizing Anderson and Tollison, Smithian competition "was compatible with any number (of competitors) as long as entry into the industry was free. Competition was essentially a rivalrous process in a sense of rivalry in a race. The case of a market-generated monopoly would be an instance of one competitor temporarily winning the race" (30).

Contemporary mainstream economic theory has served to underscore Smith's concern about the limitations of the operation of the invisible hand. In discussing this issue toward the end of this chapter, it is indicated that these limitations relate to an economy's efficiency, equity, and growth. Concerning efficiency, for example, contemporary microeconomic theory makes clear that optimal results cannot be expected from an economy where either monopolistic (one supplier) and oligopolistic (few suppliers) competition obtains. Monopolists and oligopolists, contemporary mainstream theory makes clear, are not price takers subject to the price setting of the market. Rather, they are price setters, and in their own rational self-interest they will tend to restrict supply in order to secure excess profits. In such circumstances, the invisible hand fails. It should be noted, however, that the structure of the economy in Smith's time was less concentrated. For example, agriculture had a larger role, and agriculture is often nowadays given as an example of an economic activity where the producers are price takers. On this ground, Adam Smith had more reason to subscribe to his invisible hand doctrine than we do.

None of this should conceal Adam Smith's skepticism and opposition toward positive government, especially in economic matters. Government, for Smith, does not have an active or innovative role. Winch goes on to explain that, for Smith, the legislator's main task is "to accommodate laws to the habits of men and their existing social condition" (31). But in doing this, the legislator must be governed by a sense of justice. Recall Smith's disparagement of the "man of system," the legislator who does not recognize the critical limitation on political behavior of factors like opinion (of which emotion and ignorance are dimensions).

> The man of system . . . is apt to be very wise in his own conceit; and is often so enamored with the supposed beauty of his own ideal plan of government, that he cannot suffer the smallest deviation from any part of it. He goes on to establish it completely and in all its parts, without any regard either to the great interests, or to the strong prejudices that may oppose it (32).

Smith recognizes the power of economic forces that surround governmental activity. He draws attention to the impact on government, for example, of the relative power of corporations and employers. "Whenever the legislature attempts to regulate the differences between masters and their workmen, its counsellors are always the masters" (33). Such reasons, Smith acknowledges, would frustrate the complete achievement of his system of natural liberty. Smith's recognition of the power of economic forces and special interests resonates today as the United States' executive and legislature are so thoroughly dominated by the power of such forces and interests (34), and this leads naturally to a comment on Public Choice.

III. IMPORTANCE OF THE SMITHIAN LEGACY

Adam Smith's legacy, the conceptual attitudes that can be associated with Smith, is a central feature of the contemporary world outlook. It forms part of the conceptual space for such specialties as the study of public administration and of organization; it is barely possible to practice public administration without working within the constraints of this conceptual space. This section notes the support given to the Smithian legacy by the triumphs of liberal democracy and liberal capitalism, and it comments on the legacy's encouragement of the centrality of economic relations. The importance of understanding the legacy is increased if it is recognized that it is socially constituted; it can be changed. In order to clarify the claim that Smith is wrong not to recognize that the economic sphere is socially constituted, this section considers the notions of "economics as rhetoric" and of "new economics." The importance of reconsidering the legacy is also underscored by considering the tension in Smith's view that the economic sphere is not only harmonious but also exploitative.

The Smithian legacy is currently supported by the twin triumph throughout much of the world of liberal democracy and liberal capitalism; the triumph is twin because each is considered to reinforce the other. The liberal democratic state, according to some thinkers, is now the dominant and triumphant vehicle of government. Fukuyama, for instance, has written of the end of history in the sense that the liberal democratic state now has no rivals, no alternatives (35). With the triumph of the West against communism, democracy—despite its difficulties—is now the ascendent force. Perhaps because of the long contest against communism, liberal capitalism (democracy's companion condition) is also dominant; arguably, capitalism of sorts is widely seen as part of "the American way of life" and now former communist states work toward developing market economies. Smith is an intellectual ancestor of this "triumph." Recall that WN has been described as focusing on the interrelationship of commerce and liberty (36). Smith was interested not only in the benefits of economic liberty for economic development but also in the benefits of commerce for liberty.

Economic relations have long been regarded as central for an understanding of political and social issues, by many who oppose capitalism and by many who celebrate capitalism. Smith is an important figure in moving toward this position. Macpherson describes the increasing incorporation of an economic perspective in liberal political theory from John Locke to Jeremy Bentham and to James Mill (37). Recognition of the increasing centrality of economic relations, the priority of the economic over the political sphere, is part of the legacy to which Adam Smith made an outstanding contribution. Recall that Smith would settle the problem of the American colonies in the light of the economic realities.

The important point is that a return to the words of Adam Smith reminds us of what Smith did not recognize; economic space is socially constructed. Adam Smith thought that he was identifying, in a Newtonian fashion, the underlying forces that underlie society; the equilibrating mechanism of the invisible hand explains and governs the myriad of economic phenomena that we observe in the socio-economic universe. He thought that he was dealing with givens; he thought that he was doing social physics. Newtonian physics dominated eighteenth century thought about society, and its fundamental importance in the Enlightenment is widely recognized. Consider the views of thinkers like D'Alembert, Voltaire, and Montesquieu. Newtonian science permeated the environment. During the French Enlightenment, Newtonian physics became the norm of scientific thinking. As Cassirer points out, the eighteenth century took the methodological paradigm of Newtonian physics as a starting point, and added a universal twist. It saw this paradigm as necessary for thought in general (38).

Mainstream economic theory, the theory that acknowledges Smith as its founder, has developed as a mathematicophysical enterprise. It is true that there is little mathematics in Smith's WN, just as there are few mathematical formulae in one of the other of the most important books in the history of economic theory—in John Maynard Keynes' major publication (39). But the nineteenth century saw the increasing mathematicizaton of economic theory. Throughout its history, mainstream economic theory has been generally viewed as a positivist activity, as opposed to a hermeneutic (or interpretive) enterprise (40). For one distinction, positivist science is concerned with determining causality, as contrasted with hermeneutics that is concerned with such purposes as interpreting meaning.

An alternative is to understand economic theory as rhetoric (a shocking word for those unfamiliar with Philosophy of Social Science), as a constructivist activity. The point is that the conceptual space established for public administration by mainstream economic theory can be so understood, providing more leeway for the public administration theorist and practitioner. McClosky has attracted considerable attention with his view of economic theory as rhetoric (41). Such a view would deny that the propositions of economic science can be established in such a way that the propositions have a privileged epistemological status, the sort of privileged status that is invoked when one declares, "that is a scientific fact." In the latter case, the fact is being contrasted with a fact (such as a poetic fact or a fact of everyday life) established by a method that is not regarded as scientific. McCloskey's point amounts to claiming that economic theory should be better understood as an interpretation. As Nelson writes, "The idea that economics is socially constructed should not . . . be novel to anyone with an interest in methodology or the philosophy of science or who ever heard of Thomas Kuhn (1962)" (42). She contrasts this with the view, which she rejects, of those economists who understand themselves as striving to come closer and closer to truth with a big T.

Consider the social construction of the concept of Gross National Product (G.N.P.) and compare it with the "G.N.P." that ecologists would favor. G.N.P. is an indicator that affects behavior and that governments worry about; for example, it will be recalled that the growth in G.N.P. no less than the supposed missile gap was a critical issue in President John F. Kennedy's election campaign. G.N.P. is the total value of the final goods and services produced by an economy during one year. It can be measured in two broad ways— by summing the amounts of all incomes to the various factors of production, or by summing all the sales of final goods and services. G.N.P., as now socially constituted, measures production without consideration of the "benefit" of the product to society; $2 million spent on pet rocks (or on unneeded house repairs, fraudulently contracted between dishonest repair firms and senile home owners) is counted the same as $2 million on basic food or life-saving medicine for the needy. (As an aside, it will be noted that we have passed over the celebrated paradox of value—"valuable water that costs so little" and "valueless diamonds which cost so much"—discussed by Smith and his predecessors and resolved by the neo-classical economists.) G.N.P., as now socially constituted, measures production without considering the wear and tear on the ecological assets of the country; air pollution and water pollution are not considered costs of production. In terms of G.N.P., it is irrelevant if a company produces refrigerators so designed (say, using hydrofluorocarbons) that they inadvertently widen (if they do) the hole in our world's ozone layer. Many ecologists would favor the social construction of a new concept in place of G.N.P. (the new concept sometimes called the Adjusted National Product or A.N.P.). They want a New Economics based upon a different interpretation or construction of reality. A main argument of the new economics is that, faced with finite and non-renewable resources, growth cannot continue indefinitely; and technology can do no more than postpone such problems. Many ecologists want a radical change in the conception of the economic sphere. Vincent explains that they want the growth-oriented economic order to be replaced by a sustainable economic order (43).

Smith's legacy is powerful. Of major contemporary importance in Smith and his legacy is the sense of legitimacy and priority which he has given to the market. Smith's tradition provides many public administrationists with a sense that their theorizing should be conducted within the framework of the market. The view that the market is legitimate and primary (say, over the political) is facilitated by the opinion that the market is beneficent, that it contributes toward social harmony. That is, if the market were recognized as being significantly inefficient and unfair, it would be harder to maintain that the market place should mold human society. (Of course, among the other issues impacting on this matter is one's estimate of the legitimacy of the political sphere.) Shapiro points out that there are two poles in treating the social, emphasizing harmony, and emphasizing disharmony (44). Smith is in the first category. Shapiro claims that Smith's language assumes the existence of God as the universe's author—but an author who has retired and left behind mechanisms guaranteeing that the self and the other are always congruent. Shapiro believes that this congruence is not a characteristic of the world but rather a metaphor, a trope, in the organization of Smith's writing.

Smith's own reservations about the invisible hand are typically unnoticed by believers in the Adam Smith legacy, a legacy that has acquired a life of its own. Consider Smith's view that civil society is essentially exploitative, for example. *WN* notes that, "Civil government, so far as it is instituted for the security of property, is in reality instituted for the defence of the rich against the poor, or of those who have some property against those who have none at all" (45). Some focus on understandings of the invisible hand that sustain the Adam Smith legacy. Buchanan and Tullock, for example, assert that the "great contribution" of Adam Smith lies in popularizing the notion that in "normal trade all parties gain" (46). Smith is the founder of a tradition which provides many with a sense of legitimacy about following the dictates of impersonal market forces, and it is important for public administrationists and others to return to Smith and his legacy in order to make their own evaluations of these ideas. Unexamined, the ideas will continue to constrain action in non-economic matters; alternatives, possible because any such conceptual space is socially constituted, will not be developed until the Smithian legacy is examined for validity.

IV. INCORPORATING SMITH IN THE FIELD OF PUBLIC ADMINISTRATION

The Adam Smith legacy has penetrated public organization theory and practice, just as it is part of political theory. First, significant elements of Public Choice Economics have shed important insights on public organization theory and practice, and much more can be expected in future years. Second, the general impact of economic concepts on the character of public organization theory and practice has been profound, and this may be explored by examining the centrality of efficiency (a thoroughly Smithian concept) to public administration theory and practice. The dominance of the efficiency concept, it is suggested, is an example of how the economic ethos infuses traditional public administration theory. It is suggested that this dominance is essential in capitalism, just as it is necessary in economic theory developed to predict, explain, and control activities in a capitalist context. Third, contemporary economic and other theories also suggest ways in which the Smithian legacy should be interpreted. Adam Smith does more than set the conceptual space for public administration.

This section discusses, then, these three ways in which the Smithian legacy is of particular significance for Public Administration theory and practice. The results of the Public Choice approach are discussed, explaining what it means to speak of necessary waste in government; the potential is also noted for greater use of the deductive approach. The centrality of efficiency in public administration and in the Smithian legacy is explored. The limits of Adam Smith are also emphasized, especially in terms of contemporary discussion of selected social theories and economic theory.

A. Public Choice Economics

Adam Smith is the spiritual ancestor of the use of Public Choice Economics in analyzing government. Recall that Adam Smith held that governmental institutions should be evaluated by, and should be subject to, economic standards. For example, he advocated the application of economic principles to the organization of defense and justice; he urged the use of user fees to pay for public works. Public works services should be administered in such a manner as to make effectiveness in the self-interest of administrators. Skinner points out that, for Smith, politics is like economics in being competitive. He adds that, "To this extent Smith would have been surprised to find Professor Tullock (co-founder of Public Choice Economics) referring to a *newly* established "economics of politics" which assumes that 'all the individuals in government aim at raising their own utility" (47). On the other hand, Smith has been criticized by Stigler for failing to create a "thorough-going economic theory of political behavior." Winch represents Stigler as regretting Smith's unwillingness to apply 'the organon of self-interest to political behavior' " (48).

Vincent Ostrom pioneered the application of Public Choice Economics to problems of public administration theory and practice. He advocated the establishment in the tradition of the Adam Smith legacy of "a new theory of democratic administration." Ostrom points to the theory of public goods as the central organizing concept used by political economists in studying public administration and collective action (49). Ostrom's book does not mention Adam Smith's name any more than it mentions other great economists like Ricardo, Marshall, or Keynes; instead he writes of fashioning the theory of democratic administration from "the works of Hamilton, Madison, Tocqueville, Dewey, Lindblom, Buchanan, Tullock, Olson, Niskanen, and many others" (50). As Ostrom would agree, Buchanan and Tullock—when they founded Public Choice Economics in the sixties—were attempting to apply economic concepts to the political situation. As the journal *Public Choice* notes in each issue, Public Choice is concerned with "the intersection between economics and political science." It involves, as the journal indicates, the application of essentially economic methods to political problems.

The principal impact that Public Choice has had on public administration is that it has underscored the existence of waste in public sector activity. The outcry against governmental waste has now become so commonplace that there is an understandable reaction against the outcry among those valuing public sector activity. It needs to be asserted that not all governmental activity is wasteful (obviously, it is not) and that there is waste in private enterprise as well as in public enterprise. The underscoring of what has been long recognized, however, has been significant in that it has added substance to the weight of the outcry.

Perhaps such an outcry was inevitable in a situation (even if there were no direct correlation between waste and size) where the size of governmental administration in all the advanced countries has grown during the past two centuries, especially since World War II. The statistics are undeniable. Total governmental expenditure in the United States as a percentage of gross national product jumped from 10 percent in 1929 to 34.8 percent in 1987, for example (51). All advanced countries show substantial increases. Many are concerned about governmental growth today; yet this concern is confined neither to this century nor to this country. At the 1876 centennial celebration of *WN* in London, Prime Minister Gladstone complained that,

> The full development of the principles of Adam Smith has been in no small danger for some time past; and one of the great dangers that now hangs over the country is that the wholesome, spontaneous operation of human interests and human desires seems to be in course of rapid supersession by the erection of one government department after another, by the setting up of one set of inspectors after another, and by the whole

time of parliament being taken up in attempting to do for the nation those very things which, if the teaching of the man whose name we are celebrating today is to bear any fruit at all, the nation can do much better for itself (52).

Public Choice underscores the existence of government waste by arguing that the waste is a necessary (an essential)—not an accidental—part of governmental activity. The claim is that there can be no governmental activity without waste; waste is an inevitable outcome of rational bureaucratic activity. This has been discussed elsewhere (53). When acting in a rational manner, suppliers of governmental output will choose to supply a non-optimal amount. On the supply side, Niskanen's model of the budget-maximizing bureaucrat shows the government bureau supplying twice the optimal (the most desirable) amount (54). Niskanen's model has been modified with alternative institutional and behavioral assumptions; Migue and Belanger's model is an example (55). The picture of the rationality of supply-side waste remains. This should occasion no surprise to the economist, because of the standard view in microeconomic theory of the supply and pricing behavior of the monopolist (one supplier) and the oligopolist (few suppliers). Unlike the supplier who is a price taker in conditions of perfect competition, mainstream microeconomic theory paints a picture of the rational monopolist who chooses to restrict supply in order to obtain excess profits. Governmental agencies, clearly, have monopolistic and oligopolistic characteristics.

A difference between the public enterprise and the private enterprise situation is that public officials lack the discipline of a suitable effective demand constraint. Demand signals in the private sector, while they can be criticized in terms of efficiency and equity considerations, transmit the market wishes of consumers relatively effectively. Public Choice analyses presents a different picture of the demand for public sector goods and services. Public choice analyses of alternative voting mechanisms make clear the difficulty of ascertaining what the public demands (56). This is quite separate from sorting out the demand for aggregates of multiple issues, often where individuals give contradictory answers (e.g. cut the expenditure but do not cut programs). Dealing only with small groups giving yes-no votes and considering no more than single issues, contradictory readings of public demand can be obtained by using alternative aggregation protocols (or voting mechanisms); that is, a Borda (or other) protocol may or may not give a different reading than a Cordorcet (or other) protocol of the same set of preferences expressed by the same set of people. In fact Kenneth Arrow's Possibility Theorem shows that it is impossible to specify a protocol for aggregating individual preferences (i.e. to specify what public choice economists call an axiomatic social welfare function) that can be guaranteed to satisfy even certain very minimal and basic technical conditions (57). The point is that the conditions in question are not complex items like justice or fairness. Rather, they are narrow items, like transitivity. Transitivity, it will be recalled, is the condition that, if A is preferred to B and if B is preferred to C, A is preferred to C.

Economic tools, part of the Adam Smith tradition, are useful in analyzing possible coping strategies—like privatization, agency size reduction, and budgetary squeezing. Adam Smith's own suggestions about governmental efficiency, it will be recalled, included not only keeping government out of certain functional areas but also subjecting bureaucracies (like public roads and court services) to the winds of the market place. Clearly, economic tools are part and parcel of competent public sector policy analysis. But a word should be added about the importance of being clear about the nature of the problem. The Public Choice analysis makes clear that eliminating programs (or parts of programs) is not equivalent to eliminating waste. Obviously, if an entire agency is eliminated, it is not possible for waste to occur in that agency. (However, there may be even greater waste if the consequent increase in social cost exceeds the cost of the agency. There may still be waste if the activity is completely privatized.) The point that emerges from the public choice analysis is that every single agency, to the extent that it is a bureaucratic agency, involves waste. Not even starving an agency of funds is likely to be completely successful; waste is necessary even in an impoverished bureaucracy. This presents an important challenge for public administration theory; new approaches toward public organization are required.

It is here that Public Choice can point a way for contemporary public administration theory. The traditional method of public administration has tended to be inductive, starting from individual observations and then proceeding to generalizations. The inductive approach needs supplementation by a deductive approach, the method of proceeding from the general to the particular and the method that is well developed in Public Choice and in economic theorizing. Of course, the inductive approach is valuable and it needs to be retained. Economics utilizes both approaches, with the deductive being at the center of contemporary economic theory; Adam Smith tended to favor the observational, while later theorists (some, like Leon Walras, more than others) favored the rational deductive approach. Each method, by itself, has weaknesses. Here it is noted that the inductive method, by itself, has a serious weakness. This weakness is that it tends to encourage retention of the status quo, privileging whatever exists. It was the inductive approach that Aristotle followed in his political analysis that encouraged him to justify his comments on slavery and on women. If slavery is general, the inductive approach does encourage the researcher to find a generalization that will explain (and often "justify") it; if all swans are white, there must be a reason for swans being white and a clever researcher will find or concoct a reason. Being more inclined to the deductive in his political analysis, Plato was able to be more radical; faced with objections to his ideal city, he could brush aside criticism appealing to the difficulty of ready implementation of his proposals (58). Some might argue that much of public administration Theory exhibits a weakness of being too attached to the status quo.

B. General Impact of Economics

The extent to which the Adam Smith legacy has permeated public administration theory and practice can be recognized by considering the central role accorded to efficiency, a central concept in economic theory. Despite a relative decline since World War II (59), the efficiency concept remains an important goal in contemporary public administration practice. This decline has been encouraged by writers like the Dimocks and Waldo, who have distinguished normative and descriptive senses of the efficiency concept. The Dimocks and Waldo agree that efficiency should not be an end in itself, for instance (60). The continuing importance of the concept in practice is reflected in its explicit specification as a governmental goal in Vice President Albert Gore's National Productivity Review Report; for example, the Preface explains that the Report's twin missions are "to make government work better and cost less" (61). Efficiency is a concept that also figures in much Public Administration Theory. Ostrom opposes his new theory of democratic administration against the Wilsonian Paradigm, for example, and he recognizes the role of efficiency in the latter. He characterizes the Wilsonian Paradigm as aiming for efficiency in the "perfection in the hierarchical ordering of a professionally trained public service" (62).

The claim is not that the accent on efficiency originated in economics and then infected public administration. Rather, efficiency is a modernist concept that manifested itself in a variety of ways, one of the most important being in Smithian and economic analysis. The priority given to the economic sphere in major political ideologies (liberal, conservative, and socialist ideologies, for example) contributes to the efficiency concept remaining important in disciplines like public administration. Among the other factors accounting for the influence of economics on public administration, as well as on other disciplines concerned with social concerns, is the wide acceptance of the relative boldness, coherence, and mathematical elegance of economic theory. For such reasons, it is important to come closer to the roots of the pressure to celebrate efficiency, a pressure that can be found in Smithian economics.

Baechler's comment, noted earlier, about capitalism being unique in according such a privileged position to efficiency will be recalled. Baechler advances a set of interconnected propositions on the development of capitalism, emphasizing the privileged position of efficiency in modern capitalism (63). Another proposition is that a primary condition "for the maximization of economic efficiency is the liberation of civil society with respect to the State" (64). Baechler argues that this condition can be met by the creation of a number of sovereign political units in a cultural area. It is "necessary that the value-system be modified to the detriment of religious, military, and political values, and that demand be liberated" (65). Baechler holds that such conditions have been realized only in the modern West.

Waldo is a public administrationist who has made the point about efficiency being a modernist concept. Appropriately, he has associated the rise and influence of the concept with such modernist characteristics as the world-view "popularized by Descartes and Newton," the emergence of capitalism, the development of Weberian bureaucracy, the advent of the industrial revolution, the growth of science and technology, the dominance of the power-driven machine, the development of the business ethos, and (note) the emergence of economics (66). Certainly, the genesis and triumph of efficiency are era-wide and complex phenomena. Consider the structure of capitalism, for instance. The need for control is much greater in the modernist period, where a central feature of the capitalist economic system is its free-wheeling and decentralized structure. There is a need in such decentralized and fast-moving circumstances to direct, coordinate, and control subordinates and associates, often at a distance. It is to the issue of distance that Smith's analysis speaks in particular, especially in the context of the matter of social cohesion. At close proximity, the sympathy that is described in *TMS* is able to check an individual's self-love. At a distance, there is a greater problem, met in large part by the beneficent operation of the invisible hand and also by the governmental imposition of justice requirements. This distance in the modern world is increasing in several senses; it is not merely that business is becoming more global but also that the size of populations (and thus the number of interactions) is galloping at an accelerating rate. The Smithian legacy must be considered when reflecting on the pressure to celebrate efficiency in public administration. Note that five of the items in the above list from Waldo are essentially economic in character.

Reflection on the Smithian and other roots of efficiency in public administration theory and practice highlights the matter of eras. Elsewhere, it has been argued that concepts like efficiency are culture-embedded (67). Three sets of supporting analyses are offered. First, it is argued that the efficiency concept is not a given; supposing the efficiency concept to be a feature of all possible worlds is described as false. Second, it is explained that efficiency has a latent control meaning, made more potent because it operates through an unconscious dynamic. Third, it is argued that there must be a match between the latent control feature of efficiency and societal environment. In other words, efficiency is a concept well suited to the societal conditions of modernity, the period of the past five hundred or so years. It is not at all well suited to the conditions either of the pre-modern (say, the Middle Ages) or the postmodern. All of which tends toward the important question of the extent to which American Public Administration can overcome the limitations of being a modernist project (68).

C.   Selected Social and Contemporary Economic Theories

The limits of Adam Smith's legacy should be recognized, especially if it is held that we are moving toward a postmodern condition. Adam Smith, an Enlightenment figure, was engaged in a modernist project. It is a modernist project in that, reflecting no skepticism about the power of human reasoning, Smith sought to extend the searchlight of reason more effectively into yet another corner of human activity. The conceptual space surrounding public administration is different if it is not only socially constructed but also if it is correct that we are moving into a postmodern era or situation. Properly understood, postmodernism is profound skepticism about the human capacity to know. A socially constructed concept in the modernist context refers to an underlying reality, perhaps touching this aspect (like mainstream G.N.P.) or another aspect (like ecologism's A.N.P.) of the underlying referent. Postmodern economics would go further and deny the possibility of knowing any underlying referent; some postmodernists explain that hyperreality, the idea without referent, is indistinguishable from the real (69). There is a literature discussing the application of postmodernism ideas to public administration (70), and there is no need to repeat the points here. The point is that, in the postmodern situation, the conceptual framework of public administration changes not only because the barriers between disciplines implode but also because economics (part of that imploded framework) changes. Public administration encounters economic theory where, in the postmodern context, the economic ideas without referents are hyperreal. This would be astonishing talk to Adam Smith. Through and through, Smith was an Enlightenment figure, a modernist to the core.

Others approach this differently, with a more optimistic epistemological (essentially a modernist) outlook. The historical limitations of Adam Smith are referenced by Raymond in this way, "Adam Smith said that the overall best interests of first wave society resulted from each individual entrepreneur seeking his or her own best interest, but Smith could not foresee the long-term consequences of second wave technology, and the social, environmental, and institutional characteristics of corporations" (71). This relies on Alvin Toffler's notion of waves (72). The first nature-dependent wave, coming to an end in the United States around 1870, is described as the agricultural revolution of about 10,000 years ago. The second wave, beginning to decline about 1970, is the nature-dominant Industrial Revolution. The third is described as more than increasing reliance on information and technology. It is "new forms of relating among people and between people and nature, new meanings, new forms of organization, new forms of management, a new society, and a new economy" (73). Certainly, Adam Smith did think that agriculture is more important than manufacturing. If there is a third wave, he is two waves out of reach.

Whether we are entering a new era, postmodern or third wave, will become clear only after a century or two. But it is clear enough that public administrationists must be conscious of the forces, like the Smithian legacy, that shape the lens through which they describe problems and prescribe solutions. There is a need to guard against projecting latent assumptions into our conclusions, on the same lines that Ludwig Wittgenstein is read as saying that philosophical positions are basically rationalizations of certain habits or dispositions. The Adam Smith legacy shapes the public administrationist's lens; it deserves attention.

Consider now the Smithian legacy in terms of contemporary economic theory. Each age must come to grips with the rose-colored story which Adam Smith tells and which forms part of the Adam Smith legacy. (Coming to grips is a large task; it may involve understanding why we like to tell our children fables such as that Santa Claus exists, when we know that he does not.) Smith would have us believe that, underlying the mass of diverse economic phenomena, there is a force which is not only unifying but also beneficent. This is the invisible hand that ensures (on one account) that, when each of us acts in our own self-interest, the public interest is served better than if we had acted in the public interest. There is some truth in the rose-colored contention. The market does function as a system; it does guide and it does have, as it were, a life of its own. The market, wherein individuals look out for themselves, can have unintended benefits for others. Consider any business transaction; both buyer and seller can be winners, and there does not have to be a loser. Compare the experience of buying shoes in GUM's Department Store in the former Soviet Union's Moscow with a similar experience in Bloomingdale's in New York City. Certainly, we obtain better service and products in Bloomingdale's, and a good supposition is that the reason is that Bloomingdale's was working for its own self-interest. Beyond such nuggets of truth, the invisible hand doctrine is a cultural fairy tale. The beneficence is grossly oversold. Paul Samuelson states, "After two centuries of experience and thought, however, we now recognize the scope and realistic limitations of this doctrine. We know that the market sometimes lets us down, that there are 'market failures,' and that markets do not always lead to the most efficient outcome" (74). He makes this statement in his standard introductory textbook, and this source is chosen in order to emphasize the mainstream character of the comment.

To make the mainstream point clearer, it is worth recalling the contemporary mainstream account of the causes of market failure, where the market will not operate to yield a satisfactory result and where governmental intervention is deemed necessary. The following principal sources of market failures can be identified. First, there are the failures of competition due to the existence of monopoly and oligopoly pricing. Second, there is the existence of public goods, goods which will not be supplied in sufficient quantity or at all (e.g. national defense); pure public goods have zero marginal cost for an additional consumer. Third, there are externalities, where one firm's actions result in either a benefit or a cost to others (e.g. pollution). Samuelson prescribes what he thinks are three legitimate roles in coping with the failure of the invisible hand (75). Samuelson's first category of failure, as suggested earlier and as Smith recognized, is the inefficiency that results from the existence of monopoly, externalities, and public good. This leads to governmental intervention (in such forms as the Sherman Anti-trust Laws and speed limits) and to subsidies for purposes like the weather service. Fourth, there are information failures, where private enterprise does not provide enough information. Fifth, there are incomplete markets, where individual firms do not provide a product even though the cost is less than that which individuals are prepared to pay. Sixth, there are the ravages of unemployment and inflation. Another of Samuelson's categories of invisible hand failure is instability represented by the ups and downs of the business cycles and by problems of poor economic growth it is here that the government might intervene through macroeconomic steps such as monetary and fiscal policies. Beyond this, there are the issues of redistribution and merit goods. The distribution of income in an economy may be unsatisfactory, as unattended economies do tend to lead to inordinate disparities of wealth. Gross inequalitis is yet another of Samuelson's list of categories where the invisible hand fails, leading to redistributive governmental intervention in such areas as progressive taxation and shelter and food for abandoned children. The concept of merit goods recognizes that individuals can well make decisions that are not in their fundamental best interest, and there are some items (like elementary education) that consumers should be compelled to consume.

Each public administration thinker must come to terms with Adam Smith, a writer so strong that he changed the way in which it is possible for public administrationists and others to look at the world, and with his legacy. A first challenge is to get Smith right. Adam Smith the writer has been widely misread. The success of WN has obscured the total message which he wanted to give through a reading of both WN and TMS. It is also obscured because he failed to complete the third book of his trilogy. A second challenge is to question the account he gives of the conceptual space, constituted by his view of economics, which underlies public administration and organizational theory. In particular, is the economic prior to the political? Is the economic a beneficial sphere? Are attempts aimed at the public interest doomed to encourage private gains? How adequate is the market for human needs? A third challenge is to explore in specific terms the potential for public administration of an understanding of Adam Smith and his legacy. Does economics have an appropriate influence on public organizational thinking? Is Public Choice Economics a useful tool? Are we unduly constrained by economic concepts, like efficiency? The central claim of this chapter has been that, by approaching Adam Smith and his legacy, public administrationists can assist themselves to do what they should do—examine their latent assumptions.

NOTES

1. M. Weber, *The Protestant Ethic and the Spirit of Capitalism*, Talcott Parson (ed.), New York, New York: Schribner, 1958, p. 17.
2. J. Baechler, *The Origins of Capitalism*, Oxford: Blackwell, 1975, p. 113.
3. e.g. see K. Fan, Z. Song, K. Khu, W. Guo, and Y. Chi, *An Economic History of the Major Capitalist Countries: A Chinese View*, Armonk, New York: M. E. Sharpe, 1992, p. 35.
4. M. Blaug, *Economic Theory in Retrospect*, New York: Cambridge University Press, 1978, p. 38.
5. D. D. Raphael and A. L. Macfie, *Adam Smith: The Theory of Moral Sentiments*, Oxford: Clarendon Press, 1976, p. 23. (Abbreviated as TMS.)
6. J. W. Cairns, Adam Smith's Lectures on Jurisprudence: Their Influence on Legal Education, *Adam Smith: International Perspective*, Hiroshi Mizuta and Chuhei Sugiyama (eds.), New York: St. Martin's Press, 1993, p. 66.
7. J. A. Schumpeter, *History of Economic Analysis*, New York: Oxford University Press, 1954.

8. R. H. Campbell and A. S. Skinner, *Adam Smith: An Inquiry into the Nature and the Causes of the Wealth of Nations*, Oxford: Clarendon Press, 1976, pp. 26–27. (Abbreviated as *WN*.)

9. K. J. Arrow and G. Debreu, *General Competitive Analysis*, San Francisco: Holden-Day, 1971, p. 1.

10. Jacob Viner, Adam Smith, and laissez-faire, *Adam Smith 1776–1926, Lectures to Commemorate the Sesquicentennial of the Publication of the Wealth of Nations*, 1928, p. 118.

11. Edwin G. West, Developments in the literature on Adam Smith: An Evaluative Survey, *Classical Political Economy: A Survey of Recent Literature*, William O. Thweatt (ed.), Boston, Massachusetts: Kluwer Academic Publishers, 1988.

12. *WN*, p. 456.

13. *WN*, p. 14.

14. *WN*, p. 15.

15. *WN*, p. 22.

16. *WN*, p. 22.

17. J. M. Buchanan, *Ethics and Economic Progress*, Norman, Oklahoma: University of Oklahoma, 1994.

18. B. Ingrao and G. Israel, *The Invisible Hand: Economic Equilibrium in the History of Science*, Cambridge, Massachusetts: MIT Press, 1990.

19. B. Ingrao and G. Israel, *The Invisible Hand: Economic Equilibrium in the History of Science*, p. 360.

20. e.g. see E. G. West, Developments in the literature on Adam Smith: An Evaluative Survey, *Classical Political Economy: A Survey of Recent Literature*; and D. Vickers, Adam Smith and the status of the theory of money, *Essays on Adam Smith*, A. S. Skinner and T. Wilson (eds.), Oxford: Clarendon Press, 1975.

21. *TMS*, p. 20.

22. *WN*, p. 22.

23. *TMS*, p. 61.

24. D. Winch, *Adam Smith's Politics*, New York: Cambridge University Press, 1978, p. 88.

25. *WN*, p. 795.

26. J. Viner, Adam Smith and laissez-faire, p. 118.

27. *WN*, p. 456.

28. *WN*, p. 25.

29. on one side, e.g., see G. B. Richardson, Adam Smith on competition and increasing returns, *Essays on Adam Smith*, A. Skinner and T. Wilson (eds.), Oxford: Clarendon Press, 1975; on the other, e.g., see Samuelson, A modern theorist's vindication of Adam Smith, *American Economic Review*: 2, p. 177, 1963.

30. E. G. West, Developments in the Literature on Adam Smith: An Evaluative Survey, p. 27.

31. D. Winch, *Adam Smith's Politics*, p. 88.

32. *TMS*, pp. 233–234.

33. *WN*, p. 157.

34. e.g. see Peter Navarro, *The Policy Game: How Special Interests and Ideologues are Stealing America*, John Wiley, New York, 1984; D. L. Robyn, *Braking the Special Interests: Trucking Deregulation and the Politics of Policy Reform*, Chicago, Illinois; University of Chicago Press, 1987; B. A. Forster, *The Acid Raid Debate: Science and Special Interests in Policy Formation*, Ames, Iowa: Iowa State University Press, 1993.

35. F. Fukuyama, *The End of History and the Last Man*, New York: Free Press, 1992.

36. D. Winch, *Adam Smith's Politics*, p. 70.

37. D. Winch, *Adam Smith's Politics*, p. 19.

38. E. Cassirer, *The Philosophy of the Enlightenment*, Boston, Massachusetts: Beacon Press, 1951.

39. J. M. Keynes, *The General Theory of Employment, Interest, and Money*, New York: Harcourt Brace, 1936.

40. For an account of this distinction, see P. Deising, *How Does Social Science Work? Reflections on*

Practice, Pittsburgh, Pennsylvania: University of Pittsburgh Press, 1991; and for an example of a hermeneutic interpretation of Keynes's General Theory, see e.g. P. Deising, *How Does Social Science Work? Reflections on Practice*, pp. 112–122.

41. D. N. McCloskey, *The Rhetoric of Economics*, Madison, Wisconsin: University of Wisconsin Press, 1985.

42. J. A. Nelson, Gender, metaphor, and the definition of economics, *Economics and Philosophy*: 107, 1992.

43. A. Vincent, *Modern Political Ideologies*, Cambridge, Massachusetts: Blackwell Publishers, 1992.

44. M. J. Shapiro, *Reading 'Adam Smith': Desire, History and Value*, Newbury Park: Sage Publications, 1993, p. 103.

45. *WN*, p. 715.

46. J. M. Buchanan and G. Tullock, *The Calculus of Consent*, Ann Arbor, Michigan: The University of Michigan Press, 1962, p. 250.

47. A. S. Skinner, *A System of Social Science: Papers Relating to Adam Smith*, Oxford: Clarendon Press, 1979, p. 234.

48. D. Winch, *Adam Smith's Politics*, pp. 165–166.

49. V. Ostrom, *Intellectual Crisis in American Public Administration*, University, Alabama: University of Alabama Press, 1973, p. 132.

50. V. Ostrom, *Intellectual Crisis in American Public Administration*, p. 132.

51. see e.g. D. C. Mueller, *Public Choice II*, New York: Cambridge University Press, 1989, p. 320.

52. E. G. West, Developments in the literature on Adam Smith: an evaluative survey, p. 24.

53. see D. J. Farmer, *The Language of Public Administration: Bureaucracy, Modernity, and Postmodernity*, University, Alabama: University of Alabama Press, 1995.

54. W. A. Niskanen, *Bureaucracy and Representative Government*, Chicago, Illinois: Aldine-Atherton, 1971.

55. J.-L. Migue and G. Belanger, Toward a general theory of managerial discretion, *Public Choice*: 17, pp. 17–27, 1974.

56. see e.g. D. C. Mueller, *Public Choice II*, pp 43–176.

57. K. J. Arrow, *Social Choice and Individual Values*, New York: John Wiley and Sons, 1963.

58. see Plato, *Republic*, Book 6.

59. D. Waldo, *The Administrative State: A Study of the Political Theory of American Public Administration* (2nd ed.), Holmes and Meier, 1984, p. lii.

60. M. E. Dimock and G. O. Dimock, *Public Administration*, New York: Rinehart and Company, 1953, p. 81; Dwight Waldo, *The Administrative State: A Study of the Political Theory of American Public Administration*.

61. A. Gore, *Creating a Government that Works Better and Costs Less: Report of the National Performance Review*, New York: Random House, 1993.

62. V. Ostrom, *Intellectual Crisis in American Public Administration*, p. 20.

63. J. Baechler, *The Origins of Capitalism*, p. 113.

64. J. Baechler, *The Origins of Capitalism*, p. 113.

65. J. Baechler, *The Origins of Capitalism*, p. 113.

66. D. Waldo, *The Administrative State: A Study of the Political Theory of American Public Administration*, p. lii.

67. D. J. Farmer, Social Construction of Concepts: The Case of Efficiency, *Administrative Theory and Praxis*: 16, pp. 254–262, 1994.

68. see D. J. Farmer, *The Language of Public Administration: Bureaucracy, Modernity, and Postmodernity*.

69. for discussion of this difficult notion, see J. Baudrillard, Simulacra and Simulation, *Jean Baudrillard: Selected Writings*, Mark Poster (ed.), California: Stanford University Press, 1988; and Madan Sarap, *Post-Structuralism and Postmodernism*, Georgia: University of Georgia Press, 1993.

70. see e.g. C. Fox and H. Miller, *Postmodern Public Administration: Toward Discourse*, Thousand Oaks, California: Sage Publications, 1994; and D. J. Farmer, *The Language of Public Administration: Bureaucracy, Modernity, and Postmodernity*.

71. H. A. Raymond, *Management in the Third Wave*, Glenview, Illinois: Scott, Foresman and Company, 1986, p. 73.

72. A. Toffler, *The Third Wave*, William Morrow, New York, 1980.

73. H. A. Raymond, *Management in the Third Wave*, p. 2.

74. P. A. Samuelson and W. D. Nordhaus, *Economics*, 13th ed., New York: McGraw-Hill, 1989, p. 41.

75. P. A. Samuelson and William D. Nordhaus, *Economics*, pp. 43–48.

Part III
Early Loyal Opposition
to the Modernist

HUME

In contriving any system of government, and fixing the several checks and controuls of the constitution, every man ought to be supposed a knave, and to have no other end, in all his actions, than private interest (*Treatise on Human Nature*, 1739).

BURKE

Whilst men are linked together, they easily and speedily communicate the alarm of any evil design. They are enabled to fathom it with common counsel, and to oppose it with unified strength. Whereas, when they lie dispersed, without concern, order, or discipline, communication is uncertain, counsel difficult, and resistence impracticable . . . When bad men combine, the good must associate, else they will fall, one by one, an unpitied sacrifice in a contemptible struggle (*Reflections on the Revolution in France*, 1790).

9

DAVID HUME AND PUBLIC ADMINISTRATION
Empiricism, Scepticism, and Constitutionalism

Michael W. Spicer
Maxine Goodman Levin College of Urban Affairs,
Cleveland State University, Cleveland, Ohio

Despite the fact that David Hume is not widely cited in the public administration literature, his thought has indirectly had important effects on public administration. Hume's
ideas are a creative mix of empiricism, a belief that all knowledge derives from our experience rather than our reason, and scepticism, a questioning of the reliability of our knowledge even when it is derived from experience. What I shall argue here is that while his
empiricism has indirectly, through its influence on modern philosophy, significantly contributed to empiricist ways of thinking within public administration, his scepticism may
have contributed to critiques of these ways of thinking. However, as I shall also suggest
here, Hume's most important legacy for the practice of American public administration
may be neither his empiricism nor his scepticism but rather his political writings on constitutionalism.

I. HUME'S LIFE AND TIMES

In order to better understand Hume's ideas, I begin with a brief review of his life and
times. Hume engaged in a variety of occupations during his life including being a tutor, a
judge advocate, a military aide-de-camp, a librarian, a diplomat in France, and a senior
civil servant. However, Hume, by his own account, "spent almost all" his life "in literary
pursuits and occupations" (1). Born in 1711 to what he termed a "good" but "not rich"
Scottish family, he was "seized very early with a passion for literature" which was to become "the ruling passion" of his life and "the great source" of his "enjoyments" (2). Following a university education at Edinburgh and short career in law, Hume soon "found an
insurmountable aversion to everything but the pursuits of philosophy and general learning" (3). Scholarly writing and in particular philosophical writing was the driving force in
much of Hume's life.

In his mid-twenties, Hume wrote what is now regarded as his major philosophical
work, *A Treatise of Human Nature*, which he subtitled "An Attempt to Introduce the
Method of Experimental Reasoning into Moral Subjects." In this work, Hume admitted to

"an ambition" to contribute to "the instruction of mankind" and to acquire "a name" by his "inventions and discoveries" (4). His philosophical work, however, was not highly regarded at the time by his contemporaries. Despite his attempts to advertise it by means of an anonymous abstract, this first work was ignored. It fell, as Hume termed it, "dead-born from the press" (5). Later it was sharply criticized both by philosophers and the clergy of the time for what was seen as its extreme scepticism regarding human understanding, morals, and religion. Hume attempted to recast and clarify much of his arguments in his two enquiries, *An Enquiry Concerning Human Understanding* and *An Enquiry Concerning the Principles of Morals*. However, his philosophical ideas continued to provoke controversy during his lifetime. Hume's ideas never received the academic respect to which he felt they were entitled. Indeed, he was rebuffed twice in his attempts to seek a university professorship; firstly, by Edinburgh University and then by Glasgow University.

While his academic colleagues were generally less than receptive to his philosophical work, Hume nonetheless earned a considerable world-wide reputation and celebrity as a writer, particularly in France. He also earned some measure of financial success from his many popular essays on political, moral, literary, and economic topics and from his *History of England*. In this regard, Hume was perhaps the first man of letters to write consciously for a popular audience as he benefited from the rising literacy of his age. His desire to write for a popular audience perhaps reflected his belief that philosophy was important to human affairs. He argued that "though a philosopher may live remote from business, the genius of philosophy, if carefully cultivated by several, must gradually diffuse itself throughout the whole society" (6). His works also undoubtedly reflected his own self-confessed "ruling passion," a "love of literary fame" (7).

Hume was very much a product of his times. Firstly, he was a child of the Age of Enlightenment. This was a time of great energy and optimism regarding humanity and its capacity to use reason and science to improve the human condition. Hume was exposed at university to the "new philosophy" of Sir Isaac Newton and John Locke. He clearly saw himself as a Newton of the moral sciences when he asked "But may we not hope, that philosophy, if cultivated with care, and encouraged by the attention of the public, may carry its researches still farther, and discover, at least in some degree, the secret springs and principles, by which the human mind is actuated in its operations?" (8).

Secondly, although Hume wrote sometimes in the style and with the enthusiasm of a philosopher of the Enlightenment, he was at the same time, like Locke and Berkeley, an empiricist. He rejected the belief of continental rationalist philosophers that a priori reasoning could be used to discover truths about the world. According to Hume, "the only solid foundation we can give" to the "science of man" is that of "experience and observation" (9). Hume argued that "we cannot go beyond experience" and that we should reject "as presumptuous and chimerical" any hypothesis "that pretends to discover the ultimate original qualities of human nature" (10). He saw himself as carrying forward the empiricist tradition of "my Lord Bacon" and acknowledged the influences of "Mr. Locke, my Lord Shaftesbury, Dr. Mandeville, Mr. Hutchison, Dr. Butler, who, tho' they differ on many points among themselves, seem all to agree in founding their accurate dispositions of human nature intirely upon experience" (11).

Thirdly, while rejecting Continental rationalism, Hume does seem to have been influenced by the philosophical scepticism of French thinkers, particularly Pierre Bayle. Hume argued that a degree of scepticism was "a necessary preparative to the study of philosophy, by preserving a proper impartiality in our judgements, and weaning our mind from all those prejudices, which we may have imbibed from education or rash opinion" (12). Hume clearly rejected what he termed "excessive scepticism," but he did believe that a "mitigated scepticism" was useful in encouraging "a degree of doubt, and caution, and modesty . . . in all kinds of scrutiny and decision" and in the "limitation of our enquiries to such subjects as are best adapted to the narrow capacity of human understanding" (13).

II. HUME'S EMPIRICISM

Perhaps the most important aspect of Hume's thought for modern philosophy is his empiricism. As noted above, empiricism is a belief that all our knowledge derives from experience or, as our contemporary philosophers might put it, from our sense-data. Hume's empiricism is captured most clearly in his distinction between our impressions, our "lively perceptions, when we hear, or see, or feel, or love, or hate, or desire, or will," and our ideas, "our less lively perceptions, of which we are conscious" when we reflect on our impressions (14). Hume argued that all our meaningful ideas about the world can only arise as a result of our impressions of it. For Hume, all ideas are derived from our impressions. In other words, what we understand or know of the world can only be based on the experience of our senses. As he noted, "we can never think of anything which we have not seen without us, or felt in our own minds" (15).

Since all our ideas must be derived from our impressions, Hume argued we cannot gain any knowledge of our world on the basis of a priori reasoning. For Hume, such reasoning can certainly be used to enquire into the relationship between ideas, but not into that between facts, since facts must be based in experience. The only meaningful propositions that can be derived on the basis of a priori reasoning are those of "Geometry, Algebra, and Arithmetic" (16). A priori reasoning cannot demonstrate any matter of fact since "whatever is may not be" and "no negation of a fact can involve a contradiction" (17). In other words, since nothing that is possible in fact is contrary to logic, logic alone cannot provide us with knowledge of our world.

Hume's insistence here that our knowledge of the world can only be founded in our experience was central to his most important argument regarding cause and effect. Hume argued here that "all reasonings concerning matter of fact" are based on "the relation of Cause and Effect" (18). Thus our judgments about facts inevitably involve cause and effect reasoning. "By means of that relation alone," according to Hume, "we can go beyond the evidence of our memory and senses" (18). Such knowledge of cause and effect relationships can never be based on a priori reasoning. "The mind can always conceive of any effect to follow from any cause, and indeed any event to follow upon another" (19). In other words, logic cannot dictate facts. Rather, our knowledge of cause and effect "arises entirely from experience, when we find that any particular objects are constantly conjoined with each other" (20). Our knowledge of cause and effect arises, in other words, simply as a result of our past experience of one event being followed by another.

Hume also argued that there is no reason, on the basis of logic or experience, to believe that our past experience of particular cause and effect relations between events will necessarily provide any guide to the future. As Hume observed, "it implies no contradiction that the course of nature may change, and than an object, seemingly like those which we have experienced, may be attended with different or contrary effects" (21). Furthermore, "arguments from experience" cannot prove the "resemblance of the past to the future; since all these arguments are founded on the supposition of that resemblance" (22).

Our reasonings concerning cause and effect are based, therefore, on no more than a simple inference that the past will repeat itself. For Hume, "We have no other notion of cause and effect, but that of certain objects, which have been always cojoin'd together, and which in all past instances have been found inseparable" (23).

Hume further argued that since our knowledge of cause and effect can only rest on past conjunctions of events, we cannot establish, either on the basis of logic or experience, the existence of any sort of "power, force, energy, or necessary connexion" between those objects (24). According to Hume, "When we look about us towards external objects, and consider the operation of causes, we are never able, in a single instance, to discover any power or necessary connexion; any quality, which binds the effect to the cause, and renders the one an infallible consequence of the other" (25). "One event follows another; but we never can observe any tie between them" (26).

III. THE IMPACT OF HUME'S EMPIRICISM

By basing our knowledge of cause and effect on what we experience rather than on logic, Hume is advancing an argument for an empiricist view of knowledge and, indeed, this is one reason why interest in Hume among philosophers arose in the earlier part of this century. The influence of his empiricism is especially apparent with respect to modern analytic philosophy. These philosophers, who have included logical positivists and linguistic analysts, rejected Hume's psychological and atomistic approach to knowledge. They preferred instead to examine the meaningfulness of different types of propositions or statements. However, interestingly, their views on what we can and cannot know clearly draw on Hume's empiricism. In their eyes, Hume's argument that ideas can only be derived from impressions becomes equivalent to an argument that all meaningful statements about the world must be reducible to terms which refer to our experience.

Alfred Jules Ayer, for example, made clear that his logical positivist views "derive from the doctrines of Bertrand Russell and Wittgenstein, which are themselves the logical outcome of the empiricism of Berkeley and David Hume" (27). For Ayer, like Hume, the only meaningful propositions consist of the "a priori propositions of logic and pure mathematics" and "propositions concerning empirical matters of fact" (27). According to Ayer, following Hume, such propositions "cannot be confuted [that is, proven wrong] in experience" because "they do not make any assertion about the empirical world" (27). Rather, for a proposition to express "a genuine empirical hypothesis," it is required that "some possible sense-experience be relevant to the determination of its truth or falsehood" (27). Furthermore, Ayer argues, "As Hume conclusively showed, no one event intrinsically points to any other" (28) or, in other words, "no general proposition referring to a matter of fact can ever be shown to be necessarily and universally true" (29).

Hume's ideas have, therefore, clearly influenced and encouraged modern empiricists. This being the case, not surprisingly, Humean ideas have also had an impact on public administration writing. Particularly important here is the work of Herbert Simon because of his role in advancing logical positivism in public administration and in the social sciences in general.

Simon strongly embraced the positivist idea that the only meaningful scientific statements about the world are "statements about the observable world and the way in which it operates" (30). Such statements "may be tested to determine whether they are true or false" (31). For Simon, "To determine whether a proposition is correct, it must be directly compared with experience—with the facts—or it must lead by logical reasoning to other propositions that can be compared with experience" (31). This was why he was critical of the so-called "principles of administration," terming them merely "proverbs." Simon echoes here in many ways Hume's critique of rationalism when he argues that "because . . . studies of administration have been carried out without benefit of control or objective measurements of results, they have had to depend for their recommendations and conclusions upon a priori reasoning proceeding from 'principles of administration' " (32).

Drawing on logical positivism, Simon and others strengthened the belief among many that public administration could and would become a true science by following empiricist principles. This belief has manifested itself in a variety of ways including an emphasis on behavioralist social science in the 1950s and 1960s, and an emphasis on policy analysis, cost-benefit analysis, management science, and systems analysis in the 1960s and 1970s. While this faith in the development of an empirical science of public administration is perhaps somewhat diminished nowadays, it remains an important element in the thinking of mainstream public administration.

As Dwight Waldo has observed, in public administration, "the belief that principles, in the sense of lawful regularities, can be discovered by scientific enquiry remains strong" (33). This is evidenced in the field by repeated calls over the past decade or so for more rigorous empirical and quantitative research in public administration (1). For instance, in a recent study of public administration journal publications, David Houston and Sybil Delevan argue that, "the more rigorous use of the quantitative methods advocated by mainstream social science may well be more useful in public administration than their current use suggests" (34). Although all of this empiricist enthusiasm cannot obviously be laid at the door of David Hume, a reasonable argument can be made that his ideas indirectly helped encourage a rigorous and tough-minded empiricism that is still an important part of modern public administration.

At the same time, there are important differences between Hume's empiricism and that of modern public administration writers. For one thing, the latter writers rarely if ever employ the historical approach which is so central to Hume's political analysis. Hume wrote that "history is not only a valuable part of knowledge, but opens the door to many other parts, and affords materials to most of the sciences" (35). Furthermore, modern writers' faith in empirical reasoning often seems much more pronounced than that of Hume. Would Hume, for example, have really endorsed the ambitious scientific agenda of modern writers, inspired by Simon, who seek "to design and evaluate institutions, mechanisms, and processes that convert collective will and public resources into social profit" (36). Hume, after all, observed "To balance a state or society . . . is a work of so great difficulty, that no human genius, however comprehensive, is able, by the mere dint of reason and reflection, to effect it" (37). Also, despite his claim that politics could be "reduced to a science," (38) Hume believed that "all political questions are infinitely complicated" and that "mixed and varied" and "unforeseen" consequences flow from "every measure" (39). While Hume was an empiricist, he was also keenly aware of the limits of empiricism and was, in this regard, a sceptic. It is to this scepticism that we now turn.

IV. HUME'S SCEPTICISM

Even as he advanced his empiricist ideas, Hume displayed his scepticism. He established, as noted above, there is no basis either in logic or experience for assuming either that past causal relations will be repeated in the future or that there is any type of necessary causal connection between events. According to Hume, the only basis, therefore, for our belief in causation is that of custom or habit. In Hume's view, it is custom alone "which renders our experience useful to us, and makes us expect, for the future, a similar train of events with those which have appeared in the past" (40). As Hume noted, "having found, in many instances, that any two kinds of objects, flame and heat, snow and cold, have always been conjoined together: if flame or snow be presented anew to the senses, the mind is carried by custom to expect heat or cold, and to believe that such a quality does exist, and will discover itself upon a nearer approach" (41). Furthermore, any connection, "which we feel in our minds" between a cause and an effect arises not from any impression of a force connecting events but simply because, "after a repetition of similar instances, the mind is carried by habit, upon the appearance of one event to expect its usual attendant" (42).

For Hume, custom or habit was "the great guide of human life" (40). Hume emphasized our belief that like effects will follow from like causes cannot be defended either on the basis of our reason or experience. Instead, this belief is simply a "sentiment or feeling . . . excited by nature" (43). Such a belief is distinct from "the loose reveries of the fancy" or the imagination alone only in that it is "a more vivid, lively, forcible, firm, steady conception of an object" (44). It is "something felt by the mind, which distinguishes the ideas of the judgement from the fictions of the imagination" (45). It "gives them more weight and influence; makes them appear of greater importance; enforces them in the mind; and renders them the governing principle of our actions" (46).

Hume's sceptical conclusion here is that our common belief in a world of causal relationships is nothing more than a matter of custom or habit rooted in sentiment or feeling. Our belief in facts or causal relationships is "more properly an act of the sensitive, than of the cogitative part of our natures" (47). Hume's scepticism is even more striking in his account of our ideas about the existence of physical objects. He noted that neither our senses nor our reason can justify our belief in such objects when we no longer perceive them. According to Hume, our senses "are incapable of giving rise to the notion of the continu'd existence of their objects, after they no longer appear to the senses" (48). Our reason cannot "give us an assurance of the continu'd and distinct existence of body" (49). He observed that we believe in the reality of such objects only because "we have a propensity to feign the continu'd existence of all sensible objects" which "arises from some lively impression of the memory" and "bestows a vivacity on that fiction" (50).

Furthermore, according to Hume, since our knowledge is limited to our perceptions, we cannot justify our beliefs in the existence of physical matter, the existence of a human soul, or even that of the self on the basis of either our senses, or reasoning. In regard to the self, he noted that "when I enter most intimately into what I call myself, I always stumble on some particular perception or other, of heat or cold, light or shade, love or hatred, pain or pleasure" and "never can catch myself at any time without a perception" (51). For Hume, what we think of as self or mind is "nothing but a bundle or collection of different perceptions" (51) and "the identity, which we ascribe to the mind of man, is only a fictitious one" (52).

Although discussed separately, Hume's scepticism is also apparent in his treatment of passions and morality. Hume argued that our "morals . . . cannot be deriv'd from reason" (53). Neither logic nor facts can determine what is vice or what is virtue. Reason, based as it is in either logic or facts, "is not alone sufficient to produce any moral blame or approbation" (54). For Hume, "Reason is, and ought only to be the slave of the passions" (55). In this regard, therefore, "tis not contrary to reason to prefer the destruction of the

whole world to the scratching of my finger" (56). Morals affect actions because they "ex-
cite passions" (53). "Reason of itself is utterly impotent in this particular" (53). For Hume,
morals "are not so properly objects of the understanding as of taste and sentiment" (57).

Hume, in short, argues we cannot justify on the basis of either logic or experience
everything that we take for granted in our ordinary life including; cause and effect relations, the existence of a physical world and matter, the existence of self, and the rules of
morality. All of these are based on no more than sentiments or feelings. What Hume was
really saying here and what he really proved is a matter of some dispute among modern
writers on Hume (2). Some philosophers do not see any problem in Hume's argument
that there is no necessary connection between cause and effect. They see this argument
simply as an observation that no empirical proposition can ever be logically certain. Others, however, have seen a more profound problem. According to Kant, Hume's refutation
of any a priori basis for causation "interrupted" his "dogmatic slumber" and gave "his research . . . quite a different direction" (58). Indeed, Kant's idealism was an attempt to reconcile Hume's empiricism with rationalist principles in the form of mental categories.

Hume himself certainly understood the destructive implications of his scepticism.
He observed "The intense view of these manifold contradictions and imperfections in human reason has so wrought upon me, and heated my brain, that I am ready to reject all
belief and reasoning, and can look upon no opinion even as more probable or likely than
another" (59). However, he believed that we neither could nor should embrace such extreme scepticism. He argued that in the final analysis, our own nature will not let us embrace it but rather compels us to accept and to believe what we can never prove.
According to Hume, "Nature, by an absolute and uncontrollable necessity has determin'd
us to judge as well as to breathe and feel" (60). Despite his philosophical scepticism and
because of nature, Hume finds himself "absolutely and necessarily determin'd to live and
talk, and act like other people in the common affairs of life" (61). Furthermore, extreme
scepticism is not acceptable for Hume. If men allowed themselves to be ruled by it, "all
discourse, all actions would immediately cease; and men remain in a total lethargy, till the
necessities of nature, unsatisfied, put an end to their miserable existence" (62). Thus
Hume embraced a mitigated, rather than an extreme, scepticism.

V. THE IMPACT OF HUME'S SCEPTICISM

Whatever Hume's own particular brand of scepticism may have meant to him, others have
seen it as radically undermining any type of objective claims to knowledge. Bertrand Russell, for example, saw it as inevitable that Hume's "self-refutation of rationality should be
followed by a great outburst of irrational faith" (63). Russell felt "the growth of unreason
throughout the nineteenth century and what has passed of the twentieth is a natural sequel to Hume's destruction of empiricism" (63). Consistent with this notion, Isaiah Berlin
has argued that Hume's views had an important influence on eighteenth century German
romantic philosophers, most notably Johann Georg Hamann and Friedrich Heinrich Ja-
cobi. These philosophers saw, in Hume's refutation of objective reason an opportunity for
a reaffirmation of religious faith (64).

If this is correct then, Hume perhaps can be seen as clearing a path for later philosophers. These include existentialists and phenomenologists, who, rejecting both rationalism and our immediate sensory experience as the route to knowledge of the world, have
sought other paths. Several writers have discussed the influence of Hume's scepticism on

the phenomenology of Edmund Husserl (3). Husserl saw in Hume's scepticism an affirmation of the radical subjectivity of human experience: an affirmation of the role of the human mind in giving meaning to our experience of the world. For Husserl, Hume demonstrated "the enigma of a world whose being is being through subjective accomplishment" (65). The path to universal knowledge, according to Husserl, therefore, could be found, not by direct empirical observation, but by suspending those beliefs or predispositions we bring to our observations of the world. In this way, we might arrive at a more genuine and intuitive experience of ourselves in relation to our world. We might come to better understand our shared "pre-given world" or "life-world."

The forgoing is significant because it suggests that Hume's ideas may have, at least indirectly, contributed to critiques of empiricist thinking in public administration. In this respect, the writings of contemporary radical critics of mainstream public administration, who draw on phenomenology and associated philosophies to formulate critiques of empiricist science and dominating hierarchical bureaucracies, may be seen as indirectly influenced by the scepticism of Hume. These writers urge us to suspend or put aside our preconceived ideas about bureaucracy and science. In doing so, they hope to show us their true character. Empiricist science, by focusing on preconceived cultural and political categories of experience, is seen as a barrier to authentic or genuine knowledge.

Ralph Hummel, for example, argues that phenomenology, by suspending what is "accidental and unessential" in our experience, can be used to determine what "fundamentally makes up the bureaucratic experience" (66). He accuses conventional empiricist social science of being "bureaucratic and therefore control oriented," of fragmenting organizational reality by fitting it into "preconceived categories," and of refusing "to accept the unity of experience as it is presented by living people themselves" (67). Similarly, Robert Denhart argues that the "phenomenological approach urges a radical openness to experience, a willingness to entertain all phenomena regardless of their scientific or hierarchical justifications" (68). Charles Fox and Hugh Miller, using a phenomenologist approach, likewise urge us, in considering questions of public policy and administration, "to go beyond, behind, and below the reified abstractions of our thought to our shared and indubitable experience of life" (69). They wish to move away "from the idea that there is a reality 'out there' that a value-free researcher can account for by formulating law-like generalizations whose veracity is observable, testable, and cumulative" (70).

Writers of this type emphasize the essential subjectivity of organizational and social experience. They emphasize the role of men and women in giving meaning to that experience. In doing so, they draw unconsciously on Hume's scepticism in regard to the limits of the knowledge which we derive from our immediate empirical observations of the world. However, I doubt whether Hume if alive today would accept that we either can or should, as phenomenologist writers suggest, suspend the presuppositions or preconceptions which we bring to our experience of the world. He would probably be sceptical of the idea that, by suspending these presuppositions, we can arrive at any sort of shared and real intuitive experience of ourselves and the world. Indeed, he would likely ask from what impression could we ever obtain such an idea. Hume would further see our presuppositions or beliefs in the form of our customs and traditions not as habits of perception to be suspended but rather as crucial guides to our actions. As noted already, Hume saw custom as the great guide of human life. "Without the influence of custom," he argued, "we should be entirely ignorant of every matter of fact beyond what is immediately present to the memory and senses" and "there would be an end at once of all action, as well as of the chief part of speculation" (71). The point of Hume's scepticism is not to help us transcend our customs, habits, and traditions, as phenomenologists seem to urge. Rather Hume argues we should simply accept them as inevitably shaping our experience of the world. Hume was, as Norman Kemp Smith has argued, a "naturalist" rather than a radical sceptic (72).

VI. HUME'S CONSTITUTIONALISM

Hume's philosophy has indirectly contributed then to two quite different views of public administration. One is rooted in a strong faith in empirical methods of science. The other is rooted in a radical scepticism regarding reason and observation. However, this analysis so far overlooks what is arguably Hume's most important contribution to public administration, particularly at the federal level, namely his writings on constitutionalism.

By constitutionalism, I mean the use of different institutional mechanisms to check the abuse of discretionary power by government officials. Hume articulated this idea when he suggested that, without constitutional checks and controls on power, "we shall in vain boast of the advantages of any constitution and shall find, in the end, that we have no security for our liberties or possessions" (73). Hume argued that if "separate interest be not checked, and be directed to the public, we ought to look for nothing but faction, disorder, and tyranny from such a government" (74). According to Hume, "if one order of men, by pursuing its interest, can usurp upon every other order, it will certainly do so, and render itself, as far as possible, absolute and uncontroulable" (75). He argued that "a republican and free government would be an obvious absurdity, if the particular checks and controuls, provided by the constitution, had really no influence, and made it not the interest, even of bad men, to act for the public good" (76). "A constitution" for Hume "is only so far good, as it provides a remedy against mal-administration" (77).

Hume's constitutionalism is also evident in his legal philosophy discussed in the *Treatise*. Hume argued strongly for the idea that the administration of laws must be equal and impartial. It should not take account of the merits or defects of parties in particular cases. He noted that the "avidity and partiality of men wou'd quickly bring disorder into the world, if not restrain'd by some general and inflexible principles" and that, as a result, "men have establish'd those principles, and have agreed to restrain themselves by general rules, which are unchangeable by spite and favor, and by particular views of private or public interest" (78). Hume, in his essays, saw the impartial application of general laws as an essential part of the constitutional checking of power, arguing that a government which "receives the appellation of free . . . must act by general and equal laws" (79).

Hume's emphasis here on the necessity of checking political power was consistent with his scepticism and particularly with his argument that reason must serve the passions. Especially important are Hume's observations on the power of self-love as a passion. Hume was critical of philosophers such as Bernard Mandeville who sought to explain all human sentiments and action in terms of self-love, regarding such philosophies "more like a satyr than a true delineation or description of human nature" (80). Nonetheless, Hume saw self-love as a powerful force. He noted "that men are, in a great measure, govern'd by interest, and that even when they extend their concern beyond themselves, 'tis not to any great distance; nor is it usual for them, in common life, to look farther than their nearest friends and acquaintances" (81). Indeed, it is for this reason, according to Hume, that rules of justice and government are required in a social order. As Hume observed, it "may be regarded as certain, that 'tis only from the selfishness and confin'd generosity of men, along with the scanty provision that nature has made for his wants, that justice derives its origin" (82). Hume saw the role of self-interest as particularly important in government where he believed that it is "true in politics" that "in contriving any system of government, and fixing the several checks and controuls of the constitution, every man ought to be supposed a knave, and to have no other end, in all his actions, than private interest" (83).

Hume's constitutionalism was also consistent with his emphasis on custom and tradition as a guide to action. While he went to some pains to demonstrate the logic of his constitutional principles, he saw them more importantly as part of a valued British political tradition. For Hume, "to tamper" with "an established government" or "to try experiments merely upon the credit of supposed argument and philosophy, can never be the part of a wise magistrate, who . . . though he may attempt some improvements for the public good, yet will he adjust his innovations, as much as possible, to the ancient fabric, and preserve entire the chief pillars and supports of the constitution" (84).

VII. THE IMPACT OF HUME'S CONSTITUTIONALISM

Hume's constitutionalism has undoubtedly had a significant impact on the practice of public administration, particularly at the federal level, because of its influence on the Founders. Douglas Adair showed how James Madison drew from a number of Hume's political essays to develop his arguments for an extended federal republic in the Tenth *Federalist* (85). Adair emphasized particularly Hume's essay, "Idea of a Perfect Commonwealth," in which Hume argued that in "a large government, which is modelled with masterly skill, . . . the parts are so distant and remote, that it is very difficult, either by intrigue, prejudice, or passion, to hurry them into any measures against the public interest" (86). Morton White goes even further and argues that Hume "not only influenced the political technology, and political science of the *Federalist* but also seems to have provided the authors with methodological or epistemological views concerning both of these experimental disciplines" (87).

Hume was not the only influence on the Founders, and others such as Locke and Montesquieu also played an important role. Furthermore, as Hume himself would have appreciated, the Constitution drew heavily from the British custom and law which formed the British Constitution and which shaped colonial political institutions. Nonetheless, Hume deserves considerable credit for at least reminding the Founders of some important elements of this custom and tradition. Perhaps he even inspired some of the modifications to the institutions that the Founders made.

Hume's political essays rather than his more abstract philosophical writings were his most significant contribution to modern American public administration. David Rosenbloom, (88) James Q. Wilson, (89) and others have clearly noted the importance of the Constitution to the ongoing practice of American public administration. Given the increasing pervasiveness of constitutional questions in the actions of modern public administration, it would seem clear that Hume's constitutional ideas continue to exert a significant indirect impact on such practice.

At the same time, perhaps paradoxically, public administration scholarship has itself remained remarkably free of the influence of Hume's constitutional ideas. This is because public administration writers, since Woodrow Wilson and Frank Goodnow, tend either to ignore or to be quite critical of American constitutionalism. They see the Constitution, with its many checks on power, as an impediment to effective political and administrative action. Richard Stillman, for example, argues that the Constitution, with its emphasis on checking power, promotes a "stateless" polity that not only "creates problems for building effective public administration institutions in the United States but imposes serious blinders on our capacity to think realistically about contemporary public administration theory" (90).

Admittedly, in recent years, interest has been growing in the relationship between constitutional theory and public administration. Various authors have sought constitutional legitimacy for modern public administration in the expressed views of the Founders. They argue that a strong and energetic administrative state can be justified on the basis of the Founders' writings. The administrative state for John Rohr, the most prominent of these authors, is "a plausible expression of the constitutional order envisioned in the great public argument at the time of the founding of the Republic" (91). At the same time, however, most of these writers do not give much emphasis to Hume's and the Founders' idea that political power must be checked. Rohr, for example, argues that we must "neutralize" this aspect of the Founders' argument if "we are to legitimate the administrative state" (92). In this sense, Rohr and others seek to downplay what Hume, Madison, and others would have regarded as a central aspect of constitutionalism.

VIII. CONCLUSION

While Hume is not cited frequently in the public administration literature, his ideas have had a substantial influence on public administration. They have indirectly, via their impact on modern philosophy, encouraged both support for and criticism of empiricist approaches in public administration. They have done so in ways which Hume would not necessarily approved of. Also, Hume's ideas on constitutionalism, because of their influence on the Founders' writings and design, provide what is arguably his most important legacy for the practice of public administration.

However, many public administration writers have been and continue to be uncomfortable with the idea, expressed by Hume and the Founders, that political power must be constitutionally checked. They have, therefore, ignored, criticized, or downplayed this idea. This is unfortunate since there are good reasons why we should recognize that American constitutionalism is about checking the abuse of power in our political system (93). For example, how can public administration writers argue for the constitutional legitimacy of public administration when they seem at odds with the constitutional notion of checking power? In this respect, public administration writers might profit by giving more attention to Hume's constitutional ideas and their implications for public administration. Hume, a supporter of constitutionalism and American independence and a self-confessed American in his principles, would likely be pleased by such efforts.

REFERENCES

1. D. Hume, The life of David Hume, esq: written by himself, in D. Hume, *Essays, Moral, Political, and Literary*, Liberty Press, Indianapolis, Indiana, 1987, p. xxxi.
2. D. Hume, The life of David Hume, pp. xxxii–xxxiii.
3. D. Hume, The life of David Hume, p. xxxiii.

4. D. Hume, *A Treatise of Human Nature*, (2nd ed.), L. A. Selby-Bigge, (ed.), Oxford University Press, Oxford, 1978, p. 271.
5. Hume, The life of David Hume, p. xxxiv.
6. D. Hume, *Enquiries Concerning Human Understanding and Concerning the Principles of Morals*, (2nd ed.), L. A. Selby-Bigge, (ed.), Oxford University Press, Oxford, 1963, p. 10.
7. D. Hume, The life of David Hume, p. xl.
8. D. Hume, *Enquiries*, p. 14.
9. D. Hume, *A Treatise of Human Nature*, p. xvi.
10. D. Hume, *A Treatise of Human Nature*, p. xvii.
11. D. Hume, An abstract of a treatise of human nature, in D. Hume, *A Treatise of Human Nature*, p. 646.
12. D. Hume, *Enquiries*, p. 150.
13. D. Hume, *Enquiries*, pp. 161–162.
14. D. Hume, *Enquiries*, p. 18.
15. D. Hume, An abstract of a treatise of human nature, p. 647–648.
16. D. Hume, *Enquiries*, p. 25.
17. D. Hume, *Enquiries*, p. 164.
18. D. Hume, *Enquiries*, p. 26.
19. D. Hume, "An abstract of a treatise of human nature," p. 650.
20. D. Hume, *Enquiries*, p. 27.
21. D. Hume, *Enquiries*, p. 35.
22. D. Hume, *Enquiries*, p. 38.
23. D. Hume, *A Treatise of Human Nature*, p. 93.
24. D. Hume, *Enquiries*, p. 62.
25. D. Hume, *Enquiries*, p. 63.
26. D. Hume, *Enquiries*, p. 74.
27. A. J. Ayer, *Language, Truth, and Logic*, Dover Publications, New York, 1952, p. 31.
28. Ayer, *Language, Truth, and Logic*, p. 47.
29. Ayer, *Language, Truth, and Logic*, p. 72.
30. H. A. Simon, *Administrative Behavior*, Second Edition, Free Press, New York, 1957, p. 45.
31. H. A. Simon, *Administrative Behavior*, p. 46.
32. H. A. Simon, *Administrative Behavior*, pp. 43–44.
33. D. Waldo, *The Administrative State*, Holmes and Meier Publishers, New York, 1984, p. liii.
34. D. J. Houston and S. B. Delevan, A comparative assessment of public administration journals, *Admin. and soc.* p. 268, 1994.
35. D. Hume, *Essays, Moral, Political, and Literary*, Liberty Press, Indianapolis, Indiana, 1987, p. 566.
36. R. F. Shangraw, Jr. and M. M. Crow, Public administration as a design science, *Public Admin. rev.*: p. 156, 1989.
37. D. Hume, *Essays, Moral, Political, and Literary*, p. 124.
38. D. Hume, *Essays, Moral, Political, and Literary*, p. 14.
39. D. Hume, *Essays, Moral, Political, and Literary*, p. 507.
40. D. Hume, *Enquiries*, p. 44.
41. D. Hume, *Enquiries*, p. 46.
42. D. Hume, *Enquiries*, p. 75.
43. D. Hume, *Enquiries*, p. 48.
44. D. Hume, *Enquiries*, pp. 48–49.
45. D. Hume, *Enquiries*, p. 49.
46. D. Hume, *Enquiries*, pp. 49–50
47. D. Hume, *A Treatise of Human Nature*, p. 183.
48. D. Hume, *A Treatise of Human Nature*, p. 188.
49. D. Hume, *A Treatise of Human Nature*, p. 193.

50. D. Hume, *A Treatise of Human Nature*, p. 209.
51. D. Hume, *A Treatise of Human Nature*, p. 252.
52. D. Hume, *A Treatise of Human Nature*, p. 259.
53. D. Hume, *A Treatise of Human Nature*, p. 457.
54. D. Hume, *Enquiries*, p. 286.
55. D. Hume, *A Treatise of Human Nature*, p. 415.
56. D. Hume, *A Treatise of Human Nature*, pp. 416.
57. D. Hume, *Enquiries*, p. 165.
58. I. Kant, *The Philosophy of Kant*, C. J. Friedrich, (ed.), Modern Library, New York, 1949, p. 45.
59. D. Hume, *A Treatise of Human Nature*, pp. 268–269.
60. D. Hume, *A Treatise of Human Nature*, p. 183.
61. D. Hume, *A Treatise of Human Nature*, p. 269.
62. Hume, *Enquiries*, p. 160.
63. B. Russell, *A History of Western Philosophy*, Simon and Schuster, New York, 1945, p. 673.
64. I. Berlin, *Against the Current*, Penguin Books, New York, 1982, pp. 162–187.
65. E. Husserl, *The Crisis of European Sciences and Transcendental Phenomenology*, Northwestern University, 1970, Evanston, Illinois, 96–97.
66. R. Hummel, *The Bureaucratic Experience*, St. Martin's Press, New York, 1977, p. 34.
67. Hummel, *The Bureaucratic Experience*, pp. 214–215.
68. R. B. Denhart, *In the Shadow of Organization*, Regents Press of Kansas, Lawrence, Kansas, 1981, p. 108.
69. C. J. Fox and H. T. Miller, *Postmodern Public Administration*, Sage Publications, Thousand Oaks, California, 1995, pp. 79–80.
70. C. J. Fox and H. T. Miller, *Postmodern Public Administration*, p. 79.
71. Hume, *Enquiries*, p. 45.
72. N. Kemp Smith, *The Philosophy of David Hume*, St. Martin's Press, New York, 1966.
73. D. Hume, *Essays, Moral, Political, and Literary*, p. 42.
74. D. Hume, *Essays, Moral, Political, and Literary*, p. 43.
75. D. Hume, *Essays, Moral, Political, and Literary*, p. 44.
76. D. Hume, *Essays, Moral, Political, and Literary*, pp. 15–16.
77. D. Hume, *Essays, Moral, Political, and Literary*, p. 29.
78. D. Hume, *A Treatise of Human Nature*, p. 532.
79. D. Hume, *Essays, Moral, Political, and Literary*, pp. 40–41.
80. D. Hume, *Enquiries*, p. 302.
81. D. Hume, *A Treatise of Human Nature*, p. 534.
82. D. Hume, *A Treatise of Human Nature*, p. 495.
83. D. Hume, *Essays, Moral, Political, and Literary*, pp. 42–43.
84. D. Hume, *Essays, Moral, Political, and Literary*, pp. 512–513.
85. D. Adair, That politics may be reduced to a science, David Hume, James Madison, and the Tenth *Federalist*, *Hume: A re-evaluation* D. W. Livingston and J. T. King, (eds.), Fordham University Press, New York, 1976.
86. D. Hume, *Essays, Moral, Political, and Literary*, p. 528.
87. M. White, *Philosophy, the* Federalist*, and the Constitution*, Oxford University Press, New York, 1987, p. 13.
88. D. Rosenbloom, *Federal Service and the Constitution*, Cornell University Press, Ithaca, New York, 1971.
89. J. Q. Wilson, *Bureaucracy*, Basic Books, New York, 1989.
90. R. J. Stillman II, *Preface to Public Administration*, St. Martin's Press, New York, 1991, p. 40.
91. J. Rohr, *To Run a Constitution*, University of Kansas Press, Lawrence, Kansas, 1986, p. 181.
92. J. Rohr, *To Run a Constitution*, p. 7.
93. M. W. Spicer, *The Founders, the Constitution, and Public Administration*, Georgetown University Press, Washington, D.C., 1995.

94. For authors taking this point of view and also dissenting viewpoints, see the collection of articles edited by Jay White and Guy Adams (94). J. D. White and G.B. Adams (eds.) *Research in Public Administration: Reflections on Theory and Practice*, Sage Publications, Newbury, California, 1995.

95. For good discussions of these issues by a range of authors, see the collections of essays edited by V. C. Chappell (95) and by David Livingston and James King (96). V. C. Chappell (ed.), *Hume: A Collection of Critical Essays*, Anchor Books, New York, 1966.

96. D. W. Livingston and J. T. King (eds.), *Hume: A Re-evaluation*, Fordham University Press, New York, 1976.

97. Those who see a clear link between the thought of Hume and Husserl and discuss the impact of Hume on Husserl's writings and phenomenology include R. A. Mall and Richard Murphy. According to Mall, "Edmund Husserl has given Hume the credit for being the forerunner of phenomenology" (97). Murphy argues that "Hume's historical greatness for Husserl lay in the definitive overthrow of every form of dogmatic objectivism" (98). R. A. Mall, *Experience and Reason*, Martinus Nijhoff, The Hague, 1973, p. 19.

98. R. T. Murphy, *Hume and Husserl*, Martinus Nijhoff, The Hague, 1980, p. 136.

10

EDMUND BURKE
The Role of Public Administration in a Constitutional Order

Akhlaque U. Haque
University of Alabama at Birmingham, Birmingham, Alabama

I. INTRODUCTION

Edmund Burke is probably the most influential political philosopher of the eighteenth century. Burke's work is widely read in political science, philosophy, and history. However, it is unfortunate that the implications of his ideas have been less appreciated in public administration. As a spill-over from political science, certain references to Burke's work can be found in the writings of public administration scholars (1). Also Woodrow Wilson, often regarded as the father of American Public Administration, was a great admirer of Burke who once admitted that:

> There seems to be no man to be found in the annals of Parliament, who seems more thoroughly [to] belong to England than does Edmund Burke. (. . .) His words, now they have cast off their brogue, ring out the authentic voice of the best political thought of the English race (2).

Burke is best known for his work on the French Revolution, *Reflections on the Revolution in France*, written in 1790 in reaction to the new emerging rationalism in politics that threatened the political tradition and the social order of Europe. This work was the first to have highlighted the dangers of revolutionary socialist movements, which, after his death proved what Burke had envisioned. Much of Burke's writings is devoted to politics and philosophy and in specific occasions he had focussed on public administration. It is important to understand Burke's political philosophy before going into the rudiments of his views on public administration. The first part of this chapter is devoted to Burke's life and history. In the second part I have discussed his political philosophy which connects to the later section of his views on public administration. I would try to show how Burke's ideas on human nature, tradition, law, and representation fit his ideas on public administration and how his ideas have influenced the scholars in public administration.

II. THE LIFE OF EDMUND BURKE

The importance of understanding the context and historical time is crucial to interpreting someone's work. This especially applies for Burke, who did not write a formal piece to unfold his own philosophy in a general context. Moreover, since Burke expressed his opinions as they arose, his arguments are often couched in more than one idiom, which makes it incumbent for us to discuss his era and life as it affects his writing (3).

Edmund Burke was born on January 12, 1729 in Dublin, Ireland (4). His father, Richard Burke, a modestly successful Irish attorney, descended from the family of the poet Edmund Spencer. Richard Burke converted from Catholicism to Prostestantism in 1722, seven years before Edmund's birth. His Roman Catholic mother, Mary Nagle, was of an eminent Irish family. Burke's mixed religious background had a significant effect on his intellectual, moral, and social temperament. In his lifetime Burke demonstrated a deep sense of religious tolerance. He was loyal to the Church of England and defended its privileged position, but at the same time, he intensely fought against penal laws imposed upon Roman Catholics, and civil disabilities imposed on Protestant dissenters.

Burke's learning started with his first mentor, a devoted school master, Abraham Shacklelton, and later he went to Trinity College Dublin where he graduated with a Bachelors degree in 1748. By this time Burke was a well-read young man of twenty: he had studied the classics, literature, and history, and logic, ethics, and metaphysics, as well as the rudiments of such sciences as physics, biology, geology, geography, and astronomy (5). He had also mastered Latin, Greek, and the English philosophers. In his writings, Burke used his broad range of readying and frequently mentioned Aristotle, Cicero, and Motesquieu to show that he understood the importance of morals, law, and the constitution as these political philosopher emphasized. He used Rome as a classic example to reveal the nature of governance and he paid particular heed to the order and form of Cicero's speeches. Burke, in the midst of the injustices done to his native Ireland, saw himself as Cicero who had met Verres, the corrupt ruler of Sicily. With the spirit of Cicero he wrote two pamphlets in 1749 in support of a candidate for representation in Dublin. In the pamphlets titled, *Letter to the Citizens of Dublin*, Burke asked the people of Dublin to realize the importance of freedom and to identify the enemies of freedom who he also believed to be the enemies of the British constitution.

At the age of nineteen Burke was engaged in writing *The Sublime and the Beautiful*, which was devoted to unfolding the aesthetic part of human nature. At this young age he derived ideas of the sublime and beautiful from two main principles in the human mind, one regarding passion for self and the other passion for society. The passion of self relates to the vulnerability of humans as individuals, of uncertainty and human as mortal creatures. The passions for society relate to our character who must reproduce and seek love and friendship. The former passions fall in the category of fear (because of vulnerability of the individual) and the latter into that of pleasure derived from being a part of the society. This work was the only piece that Burke had devoted to philosophy and human nature (6).

While in college Burke revealed his deep distrust of speculative reasoning in political and practical affairs, which was to become a lifelong guiding principle. He reacted strongly after reading Burgersdijk's, *Institutionum libri duo*, published in 1628. This famous compendium attacked Aristotle's logic and supported the speculative logic established by Peter Ramus, a French Philosopher. Burke refuted the metaphysical abstractions used by the speculists. Burke's reaction to Peter Ramus' writing is significant in the light of his later opposition to *a priori* reasoning in politics. He believed that "man acts from adequate motives relative to his interests and not on metaphysical speculations" and saw "geometrical accuracy in moral arguments, as the most fallacious of all sophistry" (7).

From 1750 to 1755 Burke divided his days between the study of literature and law. He acquired a profound and very extensive knowledge of European and English jurisprudence, from the ancient Roman Law and the Common Law of England down to his own age. Burke's knowledge of the law is most clearly evident in his innumerable quotations and references to the ancient records, charters, legal treatises, statutes, procedures, and decisions which comprised the common law of England. In 1757 Burke wrote "Essay Towards an History of the Laws of England," as a supplement to his *Abridgement of English History*. According to Peter J. Stanlis (3) Burke's legal erudition, which includes the traditions of Natural Law, the law of nations, English common law, criminal law, and the precedents of prescription in positive law, all infuse and inform his political philosophy, his sense of Europe as a great commonwealth of nations with common moral and legal inheritance, and his faith in the historical processes of tradition.

Burke's editorship with the *Annual Register* deserves special notice because his particular awareness of English legal history, of the Natural Law, and of the Common Law were significantly increased as he worked on book reviews and historical articles. Under his editorship *Annual Register* was a brilliant success, and some of its early issues ran to nine editions. Despite the journal's prestige and recognition in the intellectual circles, Burke preferred keeping his connection with the *Annual Register* anonymous, even after he gave up being active editor in 1765 or 1766. During this time he had correspondence with David Hume, Adam Smith, and Dr. Samuel Johnson.

Burke entered into a new phase in his life when he started his political career in early 1759 as a secretary for William Hamilton, a member of parliament. His belief in practical politics and rejection of *a priori* reasoning in governmental affairs was now being articulated in practice. He attacked Rousseau and Descartes for their speculative theories which sought the perfection of humanity through a rearrangement of social machinery. Even before he entered politics he had allied himself firmly to the ancient Classical and Christian view of humanity and society and declared war on both the scientific rationalism and the Romantic sensibility of the Enlightenment philosophy of "man and society." The arguments he used to criticize the ministers of George III, and the ideas which fill his speeches and writings on government from 1765 to his death in 1797, reveal that he remained consistent in his position throughout his life.

Burke's political career extended from 1765 to 1794 when he was actively involved in the economic reforms and parliamentary reforms in England, as well as the affairs of the American colonies, Ireland, India, and Revolutionary France. Except for a year in 1765–66 and a few months in 1782, when the Rockingham Whigs were in power, most of his twenty nine years in the parliament were spent in the opposition, often in conflict with the administration of George III, and in advocacy of unpopular causes which almost always went down to defeat. His opposition to the tax policy on the American colonies, initiated by the Grenville ministry in 1764 and supported by King George III, met with no success. His attempts to bring relief to the Catholics of Ireland from tyrannical penal laws were largely unsuccessful. His 1780 bill to reform the abuses of the royal patronage was defeated, although a large and influential measure was passed in 1782. He succeeded in impeaching Warren Hastings, Governor General of India, for his abuse of power in India. However, the trial ended in acquittal before the House of Lords, and at best served as a warning to future British governors. His opposition to radical innovation in his Whig party, earned him intense enmity from many of its members. The French crisis further alienated him from the "New Whigs," who followed Charles James Fox. Burke eventually led the anti-revolution old Whigs into a coalition with the Tory party of Pitt the Younger.

It was clear that his philosophy, since it was not dependent on popular support, was unwelcomed by the emerging Enlightenment Age.

While his political causes were frequently unsuccessful, his writings gained him lasting influence. Undoubtedly, Burke achieved the most notable success of his life with the publication of his famous work, *Reflections on the Revolution in France*, published in 1790. This book has been called the famous influential political pamphlet ever written. If we consider only Burke's immediate practical intention—to warn his people, who had cherished a traditional civil society under balanced constitutional order, against rationalism and anti-historical ideology, the *Reflection* was immensely successful.

Burke served almost thirty years as an active member of the parliament. Throughout his career he belonged to the Whig party which gained its maturity in seventeenth century, and ultimately challenged the combined authority of the crown and church. Whig political thinkers developed a theory of government around the limitation of the royal power. Burke embraced the Whig political idealism and argued that "Party divisions, whether on the whole operating for good or evil, are things inseparable from free government" and felt that the party system was important for checking power and preserving the constitution and individual liberty (8). Indeed, the idea of checks and balances were concepts that evolved in the political discourse of Whiggism. As Guttridge noted that the lovers of constitution, such as "English radicals and American colonists appealed to Locke, as political protestants to the bible of whiggism" (9). As far as Burke's philosophy goes, he re-conceptualized Whiggism in a manner consistent with the modern concepts of the constitution. Harvey Mansfield who has dealt extensively with Burke's idea on constitution, said that Burke's "view of the constitution is very similar to that of the constitution called by *The Federalist* "wholly popular"; but, unlike Madison, he never flaunts its novelty" (10).

III.   THE POLITICAL PHILOSOPHY OF BURKE

Burke's presence in the "Age of Reason" is intriguing because he did not follow the philosophical ideas of his time, which were then regarded as the key to defining politics and government in developing a rationalistic order. Since he went against the wave of the Enlightenment, he faced difficult times propagating his ideas. He said, "a certain intemperance of intellect is the disease of the time, and the source of all its other diseases" (11). Burke's greatest philosophical contribution was probably in the role of a mediator connecting the philosophical tradition of the ancient with the modern. He helped to establish the continuity on political thought, as traditional ideas were being discarded as obsolete. Burke in this sense could be appropriately called "the synthesizer," "the compromiser," or the "mediator" of philosophical discourse between the "modern" and the "ancient."

A.   Burkean Limits of Reason

One of the important features of Burke's philosophy was that he consistently rejected reason as it was applied abstractly to understanding politics. He distrusted reason because he believed human nature, tradition, and received values, as part of "natural order" are always a better guide to practical action. He understood that human beings are not purely rational creatures, and that their passions, instincts, and prejudices always play a vital role in their reasonable action. Therefore, for all practical purposes using pure reason to understand social and human behavior would be inappropriate and misleading.

> A man is never in greater danger of being wholly wrong than when he advances far in the road of refinement; nor have I ever that diffidence and suspicion of my reasonings as when they seem to be most curious, exact, and conclusive (12).

He further noted,

> politics ought to be adjusted, not to human reasonings, but to human nature: of which the reason is but a part, and by no means the greatest part (13).

Burke therefore, believed that human reason is inherently limited and the possibility of error and uncertainty should always be in the minds of a prudent observer. Because "the nature of man is intricate; the objects of society are of the greatest possible complexity," (14). For Burke, "nothing universal can be rationally affirmed on any moral or any political subject" (15). Once we accept that we can discover a "truth" we would seek assistance from pure reason. Therefore, Burke rejected all types of abstractions that are formed on the basis of *a priori* reasoning.

Burke also saw the dangers in using pure reason to guide human action. He observed that reason could well be governed by the passions of individuals, which play an important part in directing human action. Burke argued that when we allow our reasoning to guide our actions we would allow our passions to dominate. Pure reasoning to Burke, therefore is an allowance for arbitrary determination of abstract principles, which could be dangerous and misleading. Burke defended his philosophy by saying:

> The science of constructing a commonwealth, or renovating it, or reforming it, is like every other experimental science, not to be taught *a priori* (16).

Because of his skepticism to using pure reason as a guide, Burke relied on experience. He believed that, "A wise man draws all his ideas from experience rather than speculation." (17). Since "we cannot walk sure, but being sensible of our blindness," we must gather knowledge from our experience to reduce uncertainty and be "cautious and diffident" in all our decisions (18). He said, "practice and knowledge of the world will not suffer us to be ignorant that the constitution on paper is one thing, and in fact and experience is another" (19). Experience reveals latent forces operating in human affairs that seem trivial in the first place, but in the larger view, are vital. Burke believed that "(Experience) allows us to reverse our notions; makes us adopt what we rejected and reject what we were fondest of" (20).

Burke's emphasis on knowledge from experience bears some similarity to the teachings of David Hume with whom Burke had some acquaintance. Hume noted that all our reasoning about matters of fact are based upon perception of cause and effect and the knowledge of this perception does not come from *a priori* reasoning but from experience. Hume argued that experience is the foundation for all reasoning, and the foundation of our experience is custom and traditions. Burke's understanding of reason does not emanate from a rationalistic conception of human nature as Hegel understood. As Philip Selznick noted the Hegelian notion of truth "is arrived at by elaborating the logical consequences of a set of assumptions. . . . In the idealist perspective we do not learn from experience. Rather, genuine knowledge flows from the play of intellect; it is deductive in spirit if not in logic" (21). In a Burkean world "the prescriber is not an empiric who proceeds by vulgar experience, but one who grounds his practice on the sure rules of art (22) which cannot possibly fail" (23). Burke uses experience not to renovate but to revise and add to already available knowledge which directly connects to a broader part of his philosophy that emphasizes tradition.

B.   Burkean Traditionalism

As a critic of rationalism, Burke comprehended how institutions and law have evolved through a process of cumulative experience, and how human reason can grow only from within this framework. Burke rejected the premise that institutions were invented independently and antecedently through existing human reason and that civil society was formed by wise legislators. Because Burke believed that "we cannot walk sure, but being sensible of our blindness," we could take advantage from what has already been tested and proved useful. He suspected that "our stock of reason" is "small, and that individuals would be better to avail themselves of the general bank and capital of nations and of ages" (24). Tradition, to Burke, then becomes a prime source of our reasoning.

With his firm belief on tradition and institutions Burke argued, "I feel an insuperable reluctance in giving my hand to destroy any established institution of government, upon a theory, however, plausible it may be" (25). He saw traditions as the "great influencing prejudices of mankind" (26). For Burke, transmission of knowledge from one generation to the next must be unremitted, otherwise we would always have to struggle with a limited portfolio of knowledge which has not proved its worth. Burke's defense of tradition emanates from an extreme distrust of "untried speculative" ideas, a belief in a natural order which binds society. He saw the consequences of an anti-traditionalist view as having some long-term dangers. "The tested" knowledge is already embedded in traditions and institutions and therefore, it would be wise for individuals to consult and respect the usefulness of past knowledge in confronting new situations. According to Burke,

> We are uncorrupt and tolerably enlightened judges of the transactions of past ages; where no passions deceive, and where the whole train of circumstances, from the trifling cause to the tragical event, is set in orderly series before us (27).

The concept of institution is directly linked to Burke's concept of tradition and its preservation. Institution is the product of social adaptation largely unplanned which evolves out of cumulative addition of past practices. To preserve tradition would in other words mean to preserve the integrity of an institution. In this respect, Burke saw a political party as an institution of trust. All his political career was devoted to defending his party ideology and preserve its integrity. He vehemently opposed the New Whiggism being advocated by Charles Fox, who was then influenced by the French enlightenment (28). Importation of French ideals to patch up the British tradition was contrary to Burke's traditionalism and a violation of the principles of Whiggism, which included a "trust" established by tradition.

The knowledge of a constitution presupposes a deep awareness of a tradition. Burke saw constitutions as the supreme traditions which reflect the imperfect knowledge of wise and common men and women alike. He believed that we cannot understand a constitution as a mere scheme upon paper for it has a spirit and a life of its own. He argued it is indeed difficult to design a country's constitution without learning from their tradition. Indeed, this principle of traditionalism was recognized by the Framers of the American Constitution which Burke had supported (29). The Framers of 1787 did not expect to achieve perfection of human nature or of government, but used past traditions to reconcile and balance in order "to form a perfect union." The American constitution was based on a vision that is directly compatible with Burke's idea about constitutions. Russell Kirk argued that the "American Constitution recognized and incorporated a body of historical experience far older than the North American colonies: the constitutional development of England, the country with the highest degree of both freedom and order during the eighteenth century" (30). Furthermore, the Founders, by accepting the Burkean world view "rejected *a priori* theories of government, settling for politics as the art of the possible" (31). Kirk believe that there are clear signs that Burke had influenced the thinking of the Founders, at least they all share the similar views about tradition and human nature.

Carl J. Friedrich noted that Burke had made tradition a very explicit part of his philosophy. He argued "Burke's ideas on prudence as a political virtue, on the nature of society and government, on the importance of manners and religion, are all interrelated with his defense of tradition" (32). Friedrich believed that Burke thought "tradition was a better guide in politics than ratiocination" (33). He argued Burke saw the continuity of a tradition being exemplified in constitutions, "an elaborate fabric fitted to unite private and public liberty." It becomes a "thought of many minds and many ages" which therefore, "becomes the guide superior to all rational theory" (34). In the same breath, Philip Selznick argued, Edmund Burke rejected speculative reasoning because "custom has its reason that logic may not know" (35). In support of Burke's view, Selznick argued that, "the tacit knowledge of custom is often wiser than a scheme based upon explicit theorizing, which may inadequately comprehend the subtle and multiple values at stake" (36).

C.   Role of Law

Recognizing that human beings are inherently guided by passions and interests, Burke believed that checks, in the form of rules, are necessary for the purpose of control. He declared that the "The substance of the question is to put bounds to your own power by the rules and principles of law. This is, I am sensible, a difficult thing to the corrupt, grasping, and ambitious part of human nature" (37). "The source of all evil," Burke said, "is avarice" (38) and noted that "all power will infallibly draw wealth by itself by some means or other. . . . This is true in all parts of administration, as well as in the whole" (39). He called those "the enemy of GOD," who substitute "will" in place of "law" and said that "man is born to be governed by law" (40). All laws bind human kind to a constitution that is the basis of an established government and that "all good constitutions have established certain fixed rules for the exercise of their functions, which they rarely or ever depart from, and which rules form the security against that worst of evils, the government of will and force instead of wisdom and justice" (41).

Burke held that the law of morals should be the foundation for all other laws. Moral law to Burke is an expression of affection or feeling, rather than a binding rule which has been deliberately set for humans to achieve a certain end. Burke observed that moral law will necessarily limit the exercise of arbitrary action which arises from habits, customs, and inherent human prejudices. Therefore, Burke felt an essential need for a moral constitution in the civil society. He argued that, "It is a serious thing to have a connection with a people who live only under positive, arbitrary, and changeable institutions—and those not perfected nor supplied nor explained by any common, acknowledged rule of moral science" (42). According to Francis Canavan, "moral order" for Burke was the "foundation and the framework of politics" but "that moral order itself requires the existence of an intelligible world order" (43). Canavan asserted, "Burke was aware not only of the element of moral necessity in judgements, but also the vast area of contingency and mutability in them" (44).

David Hume requested Burke to comment on Adam Smith's *The Theory of Moral Sentiments*. Burke seemed to have agreed with Smith's idea on morality as understood from Burke's reviews of the book which appeared in *The Annual Register* in 1759. Burke wrote that Adam Smith's *Theory* "is in all its essential parts just, and founded on truth and nature. The author seeks for the foundation of the just, the fit, the proper, the decent, in our most common and most allowed passions" (45).

Although Burke, often regarded as a moral philosopher, emphasized moral law, given his belief in self interest as a general human nature, he argued moral law was not sufficient to limit individuals abuse of power. He understood if individuals are not governed by rules, passions are likely to control their actions. He believed once a law is established by the principles of justice, such law must be enforced and obeyed. Law which comes from necessity out of a continuous adjustment of conventions and habits has a value that can command unanimous approval from the members of the society on the basis of its usefulness. Burke's full belief in law comes from his vision that humans are motivated by passions and interests and when these passions deceive, it is a natural inclination to go by will rather than wisdom and judgment. Government, he argued, has been formed to provide for human wants, of which protection of civil liberty is one and that "society requires not only that the passions of individuals should be subjected, but that even in the mass and body, as well as in the individuals, the inclination of men should frequently be thwarted, their will controlled, and their passions bought into subjection" (46).

On one hand Burke was in favor of curbing individual freedom by giving power to the state for the betterment of the whole society, while on the other hand he was concerned about the states abuse of that power. Therefore, to limit the abuse of power of the state Burke declared one of his "maxims" by arguing "when I know of an establishment which may be subservient to useful purposes, and which at the same time, from its discretionary nature, is liable to a very great perversion from those purposes, *I would limit the quantity of the power that might be abused*" (47). Therefore, Burke argued, "I would have no man derive his means of continuing any function, or his being restrained from it, but from the laws only: they should be his only superior and sovereign lords" (48).

D.   Burkean Representation

Burke's ideas on representation are perhaps the most interesting and instructive in understanding the role of public administration in a constitutional order. Burke's classic speech in 1774 to the electors of Bristol re-asserted his notion on representation where he argued that representatives should always be concerned with broader interests rather than petty individualistic constituents demands. He believed that the "Parliament is not a *congress* of ambassadors from different and hostile interests . . . but Parliament is a *deliberative* assembly of *one* nation, with *one* interest, that of the whole—where not local purposes, not local prejudices, ought to guide, but the general good, resulting from the general reason of the whole" (49). When representatives perceive that they should have only one end to fulfill, and that is the good of the whole, they would be less likely to indulge in behavior that is good for a part but detrimental to the whole. However, Burke was not suggesting here that the wishes of the members of a constituency should be ignored, nor did he argue that constituents' concerns could not be large enough to call for action. Burke believed we must have "unreserved communication with our constituents" and their "wishes ought to have great weight" but he argued at the same time that no representatives "unbiased opinion, mature judgement" should be sacrificed. He believed representation is a "trust from Providence, for the abuse of which he is deeply answerable. Your representative owes you, not his industry only, but his judgement; and he betrays, instead of serving you, if he sacrifices it to your opinion" (50).

By basing his argument of representation on attaining the general good, Burke was able to refer to public administrators as representatives of the people whose primary objective is to look for the general good of the people to secure a balance in government.

> You [representatives] have men equally interested in the prosperity of the whole, who are involved in the general interest and the general sympathy; and, perhaps, these places furnishing a superfluity of public agents and administrators, (whether in strictness they are representatives or not I do not intend to inquire, but they are agents and administrators,) they will stand clearer of local interests, passions, prejudices, and cabals than the others, and therefore preserve the balance of the parts, and with a more general view and a more steady hand than the rest (51).

Burke also saw public administrators as representatives who form a covenant and are responsible for executing and performing a noble task. He believed the public administrators in East India Company were representatives who were "obliged to engage in a specific covenant with their masters [British government] to perform all the duties described in the covenant" (52). The idea of covenantal representation signifies the importance of trust which became crucial in the representation of India, which was an empire ruled by British representatives without any authorized government. Burke believed that the trust conferred on the representatives is "recognized by the body of the people," not because of their expertise or "ability" but because of "fidelity in representation" (53). For Burke it is a moral obligation, over and above any other obligation, that representatives must not abuse their power. He argued "it is a moral and virtuous discretion, and not any abstract theory of right, which keeps governments faithful to their ends" (54). Philip Selznick supported Burke's contention, arguing that "the theory of covenant is a theory of moral ordering; at the same time, it speaks to the nature of consent and the limits of political authority . . ." (55). He noted that "faith based on covenant might be called a constitutional faith" (56). To be in the covenant would mean to be bounded in a moral ordering and therefore, covenant is not merely a contract. On the contrary, it suggests "an indefeasible commitment and a continuing relationship" (57). The concept of representation as a trust and moral obligation is directly linked to Burke's whole idea of virtual representation. Perhaps Burke's greatest contribution to public administration is his idea on virtual representation that lays the foundation of legality for unelected representatives. Burke argued that localities without an elected representative nevertheless "have an equal representation, *because* [they] *have men equally interested in the prosperity of the whole*, who are involved in the general interest and general sympathy . . ." (58). Burke denied the need for representation always to be actual, because there are people who are never represented, not because they do not have a right to vote, but because they can rarely reached by the representatives. This extension of the idea of representation also makes all non-elected public officials "representatives" and a legitimate part of the body politic. Burke argued that any form of representation originates from the people, although they might not be elected, as "the king is the representative of the people; so are the lords, so are the judges. They all are trustees for the people" (59). He describes this as virtual representation "in which there is a communion of interests and a sympathy of feelings and desires between those who act in the name of any description of people and the people in whose name they act, though the trustees are not actually chosen by them" (60). Burke believed that virtual representation is better than actual because it is "free from many inconveniences" of actual representation and that "it corrects the irregularities in literal representation, when the shifting current of human affairs or the acting of public interests in different ways carry it obliquely from its first line of direction. The people may err in their choice; but common interest and common sentiment are rarely mistaken" (61).

A virtual representative looks at unattached interests since he or she is free from electoral obligation and the changing "affairs" and circumstances that limit literal or actual representatives. Furthermore, Burke argued in favor of virtual representation because people might choose the wrong person as their representative, who might abuse power and ignore the popular sentiments. A virtual representative on the contrary fills the gap which actual representative cannot attend. Burke said that a virtual representative is better than an actual representative because the former has more discretion to correct the irregularities of actual representation.

Representation as argued by Burke has been captured by Pitkin. Pitkin observed that Burke's "political representation is the representation of interest, and interest has an objective, impersonal, unattached reality" (62). Burke does not sacrifice his judgment to opinion but to the interests of the people. The idea of representation therefore becomes unattached in the sense that the representative would not always concur with citizens' opinions unless they serve the interest of the whole. Therefore, in Burke's view it becomes legitimate for representatives to exercise discretion when they seek to promote the interests, rather than the opinions of the people. Indeed for Burke as Pitkin observed that, "the whole electoral machinery is only the formal trappings of representation for Burke; its substance or 'virtue' is promotion of interest" (63).

IV. PUBLIC ADMINISTRATION IN BURKEAN THOUGHT

Although the role of administration in the Burkean era was limited, the significance of the executive function and the role of ministers were large enough to have been noticed by Burke. Burke specifically dealt with the issue of public administration in one of his more important works, *The Thoughts and Causes of Present Discontents*, 1770 (64). His notion of public administration can also be found in his other writings and speeches, especially the speech on Warren Hastings.

As far as public administration is concerned, there are two significant theoretical contributions made by Burke. Firstly, as noted earlier, Burke identified public administrators as virtual representatives of the people who have the moral obligation to meet larger interests of the society by being trustees of the people. Secondly, and perhaps more importantly, he linked the role of public administration with the constitution to give a legitimacy to the institution of public administration.

Burke argued, whereas the House of Commons was the "fleeting authority," the administration was the "standing government of the country" (65). He had sufficient reason to believe that the House of Commons would try to control the people, instead of being a control for the people. The House was "supposed originally to be no part of the standing government of this country. It was considered as a control issuing immediately from the people, and speedily to be resolved into the mass from whence it arose" (66). Therefore all power given to the House must be disseminated in the form of meeting constituent's demands. On the other hand, public administrators, according to Burke, were representatives of the people, who, in a sense, are much closer to the people.

> It was hoped that, [the administrators] being of middle nature between subject and government, they would feel with a more tender and nearer interest everything that concerned the people, than the other remoter and more permanent parts of legislature (67).

Here Burke recognized the role of public administrators as vital to governance because of their interaction with the public in day to day affairs. It was understood by Burke that, to make government effective, the public perception must somehow be relayed to the government. Burke found this task to belong to the public administrators, who being of the "middle nature" would capture the "feeling" and "nearer interest" of the people. Indeed he contended that, "The temper of the people amongst whom he presides ought therefore to be the first study of a statesman" (68).

Since Burke's argument of representation is based on trust and not power from the people, he was able to place an important question of legitimacy by arguing that the king who is not elected "is the representative of the people; so are the lords; so are the judges. They are all trustees of the people" (69). Furthermore, he noted that a "popular origin" does not characterize "a popular representative" (70). The idea of a popular representative "belongs equally to all parts of government and in all forms" (71). The title "representative" is dependent on how much the public can rely on representatives as trustees of the people. Clearly, Burke saw that public administrators were playing the role of virtual representatives in the British constitutional order.

The important role played by public administrators as virtual representatives led Burke to argue for a unified public administration. He argued that "the due arrangement of men in the active part of the state, far from being foreign to the purposes of a wise government, ought to be among its very first and dearest objects" (72). He envisioned the importance of an institution of administration to provide unity and discipline. Because of his fear of abuse of discretion he saw the dangers of undisciplined and diverse public administrators who could intervene in other branches of government. Their "great professional interest" as those of public administration, "must be let into a *share of representation*, else possibly they may be incline to destroy those institutions of which they are not permitted to partake" (73). At this early stage of administration, Burke was arguing to build a tradition of administration in Britain based on the constitutional principles. Burke's idea of an institution and preserving its integrity is clearly seen in his insistence on a unified body of public administrators.

A. The Burkean Unified Administration

To reduce the likelihood of the misuse of power, Burke argued that there should be only one unified administration working for one interest and that of the whole. "It is the true interest of the prince," he argued, "to have but one administration; and that one composed of those who recommend themselves to their sovereign through the opinion of their country, and not by their obsequiousness to a favorite. . . . They will be able to serve him effectually; because they will add the weight of the country to the force of the executory power" (74).

Burke points out the merits to having a single body of public servants. The argument for a unified administration rests on the idea of power emanating from a unified body; preserving the institutional integrity and tradition; and protecting the public administrators from being used as instruments to serve private or group purposes.

Burke also argued that a unified administration should not be passive in the political matters of government. He opposed the idea of Lord Bute to make public administration an apolitical institution. Burke thought "administrative neutrality" would naturally make administrators an instrument of power. He said it is the "doctrine" of "unconstitutional statesman" to argue that "all political connections are in their nature factious, and as such ought to be dissipated and destroyed" (75). Burke thought it necessary for public administrators to be "linked" together for mutual support and confidence, so as to effectively serve the body politic. Power is necessary to resist unlawful acts and also to help the executive and legislative branch to coordinate their functions. Referring to the administrators of the public Burke stated:

> Whilst men are linked together, they easily and speedily communicate the alarm of any evil design. They are enabled to fathom it with common counsel, and to oppose it with united strength. Whereas, when they lie dispersed, without concert, order, or discipline, communication is uncertain, counsel difficult, and resistance impracticable. (. . .) When bad men combine, the good must associate; else they will fall, one by one, an unpitied sacrifice in a contemptible struggle (76).

Therefore, Burke saw the importance of administrative coalitions based on definitive group principles. This he thought would subvert the pursuit of personal interest and promote the pursuit of common group interest. Clearly, Burke argued here for a unified administration in the form of an institution. The idea of an institution is not to propagate a definite group ideology or abstract idea but for internal checks based on "connection," so that the integrity of the institution is preserved by continuous group pressure. Burke argued that in any profession, except that of a soldier or a priest connections in politics is essential and "necessary for the full performance of our public duty, [who are] accidentally liable to degenerate into faction" (77). Referring to the Roman system of government Burke said that they had established "political societies" to form groups based on "such interests in the state as they severally affected" (78). Being a part of such homogeneous societies was a private honor that was to be "the foundation of public trust" (79). By way of institutional binding, Burke argued, the Romans wished their public and private virtues would not be "mutually destructive, but harmoniously combined, growing out of one another in a noble and orderly gradation, reciprocally supporting and supported" (80). In this way, public institutions, as argued by Burke, check the destructive passions and interests of individual administrators. As an additional benefit this also provides confidence and mutual support in governance.

B.   Law and Discretion

Burke said there is always a possibility that "without directly violating the letter of any law" we can work against the spirit of the "whole constitution" (81). This could be done with the discretionary power given to those who execute the laws. Burke realized that for effective administration both laws and discretionary power are equally important. He argued that laws are "a negative advantage; an armour merely defensive" (82). He contended that nations are not ruled by laws; laws are symbolic, inert, and instrumental. He believed that the same importance we give to laws must also be given to discretion because they "are next in order, and equal in importance" (83). Nonetheless, he was fearful that the door was always open for abuse of discretionary power. He stressed the importance of public principles as a guide to discretion:

> *The discretionary powers which are necessarily vested in the monarch, whether for the execution of the laws, or for the nomination to magistracy and office, or for conducting the affairs of peace and war, or for ordering the revenue, should all be exercised upon public principles and national grounds, and not on the likings or prejudices, the intrigues or policies, of a court* (84).

This he said would secure a government according to law. But he argued that laws, because of their inertness, cannot achieve the ends of the law. Burke, as Aristotle, argued that laws are necessarily defective, because they are unable to prescribe well for every situation of equity or emergency that falls under their literal meaning. Discretionary powers give all their "use and potency" to the laws. Therefore, discretion is needed to accomplish the end of the laws, that the laws themselves, because of their generality, cannot achieve. Discretion, as a remedy for the imperfections of the laws, is not an opportunity for bettering the result of the laws, but only an attempt to achieve the same result as laws in areas where laws alone cannot succeed. Therefore, Burke argued for broad discretionary powers to public administrators who give "life" to the laws. The appropriate degree of discretion, however, depends on the people themselves who execute the laws. Thus Burke formulated his most important maxims on public administration:

> The laws reach but a very little way. Constitute government how you please, infinitely the greater part of it must depend on the exercise of the powers which are left at large to the prudence and uprightness of ministers of state. Even all the use and potency of the laws depends upon them. Without them, your commonwealth is no better than a scheme upon paper, and not a living, active, effective constitution (85).

To make the constitution effective, Burke acknowledged that government ought to give public administrators broad discretionary powers. If the laws are made, discretion is inevitable for their appropriate execution. Therefore, in a Burkean world, discretion is necessary for public administrators.

Since Burke believed that, all powers, without necessary external checks, are prone to abuse, any discretionary power could be potentially harmful. Burke argued that, through their discretionary powers, ministers can very well "neglect," the laws or "ignore" and "design artfully," and cause the interest of the country to "fall into ruin and decay, without possibility of fixing any single act on which a criminal prosecution can be justly grounded" (86). Burke understood that administrators are essential for governance but potentially dangerous. For effective governance, he argued that discretionary power is essential, but it must be controlled discretion. He observed that,

> All men possessed of an uncontrolled discretionary power leading to the aggrandizement and profit of their own body have always abused it; and I see no particular sanctity in our times, that is at all likely, by a miraculous operation, to overrule the course of nature (87).

Harvey Mansfield captured this idea of law and discretion as used by Burke in his *Thoughts*. He interpreted Burke as saying that "the importance of the laws does not lie usually in the laws themselves, as they are negative and inert, but in their permeation of the realm of prudence with the idea of lawfulness" (88). He argued that prudence is not outside the laws, but only "an extension of the laws in which the laws' distrust of individual discretion is maintained and indeed improved upon, since areas where discretion should be distrusted are not distinguished from areas where it can be trusted, but tend to absorb them" (89). Therefore, Mansfield contends that discretion to Burke has no higher aim than to "enhance legality" (90). By using lawful prudence based on public principles, discretion is legitimized to accomplish the end of the laws. Mansfield notes that Burke seems to care less about the end of the laws than for lawfulness.

It must be pointed out that Burke, by allowing public administrators to use their discretionary power, did not ignore the question of administrative accountability. Burke argued that public administrators should be directly accountable to the public through their elected representatives. He believed that the "people cannot be so senseless as to suffer their executory system [public administration] to be composed of persons on whom they have no dependence" (91). He further argued "nothing, indeed will appear more certain, on any tolerable consideration of this matter, than that *every sort of government ought to have its administration correspondent to its legislature*, if it should be otherwise, things must fall into hideous disorder" (92).

It is necessary at this point to re-conceptualize Burke's thought on public administration. Burke had argued that public administration should be unified in the form of an institution. This institution based on public principles would be able to perform the representative function of government through distinctive competence. To fulfill the ends of the laws, broad discretionary power for public administrators is essential. In fact, for an effective democratic government, broad administrative discretion is inevitable. To exercise the desired level of Burkean discretion, accountability to the public and the law becomes significant. The upshot of Burke's proposal was to develop an administrative ethic or norm that would guide public administrators to become a body of public trust. Guidance to administrators is provided and nurtured through an institutional binding or internal checks and through accountability to the public and the law, which act as external checks. A public institution, according to Burke, must develop a system that allows ethical values to develop and then preserves those values through institutional binding.

V.   BURKEAN VISION AND PUBLIC ADMINISTRATION

Question might be raised as to how Burke's view of public administration connect to his political philosophy as have been presented earlier. In other words, does Burke's specific thoughts about public administration match his worldview? This section is devoted to validating the interpretation of Burkean administration from his general world view as discussed in his political philosophy.

Burke's contribution to public administration thought could be summarized in four points: first, public administration should represent the public through a unified body in the form of an institution; second, public administrators, as representatives of the people, should have broad discretionary powers to meet the ends of the laws; third, public administrators must be directly accountable to the public and the law; and fourth, public administrators must have an ethical basis which depends on national sovereignty and a universal moral order.

Burke's argument for a unified administration is consistent with his general argument concerning the importance of tradition. Through the building of precedents from past administrative actions and through the establishment of institutional ethics, a unified administration, in comparison to some fragmented form, can more easily develop a tradition which is a source of knowledge and reasoning for public administrators operating within the institution. This tradition built in the institution allows public administrators to make use of knowledge gathered in the past from day to day interactions with citizens and to learn from past practices and past mistakes. The building of such a tradition is clearly easier in a unified administration since information about past practices and norms of conduct is more easily available.

Furthermore, Burke's argument for a unified administration organized around national principles, including constitutional norms, can be seen as reflecting his general views on the fallibility of human nature and the need to check power. A unified administration, by providing strong peer pressure, can curb the natural tendency of administrators, as human beings, to violate national principles and even the law in pursuit of self-interest and, in doing so, curb their propensity to break their "covenantal" relationship with the people. A unified administration in this way can act as an internal check on abuse of power.

Burke's argument for broad administrative discretion is supported by his general view on the limits of reason. Laws made by legislators, because of limits on their reason, would necessarily have defects in terms of accomplishing their desired ends. Broad discretionary powers for administrators would help to fill the inevitable deficiencies of the law. The uncertainty and complexity of social phenomenon do not permit the design of perfect laws. Discretion, therefore, is inevitable and desirable in a Burkean world which acknowledges the limits of human reason. Moreover, Burke's argument for broad discretionary power is consistent with his idea on virtual representation. He saw representation, either literal or virtual, as a trust. Burke's argument that representatives ought to have "broad unattached" interests reinforces Burke's notion of administrative discretion. Whereas elected representatives make the law, a virtual representative understands and operationalizes the law. On the other hand, an elected representative is constrained by commitment and broad national interests and therefore, has limitations to reacting to short term changes. The fact that a representative once in office must "consider all widespread interest," is supportive of Burke's idea that virtual representatives must exercise discretion to achieve the ends of the laws.

Burke's argument that administrative discretion must be checked externally through democratic accountability is consistent with his general view that "all power lies with the people" and institutions that lose public support and confidence do not survive. It also stems from his general view that human beings are generally motivated by self-interest and hence prone to abuse their power. Burke recognized that even under the institutional norms provided by a unified administration, individual administrators might be tempted to pursue their own interests and passions at the expense of the people and so needed to be checked through accountability to elected officials and to the law.

Finally, Burke's views on the necessity of an ethical basis for administrative action is in line with his general view that a moral order, based on instinctive principles of sympathy, friendship, and love, is important in binding humans together but cannot alone ensure ethical behavior. Burke believed that such moral law alone would never guarantee that public institutions fulfill their public trust and that ethical administrative behavior must be reinforced by a commitment to national principles and respect for tradition and law.

VI. BURKEAN THOUGHT AND AMERICAN PUBLIC ADMINISTRATION

Burke's influence in public administration has been immense, although more indirectly from his conservative traditon than directly from his vision of public administration. Burke's apparent unpopularity is understood because of the rationalist movement in public administration (93). However, Burkean ideas have made significant impact in some of the important works in public administration.

As noted earlier Woodrow Wilson is the only one who claimed a direct influence by Burke and took his works very seriously as exemplified from his frequent mentioning of Burke in his political writings. In a letter to Caleb Thomas Winchester, Wilson admitted that, "If I should claim any man as my master that man would be Burke" (94). However, Niels Thorsen argued that although Wilson joined the Burkean line in words but soon left it in spirit (95). Wilson probably had difficulty in operationalizing Burke's thought, especially in regard to his views on public administration.

Wilson's theory is a significant digression from Burke's original thought on public administration. Wilson's digression becomes obvious from his classic on public administration, "The Study of Administration" (96). Unlike Burke, Wilson conceives of administration as a science and emphasizes the role of experts in administration. His attitude was to explore how the law made by legislatures, could be administered "with enlightenment, with equity, with speed, and without friction" (97). Despite Wilson's emphasis on tradition and history in political science, he de-emphasized administrative tradition as an important part of public administration. By arguing for a "business-like" administration, Wilson, unlike Burke, rejected tradition as significant guide to governance. He explicitly denounced Anglo-American administrative tradition as a source of studying future American public administration when he noted that, "Perhaps even the English system [of administration] is too much like our own to be used to the most profit in illustration. It is best on the whole to get entirely away from our own atmosphere and be most careful in examining such systems as those of France and Germany" (98).

Perhaps John M. Gaus was the first to use Burke's ideas to directly tie politics with administration (99). Gaus, by accepting the notion of representative government, used by Burke, emphasized the importance of legislative control and clear delegation of authority to public administrators. He argued that,

> the first and most basic control of government is the clear statement of the purpose and functions for which it is to be used, a statement which the heart of a constitution. (. . .) Probably the first student of politics to diagnose this problem for the representative system of government in the seventeenth and eighteenth century was Edmund Burke (100).

Gaus further contended that "Burke has made clear the immense importance of executive leadership as political leadership and for the success of the legislature in performing its function of policy determination" (101). Referring to Burke's work, in a Burkean tone, he argued that "our real problem is partly one of relating knowledge of administrators who have daily acquaintance with the application of laws to the life of the community, and the recommendations of the political executive heads, more responsibly to the legislative process" (102). Clearly, Gaus was inspired by Burke and initiated the discussion of Burkean philosophy in public administration which was not revisited until recently by the scholars known as the Blacksburgh School.

Richard Stillman, while attempting to categorize public administration thought, argued that the approach presented by John Rohr and similar writers are theories of the "modern day Edmund Burkes and Walter Bagehots who write from the point of view of evolutionary political realism, including public administration. Their thinking offers some of the most sophisticated and penetrating perspectives on the practice of public administration in the United States" (103). Stillman contention is based on the similarities he found in Burke and those scholars who treat a "state from a historical, philosophical, and evolutionary perspective" and "articulate a vision that is intricately interconnected" to constitutional and institutional roots (104). Apart from Rohr, Larry Terry's and Richard Cook's work have been directly influenced by Burke.

John Rohr in his classic work emphasizes the role of tradition and constitution in public administration and argues that public administrators are virtual representatives, whose role is legitimate and vital to democratic governance (105). Rohr argues in a Burkean vein that legitimacy is not mere legality but is also derived from tradition and history. Rohr contends that "the case for public administration should run with the grain of the American political culture, not against it" (106). He avoids theoretical abstraction and the argument of "right" to representation as sources for legitimacy. Rohr echoes Burke's beliefs when he argues that constitutions that endure, "arise from a judicious blending of reason and history or, more precisely, from the reasoning about the history of a particular people" (107). Rohr, therefore, relies more on "constitutional tradition" than abstract constitutional values (108). Like Burke, Rohr emphasizes the importance of the knowledge embedded in constitutions and argued that American Constitution "as the conclusion of the great public argument of one hundred and fifty years of colonial experience and the premise of the great public argument of the next two centuries" (109).

Paralleling Burke, Rohr also sees public administrators as virtual representatives of the people who can remove the deficiencies of actual representation. He argues, "the career civil service en masse heals the defect of inadequate representation in the Constitution" (110). With a clear concept of virtual representation, Rohr observes:

> The fact that administrators, like judges, are not elected in no way diminishes their constitutional stature. Popular election is simply one of at least twenty two ways that have been and still are approved for holding office under the Constitution (111).

Furthermore, Rohr agreed that virtual representatives must be internally checked. In a manner similar to Burke, Rohr argues that administrative discretion should be checked by institutional ethics based on constitutional principles. Discretionary power, for Rohr, is exercised by taking an oath in office and joining the covenant to "uphold the constitution" (112). Rohr's emphasis here on internal checks on administrative discretion is distinctly Burkean.

Burke saw the importance of institutions because they give power, confidence, and respect, which are important in order to exercise "Burkean discretion." This idea has also been captured by Larry Terry (113). Terry developed the concept of "Administrative Conservatorship" from Burke's ideas to emphasize the importance of institutions in public administration. To preserve the institutional integrity of public administration, Terry argued that a leadership role is important. In a Burkean tone he argued that, an administrative conservator should, through their distinctive competence, "bind institutional activities and processes to specific courses of action" (114). Burke would find it important and necessary for such a leadership role based on value commitments in certain situations, but also would find it potentially dangerous without necessary external checks.

Burke's concept of "unattached interests" as explored by Brian J. Cook, legitimize the role of public administration in a constitutive perspective (115). Cook argued that the "expertise" gained by public administration through experience and training "allows the bureaucracy to fulfill a critical representative function in modern democratic regimes" (116). He argued that expertise of public administrators allows them to fulfill the representative function of bureaucracy by representing broad, objective interests of the polity and to devising means to defend those interests.

Burke's extreme distrust in using speculative reasoning has indirectly influenced some of the conservative public administration scholars, most notably Aaron Wildavsky and James Q. Wilson. Acknowledging the fallibility of human beings and the limits of human reason, Wildavsky believed that the "human mind is drastically limited in what it can encompass" (117) and argued that "man's ability to calculate is limited, and there are few theories and no priori bases that would enable the participants to predict the consequences of alternative actions" (118). His skepticism led to his reliance on incremental budgeting which Burke would endorse. He embraced Burkean limits of human reason and argued that "life is incredibly complicated and there is little theory that would enable people to predict how programs will turn out if they are at all new" (119). In the same breath, James Wilson expresses "grave doubt that anything worth calling organization theory will ever exist" and further notes, "theories will exist, but they will be so abstract or general as to explain rather little" (120). Wilson also argued, "Experience, professionalism, and ideology are likely to have their greatest influence when laws, rules, and circumstances do not precisely define operators tasks" (121).

VII. CONCLUSION

Despite Burke's limited citation in public administration, in recent years his ideas have certainly laid the foundation for a broader role for public administration in a constitutional order. From Burke's idea about human nature, tradition, law, and representation, it has been argued here that in a Burkean world administrative discretion is essential and inevitable. By using their discretionary power, Burke emphasized that the public administrators as representatives will meet the end of the laws made by elected representatives. In a polity where laws are made by the people through their representatives, it is a duty of trustworthy administration to ensure that the laws made are thoroughly operationalized for public benefit.

Burke also argued that, given human fallibility and self-interest, the potential for abuse of this discretionary power must be checked through forming a unified administration and through the laws of the land. Burke's unified administration would have the ability to check abuse by individual administrators, as well as allow them to resist orders that are unlawful or harmful to the public. Burke argued that we must retain and recruit people of good conduct, so that the environment created by the institution would conserve such values, learned from tradition and experience that are necessary for practical governance.

Burke's insights on politics and administration and the role of administration as virtual representatives of the people continue to dominate the literature in public administration. His visions carries important implications for future public administrators. Broader knowledge and constitutional ethics, rather than technical knowledge alone, should be emphasized, especially in public administration education. Public administrators should try to uphold the constitution by preserving the integrity of their institution. A trust cannot be built without administrative values. The areas that probably need more emphasis are Burke's ideas on unified administration and conceptualizing public administration in an institutional framework that is externally checked by law. For Burke, such an approach would seem praiseworthy. Indeed, to preserve the integrity of public institutions, public administration must develop systems that will allow ethical values to be developed through institutional binding based on constitutional principles.

By the standards of immediate success and external appearances, it seemed that Burke's political career was wasted in serving lost causes. But his exemplary efforts to establish a just, orderly, free society under constitutional principles and moral ideals, were not in vain, for they provide vital insights that continue to demonstrate fruitful application in the art of governance.

NOTES

1. See for example, J. M. Gaus, *Reflection on Public Administration*, University of Alabama Press, Alabama, 1947; J. Rohr, *To Run a Constitution*, Kansas University Press, Lawrence, 1986; L. D. Terry, Leaders in the administrative state: The concept of administrative conservators, *Admin. and Soc.*: 21, 1990; B. J. Cook, The representative function of bureaucracy: Public administration in a constitutive perspective, *Admin. and Soc.*: 23, 1992.
2. W. Wilson, *The Mere Literature and Other Essays*, Houghton Mifflin, Boston, 1896, p. 105.
3. For the biographical material presented here, I am indebted to the following secondary sources: S. K. White, *Edmund Burke: Modernity, Politics and Aesthetics*, Sage Publications Inc., Los Angeles, 1994; C. C. O'Brien, *The Great Melody: A Thematic Biography and a Commented Anthology of Edmund Burke*, University of Chicago Press, Chicago, 1992; Peter J. Stanlis, *Edmund Burke: Selected Writings and Speeches*, Peter Smith, Gloucester, MA, 1968; R. H. Murray, *Edmund Burke: A Biography*, Oxford University Press, London, 1931; J. Morley, *Burke (English Men of Letters)*, Macmillan, London, 1879. For specific citation see text.
4. C. C. O'Brien in *The Great Melody*, 1992, notes that some historians believe that Burke was born in the townland of Ballywater, Shanballmore, at the house of his uncle, James Nagle. Burke might have kept his actual birth place to be secret because Shanballymore was a "Papist" rural Cork and simply not a place for a proper Protestant to be born.
5. For a details of the course followed by Burke at Trinity College, see Somerset, *A Notebook of Edmund Burke*, 1957, p. 15–17; and Francis Canavan, *The Political Reason of Edmund Burke*, 1960, pp. 197–211.
6. S. K. White explores Burke's notion of Sublime and Beautiful and argues that Burke's aesthetic reflections described in the *Sublime and Beautiful* are crucial to a full understanding of his political ideas. See Stephen K. White, *Edmund Burke: Modernity, Politics and Aesthetics*, Sage Publications Inc., Los Angeles, 1994.
7. E. Burke, *The Writings and Speeches of The Right Honourable Edmund* Burke, vol. II, Beaconsfield Edition, Little Brown and Company, Boston, 1901, p. 170. Hereinafter this would be short titled, Burke, *Writings and Speeches*, vol. 2, p. 170, unless otherwise noted.
8. E. Burke, *Writings and Speeches*, vol. 1, p. 271
9. G. H. Guttridge, *English Whiggism and the American Revolution*, University of California Press, Berkeley, Los Angeles, 1963, p. 12.
10. H. C. Mansfield, *Statesmansh and Part Government: A Study of Burke and Bolingbroke*, The University of Chicago Press, Chicago, 1965, p. 163.

11. E. Burke, *Writings and Speeches*, vol. 4, p. 49.
12. E. Burke, *A Notebook of Edmund Burke*, H.V.F. Somerset (ed.), The University Press, Cambridge, London, 1756/1957, p. 90.
13. E. Burke, *Writings and Speeches*, vol. 1, p. 280.
14. E. Burke, *Writings and Speeches*, vol. 3, p. 312.
15. E. Burke, *Writings and Speeches*, vol. 4, p. 80.
16. E. Burke, *Writings and Speeches*, vol. 3, p. 311.
17. E. Burke, *A Notebook of Edmund Burke*, p. 111.
18. E. Burke, *A Notebook of Edmund Burke*, p. 89.
19. E. Burke, *Writings and Speeches*, vol. 7, p. 77.
20. E. Burke, *A Notebook of Edmund Burke*, p. 89.
21. P. Selznick, *The Moral Commonwealth: Social Theory and The Promise of Community*, University of California Press, Berkeley, Los Angeles, 1992, p. 43.
22. E. Burke often used the word art to mean the orders of nature. See, for example, Burke's, A vindication of natural society, *Writings and Speeches*, 1, pp. 9–66.
23. E. Burke, *Writings and Speeches*, vol. 4, p. 9.
24. E. Burke, *Writings and Speeches*, vol. 3, p. 346.
25. E. Burke, *Writings and Speeches*, vol. 2, p. 442.
26. E. Burke, *Writings and Speeches*, vol. 3, p. 449.
27. E. Burke, *Writings and Speeches*, vol. 2, p. 442.
28. See for example, Burke's Speech on An appeal from the new to the old whigs, 1791, Volume 3, pp. 61–215.
29. The Framers had grown up in a decade when the parliamentary addresses of Burke and Chatham had upheld the cause of the colonies against the Crown in Parliament. Burke's famous American Speeches from 1770 to 1775 had been read and discussed by every American of the rising generation who had taken any interest in politics. He had influenced the Framers not only from his speeches but also through *The Annual Register*, for which Burke was an editor. *The Annual Register*, published every year a detailed account of the Revolution, along other details about the Thirteen Colonies. This supplied the only such reporting on either side of the Atlantic. Burke's powerful influence on the Framers of the American Constitution has been elaborately discussed in R. Kirk, *The Conservative Constitution*, Regnery Gateway, Washington, D.C., 1990.
30. R. Kirk, *The Conservative Constitution*, Regnery Gateway, Washington, D.C., 1990, p. 89.
31. R. Kirk *The Conservative Constitution*, p. 90.
32. C. J. Friedrich, *Tradition and Authority*, Praeger, New York, 1972, p. 28.
33. C. J. Friedrich, *Tradition and Authority*, p. 28.
34. C. J. Friedrich, *Tradition and Authority*, p. 28.
35. P. Selznick, *The Moral Commonwealth*, p. 395.
36. P. Selznick, *The Moral Commonwealth*, p. 395.
37. E. Burke, *Writings and Speeches*, vol. 7, p. 62.
38. E. Burke, *Writings and Speeches*, vol. 7, p. 491.
39. E. Burke, *Writings and Speeches*, vol. 2, p. 335.
40. E. Burke, *Writings and Speeches*, vol. 9, p. 458.
41. E. Burke, *Writings and Speeches*, vol. 7, p. 461.
42. E. Burke, *Writings and Speeches*, vol. 5, p. 307.
43. F. P. Canavan, *The Political Reason of Edmund Burke*, Duke University Press, Durham, 1960, p. 19.
44. F. P. Canavan, *The Political Reason of Edmund Burke*, p. 19.
45. E. Burke, *The Correspondence of Edmund Burke*, Thomas W. Copeland (ed.), vol. I, University of Chicago Press, 1958, p. 129.
46. E. Burke, *Writings and Speeches*, vol. 1, p. 492.
47. E. Burke, *Writings and Speeches*, vol. 2, p. 328; emphasis in the original.

48.   E. Burke, *Writings and Speeches*, vol. 7, p. 26–27.
49.   E. Burke, *Writings and Speeches*, vol. 2, p. 96.
50.   E. Burke, *Writings and Speeches*, vol. 2, p. 95.
51.   E. Burke, *Writings and Speeches*, vol. 7, p. 95.
52.   E. Burke, *Writings and Speeches*, vol. 9, p. 395.
53.   E. Burke, *Writings and Speeches*, vol. 1, p. 492.
54.   E. Burke, *Writings and Speeches*, vol. 7, p. 42.
55.   P. Selznick, *The Moral Commonwealth*, p. 477.
56.   P. Selznick, *The Moral Commonwealth*, p. 478.
57.   P. Selznick, *The Moral Commonwealth*, p. 479.
58.   E. Burke, *Writings and Speeches*, vol. 7, p. 99; emphasis added.
59.   E. Burke, *Writings and Speeches*, vol. 1, p. 492.
60.   E. Burke, *Writings and Speeches*, vol. 6, p. 293.
61.   E. Burke, *Writings and Speeches*, vol. 4, p. 293; emphasis added.
62.   H. F. Pitkin, *The Concept of Representation*, University of California Press, Berkeley, 1967, p. 168.
63.   H. F. Pitkin, *The Concept of Representation*, p. 63.
64.   E. Burke, *Writings and Speeches*, vol. 1, pp. 435–537.
65.   E. Burke, *Writings and Speeches*, vol. 1, p. 491.
66.   E. Burke, *Writings and Speeches*, vol. 1, p. 491.
67.   E. Burke, *Writings and Speeches*, vol. 1, p. 491.
68.   E. Burke, *Writings and Speeches*, vol. 1, p. 436.
69.   E. Burke, *Writings and Speeches*, vol. 1, p. 492.
70.   E. Burke, *Writings and Speeches*, vol. 1, p. 492.
71.   E. Burke, *Writings and Speeches*, vol. 1, p. 492.
72.   E. Burke, *Writings and Speeches*, vol. 1, p. 492.
73.   E. Burke, *Writings and Speeches*, vol. 1, p. 519; emphasis added.
74.   E. Burke, *Writings and Speeches*, vol. 1, p. 537.
75.   E. Burke, *Writings and Speeches*, vol. 1, p. 525.
76.   E. Burke, *Writings and Speeches*, vol. 1, p. 525–526.
77.   E. Burke, *Writings and Speeches*, vol. 1, p. 527.
78.   E. Burke, *Writings and Speeches*, vol. 1, p. 528.
79.   E. Burke, *Writings and Speeches*, vol. 1, p. 528.
80.   E. Burke, *Writings and Speeches*, vol. 1, pp. 528–529.
81.   E. Burke, *Writings and Speeches*, vol. 1, p. 469.
82.   E. Burke, *Writings and Speeches*, vol. 1, p. 469.
83.   E. Burke, *Writings and Speeches*, vol. 1, p. 469.
84.   E. Burke, *Writings and Speeches*, vol. 1, p. 470; emphasis in the original.
85.   E. Burke, *Writings and Speeches*, vol. 1, p. 470.
86.   E. Burke, *Writings and Speeches*, vol. 1, p. 470.
87.   E. Burke, *Writings and Speeches*, vol. 1, p. 507.
88.   H. C. Mansfield, *Statesmansh and Part Government: A Study of Burke and Bolingbroke*, The University of Chicago Press, Chicago, 1965, p. 131.
89.   H. C. Mansfield, *Statesmanship and Part Government*, p. 132.
90.   H. C. Mansfield, *Statesmanship and Part Government*, p. 132.
91.   E. Burke, *Writings and Speeches*, vol. 1, p. 471.
92.   E. Burke, *Writings and Speeches*, vol. 1, p. 471; emphasis in the original.
93.   See for example, M. W. Spicer, *The Founders, the Constitution, and Public Administration*, Georgetown University Press, Washington, D.C., 1995. Also see, A. Haque, *Edmund Burke: Limits of Reason in Public Administration Theory*, unpublished dissertation, Cleveland State University, 1994.
94.   *The Papers of Woodrow Wilson*, A. S. Link (ed.), vol. 7, Princeton University Press, New Jersey, 1966, p. 211.

95. N. A. Thorsen, *The Political Thought of Woodrow Wilson*, Princeton University Press, New Jersey, 1988, p. 158.
96. W. Wilson, The study of administration (1887) in *The Classics of Public Administration* (3rd ed.), J. M. Shafritz and A. C. Hyde (ed.), Brooks/Cole Publishing Co., California,
97. W. Wilson, The study of administration (1887), p. 12.
98. W. Wilson, The study of administration (1887), p. 23.
99. J. M. Gaus, *Reflection on Public Administration*, University of Alabama Press, Alabama, 1947.
100. J. M. Gaus, *Reflection on Public Administration*, p. 95.
101. J. M. Gaus, *Reflection on Public Administration*, p. 35
102. J. M. Gaus, *Reflection on Public Administration*, p. 35
103. R. Stillman Jr., *Preface to Public Administration: A Search for Themes and Direction*, St. Martin's Press, New York, 1991, p. 197.
104. R. Stillman Jr., *Preface to Public Administration*, p. 197.
105. J. Rohr, *To Run a Constitution: The Legitimacy of the Administrative State*, The University of Kansas Press, Lawrence, KS, 1986.
106. J. A. Rohr, Toward a more perfect union, *Public Administration Review*: 53, p. 246, 1993.
107. J. A. Rohr, Toward a more perfect union, *Public Administration Review*: 53, p. 247, 1993.
108. J. Rohr, *To Run a Constitution: The Legitimacy of the Administrative State*, p. 172.
109. J. Rohr, *To Run a Constitution: The Legitimacy of the Administrative State*, p. 173.
110. J. Rohr, *To Run a Constitution: The Legitimacy of the Administrative State*, p. 171.
111. J. Rohr, *To Run a Constitution: The Legitimacy of the Administrative State*, p. 185.
112. J. Rohr, *To Run a Constitution: The Legitimacy of the Administrative State*, p. 187.
113. L. D. Terry, Leadership in the administrative state: The concept of administrative conservatorship, *Admin. and Soc.*: 21, 1990.
114. L. D. Terry, Leadership in the administrative state: The concept of administrative conservatorsh, *Admin. and Soc.*: 21, 1990, p. 404.
115. B. J. Cook, The representative function of bureaucracy: Public administration in a constitutive perspective, *Admin. and Soc.*: 23, 1992.
116. B. J. Cook, The representative function of bureaucracy: Public administration in a constitutive perspective, *Admin. and Soc.*: 23, p. 424, (1992).
117. A. Wildavsky, *The Politics of The Budgetary Process*, Little Brown and Company Inc., Boston and Toronto, 1964, p. 10.
118. A. Wildavsky, *The Politics of The Budgetary Process*, 1964, p. 146.
119. A. Wildavsky, *The Politics of The Budgetary Process*, 1964, p. 9.
120. J. Q. Wilson, *Bureaucracy: What Government Agencies Do and Why They Do It*, Basic Books, New York, 1989, p. ix.
121. J. Q. Wilson, *Bureaucracy: What Government Agencies Do and Why They Do It*, 1989, p. 70.

Part IV
American Modernist Influence

WILSON

Unquestionably, the pressing problems of the present moment regard the regulation of our vast systems of commerce and manufacture, the control of giant corporations, the restraint of monopolies, the perfection of fiscal arrangements, the facilitating of economic exchanges, and many other like national concerns . . . It becomes a matter of the utmost importance, therefore . . . to examine critically the government upon which this new weight of responsibility and power seems likely to be cast, in order that its capacity both for the work it now does and for that which it may be called upon to do may be definitely estimated (*Congressional Government*, 1885).

PROGRESSIVISM

The scholars of this generation were republicans and reformers—middle class and middle-of-the-road. For the most part, they did not shed the American sense of freedom, and valued cooperative self-help and 'social ethics,' not socialism . . . And they still believed that policy judgements could be just as scientific as any other judgements (P. T. Manicas, *A History and Philosophy of the Social Sciences*, Oxford: Basil Blackwell, 1987).

BUREAU MOVEMENT

The efficiency movement in cities . . . began . . . in an effort to capture the great forces of city government for harnessing the work of social betterment. It was not a tax saving incentive nor desire for economy that inspired this first effort . . . but the conviction that only through efficient government could progressive social welfare be achieved (H. Breure, Efficiency in City Government, *Annals of the American Academy of Political and Social Science*: 41, 1912).

SIMON

Administrative description suffers from superficiality, over-simplification, lack of realism. It has confined itself too closely to the mechanism of authority and has failed to bring within its orbit the other, equally important modes of influence on organizational behavior. It has been satisfied to speak of 'authority,' 'centralization,' 'span of control,' 'function,' without seeking operational definitions of those terms (H. Simon, *A Study of Decision-Making Processes in Administrative Organizations*, 1947).

11

MAKING DEMOCRACY SAFE FOR THE WORLD
Public Administration in the Political Thought of Woodrow Wilson

Brian J. Cook
Clark University, Worcester, Massachusetts

I. INTRODUCTION

As the 1916 presidential campaign pressed on toward election day, Woodrow Wilson felt compelled to defend the Democratic Party against questions about its "radicalism." Such questions had arisen from business reaction to the progressive social legislation passed during Wilson's first term. To Alabama attorney John B. Knox, an at-large delegate to the 1912 Democratic National Convention, Wilson wrote: "If by radical you mean that a constant attempt is being made on the part of Democratic leaders to keep abreast of the extraordinary changes of time and circumstance, I can only say that I see no other way to keep the law adjusted to fact and to the actual economic and personal relations of our society. But radicalism is a matter of spirit rather than form and I believe that the truest conservatism consists in constant adaptation" (1).

In this brief commentary, Wilson gave expression to key elements in his political and governmental philosophy: that the nation (and the world) was in the midst of extraordinary economic, social, and political change; that public law was the principal expression of, and vehicle for, realizing the objects of what he called "political society"; that the development of law had to be guided by adaptation to new economic, social, and political facts. Despite that, Wilson felt such adaptation must nevertheless rest on deeply-rooted history and tradition. With notable adjustment and development over time, these and related components are clearly evident in Wilson's thinking, across a span of forty years, about most everything from municipal administration to world peace.

Wilson drew upon his upbringing for his views about politics, government, and administration. His formal education, and experience as an academic leader, shaped and synthesized his ideas along with his intellect and his keen powers of observation and analysis. Especially influential were the covenant theology of his Presbyterian family tutelage, and an organic view of societal and political development drawn primarily from his reading of the works of Walter Bagehot and Edmund Burke. The idea that conserving a political regime meant evolutionary change rather than stasis, and required purposeful adaptation, is particularly Burkean.

These influences reached a focal point in Wilson's awakening to the inevitability of modern mass democracy and his concern that it be guided by strong political leadership to preserve order, tradition, and principle, while facing up to the demands of an age of rapid industrial development and technological change. It was in this context that Wilson gave serious and sustained attention to questions of administration.

Wilson's life was as intense, dynamic, and complex as the nation with which he grew. Stretching from the Civil War to the Roaring Twenties, Wilson marked his span of sixty-seven years with both immense personal accomplishments, and physical and emotional pain and loss, all the while witnessing great national progress. Indeed, for at least the decade of 1910–1920, the triumphs and tragedies of man and nation were nearly one and the same.

Befitting a man of intricate intellectual and emotional make-up, whose life covered a great sweep of social, economic, and political change, characterizations of Wilson's ideas, principles, and actions are varied, and assessments of his aims and accomplishments are mixed. Moreover, with the major exception of his predecessors from the American founding (Hamilton, Jefferson, and Madison), and the minor exceptions of Machiavelli and Burke, Wilson stands alone among the individuals featured in this volume as both a man of thought and a man of action. Indeed, his writings on politics and government "were never really academic in character; they were not intended as abstract inquiries. They are more adequately described as preliminary exercises in that leadership of public opinion and constructive statesmanship to which, from the beginning, he passionately devoted his life" (2). Hence he often questioned, in both his scholarship and his political rhetoric, the value of theory unguided by facts gained through practice, experience, and historical growth.

It is therefore necessary that I begin my consideration of a portion of the elaborate spectrum of ideas embodied in Woodrow Wilson's words and actions, and their special meaning for public administration theory and practice, by placing Wilson in an informed historical context. To do so properly requires that I provide an overview of the distinctive impacts of Wilson's thought and deeds over the span of his multifaceted career. With that frame of reference, I can then trace and assess in detail the development of his political thought relevant to his ideas about administration. Finally, I can consider the influence of that thought, and the actions and accomplishments that followed from it, on public administration theory and practice. One can hope that out of this review of Wilson's work, those interested in popular government may find guides to innovation in both study and action lost over the intervening years.

II. WILSON IN HISTORICAL CONTEXT

It is easy to forget how long ago in time and how far back in cultural distance Woodrow Wilson came of age. He lived more than half his life in the 19th century. When he was born in Staunton, Virginia, his home state had not yet attempted to secede from the Union. His earliest recollection, from the age of four at his family's second home in Augusta, Georgia, was hearing that Abraham Lincoln had been elected and war would follow. In the four years that ensued, he watched his father, a Presbyterian minister, serve as a Confederate Army chaplain and coordinator for local relief efforts. The sanctuary of his father's church served as a military hospital, and the churchyard held Union soldiers as prisoners of war (3).

Equally remarkable in retrospect is that Wilson received his undergraduate degree in 1879, when Rutherford B. Hayes was president, from what was then still called the College of New Jersey. Moreover, the existence of graduate schools and the awarding of doctoral degrees in the U.S. had been firmly established, at Johns Hopkins University, for less than a decade when Wilson began his graduate study at that institution in 1883.

When *Congressional Government* appeared in print for the first time in 1885, Grover Cleveland was in his first term, and he was the first president to serve with the Pendleton Act fully in force. Over the decade following the publication of that first book, Wilson worked extremely hard on the development of his academic career. As he reached his fortieth birthday, he was well ensconced as an immensely popular professor and a faculty leader at Princeton, and he had also established a solid reputation as a public speaker. This was an entire century ago, at the same time that William Jennings Bryan delivered his "Cross of Gold" speech to the Democratic Party convention of 1896.

Following on the heels of considerable economic disruption, the 1896 election proved to be a watershed, in which "the really fundamental struggle was over whether industrialism would supersede agriculture in national priority" (4). Industrialism "won a clear victory" (4), and the twentieth century was, for all intents and purposes, underway in the U.S. Therefore, many of the distinctive forces and pressures associated with at least the early twentieth century actually surfaced in the latter decades of the 1800s, when they would have had maximum impact on Wilson's developing political, social, and economic thought. Indeed, the case is clear that Wilson's ambitions kept him well attuned to the forces of social and political commotion and change from his earliest adulthood (5).

A. Sentinel for a New Century

Despite substantial anchors in a seemingly bygone era, then, and because of his peculiar sensitivities and later accomplishments, Woodrow Wilson is thoroughly, if not exclusively, associated with the 20th century, and with modern social, economic, and political reform. Across the major segments of a multistage career, as academic political scientist and "literary" politician and historian, as university administrator and higher education leader, and as national and international statesman, Wilson embodied many of the characteristics, and substantially shaped many of the major ideas and practices, of his era and beyond.

For example, some of the central features of the progressive era—the establishment of well-defined and largely self-regulated professions, the emergence of a middle class with an increasingly professional and technical cast and thus increasingly dependent on their minds rather than their hands for their prosperity, the push for economic and social reform with a strong moralistic flavor—manifested themselves in Wilson's personal growth and development. Wilson was not classically but professionally trained—in law, history, and political science. He also "took an active part in the founding convention of the American Economic Association" (6), was a member of both the American Bar Association and the American Historical Association, and served as sixth president of the American Political Science Association. He built his initial success upon the power of his mind and his pen, and then showed how much it was true that ideas had practical, and lasting, consequences. And, immersed in Presbyterian theology throughout his youth, the spiritual and the moral were always at the center of Wilson's thought. His spirituality changed and grew over time (3), but like many of the progressive reformers, Wilson ultimately linked moral obligation and public service.

More important than how Wilson's life and personality reflected prominent features of politics and society in the early twentieth century, however, is the far-reaching imprint of his ideas and actions on political and social processes and structures. He sought to reform American democracy (and ultimately the world order), not just to meet his ideals but to prepare it for the modern age. This is the central theme of my review, in the next section, of the intellectual work associated with his attention to public administration. But it pervades most of the intentions of Wilson's political practice as well.

Thus, he is perhaps most widely remembered for his idealistic efforts to bring change, and peace, to the international order, so as to make the world safe for democracy. The articulation of his "fourteen points" formed the foundation for the Treaty of Versailles and the charter for the League of Nations. The "points" placed a stamp on international politics that endures in the ideas, structures, and practices supporting both international law, and the formal organization of a body of nation-states committed, if sometimes waywardly, to democratic self-determination, cooperation, and peaceful conflict resolution.

Wilson's foray into the international arena was for the most part an extension of the ideas and actions that he formulated and pursued, and the practical achievements he attained, as a result of his attention to American democracy and its place in the development of human civilization (2). Although a range of scholarly judgment about the extent and value of Wilson's influence exists, much recent scholarship reaches quite sweeping conclusions. Thus, in comparing Wilson's New Freedom with Franklin Roosevelt's New Deal, Charles Kesler has concluded that

> By virtue of his four elections and the peculiar distress caused by the Depression, President Roosevelt's immediate political legacy [was] more striking and long-lasting than Wilson's. But . . . in a sense Wilson's influence was greater and deeper, inasmuch as his theoretical and practical achievements made the New Deal thinkable (7).

Even more expansively, Scot Zentner has recently claimed that "Wilson's political theory underlies much of American political practice and is therefore crucial to understanding the political developments of our time" (8). And weaving Wilson even more deeply into the modern American political and governmental fabric, Stephen Skowronek has counted Wilson among the few "wild card" presidents who have embodied a "politics of preemption"—the rejection of received formulas and ascribed roles—that must be considered seriously as the emergent form of politics in the American regime. Capturing much of the essence of Wilson as both literary and actual politician, Skowronek describes political leaders in such circumstances as having little to rely on except their own "reason, talent, ideas, and character" (9).

B.   A Reformer of the First Order

Much of the support for these assessments rests on the foundation of Wilson's reformation of executive power and the place of the presidency in the American constitutional system. Thus Arthur Link, the scholar with the longest and deepest connection to Wilson, concluded that "historians a century hence will probably rate the expansion and perfection of the powers of the presidency as his most lasting contribution" (10). More recently, Jeffrey Tulis reached a similar conclusion, and again stressed the indissoluble tie between Wilson's thought and practice.

> Woodrow Wilson settled modern practice for all presidents that were to follow him. . . . More importantly, Wilson legitimized these practices by justifying his behavior with an ambitious reinterpretation of the constitutional order (11).

One cannot connect the full panoply of Wilson's ideas and actions and their influences on American society directly to his interest in constitutional reform and political leadership, and to his behavior as president. He was, for example, despite his open skepticism of science, and of a scientific study of politics, involved in the development of the social sciences as a distinct body of academic disciplines, in the professionalization of the separate social science fields, and in the "realist" orientation to the study of politics (5,12).

Although generally regarded to be an educational traditionalist, as faculty member, and then president of Princeton, Wilson nevertheless led the fight for greater rigor and order in the undergraduate curriculum, searched for new methods to encourage active learning, and pushed for the expansion of graduate education. As part of this effort he became a national spokesman for higher education and its improvement (3,13). He was also involved in general education reform as perhaps the most influential participant in the 1893 Conference on History, Civil Government, and Political Economy, part of the work of the "Committee of Ten" considering the lack of proper standards for American secondary schools (14,15).

Nevertheless, most of the changes in politics, government, and society—in structures and processes, practice and thought—associated with Wilson emanate from his lifelong concern for the reform of American government and politics. This was reform he sought so as to improve the chances of strong political leadership emerging and effective governance being realized. These reforms included Wilson's reconstitution of the theory and practice of the presidency and of political leadership under the Constitution more generally, which also concerned the role and use of the media in politics. But they also encompassed municipal government reform, political party and electoral reform, expansion of federal government responsibility and action with advances in social policy and political-economic policy, and changes in the executive organization of government and the operation of administrative systems (12,16,17,18,19).

Through all of this, Wilson's papers and public lectures plainly show, ran the vital thread of concern with democracy's development and success in the face of the challenges and contradictions of modernity. Tracing the origins and unfolding of this concern opens a broad window into Wilson's ideas about administration.

III. MODERNIZING DEMOCRACY

At the very core of Woodrow Wilson's thought and action regarding politics and public affairs was his concern for understanding and explicating the essential nature of constitutional democracy, and, once comprehending it, then adapting it to preserve it, given the realities of modern social and economic conditions. Approaching it from a historical perspective and method, Wilson characterized the development of political institutions in organic, evolutionary terms, with "democracy as the apex of the long process" (3). Recognizing "the modern reality of corporate life and mass politics and at the same keep[ing] those forces in check" became the aim of his political philosophy (20). Essentially, Wilson engaged in a shifting intellectual and practical struggle for most of his adult life to conceive, form, and bring to reality a modern administrative state resting upon a not altogether accommodating foundation of democratic individualism.

A. Origins

The sources of Wilson's strong attraction to the subject of democracy, its development, and its problems are relatively clear. He was of Scotch, Irish, and English heritage, and since boyhood he had been fascinated by British culture and traditions, and British statesmen and political institutions. At least up to the turn of the century, he regarded the British political system as the highest stage of organic development of democratic society. Furthermore, the covenant theology of his Presbyterianism stressed the existence of a "divine scheme of government of the world" (3), and "in its system of presbyteries, synods, and a General Assembly, [the] Presbyterian polity operated under the fundamental assumption that God's will for the church was determined by the church's representatives through discussion, debate, and majority votes, guided by the Holy Spirit" (3).

Together, these influences were the font, obviously, of Wilson's view that the best kind of democratic governance stressed discussion, debate, and oratory. He expressed this in his manuscript "Government by Debate," in the relatively well-known observation that "It is natural that orators should be the leaders of a self-governing people" (14). Moreover, Wilson held to the maxim throughout the rest of his life and career that discussion, debate, and the unity it could achieve were critical to modern democratic rule. To realize such unity required that constitutional barriers to it had to be overcome, either by changes in form, which he first considered, or in practice, which he ultimately expounded and attempted.

In addition, as part of his self-directed study, before he entered graduate school at Johns Hopkins, Wilson had closely read and critiqued Alexis de Tocqueville's *Democracy in America* (14). It was Tocqueville who had most clearly and forcefully made the claim of democracy's inevitable ascendancy, declaring that a "great democratic revolution is taking place in our midst," which is "universal and permanent" (21).

Finally, Wilson's first clear stirrings of political ambition came in his mid-twenties, in connection with national agitation over civil service reform. Expanding, or perhaps more accurately improving, democracy was a central plank in the civil service reform platform. Wilson envisioned himself in the thick of the reform crusade, if not actually leading it. But to do so, he concluded, required further study on his part. Thus he turned to graduate school, and "studies in politics and administration" (3,14).

The reasons for his central concern with the impact of modernity—the social upheavals and new social forms, but especially the economic and technological transformations and the emergence of new economic organizations—are less obvious. As I have already stressed, he grew up witnessing those forces at work in America after the Civil War. But he also studied political economy as both an undergraduate and graduate student, first embracing "the unthinking orthodoxy" of laissez-faire (13) while an undergraduate. He was then shaken from that embrace by Richard Ely at Johns Hopkins. Wilson took a "minor course" in political economy with Ely his first semester at Johns Hopkins (14). By the time he had completed his chapter for a collaboration with Ely and another graduate student on a history of political economy two years later, Wilson showed that he had "assimilated the assumptions of the new economics," which held that "economic theories and policies were the product of local situations and historical development" (14).

B.   Development and Fusion of Concerns

Wilson was never a full-blown populist. Yet he came to believe deeply in the power and importance of public opinion in modern government, and he championed it in his political career. He had to traverse quite a distance in his thinking about the meaning of popular rule to reach that position, however. Thus in his shorthand diary, compiled in the middle of his undergraduate years, he condemned universal suffrage as "the foundation of every evil in this country" (14). He further explored the problems of universal suffrage in an essay written in 1878 (14), and in 1879 he declared that "it is indisputably true that universal suffrage is a constant element of weakness, and exposes us to many dangers which we might otherwise escape" (14).

In the same passage of that same essay—"Cabinet Government in the United States" published in the *International Review*—Wilson also stressed that universal suffrage "does not suffice alone to explain existing evils." The real cause, previewing the argument that would find its fullest expression in *Congressional Government*, was "the absorption of all power by a legislature which is practically irresponsible for its acts" because it operates through a committee system that conceals its business behind closed doors (14). That government in a democracy was best conducted in the full light of public scrutiny was a core principle that Wilson held to as both scholar and statesman.

Underlying his harsh views about popular political participation was a concern about the cultivation of good political leadership and effective institutional management. "His influence in undergraduate organizations . . . was usually intended to reduce popular control in the interest of greater efficiency" (13). In his 1878 essay "Some Thoughts on the Present State of Public Affairs," Wilson argued that "a popular constituency" favored qualities in candidates that could only be acquired at the same time that "young men" should already be in training for legislative leadership. Hence popular influence biased the system against cultivating effective new leaders (14).

By the time of his "Cabinet Government" essay, however, Wilson was already showing signs not of a concern for the importance of restricting popular opinion to encourage the development of political leadership, but for the importance of expanding the proper expression of the popular will through political leadership. The signs grew stronger in his essay "Committee or Cabinet Government?" published in 1884 as a condensed version of the flawed and therefore never-published book manuscript "Government by Debate." In this essay Wilson continued to champion parliamentary government, but his concern was "the way it promote[d] the democratic process" and he attacked from several angles the party caucus system, in legislatures at all levels of government, that "inhibit[ed] the popular will" (13).

In *Congressional Government*, Wilson continued this stress on facilitating a properly-structured expression of the popular will, while dropping any advocacy of particular governmental alternatives and reforms. The object of his scrutiny was the congressional committee system and its deleterious impact on the nation's capacity for self-government. Indeed, Wilson was especially concerned with a properly *informed* public opinion, that then could guide "the people's authorized representatives" (22). What makes *Congressional Government* stand out, however, is the rationale Wilson offers for his inquiry, stated clearly in the "Introductory."

> Unquestionably, the pressing problems of the present moment regard the regulation of our vast systems of commerce and manufacture, the control of giant corporations, the restraint of monopolies, the perfection of fiscal arrangements, the facilitating of economic exchanges, and many other like national concerns. . . . It becomes a matter of the utmost importance, therefore, . . . to examine critically the government upon which this new weight of responsibility and power seems likely to be cast, in order that its capacity both for the work it now does and for that which it may be called upon to do may be definitely estimated (22).

Wilson thus had brought together in a single treatise the two great objects of his intellectual interest, and of his political ambition and civic concern. He sought to reveal the central facts concerning how the federal government, particularly Congress, operated. This would illuminate the weaknesses in the American system of self-government that required attention before American democracy could safely confront the economic and social forces and stresses of the modern age.

Wilson continued the development of his thinking on democracy in his next two major works, essays on "The Modern Democratic State" and "Responsible Government under the Constitution." In the former, written at the end of 1885 and published in revised form in 1889, Wilson still expressed reservations about universal suffrage. "Not mere universal suffrage constitutes democracy. Universal suffrage may confirm a coup d'etat which destroys liberty" (14). Nevertheless, he advanced substantially his organic conception of democracy and the centrality of popular opinion as the most elevated stage of human social and political development.

> Democracy means a form of government wh[ich] secures absolute equality of *status* before the law, and under which the decisive, final control of public affairs rests with the whole body of adult males amongst whom the largest liberty of opinion, of discussion, and of political choice prevails. More briefly, it is gov[ernment] by universal popular discussion. Most briefly, it is gov[ernment] by public opinion (14).

> Such a gov[ernment] really constitutes the people sovereigns. But their sovereignty is of a peculiar sort. . . . It is judicial, nor creative. It passes judgment, or gives sanction; it does not direct. It furnishes standards, not policies. Popular gov[ernment] and 'gov[ernment] by the people'; but gov[ernment] in the sense of control, not gov[ernment] in the sense of the conduct of policy (14).

> [T]he democracy which is now becoming dominant is a *new* democracy . . ., informed with a life and surrounded by controlling conditions altogether modern (14).

> Properly organized democracy is the best gov[ernment] of the few. This is the meaning of representative institutions. . . . Elections transmit the forces of thought and purpose and sentiment from every part of the vast organism to these chief, these capital organs; and the democratic constitution is at its best only when these organs respond with quick sensitiveness to the suggestions of the body (14).

> Democracy is the fullest form of state life: it is the completest possible realization of corporate, cooperate state life for a whole people. . . . The limit to the benefits of political cooperation is . . . to be found by experiment, as everything else has been found in politics (14).

Similarly, in "Responsible Government," written in early 1886, Wilson argued that American political institutions rested on "the same basis, upon no other foundations than those that are laid in the opinions of the people" (14). He found that "the heart of our whole system" rested with "the legal conscience of the people of this country" (14). And he again warned that "grave social and economic problems now putting themselves forward, as the result of the tremendous growth and concentration of our population, and the consequent sharp competition for the means of livelihood," could not be handled by an inept, unresponsive government. The "commercial heats and political distempers" already evident in the "body politic" had to be addressed by reform that provided legislation effectively "sanctioned by the public voice" (14).

With *Congressional Government* and the two major essays that followed it, Wilson had worked out key elements of his political philosophy that he would carry with him in further scholarship, and in his career as an academic and political leader. With Tocqueville, Wilson accepted the inevitable development and diffusion of mass democracy. Wilson also regarded it as the highest form of human social development, particularly because it provided the individual the best conditions for developing his full potential (8). Wilson's views in this regard are remarkably similar to what William Hudson has labeled "developmental democracy" (23).

But democracy's inevitability did not guarantee its triumph. Although Wilson's approach was organic or evolutionary, he did not see democracy's development as driven by immutable natural law. Human choice, and thus politics, was involved. Hence, again with Tocqueville, Wilson concluded that democracy had to be properly understood and explained, and his explanation was that public opinion was a *controlling* not a *deciding* force. Public opinion gave general expression to national purpose, and it placed constraints on those given the responsibility to govern. But public opinion did not decide specifically what to do. That was the domain of governors—legislators, executives, and administrators. Thus, as Wilson argued with increasing frequency, eloquence, and force in the two decades that followed, public opinion as the core of modern democracy had to be properly led, or more accurately, "interpreted" (11).

Wilson launched his further endeavors to understand the relationship between the people, as the ultimate sovereigns, and elected officials, as the immediate rulers, and how that relationship could best be structured to promote effective governance in the face of the already vast and rapidly increasing social and economic demands of the modern age, by following two lines of development. First, he promoted the systematic study of public administration with the intention of stimulating the adaptation and refinement of administrative methods that would improve the basic capacity and competence of American governments. This ultimately became an effort by Wilson to describe and establish normative principles for public administration's institutional status and role in a liberal democratic regime. In other words, he sought to reconcile modern bureaucracy with popular rule.

Second, Wilson worked further on the problems of popular political leadership, that is, the leadership of public opinion, which the design of the American system imposed. This path he ultimately followed to a thorough reinterpretation of American constitutional doctrine, placing the presidency at the center of the political system, and setting the theoretical foundation for his practices as president.

The work on administration was the more intensely scholarly of the two paths, while the work on democracy and leadership developed with Wilson's expanded career in more popular writing and public lecturing. I lend my attention in the remaining discussion of his intellectual development to his work on administration, both because it is the subject of this volume, and because it has not received the extensive dissection and interpretation it deserves, despite now twenty years of relatively easy access to the key Wilson papers. Wilson also started down the administration path first, although he worked in both areas over roughly the same period. The two intersected periodically, culminating with his final scholarly work: his Blumenthal lectures at Columbia University, published as *Constitutional Government in the United States*.

IV. THE STUDY OF ADMINISTRATION

David Steigerwald has argued that Wilson's interest in administration had its roots in his emersion and adherence to a Whig conception of public affairs, especially an emphasis on good government practice to serve the public good (20). But Steigerwald goes on to argue that Wilson's fuller turn to "an academic preoccupation with state administration . . .

proved both unsatisfying and temporary" (20). The problem, Steigerwald contends, is that in *The State,* the book in which Wilson "worked his ideas [on administration] out more fully" (20), Wilson mistakenly replaced the "self-restrained individual" with the state as the source of "balance between self-interest and the common good" (20). Thus Wilson "momentarily" characterized politics "as the give and take of everyday administration" (20). Wilson quickly realized this was not in keeping with his "Whig" tenets. He became dissatisfied with the foray into administrative study, and moved to other, more lucrative pursuits, including "a series of writings in popular history" (20).

Steigerwald is at least partly mistaken in this regard. Certainly, no evidence appears among Wilson's published papers to indicate he was disillusioned with the study of administration and abandoned it because of that. His lectures on the subject at Johns Hopkins did impose a great burden on him in time and separation from his family. He continued to teach on the subject for at least seven years after the publication of *The State,* however. The editors of his papers have made a persuasive case that Wilson's lectures on administration at Johns Hopkins and Princeton show substantial conceptual development over time. They also played an integral part in the continued development of his political ideas (14). Wilson's work on administration was not an unprofitable detour, then. Instead, it was a critical part of the overall development of his political philosophy.

A.   Initial Attention to the Subject

Henry Bragdon argues that Wilson had "begun to concern himself with administration as well as with legislation and matters of high policy" in the *Committee or Cabinet Government?* essay of early 1884. The editors of Wilson's papers locate his first writing directly on the subject to his articles "The 'Courtesy of the Senate' " and "The Art of Governing" of late 1885. Yet *Congressional Government,* which comes in between, was as much about administration as anything else, as Wilson made plain in the original preface.

There, he announced that his chief aim for the book was to make "as plain as possible the actual conditions of federal administration." He identified "two principal types" of administration, "which present themselves for the instruction of the modern student of the practical in politics: administration by semi-independent executive agents who obey the dictation of a legislature to which they are not responsible [i.e., congressional], and administration by executive agents who are accredited leaders and accountable servants of a legislature virtually supreme in all things [i.e., parliamentary]" (22). Wilson was, of course, concerned with patronage, corruption, and thus civil service reform. Yet the chief problem with "the federal administration" that Wilson found was mostly not with administration itself, but with the organization and operation of the legislature. Hence he devoted three of his six chapters to detailed analysis of Congress.

But he did address administration directly in his chapter on the executive, and his concern there, as throughout the book, was with fixing clear responsibility for the actions of administration, and giving the public every opportunity to exercise its "control" and "judgment" as a result. Moreover, at this early stage in his treatment of the subject, his conception of administration was exclusively instrumental, and from that emerged his first statement on the now famous, or infamous, politics-administration dichotomy.

Wilson characterized administration as "something that men must learn, not something to skill in which they are born. Americans take to business of all kinds more naturally than any other nation ever did, and the *executive duties of government constitute just an exalted kind of business. . . .*" (22, emphasis added). Wilson stated this in the context of his discussion of the president as the chief administrative officer, for whom he advocated adequate preparation and training. That would give individuals occupying the presidential office the time to develop their capacity for efficiency. Efficiency in turn, he insisted, "is the only just foundation for confidence in a public officer, under republican institutions no less that under monarchs" (22).

Wilson acknowledged that the president was not the entire executive. Indeed, almost all "executive functions are specifically bestowed upon the heads of the departments" (22). Wilson noted that over the course of the development of the constitutional system, these public officials had been recognized as being "independent rather than merely ministerial" (22), but that this independence was never very clearly defined. This ambiguity in the status of administrative officers violated his principle that responsibility must be clearly fixed. The separation of powers, furthermore, was a major source of that blurring of responsibility, accompanied by the development of the fragmented committee system in Congress.

As he had already argued before, much preferable was the British cabinet system, which cleaved to the principle that "the representatives of the people are the proper ultimate authority in all matters of government, and that *administration is merely the clerical part of government*. Legislation is the originating force. It determines what shall be done . . ." (22, emphasis added).

To correct the consequences of blurred responsibility required, among other things, civil service reform. But the separation of powers also blocked effective reform in the U.S. because of the same confusion it created over who was a political officer in the government and who was not. Recognizing a fundamental distinction between politics and administration thus was an independent prerequisite of reform.

> One of the conditions precedent to any real and lasting reform of the civil service, in a country whose public service is moulded by the conditions of self-government, is the drawing of a sharp line of distinction between those offices which are political and those which are *non*-political. The strictest rules of business discipline, of merit-tenure and earned promotion, must rule every office whose incumbent has naught to do with choosing between policies; but no rules except the choice of parties can or should make and unmake, reward or punish, those officers whose privilege it is to fix upon the political purposes which administration shall be made to serve (22, emphasis in original).

Questions about whether, and to what extent, Wilson contributed to the establishment of the politics-administration dichotomy have engendered considerable debate (4,12,24,25,26,27). It is difficult, however, to interpret Wilson's argument in *Congressional Government* in any other way than that politics and administration are distinct functions or activities, substantively and institutionally. Politics, he argued, involved "choosing between policies" and "fix[ing] upon political purposes," while administration was the work of bringing policies and purposes to realization. The one thing Wilson made clear was that he regarded the distinction as critically important to democratic governance, but that the separation of powers obscured it, resulting in both bad policy and bad administration.

Wilson concluded that politics and administration, although distinct realms and activities, had to be properly and securely linked. Again, the separation of powers and the congressional committee system stood in the way of achieving this linkage in the U.S., because in obscuring the distinction between the two, they weakened legislative responsibility for administration (28). This created the "forcible and unnatural divorcement of legislation and administration" (22). Such was of serious concern, because it undermined public confidence in the executive (22), left the nation "helpless to learn how it was being served" (22), and distracted "legislation from all attention to anything like an intelligent planning and superintendence of policy" (22).

In *Congressional Government*, Wilson argued quite clearly for a distinction between politics, or perhaps more accurately, legislation, and administration. They required separate institutional arrangements, but they were nonetheless linked functionally and instrumentally, with administration subordinate to legislation (28). This did not mean administration was of minor importance. On the contrary, administration could be equated with governing (" . . . legislation is like a foreman set over the forces of government. It issues the orders which others obey. It directs, it admonishes, but it does not do the actual heavy work of governing") (22).

Governing was, nonetheless, a wholly instrumental activity. It was the work of fulfilling the purposes set by politics, especially the politics of constitution making. This put Wilson squarely in the same camp as most of the American founders (29). Yet out of this initial conception, and "the universal principal of institutional change" he explicated in *Congressional Government* (22), Wilson eventually developed descriptive and normative arguments that recognized governing, and thus administration, as not merely instrumental to the polity. Much more, he concluded, law and administration were constitutive of the polity, that is, they gave new shape to the character of the citizenry, and new purpose to the regime.

B.   Toward a Constitutive Conception of Administration

The works that the editors of Wilson's papers identify as his first writings on administration appear at about the same time as "the Modern Democratic State." The editors read in these essays Wilson's first efforts to address the "problem of how democracy could make professional civil servants responsible to public opinion without impairing their efficiency" (14). They see him "working toward a definition of the field [of administration] that would be relevant in a democratic political system" (14).

Like the major theme in *Congressional Government*, Wilson directed his attention in "The 'Courtesy of the Senate' " to the importance of fixing responsibility for administration. Despite the title, Wilson found the problem of patronage and "private consultation" on executive appointments most acute in municipalities. He accepted merit selection and professionalization as a part of the remedy, but equally if not more important was to fix clearly ultimate responsibility. This in turn would fix the attention of administrators on their most important concern—efficiency. Responsibility for administration was best secured, furthermore, by subjecting appointment to the judgment of public opinion. Thus Wilson concluded that the "justice of public examination is to be preferred to the 'courtesy' of private consultation" (14).

Wilson carried these themes of the controlling force of public opinion and the clear fixing of responsibility for administration forward through "The Art of Governing" and into section II of his 1887 essay "The Study of Administration." Indeed one his most well-turned phrases therein is that "large powers and unhampered discretion seem to me the indispensable conditions of responsibility. Public attention must be easily directed, in each case of good or bad administration, to just the man deserving of praise or blame" (30).

But Wilson's field of view was even broader in the 1887 article, because at base he was still pursuing his concern for adjusting democracy to the modern age. "Old as democracy is, its organization on a basis of modern ideas and conditions is still an unaccomplished work. The democratic state has yet to be equipped for carrying those enormous burdens of administration which the needs of this industrial and trading age are so fast accumulating" (30). Hence, adjusting democracy meant improving its capacity for governance—for administration—and this posed challenges of its own. The principal difficulties lay not only in properly fixing responsibility, however, but also in adapting to democracy administrative methods whose origins rest with authoritarian regimes, and then finding the proper relationship between administration and democratic control. Thus, a more systematic study, especially a comparative study, of administration was called for.

The platform on which the proper arrangements for administration and democratic control are established Wilson made plain in *Congressional Government*, and he repeated it in the 1887 essay: the separation of politics and administration (30). As countless public administration scholars since the 1930s have argued, and as Wilson himself recognized, such a conception is descriptively inadequate. Worse, as part of the long train of development in American politics in which political and governmental theory is ever more sharply disconnected from reality and practice (31), the dichotomy is normatively pernicious. An alternative conception of public administration for democratic governance is required, and Wilson expended considerable intellectual energy in the quest, beginning with the 1887 essay.

1. The 1887 Essay Revisited

Stillman (32), Miewald (33), and Van Riper (24), among others, have concluded that Wilson's first attempt to tackle directly the subject of administration was confused, and even contradictory. This is reason enough not to treat the 1887 essay as the primary source of Wilson's ideas about public administration. But the confusion and contradiction are themselves revealing because of Wilson's central concern with the adaptation of democracy to the modern world through the adoption of effective administrative methods. He thought this possible, again, because he saw administration as amenable to systematic study. And it was so because it involved not the "dull level of technical detail," but the "lasting maxims of political wisdom, the permanent truths of political progress" that transcended even "the debatable ground" of constitutional principle (30). In this context, the first hints of further development in Wilson's thinking about what public administration was and what it should be, particularly how it was related to "policy politics" (34), emerged.

The core problem in the development of "democratic" administration for Wilson was distilling administrative methods based on those "lasting maxims" and "permanent truths," placing those methods into the hands of a well-trained administrative cadre, and giving those hands sufficient space to operate without violating the principle of popular rule, or, more accurately, consent of the governed. But the problem was further exacerbated by the challenges of modernity.

In tackling the problem, Wilson ran into the obstacle posed by a purely instrumental distinction between politics and administration. As Kent Kirwin has explained, "After asserting that administration is a separate realm and proclaiming it to be purely instrumental or mechanical in character, [Wilson] admits that 'in any practicable government' (30), it is impossible to establish lines of demarcation between administrative and political functions" (25). Part of the problem, Wilson argued, was that a "great deal of administration goes about *incognito* to most of the world, being confounded now with political "management," and again with constitutional principle" (30). In other words, politics and administration, although essentially distinct, continued to be confused. But the reason for the difficulty in establishing clear lines of separation was also that "in practice administration is deeply embedded in law" (26).

Public administration's essential instrumental quality was still at the center of attention, because to speak of it in practical terms "is to speak of it with reference to some end," and it is law "that *gives* public administration its definition, that *provides its ends*, and establishes the basis for the choice of means" (26, emphasis added). So public administration is the practice of government, the matching of "special means" to "general plans" (30). Public administration is nevertheless permeated by politics, or "the evaluative" (26), because the administrator "should have and does have a will of his own in the choice of means for accomplishing his work. He is not and ought not to be a mere passive instrument" (30). Furthermore, questions of administration do trod on political, or, more precisely, constitutional ground, because administrative questions concern both efficiency and trustworthiness, and these are inextricably linked to questions about "the proper distribution of constitutional authority" and the suitable fixing of responsibility (30).

Although the distinction between politics and administration was difficult to maintain in practice, Wilson regarded the distinction as analytically essential for normative theory and the practice of democratic government that would follow it. The central problem was "to establish structural arrangements affording an unhampered expression and an unhampered implementation of the popular will" (26). Paradoxically, public opinion could interfere with the efficient implementation of the popular will (30,14,26,28).

Eventually, Wilson concluded that a key part of the answer to the paradox was reliance on the government official closest to public opinion—the president—who therefore could direct and interpret that opinion as much as respond to it (35). But the more immediate answer was "an autonomous civil service, the members of which are obedient to their superiors who, at the top, are responsive to the representatives of the people" (26). Hence the separation of politics (the expression of popular will) from administration, and the differentiation between two types of officials fulfilling these distinct functions, was necessary.

> Steady, hearty allegiance to the policy of the government [administrators] serve will constitute good behavior. The *policy* will have no taint of officialism about it. It will not be the creation of permanent officials, but of statesmen whose responsibility to public opinion will be direct and inevitable (30, emphasis in original).

Perhaps the only clear and consistent theme in the 1887 essay is that administration should be the object of intense, systematic study, and that the results of such study had great potential for contributing to improvements in democratic governance. What public administration's relationship to democratic politics is or should be, comes across in the essay as somewhat more tangled and ambiguous. Still, Wilson was reasonably consistent in holding to the idea of a distinction between politics and administration, in which administration is the vehicle for realizing the collective aspirations of the community.

Wilson was still in the first stage of his thinking about the relationship between administration and politics, and the place that administration should occupy in constitutional government. But he was on the verge of taking the next step, because the 1887 essay shows a dawning realization on Wilson's part that administration was somehow implicated in the formation of collective aspirations, and thus in the constitution of the community. Sidney Milkis has stated it quite dramatically. "Wilson's concept of a separation of politics and administration camouflages his commitment to a very important political role for the bureaucracy—the infusing of liberal democracy with the institutional capability for a significant expansion of public action" (19). In other words, a new, self-conscious or "self-aware," (36) public administration was critical to adapting American democracy to the modern world because it would alter how citizens thought of government, particularly what they thought it should do and how they related to it.

I would not go quite as far as Milkis in my interpretation of Wilson's thinking as represented by the 1887 essay. Nonetheless, in his lectures on public administration, politics, and public law of the decade that followed, Wilson did indeed delineate a distinctive institutional domain and constitutive role for public administration in constitutional democracy.

2.   The Lectures on Administration

Wilson presaged the initial direction his lectures on administration would take in a short, unpublished essay of August 1887, in which he compared socialism and democracy. He acknowledged toward the end of the essay that socialism and democracy rested on the same essential principle: "that every man shall have an equal chance with every other man" (14). Moreover, in the "contest . . . between government and dangerous combinations [of wealth and influence]" that defined much of the character of the modern social world, democracy might admit the need "to superintend every man's use of his chance." The essential concern became how the "community . . . can act with practical advantage" in this superintendence. Socialism and democracy differed in their approaches to this concern, and thus on a "question of policy primarily, but also a question of organization, that is to say of administration (14, emphasis in original).

Wilson at this point had defined politics as a matter of what the state was to do and how it was to do it. Much the same conception is evident in his first lecture on administration organized for Johns Hopkins. Wilson observed that "We must know what, in the main, the functions of government are before we can go on with advantage to Administration's narrower questions as to the way in which they are to be performed" (14). But he also contended that, "The State in a large and increasing measure shapes our lives. . . . Business-like the administration of government may and should be—but it is not business. It is organic social life. The way in which it occupies that sphere is our subject, the subject of *Administration*" (14).

Here was a truly expansive conception of administration—it is the organization of social life, not just legal prescription and command. It should thus be studied accordingly. This suggests Wilson's abandonment of the more narrow, functionally instrumental conception of administration from the 1887 essay. If administration concerned organic social life, then it must be fundamentally political, and would have a substantial impact on the character and aspirations of the citizenry.

The editors of Wilson's papers conclude that this "first definition" of administration Wilson "embodied *en passant*" in his text *The State* (14). This is also the conception that Steigerwald concludes Wilson found untenable, and which led him to reject his foray into administration as a subject of study. Certainly, by 1890 Wilson had pulled back somewhat from what he concluded was too broad a formulation (14), but he did not reject the efficacy of the subject. Quite the opposite, he engaged in new and vigorous conceptual development on the topic after discovering the German literature on public law.

In this new conceptual development, Wilson established the essential idea of administration as law-related, but ranging beyond the boundaries of law itself. He defined the field of administrative activity as "the field of the discretionary effectiveness of institutions—the field, not of Law, but of the exercise (realization) of legalized function" (14). He continued to refine the idea of administration as institutionally a distinctive function by making fully clear that the distinction was between legislation and administration (14). But he also characterized administration as "itself a source of Law (Ordinance) i.e. of the *detail* of law" (14).

By 1891, Wilson argued that "legislation . . ., as well as Administration, may be described as the active promotion of the ends of the State" (14). He described the difference between law and administration as the difference "between origination with its wide range of choice, and discretion with its narrow range of choice," and thus that the field of administration encompassed "the field of organization, of effective means for the accomplishment of practical ends" (14). It was at this point that Wilson began to arrive at a more complete recognition that administration encompassed not only instrumental but also constitutive qualities.

Thus, in concluding that administration was part of public law, Wilson continued to argue that "Administration is indirectly a constant source of public law." He contended that it is "through Administration that the State makes [a] test of its own powers and of the public needs—makes [a] test also of law, its efficiency, suitability, etc." (14). Taking this a step further, Wilson argued that administration "is always in contact with the present: it is the State's experiencing organ. It is thus that it becomes a source of law: directly, by the growth [of] administrative practice or tradition" (14). As Wilson had argued in 1890, when the people and their legislative representatives were engaged in making choices about appropriate means, and deliberating about the effectiveness of institutions, this was best ventured "under the guidance of men trained in the observance of political fact and force." Such men were "the heads of administration" (14).

Wilson maintained throughout his lectures that administration was substantively and institutionally distinctive, and subordinate to legislating. Thus he continued to maintain that "we must make the distinction between *offices of policy and control and offices of administration proper*: the distinction between policy and administrative instrumentalities" (14). Yet administration was also an integral component of politics and the law—it was part of what made up (constituted) the law and politics of a liberal democratic regime. Hence Wilson insisted that administration "cannot be divorced from its intimate connexions [sic] with the other branches of Public Law without being distorted and robbed of its true significance. Its foundations are those deep and permanent principles of Politics which have been quarried from history and built into constitutions; and it may by no means properly be considered apart from constitutions" (14).

Another way in which he states this is in his depiction of the stages of state development. In the "law state," a stage of development the U.S. had reached, but which was short of the "constitutional state," people and administration were bound together "under a common system of law. . . . Community and government were integrated under a common power, the power of the Law." But in the constitutional state, achieved by the English constitution, administration is subject to the laws, while "not necessarily organized, energized, and commissioned at every point by the laws" (14). Indeed it is a common theme running through Wilson's lectures that administration transcends in some ways statutory law, that it "cannot wait upon legislation, *but must be given leave,* or take it, to proceed without specific warrant *in giving effect to the characteristic life of the State.* Administration rests upon customary, and so to say essential, law as well as upon legislation" (14, emphasis in original).

Miewald has determined that as Wilson's theorizing continued to develop, the "organic concept drew Wilson further away from the ideal of absolute laws of administration." Wilson moved to a position in which he saw questions of administration as regime-specific, centering on "the integration of the public service within the distinctive life of a single nation" (33). Although he may have abandoned the idea of universal laws of administration that were discoverable through systematic study, he never abandoned the notion that administration extended in part beyond statutory law, and thus had a hand in shaping the law and the public purposes law expressed.

Wilson's most compelling statement on the nature of administration and its place in a liberal democratic regime connected his understanding of its constitutiveness with his long-standing core concern for the relationship between administration and the controlling force of public sentiment.

> *Administration*, therefore, *sees government in contact with the people*. It rests its whole form along the line which is drawn in each State between *Interference* and *Laissez-faire*. It thus touches, directly or indirectly, the whole practical side of social endeavor. Its Questions are questions of *adjustment*, the adjustment of means to ends, not only, but of governmental function *to historical conditions*, to liberty (14).

Concluding the point, Wilson echoed Tocqueville, who had argued that the political effects of administration directly influenced the character of the citizenry (21). "Here lie, of course, the test [questions] as to the success or failure of government. There is *an organization which vitalizes*, and there is *an organization which kills*. If government energizes the people by the measure of assistance which it affords, it is good; if it decreases the energy and healthful independence of individual initiative, it is bad—bad just to the extent it does this" (14).

Here, it seems, is a clear statement by Wilson of a constitutive conception of administration. How the state is organized to operate—the domain of administration being organizational effectiveness, that is, the adjustment of experience and law, or facts and ideals—is vital to determining the character of its citizens, or more generally the civic vitality of the regime. To be sure, administration is still primarily an instrumentality of politics, but by virtue of the central function it performs, it invariably has a formative effect on the polity.

Wilson took one further formal step in clarifying his ideas about the relationships between politics, constitutions, and administration. It surfaced in his Princeton lectures on the "Elements of Politics" and "Constitutional Government," delivered nearly in parallel between early March, 1898 and late November, 1900, and in his last formal notes for the major scholarly work he planned but never started nor completed, the "Philosophy of Politics."

In his "Elements of Politics" notes, he characterized politics as of broader significance than political science, "because it is a study of life and motive as well as form and object" (14). He defined politics, then, as "the study of the life of States; of the genesis and operation of institutions; of the ideas, purposes, and motives of men in political society" (14).

Wilson argued that the objects of political society were many and varied because of the varied histories and political lives of nations. Yet two common objects were order and progress. Four modern political ideas have shaped the pursuit of these objects by political societies: self-government, freedom, equality, and nationality and humanity (which he alternately labeled internationality). Wilson clearly saw politics as concerned with the most basic questions of civilization, of people living in society—the motives, ideals, and purposes they have. In contrast, constitutional government, law, and administration were the integrated institutional instruments of political society, the means by which political purposes could be achieved.

Thus in his "Constitutional Government" lectures, he defined its "ultimate and essential object" to "bring the active and planning will of each part of the [government] into *accord with the prevailing popular thought and need*, and to make it an impartial instrument of all-round national development" (14), emphasis in original). As he had from *Congressional Government* onward, Wilson saw law-making and administration as distinct, but closely linked. He elaborated on the object of constitutional government as "a cordial understanding between people and government," and a most fully developed constitutional government was that "under which the cordial understanding extends *beyond questions of fundamental law* to questions of administration and policy" (14).

Although constitutions, laws, and administration were instruments of politics and the purposes polities seek to realize, Wilson left no doubt that he understood all three to exert formative effects on those purposes. He made this clear in his discussion of the "moulding and modifying power of law" in his "Constitutional Government" notes (14) in which experiment and experience, particularly in the hands of administrative experts, play a prominent role. He stated it finally and unequivocally in his last notes for his "Philosophy of Politics."

> Institutions are subsequent to character. They do not create character, but are created and sustained by it. After being successfully established, however, they both confirm and modify national character, forming in no small degree both national thought and national purpose—certainly national ideals (14).

V.   THE IMPACTS OF WILSON'S THOUGHT AND ACTION

By the eve of his selection as president of Princeton University, Wilson had attained a remarkably subtle, complex conceptualization of administration in a democratic polity. Public administration scholars and practitioners alike can share the twinge of regret that he never articulated his understanding in a completed manuscript for his "Philosophy of Politics."

As Wilson moved, year by year, deeper into the world of political action and away from the world of ideas, few if any manifestations of this understanding surface in the political rhetoric of his correspondence, essays, and speeches. He emphasized, instead, the importance of administration in carrying out the law, and its subordination to elected officials and ultimately to public opinion through political leadership and interpretation (37). And he certainly subordinated his concern for civil service reform, efficiency, and effective administrative organization to the importance of achieving and maintaining party unity in Congress and between the White House and Capitol Hill (38,39).

Of course, over time Wilson had clearly begun to position himself to realize his life's ambition. Thus more obviously practical political concerns—getting elected and reelected, promoting, explaining, and defending policy proposals, leading the nation and the world in war and peace—came to dominate his spoken and written words and his actions. It is also true, however, that Wilson's political rhetoric and practices show the unmistakable imprint of his ideas about political leadership. His speeches during the 1912 presidential campaign and as president made frequent references to leadership and the interpretation of public opinion. His actions—particularly the establishment of regular press conferences and the precedent shattering addresses to Congress direct and in person—announced even more resonantly that Wilson had made his theory of executive political leadership his practical guide.

Perhaps the disjunction between Wilson's treatment of administration in concept and his treatment of it in practice can be explained by the change in his political outlook. As both Arthur Link and John Rohr have pointed out, during the time when Wilson gave his most concentrated attention to administration, his political views were demonstrably conservative (5,40). His close affinity to the philosophy of Edmund Burke is prima facie evidence, and at this time he stressed the importance of societal order and the controlling force of law. He thus gave expression to an expansive conception of the state (3).

Following first the stroke he suffered in 1896, then the conflicts over the organization of student life at Princeton that he experienced in the second half of his university presidency, and finally the contacts from Democratic party stalwarts which suggested he might finally realize his political ambitions, Wilson turned to an increasingly progressive political orientation. Wilson's progressivism increased in strength, in fact, throughout his two terms as president. With this outlook, then, Wilson stressed the critical role and influence of the views of the mass of common men, and the importance of subordinating administration to public opinion, and maintaining control over it from above, especially in the person of the president as national leader and interpreter.

Unity, institutional cooperation, and presidential leadership of party and Congress, rather than administration, formed the centerpiece of Wilson's governing philosophy, and the foundation on which he pursued a reform program. Thus he did not make administration the core of a major transformation of the American regime in the manner of Franklin Roosevelt and the New Deal (19). Nevertheless, Wilson did lay some of the critical conceptual and practical building blocks. Thus it seems appropriate to concur with Larry Walker's conclusion that "Wilson's influence on twentieth-century public administration has occurred *least of all* through his direct influence on academic public-administration theory" (12).

In the realm of ideas, Walker argues, Wilson contributed substantially not only to the establishment of the social sciences as distinctive academic disciplines, but also to the establishment of political science as one of the premiere social sciences. He also contributed significantly, in his writings and lectures, to advances in both methods of study and pedagogy. "Through both word and example, then, Wilson promoted a dramatic revolution in political study" (12). By helping to establish securely political science as an academic subject, moreover, Wilson helped to lay down the fertile soil within which the study of public administration could grow. Wilson made a more substantial direct contribution by establishing administration as a legitimate, permanent subject of systematic study and university instruction, making him one of the three original "public administrationists" in the U.S. (12).

Through his political practices, especially as president, Wilson "had deep and lasting effect upon the administrative institutions and practices of the nation" (16). By initiating new grants-in-aid and regulatory programs, expanding the number and variety of administrative entities, and mobilizing for war, Wilson essentially set the U.S. on the path toward a modern administrative state with a scope and set of responsibilities resembling that of European governments. This activity, and the more far-reaching endeavors of the New Deal and the Second World War built in part upon it, required, of course, new administrative theory to guide and legitimate it. The structural framework for that theory was the politics-administration dichotomy, and the dispute about Wilson's place as a founder of American public administration largely revolves around the extent to which he contributed to establishment of the dichotomy and all that it has since wrought.

Surprisingly, however, the disputants generally agree that Wilson did not contribute much to the establishment and resiliency of the dichotomy (12,25). It is thus paradoxical, and frustrating, that Wilson's direct contributions to public administration theory and the practices that follow from it, link him almost exclusively, and unalterably, to the politics-administration dichotomy. The many college textbooks on American government and, separately, on public administration are the best barometers of this, for almost without exception they connect Wilson to public administration with reference only to the 1887 essay and the dichotomy idea. The principal reason is obvious. The 1887 was published, and eventually became widely disseminated through reprintings and annotated collections. In contrast, Wilson's more advanced work on administration, represented by later essays and lecture notes, was inaccessible until the systematic publication of his papers began in the late 1960s.

The result is most unfortunate, because we now know that Wilson developed the much more subtle and complex understanding of administration, especially its place in constitutional democracy, that I have described. Had this been more widely known from the very beginnings of the discipline, it might have altered considerably the development of both public administration theory, and practice, in favor of a more congenial integration of administration into the modern theory and practice of liberal democracy.

Instead, one impact has been that although a voluminous body of work interpreting Wilson exists in the scholarly literature, few if any scholars have undertaken a serious effort to build theory upon Wilson's ideas. Wilson's greater affinity for, and much more substantial contribution to, undergraduate education also helps explain this (13), for he never produced a cadre of graduate students who then went on to disseminate and embellish his ideas.

The much more perilous impact, however, is that public administration, as both an object of scholarship and a critical institutional component of a modern democratic regime, has been relegated to an instrumental, secondary status. It is left in the hands of "experts" of various kinds, and thus is of little concern to elected officials or citizens more generally, except as a problem to control. This has left a yawning chasm of misunderstanding and mistrust between the public and public administration that Wilson would never have countenanced.

The chances for a course correction still exist, fortunately, for the true legacy that Woodrow Wilson bequeathed to scholars, practitioners, and attentive citizens was fundamental. He defined anew and elevated again in importance what was perhaps the core question posed by the founding of the American regime, a question that in essence most students of public administration wrestle with in their work: what ideas, institutions, and practices properly combined produce a principled democracy that is also well administered?

REFERENCES

1. R. S. Baker, *Woodrow Wilson: Life and Letters—Facing War, 1915–1917*, Doubleday, Doran & Co., Garden City, NY, 1937.
2. H. Clor, Woodrow Wilson, *American Political Thought: The Philosophica; Dimension of American Statesmanship* M. J. Frisch and R. G. Stevens (eds.), Charles Scribner's Sons, New York, 1971.

3. J. M. Mulder, *Woodrow Wilson: The Years of Preparation*, Princeton, University Press, Princeton, NJ, 1978.
4. P. P. Van Riper, The American administrative state: Wilson and the founders—an unorthodox view, *Pub. Admin. Rev.*: 43 (1983).
5. A. S. Link, *Wilson: The Road to the White House*, Princeton University Press, Princeton, 1947.
6. R. Seidelman, with E. J. Harpham, *Disenchanted Realists: Political Science and the American Crisis, 1884–1984*, SUNY Press, Albany, NY, 1985.
7. C. R. Kesler, The public philosophy of the New Freedom and the New Deal, *The New Deal and Its Legacy: Critique and Reappraisal* R. Eden (ed.), Greenwood Press, Westport, CT, 1989.
8. S. J. Zentner, Liberalism & executive power: Woodrow Wilson & the American founders, *Polity*: 26 (1994).
9. S. Skowronek, *The Politics Presidents Make: Leadership from John Adams to George Bush*, Belknap Press, Cambridge, MA, 1993.
10. A. S. Link, *Wilson and the New Freedom*, Princeton University Press, Princeton, 1956.
11. J. K. Tulis, *The Rhetorical Presidency*, Princeton University Press, Princeton, NJ, 1987.
12. Walker, Woodrow Wilson, progressive reform, and public administration, *Pol. Sci. Quar.*: 104 (1989).
13. H. W. Bragdon, *Woodrow Wilson: The Academic Years*, Harvard University Press, Cambridge, MA, 1967.
14. A. S. Link (ed.), *The Papers of Woodrow Wilson*, 69 vols., Princeton University Press, Princeton, NJ, 1966–1994.
15. R. Hofstadter, *Anti-Intellectualism in American Life*, Alfred A. Knopf, New York, 1963.
16. H. A. Turner, Woodrow Wilson as administrator, *Pub. Admin.Rev.*: 16 (1956).
17. M. E. Dimock, Wilson the domestic reformer, *The Philosophy and Policies of Woodrow Wilson* E. Latham (ed.), University of Chicago Press; Chicago, 1958.
18. C. Noble, The Political Origins of the Modern American State, *Comp. Pol.*: 17 (1985).
19. S. M. Milkis, *The President and the Parties: The Transformation of the American Party System Since the New Deal*, Oxford University Press, New York, 1993.
20. D. Steigerwald, The synthetic politics of Woodrow Wilson, *Journ. of the Hist. of Ideas*: 50 (1989).
21. A. de Tocqueville, *Democracy in America* J. P. Mayer (ed.) (G. Lawrence trans.), Perennial Library, New York, 1988.
22. W. Wilson, *Congressional Government*, Johns Hopkins University Press, Baltimore, 1981.
23. W. Hudson, *American Democracy in Peril* (rev. ed.), Chatham House, Chatham, NJ, 1996.
24. P. P. Van Riper, "The politics-administration dichotomy: concept or reality?" *Politics and Administration: Woodrow Wilson and American Public Administration*, J. Rabin, and J. S. Bowman (eds.), Marcel Dekker, New York, 1984.
25. P. P. Van Riper, On Woodrow Wilson, *Admin. & Soc.*: 18 (1987).
26. K. A. Kirwin, Woodrow Wilson and the study of public administration: response to Van Riper, *Admin. & Soc.*: 18 (1987).
27. D. W. Martin, The fading legacy of Woodrow Wilson, *Pub. Admin. Rev.*: 48 (1988).
28. J. A. Rohr, "The constitutional world of Woodrow Wilson," *Politics and Administration: Woodrow Wilson and American Public Administration* J. Rabin, and J. S. Bowman (eds.), Marcel Dekker, New York, 1984.
29. H. J. Storing, American statesmanship: old and new, *Bureaucrats, Policy Analystsm Statesman: Who Leads?* R. A. Goldwin (ed.), American Enterprise Institute, Washington, DC, 1980.
30. W. Wilson, "The study of administration," *Pol. Sci. Quar.*: 56 (1941).
31. B. J. Cook, *Bureaucracy and Self-Government: Reconsidering the Role of Public Administration in American Politics*, Johns Hopkins University Press, Baltimore, 1996.
32. R. J. Stillman, Woodrow Wilson and the study of public administration: a new look at an old essay, *Amer. Pol. Sci. Rev.*: 67 (1973).
33. R. D. Miewald, The origins of Wilson's thought: the German tradition and the organic state,

Politics and Administration: Woodrow Wilson and American Public Administration J. Rabin, and J. S. Bowman (eds.), Marcel Dekker, New York, 1984.

34. D. H. Rosenbloom, Reconsidering the politics-administration dichotomy: the Supreme Court and public personnel management, *Politics and Administration: Woodrow Wilson and American Public Administration*, J. Rabin, and J. S. Bowman (eds.), Marcel, Dekker, New York, 1984.

35. W. Wilson, *Constitutional Government in the United States*, Columbia University Press, New York, 1908.

36. D. Waldo, *The Administrative State: A Study of the Political Theory of American Public Administration* (2d. ed.), Holmes & Meier, New York, 1984.

37. B. J. Cook, Administrative theory and residential rhetoric: Woodrow Wilson and the instruction of public opinion, Amer. Pol. Sci. Assn. Annual Meeting, 1994.

38. A. W. Macmahom, Woodrow Wilson: political leader and administrator, *The Philosophy and Policies of Woodrow Wilson* E. Latham (ed.), University of Chicago Press, Chicago, 1958.

39. S. M. Milkis, and M. Nelson, *The American Presidency: Origins and Development, 1776–1993* (2nd. ed.), CQ Press, Washington, DC, 1994.

409. J. A. Rohr, *To Run a Constitution: The Legitimacy of the Administrative State*, University Press of Kansas, Lawrence, KS, 1986.

12

PROGRESSIVISM
Critiques and Contradictions

Larkin Sims Dudley
*Center for Public Administration and Policy, Virginia Polytechnic Institute and
State University, Blacksburg, Virginia*

"We are unsettled to the roots of our being . . . personal contact and eternal authority have disappeared. There are no precedents to guide us, no wisdom that wasn't made for a simpler age . . . We are 'emancipated' from an ordered world. We drift."

> Walter Lippmann, *Drift and Mastery*, 1914,
> pp. 152–153, 196.

"Despite the success of American life in the last half-century . . . our politics is rife with discontent. Americans are frustrated with government. We fear we are losing control of the forces that govern our lives, and that the moral fabric of community—from neighborhood to nation—is unraveling around us."

> Michael J. Sandel, *Democracy's discontent:
> America in Search of A Public Philosophy*,
> 1996, Cover.

I. INTRODUCTION

None dispute the chaos of the period from 1870 to 1910 in the United States. Settlers filled the land between the Mississippi River and California, new systems of industry were created, and the urban population jumped from 9.9 million to 30.1 million. Many people of good will saw at the turn of the century that the extraordinary outburst of productive energy of the last few decades failed to produce a means of meeting human needs or controlling the social and moral upheavals that accompanied rapid physical change. Citizens looked to reform movements, particularly that called the Progressive movement, to develop the moral will, the intellectual insight, and the political and administrative agencies to remedy the accumulated evils and negligence of a period of industrial growth (1). The attempted reforms resurrected older tensions in American political life and created new ones, themes and counter themes, that still permeate the profession of Public Administration a century later.

Most Americans, administrative students included, simply "accepted" the idea of the desirability of progress throughout the first half of this century, according to Dwight Waldo's

The Administrative State (2). However, to the question, "What has been the influence of Progressivism?" Waldo asserts the answer is neither simple nor brief. No one historian has fully succeeded in capturing its many parts (3). Although disagreement exists on exactly when the genesis and flowering of Progressivism occurs, the period from approximately 1880 until the beginning of World War I appears to be the period when Progressive ideas were most influential (4). There is less agreement on what the major tenets of progressivism were and even less on how exactly the reform movement came to affect the study of public administration.

It is a mistake to exaggerate the consensus among those who chose to call themselves, Progressives. In the United States, the movement became so pervasive that many different interest groups identified with it. The word "progressivism" itself appears and disappears in the political sphere across nations, first entering British political discourse in the late 1880s, when social and municipal reformers adopted it to designate their "advanced" position within the Liberal party. (5) The term also occurs in England in 1896 when Leonard T. Hobhouse and a group of intellectuals named their journal *The Progressive Review* and in Germany in 1910 when Max Weber found a political home in the short-lived Progressive People's party. Journalists Herbert Croly and Walter Lippman identified with the "progressive movement" in 1912 when the term became widespread during the campaign to elect the Progressive's party's presidential candidate, Theodore Roosevelt.

Yet, many scholars agree that beginning in the mid-1880s, Americans experienced a period of intense creativity in political, social, and economic theory, initially removed from prevailing political institutions and practices. The world underwent an intellectual and perhaps spiritual transformation, resulting in the destruction of many of the political world's intellectual and institutional foundations (6). If one can accept that institutional relationships, practices, and purposes define political orders and distinguish one regime from another, then the period from 1890s until W.W.I was characterized by just such a change in institutions—new institutions replaced local democracy, local economy, national courts, and coalitions of political parties (6). The rise and growth of the modern university and the origination of academic social sciences provide the most obvious proof. Progressives wrote textbooks that dominated and disseminated social knowledge and trained at least two generations of academics. Among the lessons taught were that social knowledge must be cosmopolitan in origin and national in import. A new conception of citizenship was popularized that stipulated a belief in national public good not mediated by party interest, region, or sectarian religion. The University became the national church—protector of common values, meanings, and identities. From its intellectual origins in the 1880s, until the victory of Wilson and the Democratic party, Progressive thinking conquered most major cultural and intellectual bastions in America, except constitutional law, and dominated national institutions, except the courts and the party system (6). In Waldo's assessment, Progressivism was not an idea but a sheaf of ideas, old and new, at times incompatible, held together by a buoyant faith in Progress (2). According to Waldo,

> Progressivism found . . . its basis in the old democratic faith, it was stimulated by the Muckrakers and the earnest efforts of Reformers, it attempted to bring ethical absolutism into the world of science, it recruited armies of Reform sworn to march in different directions into the future, it was a welter of ideas given a monetary unity by a common basis of optimism (7).

Thus, progressivism has elements of both a social movement and a philosophical orientation. To gain a perspective on the interaction among these ideas, some of the antecedents of the movement require examination.

II. REPUDIATING THE PAST

Before 1900, public life in America was shaped by the values of classical liberalism: strong popular nationalism; a commitment to representative government and a weak central state; a belief in personal freedom; and the assumption that the natural laws governing society, as those governing the economy, were not readily altered by public policy (8). In fact, nineteenth-century America was dominated by two institutions, courts and parties (6). Corresponding to these two institutions were two dominant frameworks of thought, constitutional law and democratic individualism (6). The two frameworks were at odds with themselves. For constitutional law, the institutional framework is formal: a hierarchical system of state and federal appellate courts, systems of legal education, and professional standards. In contrast, party leaders were informally chosen and exercised a changing and bewildering number of powers prior to Progressive regulatory reforms in the twentieth century. Partisan political thought served as concessions to various interests and achieved some coherence only at the national level (6). It would seem natural that Progressive intellectuals would gravitate toward the rich tradition of constitutional law—nationalism, public service, professional autonomy, but the movement did not. Eldon J. Eisenach, author of *The Lost Promise of Progressivism*, believes this is partially due to the antilegal sentiment deeply embedded in Calvinist theology, and partially because constitutional law was considered guilty by association with the party and the excesses of democratic capitalism. Just when Progressive scholars were attempting to lower barriers, Constitutional history focused on legally constituted political institutions, thereby raising artificial barriers between politics, culture, economy, and society.

Thus, beginning in the mid-1880s, Progressive horizons were not constitutional and legal (6). Instead, the roots of American progressivism were similar to those of Britain's New Liberalism, German Social Democracy, and the Republican-Radical governments of early twentieth-century France (8). Philosophers who were one generation ahead of progressive ideas on the continent and in England searched, in John Dewey's terms, for the *via media*, the way between natural science and the ideal interests of morals and religion. These included Wilhelm Dilthey, Thomas Hill Green, Henry Sidgwick, Alfred Fouilee, and William James. These scholars contended that individual experience, conceived as radically social and unavoidably uncertain, provides the only basis for knowledge. They emphasized history as an important source of judgment, insisted that ideas must be tested in practice, and "bleached the apocalyptic vibrancy from socialism and dyed their ideas in the softer shades of reform." In short, they wanted to extend the democratic principles of participation and equality from the civil and political spheres to the entire society and the economy (9). Among the heirs to the traditions of the *via media*, those who would eventually be called progressive scholars, are Leon Bourgeois, whose doctrine of solidarity inspired a wave of solidarity in France; Leonard T. Hobhouse, who moved Britain's Liberal party from laissez-faire toward state activism; Max Weber, whose contributions did not flourish in Germany, but influenced generations of scholars, and the Americans—Herbert Croly and Walter Lippmann, editors of *The New Republic*; and John Dewey, who most clearly connects the ideas of the *via media* with the politics of progressivism (9).

Such scholars, reacting to the massive economic and social changes, became part of the new ways of viewing the structure of American society. Two ideas in particular are important in order to understand the development of the progressive period—the acceptance of the idea of progress and the rejection of the concept of American exceptionalism. First, the almost universal acceptance of the desirability of progress in the twentieth century, Dwight Waldo's premise, blinds us to the memory that the word progress itself repudiates the span of human history when most believed the future repeats the past. As recently as the late seventeenth century, the moderns asserted that the ancients' concept of adhering to the elders of the past was unjustified since the wise stood now on the shoulders of those past and became the elder (10). The main emphasis from the eighteenth century, however, associated progress as the struggle between reason and superstition. Two motifs formed from this emphasis (10). One was that science had truths and if these truths were adopted, then progress could be obtained, in morals and social sciences, as well as the physical sciences. A second motif associated progress with an unique self-corrective set of methods of science, not with a particular discourse. In this view, progress means rejecting the absolute and, instead, proposes free, experimental inquiry. A related theme is found in those ideas in historicist philosophy and in Hegel where progress is an idea embedded in a particular period of development. Here, progress would not have a definite meaning since such meaning could only be determined in the unfolding of rational purpose within a period of time.

A corollary development to the acceptance of progress was the repudiation of the idea of American exceptionalism. According to Dorothy Ross, exceptionalism is "the idea that America occupies an exceptional place in history, based on her republican government and economic opportunity" (11). Ross observes that prior to the late nineteenth century, Americans believed that the republican institutions and liberal opportunity would forestall mass poverty and the class conflict of modernity (11). As a cosmopolitan gentry moved into academia in the late 1800s, there arose recognition that Americans could no longer escape industrialization as it was known in Europe. Most scholars believed America could still escape the prolonged class conflict of Europe and the necessity for radical change. The experience of civil war and rapid industrialization along with the decline of religious assurance forced an understanding that republican ideals depended on the same forces that were creating liberal modernity in Europe: on the development of capitalism, democratic politics, and science (12). Fear that these forces were leading toward socialism led many social scientists to emphasize methods of social control. These attempts to regulate and institutionalize support historian Robert Wiebe's understanding of the period as a "search for order."

Social thought was also affected by the passion for classification so much a part of Darwinian biology. The prevailing trend was to sort humans into distinct racial, ethnic, and social groups [Frederick Jackson Turner's essay on the effect of the American frontier (1893), Thorstein Veblen's *Theory of the Leisured Class* (1898) and William Graham Sumner's *Folkways* (1906)] and to develop themes in keeping with Herbert Spencer's dictate that the basic course of evolution was from simplicity to complexity, from homogeneity to heterogeneity (13). Also, class analysis entered into American social science with the work of Charles Beard and others—as did the interest-group approach to politics with Arthur F. Bentley's *Process of Government* (1908) (13). Although European reformers did not obscure class distinctions, ideas of class conflict were only one of the factors affecting early twentieth century American social policy-making. Progressives themselves often identified with the middle class.

Thus, in American intellectual life in the late 1800s, both institutional structures and intellectual concepts were in a flux. Universities expanded and professional associations and journals grew, especially in the social sciences: the American Economic Association, the American Academy of Political and Social Science, and the American Sociological Association. From backgrounds as disparate as Marxism, Christian socialism, and utopian socialism, dissenters in the 1880s began altering the fabric of socialist philosophy and socialist politics. In line with the ferment of academia, mass circulation newspapers and muckraking magazines brought the cause of reform into every household. Books of the time grappled with the idea of what was truly American and issues of social class, e.g., Robert Grant's *Unleavened Bread*, Edith Wharton's *The House of Mirth*, and Thorstein Veblen's *The Theory of the Leisure Class* (14). Sharp criticism of unregulated laissez-fairê practices was found in Ida Tarbell's expose of Standard Oil (1904), Upton Sinclair's *The Jungle* (1906) and David Graham Phillips's *Treason of the Senate* and other investigations of corrupt alliance between the corporations and all classes of politicians (15).

Yet, the movement was certainly not without its opponents. Many scorned protest and reform and articulated a conservative defense of the status quo (16). Such claims used the so-called social Darwinism, derived by the English sociologist, Herbert Spencer, from the evolutionary theory of Charles Darwin, to oppose governmental interference in social and economic affairs. More powerful was the argument of no class conflict, the doctrine of the harmony of economic interests, or what helped one group helped everyone. Another barrier against reform was firm allegiance to the major political parties by middle class men.

III. MULTIFARIOUS IMPULSES TO REFORM

In 1900, the reform impulse was somewhat disorganized. Although the preceding populist movement had opposed the domination of the political system by eastern business interests, populist ideas did not propose a coherent philosophic alternative to laissez fair and had been defeated by William McKinley and Mark Hanna (17). Social reformers, including labor unions, also failed to design a broader understanding of social change (17). However, the broad reforms of Progressivism, the first reform movement to be experienced by the whole nation, was advanced by some socialists, by prohibitionists, and by other nonpartisan groups (17). Indeed, the movement fits well Laurence O'Toole's observations that, characteristically, American reformers assume a commonly-shared vision of the good life, reflect articulated ideology, seek to redress problems, change issues and positions regularly, and have difficulty specifying the intended beneficiaries of the reform (18). The Progressives had difficulty deciding who were their own clientele: the elite participated, the middle-class staffed beginning bureaucracies, and workers felt the movement was theirs (18).

Histories of the movement differ in locating the thrust of Progressivism. Early histories defined the Progressives as the common people—farmers, workers, and small businessmen who organized to recapture power from the railroads, large corporations, and party bosses (19). In the early 1950s, others interpreted the movement as one dominated by urban, middle professionals who wished to restore individualism and restrain the growing power of large corporations and labor unions (20). However, others viewed them as a farsighted "new middle class" of professionals who needed to impose order to solve the problems caused by industrialization. This assessment portrays the new middle class reformers as relying upon organization, the application of scientific (or social-scientific) expertise, and the values of efficiency and rationality. Robert Weibe, noted for his scholarship of the period, has declared that progressivism was driven by the ambition of the new middle class to fulfillment through bureaucratic means (21). Still others have argued that the most wealthy were the reformers and the beneficiaries of movements to regulate the economy (22).

Yet, some ideas seem to have been characteristic of most of the reformers calling themselves Progressive (23). Despite their differences, most Progressives wanted to ameliorate and improve the conditions of industrial life. Some shared a deep outrage against the worst consequences of industrialism, but they did not wish to dismantle modern economic institutions, only reform them. They had a faith in progress—in humanity's ability, through purposeful action, to improve the environment and the conditions of life. Further, most progressives preferred to work through voluntary organizations, but became convinced over time that most reform could be achieved only by legislation and public control. Most were not as comfortable with as complete an extension of state authority as was Herbert Croly whose ideas are discussed below (24).

Beyond agreement on these basics, the period can be characterized as one of intense discourse centering around themes that become part of the perennial questions for public administration. The only reasonable synthesis to these divergent views is that the period itself as well as its major tenets are best understood as a series of shifting coalitions in which major players' allegiances varied according to the issues at hand. Different groups mobilized around sets of reforms and sometimes allied themselves in puzzling ways (25).

IV. THE CONTEXT OF PROGRESSIVISM: ENCAPSULATED IN MODERNITY

Part of the shifting among coalitions in the Progressive Era is reflective of the contradictions among older and newer approaches to the world of ideas and practices. In the view of Guy Adams, Progressive ideology reflects the movement toward modernity which coalesced only within the last century in American culture (26). Following Turner (27), characteristics of modernity include: secularization, a rationality of instrumentalism, separation and specialization of life-worlds, bureaucratization, and an escalation of monetarization of values. Beginning in the Progressive Era, technical rationality, a chief component of modernity, combined scientific-analytical thinking (one of the legacies of seventeenth century Enlightenment) and a belief in technological progress (a product of the Great Transformation of the nineteenth century). Guy Adams (26) notes that technical rationality is similar to Karl Mannheim's concept of functional rationality, where tasks are organized into smaller units in the interest of efficiency and one loses the ability to understand the purposeful nature of the whole, or what Mannheim called "substantive rationality." Technical rationality is also close to what Max Horkheimer called "instrumental rationality," the narrow application of human reason for purely instrumental aims only (26). The conception of reason is narrowed from the premodern era conception of reason as a process incorporating ethical and normative concerns with instrumental aims.

In addition to the belief in technological progress and instrumental rationality, reformers constructed a critique of the abstractionism, deductivism, and formal logic of European intellectual thought. Formalism is characterized by abstraction, deductive systems of logic, and formal coherence to define a problem in reference to the system of which it is a part. Instead, the reformer sees the problem as the most important, thinks outward to solutions, and acts by re-making definitions of problems. The progressive approach relied upon historicism, the attempt to explain facts by reference to other facts, and cultural organicism, a search for explanation in all of the social sciences under the belief that all are holistically related (18). As Lawrence O'Toole explains:

The reaction against formalism, a reaction which achieved high intellectual status in the early part of the century, implied at least two significant effects for present purposes. First, the idea suggested to its proponents that they begin to tinker with the world to improve it. And, second, the reaction provided some legitimacy to those who, for whatever reason, were actively seeking to effect social betterment (28).

In the cornucopia of concepts developing at the turn of the century, O'Toole sees a broad array of ideas composed of pragmatism, new history, institutionalism, behaviorism, legal realism, and economic determinism (29). In addition, James Stever argues that the conflict between organic idealism and pragmatism was crucial to the development of thought in public administration (30). These ideas overlap, in some instances, and in others, are somewhat contradictory. However, a brief foray into some of these major ideas is necessary before discussing the critiques that provide a lasting influence upon public administration.

As the Progressive era began, organic idealism was still influential, particularly in the work of figures important to public administration, such as Woodrow Wilson and Frank Goodnow. Organic idealism, imported from the continent, was expressed in the ideas of transcendental reason, organic evolution, and the steady development of reason within human society as part of the philosophies of Friedrich Hegel, T. H. Green, Bernard Bosanquet, Francis Bradley, and Josiah Royce, the leading American idealist (30). For example, Wilson proposed that individuals possessed minimal ability to rise above their traditional past, an idea consistent with the organic-like dependency existing between individual and society. As the Progressive period developed, no group fully embraced or organized around the organic idealist position and pragmatism was displacing idealism (30).

Pragmatism, a term introduced by Charles Sanders Pierce in 1878, posited a contingent universe where meaning and truth are measured in terms of experience, which can contain subjective elements of art, emotion, and supernatural faith. In accord with the Progressive movement, pragmatism moved toward a more social view of action (31). John Dewey's "instrumentalism" contended that individuals fulfill themselves through relationships with others and stressed the value of action leading toward a "good community." Another pragmatist, George Herbert Mead, major contributor to the development of social psychology, emphasized the social basis of human reality and accepted that meaning arose from the subjective meaning actors give their actions. Consistent with the emphasis on community and social relationships, the pragmatic movement promoted numerous of the progressive causes—child-centered schools, settlement house efforts to acculturate immigrants, shared decision making among owners and workers, and economic activity explained according to institutional structure rather than classical laws.

The movement in economics supported by the pragmatists illustrates some of the ideas most dear to Progressive thinking. In close accordance with Anne Mayhew's analysis, four ideas were critical to the separation of institutionalist theory from neoclassical economic theory: evolution, culture, cultural relativity, and instrumental valuing (32). Virtually all American thought was affected by the ideas of evolution of Charles Darwin or Herbert Spencer, or of ideas attributed to them in the late 1800s. Ideas of natural selection and evolution were one means of explaining the rapid enrichment of some, as well as the lack of security for many. The ideas of society and culture as evolving systems had roots in both evolutionary thought and the increasing knowledge of human variation over time and place that became available during the nineteenth century. The recognition that morals—as well as law, custom, and art—were learned as part of a particular culture not only influenced anthropology profoundly, but other disciplines as well. The work of Thorstein Veblen and John R. Commons, scholars who began publishing in the 1890s and who are thought of as the "first institutionalists" in economics, diverged from standard economics because institutionalism rested upon acceptance of these ideas (32). Commons, from the beginning an active reformer, built a mode of process, of repetitive conflict and conflict resolution, as the driving force of social evolution. For Commons, the social theorists of the day could be divided into those who accepted a Spencerian interpretation of social evolution as something that could not and should not be consciously altered and those who were for reform, those who favored "artificial selection."

Veblen, the academic, proposed that human society not only changed, but that it was not tending to any end, spiritual or otherwise (32). To Veblen, being against or for reform was beside the point. Humans were distinguished by the employment of skills to manipulate nature as a process that changed the ways people thought about the world. He noted that people adhered to a wide variety of ideas, those both pragmatically useful and those simply accepted as part of the cultural heritage. Thus, the "cumulative change" of evolution could be driven by pragmatic adaptation, while ceremonial refusal could slow down pragmatic evaluation. His observations of the ubiquity of this duality added the idea of instrumental valuing to the ideas of culture, evolution, and cultural relativity. As Anne Mayhew notes, thus, "institutional economics diverged from other traditions in the social sciences because institutionalists placed great emphasis upon instrumental valuation as the driving force of cultural evolution" (33).

This potpourri of ideas—pragmatism, evolution, institutional economics, and most of all, technical rationality, were part of the rush to embrace modernity in all fields of academia. Intellectual leaders included those discussed by Eldon J. Eisenach in *The Lost Promise of Progressivism* (6). Eisenach examines the nineteen intellectuals who produced over one hundred and fifty books and who were the founding members of professional organizations in economics, sociology, and political and social science during the Progressive Era. Of his group of scholars, all but one had college degrees and all but two had done graduate work. They were a tightly knit group in which sociology, according to Eisenach, served both as an integrator of the new social sciences and as the major source of theoretical grounding for Progressive reforms. Included in Eisenach's list were political economists (Henry Carter Adams, John Bates Clark, Richard T. Ely, John Roberts Commons, Arthur Twining Hadley, Edmund J. James, Edwin Robert Anderson Seligman, Albert Shaw); sociologists (Franklin Henry Giddins, Edward Alsworth Ross, Albion Woodbury Small); professor of literature (Vita Dutton Scudder); and social activists (Jane Addams, Florence Kelley, and William Dwight Porter). With the field of public administration in mind, Dwight Waldo adds still other scholars to the list—J. W. Burgess, E. J. James, A. B. Har, A. L. Lowell, and F. J. Goodnow, who, according to Waldo, were stimulated by the inadequacies of the ethical approach in the Gilded Age and German universities to recreate political science as true science (2). In addition in the field of public law (particularly administrative law), F. J. Goodnow, J. A. Fairlie, and Ernst Freund advanced into realism. Obvious omissions from these lists are Charles Beard and Herbert Croly. Beard and Croly are seen as derivative in content and methods of analysis from the others with Small and Patten influencing Croly and Seligman influencing Beard. However, to trace the implication of ideas, particularly the passage from Progressivism to Wilsonian democracy and New Deal liberalism, according to Eisenach and other scholars of progressivism, Croly is absolutely essential, and is thus discussed in detail below.

V. PROGRESSIVISM AS INTELLECTUAL CRITIQUE

From the postmodernist stance of today, the significance of the turmoil of the progressive era for the field of public administration is the constructing of critiques of governing in American culture that underpin much of early public administration thought and appear and reappear in both practice and theory for most of the twentieth century. The field begins as ideas later defined as "modernity" take hold. The narratives that would give meaning to at least four generations of scholars and practitioners are constructed out of the period's devilish dilemmas. These dilemmas, many of which stem from the "wicked problems" in which public administration is immersed, define the parameters of the debates for public administration for the twentieth century.

Others have categorized the important controversies of the field or the narratives "that have been offered up to give meaning to our professional lives" (34). According to J. D. White and G. B. Adams, each of six partial narratives captures some of the field's essence, but none adequately captures the whole. They do have in common, according to White and Adams, a foundation in the "tacit, grand narrative of technical rationality" (35). Of the six themes, four are elaborated in this chapter as part of Progressivism's critique of the period's way of governing. One of White and Adams narratives, the dichotomy between politics and administration, I have subsumed below under the larger topics of the relationship between democracy and the economy and the need for an administrative state. A second, the scientific study and practice of public administration, and a third, the belief that theory informs practice, are interwoven in this chapter in the discussion on the rise of scientific methods and management in public administration. What White and Adams call the Minnowbrook narrative, the emphasis on democratic values of social equity, citizen participation, and proactive government, are considered here under the concern for citizenship. Two other narratives that White and Adams identify are mentioned only briefly in this chapter. The legitimization of Public Administration on the basis of the Constitution is not explored because many of the ideas of Progressivism were formed in rebellion to the approach of Constitutional law and because that topic is more closely associated with the work of Woodrow Wilson, the subject of another chapter in this volume. A final theme, really just re-emerging in Public Administration, after long neglect, is that of gender. Although the links among the Progressive period's general concept of gender and today's make fascinating history, the specific linkages among gender and public administration for the period are only briefly covered since that topic has been so aptly discussed by Camilla Stivers in Chapter 13 (36).

Out of these numerous narratives, perhaps the most general and familiar question from the progressive era is that of intertwining of reform and science. What shape the political economy should take is also one of the essential questions. For public administration, questions of the appropriate role of the public sector, the concept of the state, and the questions of bureaucracy in democracy owe some debt to the arguments of this period. A related set of questions centers on the relationship between a collective and citizens. Other themes include how justifications were constructed for the rise of science and scientific management and the rise of the administrative state. In choosing to focus on these dimensions as the undercurrents, and sometimes treacherous undertow, of progressivism, some of the most important themes and personalities of the period for public administration are only mentioned. Most of these, however, Pragmatism and John Dewey, George Herbert Mead, and Mary Parker Follett; Woodrow Wilson and the "New Freedom;" and the interaction among the Bureau of Municipal Research, scientific management, and municipal reform are well-covered in other chapters of this volume. Thus, the remainder of this chapter is devoted to an overview of some of the main themes of progressivism and to the critiques that take a particular form in the progressive era. These are the ones that fulfill two criteria: they both dominate much of progressive thought and continually reappear in the field of public administration.

VI.   BUILDING A CASE FOR REFORM THROUGH A CONCEPT OF SCIENCE

No matter how varied the goals of social policy makers were, the heart of Progressivism was a shared sense that the good society was efficient, organized, and cohesive. American social thinkers, placing a high value on the principle of order and organization, believed that "potentially, the greatest producer, recorder, interpreter, and user of social fact is an efficient democracy" (37). Many set out to produce just that through reforms of all sorts, coordination in organizations, the scientific method, a new role for the executive, and new, if sometimes conflicting, ideas of management.

The Progressive period was indeed an "age of reform," but it was reform infused with both religious zeal and scientific, instrumentalist language (38). Evangelical Protestantism and the natural and social sciences linked in the Progressive mind as underpinnings for their fervent hopes for reform. Ever since the religious revivals from about 1820 to 1840, evangelical Protestestanism had been a part of most American reform movements. Many Progressives believed that righting the wrongs of industrialization was their Christian duty. The Social Gospel movement spreading through the churches at the turn of the century aimed to make Christianity relevant to today's world and aligned churches on the side of the poor and working people. The stress on inner character, shared values, public opinion, social knowledge, and spiritual progress impelled the Progressives toward even deeper critiques of American constitution and party.

The same religious zeal was applied to the concept of efficiency, faith in science, and the efficacy of the scientific method (2). This efficient democracy envisioned by the Progressives required both justification and coordination. The methods of science were seen as the justification and the need for coordination was to be met by increasing centralization. Behind this idea of reform was John Dewey's concept of the empirical idealist, an adherent to a philosophy using intelligence in consideration of a desirable future and searching for the means of bringing it progressively into existence (39). Ascending concurrently in American culture, both scientific methods and public administration shared a positivist orientation, an emphasis on a range of indisputable fact and the extension of rule of law, and elimination of the metaphysical through the substitute of measurement (40).

Most of the Progressives did not envision science as the Greek concept of penetration to the hidden truth or as the Stoical capacity to safeguard oneself from that which is not under one's control (41). Rather, the Baconian idea of science became a vital part of the understanding of Progressive social science (41). Bacon was committed to the idea that knowledge was specifically for practical use, for "the relief of man's estate." As such, the Baconian features of emphasis on experiment, the amassing of data and analysis of data for patterns, and the emphasis on 'remaining close to the facts' was heartily endorsed by the reformers outside academia as well as many inside. Science in America became, then, heavily "industrialized science or technocratic science" (41).

America's first professional social scientists were Americans educated in Germany who wished to transplant German ideas about social science and the social scientist role in modern politics to North America. This fervor was combined with some ideas of Puritan redemption and bumped into the United States heritage, not only of constitutionalism, but of individualism. Although the Hegelian ideal of an organic whole was certainly influential on early writers, in practice and, thus, eventually in thought, the influence of individualism had a tempering effect (41). In the words of Peter T. Manicas,

> infused with German social science and Puritan redemption, the scholars of this generation were republicans and reformers—middle-class and middle-of-the-road. For the most part, they did not shed the American sense of freedom, and valued cooperative self-help and 'social ethics', not socialism. . . . They were German, however, in thinking of *Geisteswissenschaft* as a kind of historically oriented unified social science with overlapping, non-discrete connected concerns. And they still believed that policy judgments could be just as scientific as any other judgments (42).

However, the United States structural conditions were different from those of their German teachers. The American professoriate had to achieve authority in the face of opposition from local elite—clergymen, lawyers, and merchants (41)—and with an understanding that wealthy members of the boards of trustees had to be attracted. According to Thorstein Veblen, the academic social scientists bent to the temptation of the new order and substituted "homolectical exposition for science" (43). Instead of inquiry into nature and causes, according to Veblen, the questions became those of questions of use and a science of projected remedies (43).

Most leading reformers specialized in the new disciplines of statistics, economics, sociology, and psychology. Thus, in Mary Furmer's account, the study of society moved from the hands of amateurs at the start of the Industrial Era to those of professionals. In the 1890s and the early twentieth century, when government roles expanded, political scientists described the processes of administration while training specialists to do the administering (41). The influence of scientific naturalism and the problems of actual practice led to curiosity about how and why people behaved politically. The specialists became experts and the experts became active in the developing national bureaucracy, particularly Cornell scholars, Jeremiah Jenks at the United States Industrial Commission and Walter F. Wilcox at the United States Census Bureau. Political scientists became especially influential in developing the technical know how to administer a far-flung colonial empire in Puerto Rico and the Philippines: Jeremiah Jenks, Jacob Hollander, Thomas S. Adams, William Frank Wiloughby, Bernard Moses (41).

Reform in social policy and in governmental organization became linked to a concept of science that was primarily a concept of the scientific method, that was instrumental, and underpinned by a technocratic rationality. These themes were played out in the era at an ideological level of instrumental values permeating the arguments for democracy and at a practical level in the arguments at the workplace for scientific management. The idea of reform through science and the belief in the scientific management combined with the distrust of patronage and the party system to shore up the concept of a new leader, the expert, and a new way of organizing through regulatory commissions, management systems, and bureaucracies. Only because science is believed to be objective can one believe that regulatory commissions and professional management will not be partisan, but instead will arrive at scientific truths. The new expert, partially because of the scientific methods available in the execution of duties, is thought then to be the best hope for a true public service orientation. Most important for a conception of the political economy of reform, the subject of the next section, was the efficacy and persuasiveness of this belief in science.

VII. RECONCEPTUALIZING THE POLITICAL ECONOMY TO ACCOMMODATE LARGE SCALE REFORM

Although the discussion thus far indicates divergent currents in progressive thought, Progressive intellectuals and social reformers are credited with transforming liberal theory into progressive theory. From the "idea of natural rights culminating in the idea of noninterventionist state," these thinkers turned old liberalism into new liberalism. According to James T. Kloppenberg, they renounced atomistic empiricism, psychological hedonism, and utilitarian ethics associated with nineteenth century liberalism (5). To construct the political theory of progressivism, they discarded the idea of possessive individualism, broadened their political allegiance to include the working class along with the bourgeois, and embraced the ideals of equality and community to supplement the customary liberal commitment to individual freedom (5).

According to Edward A. Stettner, "liberal" was not a common word in the vocabulary of American political reformers in the year 1900 (3). Instead, they recognized liberalism as a philosophy emphasizing individual rights, constitutionalism, and favoring legal equality. These parts of the liberal argument were compatible with the ideas of Herbert Croly and other reformers. Other classical liberal ideas were not so appealing: the preference of many for freedom over democracy and, even more important, liberalism's close association with laissez-faire economic theory, particularly the emphasis on private property as necessary to individual liberty. However, the Republican tradition had taught Americans to fear concentrated power, whether economic or political, if the powers were thought to be hostile to liberty.

Yet a disjuncture appears. As the philosopher John Dewey observes, a theory of the freely choosing self, a voluntarist self-image, takes shape just at a time when mechanical forces and impersonal organizations begin to dominate (44). The lack of fit between the way people conceived their identities and the way economic life was actually organized led to concern about the concentration of power amassed by giant corporations (44). Following the arguments of Dwight Waldo and Michael J. Sandel closely in this section, three positions can be described. The most vocal position in academia and elsewhere was the argument that economic concentration was irreversible and that the capacity of national democratic institutions needed to be increased to control monopolies. However, a substantial number of other Progressive thinkers sought to preserve self-government by decentralizing economic power and thus, bringing it under democratic control. Finally, a solution of increasing consumer power began to emerge in the era, but does not reach substantial power until later in the century. These three positions are briefly explored below.

A. The Argument for Centralization and National Regulation

A major theme for most adhering to a Progressive philosophy was the need to use government—particularly the national government and even more particularly the national executive—to control the power of business. The national viewpoint was put forth in direct opposition to an abstract "rights-based" discourse, whether expressed as individual rights, as states rights, or as constitutional formalism (6). The nationalistic emphasis can be interpreted both as a restriction and as a release. As a restriction, nationalism placed an emphasis on substantive national goals blinding one to universal and value-neutral ideas of rights. As a release, nationalism removed the prevailing language of rights which prevented the formation of common purpose and which sanctioned the most narrow kinds of localism and civic irresponsibility (6). Thus, according to Eldon J. Eisenach, progressive nationalism is a conservative contraction of American ideals because of the emphasis on historic community, the power of the past, and collective disciplines and responsibilities required to achieve a common future. Yet, at the same time, it is a liberating call to larger life, an escape from illusory individualism trapped in a polity that thwarts civic capacity and democratic purposes (6).

A further justification for moving toward the administrative state and the sort of bureaucratic organizations spawned in the early 1900s was the vision of the state as the embodiment of moral as well as legal right. Dewey, Croly, Lippmann, Hobhouse, and Bourgeois believed that the state ought to embody ethical principles because the protection of privilege fostered by organized capitalism stood in the way of such an ethical polity (5). Thus, these progressive thinkers, as well as others, tried to channel the spirit of organized capitalism into a new politics of social responsibility. Most scholars, today, however would agree that they really only justified the expansion of state action where the shape of the state changed, but its purpose did not (45). Because these progressives stressed the themes of moral harmony and community, their position has been confused with the authoritarian organism of much conservative theory. They saw a difference in their view of social integration as the product of individual action because it was tempered by an ethic of benevolence in contrast to a paternalistic structure. Rather than imposing a set of pre-existing rules, they believed the state should manifest values of autonomous individuals conscientiously fulfilling their social responsibility (46).

The writings of Herbert Croly are an articulate exposition of the most nationalist views. Two central concepts (national community and national purpose) underpinned his progressive rationale for a more extensive reconstruction of democratic theory to accommodate new institutions and alternative practices in America. According to Croly, "the United States needed a nationalization of their intellectual life comparable to the nationalization of their industry and politics" (47). That nationalization was seen as an infusion of a national organic spirit into the culture of America (47). In Croly's words,

> The Federal government belongs to the American people even more completely than do the state governments, because a general current of public opinion can act much more effectively on the single Federal authority than it can upon the many separate state authorities. Popular interest have nothing to fear from a measure of Federal centralization (48).

To accomplish this goal, Croly in his most noted book, *The Promise of American Life*, argues Americans need to reject laissez-faire theory and accept the idea of national planning for a "better future." Drawing an emphasis on unity from the idealism of Josiah Royce, professor of philosophy at Yale, Croly asserts the ideal of a single universal national interest against the prevailing trend of developing interest groups of professionals and business and the tide of immigration (3). Croly argues for purpose that transcends the individuals and their material interest by commitment to a higher idea and asserts public interest that is political, but also moral and religious (3). In *The Promise*, Hamilton is the one to be admired as the intellectual father of the Republic (3). Thus, Croly is following the Progressive aim of a Hamiltonian national government in the service of Jeffersonian ideals (48).

Croly envisioned the American people under competent and responsible leadership deliberately planning a policy of individual and social improvement in which human nature could be raised to a higher level by improvement in institutions and laws. For Croly, democracy must stand or fall on a platform of possible human perfectibility where liberty, social interest, and equality are subordinate to brotherhood and, thus, in the long run mutually helpful (49). Croly cannot be seen as egalitarian as some of the other Progressives, in the sense of a defender of the poor or oppressed, nor is he enamored of a conception of isolated individuals armed with abstract rights. Instead, he argues for a sense of national community where popular government deliberates any action which in the opinion of the decisive majority is demanded by public welfare and which relates back to the national purpose. Although he did not describe the powers a national government should have, he did specify "regulation of commerce, the organization of labor, and the increasing control over property in the public interest (3).

Croly does see democracy as "matter of popular government," but to him, it also means more—a community in which no group granted by law any advantage over their fellow-citizens (3). On the other hand, he worries about the very able individual, and concludes, again faithful to Royce's teaching, that personal liberties are needed, but must be achieved within the common good, not for individual, selfish potential. Thus, the need is created for the democratic community, the "national democracy" allowing true equality of opportunity for able individuals to achieve full development. He identified elements normally viewed as essential to democratic theory—majority rule, universal suffrage, individual freedoms, equality . . . but his reconstructed democracy elevated the able individual—elite of talent. Here for Croly a true democracy was less a matter of popular will than popular deliberation guided by the more able—in which argument Croly is closer to Jefferson than he realized (3).

However, sensitivity to the possible perils of the expansion of the welfare state was ever present. Croly, Bourgeois, Dewey, Hobhouse, and Lippmann endorsed the expansion of government services only because they believed that the ascendancy of democratic government should enable the state to serve its citizens rather than vice versa and the antagonism between democracy and governmental action should fall to the ground (3). Most supported a "national minimum" in health, housing, education, and work. These proposals were justified by the writings of these scholars in a belief that economic power could be brought under public control through experiments in economic regulation. Hobhouse even saw regulation as a necessary means to the fulfillment of older liberal ideas.

In fact, state power increasingly became accepted as a way of restraining excessive private advantage as reformers became eager to break the ties between corporations and political parties hobbling the public interest (50). Between 1903 and 1908, forty one state legislatures created or strengthened commissions to regulate railroads and passed additional measures, such as lobbying restrictions and direct primary laws, to enlist state government as an ally in the defense of the public interest (50). At the national level, the growth of a government structure included Roosevelt (15) actions in antitrust, declaring the public stake in conservation, reinforcing the authority of the Interstate Commerce Commission, and pushing for the means to prevent the adulteration of drugs and foodstuffs and meat. This growth in regulation and bureaucratic expansion continued under

Taft and Wilson within the same ideal of dependence on the ability of government institutions to deflect private aggrandizement.

Croly, Lippmann, and Dewey endorsed regulation in a spirit of improvisation with the fervent hope at the heart of progressivism that men would govern themselves (3). Unfortunately, later assessments belie that faith as businesses did influence the regulatory bodies, who were often not experts, and either dependent on industry for technical knowledge or partisan with close ties to regulated companies.

B.   Decentralization and the Consumer Movement

With a different solution in mind, an advocate of de-centralization, Louis D. Brandeis, Supreme Court justice, thought big business threatened self-government in two ways— directly, by overwhelming democratic institutions, and indirectly by eroding the moral and civic capacities of citizens (51). To prevent the direct superiority of business, Brandeis advocated breaking up the trusts, restoring competition, and favoring locally based enterprises (52). To forestall adverse effects on moral and civic characters of workers, Brandeis recommended a full-blown "industrial democracy" that not only included assurance of better working conditions, but a share of responsibility as well as of profits. In other words, the development of citizens capable of self-government was an end, for Brandeis, even higher than distributive justice. In agreement with many of the principles of Brandeis, Woodrow Wilson wanted to restore a decentralized economy that bred independent citizens and enabled local communities to be masters of their destinies (53). De-centralizing economic power, then, was necessary to keep the communities that cultivated the virtues self-government required (51).

Finally, a third approach to the relationship of politics, economics, and citizenship arises in the Progressive era, although its full force is to be felt much later (51) and recognition of it as the dominant focus does not arise until after World War II. The growth of issues, such as streetcar fares, high taxes, air pollution, and the use of methods of direct democracy (direct primaries, initiative, and referendum) united people as consumers and taxpayers in a new mass politics based on one's consumption identity rather than one's producer or ethnic identity (51). Both Walter Lippman and Walter Weyl noted the importance of this rise and believed democracy's best hope may lie in the solidarity of the consumer. Shifting the emphasis from democracy's role in perfecting the character of citizens, Walter Weyl rested his arguments on an utilitarian theory that more equal distribution of wealth would produce higher happiness and a contractarian (voluntarist) one of the need for economic prerequisites of genuine consent; an economic equality, as well as legal, between bargains. The change is subtle and important. Both Brandeis and Croly held onto the idea of the perfectibility of the citizen, but Weyl's propositions centered around fair treatment for the citizen-consumer (51), not citizenship or self-government. These ideas become the rallying focus of the 1990s approach to government reorganization.

VIII.   THE CITIZEN'S ROLE IN REFORMING
THE STATE

In disagreement with a concept of America built on Hobbesian or possessive individualism foundations, many Progressive intellectuals shared deep opposition to Jeffersonian localism and secular constitutionalist readings of the nation (2). They articulated an ideal of a national democratic community where equality was achieved more by sharing projects in common and by participating on the basis of equal respect than by being equally protected in one's rights. Thus, most of the Progressive thinkers, whether centralists or decentralists, acknowledged that citizenship must be at the heart of the concept of the state. Two important themes pervaded the period—the need to replace parties as the educator of citizens and the need to develop alternative loci of citizenship—the development of individuals and parainstitutions.

Prior to the turning of the twentieth century, "lodge politics," where religious convictions and national origins were interwoven with party politics and elections, ruled (54). The single moment of general election gave the increasing heterogeneity of citizens unity. The badge of sovereignty was the right to vote, which transformed scattered, suspicious individuals, if only momentarily, into a governing people (54). But, popular electoral participation and party identification declined significantly at the turn of the century. Public spaces declined as ad hoc demonstrations and marches to polls, once a way of expressing loyalty in electioneering, fell victim to various reforms: the multiplication of vagrancy laws, the increase in urban police surveillance, the loss of public grazing and hunting lands, and the restriction of African-Americans from areas in the South. This closing off of public spaces diminished the act of voting as an affirmation of who one was in the community and coupled with the Australian ballot made voting an individualized private act (54). Events of the time along with Progressive ideals limited the ability of political parties to serve as the rallying focus for citizenship and citizen education.

To dissolve the unholy alliance between corrupt business and corrupt politics was seen as a task of statesmanship in the progressive movement. The democratic individualism under the blessings of constitutional property rights was repeated in economics and produced machine politics that were equally unaccountable, equally invisible, corrupting, and powerful. Thus, regulation, the development of responsible citizenship, and educating citizens was necessary. Educating citizens, a former task of political parties, was to be assumed in Progressive minds by labor unions, moral and political reform movements, settlement houses, and universities along with town, church, school, and family. The earlier roots of this ideal were early nineteenth century ideas of free institutions. These included town, church and school as well as the earlier Puritan notion of family as "little commonwealth." This formulation was expanded to make the institutions of labor unions, political reform movements, settlement houses, and universities "parastates," being supportive of government both by producing good citizens and by carrying out substantive ends desired of an ideal state. The Progressive argument envisions the party as reinforcing constitutional formalism where parastates circumvented and subverted it (2). This conception provides a thorny problem of accountability—what is the cost of locating citizenship and exercise of power outside of constitutionally mandated boundaries? The progressivism answer was that party politics is corrupt and hidden, but the parastates were visible, and thus accountable to the citizenry.

The concept of the new parastates reveals the Progressive critique of nineteenth century American regime as a national-democratic civic humanism, including a stress on public virtue and higher citizenship, but still relying upon tradition, both religious and politico-cultural (2). Civic humanism, both ancient and modern, enshrines patriotism, and patriotism requires narrative discourse and collective memory. Civic humanism asks every citizen to defend the republic and save it from degradation and despotism by making new memories emulating the old and thereby refounding the original memory. According to Eldon Eisenach,

> Both the myth of New England and its refoundings in Revolution, Constitution, and Civil War—and the biblical historical framework of evangelical Protestantism, with its jeremiad rituals of civic religion—were integral to Progressive understanding of American nationality and the public doctrines Progressives shaped (55).

Thus, citizenship was not a separate identity in the Civic Republican-Communitarian tradition in competition with a private self, but an integral part of one's personality. One cannot say that the Progressive concept of the relationship between citizen and the state immediately took hold in mainstream public administration (56). Although many scholars would fault the development of public administration for not emphasizing enough the concept of citizenship (57), the progressives' concept of citizenship is important to the critique. For Mary Parker Follet, John Dewey, and most Progressives, the state is first located in the good citizen, who, in whatever role and location, spontaneously acts according to consciously held and shared ideas of the public good. Mary Parker Follett in *The New State* (1918) gives us her concept of a true definition of liberty—a person acting as the state in every smallest detail of life (6). Where is the state? Wherever good citizens gather, organize, and act. From the ranks of Follett and Dewey, there can be no "state" without a people. Thus, the first location of the state must be an internalized idea of membership by citizens sharing values. Dewey extended this idea to that of the state as emancipator of personal capacities, securing to each individual an effective right to count in the order and movement of society as a whole (6). From the standpoint of ethics, the moral test of a practice or a law became whether it sets free individual capacities in such a way as to make them available for the development of the general happiness or the common good.

Both Follett and Dewy thought the democratic state was an achievement to be won in the future (6). Where then to exercise citizenship? First, attempts should be made to reform constitutions, government, and parties. If that fails, the good citizen participates in government institutions that contain the substantive public good. The higher ideal of citizenship as public service was enhanced by the influence of women's growing participation in public life. Whether teacher, charity worker, or mother, all were participating in the task of acting out ideals of public good and therefore "acting as the state in every smallest detail of life." A good citizen is state oriented, according to the Progressives, in the sense of seeking to achieve a larger public good in all his/her actions (6).

IX. RECONCILING DEMOCRACY AND ADMINISTRATION: ADMINISTRATION AND REFORM

Reflecting the themes proposed above and interwoven with them was an argument still at the heart of public administration—how to reconcile democracy and administration. Dwight Waldo claims that in the Progressive era, a political theory was evolved that made a virtue of the obligation to reconcile democracy and efficiency (2). In his opinion, the heart of Progressivism contained a basic conflict between those whose future vision was that of a planned and administered society, often preferring a nationalist perspective—and those who believed institutional and social readjustments would yield natural and inevitable processes to produce the greatest possible good—often preferring a decentralist or consumer perspective. The latter group continued to remain firm in the old liberal faith in an underlying harmony, and, according to Waldo, felt that the cure for democracy is more democracy. Proposed were such reforms as the initiative, the referendum, the recall, the direct election of senators, home rule, and proportional representation within the belief that the future must well up from below. In opposition were those whose patience was exhausted waiting for the good life, who had begun to think of planning and realized democracy must re-think its position and institutions and needed a strong right arm for the State in form of an efficient bureaucracy. Theirs was a belief that the future must be shaped from above. Students of administration were more drawn to the alternative of a planned and managed society in contrast to the American ideals which approved of "efficient citizens" more than "trained administrators" (2).

Exactly what role the administrators should play in the new society being envisioned differed among the thinkers of the day. The newly emerging professional middle class viewed good administration as the solution to many social and economic problems and saw civil service as a source of employment. Spokesmen for this group included Woodrow Wilson, Frank Goodnow, Thorstein Veblen, and Walter Weyl, of whom Wilson and Goodnow are most important for public administration (58). One of the concerns of Woodrow Wilson was the actions of party organizations resulting in corruption and politicization of administration and micromanagement of administrative matters. Wilson wanted to clarify the responsibility of administrators by freeing them from the kind of interference which obscured accountability. Although Paul Van Riper has observed that Wilson's famous essay, "On the Study of Administration," was not influential until after World War I, Wilson's articulation of the defense for administration exemplifies the concerns of the period (59). Contrary to most interpretations, which credit Wilson with advancing a strict separation of the two, leaving administration only to execute, recent scholarship argues that Wilson's had a broader conception of administration, including the exercise of discretion and a responsibility to public opinion (60). Van Riper asserts that Wilson wanted to advance the "partisan (not political) neutrality" of the civil service (60). James Stever maintains that Wilson joined other organic idealists in arguing that professional administrators could contribute to the stable evolution of American democracy (58). Believing the past significantly constrained social reform, Woodrow Wilson preferred incremental steps in administration and respected tradition as a guide. Thus, one reading of the "The Study of Administration" is that Wilson attempted to fit the administrator into what he viewed as the evolutionary flow of society. The "Study of Administration," in James Stever's conception becomes an exercise in reassurance, where Wilson tries to demonstrate that the integration of administration into liberal government could be painless.

Frank Goodnow, who has also been somewhat misrepresented as seeing a dichotomy, instead proclaims some continuity between the political and administrative spheres (61). Classifying government actions in two functions—the expression of popular will through legislation and the execution of that will through judicial decisions and administration, Goodnow argued that certain aspects of administration should be protected from politics. When engaged in the general executing of the law, according to Goodnow, administration must be controlled carefully by the legislature or an outside entity. Goodnow argued that the traditional political institutions should constrain administrative reform processes in order to make popular government viable (58). Like the early Wilson, portions of Goodnow's scholarship also stress the need for the evolutionary development of American liberal democracy. Goodnow thus argues that popular government need not be disrupted by competent administrative agencies and can function alongside traditional political institutions such as political parties (58).

Early interpretations of the Progressives promoted a rather naive strict separation of politics and administration. James Stever argues that Goodnow's and Wilson's message that the administrator was a safe innovation, "an instrumental technician functioning dutifully within the existing political system," was meant as a reassuring message to other elements of the Progressive coalition, such as the Populists, who were skeptical of taking power away from the people (58). From a different point, James Svara argues that both Wilson, Goodnow, and other of their contemporaries are much more worried about partisan politics in the content of their writing per se, not about legitimate involvement of administrators in policy making. Either interpretation nullifies the alleged naiveté of an insurmountable wall between politics and administration, a separation more prominent in the mechanistic writings of the twenties and thirties, according to James Svara.

In comparison to Goodnow and Wilson, the pragmatists disavowed tradition by grounding administration in analytical/scientific reason. John Dewey, Mary Parker Follett, Walter Lippmann, and Theodore Veblen continually urged the theme of casting off tradition and cooperatively applying logical reason to social problems (58). The pragmatists did not envision the administrator under the control of incrementally oriented party regulars, but instead viewed administrators as a new class skilled in logical reasoning and adept at applying the scientific method to social problems. This new pragmatic administrator was to obey the dictates of logic as well as conclusions drawn from scientific experimentation (58).

The foregoing discussion about the attempts to reconcile administration and democracy yields two interesting syntheses. One by Laurence O'Toole, is that the "orthodoxy of reform" is retained to reconcile the tensions of bureaucracy and democracy (18). He sees the field's dialogue emanating from a "continual tension-filled struggle on the part of those who are deeply committed to some vision of democracy, but who see the seeming inevitability of large-scale governmental bureaucracy" (62). The result, according to O'-Toole, is that the administrative tradition most followed was developed by individuals hostile to ideology, who banked on experience, and who simultaneously exalted the ideal of democracy and the efficiency of technique. Observations of a slightly different type are those of James Monrone who asserts that the Progressives' concept of administration actually complimented the concept of democracy (63). In other words, rather than seeing the two concepts necessarily in tension, Monrone posits they share an underlying motif. Each concept calls for operating beyond politics; each requires digging below partisan claims and clashing interests for the objective public interest of a cohesive people. The new public administration would efficiently implement the public will articulated through the newly purified democratic mechanisms. If you look at them together, the two parts do form a coherent view—one eschews subjective private interest for an objective public one; the other spurs a multitude of special constituencies for a single universalistic people (63). As James Monrone observes,

> In the recurring quest for the people, Americans redesign political institutions and rewrite political rules. The direct results have been uneven; some efforts enhance popular control, some attenuate it, some seem to manage both. Paradoxically, the unanticipated consequences are more constant. The institutions designed to enhance democracy expand the scope and authority of the state, especially its administrative capacity. A great irony propels American political development: the search for more direct democracy builds up the bureaucracy (64).

In Monrone's terms, a classical republican faith emerged with scientific experts playing a role roughly like the one of natural leaders. Thus, the republican faith becomes a view of representation, even if it is premised on an objective public interest. A formula for reconciling democracy and administration became that of substituting the division of labor and specialization of functions for separation of powers in a plan to simplify voters' tasks and make government responsible (63). Provided was a concentration of executive power and responsibility, securing for the chief executive the necessary tools for economical and efficient management, establishing the institutional devices in addition to popular elections for guarding against administrative incompetence, dishonesty (63). Principles issued included the short ballot, the increasing of executive's appointment power, abolition of overlapping terms, abortions of boards, reduction in the number of departments, and provisions for executive leadership in forming and executing the budget and the merit system. The fact that a division of labor and specialization of functions is far from the protection intended by a government of separation of powers became buried under the zeal for efficiency. This misconception of a polity as an organization sets up a misunderstanding of the role of the president in the Brownlow Committee during the New Deal. Further, administration in a polity becomes hopelessly confused with the concept of management in an organization, and particularly one type of management, "scientific management," as described below (65).

X.   REORGANIZING WORKLIFE: THE EMERGENCE OF SCIENTIFIC MANAGEMENT

One who turned the emphasis on scientific experimentation into the basis for a new management philosophy, "scientific management," was Frederick Winslow Taylor, an industrial engineer (66). Taylor attempted to inaugurate a positivist, scientific way of human interrelations, standing outside his material and contemplating an objective system of rules, workers' selection, workers' education and development, and intimate cooperation between management and men. Taylor's major thesis was that the maximum good for all society can come only through the cooperation of management and labor in the application of scientific methods (67). Both Frederick Taylor and W. H. Willoughby express belief in emergence of scientific principles from the study of data, often referred to as the "one best way," because a principle is the one best way emerging from scientific study of facts (2). There is also an emphasis on one best man because different tasks call for different qualities of inheritance and training, which can be discovered through experimentation. To maximize output, Taylor felt the scientific method had to be applied to worker selection, job determination, and the creation of proper environment. Taylor pushed for labor and management to coordinate in order to maximize the benefits for both—wages and profits. The finding of one best way and one best man are encompassed in a wide acceptance of efficiency and fact finding.

In testimony before Congress on the Eastern Rate Case in 1911, Taylor envisioned scientific management as a complete mental revolution on the part of the workingman toward their work, their fellow men, and their employers and on the part of their managers toward fellow workers and daily problems, much in the same way we hear of Total Quality Management today. Using five principles (research, standards, planning, control, and cooperation), Taylor assimilated and applied ideas that were useful to effective management. For Taylor, the first principle of scientific management is the deliberate gathering together of the great mass of traditional knowledge, recording it, tabulating it, reducing it to rules, laws, and mathematical formula. These new laws, then, are applied with the cooperation of the management to the work of the workmen. What was truly revolutionary was bringing into the business world the ideas of research, investigation, and analysis, ideas that produced more emphasis on evolutionary changes rather than abrupt revolutionary practices.

As Hindy Schachter observes (69), scientific management was most attractive to public-sector-oriented Progressive reformers, even more than to business leaders. Key progressives perceived shop management as a means for initiating organizational reform on a manageable and practical scale without damaging business. Many saw in scientific management a way to decrease the conceptual gap between the status-rich professional and the underdog workers. Taylor indicates his empathy with Progressive reformers through serializing Principles in *American Magazine*, a journal known for publishing reform writers, and fighting for American Society of Mechanical Engineers to hold a conference on air pollution. The ideas to which Justice Louis Brandeis, public manager Morris Cooke, manager and author Henry Gantt, activist Ira Tarbell, and management theorist Frank Gilbreth were attracted included Taylor's emphasis on noneconomic motivation, checking arbitrary supervisors for system gains, allowing talented mechanics to rise into planning, and the idea of training and developing men (70).

Although Taylor never published ideas directly related to Public Administration, his associate Morris Cooke, who had a distinguished public sector executive career, did link work analysis to the Progressive cause and published in several social science journals along with Charles Merriam and Harold Lasswell. Contrary to many interpretations of Taylor, neither Taylor nor Cooke, according to Schachter, posit efficiency as the goal (69). Cooke, whose contributions were to local government, believed government was basically a conversion mechanism for public demands, and, thus, citizen groups should assume the lion's share of setting organizational agendas. Although he can be justly critiqued for not being more specific about just how one would measure responsiveness, Cooke builds on Taylor's work in valuing merit for personnel selection. Cooke also tackled the question of the "expert" in administration in striving to democratize expertise by forcing the public sector engineer to put his ideas up for acceptance or disapproval by the interested public (71). Cooke does not stress the dichotomy, but instead emphasizes that some distribution channels favor one group while others favor another (72).

Frederick Winslow Taylor is the writer of the scientific management school whose ideas and name have persisted in public management. Taylor's influence has been particularly noted on the New York Bureau of Municipal Research, incorporated May 1907, and equated with the founding of the discipline. Those Charles Beard called the ABC powers, William H. Allen, Henry Bruere, and Frederick A. Cleveland and close associates, R. Fulton Cutting and Charles Beard, led what others have called the 'Municipal Reform" movement. According to Dwight Waldo, the Bureau was sensitive to appeals and promises of science; discovery of facts as solution, but tired of the moralism of the nineteenth century (2). Ardent apostles of the efficiency idea and leaders in the movement for useful education, these reformers disliked big business, but liked the business organization and pushed for many of the same principles in government that were being pushed for business with scientific management. Not only was the desire to make organizations more efficient, but to make citizens also. The Bureau pushed to educate citizens to assist them with civic awareness and militancy, efficiency, useful education, ideals that formed the core of what Dwight Waldo calls the Efficient Citizenship movement. Their vision was that true democracy consists in intelligent cooperation between citizens and those elected or appointed to serve, an ideal still present in public administration. In the efforts to organize techniques to help agencies perform task more expeditiously and to give citizens the data needed to maintain control over their governments, the Bureau reflects many of the same ideas of Taylor and his circle.

XI. RECONSTRUCTING THE RULES FOR ORGANIZING

Along with the movement to understand management from a different perspective, a movement was underway to protect the public interest through administrative expertise—in local, state, and national government. Thomas Pegram says it well,

> because the progressive understanding of democracy leaned so heavily on the ideal of the public interest, the search for responsible democratic forms led progressives away from the grassroots and into the corridors of bureaucratic expertise and executive leadership (73).

This move toward executive leadership followed the movement to thwart the spoils system, the evolution of a merit system, and the recent development of bureaucracy. During the heyday of the "spoils system," Andrew Jackson had pushed for rotation of men in and out of office in a fast growing civil service. One answer to the chaos created by rotation and fast growth was a rudimentary national bureaucracy. Under Jackson, Amos Kendall organized the postal service, with the watchwords, "organize, organize." He routinized relationships between subordinates, created an elaborate system of accounts, introduced quarterly reports and intricate systems of cross-checking, reforms that spread to other departments. Developed also were related innovations of functional specialization, executive staffs, a bureaucracy of linked offices within each agency, and efficiency records that marked officials on "competence, faithfulness, and attention" (74). These inventions permitted spoilsmen to be "placed and replaced without upsetting the integrity of the whole" (74). Thus, Jacksonians introduced new state capacities while articulating an antistatist faith. They had tried to organize recruitment to administrative service (75) and at least partially, then, the American public service was first fashioned to shore up the nineteenth-century party scramble for spoils.

In many other eyes, the major purpose of reform was to restore ability, high character, and true public spirit once more to their legitimate spheres in our public life and to make active politics once more attractive to men of self-respect and high patriotic aspirations (76). The Pendleton Act had reflected that discretionary appointments promoted spoils and that fixed rules, even if imperfect, are better than arbitrary power. The Act was considered a viable means of destroying the power base of the professional politicians who had risen to a position of dominance in national politics under the assumption that to abolish spoils, appointments must cease to be discretionary.

In the same spirit as the Pendleton Act, reformers pushed for other assurances of good government. Their previous experience in public affairs led reformers to believe that, democratic government became mostly a scramble for private advantage. To prevent that, a virtuous commitment to public interest was needed. For the reformers, efficient democratic government could not exist without trusting that commitment would come from expert members of regulatory commissions, appointive boards, and state agencies. This trust, sometimes justified, did have the effect, along with the other forces of industrialization, of distancing the affected, physically, economically, and politically from those who made decisions. An even greater consequence came from the fact that partisanship ran through the new government structure and executive stakeholders, who doubled as ambitious partisan leaders, were the ones responsible to advance the public interest (73).

At the federal level, the executive departments themselves underwent a tremendous change in the period from 1860 to 1920 (77). If we define bureaucracy as formal, hierarchical organization managed by salaried officials according to impersonal enforced, written rules, then the post Civil War federal government was far from this end. Steven Skowronek documents the systematic failures of the late nineteenth century to carry out tasks that were being routinely done by European national governments (78). After 1883, the creation of civil service contributed to the formalization of certain procedures. However, throughout the late nineteenth century, the political patronage system, the considerable power afforded low-level supervisors, and the diverse nature of federal clerical work continued to inject much of the personal and unofficial into Washington offices (79). At the turn of the century, the continual growth prompted officials to try more rationalized methods of administering offices and evaluating workers (79). For example, Richard Henry Dana's *Merit Principle of the Selection of the Higher Municipal Officers of 1903* moves concern from the theological and moral in selection to urging the necessity for experts, suggesting a separation of policy determination from execution, and testing to distinguish executive ability (80).

As the Progressive movement grew from the attacks on the parties and the spoils system, calls for reform lead to the justifications that became part of Progressive ideology. On first view, it appears that many of the Progressives appeared ambivalent about the capacity of the national government in setting norms and in administering spending and regulation programs. Remembering that many Progressives believed the "parainstitutions" would be able to perform these tasks somewhat explains this ambivalence, as some reluctantly came to realize that greater state capacity was needed for the task. Also, Americans did not then, or have they ever, had a concept of a highly educated authoritative civil service in the same way the Europeans have had.

Out of the Progressive reformers' ambivalence and the parties' desires to keep the bureaucracy from being autonomous developed another peculiar American compromise, an emphasis on a specific type of professionalism. The upper civil service became dominated by those trained in a variety of professions. The role structure centered on job descriptions and specific skills or expertise, with permeable barriers, and no clearly delineated series of positions. There were relatively wide entrance gates, allowing access based on skill levels at many points, but well-defined career paths were not numerous. Instead, technical professions were emphasized, a system of grouping positions in classes horizontally across the entire structure. These choices in organizational design limited the autonomy of bureaucracy, but still left some leadership from experts (81). Part of the justification for the specialized expert knowledge came from the growing acceptance of technical rationality. Yet, the compartmentalization of knowledge demanded by technical rationality led to a practice without context or time. Included in the model of professionalism was the development of professional associations, a cognitive scientific base, institutionalized training, licensing, work autonomy, colleague control, and a code of ethics (26).

Accompanying the emphasis on professionalism was a tendency toward centralization at both the state and local level, a tendency toward increasing the power of the executive and/or toward principles of management. In 1898, the model charter of the national municipal review recommended concentration of administrative power in the mayor and in 1917 recommended moving to a professional manager. In state reorganizations, the ex-altation of the powers of the executive branch prompted a rash of schemes for joining leg-islative and executive and/or restraining judicial and increasing the authority of the chief executive. Further, local merchants decried the inefficiency of the party state. Joined by the rising professional classes, businessmen, social workers, and lawyers wanted to see "business principles" brought into the "business of government." When the Research movement turned from bookkeeping systems to the basic relations between legislature and executive, proponents thought the efficiencies of business procedure required the business concentration of authority. These beliefs became part of the argument for the ex-altation of executive power and centralization.

In summary, the cures proposed by Progressives included rationalization, system-ization, coordination, and efficiency. Methods proposed included centralized budgets, general accounting offices, bureaus of efficiency, commissions on economy, committees on department methods, and expert leadership (63). On a more complex level, public personnel administration must inevitably reflect the regime norms and values of political system. Some scholars have stressed the lasting effects of the emphasis on neutral compe-tence in Progressive arguments to the detriment of an emphasis on representativeness and leadership (80). Yet, more recent scholarship emphasizes that the Progressives asked even more of these new experts. In a recent paper, James Svara recalls that Richard Childs, god-father of the council-manager plan, felt that mangers would be successful if they could lead their commission into great new enterprises of service. Thus, in Svara's view, the Pro-gressive image of the manager combined idealism and pragmatism. Desired was a new type of administrator with expertise and commitment to public service (81). In fact, Her-bert Croly's decision to write *The Promise of American Life* was partially a response to Robert's Grant's concern that specialized work was not properly appreciated or encour-aged in American culture. Croly captures the spirit in his call for an administrator who is "something more than an expert. He is the custodian of a social purpose . . . He must share the faith upon which the program depends for its impulse" (82).

XII. PROGRESSIVISM A CENTURY LATER

Connective links wind to, through, and from the Progressive Era and to the loose collec-tion of ideas of the turn of the century, Progressivism. Out of the multitudinous directions and ideologies of the Progressive period, I chose to emphasize above the themes of Pro-gressivism that grappled with some of the major issues of the Progressive period and that remained within the Public Administration literature as enduring controversies. Although the idea of reform was not new in American politics, the fervency with which the idea of reform was held has not often been seen in the American culture. These reformers re-peated again and again the solutions of science as expertise and instrumental rationality as the fortification for decisions.

Yet the linkage of scientific methodology to reform frayed. The professional social workers and many reformers suggested that practical education for the mass of citizenry was a more appropriate use of resources than searching for scientific law. The "peculiar" attitude of the amateur to both value truth and wish to make truth useful did not survive in most of academia. In Furmer's words, "Whether the practitioners were academics or not, a constant tension between knowledge and reform was characteristic at every stage" (83). Although the academic social scientists were as reform-minded as the amateurs, they wrapped their reform intentions in the cloak of professional prerogative and the tension was thus transformed into a conflict between advocacy and objectivity (83). Basing their claims on the objectivity of social science, the social scientists, according to Furmer, followed a path of glorification of research skills, increased specialization, developed a fundamental conservatism toward a liberal consensus, and abandoned their original mission, the comprehensive assessment of industrial society, ironically the condition that had fostered the professionalization of social science (83). Currently, the lament of forsaking the reform motif for a "social science" perspective is raised in public administration, a lament whose basis is found in the development of the social sciences within the Progressive period.

Also found in the Progressive era are both the continuance of age-old political questions and the outlines of modern debates on decentralization and citizen control. Certainly, the numerous battles surrounding the relationships of government and private power in a democracy began before the Constitution and emerge in new form almost every decade. Whether that relationship is better set through regulation from the top or through decentralization and devolution dates back at least to the Anti-Federalist-Federalist argument. The arguments about the whether and how of an American administrative state bubble up in the 1800s, but really receive a place on the national agenda in the Progressive era, again to be forcefully debated in the New Deal and from that period forward in American politics. The need for democracy to control concentrated economic power, the need for an administrative state, and the need to keep a concept of citizenship at the heart of the concept of the state all served as the basis for criticism of governing institutions at the turn of the century and continue as the basis around which controversy swirls in the theory and practice of administration. Of particular significance for public administration in this period are the arguments made by Frank Goodnow and Woodrow Wilson that for administration to execute its special duties, there must be a separation from partisan politics, an issue current enough to reappear with a new interpretation and a new solution every decade.

Another of the Progressive concerns, that the development of an educated active citizenry will be neglected, can be found in Anti-Federalist writing and even the Federalists spoke of national citizenship. Yet, the arguments of the Progressive era, at least momentarily, combined the Anti-Federalist arguments for citizen education with the Federalists' national perspective. On the surface, the arguments for democracy's control of concentrated economic power and the need for an administration state may seem to contradict an emphasis on an efficient citizen. However, what was unique in the combination was the tying of the concept of citizenship to each citizens' actions in their immediate environment through the parastates, and seeing such actions as related to citizenship in a national community. When E. J. Eisenach speaks of the "lost promise of progressivism," it is this connection to both local and national community he laments, a lament that becomes a dominant theme in the last part of the twentieth century.

On a different scale, the new ideas about management, science, and democracy become attached to the growing interest in how to organize work, an interest spurred by the tremendous growth in the economy and society. No matter whether one judges Taylor as hero or villain in organizational theory and practice, his contribution to a focus on the workplace, the relationships there, and the processes connecting what had been seen as discrete jobs is undeniable. Links from the ideas of Taylor and others of scientific management combined in multitudinous ways and interlocked with the beginning of the Municipal Bureau of Research. Its efforts to both study government and improve it, to draw in

academic expertise to governing, and to educate the citizenry to be better critics and partners of those governing are just a few of those links. From these multiple sources grew
canons of practice for both students and practitioners of administration, some of great
value and some misconceived.

The turning of the century encouraged citizens to begin thinking on a different
scale—a shift of emphasis from community to society, from ethnic and other tribalisms to
larger social units, from natural, unconscious order to a conscious social one—one subject
to social control (13). The locus of the public sphere expanded and moved away from
many smaller general spaces to increasingly distant centralized places characterized by specialization and professionalization. The movement away from parties as an unifying theme
went in many directions—toward greater participation in neighborhoods, in communities,
in volunteer groups, in formal work organizations, toward a sense of national citizenry, and
toward nonparticipation. Yet, the real locus of the public sphere—balanced precariously in
many reformers' minds in the informed citizen—moved away from individuals and toward
more professional management at the city and state level and toward more formal organizations and institutions at the national level. The belief that the executive was more likely
to carry out the public good helps explain to some extent some of the fascination with autonomous political executives, e.g., strong-mayor or city-manager forms of urban government. Accompanying that belief was the dissemination of much of the public dialogue of
the island communities of the 1800s to more specialized niches within public organizations, bureaus, agencies, and local governments. In many cases, the sense of being connected to publicness lost a concrete referent in actual physical space and abandoned some
of its immediacy and intimacy in a trend toward an abstraction of "the public" and lack of
citizen involvement that would be again regretted at the approach of a new century.

Although an interplay among the elements of Progressivism and pluralism defined
much of the content and led to many of the conflicts that shaped early twentieth-century
American social policy-making, Progressive attitudes did face two powerful counterforces.
First, in issue after issue, the search for ways of enhancing social conformity collided with
American pluralism, as a variety of ideas emerged from the same economic and social developments. Another countering force was the weight of the past, the persistence—even
the strengthening—of the traditional social values and beliefs which found expression in a
variety of forms: localism, individualism, religious fundamentalism, and laissez-faire (13).
Partially because of this resistance, the thoughts of major progressive intellectuals, such as
Edward A. Ross, were characterized by a belief in and search for policies designed to restore an American social cohesion whose loss they regarded as a major casualty of modern
times. To replace the rejection of individualism and socialism, the answer of Ross was "the
principle of order and organization," applied to the improvement of individuals and institutions (13). This answer, what historian Robert Wiebe calls, "The Search for Order" is repeated over and over again in the Progressive dialogue.

The answer of order and organization to pluralism's demands brings us into the
realm of what Dwight Waldo calls insoluble problems (2). Whether couched as a question
of the relationship between art and science, self and community, citizen and nation, or
politics and administration, the turn of the century philosophers, thinkers, scientists, administrators, and citizens appeared caught up in reforms that gave somewhat different answers to how one reconciles freedom and order. Laurence O'Toole makes a strong case
that the notion of reform itself seems to provide an organizing idea which transcends the
dogmas of earlier days. He, along with political theorist Michael J. Sandel, speculate that
any solution to the freedom-order debate will demand large-scale normative political the-

ory. Eldon J. Eisenach finds the same controversies emerging in the revival of Communitarian thinking and believes re-examination of the relationship between individual rights and community would be a good beginning for a more satisfactory understanding of the dialectic between freedom and order.

Whether or not current political dialogue leads us to better synthesis of the demands for freedom and the demands for order (84), we can credit the Progressives for enhancing the debate. They sharpened the credibility of polar positions, and momentarily proposed several solutions: those of increased nationalism and those celebrating decentralization and localism, those enhancing direct democracy and those increasing bureaucracy, those favoring development of social self and of scientific management. Although the delicate balancing leaves us somewhat perplexed, that is characteristic of a nation which always yearns for the direct rule and communal nature of an agrarian colony in the midst of a dense postindustrial society (63). As James Monrone so aptly reveals:

> At bottom, however, the Progressive reform turned on two apparently contradictory ideals: First, the reformers would strip public power from corrupted political officials and vest it directly in the people . . . At the same time, experts would be responsible for administration; they would shun politics for scientific facts. At the heart of the Progressive agenda lay a political paradox: government would be simultaneously returned to the people and placed beyond them, in the hands of the expert . . . Both their administrative science and their direct democracy rested on the assumption of united, virtuous, communitarian people sharing an objective public interest. Once again, the ambiguous image of "the people" served to meld an uneven coalition of interests and philosophies. . . . they embraced the democratic wish, seeking communal constituencies that were part memory and part myth (85).

In doing so, out of Progressivism came both the scaffolding for the administrative state and the dread of it, and most of all, a founding dialogue about public administration, out of part memory and part myth.

NOTES

1. R. Hofstadter, *The Progressive Movement, 1900–1915*, Englewood Cliffs, NJ: Prentice Hall, Inc., 1963.
2. D. Waldo, *The Administrative State*, New York: Holmes and Meier Publishers, Inc., 1984.
3. E. A. Stettner, *Shaping Modern Liberalism: Herbert Croly and Progressive Thought*, Lawrence, Kansas: University Press of Kansas, 1993.
4. R. Hofstadter, 1963; E. J. Eisenach, *The Lost Promise of Progressivism*, Lawrence, Kansas: University Press of Kansas, 1994; and M. Keller, *Affairs of State: Public Life in Late Nineteenth Century*, Mass, Harvard University Press, Cambridge, 1977.
5. Weber believed the risks involved in equating politics with morality might outweigh the potential benefits. J. T. Kloppenberg, *Uncertain Victory, Social Democracy and Progressivism in European and American Thought*, 18701920. New York:, Oxford University Press,1986.
6. E. J. Eisenach, *The Lost Promise of Progressivism*, Lawrence, Kansas: University Press of Kansas, 1994.
7. D. Waldo, 1984, p. 18.
8. M. Keller, *Affairs of State: Public Life in Late Nineteenth Century*, p. 2.
9. J. T. Kloppenberg, 1986, p. 199.
10. R. Audi (ed.), *The Cambridge Dictionary of Philosophy*, Cambridge: Cambridge University Press, 1995.

11. D. Ross, *The Origins of American Social Science*, Cambridge: Cambridge University Press, 1991, p. xiv.

12. D. Ross, 1991, p. xv.

13. M. Keller, 1977, pp. 2–4.

14. See M. Keller, 1977, for details.

15. See M. Keller, 1977, for fuller bibliographic information.

16. See R. S. Silberman, *Cages of Reason: The Rise of the Rational State in France, Japan, the United States, and Great Britain*, Chicago: The University of Chicago Press, 1993.

17. E. A. Stettner, 1993, pp. 2–3.

18. L. O'Toole, Jr., "American Public Administration and the Idea of Reform," *Administration and Society*: 16; 141–166, (1984).

19. B. P. DeWitt, *The Progressive Movement*, New York, 1915 and C. A. and M. R. Beard, *The Rise of American Civilization*, 2 vols., New York, 1927.

20. G. Mowry, *The California Progressives*, Berkeley, Cal., 1951; A. D. Chandler, Jr., "The Origins of Progressive Leadership", *The Letters of Theodore Roosevelt*, (E. E. Morrison, ed.) 8 vols., Cambridge, Mass., 1951–54; and R. Hofstadter, *The Age of Reform: From Bryan to F.D.R.*, New York, 1955.

21. R. Wiebe, *The Search for Order*, 1877–1920, Greenwood Press, 1967.

22. G. Kolko, *The Triumph of Conservatism*, New York: Free Press, 1963. Reprint, Quadrango Books, Chicago, 1967.

23. A. S. Link and R. L. McCormick, *Progressivism*, Illinois: Arlington Heights, 1983.

24. Finally, one stream that did associate itself with the progressivism movement is not considered here. Some wished to return the nation to what was considered its destiny of white Anglo-Saxon Protestantism through prohibition, immigration restriction, and racial segregation, a theme that reappears in the history of the nation, but does not receive serious philosophical consideration in the field of public administration.

25. J. T. Kloppenberg, p. 313.

26. G. B. Adams, "Enthralled with Modernity, The Historical Context of Knowledge and Theory Development in Public Administration," *Pub. Admin. Rev.*: 52; 363–373 (1992).

27. B. S. Turner, ed. *Theories of Modernity and Postmodernity*, London: Sage Publications, 1990. Quoted in G. B. Adams, "Enthralled with Modernity," 1992.

28. L. O'Toole, "American Public Administration," 1984, p. 145.

29. M. White, *Social Thought in America*, Beacon Press, Bost, 1957, quoted in G. B. Adams, "Enthralled in Modernity," 1992, p. 374.

30. J. Stever, "The Dual Image of the Administration in Progressive Administrative Theory," *Admin. Soc.*: 22; 39–57.

31. See J. L. Stafford, *Pragmatism and the Progressive Movement*, Lathem, Maryland: University Press of America, 1987; and D. N. Shalin, "G. H. Mead, Socialism and the Progressive Agenda," *AJS*: 93;913–951 (1988).

32. A. Mayhew, *Journal of Economic Issues JEI*: 21; 971–998(1987). See also Philip Mirrowski, "The Philosophical Bases of Institutionalism," *JEI*: 21;1001–1038 (1987). J. E. Jackson (editor), *Institutions in American Society: Essays in Market, Political and Social Organizations*, The University of Michigan Press, Ann Arbor, 1993; and the fall 1995 issue of *Polity*, volume XXVIII for a discussion of early institutionalism.

33. A. Mayhew, p. 992.

34. J. D. White and G. B. Adams, *Research in Public Administration: Reflections on Theory and Practice*, Thousand Oaks, CA.: Sage Publications, 1994.

35. See also John J. Hirlin, "The Big Questions of Public Administration," Unpublished Manuscript. School of Public Administration, University of Southern California, August 1995.

36. C. Stivers, *Gender Images in Public Administration: Legitimacy and the Administrative State*, Newbury Park, CA: Sage Publications, 1993.

37. M. Keller, pp. 4–5.

38. M. Keller, p. 5.

39. See J. Dewey, *Principles of Psychology*, 1890 and Morton G. White, *Social Thought in America: The Revolt Against Formalism* (1949).

40. The rise of scientific methods is discussed in P. T. Manicas, 1987, Dorothy Ross, 1991, and M. O. Furner, *Advocacy and Objectivity: A Crisis in the Professionalization of American Social Sciences, 1865–1905*, The University Press of Kentucky, 1975.

41. See M. O. Furmer 1975 and P. T. Manicas, 1987. The conditions for a technocratic kind of social science were almost perfect in the United States—a lack of a class based professorate, fantastic new growth including possibilities for a professional, practical social science, and the belief that all problems could be solved. In the Progressive mind, what was needed was a solid science basis not only for the technical arts and learned professions, but for commerce, government, and social relations.

42. P. T. Manicas, *A History and Philosophy of the Social Sciences*, Oxford: Basil Blackwell, Ltd., 1987, p. 211.

43. T. Veblen as quoted in P. T. Manicas, 1987, p. 215.

44. M. J. Sandel, *Democracy's Discontent: America in Search of a Public Philosophy*, Cambridge, Mass.: Harvard University Press, 1996.

45. Kloppenberg observes that there is a gap between theory and practice. Although the values proposed were laudatory, e.g., benevolence, the scholarship of our time reveals that the Progressive theorists did not dwell long enough on the concept of power and how it may slip between theory and practice. In other words, interest groups often bent policies to their own aggrandizement

46. Max Weber, whose writings are not influential to public administration until much later, doubted the people's ability to mobilize around a nonpartisan public interest. Separate from other theorists of progressivism by his pessimism, Max Weber feared that concentration of power in corporate capitalism and a new class of managers would not lead to social harmony and public ownership, but instead to the domination of society by bureaucrats. Weber reasoned that the locus of struggle would simply shift, for regardless of the economic system, he concluded, "politics means conflict."

47. H. Croly, "The New World and the New Art," *Architectural Record*, 12; 53 (1902) In the spirit of nationalism further to be admired by many progressives was Theodore Roosevelt whom Croly saw as "Hamiltonian" with a difference . . . adding in the other half of the ideal of which Hamilton was afraid, the people. Croly supports Roosevelt fully in his first term, but falls in and out of favor with Roosevelt during the Progressive era.

48. H. Croly, *The Promise of American Life*, Macmillan, 1909. Reprint, Archon Books, Hamden, Conn., p. 278.

49. Croly takes the French triad—Liberty and equality are contradictory, but fraternity could conciliate the principles.

50. T. Pegram, *Partisans and Progressives: Private Interest and Public Policy in Illinois, 1870–1922*, Urbana, IL: University of Illinois Press, 1992.

51. See the discussion in M. Sandel, 1995.

52. Some beginning references for the study of local government in the Progressive era include; R. J. Stillman, II, *The Rise of the City Manager*, University of New Mexico Press, Albuquerque, 1974 and J. H. Svara, "*Progressive Roots of the Model Charter and the Manager Profession: A Positive Heritage*", N.C.R. 78 (Sept./Oct.), 339–355. L. White, *The City Manager*, Chicago: University of Chicago Press, 1927.

53. This dialogue between decentralists and centralists illustrates well why John Rohr calls the Progressive period the founding of American Public Administration in thought and the New Deal the founding in deed. See J. A. Rohr, *To Run A Constitution: The Legitimacy of the Administrative State*, Lawrence, Kansas: University Press of Kansas, 1986.

54. R. Wiebe, 1995.

55. E. Eisenach, p. 52.

56. The positivistic orientation and the beginning of the pluralistic position counter the acceptance of this orientation. See Richard Stillman for a good discussion of the state.

57. C. M. Stivers, "Refusing To Get It Right: Citizenship, Difference, and the Refounding Project", *Refounding Democratic Public Administration: Modern Paradoxes, Postmodern Challenges*, G. L. Wamsley and J. F. Wolf, (eds.), Thousand Oaks: Sage Publications, 1996.

58. See J. Stever and D. W. Noble, *The Progressive Mind, 1890–1917*, Minneapolis: Burgess Publishing Company, 1981.

59. P. O. Van Riper, "The Politics Administration Dichotomy: Concept of Reality?" in Jack Rabin and James S. Bowman (eds.), *Politics and Administration: Woodrow Wilson and American Public Administration*, New York: Marcel Decker, 1984.

60. J. S. Svara, "The Politics—Administration Dichotomy Model as Aberration," Paper Presented at Public Administration Theory Network National Symposium, February, 1996.

61. F. Goodnow, *Politics and Administration: A Study in Government*, The Macmillan Company, New York, 1914.

62. O'Toole, p. 149.

63. J. A. Monrone, *The Democratic Wish: Popular Participation and the Limits of American Government, Basic Books, 1990.*

64. J. A. Monrone, 1990, p. 1.

65. G. L. Wamsley and L. S. Dudley, "From Reorganizing to Reinventing: Sixty Years and "We Still Don't Get It," forthcoming in the *International Journal of Public Administration.*

66. Other important figures of the period who contributed to the movement included Henry L. Gantt, Hugo Munsterberg, Walter Dill Scott, Harrington Emerson, Harlow S. Person, and, not reaching American scholars until the 1940's, Henri Fayol. Some of these understandings filtered into public administration through the works of F. A. Cleveland and W. E. Mosher, J. M. Pfiffner, L. D. White, Luther Gulick, and D. C. Stone.

67. C. S. George, *The History of Management Thought*, Prentice-Hall, Inc., Englewood Cliffs, New Jersey, 1972 and H. L. Schachter, *Frederick Taylor and the Public Administration Community: A Reevaluation*, Albany: State University of New York Press, 1989.

68. F. W. Taylor, "The Principles of Scientific Management" *Bulletin of the Taylor Society, 1916.* Reprinted in *Classics of Organization Theory*, J. M. Shafritz and J. S. Ott, (eds.) Pacific Grove, California: Brooks/Cole Publishing Company, 1987, pp. 69–80. For example, that shovelers using shovels that averaged twenty-one pounds was most efficient is an example of what Taylor meant by a scientific fact (68). Further, an example of what is meant by the true revolution is Taylor's idea that the manager under scientific manager would become a welcomed teacher, rather than a feared monitor whom workers would try to dupe. Although emphasis was placed on discovering the one best way, that way could be modified after workers understood it (68).

69. H. L. Schachter, 1989.

70. There were, however, opponents to the system. These included old-line plant managers objecting to higher wages and company-sponsored training, and foremen jealous of traditional prerogatives. The American Federation of Labor also was in opposition because of fear of breaking members' monopolies on shop expertise. Part of the difficulty lay in Taylor's own idealism which lead him to give too little thought to situations where it was difficult get worker-manager cooperation, where there was realistic fear that pay gains would lead to subsequent rate cuts, or mixed motives situations, where the impetus for mutually beneficial cooperation coexists with a conflict over how to cooperate. (Schacter, p. 69).

71. As for the differences in public and private, Henry Metcalfe's formulations were the source used, since Wilson was not cited in the public administration literature before the war. Metcalfe did posit a distinction between private management judged on efficiency and government administration evaluated also on legislative accountability. (From H. Schacter, 75–76).

72. Schachter makes a good case that Cooke, and in many cases, Taylor, were not top-down theorists, but, instead, advocated noneconomic motivational strategies and understanding worker

sentiments, saw the importance of viewing work as play, realized the importance of persuasion as the key to internal efficiency, and stressed the role of information for management a good ten to fifteen years before the insights of the Hawthorne group, Douglas McGregor, and Chester Barnard. Although there may have been sentiments held in common by Taylor and later management theorists, the difference in emphasis is important, and perhaps, underemphasized by Schachter. Taylor and Cooke stressed the process of scientific management, the role of information, and productivity while the later human relations school emphasized leadership and employee relations. Further, although explained away by many later biographers, some of Taylor's comments about workers are still very paternalistic.

73. T. Pegram, p. 218–219.
74. J. Monrone, p. 92–93.
75. See B. Silberman, 1993 and A. Hoogenboom, *Outlawing the Spoils*, Urbana, Ill.: University of Illinois Press, 1968.
76. The role of the administrator per se, was dominant in the ideas of a limited number of Progressive groups. One was the Mugwumps, the educated old gentry of the Northeast who wished to curb the excesses of the political machines and the new men of wealth. Spokesmen included Carl Shutz, George Curtis, and Charles Bonaparte.
77. See C. S. Aron, *Ladies and Gentleman of the Civil Service: Middle-Class Workers in Victorian America*, New York: Oxford University Press, 1987. From the point of view of the civil servants themselves there were advantages and disadvantages to the increasing bureaucratization. Prior to civil service reform, jobs were insecure causing men and women both to subjugate themselves to power to obtain a position. Both found it somewhat degrading—women expressed concern over the compromising of their moral virtue; men often felt their manhood impugned. Without standardized criteria and rules, autonomous officials were free to exercise anti-female biases and women found they couldn't advance because supervisors refused to promote women. Both men and women were sometimes subject to tyranny of petty supervisors who wielded extraordinary amount of discretionary power. On the positive side, the new merit system did open clerkships to those who could never have had advantage. Competing and succeeding offered middle class men a sense of proven expertise. For women, it is less clear as women were still hired for only low status. The somewhat decentralized day to day functioning and power of low level supervisors meant middle class workers found some relief from routinized jobs and closely controlled work routines. Often women won in this ad hoc decentralized system because they could take risks and do men's jobs.
78. S. Skowronek, *Building A New American State: The Expansion of National Administrative Capacities*, 1877–1920, Cambridge: Cambridge University Press, 1982.
79. The tradeoff for the greater protection and insurance of more equitable treatment of the increasing formalization and routinization was the sometimes arbitrariness of the rules and classifications themselves.
80. D. H. Rosenbloom, *Century Issues of the Pendleton Act of 1883: The Problematic Legacy of Civil Service Reform*, New York: Marcel Dekker, 1982.
81. See B. L. Silberman, 1992.
82. Quoted in J. Svara, "The Politics-Administration Dichotomy Model as Aberration," p. 7.
83. M. O. Furmer, p. 322.
84. For a recent examination of these issues, see G. L. Wamsley and J. F. Wolf, (eds.), *Refounding Democratic Public Administration: Modern Paradoxes, Postmodern Challenges*, Thousand Oaks: Sage Publications, 1996.
85. J. Monrone, pp. 98–99.

13

THE BUREAU MOVEMENT
Seedbed of Modern Public Administration

Camilla Stivers
Levin College of Urban Affairs, Cleveland State University, Cleveland, Ohio

I.   INTRODUCTION

During the early twentieth century, groups of Progressive reformers established privately sponsored bureaus of municipal research, intending to use systematic investigation to improve municipal agency management practices and loosen the hold of party bosses on urban politics and policy-making. So homogeneous were the outlook and approach of the bureau researchers, and so ardent their commitment, that they were dubbed a "movement" by their early chroniclers (1,2,3).

In general the field of public administration, particularly in the U. S., has been remarkably inattentive to its historical development (4), a pattern one hopes the present volume will help change. To the extent that we do have an intellectual history, municipal research bureaus are widely regarded as a (sometimes the) principal point of origin for scholarship and professional education in public administration (5,6,7). Yet the nature of their enterprise and the extent of its influence to the present day have not been examined thoroughly.

This chapter will trace the history, philosophy, and influence of the bureau movement on modern public administration. As its title indicates, the chapter adopts the viewpoint of earlier histories that the ideology and tactics of bureau advocates had a profound effect on the development of the field. It will maintain, however, that the impact in question is both worthy of deeper reflection and more equivocal than the relatively cursory and sanguine accounts in the literature of public administration to this point might lead one to conclude.

II.   HISTORICAL DEVELOPMENT

By the early twentieth century, industrialization, mechanization, and successive waves of immigrants from Europe had increasingly concentrated the U. S. population in ever larger cities. There, growing demands for basic infrastructure and services strained the capacity of municipal governments organized in the nineteenth century to cope with the problems of a simpler time. The urban political machine "by default . . . as much as by design" had

259

become the "one mechanism capable of coordinating public policy in the industrial city" (8). The machines operated on the basis of quid pro quo politics that rewarded members' loyalty at the polls with government jobs, especially on the police force (9), and met the policy needs of business elites—a relatively stable economic climate and access to government contracts and franchises—in return for campaign contributions and, at times, outright bribes.

Left out of this equation was a growing group of educated middle-class professionals, hostile to machine politics, who organized themselves to press for improvements in the workings of municipal governments. Much has been written about the motivations of this group, to which the bureau researchers belonged, and scholarly treatments of them vary tremendously. The literature of public administration tends to portray them as selfless and principled, and accepts their diagnosis of government ills as accurate. Historians, on the other hand, have stressed the reformers' own interests: their middle-class "status anxiety" (10), their "search for order" in a time of social unrest (11), or their frank interest in government jobs for themselves (12). The probable truth is that, like most human beings, the reformers' motives were mixed. They were both genuinely concerned to ameliorate social problems and interested in increasing their own influence on urban policy and administration.

Certainly the difficulties of the 1890s, including a serious depression, farmer and worker protests, currency troubles, and the closing of the frontier, produced growing unease among the middle and elite classes, a sense that, as the title of one account suggests, American society might be "standing at Armageddon" (13). In any case, beginning as early as Woodrow Wilson's well-known essay, "The Study of Administration" (14), administrative reformers based their arguments in favor of efficiency and expertise on the premise that party-controlled governments were inadequate to the complex challenges they faced.

As the nineteenth century drew to a close, the municipal reformers began to turn away from "throwing the rascals out"—ousting machine politicians at the polls and replacing them with good government candidates—largely because success in voting in one reform mayor would be reversed at the next election. A panoply of civic reform clubs and organizations developed, based on the idea that "[e]ven 'bad' men in government could be led down the path of municipal righteousness and if properly guided serve as the instruments of good government" (15). Instead of frankly opposing machine politicians and agency personnel, reformers would try to work with them, offer expert advice, present study results, and defend the needs of agencies at budget hearings.

These organizations quickly became an important outlet for reform energies. As early as 1894, a national conference on good government drew representatives from nearly 250 municipal reform clubs, and the formation shortly thereafter of the National Municipal League linked like-minded reformers from a variety of clubs and locales. While some clubs were concerned with the broad spectrum of municipal problems, others concentrated on specific needs like education, public health, recreation, or crime prevention. Both men and women were involved, with women's clubs providing a protected framework within which educated and well-to-do women, barred from the polls as yet, could put their talents and activism to work on public concerns.

Among the many reform groups, the organizers of the bureaus of municipal research emerged in the early twentieth century as a distinctive approach to civic reform. The first bureau was incorporated in New York City in 1907. Its principal organizer, William H. Allen, was a social worker and general agent for the Association for Improving the Condition of the Poor, a charity organization noted for the application of efficiency precepts to philanthropy. Allen's experience with the AICP had convinced him that efficient administration made for more effective charities and that this lesson could be applied to government as well. He suggested to R. Fulton Cutting, president of the Citizens' Union, that a non-partisan agency of experts could research the best administrative methods for city government. In 1905 Cutting and Allen established the experimental Bureau of City Betterment as an arm of the Citizens' Union. As director, they recruited Henry Bruere, a former settlement house worker and welfare secretary for Chicago's McCormick Works.

As the new Bureau was establishing itself, the reform-minded mayor of New York City, George B. McClellan, had appointed a commission to look into the financial and accounting practices of city agencies. The commission's investigative efforts were stalled, however, due to lack of cooperation on the part of agency officials. In an brilliant end-run around the bureaucracy, Bruere conducted a field study of the condition of Manhattan streets, comparing first-hand observations with available repair records. The shocking state of the streets, which contradicted reported repairs, was publicized in a pamphlet entitled "How Manhattan is Governed." Bruere's report hit New York like a bombshell. As a direct result, Governor Charles Evans Hughes dismissed the Manhattan borough president on the grounds of incompetence. Together with Frederick Cleveland, chair of the mayoral commission, Allen and Bruere succeeded in attracting funding from several wealthy benefactors, including John D. Rockefeller and Andrew Carnegie, for the formation of an independent bureau of municipal research, inaugurated in 1907 with the three organizers as co-directors.

The early success of the New York Bureau quickly led to the formation of similar bureaus in other cities around the U. S., twenty of them by 1915. The New York Bureau served as a direct catalyst, with New York men traveling to other cities to offer advice and technical assistance. In 1911, the New York Bureau established a training school to prepare professional administrators. The school produced many graduates who became directors or staffers at bureaus in other cities and thereby promoted the homogeneity of the bureau movement. Bureaus in Philadelphia, Cincinnati, Milwaukee, Dayton, Kansas City, and San Francisco were among the best organized and most active.

With some ebbs and flows in their fortunes during World War I and the depression, municipal research bureaus remained active until the 1940s. By that time universities, legislatures, and state and local governments had established their own research institutes, whose work gradually diminished the perceived need for private, non-profit organizations in this arena. The Institute for Public Administration, into which the New York Bureau was organized in the early 1920s, is still active.

According to Gill (16), more than half the trustees of municipal research bureaus were manufacturers, bankers, lawyers, merchants, realtors, insurance brokers, and financiers. As Gill notes, labor and professions other than the law were virtually unrepresented; more than 80% of trustees came from the business world. There were only a handful of women.

Following the pattern established in New York, the bureaus were dependent upon the support of a few key benefactors. While they received large numbers of $10-and-under contributions, these made up less than five per cent of the total amount. Contributions of over $100 constituted nearly three-quarters of bureau support. In New York, seven donors gave nearly half of Bureau's total operating funds during its first decade of operation. Gill (16) suggests that the bureaus' reliance on large donors, together with dominance of their boards by business interests, led researchers to stress the "business-like" quality of their approaches and recommendations, even when the ideas came not from business but from the public sector or from the researchers' own creativity.

III. TYPICAL ACTIVITIES

Municipal research bureaus engaged in a wide range of efforts to improve public management practices. These included the development of municipal budgeting and uniform accounting methods; the establishment of guidelines for the preparation of statistical charts; standardization of personnel procedures such as time sheets, job descriptions, work routines, performance assessments, and retirement systems; the design of organization charts; uniform crime statistics; in-service training of city employees; revamped billing procedures for public utilities; improved garbage collection and sanitary inspection methods; improved purchasing and inventory control; reforms in housing inspection, milk inspection, and medical inspection of school children; and the systematization of records in all areas of government.

The centerpiece of bureau activity, however, was the development of the executive budget. Prior to the bureaus' efforts, government expenditures were typically authorized by city councils on a piecemeal basis. Appropriations were routinely made without systematic reference to available revenues or total projected expenses. Special revenue bonds took care of any shortfalls. In general, the bureaus saw the lack of a comprehensive executive budget as the root cause of inefficient administration. As a result, executive budgeting and the accounting methods it requires became their central concern. Supporting this focus, as we shall see, was an entire political philosophy that entailed shifting power from the legislature to the chief executive in order for the latter to be able to propose and execute effective policies.

According to Dahlberg (17), the first municipal agency budget in the United States was adopted by the New York City Department of Health in 1907, after a requested study by the New York Bureau demonstrated the need for it. Bruere's earlier report on Manhattan streets had made clear how agencies had to exaggerate their expenditure requests in order to ward off automatic cuts by the Board of Estimates and Apportionment. In response to this report, health department director Hermann Biggs asked Bruere to help his department develop a budget. Biggs was convinced that a budget was the best strategy for securing adequate funding by documenting the department's need. Bruere recognized that a health department budget would be a high-profile project since the department's work affected the entire community directly and involved well-publicized issues like the safety of milk and protection against tuberculosis. Bruere modeled the budget after the AICP budgeting process described in Allen's book, *Efficient Democracy* (18).

Acting on an aldermanic resolution, the Board of Estimates and Apportionment not only approved the health department budget but directed that all city agencies should follow a similar procedure thereafter. Thus, two principles were established: specification of the purposes for which requested funds were to be spent, and the appropriation of specific sums for specific purposes.

Citizen education was another of the bureaus' key activities, on the theory that informed citizens would hold governments accountable and demand economical and effective use of tax dollars. Many of the bureaus published periodic bulletins describing their research findings or alerting the public to important policy issues. Bureau staff members also addressed civic groups and some bureaus maintained public information services. Combining public education with their interest in budgeting, some bureaus organized budget exhibits, displaying graphs that showed the costs and benefits of various government activities, along with more tangible items like six-cent hat hooks for which the city government had paid 65 cents apiece. The first such exhibit, held in New York City in 1908, drew 50,000 people and received considerable press coverage.

IV. PHILOSOPHY

Bureau reformers employed a rhetoric of non-partisan neutrality based on their belief in the ability of objective, scientific fact-finding to demonstrate the most effective and efficient way of managing public agencies. The extent to which either effectiveness or efficiency took precedence in the minds and hearts of the bureau men is a matter of some debate in the literature. The bureau researchers themselves maintained that efficiency was the instrument of effectiveness, to be able to accomplish more for a given expenditure. For example, Bruere (19) commented;

> The efficiency movement in cities . . . began . . . in an effort to capture the great forces of city government for harnessing the work of social betterment. It was not a tax-saving incentive nor desire for economy that inspired this first effort . . . but the conviction that only through efficient government could progressive social welfare be achieved, and that, so long as government remained inefficient, volunteer and detached effort to remove social handicaps would continue a hopeless task.

The bureau publications of the time are filled with similar statements to the effect that solving problems of city life was the first priority and efficiency the means to that end. Schiesl (20) supports the idea that the bureaus were sincerely interested in social welfare.

Numerous other commentators, however, have pointed out that, while effectiveness may have come first to start with, efficiency gradually displaced it. As Crane (21) saw the bureaus, their primary aim was to promote governmental economy and efficiency. Better service was a secondary goal, a stance Crane argued was made necessary by the bureaus' reliance on the financial support of private business interests. Gill (16) agreed, suggesting that the bureau emphasis on science and fact-finding eventually became an end in itself. Waldo (22), after quoting both Allen and Bruere, observed that, over time in the movement, "research and facts have come to be regarded less and less as devices of citizen cooperation and control and more and more as instruments of executive management." Karl (23) argued that the New York Bureau came to define "fiscal reform as the real reform"— in other words, to make the improvement of government methods an end in itself.

At the very least, bureau reformers believed, first, that it was possible to distinguish ends from means, so that the methods of government could be seen as neutral (non-political, value-free), and second, that democratic accountability would be served by administrative practices that made efficient use of available resources. They adopted the politics-administration dichotomy especially as formulated in Frank Goodnow's *Politics and Administration* (24). Goodnow argued in favor of a separation of government *functions*, with the legislature handling the expression of the popular will and the executive responsible for its execution, rather than the separated *powers*, checks and balances theory of the framers of the Constitution.

The bureau men moved toward a view of government that emphasized the need for centralized control and rational decision-making, hence the desirability of a stronger chief executive. They saw separated powers as weakening the executive branch by depriving it of a policy role, and called for such reforms as the executive budget and staff-versus-line distinctions in order to make it possible for the executive to centralize and systematize control over government processes. In this respect, the bureau philosophy represents a fulfillment of Alexander Hamilton's interest in promoting "energy" in the executive in order to make government capable of strategic action and in order for the executive to check the power of the legislature, an interest that had been in abeyance during the Jacksonian era.

Dahlberg points to the New York Bureau's report to the 1915 state constitutional convention as a clear example of this Hamiltonian political philosophy. In her view the crux of the bureau philosophy was the idea that "greatest responsibility and responsiveness is found where the executive is responsible for leadership and administrative direction, and where the electorate must decide when irreconcilable differences arise between the legislature and the executive" (25). Dahlberg, a friendly analyst of the bureau approach, calls the lack of a provision for such clear assignment of functions to different branches in U. S. government a "historical accident." The politics-administration dichotomy, she notes, would correct this misstep, producing a government with each part in harmony with the rest, "adapted to perform the service for which it was intended." The proper function of the legislature would be to "control the executive and call him to account for his expenditures" (26), a process aided by the executive budget and a corps of staff specialists serving the chief executive's policy and management information needs.

Charles Beard's introduction to the Bureau's constitutional report observed that government to that time had been based on the mistaken idea that legislatures should govern rather than simply call the executive to account by submitting to the people disputes between the two branches. Interestingly, though the new constitution was defeated at the time of the convention, the cause was taken up again several years later by Governor Al Smith. He appointed his own constitutional commission, headed by Robert Moses and staffed by A. E. Buck and John Gaus, all of them New York Bureau "graduates." Most of the bureau's recommendations of 1915 were adopted in the election of 1925 (17).

The question of democratic accountability was one the bureau reformers emphasized consistently. In their view, inefficient, wasteful government could not serve democracy well. Officials were responsible to the people for expenditure decisions. Such accountability was impossible with antiquated financial management techniques. Agencies staffed with trained experts rather than people whose main qualification was party loyalty seemed to the bureau men both a basic requirement and fulfillment of democracy. From their perspective, the average citizen was more interested in well-run government than in direct involvement (again, a Hamiltonian argument). They reasoned that if trained public administrators executed legislative mandates in an effective and efficient manner, democracy would be well served.

Administrative accountability would be supported by what the bureau reformers called "efficient citizens," who would rally round agencies if they had the information necessary to understand administrative action. The bureaus' information bulletins and budget exhibits were based on this premise. As William H. Allen put it:

> Without . . . facts upon which to base judgment, the public cannot intelligently direct and control the administration of township, county, city, state, or nation. Without intelligent control by the public, no efficient, progressive, triumphant democracy is possible (27).

Allen saw citizen reformers unarmed with systematic knowledge as well-meaning but in-effective do-gooders—"candles under a bushel"—who could be transformed by the acqui-sition of facts.

Although the rhetoric of efficient citizenship has an appealing ring, the bureau men's understanding of "the public" was limited. It was shaped by the Progressive ten-dency to define "the public" in distinction from either capital or labor. As Dawley notes, for Progressives the public consisted of "social workers, journalists, lawyers, educators, and other middle-class opinion makers who were supposed to represent some disinter-ested general will" (28). The rejection of political parties by educated middle-class people can be traced to their sense that the Democratic party served working-class immigrants and the Republican party big business and finance capitalists. This left no place for the new professionals—hence their stress on being "non-partisan." Many of the Progressive reform proposals were premised on the need to harmonize and reconcile class differences. This aim was served by ideas of "the public" and "the public interest" that took hold dur-ing this period. Ehrenreich (28) points out that, after setting aside capital and labor, the only public left is the middle class. For Progressives, "the public" symbolized the idea of a classless society, where differences could be transcended under the rationalizing and har-monizing guidance of expert professionals.

For the new professionals, conflict of any kind and especially among classes consti-tuted a failure to find the best solution to an issue, a position outlined most clearly in the work of Progressive management thinker Mary Parker Follett (30,31). The bureau men's reliance on scientific investigation as the basis for building working relationships with public agency incumbents embodies the sense of Follett and others that the facts of the situation could point toward an approach that all interests would recognize as best. In ad-dition, as Dahlberg (17) suggests, bureau reformers believed that ordinary folk were by and large uninterested in the workings of government, making it the responsibility of en-lightened citizens to see to it that government was well run.

In their focus on administrative decision-making based on factual analysis, the bu-reau approach anticipated Herbert Simon (32) by some forty years. The movement away from "good men" toward "good methods" (3) also prefigures Simon's emphasis on reject-ing unproven principles of administration in favor of the results of scientific investigation, but with more trust than Simon was willing to put in day-to-day experience. Bureau re-searchers held that careful analysis of actual practice in agencies could yield useful infor-mation, data that would be reliable because systematically acquired, an approach largely derived from Frederick Taylor's (33) method of identifying principles of scientific manage-ment by painstaking study of ongoing work.

V. THE SURVEY APPROACH

The bureau men were interested in examining existing practices in order to improve them. This led them to adopt what was called the "survey approach," an epistemological orientation that later commentators (5,6) have seen as both the centerpiece of the bureau perspective and the taproot of the modern field of public administration. Historians of public administration see the survey method as a sign of the scientific orientation of the bureaus. In the early twentieth century, however, surveys had not reached the level of methodological sophistication now taken for granted, nor did they entail the kind of de-tachment expected today. For Progressive reformers, the word "survey" connoted a systematic approach to gathering facts about a neighborhood or community for the express purpose of problem solving.

Although their contributions to the survey method remain unacknowledged in the literature of public administration, the pioneers of the approach in the United States were the settlement houses. The first survey was conducted by residents of Chicago's Hull House (34); it exhaustively delineated socioeconomic characteristics and problems of the immediate area. The Hull House survey report was notable for its detailed maps, documenting the concentration of various ethnic groups in certain blocks, the relationship between ethnicity and weekly income, the relegation of the very poor to crowded rooms in the rear of tenements while those with more resources clustered at the front. The report provided house by house information, as well as a number of special reports on issues like sweatshops, child labor, and charities in Cook County.

Other surveys quickly followed, including two conducted under the auspices of South End House in Boston. In 1907, the survey approach broadened from the neighborhood level to an entire community. The Pittsburgh Survey, sponsored by the Russell Sage Foundation, sought to describe the conditions of an entire city as they were being affected by industrial development. Over sixty researchers spent a year collecting statistical data on urban problems and interviewing steelworkers, managers of steel plants, women workers, clergy and real estate brokers. As Cohen (35) notes, "The Pittsburgh Survey was part of the political arsenal used by urban reform groups against political machines." Its findings were used to consolidate 27 wards into nine at-large districts, thus breaking the hold of the Pittsburgh machine. The survey also documented, using the steel industry as an example, how the unregulated workings of capitalism undercut the capacity of citizens and communities to participate in democratic institutions (36).

Bureau researchers took the Pittsburgh Survey as their model, though it is likely they were more attracted to the machine-busting side of the effort than its critique of capitalism. Both Charles Merriam's (37) progress report on municipal research and Luther Gulick's (7) retrospective cite Pittsburgh as the exemplar even though Bruere's 1906 survey of Manhattan streets predated the Pittsburgh research by a year and the publication of its findings by three. In any case, the idea that systematic investigation could be the key to loosening the hold of political machines on the workings of city agencies quickly became the centerpiece of the bureau approach to reform.

Reporting in 1928 on the work of the New York Bureau and the National Institute of Public Administration that grew out of it, Gulick (38) admitted that, in the hands of bureau researchers, the "survey method" became rather loosely applied to a wide variety of investigations in order to connote rational, non-partisan analysis:

> The term "survey" was used to describe the Bureau's studies of city government because it conveyed the idea of the inclusive, objective, and scientific approach which the Bureau applied to its work. . . . The term was not original with the Bureau. It was being used at that time in the same sense by the Russell Sage Foundation in its "Survey of Pittsburgh."

As Gulick goes on to describe, a typical bureau survey entailed descriptive analysis of the organization and functioning of a government department, or indeed, an entire government. The analysis would encompass applicable constitutional and statutory provisions, scope of work, major activities, budget, personnel, and interactions with other agencies. It sought to uncover objectives, need for the work, methods, division of labor, and record-keeping in order to arrive at a judgment as to whether the agency or government was meeting existing need efficiently and was prepared to cope with future demands. Such research projects were actually more like today's case study than the modern social science survey. In many respects—particularly in questioning the agency's need to exist and the extent to which it accomplishes its purposes—today's performance measurement movement echoes many of the dynamics set in motion by the bureau surveys. Certainly the latter established as a precedent the notion that systematic investigation could determine the worth of public administrative work.

To sum up the philosophy of the bureau movement, one can do no better than Waldo's assessment, which is worth quoting at length:

> The spirit of the Bureau movement has deeply affected public administration. The Bureau movement was a part of Progressivism, and its leaders were leaders of Progressivism. They were tired of the simple moralism of the nineteenth century, although paradoxically they were themselves fired with the moral fervor of humanitarianism and secularized Christianity. They were stirred by the revelations of the Muckrakers, but despaired of reform by spontaneous combustion. They were sensitive to the appeals and promises of science, and put a simple trust in discovery of facts as the way of science and as a sufficient model for solution of human problems. They accepted—they urged—the new positive conception of government, and verged upon the idea of a planned and managed society. They hated "bad" business but found in business organization and procedure an acceptable prototype for public business. They detected politicians and were firm in the belief that citizens by and large were fundamentally pure at heart, desirous of efficient and economical government, and potentially rational enough to "reach up" and support a vigorous government, wide in its scope, complex in its problems, and utilizing a multitude of professional and scientific skills. . . . They caught the vision that "true democracy consists in intelligent cooperation between citizens and those elected or appointed to serve" [The quotation is from Frederick A. Cleveland, *Chapters on Municipal Administration and Accounting*, New York: 1901].

The municipal research bureaus represented the quintessence of the tension between democracy and efficiency in terms of which Waldo summed up the forces of reform that produced the field of public administration. Waldo held that the administrative reform challenge was to reconcile the desire for managerial efficiency, derived from science and achieved by experts, with democratic values. The bureaus' particular strategy was to argue that efficient management was democratic, first, because corruption and waste were not in the public interest, and second, because management carried out the will of the people as expressed by the legislature and had no politics of its own. Both of these are still live arguments in the field, as will be suggested below. Certainly the tension between efficiency and democracy is not only an ongoing but a constitutive one, as Waldo noted.

VI.   FROM TRAINING TO EDUCATION

How was it that the bureau approach became a central influence in the development of the field of public administration? The link was forged out of the interest of bureau men in preparing competent experts to assume responsibility for efficient management in public agencies. A small-scale training effort by the New York Bureau evolved in a relatively short time into full-fledged professional education under university auspices, and the connections between them were direct.

The spark was lit when the bureaus' growing recognition of the need for training met its financial angel, Mrs. E. H. Harriman. Harriman, whose husband was a generous supporter of municipal research, became interested in modeling the American civil service on the professional services found in England and France, but her offer to fund the necessary educational program was rejected by Harvard, Yale, and Columbia on the grounds that "politics" were "dirty" and "unacademic" (40). At the same time, leaders of the New York Bureau, especially William H. Allen, conceived of the idea of a training school. Allen and Harriman joined forces in 1911 to launch the school, with Harriman writing letters to well-connected men requesting their financial and moral support (according to Dahlberg, the only one who doubted the need for the school was Woodrow Wilson!). Some 485 applications were received from 106 cities in 25 states for the first class of 25 students. The first group included men with academic or practical backgrounds in finance, several engineers, a lawyer and a school superintendent.

The training was extremely practice-oriented at first, with each student paired with a Bureau member and assigned to research a particular agency or function. One typical assignment: "Work out a report with recommendations covering the civil service in New York City, including conditions governing employment, development of individual efficiency, reward of efficiency through proper compensation, proper discipline, welfare, etc." (41) All trainees took an accountancy course. The normal length of training was two years, and focused on whatever issues or needs were current in municipal government at the time. Required reading included Frederick Cleveland's book on municipal accounting, Bruere's *The New City Government*, Allen's *Efficient Democracy*, and perhaps inevitably, Frederick Taylor's *Principles of Scientific Management*. Although there were few organized classes and virtually no lectures at first, over time the training began to assume a more conventionally academic format.

Charles A. Beard's evaluation of the school after its first year said that it met "every requirement of a university" but added the "practical contact with the world of affairs" that universities were not offering (42). As a result of Beard's report, Columbia, the University of Pennsylvania, New York University and the University of Michigan began granting graduate credit to trainees. Beard became director of the school in 1915, after which the training became more systematic and academic, with requirements in budgeting, accounting, municipal politics, and law. When Beard assumed directorship of the New York Bureau in 1918, Luther Gulick took over as head of the training school. Among the better-known graduates of the school were Robert Moses, A. E. Buck, Lent Upson, Luther Gulick, and Mabel Newcomer.

In 1914, the University of Michigan began offering an M. A. in public administration, a program headed by former New York Bureau men, and several other master's and bachelor's level programs followed, all directly or indirectly linked to the training school (6). When the Maxwell School was established at Syracuse University in 1924, the first class consisted of students who transferred there from the training school along with its then-director, William E. Mosher, who became dean. Mosher continued to bring Maxwell School classes to New York for three-month internships until 1930, and approval by the New York staff was required before Maxwell students received their master's degrees.

The roots of public administration as an academic discipline, then, are firmly planted in the bureaus of municipal research, pre-eminently in the New York Bureau. Ridley and Moore's (43) progress report on training for the public service cited the Maxwell School for its "conviction that administration per se has a definite content which can be taught," and Stone and Stone's (6) history of public administration education makes clear the ties between university-based and training school approaches. Certainly the political philosophy represented in the bureau approach still shapes the field of public administration in fundamental ways.

VII. THE INFLUENCE OF THE BUREAUS

In his assessment some 45 years after the founding of the New York Bureau, George Graham (44) identified several beliefs that he felt guided academics in the teaching of public administration. They included the power of reason, the rationality and factual correctness of Western cultural values, the essentially administrative nature of the application of reason, and the possibility of finding equitable solutions to public problems—all tenets that the bureau men would likely have endorsed or did so explicitly. Graham's perspective perpetuated important aspects of the bureau approach: while he rejected the politics-administration dichotomy on which the bureaus relied, he fully accepted their faith in strong and competent administrative leadership and echoed their questioning of the doctrine of separated powers, which he suggested might usefully be left to "rest uninterrupted in antiquarian splendor" (45). For those who believe that bureaucrat-bashing is of recent origin, Graham's observation that for a generation "public administrators have been on the 'hot seat' of professional and public criticism" is noteworthy (the more things change . . . etc.).

As the present essay is being written, the field of public administration is at about the same remove from Graham as his report was from the field's source in the bureaus of municipal research. While a thorough review of the philosophy and practice of contemporary public administration is well beyond the bounds of my chapter, I want to conclude by suggesting, at least, that the bureau men's philosophy is still central to the field. While my case example, the reinventing government movement, is far from the whole of public administration today, the ardor with which contemporary reformers have embraced the reinvention frame of reference suggests that today's fundamental administrative values are much like those of the bureau reformers and that the implications of that continuity may deserve more attention than they have yet received.

VIII. REINVENTION: FORWARD TO THE PAST?

When looked at in light of information about the bureau movement and its role in shaping something called "public administration," the call to reinvent government (46) and the speed and enthusiasm with which it has been taken up at both the federal and state levels reveal nuances that are not apparent when they are considered out of historical context. Examined within this context, not only does reinventing government seem less new than it might otherwise, but indeed, its major proposals begin to sound terribly familiar. If we accept the arguments of historians that municipal reformers acted not only out of altruistic concern to improve government but also for various self-interested motives, and if reinventing government reflects, as I will try to show, many of the same features as the bureau reformers' proposals, parallels between the two movements may suggest that they serve similar aims and thus reveal aspects of the current reinventing fervor we might otherwise miss.

For simplicity's sake let us take the Gore Report as our example of reinventing government. Its recommendations are based on the premise that "the central issue we face is not *what* government does, but *how* works;" the main problem is "good people trapped in bad systems" (47). Both of these ideas echo the perspective of the bureau reformers. The first accepts the bureau notion that how government does its work can be separated from what it does and that the one can therefore be addressed without creating implications for the other. In other words, as of old, means can be separated from ends. The second adopts the bureau men's reform strategy, which was (as Waldo held) to seek good methods rather than good men—that is, to rely on administrative rather than political solutions (again, assuming the two can be separated).

Reinventing government in fact resurrects the politics-administration dichotomy on which bureau reformers relied but which public administration thinking ostensibly banished several decades ago, and relies on it for the same reason: to strengthen executive branch power at the expense of the legislature. The Gore Report's indictment of red tape is a reflection of the administrative expert's dislike for politically-imposed controls. It is defended on much the same ideological basis as the early twentieth century reformers called for "scientific" approaches to public management: that is, politics-as-usual is ineffective; it doesn't ensure results and it wastes the public's money.

The Hamiltonian idea that what people want is not participation in government but results, that is, services that work well and don't cost very much, is reflected as strongly in arguments for reinvention as it was in the bureau perspective. Both strengthen the administrator's hand. Today this is done in the interests of managerial "creativity" and "entrepreneurialism." Formerly, it was done for the sake of being "scientific" and "businesslike." Again, just as the bureau men argued for "efficient citizens" armed with facts to rally round expert administration, today advocates of reinventing government suggest that "customer service" will win the hearts and minds of a disenchanted public. In the same way as the bureau men once argued that democratic accountability would best be served by getting government to work efficiently, the identical argument is now made on behalf of the National Performance Review and similar reinvention efforts.

In sum, the difficulty that Waldo saw in the Progressive reform approach to early public administration exists today: reform is based on an unacknowledged theory of governance masquerading as a set of management techniques. Today we are not only absorbed with reinventing government but our decontextualized enthusiasm for procedural strategies like total quality management, productivity improvement, and performance measurement suggest continuing reliance on Progressive orthodoxy in early public administration. As Waldo observed, the most basic postulate among public administration's founders was "that true democracy and true efficiency are synonymous, or at least reconcilable" (48). The contemporary field of public administration is excessively concerned, just as the bureau men were, with finding the right management technique and as insufficiently sensitive to the political dynamics that inhabit every public administrative procedure—even the most apparently innocuous.

Reminding ourselves of public administration's roots in the bureaus of municipal research presents an opportunity to become more sensitive to the intertwining of facts with values, of policies with implementation methods, of politics with administration. The question Waldo posed is still relevant: "Are students of administration [including its practitioners and its theorists] trying to solve the problems of human cooperation on too low a plane?" (49) Without rejecting the bureau men's dedication to improved methods, we might also raise our sights more fully and more regularly to the substantive dimensions of public administrative work, that is, its inevitable implication in questions of the public good.

REFERENCES

1. J. M. Gaus, *A Survey of Research in Public Administration*, Social Sciences Research Council, New York, 1930.
2. J. M. Pfiffner, *Municipal Administration*, Ronald Press, New York, 1940.
3. D. Waldo, *The Administrative State*, Ronald Press, New York, 1948.
4. G. B. Adams, "Enthralled with modernity: The historical context of knowledge and theory development in public administration," *Pub Admin Rev:* 52; 363–373 (1992).
5. F. C. Mosher, "Democracy and the Public Service," Oxford University Press, New York, 1968.
6. D. C. Stone and A. B. Stone, "Early development of education in public administration," *American Public Administration: Past, Present, Future* F. C. Mosher (ed.). University of Alabama Press, University, AL, 1975, pp. 11–48.
7. L. H. Gulick, "Reflections on public administration, past and future," Pub Admin. Rev. 50; (1990).
8. R. F. Pecorella, *Community Power in a Postreform City: Politics in New York City*, M. E. Sharpe, Armonk, NY, 1994, p. 31.
9. J. C. Teaford, *The Unheralded Triumph: City Government in America, 1870–1900*, Johns Hopkins University Press, Baltimore, 1984.
10. R. Hofstadter, *The Age of Reform: From Bryan to F. D. R.*, Vintage Books, New York, 1955.
11. R. H. Wiebe, *The Search for Order 1877–1920*, Hill and Wang, New York, 1967.
12. R. Muncy, *Creating a Female Dominion in American Reform 1890–1935*, Oxford University Press, New York, 1990.
13. N. I. Painter, *Standing at Armageddon: The United States 1877–1919*, W. W. Norton, New York, 1987.
14. W. Wilson, "The study of administration," *Pol. Sci. Quart.:* 2; 197–222 (1887).
15. R. Skolnick, "Civic group progressivism in New York City," *New York History:* 51; 418 (1970).
16. N. N. Gill, *Municipal Research Bureaus*, American Council on Public Affairs, Washington, 1944.
17. J. S. Dahlberg, *The New York Bureau of Municipal Research: Pioneer in Government Administration*, New York University Press, New York, 1966.
18. W. H. Allen, *Efficient Democracy*, Dodd, Mead, New York, 1907.
19. H. Bruere, "Efficiency in city government," *Annals of the America Academy of Political and Social Science:* 41; 93 (1912).
20. M. J. Schiesl, *The Politics of Efficiency: Municipal Administration in America 18880–1920*, University of California Press, Berkeley, 1977.
21. R. T. Crane, "Research agencies and equipment," *Amer. Polit. Sci. Rev.:* 17; (1923).
22. Waldo [3], p. 33n.
23. B. D. Karl, *Executive Reorganization and Reform in the New Deal: The Genesis of Administrative Management 1900–1939*, Harvard University Press, Cambridge MA, 1963.
24. F. Goodnow, *Politics and Administration*, McMillan, New York, 1900.
25. Dahlberg [17], p. 97.
26. Dahlberg [17], p. 98.
27. Allen [18], p. ix.
28. A. Dawley, *Struggles for Justice: Social Responsibility and the Liberal State*, Belknap Press of Harvard University Press, Cambridge MA, 1991, p. 154.
29. J. H. Ehrenreich, *The Altruistic Imagination: A History of Social Work and Social Policy in the United States*, Cornell University Press, Ithaca NY, 1985.
30. M. P. Follett, *The New State: Group Organization the Solution of Popular Government*, Peter Smith, Gloucester MA, 1965, [1918].
31. M. P. Follett, *Creative Experience*, Peter Smith, New York, 1951 [1924].
32. H. Simon, *Administrative Behavior*, The Free Press, New York, 1945.
33. F. W. Taylor, *Principles of Scientific Management*, Harper, New York, 1911.

34. [Residents of Hull House], *Hull House Maps and Papers: A Presentation of Nationalities and Wages in a Congested District of Chicago, Together with Comments and Essays on Problems Growing Out of the Social Conditions*, Thomas Crowell, Boston, 1895.

35. S. R. Cohen, "The Pittsburgh Survey and the social survery movement: A sociological road not taken," *The Social Survey in Historical Perspective 1880–1940*, M. Bulmer, K. Bales and K. Sklar (eds.), Cambridge University Press, Cambridge, England, 1991, p. 249.

36. S. R. Cohen, "From industrial democracy to professional adjustment: The development of industrial sociology in the United States, 1900–1955," Theo and Soc.: 12; (1983).

37. C. E. Merriam, "The next step in the organization of municipal research," Nat. Mun. Rev.: 11; (1922).

38. L. Gulick, *The National Institute of Public Administration: A Progress Report*, National Institute of Public Administration, New York, 1928, p. 31.

39. Waldo [3], pp. 32–33.

40. Dahlberg [17], p. 117.

41. Dahlberg [17], p. 125.

42. Dahlberg [17], pp. 131–32.

43. C. E. Ridley and L. S. Moore, "Training for the public service," *Ann. Amer. Acad. Polit. and Soc. Sci.*: 189;(1937).

44. G. A. Graham, "Trends in teaching of public administration," Pub. Admin. Rev.: 10;(1950).

45. Graham [44], p. 74.

46. D. Osbourne and T. Gaebler, *Reinventing Government*, Addison-Wesley, Reading MA, 1992.

47. Executive Office of the President, *National Performance Review*, Government Printing Office, Washington, 1993.

48. Waldo [3], p. 206.

49. Waldo [3], p. 211.

14

OF PROVERBS AND POSITIVISM:
THE LOGICAL HERBERT SIMON

Peter L. Cruise
Golden Gate University, San Francisco, California

I. INTRODUCTION

Perhaps no movement or school of thought had more effect upon the field of Public Administration in the mid-twentieth century than did logical positivism. In the late 1930s just as the field was beginning to flower both as a profession and as an academic discipline—due in large part to the pioneering work of Classical Period writers such as Frank Goodnow, Leonard White, W.F. Willoughby, Luther Gulick, and Lyndall Urwick—the seeds of the logical positivist perspective had been planted. These seeds, mainly in the form of works published by Chester I. Barnard, were already questioning basic tenets propounded by Gulick and Urwick and, by implication, the writings of the field's first serious scholar Woodrow Wilson. The attacks were further refined and led most notably and articulately by a young University of Chicago doctoral student named Herbert A. Simon. During the late 1940s and early 1950s, these attacks would be responsible for a such a fundamental shift in the locus and focus of the study of the discipline that, for a time, even the name "Public Administration" seemed to disappear from the academic and professional landscape (1). Although over 50 years and millions of critiquing words have passed since the start of the logical positivist revolution, its after effects-like lingering radiation from an atomic bomb-resonate in the discipline today as the twenty-first century dawns.

This chapter will explore the rise of the logical positivist perspective in the field of Public Administration, its heyday, and finally its diminution. Epistemology and important epistemological and philosophical antecedents to logical positivism, such as Empiricism, Modern Science, the Scientific Method, and Logical Atomism will be reviewed. Within these schools of thought, writers such as Alfred North Whitehead, Bertrand Russell, Ludwig Wittgenstein, and the writers in the Vienna Circle will be examined.

Once these European philosophers began to influence American writers, especially Chester Barnard, logical positivism and Public Administration were to remain strange bedfellows for a number of decades. The most significant individual, and to whom logical positivism is most identified, is Herbert Simon. Although Simon has long since left writing about the discipline, his early writings marked the dramatic shift from the Classical to the Behavioral Period in Public Administration (1,2). The theories propounded by Simon and the subsequent effect of his writings are still present in the field and will be examined in this chapter.

The dominance of the logical positivist perspective in Public Administration would result in many strange things: an early split in field that explains why university Public Administration departments are located where they are today; a decline in the 1950s and early 1960s in Public Administration as an academic field of study (in favor of Political Science) so severe that a separate identity for the discipline nearly vanished from American colleges and universities; an early 1970s counterrevolution against logical positivism, which began with the New Public Administration champions at Syracuse University and resulted in a reinvigoration of the field; and in the 1980s and early 1990s, in a touch of irony, the acceptance of alternative, anti-logical positivist approaches to research in the field, such as Phenomenology and qualitative methods. The chapter will conclude with an exploration of these reactions to the close relationship between logical positivism and Public Administration. If the two were indeed strange bedfellows in the middle of the twentieth century, they are now, in the late 1990s, perhaps still in the same house but occupying separate bedrooms.

II. EPISTEMOLOGY AND THE PHILOSOPHICAL ANTECEDENTS OF LOGICAL POSITIVISM

A.   A Definition of Epistemology

Epistemology is the branch of philosophy concerned with the theory of knowledge. Traditionally, central issues in epistemology are the *nature* and *derivation* of knowledge, the *scope* of knowledge, and the *reliability* of claims to knowledge (3). According to Thomas D. Lynch, an inquiry of knowledge in the study of Public Administration is heavily influenced by what the academic community believes are the proper means to decide what gets included in the literature of the field. Students and academics interested in exploring the major epistemological views in Public Administration typically ask questions like: How does each view largely define accepted knowledge? What are the implications to Public Administration? Are any of the views dysfunctional? In what ways? What are the implications to the development of the field or discipline?*

Philosophers have frequently been divided over the nature and derivation questions in epistemology. For example, Rationalists (i.e., Plato and Rene Descartes) have argued that ideas of reason intrinsic to the mind are the only source of knowledge. Empiricists, on the other hand, (i.e., John Locke and David Hume) have argued that sense experience is the primary source of our ideas (or knowledge). The debate between the Rationalists and Empiricists continued for quite some time and later took a significant turn with Immanuel Kant's discussion of whether there could be synthetic a *priori* knowledge, that is, knowledge not based on experience but which is a condition of the comprehensibility of experience (4). Kantian philosophy, however, is not a focus of this discussion and is covered in greater detail in another chapter. Kant, although anti-empiricist in the derivation of knowledge question, agreed with the Empiricists in

---

*Course outline for PAD 7005, Conceptual Foundations for Public Administration. Copies available from the author.

the scope of knowledge question in that knowledge is limited to the world of experience (4,5).

Regarding the question of the reliability of knowledge, a significant influence in the history of epistemology has been the role of the skeptic in demanding whether any claim to knowledge can be upheld against the possibility of doubt. As early as Rene Descartes (1596–1650), who set aside any claim that was open to doubt, the role of the skeptic was to increase the level of rigor and precision necessary to posit knowledge (3). Postmodernist perspectives notwithstanding, in contemporary epistemology the role of the skeptic has been somewhat diminished. Even Descartes and Modern Science would propose at least one basic truth with his statement: *cogito, ergo sum* (I think, therefore I am) (3,4). As will be discussed later, individuals such as George Edward Moore and Ludwig Wittgenstein have been influential in redirecting attention from the defense of claims to knowledge against doubt to an analysis of their meaning.

B.   Philosophical Antecedents to Logical Positivism

To understand how logical positivism answers the basic epistemological questions discussed earlier, we must first focus on aspects of the philosophical perspectives of two earlier movements: *Empiricism* and *Modern Science*. Aspects of these two movements form the foundations upon which much of logical positivism rests.

1.   Empiricism and Modern Science

A good understanding of the empiricist perspective can be determined from the word itself-the term comes from the Greek word *emdeiria*, meaning experience. The basic tenet of Empiricism is that legitimate human knowledge arises from what is provided to the mind of the individual by introspective awareness through the vehicle of experience. It is: 1. a *rejection* of other doctrines (such as Platonism) that state that when the human mind first encounters the world its is already furnished with a range of ideas or concepts which have nothing to do with experience; and 2. an *acceptance* of the idea that, at birth, the mind is a "white paper," or *tabula rasa*—void of all characters and that only experience can provide it with ideas (3). Interestingly, these statements are in sharp contrast to aspects of Modern Science as espoused by Descartes who said that man has certain innate seeds, that if properly cultivated, would grow into knowledge. However, the similarities between Empiricism and Modern Science, and their collective contribution to logical positivism, are more important than their differences and will be discussed later.

Empiricism has taken many forms, but one common feature is that it starts from experimental science as a basis for understanding human knowledge (3). This is opposed to the Rationalist approach, which starts from pure mathematics as the basis for understanding human knowledge. Empiricism and its major proponents developed during the seventeenth and early eighteenth centuries, most directly as a result of the growing success and importance of experimental science and its gradual identity separate from pure mathematics and other disciplines. Major early proponents of Empiricism, known collectively as the "British Empiricist School of Philosophy," were Francis Bacon, John Locke, Bishop Berkeley, and David Hume. Later individuals, also usually classified as Empiricists, in the nineteenth and early twentieth centuries include John Stuart Mill and Bertrand Russell (5). Russell's inclusion in this list provides one of the major personality links between the classical British Empiricists and the beginnings of logical positivism in the twentieth century.

Empiricism's earliest days can be traced to ancient Greece and the first declared empiricist Epicurus (341 BCE–270 BCE). Epicurus maintained that the senses are the only source of knowledge. He was also an extreme atomist and held that sense perception comes about only as a result of contact between the atoms of the soul and the films of atoms issuing from bodies and objects around us. According to Epicurus, all sensations are true and there is no standard other than sensation to which we may refer our judgments about the world (3). Implicit with Epicurus's description of knowledge is that humanity cannot discover the real, indubitable truths of the universe, one can only develop probable hypotheses about the world around them.

The inductive knowledge-from-observation and hypotheses development and testing motifs that undergird Empiricism flowered more fully during the time of the British Empiricists in seventeenth-century England. Hypotheses development and subsequent experimentation by individuals such as Robert Boyle (i.e., Boyle's Law) and Isaac Newton (i.e., Laws of Thermodynamics) necessary for Empiricism to be accepted were expanding rapidly in the physical sciences in seventeenth and eighteenth-century Europe. Empiricism sees the acquisition of knowledge as a slow, piecemeal process, endlessly self-correcting but limited by the possibilities of experimentation and observation (5).

Modern Science, as developed by Descartes, has a number of parallels to Empiricism and these parallels are important to the development of logical positivism. According to Descartes, the solutions to the questions posed by epistemology lay in the systematization of knowledge. In the ideal method described by Descartes, man would start with basic axioms whose truth was clear and distinct, setting aside anything which can supposed to be false until he arrives at something that cannot be supposed to be false. Critical to this basic analysis is that nothing should be accepted as true unless it was clear and distinct. Next, one should analyze the basic axiom, starting with simple thoughts and only later proceeding to more complex thoughts. Following these steps, one should review the entire process so that no possible consideration is omitted (4).

The most important similarities between Modern Science and Empiricism include the need to systematize the acquisition of knowledge, thereby avoiding the introduction of extraneous variables which could confuse and cloud the final product and the need for careful self-correction and comprehensiveness throughout the process to avoid overlooking or omitting important variables which could affect the final product. The most important difference between the two perspectives includes the issue of the existence of certain innate truths. Modern Science and Descartes propose that the universe can be explained in terms of absolute properties or truths. By employing the appropriate procedures described above, we can discover knowledge that, under no circumstances, can be false. Empiricists, on the other hand, say even if systematized procedures for the acquisition of knowledge were employed, man cannot discover absolute truths, but can only develop probable hypotheses about the universe. Within certain confidence intervals and at certain levels of significance, man could work out a theory of knowledge, but only within the bounds of the actual achievements of scientists. Discussion of "limits" and "bounds" along with the disputation that certain organizational absolute "truths" were, in fact, proverbs would resonate strongly nearly a century after they were first discussed when logical positivists like Herbert Simon would examine behavior of individuals within organizations with concepts such as "bounded rationality" and "satisficing."

Just as logical positivism owes much to Empiricism and Modern Science, it is useful to examine the thinking and writings of several early twentieth-century philosophers and scientists who were not only the bridges between the eighteenth- and nineteenth-century perspectives of Empiricism and Modern Science but contributed their own important concepts to logical positivism as we know it today. Before embarking upon an examination of the twentieth century philosophers important to the development of logical positivism, it is useful to explore several aspects of contemporary philosophy to gain an understanding of the context in which these individuals developed their various perspectives regarding philosophy and epistemology.

Philosophy and the philosophical tradition is nearly 3000 years old in the Western World. Even with this long history, the exact nature of philosophy is still a matter of debate. For example, the early Greek thinkers thought of philosophy as we might now think of contemporary science. These individuals thought that through philosophical reflection alone the nature of the universe would be revealed to them. The explanations of the universe gained through philosophical reflection gradually grew more complex and grandiose. For example, in Ancient Greece in the fourth century BCE, Democritus worked out a crude version of atomic theory 2000 years before empirical verification of it was possible (4).

Over time, as man's curiosity of nature grew and as knowledge of it increased, the study of nature became an activity which broke away from philosophy and became the new discipline of "science." This breakaway is a comparatively recent event, however, because as recently as the nineteenth-century university physics courses were still described as "natural philosophy" courses (1). The current practice of universities awarding Doctorates of *Philosophy* to individuals in the physical sciences (as well as in many other fields of study) is another example of the early dominance of philosophy over science. Although science is a broad descriptor encompassing many aspects of the physical and natural worlds, all activities associated with science utilize a common methodology. This methodology still includes the ancient philosophical stance of thoughtful reflection of the world, but also involves the careful observation and experimentation with it. This process became known as the "Scientific Method" (3). Further, according to proponents of this perspective, true knowledge of the world can only be acquired through the use of the Scientific Method.

With the break away of science from classical philosophy in the late nineteenth century, obvious questions developed: What is philosophy apart from science? What kind of knowledge does philosophical activity result in? Is philosophy different from science? Does philosophical activity result in any knowledge at all (4)? In the twentieth century several influential philosophical movements developed each with answers to these and other important questions in philosophy and science. Important to the development of logical positivism was perspective of Logical Atomism and the works of Whitehead, Russell, and Wittgenstein, and eventually, the Vienna Circle.

2. Logical Atomism

Logical atomism is an extremely complex philosophical perspective, based primarily on highly technical mathematical or symbolic logic as developed by Alfred North Whitehead and Bertrand Russell during the period from 1910 to 1913. This section will deal with just a few of its fundamental propositions important to the subsequent development of the works of Ludwig Wittgenstein, a student of Bertrand Russell, and Wittgenstein's influence on the early logical positivists.

a. ALFRED NORTH WHITEHEAD, BERTRAND RUSSELL, AND *PRINCIPIA MATHEMATICA.* After more than ten years of work, Whitehead and Russell, in a series of three volumes entitled *Principia Mathematica*, described a new type of logic, broader in scope than the then standard and accepted logic system based of the works of the Greek philosopher Aristotle. This new system of logic described the relations of symbols to each other (symbolic logic). The importance of the work by Whitehead and Russell lay in the fact that it did not reject the centuries of work by philosophers since Aristotle, but refined it, through mathematics, to a degree of precision never before seen. This symbolic logic could also be used to develop a precise new symbolic language, beyond that of natural languages like French, English, or Spanish, that could clarify the meanings of sentences for further philosophical analysis (4).

Principia Mathematica and the writings of Whitehead and Russell would receive even further explanation and elaboration with Ludwig Wittgenstein (1899–1951), whom many regard as the greatest philosophical genius of the twentieth century. Wittgenstein, among other things, thought of philosophy as an autonomous discipline (e.g., separate from science) dealing with its own sort of particular problems. He did not believe that science could solve philosophical problems and, in later life, would say that even philosophy could not provide any factual information about the world (4). It is only one part of Wittgenstein's great body of work, however, that would launch the logical positivist movement. Several statements contained in Wittgenstein's 1922 work *Tractatus Logico-Philosophicus* would be responsible for a small group of students in Austria, led by a University of Vienna professor named Moritz Schlick, to describe this new philosophical perspective.

b. LUDWIG WITTGENSTEIN AND *TRACTATUS LOGICO-PHILOSOPHICUS*. The logical atomist perspective of Whitehead and Russell received its most comprehensive explanation in this work of Wittgenstein. Wittgenstein's version of logical atomism became known as "Picture Theory." Continuing with the previous examination by Whitehead and Russell of logical precision in language, a perfect language, according to Wittgenstein, is like a map, as it pictures or mirrors the structure of reality. As philosophers attempt to utilize the logical atomistic perspective and symbolic logic to develop aspects of the structure of reality, they would be *actively engaged* in the process, not in a merely passive and reflective stance as in the past (6). This single part of Wittgenstein's massive work would become extremely significant for the eventual development of logical positivism. Wittgenstein's contention that philosophy is a genuine activity, just as science is, would become a major focus for the Vienna Circle. But unlike science, philosophy does not discover new facts or new knowledge. Philosophy describes the structure of the world, and how its basic ingredients are constructed. This is knowledge, but not the same kind that science develops (4). The philosophical system of logical atomism was a metaphysical system in the traditional sense, and as such, it would be rejected shortly by thinkers who would use the same symbolic logic developed by logical atomists to contend that metaphysical knowledge developed by such thinking was nonsense (6).

C.   "Philosophy as Activity" and the Rise of the Vienna Circle

As has been described, logical positivism is often thought to have been initiated by the remark of Wittgenstein in the *Tractatus Logico-Philosophicus* to the effect that philosophy is not a theory, but an activity. The group associated with the beginnings of the movement were individuals meeting in seminars in Vienna, Austria conducted by Moritz Schlick in the early 1920s. The original members of the group were committed to science either by scholarship or profession, and philosophy was more of an avocation. Among its members were Hans Hahn, Fredrich Waismann, Herbert Feigl, Otto Neurath, and Rudolf Carnap.

The original focus of the group was Empiricism, however they were heavily influenced first by Whitehead and Russell and then, more profoundly, by Wittgenstein (7).

In elaborating upon Wittgenstein's view that philosophy was not a theory but an activity, the Vienna Circle held that philosophy does not produce propositions which are true or false; it merely clarifies the meaning of statements, showing some to be scientific, some to be mathematical, and some to be nonsensical (8). Four principles of logical positivism were eventually developed by the Vienna Circle. The first principle is that of *logical atomism*, which says that all complex statements depend on their truth based on simple statements about what may be sensed, and that none of these simple statements can entail any others. The second principle is the *verifiability theory of meaning*, in which only those propositions which can be given meaning verifiable by scientific methods could be said to be either true or false. Therefore anything else, especially metaphysical philosophy has no genuine meaning. George Edward Moore, and individuals at the Cambridge School of Analysis, are most closely identified with verification theory. For a time, a second center of logical positivism flourished in England, rivaling the one in Vienna. The third principle of logical positivism is the *analytic character of a priori knowledge*, which holds that all necessary statements reveal the contents of our ideas, rather than reporting truths about the world. Finally, the fourth principle describes the *emotive theory of values,* where statements of value are neither true or false, but are simply expressions of attitude (7,8).

Of the four principles of logical positivism described by the Vienna Circle and the Cambridge School, it can be argued that the two principles that describe the verification principle and the emotive theory of values would have the greatest impression on the budding career of Herbert Simon and, subsequently, a profound effect on American Public Administration. It is not a great leap to see that Simon's attack on the work of Gulick and Urwick in *Principles of Administration* and his promotion of the "fact-value dichotomy" in his own work *Administrative Behavior* are direct extensions of these basic principles of logical positivism as developed in the Vienna Circle and the Cambridge School of Analysis. Although Simon was not the first to challenge the direction of the new discipline of Public Administration, by building upon the tenets of logical positivism he would force a major shift from what was then the Classical perspective to the Behavioral perspective in Public Administration (2). Although Simon used the logical positivist perspective as developed by the Vienna Circle in the 1920s to mount much of his subsequent work in Public Administration, we have seen that the philosophical traditions of logical positivism actually stretch back through Logical Atomism, the Empiricist and the Modern Science schools of thought of the fifteenth and sixteenth centuries and actually begin in Ancient Greece with the first declared atomist and empiricist, Epicurus.

III.   LOGICAL POSITIVISM AND PUBLIC ADMINISTRATION THEORY: THE RISE OF HERBERT SIMON

By the time the Vienna Circle was meeting and discussing the theory of logical positivism in 1920s Austria, President Woodrow Wilson was already dead and his famous, Public Administration-founding essay *A Study of Administration* was over thirty years old. In this essay, along with a discussion of a necessary separation or dichotomy between politics and administration, was a clear call for the serious study of the new field of Public Administration (9). Twelve years after Wilson's essay, in 1900, books discussing the emerging discipline of Public Administration were written by Frank Goodnow and Leonard White and further developed the concept that the activities of administration in government should be separate from politics or political influence. If this occurred, said these individuals, the concepts of efficiency and the "one best way," both developed through the work of Frederick Taylor and the Scientific Management movement, could be brought into administrative activities (1).

By the early 1920s, the Bureau Movement in the United States was also in full flower. As an outgrowth of the Progressive Movement's desire to reform government at the municipal level, the establishment of New York City's Bureau of Municipal Research (BMR) in 1906, in particular, was to bring forth a number of major figures in Public Administration which would later be attacked by the adherents of logical positivism (10). The early BMR writers, who collectively became known as the ABCs, were William Allen, Henry Bruere, and Frederick Cleveland. Each of the ABCs dealt with aspects of municipal government administration that had been open to problems and corruption in the past. Their works collectively, like the mission of the BMR itself, called for the promotion of efficient and economical government; the adoption of scientific methods of accounting and reporting the details of municipal business; and the collection, classification, analyzation, correlation, interpretation, and finally publication of the resulting data related to the administration of municipal government (11,12,13). The activities of the BMR were designed to direct government energy effectively and efficiently for ultimate social betterment. It is not difficult to see aspects of Empiricism and Modern Science contained within the works of the ABCs and in the mission of the BMR. Each had ideas on systematization of knowledge, a reliance on observation and data collection, and a search for innate truths (i.e., the one best way) among other things. Although it shared this common philosophical ancestry with logical positivism, also contained within the Bureau Movement were concepts abhorrent to the logical positivist perspective.

The philosophy of writers who came from the Bureau Movement perhaps best explains their eventual conflict with logical positivism. The founders of the BMR, for example, were social idealists in the sense that they were philanthropists and Settlement House workers concerned with getting the fullest amount of benefit for the public with altruistic, rather than economic motives. The founders, as part of the Progressive Movement, were concerned with ways of increasing government responsibility that reflected an interest in social control of economic life and in making the expanding industrialism in the United States subject to a rational and benevolent democratic program. Government officials had to be responsible to the citizens which elected them to office. Citizens also had to be responsible by insisting that their elected officials be accountable to them (14). A strong value base undergirds these relationships and, indeed, the entire Bureau movement. This strong value base, along with pronouncements of "the best way" to do this or that discussed by later Bureau movement writers Luther Gulick and Lyndall Urwick in their book *Papers on the Science of Administration* would provide ammunition for a young doctoral student at the University of Chicago, Herbert Simon (15).

A. The Influence of Chester Barnard

Although the history of the development of Public Administration was certainly altered dramatically by the writings generated by Herbert Simon during the late 1940s and through the 1950s, Simon owes an intellectual debt to the works published in the 1930s by Chester Barnard. However, Barnard was certainly not a logical positivist. Barnard was an empiricist whose empiricism was derived from experience and observation (2). It could be argued that his work, especially when discussing executive decision making in organizations, was rooted in the trait theory of leadership school. When Barnard describes the development of executives within organizations, he de-emphasizes intellectual ability and academic training and emphasizes intuition, know-how, hunches, and other characteristics related to intensive experience. This early description of managers in organizations would have effects beyond Simon, when, in the early 1970s Henry Mintzberg, in *The Nature of Managerial Work*, would describe through data developed through qualitative methods the decision making process of managers in a variety of organizational settings (16).

Herbert Simon would adopt major aspects of Barnard's work as he began to describe decision making within organizations. For example, Simon agreed with Barnard's conceptualization of the organization as a system of exchange and the definition of authority suggested by that conceptualization (2). Although disagreeing with his conclusions as to its source, Simon also adopted Barnard's atomistic approach that complex formal organizations evolve from, and consist of, simple formal organizations (2). This atomistic thinking by Simon continued with his research methodology. The unit of analysis in Simon's work became decision premises, rather than the decisions themselves (2). Finally, Simon builds on Barnard's description of human nature and the ability to choose among alternatives within an organizational setting (2). Barnard felt that individuals are limited in their power to choose by physical, biological, and social factors. According to Barnard the organization's role, as defined by its purpose or mission, also helps to prescribe a set of alternatives among which individuals can choose (17). Simon's "Satisficing Man" model with its *bounded rationality* is firmly rooted in Barnard's explanation of individual behavior.

Perhaps the most important departure from the work of Barnard is Simon's promotion of the logical positivist's "value free" zone required for the development of a science of administration. Simon argued that facts (i.e., statements about the observable world and the way in which it operates and can be either true or false) could be logically separated from values (i.e., statements about what "should be" or preferences for desired events and cannot be true or false, or even studied) and analyzed in a value-free zone (18). Unlike Simon's approach, underlying Barnard's writings in Public Administration is a motif of an "open system" in which all social phenomena must occur. Although the complexity of each subsystem limits our understanding of cause and effect, Barnard felt that all subsystems (e.g., facts and values; politics and administration) are connected to the system and even a larger supersystem. They interact and are at the same time determined and determining forces in the system (17). Under Barnard's explanation, and in direct conflict with Simon's work, no decision making or value free subsystem could be artificially carved out or isolated from any other part.

B.   Attacks on the Works of the Classicists

Although interest had been growing for some years since the 1920s and 1930s to expand upon the work of the Classical Period writers who attempted to develop a more scientific approach to the study of Public Administration, Herbert Simon's formidable responses did not come until the late 1940s. In 1946 Simon, a recent graduate of the University of Chicago's doctoral program in political science, in that year published an article entitled "The Proverbs of Administration" in *Public Administration Review* (PAR) in which he sharply criticized the previous work in administrative theory, and then outlined several requirements for an inductive and scientifically-based theory of administration based on the tenets of logical positivism (19). This article was subsequently reprinted as a chapter in Simon's first book, *Administrative Behavior: A Study of Decision-Making Processes in Administrative Organization*, which was published in 1947 and was based on his doctoral dissertation (18).

In his PAR article, Simon was critical of the much of the previous work by writers such as Gulick and Urwick, when he described aspects of it as "proverbs" and often in contradiction with itself. The attack focused on four principles promoted by Gulick and Urwick in *Papers on the Science of Administration*. The very inclusion of the term "science" in the title of the book seemed to disturb Simon as he mounted his attack on the Gulick and Urwick principles. The principles were specialization; unity of command; span of control; and organization by purpose, process, clientele, and place. Although Simon agreed that these ideas were acceptable as "criteria for describing and diagnosing administrations," he felt that when they were treated as immutable laws, they were often in contradiction. Simon cleverly went on to analyze them as laws and attempted to prove their contradictory nature. In summarizing his position, Simon wrote:

> Administrative description suffers from superficiality, oversimplification and lack of realism. It has confined itself too closely to the mechanism of authority and has failed to bring within its orbit the other, equally important modes of influence on organizational behavior. It has been satisfied to speak of "authority," "centralization," "span of control," and "function" without seeking operational definitions of those terms (19, p. 56).

In his book *Administrative Behavior*, Simon undertakes the task of laying out a comprehensive theory of administrative organization based upon a logical positivist view of knowledge acquisition. Simon argues that the role of the scientist is the examination of factual propositions, specifically those based upon the observation of manifest behavior or those logically inferred from observation. Simon proposed that neither the values of the scientist nor those of the person being observed should enter into research or theory building, as no knowledge of the world can be developed from value laden or "should be" statements (18).

C.   The Models of Man: Rational, Administrative, and Satisficing

The rational model of administration and its associated terminology, as first proposed by Simon over 50 years ago, have entered the lexicon of Public Administration. Terms developed long ago and often still used today include: Satisficing Man; bounded rationality; and Administrative Man. According to Simon, at the basis of administrative organization is the concept of rationality. Organizations are created in order to enhance human rationality and structure human behavior so that it may approximate rationality (20). Like the Epicurus and the Empirical school but unlike Descartes and the Modern Science school, Simon felt that absolute or pure rationality could not be achieved, only approached. Following this line of reasoning, individuals are also limited in their capacity to respond to complex problems. Due to this limitation, individuals find it necessary to join together in groups and organizations to deal effectively with the world around them (20). And in a continuation of this thinking evidently inspired by G. W. F. Hegel, Simon felt that only through organizations can an individual approach rationality.

Simon's Administrative Man was developed to replace the classic Economic Man (who was basically a utility maximizer) and exists whenever an organization's values displace the individual's own values or the organization substitutes for the individual's own judgment and decision-making process (18). Because true rationality cannot be achieved, an individual is limited (i.e., bounded) in his perception of rationality. When decisions are necessary, his cognitive and analytic abilities are also made under the operating system of bounded rationality and he "satisfices;" he makes limited decisions that are merely satisfactory and sufficient for the situation (2).

Simon discussed the rational model of administration once more in 1957 the book *Models of Man*. In the years after and continuing into the 1990s, Simon has turned increasingly toward the social psychology of decision making, then to information technology and the processes of cognitive development.

IV. SIMON AND LOGICAL POSITIVISM'S EFFECT ON PUBLIC ADMINISTRATION

Perhaps Dwight Waldo best summarized Herbert Simon's early effects on the discipline of Public Administration. According to Waldo,

> [Simon] replaced the [Wilsonian] politics-administration dichotomy, and offered in its place the fact-value distinction of logical (positivism). He revealed the shallowness of the claims to science, but offered "genuine" science. He demonstrated the "principles" to be rules-of-thumb, folklore, but held out the hope of arriving at empirically based knowledge that would pass the test of true science. Simon is . . . the strongest intellect to address our core problems (in Public Administration) in the past generation. If he could not give us a new set of firmly held orienting beliefs to replace the old ones, then we are not likely to have a replacement (21, p. 78).

However, Simon's early challenge to Public Administration and his call for a "genuine" science of administration based on social psychology principles conducted in a value-free zone made many in the field uncomfortable. In the midst of this discomfiture, political scientists added to Simon's challenge by attacking the action-orientated, practice base of the field. Noted political scientists even called for a "continued dominion of political science over public administration." (1, p. 30) Public Administration began to decline as a separate identity at many colleges and universities, often becoming only an area of emphasis within larger Political Science departments. However, during the period from the mid 1950s until the early 1960s, an important shift was also taking place with the discipline of Public Administration that would eventually lead to is rebirth. As political scientists and the progeny of Herbert Simon grew and dominated, what was left of Classic Public Administration—specifically those individuals unsatisfied with Simon, logical positivism and Behaviorism generally—began to seek shelter elsewhere. The unifying epistemological perspective became General Management, and the port in the storm became Schools of Business (1).

With the inauguration of School of Business and Public Administration at Cornell University in the 1950s, individuals who still believed in the necessity of the discipline of Public Administration to address real world, value laden issues would gain a foothold and began the long climb back to a place in the sun. Eventually, the rapid expansion of government programs during Lyndon Johnson's Great Society, the founding of the National

Academy of Public Administration, and with the rise of the "New Public Administration," colleges and universities with autonomous schools and departments of public administration grew rapidly and now account for the majority of all such programs in the United States (1).

V. THE PUBLIC ADMINISTRATION COUNTERATTACKS ON LOGICAL POSITIVISM

It is certainly reasonable to say that the growth of logical positivism brought about the (temporary) abandonment of the core values of Public Administration inculcated by those individuals in the Progressive and Bureau movements in the then-budding discipline. The shift away from value based considerations weakened and split the field and left a lasting mark that today still haunts the discipline. A section from a recent paper by Robert Berne, Dean of the Wagner School of Public Service at New York University, in which he discusses public service needs for the twenty first century at a National Association of Schools of Public Affairs and Administration (NASPAA) conference highlights the continuing effects of Herbert Simon and logical positivism

> just as there is no way to separate policy from administration, there is no such thing as value free work in public service. Like it or not, the public sector is all about values and I believe that some of our current problems (in public administration) stem from our inability (as academics) to address the role that values play (22, p. 85).

This is only one of the latest calls for a return to value based approaches to the discipline of Public Administration.

As early as 1955 in the book *The Study of Public Administration*, written at the height of its dominance over Public Administration, Dwight Waldo attempted to force the discipline away from logical positivism (14). It would take thirteen years and a more organized and concerted effort on the part of Waldo to achieve his desired impact on logical positivism.

A.   The New Public Administration: Values are Important

The return to a value-centered approach to the discipline of Public Administration began in earnest in 1968 when Dwight Waldo, Director of the Maxwell School, invited a group of young intellectuals to Syracuse University to discuss the state of the discipline. Unrest and turbulence, present on the American scene at the time, also highlighted the conference. The resulting book, *Toward A New Public Administration*, consisted of papers presented at the conference as well as commentary and several chapters assessing the impact of the movement. Called alternatively the "Minnowbrook Perspective" or just "New Public Administration," the common themes among the diverse perspectives presented include the wish for a "proactive administrator" with positive values to supplant the so-called "impersonal" or value-free bureaucrat; the desire that "social equity" at least match efficiency as the goal of public administration; the emphasis upon adaptive and client-centered organizations rather than bureaucracies; and the revolt against "value-free" social science, to be replaced by social relevance (23).

In the years after the Minnowbrook Conference the literature of Public Administration began to echo many of the themes raised by the participants. For example, H. George

Frederickson and Frank Marini, among others, first discussed the potential future of Public Administration as an outgrowth of the Minnowbrook Conference, describing the importance of concepts such as social equity and value premises (23). Frederick C. Mosher and others wrote about the need for strengthening codes of ethics for elected officials in the wake of the Watergate scandal (24). Samuel Krislov introduced the concept "representative" when addressing the structure and composition of bureaucracy and the need for it to reflect the diversity of its clientele (25). The number of Public Administration writers who presented value based reasoning in their works continued to grow throughout the 1980s and 1990s. By the 1990s Simon's long-ago call for value free zones in which to develop knowledge central to the field of Public Administration, if not lost in the mists of time, was certainly out of the mainstream of the discipline.

With the return to a value base in Public Administration, new perspectives, methods and tools for academics and researchers were necessary. These needs led to the growth and acceptance of alternative research perspectives within the field.

B. The Growth of Alternative Research Perspectives: Phenomenology and Qualitative Research Methodology

Phenomenology is a school of thought whose principal purpose is to study phenomena, or appearances, of human experience while attempting to suspend all consideration of their objective reality or subjective association (4). The atomistic, knowledge through experience, and tabula rasa nature of humanity motifs, first proposed long ago by Epicurus, are present in this school of thought, although Phenomenologists would never classify themselves as Empiricists. Phenomenology's major writers include a combination of the works of Søren Kierkegaard (1813–1855) and aspects of the philosophy of Friedrich Nietzsche (1844–1900). Edmund Husserl (1859–1938) and later his student Martin Heidegger (1889–1976) expanded on Kierkegaard and Nietzsche through works published early in the twentieth century. They are responsible for what we now recognize as contemporary Phenomenology. They believed that philosophy could be an exact science, based on certainty which rested on no presuppositions. In a return to the Modern Science of Descartes and a rejection of Empiricism, Phenomenology searches for absolute truths through a "phenomenological reduction" of consciousness and, through this process, uncovers what is intuitively certain along with the essences of experience (4).

The appearance of the Phenomenological perspective in Public Administration can be first seen in the *case method*, which began in the 1930s when, under the aegis of the Committee on Public Administration of the Social Science Research Council, case reports were written by practicing public administrators on managerial problems and how they solved them (1). The popularity of the case method, although diminished by the general diminution of the field under the assault of the logical positivists, returned as the field expanded in the late 1960s and flourishes still today.

As the field of Public Administration again embraced value-based research, alternative methods of data collection and analysis were also necessary. The Phenomenological perspective, now combined with *Ethnography* and *participant-observation*, were utilized more frequently, especially in the production of doctoral dissertations in Public Administration. The expansion of alternative methods of research design, data collection, and analysis in the field has not been welcomed by all, however. Guy Adams and Jay White, building on the earlier work of Howard McCurdy and Robert Cleary, feel that the quality of doctoral dissertations in Public Administration throughout the 1980s has been poor, as evidenced by the subsequent lack of appropriate, main stream, peer-reviewed Public Administration publications by the newly minted doctoral degree holders (26,27). According to Adams and White, this situation has contributed to a lack of knowledge and theory development within the field. Perhaps Herbert Simon and logical positivism are not as far back in the mists of time as we thought.

VI.   POSTSCRIPT: THE LEGACY OF HERBERT SIMON AND LOGICAL POSITIVISM FOR PUBLIC ADMINISTRATION

Inasmuch as logical positivism attacked and weakened Public Administration for a time, it is also fair to say that the writers in the field during the Classical Period provided their attackers with plenty of ammunition. By overstating their positions in search of universal truths and absolutes, the Classical Period writers, however well intentioned and well meaning, provided Herbert Simon and others large targets that were easy to strike.

In his defense, by demanding higher standards for proof of knowledge development and proposing a multivariate approach to the study of Public Administration, Simon forced the field into a period of introspection and reevaluation from which it has emerged, perhaps still suffering from its long-standing identity crisis, but certainly more robust and more willing to deal with value-based issues than ever before.

REFERENCES

1.   N. Henry, *Public Administration and Public Affairs*, Prentice Hall, New Jersey, 1995.
2.   B. Fry, Herbert Simon, *Mastering Public Administration: From Max Weber to Dwight Waldo*, Chatham House Publishers, New Jersey, 1989.
3.   P. Edwards (ed.), *Encyclopedia of Philosophy*, Macmillan, New York, 1967.
4.   R. Popkin and A. Stroll, *Philosophy,* Heinemann Professional Publishing, Ltd., England, 1990.
5.   L. Beck, *18th-Century Philosophy*, The Free Press, New York, 1966.
6.   G. Bergmann, *The Metaphysics of Logical Positivism*, The University of Wisconsin Press, Wisconsin, 1967.
7.   B. Gross, *Analytical Philosophy: An Historical Introduction*, Pegasus Press, New York, 1970.
8.   A. Wedberg, *A History of Philosophy*, Clarendon Press, England, 1984.
9.   W. Wilson, The study of administration, *Polit. Sci. Quart.: 2,* 1987 (1887).
10.   D. Pugh, ASPA's history: Prologue, *Pub. Admin. Rev.:* 45, p. 475, 1985.
11.   W. Allen, *Efficient Democracy*, Dodd, Mead and Company, New York, 1907.
12.   H. Bruere, *The New City Government: a discussion of municipal administration, based on a survey of ten commission governed cities*, D. Appleton and Company, New York, 1912.
13.   F. Cleveland, Chapters in municipal administration and accounting, *Funds And Their Uses*, D. Appleton and Company, New York, 1913.
14.   D. Waldo, *The Study of Public Administration*, Doubleday and Company, New York, 1955.
15.   L. Gulick and L. Urwick (eds.), *Papers on the Science of Administration*, A.M. Kelley, New York, 1969 (reprint).
16.   H. Mintzberg, *The Nature of Managerial Work*, Prentice-Hall, New Jersey, 1973.
17.   W. Wolf, *The Basic Barnard*, Cornell University Press, New York, 1974.
18.   H. Simon, *Administrative Behavior: A Study of Decision Making Processes in Administrative Organization*, The Free Press, New York, 1947.
19.   H. Simon, The proverbs of administration, *Pub. Admin. Rev.:* 6, p. 53, 1946.

20. R. Denhardt, *Theories of Public Organizations*, Brooks/Cole Publishing, California, 1984.
21. D. Waldo. *The Enterprise of Public Administration*, Chandler & Sharp Publishers, California, 1980.
22. R. Berne, Public administration in the twenty-first century: Beyond the prescriptive buzz-words, Proceedings of NASPAA, Austin, Texas, 1995, pp. 82–87.
23. F. Marini (ed.), *Toward a New Public Administration: The Minnowbrook Perspective*, Chandler Publishing Company, New York, 1971.
24. F. Mosher and Others, *Watergate: Implications for Responsible Government*, National Academy for Public Administration, Washington, D.C., 1974.
25. S. Krislov, *Representative Bureaucracy*, Prentice-Hall, New Jersey, 1974.
26. G. Adams and J White, Dissertation research in public administration and cognate fields: An assessment of methods and quality, *Pub. Admin. Rev.*: 52, p. 363, 1994.
27. H. McCurdy and R. Cleary, Why can't we resolve the research issue in public administration, *Pub. Admin. Rev.*: 44, p. 49, 1984.

Part V
Later Modernist Opposition

DIMOCK

The successful executive, therefore, is he who commands the best balance of physique, mentality, personality, technical equipment, philosophical insight, knowledge of human behavior, social adaptability, judgement, ability to understand and get along with people, and sense of social purpose and direction (*Executive in Action*, 1945).

PHENOMENOLOGY

It is we who are genuine positivists. In fact, we permit *no* authority to deprive us of the right of recognizing all kinds of intuition as equally valuable sources for the justification of knowledge, even that of 'modern natural science' (E. Husserl, *Ideas*, W. R. B. Gibson trans., 1962).

SARTRE

Hell is other people (*No Exit*, 1947).

RAWLS

Implicit in the contrasts between classical utilitarianism and justice as fairness is a difference in the underlying conceptions of society. In the one we think of a well-ordered society as a scheme of cooperation for reciprocal advantage regulated by principles which persons would choose in an initial situation that is fair; in the other as the efficient administration of social resources to maximize the satisfaction of the system of desire constructed by the impartial spectator from the many individual systems of desires accepted as a given. (*A Theory of Justice*, 1971).

15

MARSHALL DIMOCK'S DEFLECTIVE ORGANIZATIONAL THEORY

James A. Stever
University of Cincinnati, Cincinnati, Ohio

Marshall Dimock offers students of organizational theory a large and sprawling landscape of concepts, approaches, and arguments. At first glance, these disparate elements present a dizzying array, particularly when the relationships between the major components of his theory seem to be riddled with internal contradictions and inconsistencies. The intent of the following review of Dimock's scholarship will be to build the case that his contributions to the discipline are best understood as a gradual deflection away from conventional organization and administration theories and toward an embrace of premises that were not shared by the milieu in which he operated. Whereas Dimock's early career can be characterized as an endorsement of prevailing public administration norms, his writings during the 1950s began to contain a discernible rejection of the direction that many of his colleagues in public administration and political science were taking. By the 1970s, Dimock had acquired an iconoclastic reputation. By the 1980s, he consolidated and articulated his reasons for embracing what proved to be a novel and unique perspective on the role of organization and administration in modern society. His legacy to organizational theory is an alternative approach that challenges conventional wisdom.

Dimock's deflection away from the organizational theory of his peers can be illustrated by following his intellectual migration through five distinct historical contexts. Within each, he moved further away from what he regarded as wrongheaded prevailing norms and closer to what has become characteristic of his unique approach to organizational and administrative theory. These five contexts are:

The founding of the public administration profession and the establishment of American administrative state,
The New Deal era,
The era of the imperial presidency,
The behavioral era of Political Science, and
Problems of the administrative state during the 1980s.

I. THE CONTEXTS OF MARSHALL DIMOCK'S SCHOLARSHIP

The professional career of Marshall Dimock spanned not only the founding era of the public administration profession in America, but the rapid growth of the administrative state, the New Deal era, the consolidation of power within the American presidency, the behavioral revolution within political science, and the decline of the administrative state in the 1980s. His 1903 birth in San Bernardino, California occurred amidst the rapid industrialization and urbanization that spawned the Progressive movement. By 1928, he earned his Ph.D. from Johns Hopkins University with a specialty in political science and economics. He wrote his dissertation on congressional investigating committees. At the time of his death at age 88 in 1991 on his farm near Bethel, Vermont, he remained active in scholarly, professional, political, and community affairs. Each of these successive contexts progressively shaped his thinking, and the lessons he drew from them were often at odds with those learned by his peers and contemporaries.

The entry into professional life for many turn of the century American leaders was an education at a Northeastern university. Institutions such as Harvard and Johns Hopkins dominated American intellectual life throughout the nineteenth, even early twentieth century. The professors in these universities were steeped in European culture, idealism, constitutionalism, and committed to noblesse oblige. Though born in California, Dimock's graduate school experience was at Johns Hopkins, and it transformed him. The geographic center of his life became the Northeast—where he settled eventually on a Vermont farm. He developed an abiding affinity for the Northeastern political culture and tradition—remarking that Woodrow Wilson and Franklin D. Roosevelt were his two favorite presidents (1).

By virtue of obtaining a graduate education at Johns Hopkins, Dimock acquired a classical, liberal arts mindset about administration. This education placed him in direct contact with many leading figures in twentieth century government including Arthur O. Lovejoy, W. W. Willoughby, W. F. Willoughby, and Frank J. Goodnow. These scholars manifested an abiding concern for the American constitutional tradition. Their intent was to render it compatible with the rapidly growing administrative agencies within the American State. These scholars were not administrative technicians and specialists, but rather concerned for constitutional, ethical, and cultural issues generated by the introduction of administrative agencies into the traditional liberal state. Rejecting the pessimism of Durkheim and Weber about modern administration, this tradition, with Woodrow Wilson as its chief spokesman, believed that constitutionally constrained administration could be a positive contribution to American liberal democracy.

Dimock was one of the charter members of the American Society for Public Administration. These founders understood professional public administration as an enterprise steeped in political theory and rejected the later premise that administration could be a free standing, specialized, technical profession. Public administration was to be externally grounded; guided by the principles of liberal constitutionalism, political economy, philosophy, and statecraft. Woodrow Wilson's question, articulated in *The Study of Administration*, was actively pursued by the founders: Can the American constitutional tradition be reconciled with administrative principles so that the resulting administrative state enhances the political economy and culture of America?

After receiving his Johns Hopkins Ph.D. in 1928, Dimock taught at the University of California at Los Angeles from 1928 to 1932. His move to the University of Chicago was providential, placing him in a political science department that became one of the architects of the New Deal. Supported by Charles E. Merriam, Rockefeller funds, and colleagues who were on the cutting edge of governmental reform, Dimock became one of the central brain trust members who traveled on designated Pullman cars from Chicago to Washington, D.C. to frame the outlines of Franklin D. Roosevelt's New Deal (2).

The period from 1932 to 1945 was one in which Dimock served with distinction and without dissent. He left the University of Chicago in 1937 to serve the Roosevelt administration in a variety of distinguished positions: in the Immigration and Naturalization Service under Frances Perkins, as Assistant Secretary of Labor, and as chief executive of the Sea-Going Manpower Program in the War Shipping Administration. With the survival of the country at stake, Dimock functioned as a loyal servant of the state. There were no indications in this period that he harbored reservations about the administrative state or that he harbored alternative approaches to public administration and organization. During this thirteen year period, he worked to assure that the administrative state not only developed apace, but functioned smoothly and at peak efficiency.

Conventional professional wisdom during the New Deal and World War II supported a larger and more powerful presidency; one that was substantially in control of federal administrative agencies. Arthur M. Schlesinger labeled the presidency that emerged the "imperial presidency" (3). For many scholars and practitioners of public administration, the development of the presidency became synonymous with sound governmental management. From the beginning of his work within the Roosevelt administration, Marshall Dimock's was professionally associated with groups supporting a strong presidency. However, by the mid 1950s, he began to challenge whether the presidency could be significantly strengthened through organizational means. Though his autobiography, published in 1980, defends the original contributions of Louis Brownlow's Committee on Administrative Management (4), he challenged the successive attempts to strengthen the presidency—arguing that, large and powerful presidential staffs interfered with the personal ability of presidents to govern. Frank Sherwood argues that Dimock eventually came to the position that strengthening the Executive Office of the Presidency was a "limited solution carried to excess" (5).

In addition to their support for the imperial presidency, Dimock had other concerns about administrative professions in the post war era. The behavioral revolution presented a dilemma for many classically trained political scientists. As a Johns Hopkins graduate, Marshall Dimock believed that the foundations of politics and administration were intellectually grounded in law, philosophy, and religion. Traditional political science was the basis for his approach to organization and administration. He served in the University of Chicago Department of Political Science, 1932–41, as a professor of political science at Northwestern University, 1945–48 and as head of New York University's Department of Government from 1955–62. In contrast to many of his peers who adapted and assimilated the few behavioralist assumptions of the 1950s, Dimock rejected this approach from the outset. He opposed its premises about the origins of human behavior as well as the implications of this approach for organizational management. Thus, Dimock did not follow Elton Mayo and Herbert Simon into the new world or organizational behavior.

Finally, as the large governmental organizations constituting the American administrative state came under heavy criticism during the late 1970s and 1980s, Dimock's later scholarship searched for ways to reestablish their legitimacy as an integral part of liberal government. On one hand, Dimock insisted that administrative agencies were necessary to integrate and implement government policy. On the other, he acknowledged that the administrative state had become distended and intrusive. As a remedy, he proposed to shrink the administrative state long before this reduction became fashionable. To accomplish this, he urged the citizenry to accept more personal responsibility. His later scholarship argued that the failure of administrative organizations could be traced to leadership. His solution was the restoration of political leadership as a first step toward the revitalization of governmental organizations. Dimock's last published work was devoted to an exploration of ways to restore the administrative state to its former grandeur and promise (6).

At the time of his death in 1991, he was actively pursuing the revitalization of the administrative state by: attending professional conferences, speaking before professional associations and civic groups, as well as producing manuscripts and articles. His last work (unpublished) was titled *A Philosophy of Administration*. Though he had written a book by the same title in 1958 (7), this second book on the subject represented a second, original attempt to clarify his thinking about the philosophical basis of administrative organizations. This last manuscript presented an alternative basis for modern-organizational theory. It extrapolated and clarified themes that began to surface in his published works on organizational theory during the late 1940s.

Dimock's scholarship can be divided into two periods: early and mature. The early period extends from 1928 to 1945; the mature from 1945 to 1991. From 1945 onward, his scholarship was iconoclastic, providing an atypical philosophical prism through which to view the modern organization. This post World War II scholarship commenced with the publication of *The Executive in Action* in 1945 (8). During the subsequent four decades, he produced a series of books devoted to organizational theory. Closer examination of these books will illustrate Dimock's progressive embrace of organizational principles that originated in premodern, as opposed to modern philosophy.

II. MAJOR WORKS

From the publication of his first book, *Congressional Investigating Committees*, in 1923 to the end of World War II. Dimock had published ten books and 57 articles on various institutional aspects of public administration. During this early period he worked with other colleagues to develop public agencies that served overarching public interests. He promoted, along with other colleagues, the constitutional basis of public administration, and accepted the premise that the ends of public organization must be democratically determined. If there were a distinguishing trait to his scholarship during this early era, it that Dimock proposed alternative means for developing and controlling the American administrative state. Whereas the Brownlow Committee suggested that the executive should be the primary unit within the federal government to control and supervise administrative agencies, Dimock argued that the Congress was the more appropriate locus of control (9). This issue was particularly controversial in the case of government corporations. Their quasi public, quasi private status placed them at the margins of the federal government, but raised questions about supervision and control. Dimock acquired expertise on such issues and explored the problems associated with integrating these corporations into the federal administration. His focused on a range of public corporations including public utilities, the Panama Canal, and the Inland Waterways Corporation. In the case of the Panama Canal, her argued: "Every Policy affecting the Canal administration is an appropriate subject for Congressional attention" (10). This insistence on congressional management differed from that of the approach taken by the Brownlow Committee—one which placed management and operational control under the executive branch and giving the Congress indirect, broad influence. However, these were means-oriented, technical issues among professional colleagues characteristic of the internal tensions found within any profession. Dimock's broader, more fundamental and foundational departure from the conventional norms of the profession began with the publication of *The Executive in Action* in 1945.

The Executive in Action inaugurated a new era in Dimock's scholarship, one in which the practical, technical, and instrumental questions of administration gave way to questions and themes of a philosophical, theoretical nature. This landmark book represented Dimock's attempt to communicate directly to those who aspired to manage large organizations. It offered advice on predictable management problems such as meshing line and staff, delegating, maintaining unity of command, and building the organization. This book was addressed primarily to practicing organizational executives, and it served as the platform for Dimock's subsequent management consulting career. Yet, simmering beneath this seemingly practical book was a challenge to the popular systems theory and behavioral approaches that were gaining popularity in the post war management milieu.

The introduction to the book laid out two claims. The *first* was that organizational managers were destined to be the leading statesmen of post war industrial nations. It recognized the growing power of large organizations. This was a theme reminiscent of diverse types of literature in the post-progressive period—arguments advanced elsewhere by Mayo, McGregor, and Burnham, Mannheim, and Veblen. The *second*, though, was original; expressing Dimock's own assessment of the relationship between organization and leader. Whereas the period literature—ranging from Marxist literature to management literature—acknowledged the growing power of organizations, their assessment was that the inherent power of organizations explained why organizational executive were powerful. Dimock stood this argument on its head—arguing that organizations were epiphenomenal, deriving their vitality and energy from that of their leader. Though the philosophical base for this original perspective on organization was not established by *The Executive in Action*, subsequent post war works elaborated and justified this point of view.

Free Enterprise and the Administrative State signaled a clearer philosophical departure from the conventional wisdom on the administrative state. Whereas Dimock's pre-war writings differed with colleagues over the appropriate means by which to advance the administrative state, this work challenged both the necessity and desirability of such a state. *Free Enterprise and the Administrative State* was written by an author who had undergone a fundamental change of mind. Also, whereas earlier works were written to a professional audience, this work was written to executives, businessmen, and the broader public.

The opening line of *Free Enterprise and the Administrative State* conveyed Dimock's shift: "The Free Enterprise System is said to be losing ground in the United States and to be giving way to an all powerful 'administrative state.' " The remainder of the book depicts a dialectical relationship between free enterprise and the regulation promulgated by the large organizations of the administrative state. Dimock urged his business audience to conduct their affairs responsibly—on a small scale—in order to dispel the argument that business requires government regulation. Only irresponsible, power hungry businessmen who rampantly use technology to create corporations that abuse the public trust require government regulation. Such an argument set Dimock apart from his colleagues who assumed the inevitability and growth of the administrative state—one that would inevitably displace the old individualistic, free enterprise approach to business organization.

Whereas the public administration profession of the 1950s was attempting to fashion a humane, democratic administrative state, Dimock was trying to squelch the need for such a state in order to maintain nineteenth century values that he regarded as superior to any that could develop in large administrative organizations.

How can this shift be explained? One way is to consider Dimock's changing personal situation. After the war, he retired from active government service and entered the academy—serving from 1945–1948 as Professor of Political Science at Northwestern University, then served from 1949–1950 as a Vermont State Legislator. He also turned to farming as an avocation. However, to dwell on these career shifts is to overlook the more fundamental explanation, a shift in intellect. This shift can be summed up as a movement away from modern philosophy combined with a progressive embrace of premodern philosophy.

Prior to 1945, he worked within the American constitutional tradition, a perspective that was fundamentally modern. Like other constitutionalists, he acknowledged that shifting circumstances obviated old constitutional arrangements. Constitutionalists are modernist in the sense that the constitution becomes an instrumental document by which to progressively improve society and the human condition. This historicist faith that society can be perpetually improved clashes with premodern perspectives which view the human condition as one in which social structure and human personality are influenced, even determined by nature. For example, from Aristotle's perspective, human character and the polity grew in the same organic fashion as trees and other natural phenomena. In migrating to the premodern perspective on organization, Dimock began to doubt whether the professions could use their knowledge and the administrative state as instruments for the improvement of American democracy. Instead, he began to develop a theory of organization and administration which viewed organizations and individuals as natural products. Hence, the task becomes that of understanding how organization and administration are influenced by nature—how they grow and decline in accordance with natural rhythms.

Vestiges of this premodern philosophy emerged first in *A Philosophy of Administration*, published in 1958, a book that he regarded as a sequel to *The Executive in Action* (11). In contrast to the functional and mechanistic POSDCORB principles of administration (planning, organizing, staffing, directing, coordinating, reporting, and budgeting), Dimock proposed naturalistic principles of administration and urged leaders to grow the organization in organic fashion while maintaining balance an harmony among the institution's constituent parts. Dimock was fully aware of the differences between his organizational philosophy and other approaches. In making his case for an alternative approach, he criticized contemporary approaches for attempting to reduce organizations to little more than orderly interactions that produced decisions in machine-like fashion (12). Biology, he argued, was the appropriate foundation for administration. To him, the behavioral approaches to administration were misguided in their engineering attempts to identify the essential parts of organizations, and standardize their operation, including their interaction with other constituent parts.

The casual reader of Dimock's philosophy might assume the origins of his organic philosophy extend back only to nineteenth century idealism; that he was merely reviving the early modern Germanic or British organic approach to statecraft and applying it to administration. Such a reading would overlook Dimock's basic skepticism about the possibility of a distinctly modern approach to administration. His criticism was that administration was an enduring feature of the human condition, an essential enterprise involving the integration of basic parts of any given society. He denied that modern science could develop forms of administration that were substantive improvements over those that developed in ancient civilization. Dimock argued that balance within an administrative organization is an enduring task confronted by virtually all administrators throughout history. And, balance within administrative organizations is akin to balance within biological systems—a continual, delicate process (13). The only difference is that within administrative systems there is no organ such as the brain that assures balance. It is the judgement of the leader that assures the organization is properly integrated and synchronized.

In *Administrative Vitality*, Dimock's premodern approach to administrative theory was elevated to high art (14). The book, published in 1959, used premodern organic philosophy to construct a theory of organization. Challenging Weber's pessimistic prognosis for modern organization, Dimock argued that organizations are not inherently predisposed to either bureaucratic rigidity or to decay (15). He also stopped short of endorsing the classical argument that human institutions are subject to the same rhythms found in nature. Rather, using Toynbee, he observed that "the gifted individual is able to harmonize all the diverse elements of his environment into an effective whole" (16). The gifted individual Dimock was referring to was the administrator; the "whole," the organization. Rather than place faith in organizational structure or design, as were many of his contemporaries, Dimock relied on the administrator. He understood that organizations decline when they become introverted, rule ridden and otherwise blind to the needs of their environment. In contrast, organizations remain vital when their leaders use authority to resist these enervating tendencies or when employees voluntarily respond to environmental challenges (17).

With the premodern approach Dimock swam against the current of modern organizational theory—a current depicting the organization as inherently powerful, as a superior institutional form by which to accomplish the work of the modern era. His later works revisited, amplified, but never departed from this theme. For example, 18 months before his death, he published "The Restorative Qualities of Citizenship" in *Public Administration Review* (18). This article argued that the foundations of governmental renewal lay in restoring the virtues and vitality of individual citizens. Governmental institutions cannot compensate for irresponsible, weak individuals. His last major manuscript, currently unpublished, was a book devoted to administrative philosophy. It argued that organizations must conform to nature, that they wither if they do not take account of the natural qualities and inclinations of their employees or the principles of nature such as balance and integration.

At the time that he crafted this approach to administrative organizations, Dimock's ideas were not in vogue, but rather at odds with the dominant modern approaches then in fashion: e.g., systems theory, cybernetic theory, structural approaches, and the managerial school founded by Barnard and Mayo. Locating Dimock within this array of twentieth century administrative and organizational theory is an challenging task; largely because Dimock himself staked out his novel positions with relative indifference to other theories. He wrote for practical businessmen and the educated public with minimal concern for the academic enterprise of staking out the relationship between his theory versus others. This difficulty notwithstanding, his theory can be understood by comparing it to other recent premodern theories that have developed. Also, his theory stands in sharp contrast to the managerial theory of Mayo, and the behavior theory of Herbert Simon.

III. RELATIONSHIPS TO OTHER THEORIES

Other premodern theories with naturalistic overtones have surfaced after Dimock's approach paved the way during the 1950s. For example, during the 1970s, the entrepreneurial approach shifted attention back to the natural qualities of leaders. It became fashionable to attribute the success of any given organization to the creative talents of its founder. In this vein of thought, Eugene Lewis defined the public entrepreneur as "a person who creates or profoundly elaborates a public organization so as to alter greatly the existing pattern of allocation of scarce public resources" (19).

Premodern, naturalism also entered the spectrum of organizational theory through the power approach to organization. Eschewing structural explanations for the subordinate place of women in organization, Rosabeth Kanter argues that women must learn to wield power (20). Others besides Kanter have acquired an appreciation for the role of nonrational factors in the organization. Jeffrey Pfeffer finds that leaders share certain natural qualities enabling them to rise to positions of prominence within organizations: e.g., energy and physical stamina, sensitivity to others, charisma, and an ability to tolerate conflict (21). These are natural endowments that affect individual success having little to do with traditional modern explanations for leadership success such as mastery of leadership technique or rationality.

In retrospect, Dimock's pioneering premodern approach to organizational theory was a novel approach, the first of its kind. His attempt to introduce biology as an explanation for organizational dynamics occurred amidst a skeptical milieu of modern theory, and these rival theories understood organizations in radically differing terms. It is certain, though, that Dimock would not have agreed with either the entrepreneurial or the power approaches. For all of his emphasis on the natural qualities of the leader, he placed an abiding emphasis on ethics and morality as the sine qua non of leadership, qualities that entrepreneurial and power theories seldom stress. Dimock defined strength as strength of character as opposed to strength defined strictly in power oriented terms. One can anticipate that Dimock's response to Pfeffer and Kanter would be that leaders who attempt to lead without ethical and moral consideration for others alienate rather than stimulate trust and cooperation within the organization. Dimock sought to avoid any religious or transcendental argument for ethical leadership. Rather, he concentrated on the salutary impact that ethics had throughout the organization (22).

The rival organizational theories most prominent on Dimock's horizon were those advanced by the managerialists. The major theorists in this tradition were Lawrence J. Henderson, Elton May, Fritz Roethlisberger, George C. Homans, T. N. Whitehead, and Chester Barnard. Collectively, they believed that modern organization itself was a superior institutional form that should be used to refit industrial society for the challenges of the twentieth century. Unlike Max Weber, they adopted a positive approach toward organization, believing that it was a resource, not something that was destined to detract from the quality of life available to the modern individual. Though Herbert Simon was not an integral part of this school, Dimock considered Simon and the managerialists to share a common fault. Each encouraged dependence upon the organization—treating the organization as an aid or as a crutch to rationality and creativity. This violated Dimock's own approach, one which viewed individual character and creativity as prior to organization, not created and enhanced by it. His criticisms of Simon were quite direct. In *Administrative Vitality*, he argued that Simon assumed erroneously that organizations could enhance individual rationality and aid their power to reach rational decisions. Such a strategy was flawed because, from Dimock's perspective, organizations ought to encourage individuals to think in creative ways. They should not depend upon accepted organizational canons of rationality (23).

It was Simon as well as managerialism's view of the individual that differed most sharply from Dimock's own assessment. Both believed individuals and the concept of freestanding individual rationality to be an outworn, nineteenth century approach to modernity. For individual rationality, both Simon and the managerialists sought to move the locus of rationality from individual to organization. Mayo, for example, repeatedly argued that individuals, left to their own devices were ill prepared to cooperate effectively with others. For Mayo and the managerialists, individuals not only had to be taught to cooperate, but they required an organization which would perpetually socialize and otherwise constrain them to cooperate. Believing that the work in the twentieth century was destined to be performed by collectives of specialists rather than by discrete, talented and skilled individuals, Mayo and others turned to organizations as the ongoing instrument for rational effective cooperation.

This vision of collective rationality and collective work ran counter to Dimock's own assessment of the twentieth century. For him, the twentieth century, like all centuries before it was a period in which a few gifted individuals integrated other individuals into effective organizations. However, this integration was based on cognitive volition, trust, and ethical relationship. Dimock viewed the Simon and the managerialists as resorting to behavioral trickery because they harbored far too dismal an assessment of the cognitive and moral faculties of the average man. Hence, administration becomes an enterprise too heavily laden with an emphasis on non-cognitive behavioral control. Dimock encouraged leaders to manage by intellectual and ethical methods that appealed to mankind's more noble, higher abilities and characteristics.

In spite of his many strident disagreements with fellow colleagues, Dimock remained active in the professions and close friends with many of the leading intellectual figures of his era. He routinely corresponded with and visited, for example, Luther Gulick, who developed the more functional POSDCORB approach to administration. He actively corresponded with friends and colleagues in government service throughout the world. His death triggered a torrent of tributes and eulogies testifying to his personal as well as intellectual impact.

The definitive assessment of his contributions and legacy has yet to be written for several reasons. First, the corpus of his intellectual contribution is vast: 47 books, hundreds of professional articles, and an extensive but important array of non professional publications such as his popular animal stories. All of these must be synthesized and will have a bearing on any authoritative assessment. Second, his unpublished manuscripts await final editing, publication, and assimilation into the professional milieu. Hence, any assessment of Dimock's legacy must be a qualified assessment.

IV. IMPACT AND LEGACY

Dimock's most significant impact on the professions occurred from 1930 to 1950. From 1950 onward, his primary impact was on organization theory and philosophy. The behavioral revolution passed him by, both in public administration and in political science. During the twenty year period between 1930 and 1950 when he was at his professional zenith, he helped frame the intellectual issues that affected the institutions and public policies of the New Deal and World War II era. Once the study of organizational behavior effectively displaced the classical approach to organizations that he learned at Johns Hopkins, he developed a new audience appealing primarily to businessmen as opposed to professionals.

In the long run, though, the new intellectual foundation that he laid for organizations as an outsider from 1950 onward may outweigh his early professional influence as an insider. His writing during the 1950s challenged professional orthodoxy and it remains to be seen whether this challenge will grow into a major paradigm affecting the study of organizations. He argued that the enduring basis of the modern organization is the individual rather than the inherent rationality imbedded in the structure and processes of the organization.

Dimock's organizational individual was at odds with the vision of the employee that emerged in Herbert Simon's neoclassical approach or from the writing of managerialists such as Mayo or Barnard. The neoclassical and managerial approaches depicted the average employee as prone to habit, and inclined to take orders so long as these orders did not violate deeply held convictions or moral norms. These approaches also painted the average employee as one in need of guidance and assistance from the organization. Hence, the rational organizational aided the individual in adjusting to the technical, complex world of the twentieth century.

In contrast, Dimock reversed the image—arguing that the organization depended more on the individual than the individual on the organization. Left to their own devices, Dimock argued, organizations would become ossified, rule ridden, and bureaucratic. Organizations depend on the vitality of individuals.

The debate that Dimock opened, though, is more significant than simply to cavil about individual versus organization. His writings challenged the pervasive assumption that organizations, *sui generis*, were destined to displace individuals as the dominant actors of modern society. The Progressive movement planted the seeds of this faith in organization, that somehow administrative organizations, once attached to government, would eliminate patronage and usher in an era of good government. The classical, managerial, and neoclassical approaches to organization encouraged this faith. Dimock was among the first administrative theorists to challenge the foundations of this dominant point of view.

The record will undoubtedly show that Dimock lodged this challenge without resorting to radicalism or skepticism. Finding no audience within the profession, he used his considerable talents to carve out a new career in business consulting. However, throughout his career, he remained loyal to the ideal of a progressive political economy, one governed by well-administered, vital organizations. To this extent he was a modernist. Yet, he recognized that for modernity to persist and flourish it could not succumb to faith in exotic organizational technologies. Rather, the strength of any organization lay in its leadership and in the character and creativity of individuals who worked within the organization.

One of the pillars of Dimock's legacy is that he sketched out not only an alternative basis for the organization, but an alternative route by which modernity could advance—one that relied extensively on premodern philosophy. The impact of his scholarship will inevitably depend on how it is perceived by scholars who are themselves disenchanted with conventional modern organizational theory. One alternative has been to embrace Postmodern philosophy and reject modern organization altogether. Dimock has little to say to those who accept this alternative. He chose premodern, not Postmodern thought.

Yet, Dimock's premodern organizational theory is, in many respects, more satisfying that genre of premodern organizational theory which resurged in the 1970s. This 1970s theory attempts to deflate conventional modern theory by arguing that no modern organization management technique is immune from old fashioned power principles. Hence, 1970s premodern theory argues that power is the common denominator of all organizations throughout time. Dimock's premodern theory rejects power as the basis for organization. Nor is Dimock skeptical of the positive role that organizations can play in advancing modernity and improving the standard of living for the masses. Instead, Dimock argues that organizations must be founded on individuality and ethics, not on techniques of influencing and molding organizational behavior. This was the essence of Dimock's scholarship—one that sought to correct the professional excesses of his time.

Dimock's peers, professional colleagues, and friends understood that he was writing from an unconventional perspective. This unconventional reputation was well deserved. Whereas the dominant professional ethos of Dimock's milieu was modern, his approach was not modern. At some junctures, his observations about organizations were anti modern. These observations lead to be broader question: how can Dimock's scholarship be categorized? The previous narrative has used to term "premodern" to describe his philosophical approach to organizations. Yet, this term can include a wide variety of medieval, antimodern, ancient, and classical perspectives. The following section will consider Dimock's premodern orientation more closely and will argue that Dimock's work ultimately rested upon classical foundations, themes, and convictions.

V. CLASSICAL FOUNDATIONS

The classical worldview is one seldom linked to organization theory. Systematic, scientific study of organizations is largely a modern phenomenon. Though, from a Weberian perspective, vestiges of organizations in the form of bureaucracy can be traced back into ancient societies, the ubiquity and intensity of theory devoted to organization per se, is coterminous with the developing of modern philosophy and the exigencies associated with modern society. Organization theory, driven by modern philosophy, becomes, scientific, technical, empirical, and experimental, and, above all, rational. In contrast, the classical orientation evokes images of gods and goddesses, marble temples, and a philosophical approach to life. The Greeks, though they understood some scientific concepts, did not apply them to organizations. Moreover, the modern concept of efficient, rational organization was not a part of classical thought.

Prior to Dimock, conventional wisdom dictated that classical thought was an unsuitable platform for modern organizational theory, and there were sound reasons for this conclusion. The distance between original classical thought and organization theory can be illustrated by considering briefly the nature of classical thinking. The earliest manifestations of the classical worldview can be found in the epic poetry of a blind poet named Homeros who wrote in the eighth century BC (24). The resulting genre of Homeric epic poetry depicted ordinary, straightforward people in the grip of cosmic forces and challenges. The mindset commonly associated with the philosophy of the classical period was originated in the fifth century BC under the influence of Plato. Platonic philosophy cast the individual and conventional society as the reflection of transcendental forms. Hence, the structure of society and even individual behavior itself was driven the factors that were beyond the cognitive capabilities of even the best and brightest individuals. Plato did hold out the hope that elite philosopher kings could attain some fragmentary knowledge by studying how these forms shaped and molded human behavior and experience.

Even the challenge to Platonic thought from Aristotle in the fourth century did not change the dominant parameters of classical thought. Though Aristotle challenged the existence of transcendental forms, he nevertheless accepted the individual as a product of nature that grew and developed according to predetermined natural processes. Aristotle also explained politics in the same way. The politics of a given society was shaped, influenced, and determined by the quality of the people in the society. This explains Aristotle's explanation for democracy. He argued that common people (the *demos*) prefer democracy because such a governmental form suits their inherent natures.

Dimock was the first prominent modern organizational theorist to consciously renounce modernist presuppositions but to attempt a linkage between classical philosophy and organization theory. His efforts resulted on a corpus of organizational theory with classical, not modern philosophical foundations (25). There are two pervasive indicators within the corpus of this theory that suggest the presence of classical foundations: 1. his theory of organizational leaders, 2. his rejection of modern idea of progress and affinity for classical growth/decay explanations for organization development.

Written in 1945, *The Executive in Action* was the first indicator that Dimock was moving away from the modern ideal of a professionally trained, technically adroit manager. Chapter one of this work depicts the manager in Aristotlean terms, as an individual who must be balanced. In Dimock's words:

> The successful executive, therefore, is he who commands the best balance of physique, mentality, personality, technical equipment, philosophical insight, knowledge of human behavior, social adaptability, judgement, ability to understand and get along with people, and a sense of social purpose and direction (26).

He was careful to soften this classical rhetoric with the qualification that managers were not natural elites, because they were they born with natural leadership qualities.

However, thirteen years later in his *Philosophy of Administration*, Dimock moved closer to the classical theory—arguing that those who influenced society most were gifted individuals with natural gifts. Consider the following passage:

> Administration is outstanding individuals. Individuals who in their personalities and character exhibit an integration of universal values, such as wisdom and reverence, honesty and integrity, devotion to human interests, as well as those traditions which are favored in the cultural stream of particular civilization, such as the American where dynamism and decisiveness, logic and objectivity are given special attention (27).

In this work he also refers to administrators as constituting a "class" who, acting through institutions shape the society of which they are a part (28). These statements about leadership are strikingly reminiscent of Plato's conviction that the gifted rule. Moreover, it echoes a pervasive classical theme—that an individual's character is naturally given and cannot be significantly altered through training or through the acquisition of skills techniques.

A second indicator of Dimock's classical word view is his naturalistic analysis of organizational behavior and development. Greek philosophy gave the principles of growth and decay center stage. Physis (growth) was a central analytical principle present in Aristotle's *Politics*. *Administrative Vitality*, published in 1959, was the first credible book on organization theory to build a theory of organization around classical growth/decay principles. In the opening chapters of the book, Dimock makes it clear that growth and decay are fundamental, universal principles. Predictably, organizations are subject to these principles. The task of the managers is to understand how to maintain the vitality of organizations and avoid debilitating decay in which the organization acquires rigid bureaucratic-like traits that results in its ossification. *Administrative Vitality* was a series of instructions to managers on how classical principles of growth and vitality can be enhanced by wise leadership.

In the final analysis, the organization theory of Marshall Dimock should be understood as a pioneering effort to recast the foundations of conventional modern thinking about organizations. Like all pioneers, his work was often misunderstood and occasionally opposed because it challenged the prevailing professional wisdom. Moreover, though he forged a linkage between classical philosophy and organization theory, he did not produce a systematic, definitive explanation of the full relationship between these two modes of thought. That task must inevitably be left to future theorists capable of applying classical wisdom to modern concepts.

REFERENCES

1. M. E. Dimock, *The Center of My World*, Taltsville, Vermont: Countryman Press, 1980, p. 110.
2. *The Center of My World*, p. 50.
3. A. M. Schlesinger, *The Imperial Presidency*, Popular Library, New York, 1974.
4. *The Center of My World*, p. 95.
5. F. P. Sherwood, "A Limited Solution Carried to Excess," *Int. Jour. of Pub. Admin.* 17, pp. 2085–2107, 1994.
6. M. E. Dimock, *Crisis Management*, published as a special volume of *Int. Jour. of Pub. Admin.*: 14, pp. 499–762, 1991.
7. M. E. Dimock, *A Philosophy of Administration*, Harper & Row, New York, 1958.
8. Dimock, Marshall E., *The Executive in Action*, Harper & Row, New York, 1945.
9. Seidman, Harold "Dimock's Philosophy of Administration," *Int. Jour. of Pub. Admin.*: 17, pp. 2025–2035, 1994. 17(11): 2025–2035.
10. M. E. Dimock, *Government-Operated Enterprises in the Panama Canal Zone*, University of Chicago Press, Chicago, 1933, p. 33. Louis Brownlow wrote the introduction to this work; observing that Dimock's ideas on the subject were "food for thought." Though Dimock's ideas departed from Brownlow's own maxims for sound government administration, he gave Dimock intellectual freedom to explore alternative approaches.
11. *A Philosophy of Administration*, p. 19.
12. *A Philosophy of Administration*, p. 19.
13. *A Philosophy of Administration*, p. 41.
14. M. E. Dimock, *Administrative Vitality: The Conflict with Bureaucracy*, Harper & Row, New York, 1959.
15. *Administrative Vitality*, p. 87.
16. *Administrative Vitality*, p. 49.
17. *Administrative Vitality*, 93, see also Chapter 12 entitled "Integrative Leadership." In this chapter Dimock argues that the leader is responsible for keeping the organization in balance and out of destructive cycles.
18. M. E. Dimock, The restorative qualities of citizenship, *Pub. Admin. Rev.*: 50, pp. 21–25, 1990.
19. E. Lewis, *Public Entrepreneurship: Toward a Theory of Bureaucratic Political Power*, Indiana University Press, Bloomington, 1984, p. 9.
20. R. M. Kanter, *Men and Women of the Corporation*, Basic Books, New York, 1977.

21. Pfeffer, J. *Managing With Power: Politics and Influence in Organization*, Harvard Business School Press, Boston, 1992, pp. 79, 165–88.
22. For an elaboration of Dimock's pragmatic approach to ethics, and the tendency of ethical leadership to stimulate cooperation rather than dissension, see *A Philosophy of Administration*, pp. 52–61.
23. *Administrative Vitality*, p. 111.
24. A. Dihle, *A History of Greek Literature*, Routledge, New York, 1994, p. 10.
25. For a full elaboration of the classical principles embraced by Dimock, see J. A. Stever, Nature and administration, *Int. Jour. of Pub. Admin.*: 17, pp. 2109–2135.
26. *The Executive in Action*, p. 11.
27. *A Philosophy of Administration*, p. 5.
28. *A Philosophy of Administration*, p. 2.

16

PHENOMENOLOGY

William L. Waugh, Jr.
Georgia State University, Atlanta, Georgia

For the last half century or more, critics of logical positivism have pointed out the inherent limitations of empirical research and offered alternative philosophies and methods for examining phenomenon that cannot be empirically verified and measured. One of the groups of critics, the *phenomenologists*, have argued that the research methods of the physical sciences are ill-suited to the study of human behavior and the human "world." They have maintained that to understand human behavior one must recognize that perceptions differ and how one perceives the world defines how one acts. Reality is a social construct. *Phenomenology* gained considerable popularity as a philosophical alternative to logical positivism and as a scientific approach during the postwar period and still has its proponents in the academic and philosophical communities.

Phenomenology is derived from the Greek words "phainomenon" ("appearance") and "logos" ("reason" or "word") and can be loosely translated as "reasoned inquiry" (1). Phenomenology is not a school or a uniform philosophic discipline. Phenomenological purists would call it a return to the methods of classical Greek philosophy rather than a separate, new approach to philosophy or simply a reaction against the philosophy of logical positivism (empiricism). A simplistic definition of phenomenology would be that it is a philosophical perspective arrived at by the elimination of one's assumptions and biases concerning everything except perceived reality. Since the early decades of this century, phenomenological approaches have been debated. The resultant philosophical approach has had considerable appeal and has been applied to every field from ethics to music and from aesthetics to social behavior. Strands of phenomenology underlie the existentialist works of Jean-Paul Sartre and Albert Camus and in the approach to psychology of Viktor Frankl (2).

The philosophical roots of phenomenology, as an analytical method and as a framework for describing and explaining social relationships and psychological orientations, can be found in the works of Edmund Husserl (1859–1938). Husserl felt that a critical error had been made in philosophy when René Descartes (1596–1650) distinguished between the activity of the conscious mind (*reas cognitans*) and the objects of conscious thought (*reas extensa*) and subsequent thinkers assumed the activity and the objects to be separable. Husserl argued that the activity of consciousness and the objects of conscious thought are inseparable aspects of human experience. By separating the activity and the objects, philosophers and scientists are attempting to treat consciousness as an empirical phenomenon amenable to investigation by the quantitative methods of natural science. This propensity to treat the subjective as an objective reality is rejected by phenomenologists on the basis that: "1. consciousness itself is not an object among other objects in nature, and 2. there are conscious phenomena which cannot be dealt with adequately by means of the quantitative methods of experimental science" (3). Phenomenologists attempt to account for those subjective qualities that either are assumed by empiricists to be unreal or are treated as objective, observable phenomena when they are not. They seek to divest themselves of their assumptions concerning what is real and what is not and to begin with the content of the human consciousness as the focus of their investigations. In short, they seek to shift from questions of reality to questions of the meaning of phenomena.

While Husserl was not the first to posit the relationship between reality and human consciousness, he is generally credited with laying the philosophical foundation for phenomenology and has been described as the "father of pure phenomenology." Subsequent writers, including Alfred Schutz (1899–1959) and Martin Heidegger (1889–1976) expanded upon those ideas, but they seemingly are as often called heretics as heroes of the movement. Indeed, there is no single definition of phenomenology. While Husserl's writings are generally the starting point for a discussion of the philosophy, his own view of phenomenology changed over time and according to the nature of his inquiries and agreement on phenomenology's underpinnings has been lacking since his initial work.

Notwithstanding the evolution of his philosophy and its ultimate form, and at the risk of oversimplification, Husserl argued for a *transcendental phenomenology*. That is, he presented an argument for the importance of subjective interpretations of reality and a methodology for determining the true *essence* of reality through an understanding of the perceptual filters that influence how individuals and groups take in, store, and interpret information on social and physical phenomena. As stated by Ralph Hummel, the best known contemporary proponent of phenomenological methods in American public administration, Husserl and his disciples argued that the "ways of knowing define reality" (4). Consciousness is the beginning place according to Husserl, although Heidegger and others have argued that a more abstract state of being is the beginning place.

While phenomenology became somewhat popular among American scholars during the 1960s and 1970s, it was a product of an earlier period of social and political turmoil. Nonetheless, it is still a subject of considerable philosophical debate. For that reason, it is useful to examine its origins and evolution before looking at its basic principles and its early and current influence on the social sciences in general and on public administration research and practice in particular.

This chapter examines the philosophy from its roots in the "Phenomenological Movement;" provides an overview of its philosophical underpinnings, focusing on its challenge to logical positivism and its defense against the empiricists' critique; the application of phenomenological methods in the social sciences; and, the influence of phenomenology on public administration theory and practice.

I.   THE PHENOMENOLOGICAL MOVEMENT

Our dominant scientific method has long been rooted in logical positivism (empiricism), a reliance on sensory experience to define and study the social world. With some adaptation, the tools of the natural sciences have been taken up by researchers in the social sci-

ences, often with little regard for problems of application when dealing with human behavior and often with far too much confidence in empirical method. In short, for positivists, if phenomena could not be observed and measured, they were often discounted
and seldom studied seriously. Despite those obvious limitations, alternatives to positivist
methodologies have been elusive. But, when Immanuel Kant (1724–1804) opened the
door with the notion of subjective reality, i.e., that a subjective ordering of data determines the interpretation of empirical reality (5); the debate was joined. A product of that
philosophical debate was phenomenology.

Herbert Spiegelberg has referred to "phenomenology" as a "moving . . . philosophy
with a dynamic momentum" (6). In fact, the origins of the term itself are ambiguous
enough to complicate the history and tenets of the philosophy. Despite the meanings
given the term by a number of other philosophers, for the past half century or more it has
come to be associated with the Phenomenological Movement and Edmund Husserl.
Nonetheless, it should also be noted that there are several major streams in the philosophical debate and some rather fundamental differences among them. As Spiegelberg warns,
while Husserl may be identified as a central figure in the Phenomenological Movement,
his own interpretation changed over time and his students tended to be "flung off at a tan-
gent" following currents initiated by Husserl's own work (7). The resultant lack of a clear
line of succession from Husserl to one or more of his students or to another proponent of
the philosophy also complicates the history. Indeed, while early philosophical threads associated with phenomenology can be traced to his teacher, Franz Brentano (1838–1917),
and Carl Stumpf (1848–1936), Husserl is still considered the major impetus for the
movement. A fluid series of relationships characterized the movement rather than a
clearly identifiable core of philosophers and students. Initially, the center of the phenomenological debate was in Germany, particularly among widening circles of scholars in
Göttingen and Munich (8). The coeditors of the *Jahrbuch für Philosophie und Phänomenolo-
gische Forschung,* which was published from 1913 to 1930, provided some focus for the
discussions in Germany, but the changing political climate under the Nazi regime and the
resultant movement of students and scholars to universities and other institutions outside
of Germany widened the circle of participants in the discussion.

French existentialist writers, such as Jean-Paul Sartre and Maurice Merleau-Ponty,
and the International Phenomenological Society founded in the U.S. in 1939 picked up
and offered some focus for the philosophical debate, but provided little coherence for the
philosophy itself. In the 1960s and 1970s, phenomenological societies were founded in
the U.S., Great Britain, and Germany as existentialist and transcendentialist thought was
again in vogue. Alfred Schutz brought the discussion of phenomenology to the U.S.
through his teaching and the publication of some of his early works in English, particularly *Phenomenology of the Social World,* originally published in Germany in 1932 and not
published in the U.S. in English until 1967 (9). While Schutz became a central figure in
the American Phenomenological Movement, many still look to Martin Heidegger, who
was chosen by Husserl as successor to his faculty chair at the University of Freiburg, as his
"legitimate heir." Serious disagreements between the two men, as well as conflict related
to the exclusion of Jewish faculty from the university during the Nazi period when Heidegger, a member of the Nazi party, served as rector, suggest that Heidegger's work diverged significantly from that of Husserl. In fact, Heidegger worked on topics other than
phenomenology for a time. But, subsequent writings, particularly in the 1960s, indicate
Heidegger experienced a renewed interest in phenomenology as a method of scientific inquiry and embraced many of the Husserl's principles in his own interpretation of phe-

nomenology. Whether or not his interest was genuine or opportunistic is uncertain (10). Regardless of Heidegger's intentions, his later work still provides methodological foundation for social science researchers (11).

In some measure, the development of the Phenomenological Movement may have been related to the political and intellectual ferment of the early twentieth century, fueled by war and economic depression. The major impetus may have been the growing concern that the science rooted in logical positivism was not addressing the practical needs of society and that philosophical tools were not being brought to bear on the issues of the day. It was hoped that phenomenology would help fill in the gaps in scientific inquiry, rather than supplant positivist scientific method entirely, and reaffirm the importance of philosophical approaches to inquiry in social science.

II. THE PHENOMENOLOGICAL PERSPECTIVE

Despite rather fundamental differences among some of the streams of philosophical discussion, there are generally agreed upon principles that define phenomenological method and reasoning. According to phenomenologists, there may or may not be an objective reality, but there is an *essence* that may be widely accepted as representing reality. The operational reality, the *Lebenswelt* or *lived-world*, within which an individual acts, is defined by that individual and may differ according to his or her perceptions (12). The world of human beings is defined in large part by our senses with all their inherent limitations: We are somewhat limited in our capabilities to hear and see, for example. Some of us have broader ranges in our perceptions of sound or clearer vision, but, for the most part, all of us hear and see approximately the same things. That is true of our perceptions of social phenomena, as well. In a sense, we each have our own "realities" and, thus, have our own imperatives for action. But, we generally have common perceptions of social and physical phenomena that permit us to interact reasonably coherently, particularly if we understand the perspectives of those with whom we are interacting. In other words, our consciousness of the world is the logic by which reality is defined. Ideology, religion, experience, milieu, and other social and psychological factors, as well as the tools with which we observe and comprehend what goes on around us, such as language and ethics, affect our perceptions of reality. At what level those perceptions are biased is a matter of debate among phenomenologists, but most would agree that the focus should be on rather fundamental values, one's *Weltanschauung*.

The idea that one can divest oneself of assumptions and biases is predicated on the phenomenological view that one begins with a *natural attitude*; an understanding at birth that the surrounding world is real, that the individual his or herself is real, and that other people are real. According to Husserl, one's understanding is common-sensical and not needing empirical verification or logical inference. For the phenomenologists, this *natural attitude* should be the beginning place of philosophy, just as it was with the classical Greek philosophers. They seek to return to the state in which one has no biases or assumptions about one's social world or *lived-world*, thereby assuming the *philosophical attitude* in which all things (except reality) are open to question and investigation. It is not necessary to return to the *natural attitude* in all philosophical or scientific inquiry, but it should be the ultimate starting place. The process of divesting oneself of beliefs, biases, etc., Husserl variously called *phenomenological reduction, phenomenological epoche*, and *bracketing* (13).

The conceptualization of the consciousness is the foundation of the approach. For the phenomenologist, the world and consciousness are interdependent, neither having meaning without the other. The link between the conscious mind and the object of that consciousness is *intentionality*; that is, conscious activity is consciousness of a thing (an object). A *phenomenon* is any "thing" of which one is conscious (and any phenomenon is a legitimate concern for philosophy or science). *Experience* of a phenomenon, then, is more than simply sensory perception; it is concerned with any thing, any phenomenon, of which one is conscious, be it physical object or idea. *Seeing* for Husserl did not mean only with the eyes. It meant perceiving with the mind as well. The non-empirical *seeing* Husserl called *intuition* (14).

Taking a slightly different tack, it can be said that phenomenologists believe that all phenomena are intimately knowable. Reality is not restricted to those things that can be empirically verified or logically inferred, rather reality is based on an understanding (*verstehen* or common-sense knowing) of the social world. Each person, according to phenomenologists, has a *Lebenswelt* or *lived-world*, a common sense knowledge of everyday life which does not necessitate the questioning of reality. Nor should reality be a focus of scientific or philosophical inquiry—reality is a given of the *natural attitude* (15).

Using Max Weber's ideal types and concepts of action as a reference point, Alfred Schutz formulated the framework of an *existential phenomenology*. Experience, according to Schutz, creates a complex social world. Our perceptions are based upon how we view the world and our participation in social relationships. Those with whom we interact or can interact with directly represent a world of *consociates*. Within this grouping, we may participate in *Thou*, *We*, or *They* relationships in terms of whether we view ourselves as participants in projects (directed action) and whether we view others as subjects or objects of action. In *We* relationships there is great potential truly to understand the motives and interests of others. According to Schutz, there is also a distinction between what is "here" for the individual and what is "there." In other words, individuals have an internal understanding of their world and the world that is outside (16).

Perspectives on phenomena may change in space and time and may be shared. Perceptual meaning is all important. For example, a hammer can be viewed as an object and as a means of hammering a nail. When we see a hammer, we generally perceive it in the broad sense. In other words, the content and context of phenomena are part of our consciousness. By way of application, participant-observation, for example, might afford a researcher a useful vantage point for observing and understanding how a community or organization is acting. Rather than simply observing a community's actions, the researcher develops an understanding of why they are acting and what it means broadly for them. For that reason, phenomenological methods were adopted by anthropologists, sociologists, and others studying group behaviors. By contrast, as relationships become more distant, farther from our own understanding, we tend to create abstract explanations. We interpret, extrapolate, and develop *ideal types* to explain the motives and actions of others and, thus, lose fundamental understanding of perceptions and perspectives (17).

In effect, the *They* perspective or orientation separates the observer from the actors being studied and he or she has to interpret actions without necessarily having the advantage of understanding the reality that is driving them. The observer may also be biased by his or her own reality. The result may be a process of *typifying* the world (18) because of the tendency to relate observed phenomena with facts or objects already known through prior experience and interpretations shared within a society or smaller social grouping. There are conventions that reflect selectivity in attention and these pose a limitation or obstacle for the scientist.

A.   The Phenomenological Critique of Logical Positivism

Some of the major areas of contention have already been mentioned in passing, but the implications of the phenomenological perspective are more subtle. Phenomenological reasoning is not diametrically opposed to that of logical positivism. Phenomenologists, for the most part, do not attack empiricism as being invalid as a scientific method, rather they often insist that it be recognized that empiricism presents a very narrow view of the social world.

Logical positivism offers a narrow view in several ways, according to the phenomenologists. Alfred Schutz identified most of the problems that he found with logical positivism in the following way:

1.   The primary goal of social sciences is to obtain organized knowledge of social reality.
2.   All forms of naturalism and logical positivism simply take for granted this social reality, which is the proper object of the social sciences.
3.   The identification of experience with sensory observation in general and of the experience of overt action in particular excludes several dimensions of social reality from all possible inquiry.

   a.   Even an ideally refined behaviorism can . . . merely explain the behavior of the observed, not of the observing behaviorist.
   b.   The same overt behavior . . . may have an entirely different meaning to the performers.
   c.   The concept of human action in terms of common-sense thinking and of the social sciences, includes what may be called 'negative actions,' i.e., intentional refraining from acting, which, of course, escapes sensory observation.
   d.   Social reality contains elements of beliefs and convictions which are real because they are so defined by the participants and which escape sensory observation.
   e.   The postulate of sensory observation of overt human behavior takes as a model a particular and relatively small sector of the social world, namely, situations in which the acting individual is given to the observer in what is commonly called a face-to-face relationship. But there are many other dimensions of the social world in which situations of this kind do not prevail (19).

The first argument is that the logical positivists take for granted social reality while dismissing as unreal and unobservable the meaning of human activity (the social reality of the actor). Logical positivists also attempt to deny their subjectivity, hiding behind objective measuring devices borrowed from natural science. Above all, according to Schutz, the logical positivists miss the *essence* or meaning of what they are trying to observe.

According to Schutz, there is a basic difference between social and natural science, and that difference is man. The natural scientist can *bracket* or draw boundaries for his own relevant part of the social world (and it is social for the scientist), but the social scientist cannot interpret the behavior of others without knowing what their realities are, what their *lived-world* is. After all, the behavior of the observed actors is predicated on their own purposes and meanings, not those of the observing scientist. The imposition of natural science logic and method ("monopolistic imperialism" according to Schutz) does not leave room for interpretation of the meaning of conscious activity in any case (20).

As well as being unsuited to the interpretation of meaning in phenomena, logical positivism, according to the phenomenologists, attempts empirically to verify largely subjective phenomena. Beliefs, orientations, and motivations are not observable phenomena, nonetheless they are phenomena. Empiricists often attempt to make the unobservable observable with the result that they ascribe their own beliefs, orientations, and motivations to the observed actors. The result is the same whether the observers are focusing on the actors or the phenomena. Phenomenology requires that the focus be on both, as inseparable aspects of the phenomena—the conscious mind and the world.

In summary, phenomenologists believe that the logical positivist approach is too narrow, though valid for genuinely observable phenomena perhaps. They assert that each phenomenon must be recognized for what it is without imposing a methodology that is inappropriate to the subject matter. Subjective subjects must be approached with subjective methodologies, i.e., phenomenology (21).

B.   The Phenomenological Defense Against Logical Positivism

By far the greatest attacks on phenomenology by logical positivists are based on the issue of subjectivity. Objectivity has become almost synonymous with empirical science and subjectivity with bias and nonscientific methods. What of the phenomenologists' subjectivity then?

Phenomenologists hold that all social scientists "abstract" from the world according to the problem being studied. The abstractions made by empirical scientists are themselves subjective. The generalizations, formalizations, idealizations, and all the other analytical and theoretical constructs are removed from the reality of the phenomena observed. According to Schutz, "Strictly speaking, there are no such things as facts, pure and simple . . . [t]hey are . . . always interpreted facts" (22).

What of the subjective meaning of behavior that the phenomenologists wish to ascertain in their research? They contend that one can know to a certain extent the motivations of another, if one knows the circumstances or *lived-world* of the other. The process of *self-typification* allows phenomenological researchers to approximate a perception of the actors' social world to supplement their commonsense knowledge of that same world. The researcher's commonsense knowledge of the actor's social world is predicated on what Schutz called the *Thou* orientation, the perception of others in one's own social world and the feeling of *community* with others whom one shares a social world (including past and present generations). In short, phenomenologists believe that a bond of humanness, intersubjective knowledge, provides a basis for understanding the *lived-world* of another (23). Also, to approximate a perception of the actor's *lived-world*, phenomenologists can make determinations based on the actor's degree of socialization. The more socialized the actors are, the more predictable their behavior will be and the more decipherable their motivations should become. The commonsense knowledge of the actors, as developed through the process of socialization, is much more readily accessible through observation by the researcher due to his or her inherent empathy (the *Thou* orientation). The test of the researcher's findings from objective validity should be the logical consistency of the findings with the actor's commonsense knowledge (24).

III. THE PHENOMENOLOGICAL APPROACH TO SOCIAL SCIENCE RESEARCH

In phenomenological social science research the purpose is to "make explicit what is implicit in the social action of members of a given society" (25). Stewart and Mickanus offered a brief characterization of the phenomenological view of society stating that:

> Phenomenology views society as comprising free persons making choices within the context of the value system of the society. It sees the structures and institutions of society not as the product of material conditions or deterministic forces but the outcome of value considerations. Hence, to understand the structures of any society, it is necessary to understand the values which gave rise to the directions, goals, and meaning of the structures. One may change the material aspects of society's institutions, but if the values are not changed, the institutions remain the same. Or one may retain the material aspects of society's institutions while changing the values upon which they are based, with the result that one will experience them as different institutions (26).

The key, then, to phenomenological research in the social sciences is value structures. While values are not viewed as absolute by many phenomenologists, they are most often seen as identifiable "object-like" phenomena. While basic values change, they are "nearly universally experienced" and, as transcendent phenomena, can be isolated or *bracketed* through intuitive inquiry (27). The important methodological question is how are researchers to understand the values of other human beings and their societies?

The literature of applied phenomenology in the social sciences is somewhat limited, but very innovative. The applications in fields outside of philosophy are also limited. Perhaps the best known application technique in the social sciences has been the anthropological and sociological uses of participant-observation as a means of gaining insight into the motivations and values of subject-actors. Biologists have even used the same technique to observe animal behavior by placing researchers within animal herds and other social groupings. Cultural anthropologists have used it to gain the confidence of and insight into primitive societies. The researcher seeks to achieve commonsense knowledge of the observed actors by interacting within their social world, with or without the subject-actors knowing that they are being observed. A major facet of the phenomenological critique of behavioralism is the presumed connection between attitudes and behavior. Behavioralists "psychologize" phenomenon, in other words (28). Phenomenologists do not make the distinction between cognition and action, both are part of the same process.

Other applications of phenomenological techniques have been personal interviewing, usually unstructured interviewing, and the study of personal documents, such as letters, autobiographies, and diaries to understand the *lived-world* of actors (29). An application in the study of history, for example, would involve the researcher becoming immersed in the literature, including diaries and other personal accounts of events, in order to understand why individuals and groups behaved as they did during a particular period of time or in response to a particular stimulus.

The research methodology for phenomenological, qualitative research is primarily concerned with the problems of how to control the impact of the observer on the observed, how to assume the *natural attitude*, how to interpret behavior objectively, and how not to empathize so much with the subjects of the inquiry that the researcher jeopardizes objectivity, as well as the technical aspects of research design, data gathering, and analysis of findings.

More specifically, phenomenologists seek the *natural attitude* by which the everyday world can be defined free of the biases of history, notions of causality, and intersubjectivity. Only by stripping away the experiences that create a false or, at minimum, an erroneous picture of the world can the social scientist understand phenomena. At what place in human consciousness the essence of reality is to be found is a matter of conjecture and debate. For Husserl and the *transcendental* phenomenologists, intuition is the source of the *natural attitude*. For the *existentialist* phenomenologists, peeling away the biases created by experience is the means of achieving the *natural attitude*. Again to oversimplify, phenomenologists argue that there is not simply an idiosyncratic definition of reality, rather human experience colors how the world is perceived and one has to peel away the biases created by one's psychological, social, and political predispositions to uncover the "truth." Natanson refers to this as a process of "self-scrutiny," to "practice the natural attitude" (30). Finding the common ground, the shared reality, will then permit researchers to examine phenomena objectively.

The notion of subjective interpretations of reality being essential to an understanding of social and physical phenomena would simply seem intuitively logical. The adage of "walking a mile in another's shoes" in order to understand that person's motivations and values is certainly consonant with this idea. Similarly, the adage of "where one stands depends upon where one sits" captures the notion of values based upon perspective. In some measure, phenomenology recognizes differences in perspective. However, more precisely, phenomenological analysis focuses not simply on the points of view of actors but on developing a thorough understanding of the world in which they live. The real appeal of phenomenology is the promise of a philosophical tool for achieving an unbiased view of social phenomena. Philosophers and writers such as Heidegger, Sartre, and Merleau-Ponty certainly subscribed to that notion.

Phenomenology also appealed to the sensibilities of many social scientists in the 1960s and 1970s as the limitations of behavioralism were becoming more and more apparent. The proponents of logical positivism and, by extension, behavioralism promised a value-free, objective social science (31). Post-behavioralists, including the proponents of phenomenology in its several forms, pointed out the problems of individual and social biases. They influence not only how social phenomena are interpreted and but also decisions concerning which phenomena scholars and scientists examine and in what context. There were practical problems of analyzing intangible and difficult to measure phenomena such as power. Certainly, during the turbulent 1960s, there was also a political backlash against science's presumed objectivity and its lack of socially sensitive values. Denunciations of science were common in the political literature of the time, particularly as science often appeared to offer support for the policies of the incumbent elites rather than answers for the problems of the poor and disadvantaged. Indeed, the promise of a new scientific method that recognizes the need to address social problems directly and at an individual level made phenomenology all the more attractive to social scientists. Apart from the political baggage of logical positivism, the science of the day was viewed as a sterile god, based upon analogies far removed from the reality of society and addressing questions of little direct importance to modern society (32).

Clearly, the allure of phenomenological approaches to social science research was enhanced by the milieu. Literature, political commentary, and scholarly debate focused on the perceived inadequacies of the social, economic, and political structures of the time and appealed for new scientific and philosophical approaches. The problems of the day were attributed to economic and political elites, nationalism, ideological conflict, class struggle, colonial domination, and so on. From the writings of Jean-Paul Sartre and Albert Camus to those of C. Wright Mills and Herbert Marcuse, officials, citizens, and scholars were encouraged to break the bonds of their cultural and political value systems and to examine the realities of others in society. For example, in 1963, Frantz Fanon's *The Wretched of the Earth* (33) put a human face on the struggle against colonialism and provided a philosophical justification, even a strong argument, for violent responses to political oppression. Moreover, as Westerners discovered the transcendentalism of South and East Asian religions and philosophies, they were encouraged to seek out perspectives quite different from the old. It was a time for questioning the rationality, including the science, of the state.

The notion of subjective reality, supported by existentialist and transcendentalist philosophies, encouraged attention to phenomenology as a research tool for post-behavioralist research. Phenomenology rests on a line of reasoning that does not entirely deny objective reality, but assigns great significance to reality as defined subjectively. The task of the researcher is to sift through the preconceptions born of experience, world view, or ignorance to identify the *essence* of reality. In short, the phenomenological perspective finds support in the notion that we all assign different values to reality. Phenomenologists put a premium on understanding the values that one uses consciously or unconsciously to interpret one's surroundings and to guide one's actions. In some measure, research requires selecting a perspective and having some understanding of the importance of experience to the development of a thorough understanding, what Wilhelm Dilthey calls *verstehen* (34), of social and physical phenomena. An internalized understanding on the part of the researcher facilitates reconstruction of the perspectives of participants in particular events and thus affords a perspective from which the rationality of their actions can be understood and assessed. In action terms, intersubjectivity or understanding the perceptions and perspectives of ourselves and those with whom we are interacting greatly facilitates understanding. In that way, phenomenological methodologies provide a vehicle for moving from the philosophical level to the practical, from the abstract to the concrete.

The criteria for defining the boundaries of the Phenomenological Movement, to identify those using phenomenological methods, according to Spiegelberg, are: 1. the use of "direct intuition . . . as the source and final test of all knowledge, to be formulated as faithfully as possible in verbal descriptions . . . insight into essential structures as a genuine possibility and a need of philosophical knowledge;" and 2. "conscious adherence . . . to the movement . . . full awareness of these methical principles" (35). As Carl Friedrich has described it, one should try to describe phenomena in as general terms as possible, "asking . . . for the essence of it" (36). The objective is to focus on the *essence* of the phenomenon, rather than to seek a conceptual clarity that may distort the meaning of the phenomenon under study. Put another way, the phenomenon is more important than the words used to describe it in measurable terms.

The concern with the use of language is central to the phenomenological critique of logical positivism, but, more importantly, it is central to the phenomenological view of man's understanding of the world. The phenomenological literature devotes considerable attention to hermeneutics, the connection between language and knowledge (37). Clearly, language serves a critical role in conceptualizing and understanding the world. While translation may provide an approximate meaning, the conceptualizations and analogies inherent in language have an impact on how phenomena are experienced and remembered and on how they affect future behavior.

As well as focusing on the impact of language, the procedures for applying phenomenology to inquiry include:

1. investigating particular phenomena;
2. investigating general *essences*;
3. apprehending essential relationships among *essences*;
4. watching modes of appearing;
5. watching the constitution of phenomena in consciousness;
6. suspending belief in the existence of the phenomena; and
7. interpreting the meaning of phenomena (38).

Spiegelberg went on to note that the first three procedures underlie the work of all affiliated with the Phenomenological Movement and that the remaining four procedures were not as commonly accepted or applied (39). The defining criteria of phenomenologists were to accept the notion of *essences* distinct from the empirically observable and to employ intuition in examining those *essences*. However, the practical problems of how to frame research questions in a manner consistent with the precepts of phenomenology and the nature of the intuitive investigation have generated considerable debate among phenomenologists. Alfred Schutz suggested focusing on the *natural attitude*, examining how meaning developed and reconstituting the social and psychological environment that affects how we perceive and value phenomena. Maurice Merleau-Ponty, on the other hand, focused on the differences between what we perceive and the *essence* of the phenomena (40).

In reference to the latter approach, one method of applying phenomenological principles is through *imaginative variation*. According to Mohanty, the researcher should:

1. Start with an actual or imagined instance of the sort under consideration. This *arbitrarily* chosen example will serve as the model.
2. [Develop] an intuitively open multiplicity of variants upon it, which are to be produced in imagination voluntarily and arbitrarily.
3. [A]s 2 proceeds, a unity, an invariant structure shows itself as that but for which the example arbitrarily chosen as example (or the sort of thing under consideration) would not be thinkable as an example of its kind. Transforming actual phenomena into possibilities and reducing the possibilities into an essence, a transcendent reality (41).

The imagined phenomenon provides an *ideal type* as the researcher intuitively sorts through possibilities in order to arrive at a reasonable *essence*, a *transcendent reality* in Mohanty's terms.

Understandably there is some conflict between social scientists employing empirical methods and those using phenomenological methods. The verifiability of research findings is a major issue. Although the phenomenologist may document his or her understanding of social phenomena and the reasoning may be examined, there may be little or no empirical evidence to substantiate the conclusions. "[P]henomenology and empirical science operate at qualitatively different levels," according to Natanson (42).

Existential phenomenology very much affected the development of the "growth psychology" movement of the 1960s and 1970s. The notion of using self-revealing behaviors to encourage and clarify interpersonal relationships and thereby to encourage personal growth is an extension of the *We* relationship Schutz described. Sharing one's perceptions permits others to understand the reality that is guiding behavior and that sharing results in a social or *We* perspective that facilitates the setting of personal goals that are consonant with the group. In the process communication is improved and less effort is expended in behaviors designed to hide feelings. Client-centered therapies were also a logical application of the methodology. Abraham Maslow's self-actualized-self-transcendent state, with individuals responding to more than their own basic needs, identifying with their jobs and comfortable with themselves, was also a product of the phenomenological perspective (43). Organization theory had butted up against the Weberian model. While questions were raised about how well the Weberian ideal type fit bureaucratic reality in many cases, there had been very little challenge of its basic assumptions or explanation of how to incorporate organizational change into the static model (44).

At this juncture public administration scholars began to explore the utility of phenomenology as a tool of social science research and as a vehicle for understanding fundamental changes that were taking place in American society in order to guide policy making and government administration.

IV. PHENOMENOLOGY AND PUBLIC ADMINISTRATION

In large measure, phenomenology's impact on the study of public administration has been derived primarily from its impact on social science research in general. Public administration scholars have been as prone to the same frustrations with the dominant positivist scientific method as have other social scientists. In fact, Dwight Waldo criticized logical positivism in an article in the *American Political Science Review* as early as 1952, although alternatives to positivist approaches were scarce at that time—at least in the U.S. (45).

The clearest proposition of a phenomenological perspective in public administration was made by Larry Kirkhart in his contribution, "Toward a Theory of Public Administration," to the landmark 1968 Minnowbrook Conference (46). The participants in that conference struggled to understand the changes that were taking place in American society and the role of public administration in addressing social needs. As Dwight Waldo, sponsor of the conference, states in his Foreword to the edited volume of Minnowbrook papers, the meeting was intended to address the study and practice of public administration in a time of "mounting turbulence and critical problems" (47). The papers by Kirkhart and Frank McGee related public administration to the social science theories of the day. Then, as now, the field of public administration was amorphous, albeit somewhat constrained by the boundaries of the discipline of political science in which most of its theorists were trained. Logical positivism was the dominant scientific orientation and dictated a research methodology based on empirical investigation. Experimental designs were generally viewed as a goal that social scientists should pursue.

Within the behavioral sciences, the clear objective was to minimize subjectivity and thereby to assure or, at minimum, to increase objectivity. For public administration scholars, concepts and theories were borrowed from a wide variety of fields, but the social science research tradition tended to come from political science. As Kirkhart pointed out, a clear definition of "public administration" was elusive at the time of the Minnowbrook conference. Such a definition would likely have helped public administration researchers clarify their values and would have provided a clearer understanding of the field. Nonetheless, the philosophical and scientific turbulence that was overtaking traditional social science thinking held promise for public administration research and Kirkhart addressed that potential. For the Minnowbrook participants, the challenges to logical positivism were both intriguing and frustrating. Phenomenology was identified as a major movement relatively new to the U.S. and the U.K. that offered a methodology to guide social science research rather than a philosophy to define its parameters.

The subjectivity of reality and truth has profound implications for public administration. Understanding the impact of public organizations on their employees and clients requires an understanding of the perspectives of those actors, including the values and perspectives of the society as a whole. The observer, whether a researcher or a practitioner seeking to improve administration, has to understand the meanings attached to programs and processes by the individuals. A favorite topic in the literature of public management is the notion of a "bureaucratic personality" creating perverse incentives contrary to effective decision making or efficient administration yet supportive of organizational or personal interests. The "administrative man" model is certainly a frequent topic in public administration education.

The idea that cultural and professional values influence problem definition, the range of decision options that are considered, and the ultimate selection of a course of action also has some currency in the literature. That lawyers tend to view policy and administrative problems in terms of applications of law and that engineers may be biased toward engineering solutions to problems should be rather obvious. However, it is perhaps less obvious that the values of individualism, egalitarianism, and competition limit the search for solutions for social problems in the U.S. because Americans are somewhat predisposed to certain kinds of solutions, even when they intuitively appear wrong. That observation, of course, is based on the assumption that Americans have common perceptual filters. Gender, ethnic, and other differences may well broaden the perspectives of Americans, although other cultural influences may constrain them.

There are also problems when bureaucrats or technocrats assume the *They* perspective, rather than viewing themselves as part of the society they serve and as having responsibility for addressing the issues that society feels are important. As Ralph Hummel argues, public employees need to redirect their energies from serving their "technical systems" to serving the public (48). Bureaucrats, according to Hummel, develop broad policies that represent imperfect analogies or models of the *lived-world* in which their clients function and implement narrow procedures that fail to respond to the unique and varied interests and needs of the clients. Bureaucrats try to fit their clients to models designed to serve the needs of the bureaucracy itself (49). Efficiency and other organizational values supplant individual understanding of the physical world, affecting clients and employees alike (50). These ideas are certainly not new, although Hummel's framing them in phenomenological terms may be.

Norton Long noted over forty years ago (51) that the objectives of public administration had seemingly drifted from a concern with the public interest to a preoccupation with organizational efficiency and control. Professionalization, bureaucratization, technical proficiency, and isolation from public scrutiny and accountability have discouraged attention to the broader public interest in favor of a highly rationalized system of administration. Long noted, too, the negative impact on the Presidency when the symbolism of the position is ignored as officials pursue more partisan self interests (52).

Even today, many public administrators and public administrationists do not see the inherent political nature of management reforms and how they may distract organizations from their mission to serve the public. In 1954, Long pointed out the importance of having a "representative bureaucracy" to help inform policy making by broadening the perspective and clarifying the public interest, but he has more recently concluded that that role seems to have fallen prey to partisanship.

Indeed, Frank Sherwood, in responding to Long's 1954 article and a 1996 follow-up in *Public Administration Review*, argues for a renewed public administration role in formulating the policy agenda by identifying important issues and helping policy makers and the public make informed choices (53). Robert B. Reich suggests much the same role for public administrators in his book *The Power of Public Ideas* (54). In some measure, Sherwood and Reich may be suggesting that public administrators help elected officials and the public find the *natural attitude* by structuring the policymaking process so that the public can understand important issues and express their interests.

The impacts of individual and organizational perspectives on problem definition (55) and policymaking (56) are also widely accepted. Professional training, predispositions toward certain administrative styles and roles, language, and other aspects of organizational culture can profoundly affect the willingness of individuals and their organizations to trust and cooperate with others involved in multiorganizational and intergovernmental programs and, thus, determine the effectiveness of joint efforts (57).

Ethics, by phenomenological reasoning, is also a social construct and, as such, based upon shared views of right and wrong rather than values external to individuals or social groupings. Individuals and societies create systems of ethics, either consciously or unconsciously, based upon experience or need. While there are some generally accepted norms of behavior, such as not stealing from one's organization or ignoring the needs of clients, there are certainly many less agreed upon values in our typical codes of ethics and standards of performance.

Action theory is associated with the post-behavioralist movement and phenomenology (58). Michael M. Harmon (59) outlined the application of action theory to public administration and argued for a new paradigm encompassing such aspects as an "active-social" concept of self, intersubjectivity (the meaning of actions of self and others), the *We* relationship, the compatibility of decision rules, the need for personal responsibility in administration, the desirability of a "proactive" administrative style, and the importance of "moral-ethical" administrative practice.

To the extent that action theory has influenced current studies of organizational culture and learning, phenomenological methods are continuing to have a major impact on public administration. The notion of a social construction of reality within organizations is explicit within that literature. "Organizational culture is the shared set of meanings and perceptions of realities that are created and learned by organization members in the course of their social interactions," according to Steven Ott (60). Robert Golembiewski's "ideal-type" of a culture characterized by openness, self knowledge, and trust, as prerequisite to a "regenerative system," is explicitly connected to the phenomenological literature (61). A clearer connection between the principles and practice of phenomenology can be found in the literature relating to action theory and research.

In essence, action theory may be construed as empirically focused, but relying more on "local" values. The goals are empirically testable questions and generalizable answers, but the emphasis is on what works in a specific locale and a specific time. Individual and group perspectives and values, i.e., "realities," are important variables in the success or failure of an organization or program (62). In some measure reality is defined by individuals, but in group and organizational settings shared meanings may develop that provide a framework for understanding what actions mean and whether they are good or bad or neither (63). The challenge to practitioners is to recognize and manage the culture (64).

Michael Vasu, Debra Stewart, and G. David Garson (65) point out the phenomenological perspective on the impact of technology on organizations and individuals. Citing writers such as Peter Lyman, they describe the view that we are in danger of "technical hegemony." While the studies cited in response to the phenomenological critique indicate that computers do not appear to be having a negative impact on workers, there are indications that the "technical culture" created by computer technology is affecting the power structure within organizations. Certainly philosophical critiques of technological innovation are not uncommon. Nor are warnings that technology threatens our culture (66). The phenomenological critique, however, encourages a close examination of technology and its social impact and challenges the attitude that technology and rational decision processes are value-neutral.

In some measure, Ralph Hummel raises some of the same issues by focusing on the "intentions and beliefs of workers," including the common perceptions and the conventions of language and symbol. There is also a strong normative component in his analysis which encourages efforts to empower employees, rather than manipulate or coerce, and to develop "circle" rather than "pyramid" managers. He argues for less hierarchical relationships, more empowerment of workers, "open" bureaucracies, and role flexibility. "The first step on the way to becoming the circle manager of post-modernity is to recognize the ways of understanding where they already exist" (1990: 215). He goes on to extol the virtues of synthesizing methods of understanding "because they connect science and reason to practicality" (67).

V. CONCLUSIONS

While phenomenology has not been widely embraced by practitioners and scholars, it has had a profound influence on public administration practice and research. Phenomenology has been absorbed into the literature and language of the field and has had a significant influence on theory, research, and practice. As a practical matter, phenomenological reasoning encourages attention to how people relate to bureaucratic organizations and government programs, as well as to each other. For example, as Hummel and others have pointed out, the tendency to "objectify" people in social science research and in government administration may have serious repercussions. The apparently low public regard for government agencies and officials may well be a reflection of how insensitive and unresponsive many agencies and officials have been in recent decades. As Hummel suggests, the assumption of a We perspective in which the public, the clients, become subjects rather than participants in public programs, creates perceptual barriers that reduce the capacities of agencies to understand and address social problems. Professionalization, too, often creates distance between public employees and their clients and among employees themselves that may alienate support. Even more fundamental, as David Rosenbloom has pointed out, bureaucracy is a middle-class institution (68) and others, particularly lower income Americans, may be alienated by its processes and confused by its organizational complexity.

Public employees themselves often feel alienated, as well. Administrative reform seems to have taken on a life of its own. In some measure it is a problem that economics has apparently become the language of administration and policymaking with the result that economic values are preempting all others. In other words, economic needs are increasingly supplanting other human needs. And, there are indications that public and private sector organizations will suffer in the long term for their lack of attention to noneconomic needs. Nonetheless, even the language of administration is designed to promote economic values. For example, thousands of employees have lost their jobs in recent years and the language of job termination has been sanitized to downplay the impact on individuals and to emphasize the organizational rationale for the terminations. Organizations changed the terminology from "lay-off" to "reduction-in-force" to "down-sizing" and, finally, to "right-sizing." The latter term suggests that terminations are a positive phenomenon, but, from the perspective of the employees who lose their jobs and the coworkers who have to assume their responsibilities, that is certainly untrue.

Phenomenology offers a useful set of tools and perspectives for public administration researchers and practitioners. Researchers may fail to recognize the important issues that need to be addressed because they are not sensitive to the realities with which people and communities have to contend. Officials may well alienate public support for programs due to the depersonalization of administrative processes and the failure to respond to the problems that the public feels are important. Although the *consociated* model, more particularly public administrators' *verstehen* of social needs and their identification with the public, may only be a "wish-thought" (68), consistency between administrative values and societal values is essential.

The decline of public support for government services strongly suggests a need to reevaluate current preoccupations with cost-efficiency and managerial reform, particularly when they are inconsistent with the need to address societal problems. Interestingly, phenomenologists have warned about misuses of Max Weber's bureaucratic model, indicating that public administrationists and administrators need to be aware of the abstract nature of *ideal types*. Weber's classic bureaucratic model was intended to help the researcher understand relationships among variables and help practitioners understand bureaucratic processes. The model does not represent reality. As pointed out during the Minnowbrook conference in 1969, it is a problem in the field of public administration that the Weberian model has been taken by positivists to be a goal, rather than a device for understanding bureaucratic structures better. The tendency is to use it as a model of reality that simply will not work and certainly would not be desirable.

Weber was cognizant of the subjectivity of bureaucratic behavior, including individual orientations toward social relations, the group, power and authority, and the role of the state in society (70). In fact, Weber was a contemporary of many of those involved in the Phenomenology Movement. While he differed with them on some important issues, he too was influenced by their discussion. The Weberian ideal-type was not intended to be a normative model.

The phenomenological perspective supports a *consociated* model of bureaucracy in which project teams replace strictly hierarchical structure, decision making is decentralized, leadership is situational, clientele are represented in the organization, and employees are highly professional and mobile (71). In that regard, phenomenology supports a normative model of administrative organization and behavior. In fact, Hummel (72) suggests that the traditional, "pyramid" or hierarchical manager, and the classical Weberian bureaucratic model, will become dysfunctional in an age in which information flow and role flexibility are far more important than administrative control. He and others predict changes in administrative structure and process as we find ourselves in a world of shared power with increasing demands for multiorganizational responses to problems, collaborative administrative arrangements, and participative decisionmaking. The movement away from "command and control" structures, with their centralized executive authority, to more collaborative and cooperative arrangements suggests profound alterations in how people relate to each other and to their organizations (73).

Lastly, phenomenology offers a means of reaffirming the importance of philosophy to social science and the importance of understanding "man in the actual context of his immediate experience, his life-world" (74). Phenomenology poses interesting questions about the nature of contemporary social and natural science. While there is a certain attraction to the seeming simplicity of reducing social phenomena to numbers and thereby divining society's future, phenomenology makes one aware of the limitations of science as it is currently practiced. That there are phenomena that defy observation, few would disagree. That there are subjective elements in logical positivist science, most would agree. Subjectivity is not necessarily bad. Phenomenology offers a pragmatic approach to scientific inquiry that is sometimes lacking in empiricism. About that pragmatism, Husserl said:

> It is *we* who are genuine positivists. In fact we permit *no* authority to deprive us of the right of recognizing all kinds of intuition as equally valuable sources for the justification of knowledge, not even that of 'modern natural science' (75).

Phenomenology is viewed as a supplement or complement to empiricism, another tool to help understand social and physical phenomena, and it has had and continues to have a significant impact on the social sciences, including public administration. As Carl Bellone and Lloyd Nigro pointed out in 1980, although positivist science has its limits, it does have value in administration and policymaking (77). Scientists and administrators need to be reminded that human values are the central values. Administration is not simply a process of rational, value-neutral action. It has normative bases and effects.

REFERENCES

1. D. Stewart and A. Mickunas, *Exploring Phenomenology: A Guide to the Field and Its Literature,* American Library Association, Chicago, 1974.
2. See, e.g., H. Spiegelberg, *The Phenomenological Movement: A Historical Introduction,* 2nd Ed., Volume 1, Martinus Nijhoff, The Hague, 1969.
3. D. Stewart and A. Mickunas, *Exploring Phenomenology,* p. 4.
4. R. P. Hummel, *The Bureaucratic Experience: A Critique of Life in the Modern Organization,* 4th Ed., St. Martin's Press, New York, 1994, pp. 15–16.
5. M. M. Harmon and R. T. Mayer, *Organization Theory for Public Administration,* Little, Brown, and Company, Boston, 1986, p. 291.
6. H. Spiegelberg, *The Phenomenological Movement: A Historical Introduction, Student Edition,* 3rd Ed., Kluwer Academic Publishers, Dordrecht, The Netherlands, 1994.
7. H. Spiegelberg, *The Phenomenological Movement,* p. 2.
8. H. Spiegelberg, *The Phenomenological Movement,* pp. 165–67.

9. Translated by G. Walsh and F. Lehnert, Northwestern University Press, Evanston, Ill., 1967.

10. H. Spiegelberg, *The Phenomenological Movement*, pp. 339–47.

11. See, e.g., R. P. Hummel, *The Bureaucratic Experience*, 1994.

12. D. Stewart and A. Mickunas, *Exploring Phenomenology*, pp. 24–26.

13. D. Stewart and A. Mickunas, *Exploring Phenomenology*, pp. 24–26.

14. D. Stewart and A. Mickunas, *Exploring Phenomenology*, pp. 8–9, 22–23, 40, 43; and E. Husserl, *Ideas: General Introduction to Pure Phenomenology*, (W. R. B. Gibson, trans.), Collier Books, New York, 1962, pp. 75–76.

15. D. Stewart and A. Mickunas, *Exploring Phenomenology*, p. 126; and A. Schutz, Common-sense and scientific interpretation of human action, M. Natanson (ed.), *Philosophy of the Social Sciences*, Random House, New York, 1963, pp. 339–341.

16. M. Natanson, Alfred Schutz on social reality and social science, M. Natanson, (ed.), *Phenomenology and Social Reality: Essays in Memory of Alfred Schutz* Martinus Nijhoff, The Hague, 1970, pp. 101–122.

17. L. Kirkhart, Toward a theory of public administration, F. Marini (ed.), *Toward a New Public Administration: The Minnowbrook Perspective*, Chandler Publishers, Scranton, Penn., 1971. pp. 93–121.

18. M. Natanson, Phenomenology and the social sciences, M. Natanson (ed.), *Phenomenology and the Social Sciences*, Volume 1, Northwestern University Press, Evanston, Ill., 1973, pp. 16–22.

19. A. Schutz, Concept and theory formation in the social sciences, M. Natanson (ed.), *Philosophy of the Social Sciences*, Random House, New York, 1963, pp. 236–38.

20. A. Schutz, "Concept and theory formation in the social sciences," p. 232.

21. D. Stewart and A. Mickunas, *Exploring Phenomenology*, p. 23.

22. A. Schutz, Common sense and scientific interpretation of human action, p. 304.

23. A. Schutz, *The Phenomenology of the Social World*, pp. 97–98.

24. A. Schutz, Concept and theory formation in the social sciences, pp. 244–248.

25. L. J. Goldstein, The phenomenological and naturalistic approaches to the Social, *Philosophy of the Social Sciences*, M. Natanson (ed.), Random House, New York, 1963, p. 295.

26. D. Stewart and A. Mickunas, *Exploring Phenomenology*, pp. 128–29.

27. C. J. Friedrich, Phenomenology and political science, M. Natanson (ed.), *Phenomenology and the Social Sciences*, Volume 2, Northwestern University Press, Evanston, Illinois, 1973, pp. 182–83.

28. C. J. Friedrich, Phenomenology and political science, p. 179.

29. R. Bogdan and S. J. Taylor, *Introduction to Qualitative Research Methods: A Phenomenological Approach to the Social Sciences*, John Wiley and Sons, New York, 1975, pp. 4–7.

30. M. Natanson, Phenomenology and the social sciences, p. 8.

31. M. M. Harmon and R. T. Mayer, *Organization Theory for Public Administration*, p. 227.

32. See, e.g., R. P. Hummel, *The Bureaucratic Experience*, p. 211.

33. Fanon, *The Wretched of the Earth: The Handbook for the Black Revolution that is Changing the Shape of the World*, with an Introduction by J.-P. Sartre, Grove Press, New York, 1963.

34. M. M. Harmon and R. T. Mayer, *Organization Theory for Public Administration*, p. 293.

35. H. Spiegelberg, *The Phenomenological Movement*, pp. 5–6.

36. C. J. Friedrich, "Phenomenology and Political Science," pp. 175–76.

37. J. N. Moharty, *Transcendental Phenomenology: An Analytical Account*, Basil Blackwell, Oxford, U.K., 1989, p. 21.

38. H. Spiegelberg, *The Phenomenological Movement*, p. 659.

39. M. Natanson, Phenomenology and the social sciences, p. 24.

40. M. Natanson, Phenomenology and the social sciences, pp. 27–30.

41. J. N. Mohanty, *Transcendental Phenomenology*, p. 29.

42. M. Natanson, Phenomenology and the social sciences, p. 34.

43. L. Kirkhart, Toward a theory of public administration, pp. 142–43.

44. L. Kirkhart, Toward a theory of public administration, pp. 144–45.

45. D. Waldo, Replies and comment, *Am. Pol. Sci. Rev.:* 46, p. 503, 1952 Also see: D. Waldo, *The Enterprise of Public Administration*, Chandler and Sharp Publishers, Novati, Calif., 1980.

46. See F. Marini (ed.), *Toward a New Public Administration*.

47. "Foreword" to F. Marini (ed.), *Toward a New Public Administration*, p. xiii.

48. R. P. Hummel, *The Bureaucratic Experience*, p. 23.

49. R. P. Hummel, *The Bureaucratic Experience*, p. 212.

50. R. P. Hummel, *The Bureaucratic Experience*, pp. 19–20.

51. N. E. Long, Public policy and administration: The goals of rationality and responsibility, *Pub. Admin. Rev.:* 14, 1954, reprinted in *Pub. Admin. Rev.:* 56, 149–52, 1996.

52. N. E. Long, Public administration and the goals of rationality and responsibility, *Pub. Admin. Rev.:* 56, 152–54, 1996.

53. F. P. Sherwood, An academician's response: The thinking, learning bureaucracy, *Pub. Admin. Rev.:* 56, 154–57 (1996).

54. R. B. Reich (ed.), *The Power of Public Ideas*, Harvard University Press, Cambridge, Mass., 1988.

55. See, e.g., D. Dery, *Problem Definition in Policy Analysis*, University Press of Kansas, Lawrence, 1984.

56. See, e.g., W. L. Waugh, Jr., *Terrorism and Emergency Management: Policy and Administration*, Marcel Dekker, New York, 1990; and, W. L. Waugh, Jr. (1989). Informing policy and administration: A comparative perspective on terrorism, *Int. Jour. of Pub. Admin.:* 12, 477–99, 1989.

57. W. L. Waugh, Co-ordination or control: Organizational design and the emergency management function, *Int. Jour. of Dis. Prev. and Manag.:* 2, 17–31, 1993.

58. See, e.g., J. G. Gunnell, Political inquiry and the concept of action: A phenomenological analysis, Natanson (ed.), *Phenomenology and the Social Sciences*, pp. 197–275.

59. M. M. Harmon, *Action Theory for Public Administration*, Longman, New York, 1981. Also see: Harmon, Toward an active social theory of administrative action: Some empirical and normative implications, in *Organizational Theory for the New Public Administration*, C. J. Bellone (ed.) Allen & Bacon, 1980, pp. 176–218.

60. Ott, *The Organizational Culture Perspective*, Dorsey Press, Chicago, 1989.

61. R. T. Golembiewski, OD perspectives on high performance, R. B. Denhardt and B. R. Hammond (ed.), *Public Administration in Action: Readings, Profiles, & Cases*, Brooks/Cole Publishers, Pacific Grove, Calif., 1992, pp. 324–331.

62. R. T. Golembiewski, The future of public administration: End of a short stay in the sun? Or a new day A-dawning?, *Pub. Admin. Rev.:* 56, 139–48, 1996. Also see, C. Argyris, R. Putnam, and D. McL. Smith, *Action Science*, Jossey-Bass Publishers, San Francisco, Calif., 1985.

63. P. L. Berger and T. Luckmann, *The Social Construction of Reality*, Doubleday, Garden City, New York, 1966.

64. H. F. Gortner, J. Mahler, and J. B. Nicholson, *Organization Theory: A Public Perspective*, Dorsey Press, Chicago, 1987.

65. M. L. Vasu, D. W. Stewart, and G. D. Garson, *Organizational Behavior and Public Management*, Second Edition, Marcel Dekker, New York, 1990, pp. 319–21.

66. See, e.g., N. Postman, *Technopoly: The Surrender of Culture to Technology*, Vintage Books, New York, 1992.

67. R. P. Hummel, Circle managers and pyramid managers, p. 215.

68. D. H. Rosenbloom, *Public Administration: Understanding Management, Politics, and Law in the Public Sector*, Random House, New York, 1986, pp. 389–92.

69. F. McGee, Comment: Phenomenological administration—A new reality, F. Marini (ed.), *Toward a New Public Administration*, p. 168.

70. L. Kirkhart, Toward a theory of public administration, pp. 148–55.

71. L. Kirkhart, Toward a theory of public administration, pp. 158–64.
72. R. P. Hummel, Circle managers and pyramid managers.
73. Waugh, Co-ordination or control.
74. M. Natanson, Phenomenology and the social sciences, pp. 42–43.
75. Husserl, *Ideas*, p. 787.
76. C. J. Bellone and L. G. Nigro, Theories of value formation and administrative theory, *Organization Theory and the New Public Administration*, pp. 52–67.

17

JEAN-PAUL SARTRE

William L. Waugh, Jr.
Georgia State University, Atlanta, Georgia

Jean-Paul Sartre and the French existentialists offered an alternative to the dominant scientific and philosophical paradigms of the postwar period and they were embraced by scholars, students, and others frustrated by the inability of government and business to address the ills of society. Existentialist philosophy encourages stripping away ideological, economic, and personal biases to expose the causes of conflict, poverty, and suffering and relying upon individual responsibility to find remedies. While Sartre and the existentialists had only a limited direct impact on public administration, their notions that individuals bear responsibility for their own actions and that individuals are not trapped by their past, but can be defined in terms of their potential, have had lasting influences.

The influence of existentialism on public administration is expressed most clearly in an article entitled "The Existential Executive" which appeared in a 1970 issue of *Public Administration Review* (1). The author, Anders Richter, pointed out the increasingly apparent failure of American policy in Vietnam, growing domestic economic problems resulting from the attempt to wage the Vietnam War and the War on Poverty at the same time, heightening racial tension and conflict, and increasing intergenerational conflict fueled by accelerating social change. The litany of crises in the 1960s was long and familiar and Richter anticipated that the solution might be a revolution "from the top" in American government. Drawing upon the literatures of existentialism and humanistic psychology, he argued that senior public administrators were under increasing pressure to address the serious problems facing the U.S. and, indeed, had the technical expertise effectively to do so. Grounding his argument in Jean-Paul Sartre's contention that individuals have a responsibility to exercise their freedom to act to preserve individual and societal options for the future, Richter suggested that public administrators have a responsibility to themselves and, by extension, to society at large to understand the true *essence* of the world around them and to initiate action to alleviate conditions that constrain freedom of action.

That article demonstrates the promise that existentialism engendered during the 1960s and 1970s. It was widely felt that American society was undergoing revolutionary transformation and that fundamental changes required new perspectives. For that reason, the perspectives offered by existentialist writers on the direction and extent of the social and political change were met with considerable excitement. Their books were widely read and discussed on college campuses and they were invited to speak and to comment on the issues of the day. The group was not large. Jean-Paul Sartre was the acknowledged leader of the Existential movement following World War II and, along with Albert Camus (1913–1960), Maurice Merleau-Ponty (1908–1961), and Simone de Beauvoir (1908–1986), provided the core of the French existentialist literature. In large measure, Sartre borrowed many of the existentialist concepts generated during the 1920s by German idealists and made existentialism a subject of literary commentary and social debate. That debate was very much a part of the milieu of the 1960s, fueling the political discussions and encouraging political activism among students and scholars in Europe and North America.

In suggesting the applicability of existentialist principles to American public administration, Richter argued that bureaucrats, as they gain more and more knowledge about cause-effect relationships and policy options and develop skills in applying that knowledge, have a social obligation to exercise their *free will*, their *choice*, in the public interest. Indeed, they have an ethical responsibility to act. The primary question should be how to assure *objectivity* so that they are responding to the true *essence* of the phenomena. At issue then, is how can public administrators assure that they are responding to objective conditions, rather than to erroneous perceptions of reality fostered by cultural and organizational biases? Just as the U.S. Department of Defense fostered an orthodox perspective on the Vietnam War and the foreign policy establishment fostered a belief in the fundamental conflict between communism and capitalism, professional and organizational contexts color perceptions of reality and the range of "acceptable" policy options. Conformity with the accepted agency value systems and the dominant political perspectives was strictly enforced. Deviance, even when supported by knowledge, was discouraged and deviants were severely punished. Thus, public administrators, even when they discerned conflict between what they knew to be true and what their agencies averred to be true, were constrained in their freedom to act upon their knowledge and experience (2).

Richter went on to argue that administrative approaches are dominated by the technology and values of the new administrative professions. He concluded that: "The enemy of true reality is ultrapracticality" (3), meaning that impersonal, scientifically derived, and programmed decisionmaking is too far removed from human experience to be objective. Indeed, rather than being value neutral tools of administration, the techniques of rational analysis and decisionmaking very much determine the ends and means of administrative action and policymaking. Those rational methods got us into Vietnam and kept us from understanding and correcting what we were doing. Conformity with organizational culture, fear of job loss, habit, indifference to society's needs, excessive reliance on standard operating procedures and regulations, and a plethora of common technical tools and behaviors are distracting us from understanding the *essence* of reality and acting to achieve our goals. Public administrators, according to Richter, should be seeking *authenticity*. In the vernacular of the day, they should be seeing and "telling it like it is," discarding the organizational filters and professional arrogance that cloud our understanding of social and economic problems. "We must discover proactive administrators who possess the objectivity to make responsible choices" (4) and who can accept the consequences of their actions.

Citing Sartre's observation that one's freedom rests on the freedom of others, Richter argued that public administrators have a fundamental and compelling responsibility to act. Freedom is defined in terms of options for the future and public administrators should act to preserve options for themselves and for society. That freedom, according to the existentialists, is rooted in individual responsibility. "The existentialist executive makes his own choices. . . ." (5). Richter also pointed out the importance of the generalist administrator with a broad perspective, citing Abraham Maslow and the organizational humanists, who can see beyond the minutae, beyond the technical details, and understand the options that the future will offer to individuals and to society as a whole. The value of *authentic* organizations, meaning those sensitive to the true *essence* of reality and focused on long-term goals and options, was also pointed out. Such organizations, under the leadership of skilled and ethical administrators, were seen as the best chance to preserve society's options for the future (6).

Richter's advocacy of a more proactive bureaucracy was predicated on his experience at the Federal Executive Institute. Interacting with other federal executives, he noted the frustration born of failed programs when their shortcomings were indeed correctable, as well as the misplaced confidence encouraged among many executives by technical skill and scientific method (7). Richter's contention that organizations inhibited the freedom of their members to exercise individual responsibilities was not particularly controversial, even for the period of time in which it was expressed. Several well publicized cases of whistleblowing, such as Daniel Elsberg's release of the Pentagon Papers to the media, provided ample evidence that most administrators could not be considered free to express their own opinions or to act upon them. The cases demonstrated that at least a few public officials viewed it as their responsibility to act, but they also demonstrated that the choice might be a very costly one for each of them. That argument for the existence of individual responsibility for ethical conduct is perhaps the most lasting legacy of the existentialist philosophy for public administration.

Richter's article was very much a product of the debate over existentialism that Sartre and his colleagues encouraged. The existentialists, as well as the prophets of the New Left, blamed big government and big business for the social and economic problems of the day and the insensitivity and arrogance of scientists and technicians for the policy failures. The policy debate was distilled into a philosophical debate about individual and societal goals and how to achieve them. When the debates cooled off, as the Vietnam War wound down and racial and generational conflict appeared to wane, popular interest in existentialist philosophy also appeared to decline in the U.S. Nonetheless, while the impact of existentialism on American public administration was not great, notwithstanding Richter's article in *Public Administration Review*, the alternative perspective was absorbed by scholars and practitioners in the field and, undoubtedly, has had a significant, albeit indirect, effect. Existentialism, particularly in conjunction with the phenomenological approach to the study of administration, was discussed at the Minnowbrook Conference in 1969 and in the public administration literature into the 1980s. While arguments that public administrators become political activists are far less frequent than they were during the 1960s and early 1970s, existentialist thought can still be found in the literature of the field, particularly in the more humanist writings. Certainly existentialism has had an impact on the discussion and application of codes of ethics, as well as on the advocacy of social and political causes by bureaucrats encouraged by proponents of the "new public administration" (8).

This chapter examines the development of Sartre's existentialist philosophy and how it related to the philosophies of others, the basic tenets of existentialist thought, the relationship between Sartre's views on existentialism and Marxism (because his Marxism, in part, defined his celebrity in Europe and North America), and the influence of existentialist writings on the literature and practice of public administration. The objectives are to focus on 1. how existentialism affected philosophical and policy debates in general and 2. how it affected the debate over the role of public administration in American society in the 1970s.

I. SARTRE THE EXISTENTIALIST

Existentialist thought has evolved over time and its tenets vary from writer to writer. While there are common elements, a variety of perspectives are generally subsumed by the label. The philosophical orientation changed over time in Sartre's writings, too, as he worked out a justification for political action and reconciled his earlier writings with the options he encountered later.

Expanding upon the existential thought of Martin Heidegger and other German phenomenologists, Jean-Paul Sartre helped elevate existentialism from a theological and philosophical movement, within academic and philosophical circles, into a literary movement accessible to a much broader audience. The impact of existentialist thought was felt in Europe in the period of intellectual ferment prior to World War II and, in the immediate aftermath of the war, became a major subject of academic and philosophical debate. As exemplified by Anders Richter's attention to the value of existentialism to American public administrators, the discussion reached the U.S. in the 1950s and 1960s and encouraged a broad re-examination of our dominant philosophical and scientific paradigms.

In some measure, understanding existentialism requires some understanding of Jean-Paul Sartre and his colleagues. Sartre was very much a product of his milieu. He was born in Paris on June 21, 1905. His father died the next year and he lived with his mother and grandparents until 1917 when his mother remarried and the family moved back to Paris. After studying in Paris, he taught at several high schools and began writing for a variety of publications. The early writings generally reflected the philosophical debate current at the time. He served in the military from 1929 to 1931 and then returned to teaching. While on a grant to study at the French Institute in Berlin during 1933–34, Sartre was introduced to the phenomenology of Edmund Husserl and was undoubtedly able to read the works of the German idealists before they were translated into French and made more broadly available. He held a series of teaching positions, wrote, and lived a bohemian lifestyle with Simone de Beauvoir until drafted back into the military in 1939. He was captured by the Germans in 1940 and escaped the following year. The remainder of the war was spent in the Resistance, initially in a small group co-founded by Merleau-Ponty and later in a teaching position. He founded the literary journal *Les Temps modernes* in 1944 and, as his writings gained popularity, he toured and lectured in the U.S. and other countries (9).

Sartre was in the middle of the major philosophical debates of the 1930s and 1940s and was profoundly affected by both World War I and his own military experience in World War II. In that sense, he was a product of his time and very much caught up in the search for alternative philosophical and political perspectives. The existentialist philosophy picked up during his studies in Berlin in the 1930s was slowly expanded upon and he gave it a distinctive flavor.

Politically, he and Merleau-Ponty embraced much of the humanist philosophy of Marxism, but denounced the deviance reflected in the Soviet Union's oppression of the populations of Russia and Eastern Europe in the late 1940s and early 1950s. In the years following that break with the Soviet Union and with the French Communist party, Sartre's work became increasingly topical and international. He promoted international peace organizations and expressed strong opposition to the Soviet invasion of Hungary in 1956, French violations of human rights in Algeria, apartheid in southern Africa, Soviet actions in Czechoslovakia and elsewhere in Eastern Europe, U.S. involvement in Vietnam, the Biafran civil war, and the Yom Kippur War. In the latter case, he supported Israel. He encouraged public attention to the plight of the boat people from Vietnam and to other causes of the day (10). His writings included the preface of Frantz Fanon's *Wretched of the Earth* (1963) in which he explained why Fanon's argument for violent overthrow of colonialist oppressors was justified. Addressing the French people, he made the case both for collective guilt for the exploitation of colonial peoples, and the atrocities committed by the French military in Algeria, and for individual action to rectify the sins of colonialism. To those who felt no guilt, he stated:

> Try to understand this at any rate; if violence began this very evening and if exploitation and oppression had never existed on the earth, perhaps the slogans of non-violence might end the quarrel. But if the whole regime, even your non-violent ideas, are conditioned by a thousand-year-old oppression, your passivity serves only to place you in the ranks of the oppressors (11).

It was not enough to acknowledge the atrocities committed against the people of Algeria, Indochina, and other parts of the developing world and to urge peaceful solutions. One had to understand one's part in that oppression and take an active role in alleviating its effects. To the French people, Sartre declared: "With us, to be a man is to be an accomplice of colonialism, since all of us without exception have profited by colonial exploitation" (12).

Sartre was awarded the Nobel Prize for Literature in 1964, but declined the award because he felt that acceptance would represent compromise with a societal perspective on individual action. He refused to be co-opted. Following a very active decade of political activism, his health began to fail in the early 1970s and he died on April 15, 1980 (13).

In large measure, Sartre mirrored his time, incorporating new philosophical perspectives, pursuing individual freedom, and commenting on the major social and political issues of the day. His was an evolving philosophy, from atheistic phenomenology; to Marxism; to a more applied form of existentialism. As a result, he became a target of critics from the Right and the Left and was in the middle of much of the social and political debate of the 1960s and 1970s.

During the postwar period, writers, philosophers, and political commentators were decrying the depersonalization of Western societies. Political ferment brought on by the collapse of colonial empires and the creation of ideological blocs, dislocation and relocation brought about by rapid urbanization and industrialization, rapidly changing social values and norms of behavior, mechanistic organizational structures, and seemingly blind confidence in science and technology provided fertile ground for alternative philosophical perspectives. Socialist, existentialist, and a variety of transcendentalist philosophies attracted adherents in the U.S.

II. THE EXISTENTIALIST PHILOSOPHY

> Sartre's philosophy is usually taken as the paradigmatic example of existentialist philosophy, and other figures are considered existentialists insofar as they resonate with certain Sartrian themes—his extreme individualism, his emphasis on freedom and responsibility, his insistence that we and not the world give meaning to our lives (14).

In simple terms, existentialists argue that the perspectives of individuals are the proper vantage point for expressing and solving human problems. Through the exercise of *free will*, individuals shape themselves and are responsible for their own actions. It is on the level of individual human existence that the past, present, and future are given meaning. Purpose and meaning are not externally derived, according to Sartre, from God or society.

Martin Heidegger's (1889–1976) *Dasein*, meaning that "its existence precedes its essence" provided a point of philosophical departure for the existentialists and for Sartre in particular (15). The notion of *existence preceding essence* is that one may imagine and act upon a phenomenon, meaning it exists, before it becomes real or tangible. In other words, we respond to and act upon options that we anticipate. Hegel's, and later Marx's, *dialectic* posited the idea of future options or phenomenon being products of the past and present. Sartre's philosophy emphasized the importance of understanding the *essence* of the past and the present in order to anticipate the future.

The *Self* is defined not as static and knowable, rather it is defined in relationship with the world in which one lives. Moreover, the *Self* is not so much the product of that world as it is the possibilities that the world provides. It is through experience, through action, that the *Self* is defined. As described by Sartre, "Man makes himself" (16). Central to this notion for Sartre was the freedom to choose and the desirability of *authenticity*, truthfulness to one's self and one's responsibility to act (17).

While Soren Kierkegaard (1813–1855), a Danish philosopher, is often acknowledged as the first existentialist, Edmund Husserl's phenomenological method provided the foundation for much of Sartre's work, although he disagreed with Husserl's view that the world is a construct defined by the consciousness. The self and the world are distinct, according to Sartre, although the self is found in the world. Consciousness is selfless, "pre-reflective." Sartre and the other French existentialists made the distinction between the "being-for-itself" or for consciousness and the "being-in-itself" or of the physical world, the rational man and the meaningless world. For Sartre and his colleagues, the indifferent world was without God. Not all existentialists were atheists, however. They also differed on the possibility of meaning and Albert Camus, for one, judged the "Absurd" world to be devoid of meaning. That did not mean he believed people should lack purpose, rather that being human was in itself sufficient motivation for individuals to act (18).

At issue for the existentialists was not a method of inquiry to study the world, as it was for the German phenomenologists, rather it was the fundamental nature of man. Sartre and his colleagues generally argued that the nature of man is neither good nor bad, that man has the freedom to choose and, therefore, can be what he chooses to be. Moreover, one is responsible for one's choices, regardless of the reasons they were made. For Sartre, that meant that one is always responsible for one's choices, even when they are coerced or misinformed. Camus and Merleau-Ponty, on the other hand, were more forgiving in that their interpretations accepted that circumstances may limit or force choices and some actions can be excused as not being voluntary (19). The individualism of the philosophy appealed to those wishing to assign blame for actions taken during World War II and its immediate aftermath and helped shape the post-war milieu. In large measure the notion of individual responsibility was a reaction to Sartre's own experiences as a prisoner of war and in the Resistance during the war. To his mind, excuses for being a Nazi or submitting to Nazi domination or any number of acts of violence were without merit. There was no excuse and, ultimately, according to Sartre, people are responsible for choosing to commit those acts.

Consciousness is "nothingness," an awareness capable of seeing "the world as it is or as it might be, as well as the way it is" (20). Consciousness is not distinct from the world. *Facticity*, a concept Sartre borrowed from Heidegger, represents one's past and its potential implications or impact on one's future. It is essential to understand and accept one's past, but not to be constrained by it. For Sartre, the past may be used or overcome, but it cannot be ignored because it helps shape future opportunities. *Transcendence* is one's ability to envision the future and to formulate intentions to act to realize the desired future. *Fallenness* is the tendency to betray one's potential, one's *Self*, by denying that one has choices or by denying one's past. Sartre argued that one should understand one's past but, rather than be trapped by it, one should use it as a starting place to achieve one's potential (21). To act in *good faith* is to act in a manner consistent with one's *Self*. In short, the goal is to be truthful to oneself, to understand one's past and one's current and future options, and to exercise one's freedom to choose one's own future. That is our responsibility to ourselves and to society. Subconscious or unconscious motives are rejected as impossible or irrelevant.

The ultimate value is freedom in terms of both exercising one's own choice and defending the choice of others. Success or achievement, too, is less important than the intention, the action (22). The idea of acting for a larger social end came relatively late to Sartre. He began to formulate his social philosophy in *Critique of Dialectical Reason* (1960). However, the individualist focus of existentialism made it unclear how one should reconcile the understanding of one's *facticity* and *transcendence* and the exercise of one's free will with the needs of society or one's organization (23). As Sartre stated in *No Exit* (1947), "Hell is other people," and certainly his philosophy did not easily accommodate the freedom and responsibility of others. Others tend to constrain our actions and affect our understanding of ourselves. Moreover, we tend to see ourselves as others seem to see us and to respond to the perceived expectations of others is to act in *bad faith*. The issue is how to assure that we are being *authentic* and yet choose actions that support a collective good. That distinction marked a fundamental change in Sartre's philosophy, the reconciliation of individual and social action. It was easier to justify support for political revolutionaries, because their struggles against colonial oppression, political repression, or capitalist exploitation were to gain freedom and were consistent with their own responsibilities to act, than it was to justify support for an organization or a political party with more ambiguous goals. That apparent conundrum may also explain why Sartre seemed more comfortable with the early works of Marx with their focus on broad revolutionary goals and with their dialectical justification than he was with the later works and their application in the Soviet Union and other Communist regimes.

III. SARTRE THE MARXIST

Jean-Paul Sartre's brand of Marxism was far more humane than those practiced by communist regimes of his time. Nonetheless, his connection to those regimes and to Communist parties in France and elsewhere is an important factor in considering his impact on American society in general and American public administration in particular. As Daniel Bell noted in his classic *The End of Ideology* in 1962:

> Europe, in legend, has always been the home of subtle philosophical discussion; America was the land of grubby pragmatism. Questions laid to rest in Europe found their reincarnation (an old quip had it) twenty years later in the United States. Whatever the truth of the remark once, the reverse is true today. . . . But while in Europe only a small number of intellectuals left the Communist orbit before the war, in the United States almost the entire group of serious intellectuals who had been attracted to Marxism had broken with the Communist party by 1940. Thus, as an intellectual problem, Bolshevism disappeared from the American scene almost twenty years ago (24).

In terms of party affiliation, Marxism did not enjoy a wide following in the U.S. during the 1960s. To the extent that there were Marxists among the intellectual community in the U.S., the attachment to Marxist principles tended to be philosophical, more abstract than partisan. To some degree, Sartre's attachment to Marxist philosophy and his criticism of Soviet actions likely made him a more attractive figure among European and North American students and intellectuals. In a time when most were asked to choose one side or another, it kept him ideologically isolated from both Cold War establishments. That suited his personality, as well as his role as social and political commentator. He was very much a loner, notwithstanding his long relationship with Simone de Beauvoir, and even tended to alienate his friends and colleagues. While Sartre was a Marxist, he was not a member of the Communist Party. He liked the communalism inherent in communist philosophy, but rejected the notion of economic determinism. Blaming the economic system for the failures of the social system was, to Sartre, an unacceptable excuse for action (or inaction) (25). Moreover, because he was suspicious of social groupings of any sort, he was uncomfortable dealing with political parties and other organizations. He was not inclined to be co-opted by one side or the other and his individualist philosophy discouraged membership in such organizations.

The Hegelian *historical dialectic* also had appeal. The understanding of the past and present and their inherent potential for the future was very much an existentialist view. Sartre likely encountered the *dialectic* during this studies in Germany and it very much fit into the existentialist frameworks he found in the writings of Edmund Husserl and the German phenomenologists.

Sartre was also attracted to Marxist humanism, the belief in man's responsibility for man and the responsibility to free man from oppressing conditions. Man creates his own world (26). Sartre had a series of intellectual rapprochements with the French Communist party and other Marxist groups, including the Soviet Communist party, but each was interrupted by disagreements over Soviet political and military actions. He decried the distortion of Marxism by Stalinists and, through speeches and writings, attempted to reaffirm the underlying humanism of Marxist philosophy. That view of Marxist humanism was summed up by Erich Fromm in the introduction to *Marxism and the Human Individual* (1970) by the Polish scholar, Adam Schaff:

> Marx was one among the great humanist philosophers who, like the humanists from the Renaissance up to those of our day, have stressed the idea that all social arrangements must serve the growth and unfolding of man; that man must always be an end and never a means; that each individual carries within himself all of humanity; that human progress in science and in arts depends on freedom; that man has the capacity to perfect himself in the process of history (27).

Raymond Aron who was a school mate of his suggests that Sartre's view of Marxism drew principally upon the earlier writings, before the philosophy of *Das Capital* was fully formulated (28). It also reflected the idealism of the Marxist revolution, before the abuses of Stalin and others. That view is consistent with others and may well reflect a broader dissatisfaction among French Marxists with the dogmatism of the French Communist party, as well as the oppressive actions of the Soviet government (29).

In short, while Sartre's defection from the Marxist intellectual camp was much heralded in Europe, it likely had little impact in the U.S. because Marxism did not enjoy the same currency among American intellectuals. However, the defection did reaffirm the choice made decades earlier and, for that reason, Sartre's sincere concern over the abuses of power by the Soviet government was well received on both sides of the Atlantic. As he stated in *Existentialism and Humanism*: "Nor does this mean that I should not belong to a party, but only that I should be without illusion and that I should do what I can" (30). *Authenticity* was all important.

IV. EXISTENTIALISM AND PUBLIC ADMINISTRATION

In a recent analysis of the state of the field of public administration theory, Robert Denhardt noted a shift in public administration theory during the 1980s toward a more subjective orientation, citing the works of Dwight Waldo, Robert Golembiewski, Ralph Hummel, Frederick Thayer, and others, including himself. The use of psychoanalytical, phenomenological, and other alternative (to positivist) approaches promised to provide new knowledge of individual and organizational action. The immediate postwar period was dominated by more objectivist theories of public organization, including those by Herbert Simon, Vincent Ostrom, Graham Allison, Anthony Downs, and Gary Wamsley (31).

Indeed, while there was no ground swell of support for existentialist perspectives on public administration, the philosophy did have its impact. Some well-known public administrationists expressed concerns about the dominant scientific and philosophical paradigms of the time and they suggested alternatives. For example, Dwight Waldo, then editor of *Public Administration Review*, argued in a 1968 issue that public administrators bore some responsibility for the turmoil of the time. He focused on the role of public administrators in the "revolutions" of the 1950s and 1960s, observing that:

> Perhaps we in public administration helped to create the present situation by our *failures* as well as by our *successes*. Perhaps we ought to have taken the initiative in moving sooner on a number of problems that are now in the center of the stage . . . *If* we have so much wealth, and *if* we have so much know-how—and we brag a lot about both, you know—why can't we create a livable environment, shackle violence, abolish poverty, and generally secure equal treatment and justice? (32).

Citing Albert Camus' bureaucrat character in *The Plague*, Waldo went on to suggest that reliance on routinized processes in the face of events requiring action and creativity was ineffective at best and a failure to live up to the public administrator's responsibility to act on the basis of expertise and in the public interest at worst. While noting the value of the image of bureaucratic neutrality, he called for more *self-conscious* action in the face of mounting revolutionary change and warned that rational processes, such as PPBS, cause a "undue restriction of vision, leads to overnarrow parameters and oversimplication of premises" (33). He concluded by warning that more involvement in politics and policy-making by public administrators certainly was risky, but that it was also risky to defend the status quo while pressures for fundamental change were building.

Not surprisingly given Waldo's central role in organizing the conference, Michael Harmon's contribution at Minnowbrook in 1969 found support in the existential literature for activist public administrators, as well. He wrote that the public administrator needs to try to understand the relationship between his or her own choices and those in the public interest. One's freedom rests on the freedom of others, as Sartre had observed. Ethical and political neutrality is an abdication of responsibility to oneself and to society, according to Harmon (34). To fail to use one's expertise and experience to assure effective government responses to socioeconomic problems is unprofessional, as well as being poor citizenship.

Notwithstanding that argument, the suggestion that public administrators be active participants in policy making, exercising their freedom and responsibility, was roundly criticized at Minnowbrook by John Paynter. He argued in terms of whether such activism would "meet the conventional democratic test of administrative responsibility" (35). The politics-administration dichotomy, however discredited as a defining principle of public administration by that time, supported a more reactive role for public administrators.

This was the context within which Anders Richter advocated a more proactive and politically involved bureaucracy and warned against overly rational administrative processes and tools. Public administration scholars had noted the appropriateness of existentialist and phenomenological approaches at Minnowbrook and at least a few practitioners were noting their utility in public administration practice.

By contrast, while they may have acknowledged the potential of individualist approaches, others argued for more objective or empirical methods of determining social and political options. For example, Vincent Ostrom argued in a 1980 *Public Administration Review* article that organizations are artifacts, "works of art," that represent intentions to pursue specific ends and that there are two methods of accounting for the strategies chosen to pursue those ends. He suggested that:

> One is to rely upon the presumption that human beings share a basic similitude of thoughts and passions, and by taking the perspective of others, attempt to understand the basic structures and logic of their situation and infer the strategy that they are likely to pursue. This is essentially the strategy that is inherent in methodological individualism (36).

However, the other method he described involves "elucidating the appropriate information," i.e., communicating personal and organizational preferences, through market pricing and other conventions. That function, he observed, is more often the province of organizations (37). While, like the existentialists, he concluded that language and other communication vehicles are often ambiguous, imprecise, and value-laden and certainly affect administration and the science we use to understand it, he chose a different course altogether. He went on to say that: "The alternative to developing a value-free science of administration is to become explicitly aware of the fundamental role that values play in all forms of artisanship in general, and in the forms of artisanship involved in the organization of human societies in particular" (38). To accomplish that he suggested that we need a far better understanding of individual and social purpose which may be achieved by more self-examination. Unlike the existentialists, however, he felt that our understanding of others may best be found in an understanding of ourselves, i.e., that social purpose is paramount and that it may be devined through individual self-scrutiny. This perspective is essentially diametrically opposed to that of the existentialists. The existentialists argue for a focus on individual purpose and, perhaps, suggest that an understanding of human purpose may be found through examination of social action.

In short, the importance of individual values and perspectives and the need for self-scrutiny was acknowledged, but the answer to the question of how to understand reality is to be found in our shared values, rather than within each of us. And, our shared values are manifested in the artifacts, the organizations, of our society, rather than to be devined from experience and philosophical reflection. The belief in an objective reality, distinct from and independent of human consciousness, even more clearly differentiated his philosophy from that of the existentialists.

The vestiges of existentialist philosophy can also be found in more recent works. Existentialist phenomenological approaches are rare in the public administration literature, but there is increasing attention to the importance of human perception and organizational predispositions to the definition of policy problems (39). Policy problems are not part of an objective reality; there is a subjective, constructionist, element in their definition. I, for example, have suggested that the phenomenon of terrorism can be defined in terms of its essential elements, but that individuals and agencies tend to defined the violence in terms that fit their own cultural and political orientations and design policies based upon the assumptions inherent in those interpretations. National security personnel and agencies see terrorism in international terms with nations being the basic unit of analysis. Law enforcement personnel and agencies see terrorism in terms of human victims and have their own predispositions toward particular methods of alleviating the problem. Scholars and theoreticians may view the phenomenon as revolutionary challenges to the status quo, and so on. On one level, the phenomenon has different meanings to different people. On another level, however, the phenomenon has an *essence* that is common. Moreover, the concept of terrorism has intensely political connotations that affect its application. Only by cutting through the misperceptions or biases to focus on the essence of the phenomenon can one find a policy that may address the problem effectively (40).

V. CONCLUSION

Richard Page has suggested that both pragmatism, with its particular appeal to American sensibilities, and existentialism have been the "[t]wo major philosophical efforts that have matured in the twentieth century" (41). While pragmatism provides philosophical foundation for communitarian states, "existentialism is supremely individualistic" (42). Despite the seeming incompatibility, both pragmatism and existentialism appealed to Americans. Page judged that existentialism encouraged individuals "to soar above reason in an individualistic response to the wrongs of society" (43). In some measure, that may be an appropriate description of existentialist interpretations of public administration, but the expression of existentialist perspectives in the field also captured the excitement and enthusiasm of the time for alternatives to the status quo. The search of answers to critically important social and economic problems was compelling and the appeal of individualistic philosophies was easy to understand. The 1960s and 1970s were also a period of growth for American government and the activist orientation of the existentialists appealed to those seeking socially meaningful roles in public agencies and personal growth through the exercise of those roles.

John Raulston Saul suggests that the brief popularity of existentialist philosophy was due to the fact that Westerners, in general, are uncomfortable with a philosophy that encourages people to be judged by their actions, rather than by their power or position (44). That may be all the more true when the actions upon which someone is judged are based upon individual interests or needs rather than upon a broader social interest. The popularity, however, was likely fueled by a compelling need for political action to address the ills of society, considerable frustration with governmental and societal inertia, and the growing distrust of large and complex organizations of all sorts. The impersonality of organizational technologies and the subordination of personal values to the technical were also likely factors. This was a time in which science and technology were associated with the status quo, perceived to be dehumanizing, and thus were subjected to political and social attack. Phenomenological inquiry, reasserting the importance of the subjective and, in large measure, rejecting the positivist subjective/objective dichotomy (45) was similarly in vogue, although certainly not as popularly embraced.

For a time, albeit brief, existentialist philosophy found fertile ground in public administration theory and encouraged alternative views of public organizations and the roles of public administrators. The writings of Sartre, Camus, and others were the vogue on college campuses and among scholars. The publication of Richter's "The Existentialist Executive" exemplified that interest in alternative perspectives and was an acknowledgment of the frustration among public administrators about the state of American policy in Vietnam and regarding the social and economic problems of the day. To some extent, the call for adminstrators to exercise their moral responsibilies to the public is still relevant. Certainly the idea that ethics are derived from individual responsibility to the public is current and public administrators are expected to act upon that responsibility by blowing the whistle when corruption or incompetence interfere with the pursuit of public purposes, as well as by recommending policy change when inefficiency or ineffectiveness threaten. More importantly, for public administrators to judge whether actions are right or wrong based upon their own values, perhaps with some self-examination of those values before acting, is certainly desirable.

Existentialism has also had a lasting impact on public administration research. Existentialist and transcendentalist phenomenology, for example, provided a welcome alternative to empirical social science and, at least to some extent, can still be found in the works of Ralph Hummel and a few others who choose to "soar above reason" (as Page suggested). Perhaps inevitably, existentialist perspectives succumbed to the dominance of logical positivism as those in the field of public administration became enamored of quantitative techniques and seduced by economic conceptual frameworks. Nonetheless, interest in alternative philosophies, as well as critical theories, does appear to be increasing. As has been the case with other philosophical views, existentialism has had a lasting impact on the theory and thought of public administration, particularly in terms of the importance it assigned individuals in determining and applying ethical standards and, perhaps to a lesser extent, in its charge to public employees to act proactively to preserve individual and collective freedom.

REFERENCES

1. A. Richter, The existentialist executive, *Pub. Admin. Rev.*: 30, 415–422, 1970.
2. A. Richter, The existentialist executive.
3. A. Richter, The existentialist executive, p. 418.
4. A. Richter, The existentialist executive, p. 420.
5. A. Richter, The existentialist executive, p. 421.
6. A. Richter, The existentialist executive.
7. A. Richter, The existentialist executive.
8. See, e.g., H. G. Frederickson, *The New Public Administration*, University of Alabama Press, Alabama, 1980.
9. C. Howells, ed., *The Cambridge Companion to Sartre*, Cambridge University Press, Cambridge, U.K., 1992, pp. ix–xvi.
10. C. Howells (ed.) *The Cambridge Companion to Sartre*. Also see; G. A. Schrader, Jr. (ed.), *Existential Philosophers: Kierkegaard to Merleau-Ponty*, McGraw-Hill Book Company, New York, 1967;

J. S. Catalano, *A Commentary on Jean-Paul Sartre's Being and Nothingness*, University of Chicago Press, 1985.

11. J.-P. Sartre, Preface to F. Fanon, (C. Farrington trans.), *The Wretched of the Earth*, Grove Press, New York, 1963, p. 25.

12. J.-P. Sartre Preface to *Wretched of the Earth*, p. 25.

13. C. Howells (ed.), *The Cambridge Companion to Sartre*, pp. xix–xvi.

14. R. C. Solomon and K. M. Higgins, *A Short History of Philosophy*, Oxford University Press, New York, 1996, p. 277.

15. R. C. Solomon, *Continental Philosophy Since 1750: The Rise and Fall of the Self*, Oxford University Press, Oxford, U.K., 1988, 160.

16. R. C. Solomon, *Continential Philosophy Since 1750*, p. 174.

17. See, e.g., R. C. Solomon and K. M. Higgins, *A Short History of Philosophy*, p. 275.

18. Solomon, *Continential Philosophy Since 1750*, pp. 174–176; Solomon and Higgins, *A Short History of Philosophy*, pp. 277–282.

19. R. C. Solomon, *Continential Philosophy Since 1750*, pp. 178–179.

20. R. C. Solomon, *Continential Philosophy Since 1750*, p. 181.

21. R. C. Solomon, *Continential Philosophy Since 1750*, pp. 182–185.

22. R. C. Solomon, *Continential Philosophy Since 1750*, pp. 189–190.

23. See, e.g., R. Aron, *History and the Dialectic of Violence: An Analysis of Sartre's Critique de la Raison Dialectique*, Harper and Row, Publishers, New York, 1975, pp. 209–210.

24. D. Bell, *The End of Ideology: On the Exhaustion of Political Ideas in the Fifties*, The Free Press, New York, 1962, 309–310.

25. R. C. Solomon, *Continential Philosophy Since 1750*, pp. 191–193. See also, J. S. Catalano, *A Commentary on Jean-Paul Sartre's Critique of Dialectical Reason*, University of Chicago Press, 1986. Catalano argues that the initial appeal of Marxism for Sartre was the concern with alienation, rather than the dialectic (p. 21).

26. A. Schaff, Introduction by E. Fromm. *Marxism and the Human Individual*, McGraw-Hill Book Company, New York, 1965, pp. 168–170.

27. A. Schaff, *Marxism and Individualism*, p. x.

28. R. Aron, *History and the Dialectic of Violence*, pp. 207–208.

29. See, e.g., A. Dobson, *Jean-Paul Sartre and the Politics of Reason: A Theory of History*, Cambridge University Press, Cambridge, U K., 1993, pp. 9–15.

30. J.-P. Sartre, (P. Mairet trans.) *Existentialism and Humanism*, Methuen, London, U.K., 1957.

31. R. B. Denhardt, Public administration theory: The state of the discipline, in *Public Administration: The State of the Discipline*, N. B. Lynn and A. Wildavsky (eds.), Chatham House Publishers, Chatham, N.J., 1990, 54–63.

32. D. Waldo, Public administration in a time of revolutions, *Pub. Admin. Rev.*: 28; 365, 1968.

33. D. Waldo, "Public administration in a time of revolutions," p. 367.

34. M. M. Harmon, Normative theory and public administration: Some suggestions for a redefinition of administrative responsibility, in *Toward a New Public Administration: The Minnowbrook Perspective*, F. Marini, (ed.), Chandler Publishing Company, Scranton, Pa., 1971, 181–182. Elements of existentialist phenomenology are also discussed in L. Kirkhart, Toward a theory of public administration, in *Toward a New Public Administration: The Minnowbrook Perspective*.

35. J. Paynter, Comment: On a redefinition of administrative responsibility, *Toward a New Public Administration: The Minnowbrook Perspective*, pp. 185–187.

36. V. Ostrom, Artisanship and artifact, *Public Admin. Rev*: 40, 310, 1980.

37. V. Ostrom, Artisanship and artifact, pp. 310–311.

38. V. Ostrom, Artisanship and artifact, p. 315.

39. See, e.g., D. Dery, Introduction by A. Wildavsky, *Problem Definition in Policy Analysis*, University Press of Kansas, Lawrence, 1984.

40. W. L. Waugh, Jr., *Terrorism and Emergency Management*, Marcel Dekker, New York, 1990.

41. R. S. Page, The ideological-philosophical setting of American public administration, *Public Administration in a Time of Turbulence*, D. Waldo (ed.), Chandler Publishing Company, Scranton, Pennsylvania, 1971, p. 64.

42. R. S. Page, The ideological-philosophical setting of American public administration, p. 65.

43. R. S. Page, The ideological-philosophical setting of American public administration, p. 65.

44. J. R. Saul, *Voltaire's Bastards: The Dictatorship of Reason in the West*, Vintage Books, New York, 1992, p. 287.

45. See, e.g., R. B. Denhardt, *In the Shadow of Organization*, University Press of Kansas, Lawrence, 1981, pp. 99–108; and, H. Y. Jung, A critique of the behavioral persuasion in politics: A phenomenological view, *Phenomenology and the Social Sciences, Volume 2*, M. Natanson (ed.), Northwestern University Press, Evanston, Illinois, 1973.

18

JOHN RAWLS AND PUBLIC ADMINISTRATION

Stephen L. Esquith
Michigan State University, East Lansing, Michigan

On its face John Rawls's political philosophy seems to be unconcerned with, if not openly hostile to, Public Administration. In Rawls's ideal democratic society almost all adult members are property owners (1) and free to participate in a "social union of social unions" (2) while striving for "meaningful work in free association with others." (3) And in defending this ideal, Rawls has little directly to say about the study or practice of governing through complex organizations. His account of government institutions is limited to traditional constitutional principles like separation of powers and the rule of law. As for the functions of government, he distinguishes between a handful of economic tasks but warns: "These divisions do not overlap with the usual organization of government but are to be understood as different functions" (4) that presumably can be carried out apart from and under the control of the deliberative, more democratic processes of repre sentative government.

Nor does Rawls treat administrative decision making as a special form of political reasoning with its own peculiar "burdens" or limitations (5). As the veil of ignorance is gradually lifted, that is, once a just constitution and the laws pursuant to it have been made, Rawls argues, then these higher rules can be applied with full knowledge by judges and administrators, and followed by citizens "generally." Administrative decision making occurs against the same background of principles, laws, and facts that judicial decision making does and, for that matter, that the choices and judgments of citizens do when they face fundamental questions like whether or not to obey a military order (6).

What Rawls does say about administration, at a high level of abstraction, suggests that a society that is too dependent upon a public administration informed by classical utilitarian principles, would not be acceptable to him.

> Implicit in the contrasts between classical utilitarianism and justice as fairness is a dif ference in the underlying conceptions of society. In the one we think of a well-ordered society as a scheme of cooperation for reciprocal advantage regulated by principles which persons would choose in an initial situation that is fair, in the other as the effi cient administration of social resources to maximize the satisifaction of the system of desire constructed by the impartial spectator from the many individual systems of de sires accepted as given (7).

Two things stand out in Rawls's general criticism of utilitarian administrative politics. First, he rejects the idea that the institutions that form the basic structure of a well-ordered society (its government, economy, and social life) should be designed to manage society's social resources as efficiently as possible. Second, by efficient administration he means arranging these institutions for the maximal satisfaction of the existing desires of an artificial body as seen from the point of view of an allegedly impartial spectator. If *public* administration consists simply in the efficient administration of government agencies and bureaus with this maximal end in mind, then clearly Rawls is opposed to it.

Has public administration been utilitarian in this sense? Twentieth-century attempts to conceptualize public administration began this way, but classical utilitarian principles have been subjected to a variety of criticisms as both prescriptions for and descriptions of what public administrators do for the last fifty years.

The early Wilsonian belief that public administration could and should be separated from politics had as one of its corollaries that efficient administration was desirable but only possible when administrative and political "functions" were not carried out within the same organizational structure. But even within a purely adminstrative structure, Luther Gulick added in 1937, to be efficiently carried out the functions performed must be "homogeneous." Where they are "non-homogeneous" (for example, water supply and education) unwanted technical inefficiencies will occur if they are carried out within the same administrative unit (8).

Gulick and other less sophisticated adherents to Frederick W. Taylor's theory of scientific management clearly believed that efficiency was "the single ultimate test" of good public administration. These early writers on public administration, however, soon were vigorously criticized by academics not unsympathetic to the idea of public administration. As Robert Dahl argued in 1947, even Gulick had trouble remaining faithful to the belief in efficiency given what he knew about political reality.

> It is far from clear what Gulick means to imply in saying that "interferences with efficiency" caused by ultimate political values may "condition" and "complicate" but do not "change" the "single ultimate test" of efficiency as the goal of administration. Is efficiency the supreme goal not only of private administration, but also of public administration, as Gulick contends? If so, how can one say, as Gulick does, that "there are . . . highly inefficient arrangements like citizen boards and small local governments which may be necessary in a democracy as educational devices (9).

Not only have academic writers on public administration questioned the value of efficiency as the sole or even primary measuring stick for judging the legitimacy of government, they have also questioned the possibility of impartial administration and the separation of politics and public administration. Perhaps the most powerful rejection of scientific management and the politics-administration dichotomy was Dwight Waldo's 1948 study, *The Administrative State: A Study of the Political Theory of Public Administration*. The internal workings of public bureaucracies, like their conduct within the larger political system as a whole, were also subjected to a political analysis. Philip Sezlnick's 1948 study, *TVA and the Grass Roots*, made it clear that the development of a career bureaucracy is a political process not a scientific creation.

Finally, students of public administration have recognized that public administrators, even as political actors, do not make rational decisions based upon some encompassing or overarching conception of the good the way a utilitarian would want. They are not spectators any more than they are impartial observers of the political process. They are entangled in a complex process of empirical analysis and evaluation that allows them, at best, to "muddle through" one problem after another. According to Charles E. Lindlbom writing in 1959, the public administrator at best "focuses his attention on marginal or incremental values. Whether he is aware of it or not, he does not find general formulations of objectives very helpful and in fact makes specific marginal or incremental comparisons" (10).

Public administrators have not ignored efficiency or impartiality entirely, but they continue to temper these values with concerns for effectiveness, due process, the political imperatives of labor-management relations, and the fair distribution of public goods and services. Both academic and practicing public administrators do not simply assume that an impartial spectator can aggregate the existing desires of citizens, or even that they should try. Administrators, like all other political animals, are participants with vested interests, past associations, and career plans. Public administrators have probably always known this and gradually students of public administration have come to take it more seriously. In addition an equally important fact is that citizens often want to play an active role in the formulation and implementation of public policies, and in the process sometimes critically reflect on their existing desires. It is simply impossible to conflate citizen desires at any one time into a single meaningful index. Citizen are often aware of the contingent nature of their desires and act with this in mind.

In short, the classical utilitarian myth of an impartial spectator who sets the rules of government and the myth of a totally passive constituency that only wants its transparent, fixed desires satisfied have little to do with either the theory or practice of public administration. In the real world of public administration, the ideal of social cooperation envisioned by classical utilitarians like Bentham and Sidgwick became largely irrelevant at about the same time Rawls began to publish his work in political philosophy.

In this real world of public administration, I want to consider Rawls' theory of justice from two converging angles: 1. the role that Rawls' theory already has played in the evolution of public administration in this post-War period and 2. the additional contributions the theory can make.

When speaking of Rawls's theory of justice, I will be primarily concerned with Rawls' own writings, especially *A Theory of Justice* (1971) and *Political Liberalism* (1993). These two books express the essentials of a lifelong project that include many articles and lectures that often diverge in their details from the two books but not, I believe, in their overall significance. Another feature of Rawls' corpus is that like other important philosophers, Rawls's work has been carefully interpreted, criticized, and in some cases extended (11). It is often difficult to draw the line between his own exposition of his theory and the meaning of the theory as it has been elaborated by others. This is especially true in an area like public administration where Rawls's views are for the most part implicit or only suggested. In speaking about the relevance of his theory for public administration I will often rely on others who have sought to make Rawls' views more explicit or extend them in this direction.

Many scholars in the field of public administration have cited Rawls and consider his work relevant to their own. In this essay I have chosen to focus on only a few, with special emphasis on the work of H. George Frederickson. I do not mean to suggest that only Frederickson has gotten Rawls right or even that he makes the best arguments for extending Rawls in this direction. However, his work, I will argue, provides a very effective way of dealing with the diffuse subject of intellectual influence. Frederickson has been a key figure in public administration in the United States over the past half-century and his references to Rawls are both thoughtful and wide-ranging (12).

I. RAWLS'S THEORY OF JUSTICE

The entry of Rawls's theory of justice into the discourse of public administration was prepared three years before the publication of *A Theory of Justice* when the first Minnowbrook conference was held in September 1968 at Syracuse University. At this conference young academics in the field of public administration gathered to assess the strengths and weaknesses of the field and plot a "new" course. The organizing force behind the conference was Dwight Waldo who realized that in such turbulent times public administration was already being transformed and public administrators were facing new and difficult issues (13). While not a participant at the conference, H. George Frederickson presciently noted at the time that a key, if not *the* key feature of the New Public Administration was "social equity." "Conventional or classic public administration," Frederickson wrote, "seeks to answer either of these questions: 1. How can we offer more or better services with available resources (efficiency)? or 2. How can we maintain our level of services while spending less money (economy)? New Public Administration adds this question: Does this service enhance social equity" (14).

Looking back on Minnowbrook I, Frederickson wrote in 1989 that the conference identified nine important themes that subsequently became central aspects of public administration. Three of these themes, in particular, including "social equity," define the areas within public administration that Rawls' theory of justice has proved to be most relevant. Quoting from Frederickson's list:

> —Social equity has been added to efficiency and economy as the rationale or justification for policy positions. Equal protection of the law has come to be considered as important to those charged with carrying out the law (public administrators) as it is to those elected to make the law.
> —Ethics, honesty, and responsibility in government have returned again to the lexicon of public administration. Career service bureaucrats are no longer considered to be merely implementors of fixed decisions as they were in the dominant theory of the late 1950s and the early 1960s; they are now understood to hold a public trust to provide the best possible public service with the costs and benefits being fairly distributed among the people.
> —Effective public administration has come to be defined in the context of an active and participative citizenry (15).

These three moral themes in the New Public Administration represent, roughly, the contact points between Rawls's theory of justice and public administration. For convenience, I will call them distributive justice, administrative ethics, and participation.

Frederickson, perhaps more than anyone else inside public administration, has worked tirelessly to keep these themes alive and support others in the endeavor. In *New Public Administration* (1980), there is a distinct tone of urgency. According to Frederickson, a public admininstration that does not actively seek to correct the inequities and suffering in modern democratic societies like the United States will inevitably exacerbate these problems because it "will eventually be used to oppress the deprived" (16). Citizens must be given a greater amount of choice in public services, bureaucracies must be decentralized so as to be more responsive, neighborhood councils must be formed with real power to influence outcomes, and, most of all, public services must be equitably distributed, especially across racial and economic class lines. It is on this last measure of equity that Frederickson turns directly to Rawls for a more detailed set of principles of social equity.

Frederickson quickly summarizes Rawls's method of moral reasoning from behind a "veil of ignorance" and restates the principles of justice as fairness chosen in this "original position" equal liberty, fair equality of opportunity, and the difference principle (that holds that only social and economic differences that are to the benefit of the least advantaged are permissible). Frederickson then endorses David K. Hart's interpretation of Rawls that highlights his relevance for the New Public Administration (17).

Following Hart, Frederickson argues Rawls's principles of justice ensure that organizational needs never override individal liberties or needs for primary goods. Frederickson says,

> The problem is one of making complex organizations responsible to the needs of the individual. This requires rising above the rules and routines of organization to some concern for the self-respect and dignity of the individual citizen. Rawls' theory is designed to instruct those who administer organizations that the rights of individuals would be everywhere protected (18).

In an earlier article, written two years after Hart's, Frederickson includes this revealing gloss on Rawls's relevance for public administration. Not only do the principles of justice as fairness serve as ideal guides for legislative and constitutional decisions, they are especially important in a political society in which electoral politics does not exhaust political activity.

> The reason this [Rawlsian] perspective is so central to modern public administration is that public officials are in positions of implementing public programs; therefore, they have power over patterns of service distribution. . . . Modern public administration should seek to activate a kind of democracy in which majority rule through electoral process and the general patterns of "pluralism" are combined with protection for minorities, not only by the courts, but by the organizational structure or designated powers used in public administration and by the normative or ethical behavior of public servants (19).

Second, Frederickson argues that public administrators should be held to a higher ethical standard than other citizens. Rawls makes the distinction between the natural duty to advance justice as fairness which all persons with a sense of justice have and the additional obligation which those who hold public office or have benefited from being in a well-ordered society have. According to Rawls,

> The thing to observe here is that there are several ways in which one may be bound to political institutions. For the most part the natural duty of justice is the more fundamental, since it binds citizens generally and requires no voluntary acts in order to apply. The principles of fairness, on the other hand, bind only those who assume public office, say, or those who, being better situated, have advanced their aims within the system. There is, then another sense of *noblesse oblige*: namely, that chose who are more privileged are likely to acquire obligations tying them even more strongly to a just scheme (20).

Again following Hart, Frederickson suggests that one element of this new "noblesse oblige" is a duty to perform public service. Because not all persons are genetically "equal," the more advantaged have a moral duty to serve all others including the disadvantaged, not for altruistic reasons but because of the significance of interdependence (21).

This seems to go beyond Rawls's argument. Rawls's conception of political obligation is that those who are in public service or who have benefited from the principles of justice as fairness have an obligation to follow these specific principles. This is a stronger constraint on their conduct than the natural duty to advance and uphold just institutions that those who are more passively and less advantageously a part of even a well-ordered society have. Frederickson and Hart want to add that public administrators are not only obliged to follow the letter of the principles of justice themselves but also put themselves at the service of the less advantaged. Why? Frederickson suggests that without the willing cooperation of the less advantaged, those who are better off would be worse off. In order to sustain this cooperation, they must serve as public administrators. This is a creative extension of Rawls' own argument for the difference principle based on the dynamics of social cooperation (22). Hart suggests that it is through this kind of "fraternal" work as public administrators that a higher form of self-respect becomes possible. Public administrators serve in order to enhance their own self-respect as well as the self-respect of others through the provision of some public primary goods and the protection and maintenance of others (23).

Frederickson adds one more point in this initial effort to extend Rawls to public administration. The model for Rawlsian public administration is not to be found in legislative or executive action, but in judicial decisions (24). The distribution of public services and job opportunities has been the subject of several important court decisions. Unlike judges, however, for public administrators to fasten onto an appropriate operational conception of social equity, they must take a very different stance toward their clients and consumers.

> It is difficult to know of citizen needs if the public administrator is not in direct and routine interaction with elected officials and legislative bodies. Thus, participation and political interaction are critical to the development of the concept of social equity. The public official will come to be understood as a processor and facilitator with elected officals of government response to rapid social, economic, and political change. In fact, an ability to mobilize government institutions to change may well come to define leadership in the future (25).

Although Rawls takes a very strong stand in defense of the fair value of political liberty, his principle of participation does not go this far. Rawls would clear away direct and indirect obstacles to political participation such as unequal educational opportunities and discriminatory voting laws, but, according to Rawls, there is no duty to participate in public life or to stimulate others to participate. Public administrators that encourage or prod citizens into greater participation, then, might be exceeding the bounds of office from Rawls' point of view, but this is a matter of speculation since Rawls does not treat it explicitly (26).

The new public administrator is not only guided by Rawlsian principles of justice and bound by a strong obligation to serve as a public administrator. The new public administrator must also be an active participant in a public dialogue that includes citizens themselves as well as legislators and other elected political officials about the needs of citizens. How should this public dialogue be conducted? What method of moral reasoning is appropriate in this forum? Frederickson alludes to one possible answer: "The theory of justice would provide a means to resolve ethical impasses (the original position)" (27). Frederickson does not discuss exactly how the original position could serve as a device for guiding moral arguments, but as we shall see below, this becomes a primary concern of Rawls in *Political Liberalism*.

Frederickson has not remained content simply to champion the positions he developed during the 1970s. Since *New Public Administration*, he has self-critically re-examined his views. This voice has been joined by others within public administration who feel the need to clarify its ethical foundations and principles.

We can begin with an interesting article by Frederickson and Hart published in 1985 that returns to the concept of "noblesse oblige." Throughout the 1980s, public administrators and government workers in general were subjected to virulent attacks, especially from the Right. Middle class tax revolts, corporate anti-union campaigns, and a more diffuse hostility toward "big government" put public administrators on the defensive. Where the New Public Administration called for more equal service delivery and citizen participation in public administration, the public agenda in the 1980s was dominated by demands for privatization and greater consumer choice (28).

In defending the profession in this context, Frederickson and Hart shifted away from a primary concern with social equity and citizen participation. Instead he emphasized the need for a new civic humanist conception of administrative ethics. What virtues, what kind of moral character, they asked, should public administrators have to merit the trust of their "constituents?" Relatedly, what kind of civic virtue should public administrators seek to cultivate in citizens in general so that they can trust these professionals?

Influenced by the conservative strategy of legitimating professional discourses by tracing them back to the American Founders' original intentions, Frederickson and Hart turned to Jefferson and other selected Founders. They argued for an ethic of civic humanism centered on the virtue of "benevolence." Frederickson and Hart realized that in an important sense this diverged from Rawls's earlier conception of noblesse oblige and political obligation, (29) but they apparently felt that the times required it. Before examining this administrative ethic in more detail, a further comment is necessary on the context in which the need for administrative ethics had become so pressing.

One way of thinking of this need for an administrative ethic is to recognize that what public administration needed was a discipline of its own. However, the word "discipline" is intentionally ambiguous (30). In one sense public administration was still struggling to be an academic discipline like political science, law, and economics. It was still searching for its own particular corpus of knowledge, research methods, classical texts, and equally important, its institutional bases in universities, publicly funded research institutes, and private foundations. In this sense it was a discipline in friendly competition with other new professional, disciplines like policy analysis. In a more distant manner, it was a vaguely hostile competition with new academic programs like women's studies, Black studies, and other cultural studies programs.

Simultaneously, this emerging institutional discipline was also a discipline in the ethical sense. As a body of knowledge it prescribed a training regimen for practitioners, a method of cultivating the habits of heart and mind needed to bear up under the pressures of public office. Research methods and modes of engagement with other professionals provided some of the disciplinary training needed to get public administrators into fighting form: public administrators had to learn what it takes to do your duty. Hence, the emphasis on administrative ethics. In this regard public administration was no different from other professional disciplines. Medical ethics, legal ethics, and then scores of other professional ethics had been created in the 1970s to cope with consumer dissatisfaction and inter-professional turf battles (31). Public administrators realized that they too would have to discipline their forces if they were to hold on to their tenuous place within the academic and professional labor markets.

The question becomes now, what did Frederickson and Hart mean precisely by a civic humanist ethic for public administrators? First, they argued that one of the things that got public administrators into trouble was the perception that they were devoted, above all, to their own individual bureaucratic careers. Using the striking comparison between Nazi bureaucrats and Danish civil servants during World War II, they argued that while the former had lost any feeling of moral responsibility to a regime that was a corrupt charade, the Danes under Nazi occupation continued to feel a "profound commitment to the democratic values of their nation and genuine love of the people" (32). The protective acts taken by Danish bureaucrats for Jewish citizens were done not as extraordinary individual acts of moral courage, but as acts of civic duty. For them, all Danish citizens, including Jewish citizens, deserved the equal protection of the laws, individual freedom, and the other rights detailed in the Danish constitution. It was the patriotic duty of bureaucrats to see that these "democratic values" were upheld. Here was a model of the ethical bureaucrat that other citizens could trust.

> Therefore, we define the primary moral obligation of the public service in this nation as the patriotism of benevolence: an extensive love of all people within our political boundaries and the imperative that they must be protected in all of the basic rights granted to them by the enabling documents. If we do not love others, why should we work to guarantee the regime values to them? The "special relationship" that must exist between public servants and citizens in a democracy is founded upon the conscious knowldege about the citizens that they are loved by the bureaucracy (33).

To recover this ethic of benevolent patriotism, Frederickson and Hart turned to the American Founding. Emphasizing the influence of the "moral sense" school of the Scottish Enlightenment on the Americans, they argued that statesmen like Thomas Jefferson and James Wilson recognized that human beings were not narrowly self-interested egoists. They possessed a keen moral sense, and "both citizens and public servants [were] possessed of an extensive and active love for others—in other words, they possess a sense of benevolence" (34).

In the case of public administrators, the patriotic duty to act benevolently involves more than a vague "sense of benevolence." In fact, Frederickson and Hart argued, public administrators must be "both moral philosophers and moral activists." They must be able to interpret the fundamental "regime values" of the country and measure any policies they are enjoined to carry out against these values. For example, they should not permit the value of equal educational opportunity to be subverted through executive orders and less forthright forms of bureaucratic inertia. While elected officials have a similar responsibility, the fact that public administrators are around longer and have responsibility for the "day to day implementation of public policy" means that they have an even more stringent duty to uphold these values (35).

Frederickson and Hart close their argument by noting that Rawls did not rely so heavily on the virtue of benevolence in his theory of justice. It is unfortunate, they suggest, that he did not realize, as Jefferson did, that democratic government depends upon the heroic benevolence of a committed bureaucracy. Public administrators, they conclude, should not settle for less (36).

In 1988 Minnowbrook II was held, and the papers published in *Public Administration Review* by participants in this 20th anniversary conference reflect the defensive shift away from social equity and participation toward a disciplinary administrative ethic. In his introduction to this issue, Frederickson compares the two conferences along several dimensions. One difference is in the "mood, tone, and feeling of the two conferences."

> The 1968 conference was contentious, confrontational, and revolutionary. The 1988 conference was more civil, more practical. Both conferences were theoretical, but the 1968 conference dialogue was decidedly anti-behavioral, while the 1988 conference was more receptive to the contributions of behavioral science to public administration (37).

This is arguably a promising sign for a young profession. Public Administration is no longer simply opposed to the existing political order, but is now searching for a way to make its case more effectively from the inside and, where possible, in alliance with neighboring professions such as economics and policy analysis. But there is another way to read this change in "mood, tone, and feeling." To do this, let's take a closer look at David K. Hart's opening article which pursues the theme of administrative virtue.

Hart reiterates the claim he and Frederickson had already made that people are by nature capable of benevolent love for others as well as self-love. He describes this capacity not just as a potential virtue but as a need: "all individuals have an innate need to love others" just as strong as the need to love themselves (38). In the case of public administrators, this need should be fulfilled in four ways. The first three are fairly noncontroversial. Public administrators should use their discretion and good judgment to ensure that individual civic autonomy is not sacrificed to some greater good. Second, they should "govern by persuasion." That is, they should argue honestly and eloquently in their capacity as public servants, and not deceive or arrogantly try to impose their will. Third, they should resist corruption, especially the subtler forms of corruption that accompany the "tyranny of expertise." Mutual trust, not fear, should motivate their relationships with citizens. Finally, and this is the virtue I want to underscore, public administrators should stand as "civic exemplars." According to Hart,

> Because so many of those who have power are so inaccessible and their power is so great, their qualities of character must be made constantly evident to the people. A people who would be free and virtuous need the reinvigoration that comes from seeing exemplars of civic courage (39).

In demonstrating their "fidelity to the Founding values," exemplary public administrators encourage citizens to trust the more powerful public administrators among them who are "inaccessible." This is an odd argument, not because exemplary figures cannot have this effect but because of what it suggests about Hart's own purpose. The "tone" of the argument is very different from that of Minnowbrook I. Rather than ask how powerful bureaucrats can be made more accessible, Hart is suggesting that the estranging effects of their inaccessibility can be partially mitigated by other bureaucrats on the frontline who present themselves in a benevolent, discursive, and trustworthy manner.

Hart says that what is needed is a "partnership in virtue among all citizens." By acting autonomously, valuing persuasion, avoiding the arrogance of expertise, and exemplifying, at least on the frontline, fidelity to the Founding regime values, public administrators can show citizens that they are willing and able to act with benevolent love toward them. In return, perhaps, citizens will show the same respect toward bureaucrats and join in this "partnership in virtue." The tone here is not simply one of greater cooperativeness and openness to behavioralism. What Hart suggests in this call for a "partnership in virtue" is that we should trust the exemplars of benevolence and not press those who wield the most power to share it more broadly or exercise it more openly. It is a partnership in virtue, not in power. This modern version of civic humanism, in fact, comes much closer to the elitist Ciceronian model Hart invoked at the outset of the paper than he may have realized.

After Minnowbrook II what remained of the original New Public Administration made something of a comeback. Administrative ethics did not cease to be a pressing legitimating concern for public administration. Frederickson, however, was drawn back to the other earlier concerns of equity and participation. In 1990 he published yet another article on social equity and acknowledged that Rawls was still the philosophical inspiration for this theme in the New Public Administration. Frederickson also admitted that "the theory thus far has been of limited use in the busy world of government" (40). What was needed was a more fine-grained descriptive theory that distinguished between different public goods and services. Equality or equity in one area may not be the same as equality or equity in another. Second, public administration must make use of the techniques of policy analysis in order to identify more precisely which bureaucratic structures and decision rules influence the distribution of particular goods and services. Sometimes rules that seem to be designed strictly for organizational efficiency and effective service delivery have unintended distributional effects. It is (once again) urgent that these techniques be applied in the field of public administration given the increasing inequalities in the distribution of goods and services over the past decade (41).

This urgency is acutely felt in the area of environmental policy making. Frederickson suggests that equity requires that public administrators have a special duty to look out for the interests of future generations, both proximate and far into the future. Reliance on markets to solve policy problems such as toxic waste disposal and the proper use of wetlands inevitably disadvantages future generations.

Even in areas such as education and transportation, highly complex issue exists of how much the present generation should pay for the well being of future generations. Frederickson seems to agree with Rawls's philosophical justification for a strong principle of inter-generational justice. However, he argues that its application must be tailored to specific policy areas (42). While Frederickson skims over a large number of philosophical views in this article, he shows creativity in applying his own differentiated view of equity to several different problems, and he does it with newfound enthusiasm. Clearly Rawls's theory continues to influence him and his own personal commitment to social equity in public administration has not flagged.

Frederickson undoubtedly now feels the need to apply moral principles to particular cases and refine them in light of these cases. He hints that this, more than philosophical speculation, is the first order of business for public administration (43). The relationship between moral principles and cases is similar to Rawls's concept of reflective equilibrium, but for Rawls the test of moral principles is how well they cohere with considered moral intuitions against a background of just institutions (44). The parallel to Frederickson's turn to case studies is admittedly loose, but some philosophers have developed a similar point using the concept of moral casuistry. We might say that Frederickson overlooked an opportunity to apply Rawls's conception of reflective equilibrium to the pragmatic turn in his own work at this point (45).

I want to consider one last article by Frederickson that raises a slightly different theoretical issue, the meaning of the word "public" in public administration (46). This will take us back to Frederickson's earlier passing comment on the original position as a method of moral reasoning.

In this 1991 article Frederickson surveys the competing theories of public administration and suggests four "requisites" for any general theory of public administration. First, any sound theory of public administration must be grounded in the "regime values" of the Constitution. This means that the theory must specify the highest moral obligations of public administration in terms of values to which every citizen is committed. Rawls holds a similar view in *Political Liberalism* where he emphasizes that his theory draws upon the "fundamental ideas . . . implicit in the public political culture of a democratic society" (47).

Second, the theory must endorse an "enhanced" conception of virtuous citizenship like Hart's conception of civic humanism. Virtue here is not simply a non-cognitive feeling or emotion. Frederickson makes it clear he believes that the virtuous public administrator is someone capable of philosophical reflection on and critical judgments about contested terms like equality and equity as well as someone who wants to do this for the public's good. Third, public administration theory must spell out ways of responding to the collective interest and also inchoate public interests, not just the individual and group interests of private citizens. Collective interests include the unexpressed interests of future generations to a clean environment and a rich cultural heritage; inchoate public interests include the interest in equal treatment under the law. Finally, Frederickson asserts, a theory of public administration must characterize the relationship between public administrators and their public in terms of love and benevolence, not only self-interest.

Looking back over these four requisite conditions for a sound theory, Frederickson concludes that they contain a vision of the public that public administrators serve and that bears partial resemblance to the implicit publics in each of the five competing theories (pluralist, public choice, representative government, clientist, and "citizen" theories). It is the last, the citizen theory of public administration, that comes closest to satisfying all four requisite conditions for a conception of the public as Frederickson defines them. Pluralist, clientist, and public choice theories are only responsive to organized interest groups and those with enough private resources to be heard. The theory of the public as a body of represented voters is more promising, but not sufficient: it ignores the need for an ongoing day to day relationship between citizens and bureaucrats. Only the conception of the public as a body of citizens rather than clients, consumers, constituent voters, or special interest groups seems to match up fairly well on all four counts.

While this comes as no surprise, what is interesting is Frederickson's attempt to find a meta-language for comparing and synthesizing these competing theories. He wants to develop a language about the public that they all share even though they seem to approach this amorphous concept from very different directions. In other words, Frederickson is searching for a method of moral reasoning that would allow us to weigh the strengths and weaknesses of the five competing theories in a moral way.

In Rawlsian terms, this could be done using the original position. If you didn't know whether you belonged to a strong interest group, a powerful voting block, a rich lobbying group, or a well-respected professional organization, what virtues and principles would you choose in your theory of public administration? This use of the original position, I think, is a legitimate extension of Rawls's characterization of it as a device for "public reflection and self-clarification" (48). It is a method of "public reason," not just a technical philosophical tool, that can be used to discuss vexed public questions as long as there is some "overlapping consensus" to begin with.

That Frederickson had sensed this earlier but not explored it is understandable. In constructing his framework for a theory of public administration in 1991 he has, in fact, found a way to make good use of perhaps the most essential part of Rawls' theory, the original position. More important than Rawls's preferred moral principles, the method of reasoning from behind a veil of ignorance serves as a way of representing particularistic preferences so that their public values can be critically compared. This is what Frederickson wants to do. Even though all five competing theories have a different degree of public worth for him, they all have some public merit.

The consumer model of the public that public choice theorists presuppose, perhaps the least favored from Frederickson's own perspective, has to be granted some legitimacy.

While programs like school vouchers threaten to worsen social and economic inequality, it is also true that many public schools have been unresponsive to the need for self-respect, especially among poor minority students. If special publicly chartered and publicly funded schools that emphasize minority cultural traditions can enhance self-respect without discriminating against majority students or neglecting other educational goals, then providing families with this option seems to have a certain prima facie legitimacy from a Rawlsian point of view. Care would have to be taken so that the quality of mainstream public education did not suffer, but the point is that this sort of "public choice" is not necessarily unjust. Freedom and self-respect are no less "regime values" than equality.

What I am suggesting is that Frederickson, in so many words, has called for the use of what Rawls calls "free public reason" to the internal theoretical debates in public administration. Public reason is the manner in which we settle disagreements about "the good of the public and matters of fundamental justice" in the public domain among citizens (49). Public reasons are those, given in this context, that avoid appeals to controversial moral, religious, and philosophical doctrines. This address only the "constitutional essentials" of the political society (50). They are reasons offered in a fair minded, civil, and tolerant way. And they are reasons guided by "principles of reasoning and rules of evidence in the light of which citizens are to decide whether substantive principles properly apply and to identify laws and policies that best satisfy them" (51).

There is an "overlapping consensus" that Rawls claims exists in liberal democratic societies over liberty and equal opportunity. Thus reasonable persons with different comprehensive moral views of the good society and the good life can agree, by using public reason, on principles governing the basic political structure of that society. This has its analog in the consensus Frederickson hopes to identify among the five competing theories of public administration. Although these theories rest on a different metaphysical conception of the person and "the public," they all accept the regime values of a liberal democratic society. On the basis of this overlapping political consensus, advocates for the competing theories can discuss the meaning of administrative virtue, responsibility, and discretion. Such a discussion, then, would be an example of the use of free public administrative reason.

In extending Rawls's account of public reason in this direction I have linked it with his earlier formulation of the original position and the later notion of free public reason. The two methods of reasoning are not obviously identical and some commentators have even argued that Rawls's shift to free public reason is a mistake. However, public reason is less precise than the original position. Its avoidance of strong truth claims seems to surrender the ideal of impartiality that motivated *A Theory of Justice* (52). On its own terms, it may not be enough to sustain an "overlapping consensus" among deeply opposed parties in a liberal democratic society (53).

Although Rawls does sometimes describe the original position in decisionist terms, he has gradually adopted a different way of characterizing it as device of representation and a method for "public reflection and self-clarification" (54). That links it directly to the seemingly more broadly based method of public reason. Rawls did not believe all citizens must rely on the original position to make all of their political decisions. To step behind the veil of ignorance every time a political decision has to be made is cumbersome. However, for public administrators, judges, and citizens facing significant political issues like civil disobedience, the original position in this less decisionist sense is a prerequisite for identifying and fine-tuning the guidelines for free public reason. If public administrators must have a philosophical frame of mind, as Frederickson argues, then theirs should enable them to deliberate behind the veil of ignorance. Ordinarily, most citizens can simply be taught to respect these guidelines of public reason. However public administrators must be able to adjust and interpret these guidelines as well on a day to day and case by case basis. This means they should be able to use the original position as a device for representing the public content of competing views when parties disagree.

> In justice as fairness . . . the guidelines of inquiry of public reason, as well as its principle of legitimacy, have the same basis as the substantive principles of justice. This means in justice as fairness that the parties in the original position, in adopting principles of justice for the basic structure, must also adopt guidelines and criteria of public reason for applying those norms (55).

The constraints on knowledge and motivation in the original position must be adjusted to bring considered judgements and principles into reflective equilibrium. In addition, public administrators must adjust these constraints by trying to find a socially acceptable set of guidelines for free public reason, one that all the (reasonable) parties involved will accept. In the debate between public choice theorists, representative democrats, constitutionalists, and virtue ethicists over the purposes of public administration, the mediating public administrator can find agreement on the guidelines governing public reason. They must rely on the original position or something like it to clear away the conceptual confusions and false problems. In this sense the theorists of public administration can be characterized as political educators. They teach those in government how to think about basic issues like responsibility, participation, and equity (56).

II. CONCLUSION

To summarize, I have called attention to three areas in which Rawls's theory of justice has had a direct relationship to recent work in public administration: 1. the extensions of Rawls's theory that public administrators such as Frederickson have suggested (for example, the extension of the obligation of noblesse oblige and the principle of participation), 2. the refinement of the Rawlsian conception of equality as applied to different public services, and 3. the development of a complex theory of administrative virtue that reaches beyond Rawlsian civility to benevolence.

In addition, I have argued that the search for common ground among competing theories of public administration, not just Frederickson's own preferred theory, relies on something like Rawls's device of the original position. The original position, which Frederickson asserts is a model of moral reasoning public administrators should follow, is designed to specify guidelines for free public reason (and not just pick out particular regulative principles of justice). In this capacity the original position can mediate between competing theories of public administration, themselves already attempting to mediate conflicts between bureaucrats and their clients and constituents.

This second order mediating function that Frederickson would like Rawls's theory to perform for public administration has already occurred in other spheres where professional ethics and policy analysis are more complexly articulated. In medicine, for example, we can distinguish three levels of political activity. The first level is that of the social practice of medicine itself. This social practice includes the professional-client relationship between doctors and patients. However, it also includes the lobbying activities of professesional medical associations, the expert testimony medical professionals give in legislative and judicial hearings, and the organized activities of patients and others concerned about the power of the medical professions.

As conflicts between doctors and patients (both individual clients and organized consumers of medical services) erupt and develop, two kinds of mediating forces have emerged in response. One force is expressed in the language of policy analysis. Experts in epidemiology, for example, have been enlisted to mediate conflicts such as the availability of experimental drugs for certain contagious diseases. How should clinical trials be run? How quickly can new drugs be made available commercially? Doctors, patients, drug companies, and consumer groups are unable to solve problems like these themselves and must rely on policy analysts to help them out. The other force is expressed in the language of professional ethics. These less quantitative and scientific questions concern the moral duties of professionals and rights of corporations, clients, and consumers. For example, what is the "informed consent" of a patient? In this case the mediating force is wielded by medicial ethicists who, like policy analysts, provide some help in resolving the conflicts between professionals and their clients and consumers (57).

Realistically, these efforts at mediation often fail. Policy analysts disagree among themselves about what counts as an emergency and how new drug trials should be structured. Professional ethicists certainly do not all speak in one voice. To mediate among them, a second order mediation sometimes comes into play. At this more abstract level, philosophical methods of reasoning like the original position or the impartial utilitarian spectator are enlisted. They help professionals, the advocates of clients and consumers, policy analysts, and professional ethicists construct a provisional consensus that will see them through the problem or conflict at hand.

I am suggesting that the disciplinary social practice of public administration, in a rudimentary way, is beginning to show signs of the same kind of three-tiered differentiation. Public administrators, like physicians and other medical professionals, often find themselves embroiled in rigidified conflicts: businesses threaten to leave town, unions go on strike, clients file embarrasing lawsuits, and consumer groups occupy public spaces. As street-level bureaucrats, public administrators have to deal with individual clients; teachers have their students, social workers their cases. Above the street-level public administrators must still face organized consumer groups, from taxpayers in revolt to neighborhood associations demanding better municipal services, either in the press or in court.

These first level conflicts can be partially resolved by policy analysts and codes of administrative ethics. The former can help by calculating just how much money is needed, say, for a new sewer system. The latter can help by spelling out just how far an assistant principle can and should go in disciplining unruly students. But as in the case of medicine, policy analysts and administrative ethicists will disagree. Again, some method of reasoning is needed to decide how to iron out these conflicts.

Frederickson's attempt to find some common ground that different conceptions of "the public" in public administration theories can occupy, addresses these second tier conflicts from yet a third level. Rawlsian guidelines of public reason chosen behind a veil of ignorance might be able to set the ground rules for debates among competing theories of administrative effectiveness, social equity, and participation.

In the case or publicly chartered schools mentioned above, only public discussions of the issue after the facts and possible consequences are on the table are likely to settle the matter. The costs to taxpayers, parents, teacher unions, and other students and the benefits to students in the charter schools will not be weighed by policy analysts and ethicists alone. Because there will be disagreements about the facts, possible consequences to the school system, and the morality of this kind of cultural education in the public schools, guidelines for public debate among these parties will have to be set. If, that is, the issue is to be resolved in a deliberative manner among administrators and the directly interested parties.

There is no reason, at least in principle, to think that this kind of second order mediation cannot work in public administration just as well as it has in medicine. Is it the right thing to do? From the point of view of preserving professional authority and satisfying client and consumer needs, it seems to be the right thing to do. But, are these the only relevant perspectives? Should we simply assume that what is good for professionals, clients, and consumers is good for a democratic society as a whole? The appropriate moral limits of professional authority and the reasonable needs of clients and consumers may not be limits that can be defined behind the veil of ignorance. Public administration, like other disciplinary social practices, may be moving in a Rawlsian direction even though Rawls's particular principles of justice as fairness remain controversial. Whether this is a good thing from a democratic perspective is a difficult problem that requires that we think about the voices as well as the images that can be seen and heard behind the veil of ignorance (58).

NOTES

1. J. Rawls, *A Theory of Justice*, Cambridge: Harvard University Press, 1571, p. 274.
2. Ibid., p. 529.
3. Ibid., p. 290.
4. Ibid., pp. 275–76. Rawls follows R. A. Musgrave in dividing government into allocation, stabilization, transfer, and distribution branches, later adding a special exchange branch to deal with public funding of public goods (p. 282).
5. J. Rawls, *Political Liberalism*, New York: Columbia University Press, 1993, pp. 54–58.
6. Rawls, *A Theory of Justice*, p. 199.
7. Ibid., p. 33.
8. L. Gulick, Notes on the theory of organization, reprinted in *Classics of Public Administration*, J. M. Shafritz and A. C. Hyde (eds.), Oak Park, Illinois: Moore Publishing Co., 1978, p. 44.
9. R. A. Dahl, "The Science of Public Administration: Three Problems," (reprinted in Shafritz and Hyde, eds.), p. 124.
10. C. E. Lindblom, The science of 'muddling through,' (reprinted in Shafritz and Hyde, eds.), p. 206.
11. "The problems of extension" Rawls mentions include health care, particularly for those with special needs, international relations (or what he calls "the law of peoples"), duties to future generations, and the application of justice as fairness to other species and the environment. Extending the theory involves more than simply the mechanical application of Rawls' principles of justice as fairness to particular policy problems. Rawls, *Political Liberalism*, p. 20, 244. For an example of an extension of the theory to health care that Rawls seems to accept, see N. Daniels, *Just Health Care*, Cambridge: Cambridge University Press, 1985.
12. For other references to Rawls, see K. G. Denhardt, *The Ethics of Public Service: Resolving Moral Dilemmas in Public Organizations*, New York: Greenwood Press, 1988; and for other approaches to public administration from a moral point of view see, *Ethical Frontiers in Public Management: Seeking New Strategies for Resolving Public Dilemmas*, J. S. Bowman (ed.), San Francisco: Jossey-Bass Publishers, 1991; J. A. Rohr, *To Run a Constitution: The Legitimacy of the Administrative State*, Lawrence: University Press of Kansas, 1986; R. A. Chapman, *Ethics in Public Service*, Ottawa, Canada: Carleton University Press, 1993; and R. C. Chandler, *Civic*

Virtue in the American Republic: Essays on Moral Philosophy and Public Administration, Kalamazoo, Michigan: Western Michigan University Press, 1987.

13. Proceedings were published in *Toward a New Public Administration: The Minnowbrook Perspective*, Frank Marini (ed.), Scranton, PA: Chandler Publishing Co., 1971.

14. Ibid., p. 311.

15. H. G. Frederickson, Minnowbrook II: Changing epochs of public administration, *Public Admin. Rev.*: 49, 97, 1989.

16. H. G. Frederickson, *New Public Administration*, University, Alabama: University of Alabama Press, 1980, p. 38.

17. D. K. Hart, Social equity, justice, and the equitable administrator, *Pub. Admin. Rev.*: 34, 3–11, 1974.

18. H. G. Frederickson, *New Public Administration*, p. 41.

19. H. G. Frederickson, The lineage of new public administration, *Admin. and Soc.*: 8, 171, 1976.

20. J. Rawls, *A Theory of Justice*, p. 116.

21. H. G. Frederickson, *New Public Administration*, p. 41.

22. "Now what can be said to the more favored man? To begin with, it is clear that the well-being of each depends on a scheme of social cooperation without which no one could have a satisfactory life. Secondly, we can ask for the willing cooperation of everyone only if the terms of the scheme are reasonable. The difference principle, then, seems to be a fair basis on which those better endowed, or more fortunate in their social circumstances, could expect others to collaborate with them when some workable arrangement is a necessary condition of the good of all." Rawls, *A Theory of Justice*, p. 103.

23. D. K. Hart, Social equity, justice, and the equitable administrator, pp. 8–9.

24. J. Rawls also considers Supreme Court decisions, at the best, exemplars of "free public reason." *Political Liberalism*, pp. 231–40.

25. H. G. Frederickson, *New Public Administration*, p. 46.

26. "What is essential is that the constitution should establish equal rights to engage in public affairs and that measures be taken to maintain the fair value of these liberties. In a well-governed state only a small fraction of persons may devote much of their time to politics. There are many other forms of human good. But this fraction, whatever its size, will most likely be drawn more or less equally from all sectors of society. The many communities of interests and centers of political life will have their active members who look after their concerns." Rawls, *A Theory of Justice*, p. 228.

27. Ibid., p. 42.

28. The complex causes for these new sentiments and demands are rooted, I believe, in a changing global political economy. But this is a subject that goes far beyond the boundaries of the present paper.

29. Rawls rejects civic humanism in general, not just benevolence as a political virtue. Civic humanism, he argues, is a "form of Aristotelianism" that requires political participation for achieving the good life. *Political Liberalism*, p. 206.

30. Here, obviously, I am drawing on the work of Michel Foucault, especially *Discipline and Punish: The Birth of the Prison*, (Alan Sheridan trans.), New York: Pantheon, 1977.

31. See M. Davis, The ethics boom, what and why, *Centennial Rev.*: 34, 163–86, 1990.

32. H. G. Frederickson and D. K. Hart, The public service and the patriotism of benevolence, *Public Admin. Rev.*: 45, 549, 1985.

33. Ibid., p. 549.

34. Ibid., p. 550

35. Ibid., p. 551.

36. Ibid., p. 552.

37. H. G Frederickson, Minnowbrook II: Changing epochs of public administration, *Pub. Admin. Rev.*: 49, 99, 1989.

38. D. K. Hart, A partnership in virtue among all citizens: The public service and civic humanism, *Pub. Admin. Rev.*: 49, 102, 1989.

39. Ibid., p. 104,

40. H. G. Frederickson, Public administration and social equity, *Pub. Admin. Rev.*: 50, 230, 1990.

41. Ibid., p. 536.

42. H. G. Frederickson, Can public officials correctly be said to have obligations to future generations? *Pub. Admin. Rev.*: 54, 458, 1994. The summary of Rawls's argument here is a bit misleading in that Frederickson fails to emphasize that if the difference principle was simply applied to generations, the result, as Rawls notes, would be a zero savings rate where the first generation is (likely to be) the least advantaged generation. Hence the need for a special just savings principle. See *A Theory of Justice*, p. 291. But see *Political Liberalism*, pp. 273–74.

43. *Ethics and Public Administration,* H. G. Frederickson (ed.), Armonk, NY: M.E. Sharpe, 1993, pp. 9–10.

44. J. Rawls, *A Theory of Justice*, pp. 20–22, 48–51 and *Political Liberalism*, p. 8.

45. On the subject of moral casuistry and its relationship to Rawls, which comes closer to Frederickson's view here, see Albert R. J. and S. Toulmin, *The Abuse or Casuistry: A History of Moral Reasoning*, Berkeley: University of California Press, 1988, pp. 285–93.

46. H. G. Frederickson, Toward a theory of the public for public administration, *Admin. and Soc.*: 22, 395–417, 1991.

47. Rawls, *Political Liberalism*, p. 13.

48. Ibid., p. 26.

49. Ibid., p. 213.

50. Ibid., p. 217.

51. Ibid., p. 224.

52. B. Barry, *Justice as Impartiality*, New York: Oxford University Press, 1995.

53. S. Scheffler, The appeal of political liberalism, *Ethics*: 105, 4–22, 1994.

54. Rawls, *Political Liberalism*, p. 26.

55. Ibid., p. 225.

56. For an uncritical view of this mediating role, see D. F. Thompson, Paradoxes of government ethics, *Pub. Admin. Rev.*: 52, 254–59. Thompson describes the "main business of government ethics" as an "education in democracy." p. 255.

57. Dan W. Brock argues that the deliberations of ethics commissions on subjects like euthanasia should not be guided by either deductivist moral theories are particular moral judgments. Instead, these commissions like other public policymaking bodies, should reach "considered moral judgments" through the Rawlsian methods of reflective equilibrium and public reason. "The task of ethics commissions is often to try to find a common public moral discourse that can yiedl a consensus on which pubilc policy can be formed among individuals and groups otherwise in disagreement on many important matters." See Public moral discourse, in *Society's Choices: Social and Ethical Decision Making in Biomedicine*, Washington, D.C.: National Academy Press, 1995, p. 238.

58. My own view is that Rawlsian theory does indeed operate as a political education for participants in administrative politics, but it is tone deaf to the ways in which this politics of policy making domesticates and disarms many citizens on the margins within neo-corporatist societies. I have discussed the democratic limitations of Rawls's theory and the original position in particular in *Intimacy and Spectacle: Liberal Theory as Political Education*, Ithaca: Cornell University Press, 1994.

Part VI
Rise of Postmodernism

WITTGENSTEIN

I do not want my writing to spare other people the trouble of thinking (J. F. M. Hunter trans., *Understanding Wittgenstein*, Edinburgh: Edinburgh University Press, 1985).

POSTMODERNISM

We no longer believe that the truth is true when all its veils have been removed. (Jean Baudrillard, *Simulacra and Simulation*, Sheila Faria Glaser, trans., Ann Arbor: University of Michigan Press, 1994).

19

FROM POSITIVISM TO POST-POSITIVISM: AN UNFINISHED JOURNEY

Laurent Dobuzinskis
Simon Fraser University, Burnaby, British Columbia, Canada

Today, the legitimacy of public bureaucracies is more and more often challenged by an increasingly individualistic citizenry and by new political forces (e.g., the Republican majority in Congress). Public servants in most western democracies must deal with many new demands and expectations. At the same time, they also face severe financial restrictions. Indeed both the scope and the role of government have become very problematic in the United States and around the world. Original ideas and reform proposals have been advanced in recent years; they reflect a new understanding of policy analysis and public sector management more suited to the problems of "postmodern" societies. Much talked about reforms have been implemented in the United States and other countries. Does this mean that public administration has been radically transformed or are these changes merely the outcome of yet another fad? Have we really entered the age of postmodern government?

Before answering that question, a few definitions need to be provided. To begin with, the phrase public administration is less simple than it may appear. Public administration is both an art and a science. It is a practical activity, with its own rules of professional conduct and criteria of excellence, as well as an academic discipline, with its own theories and methodological precepts. (There are even dissenting voices claiming that public administration is neither a discipline nor a profession, or maybe is one, but not the other (1).) The discipline of public administration is itself composed of two camps: one, centered in political science or sociology departments, which does basic research on bureaucracy; another, centered in professional schools, which is more concerned with problem-oriented research (2). The two sides of public administration do not always match. Thus any generalization about trends in public administration must be examined very critically.

Moreover, the socio-cultural context of public administration greatly influences its intellectual content and its tacit values. This chapter is concerned primarily with public administration in a North American context (i.e., the United States and Canada). Within this context there are obvious and not always reconcilable differences between national, state, provincial, and municipal governments—even within any single level of government there usually are significant variations among departments, commissions, and so on.

The heterogeneity of public administration being granted, there clearly exist some concepts, values, and goals which cross institutional and disciplinary boundaries. The formative period was marked by a generally positivist understanding of how human organizations function and of the psychology of their members. Now positivism is another vague term that has been rendered almost meaningless by critics who equate it with whatever methodology they reject. But, as a starting point, it can serve as a convenient umbrella for a range of approaches that were (or are still) characterized by a. their emphasis on objective, as opposed to normative, analysis—the assumption being that the observer can achieve a critical distance from the observed and independently constituted realities under examination; and b. the notion that law-like regularities can be identified for the purpose of explaining and predicting both natural and societal phenomena.

Post-positivist approaches challenge both these assumptions. Post-positivism, however, does not constitute a well integrated, coherent doctrine. Postmodernism, of which post-positivism is an aspect, is even more difficult to pin down. It included various philosophical currents opposed to the rationalist doctrines that form the intellectual legacy of the Enlightenment. In its most radical expression, postmodernism undermines all hierarchical orderings: there are, according to this view, no foundations upon which either theoretical knowledge or societal structures can be safely grounded. In a less strict sense, postmodernism refers to societal trends that pose a challenge to the set of institutions and cultural patterns we have inherited from industrial society as it existed prior to the emergence of the information revolution (circa 1960). As such, postmodernism encompasses many areas of cultural life which bear little or no relationship to the practical concerns of government officials. However, societal changes and cultural trends do have consequences for policy-making and public sector management.

Although it may not be helpful to speak about postmodern politics or government as if these were factual realities, there is little doubt that public administration is in ferment today. The positivist certainties of a few generations ago no longer provide the solid ground upon which the discipline can grow. Not everything that happens in the world of public administration can be interpreted as an aspect of the emergence of postmodern values, but the term post-positivism describes rather well some of the new directions in public administration. And yet the shift from positivism to post-positivism in public administration is neither complete nor entirely evident. This chapter provides a general perspective on the circumstances and effects of this complex dynamics.

Over the course of the last two decades, we have witnessed the emergence of a critical discourse that challenges the idea that objective, empirical models are appropriate for dealing with political and organizational phenomena. Doubts have also been raised about the degree to which actual scientific practice corresponds to the idealized model proposed by positivistic accounts of "the" scientific method. This chapter attempts to show, that it would be wrong to describe this evolution as being a simple and unambiguous shift from one paradigm to another. Whether other disciplines (e.g., political science), have also evolved from a positivistic to a post-positivistic stage is a moot point, the hope is to show that public administration has never been unambiguously positivistic nor has it become wholeheartedly post-positivistic. As far as public administration is concerned, the positivistic discourse never became a coherent and all-encompassing "grand narrative," as Lyotard[1] would say (3). Here we encounter an interesting paradox: with its partial narratives, its succession of incompletely formulated, or only superficially applied paradigms, public administration has always been standing "on the brink of the postmodern condition" (4).

The first section traces the origins of public administration back to a political and cultural climate that was very receptive to the idea that science could provide answers to the problems of the time. The second section examines the extent—although limited—to which this outlook meshes with the view that organizations are like machines which can be designed and controlled by experts. The third section raises the question of whether efforts undertaken over the last two or three decades to apply the methodology of public choice to the study of bureaucracies mark a qualified return to positivism. The fourth section examines the circumstances that have led to a renewed emphasis on citizen involvement in administrative and policy matters, and on the design of flexible, adaptive organizations. One can discern in these developments at least an echo of postmodernism. The final section examines new currents in scientific thinking which suggest that a more adequate science of public administration can be developed from a post-positivistic perspective.

I.   DISCIPLINING ADMINISTRATION

The nineteenth century was the age of positivism. Empirical observations and logical deductions came to be seen as the only legitimate sources of knowledge. Science and technology appeared to provide rational grounds for the establishment of a new social, moral and political order. Auguste Comte, for example, argued that "the development of all sciences followed from mathematics, through astronomy, the physical and biological sciences, and reach their apogee in the rise of the social sciences" (5). Even if Comte coined the term "positive philosophy," he was certainly not the only thinker who contributed to its development. Most of the social philosophers and pioneers of the early social sciences shared the view that social realities can be known objectively, i.e., that separating facts from values is both possible and desirable. This was true of John Stuart Mill, Herbert Spencer, Emile Durkheim, and Max Weber, to name some of the most important ones, and in a more qualified sense, this was true also of Marx (6).

   The practical effects of this new faith were not immediately visible. However, the political and bureaucratic elites in western Europe undertook to reform their administrative systems early in the second half of the century. For example, in Great Britain the Trevelyan-Northcote report of 1857 marked the first step toward the creation of a professional civil service; by 1870 a politically neutral Civil service Commission was in charge of recruiting the members of the British professional administrative elite, and a rudimentary system of classification was in place. When Max Weber wrote his classical analysis of bureaucracy, the institutions he was describing existed in most countries of continental Europe. Administrative reforms in North America took a little longer to produce noticeable effects. In both the United States and Canada, the British example inspired many active reformers; books and articles were published on this topic (7). But the practice of political patronage was so well entrenched—indeed Jacksonian democracy had made a virtue out of political patronage—that it became necessary for the reformers to mobilize political support. While administrative reforms in Britain and in other European countries came about as a result of a top-down process, it was a bottom-up process in the United States as various groups, notably the National Civil Service Reform League, took up that cause. Their campaign for a professional civil service had very practical objectives. Their discourse, however, revealed an underlying commitment to "science" defined less as a specific activity than as a mythical force. In an age when there was still no reason to doubt that science and technology might bring anything other than "progress," one could believe that technological rationality ought to guide social and political matters.

The momentum toward administrative reforms gathered up speed during the Progressive era (1896–1920). However, movement in that direction had begun even earlier. In the 1870s and 1880s political pressures and theoretical reflections converged; at both the practical and the theoretical levels, the ideal of a professional public service took shape. It became evidently clear to a variety of interests that the requirements of a modern industrial society in a phase of rapid expansion could be met only by a professional public service dedicated to rational principles of efficiency and non-partisanship. It was "getting harder to *run* a constitution than to frame one" (8) as Woodrow Wilson wrote in 1887; Wilson, in fact, was involved in the reform movement. Thus Congress passed the Civil Service Act (Pendleton Act) in 1883 which marked a decisive step toward the implementation of the merit principle in the U.S. government.[2] Throughout the following decades the scope of the merit system continued to expand at the federal level as well as in many states. Also the budgetary process was rationalized by the introduction of line item budgeting. At the municipal level, many cities adopted the city manager system; indeed some reformers tried to push the idea of a state manager as a counterweight to the governor (9).

In this context, public administration emerged as a discipline. Of course, the study of government and the search for scientific principles of administration can be traced back to much earlier times. The term "bureaucracy" itself dates back to eighteenth century France when it was first used in its modern sense by Vincent de Gournay (10); he could have had in mind the "Physiocrats" (e.g., Turgot, Quesnay) who had posed some of the very first maxims of rational governance. Classical political economy, as originally conceived by Adam Smith and David Ricardo, further advanced the idea that managing the affairs of the state is something that should be guided by demonstrable principles instead of being left to the caprice of the sovereign. However, public administration as we know it today in North America originated in the last decade of the nineteenth century and in the first two or three decades of the twentieth century.

Woodrow Wilson's 1887 seminal essay "The Study of Public Administration" is ritualistically cited as the historical foundation of the discipline. According to Paul van Riper, who looked at the citations in the public administration literature between the 1890s and the First World War, Wilson's paper actually had little impact at the time it was published (11,12). Regardless of its practical influence, Wilson's article eloquently conveys the values that inspired the pioneers of the discipline; they defended and promoted these values in a number of classical texts (e.g., Frank J. Goodnow's *Politics and Administration*, 1900, or W. F. Willoughby's *Principles of Public Administration*, 1927). What Wilson did was to provide an application to public administration of the positivist dogma that facts must be separated from values by proclaiming that politics and administration belong to different spheres. From that perspective, the task of public bureaucracies is purely instrumental; it is strictly concerned with the efficient implementation of policies and programs.

The instrumental quality of bureaucracies was also an essential element of Max Weber's analysis (13). Although references to his writings on the subject now appear in most textbooks, North American scholars were not familiar with them until the mid-1940s. However, despite this chronological discrepancy, Weber's ideal bureaucracy deserves to be at least briefly mentioned in the context of this discussion of the positivist nature of the foundations of public administration.

The politics/administration dichotomy has long ceased to be embraced as an empirical reality. Middle and upper-level bureaucrats have become accepted as policy-makers in their own right since the 1940s. With the considerable extension of the responsibilities of the state which began in America during the New Deal, elected officials have been unable to compete with the expertise and know-how of their bureaucratic officials. The same holds true for Canada; indeed in the 1950s it was common to say in Canada that the top-ranking bureaucrats of that era—the so-called "mandarins"—were running the country.[3] In both countries, the policy-making role of senior bureaucrats has been curtailed in more recent year by political leaders determined to reduce public expenditures and to ensure stricter accountability. But even the achievement of these goals is conditional, in part at least, on the cooperation of senior bureaucrats.

The positivist separation of facts and values resurfaced under a new form with the triumph of strategic planning in the early 1960s. Policy analysis in the age of Planning Programming Budgeting System (PPBSJ)[4] was trumpeted as a rigorous, scientifically-based exercise in fact finding and program evaluation, while politics was described as irrational and disruptive. This more modern version of the politics/administration dichotomy itself collapsed under the weight of evidence showing that strategic planning has failed in both the private and the public sectors (14,15,16). As Henry Mintzberg explains (17), the idea that large organizations should pursue strategic goals is not problematic; rather the problem lies the professional planners' conviction that strategy formation should be the product of a controlled process of analysis and reporting, a "system" that functions independently of the contingencies of the market or of politics.

Thus supposedly revolutionary concepts and methods often turn out to be recycled ideas. To put it in less polemical terms, a historical perspective is too often lacking in public administration, as Guy Adams notes (19). We need to follow an historically informed and perceptive approach in order to evaluate Harold Lasswell's contribution to the discipline, and to appreciate the tradition he represented. On the one hand, his efforts to create new interdisciplinary "policy sciences" (20,21) often seem to run parallel to the reformulation of the old politics/administration dichotomy into a technocratic politics/policy distinction. The epistemology of the proposed policy sciences shares with the behaviorist social sciences of the 1950s and 1960s a commitment to linear causal modeling using statistical methods. On the other hand, Lasswell insisted that the policy sciences are not simply applied social sciences (22). The positivism inherent in his methodological prescription was balanced by a contextual orientation that took values as an integral part of the analytical process. The policy sciences he envisioned were to be "the policy sciences of democracy." Democracy needs both enlightened leadership and the freedom to engage in critical debates. The Lasswellian scheme achieved a synthesis of both aspects. The policy advisor or public sector manager who would wish to be guided by it would have to be both priest and jester, to borrow a metaphor from Douglas Torgerson. The priestly function is that of the professional analyst carefully collecting data according to the best methodological rules. Lest he or she confuses these data with the "real" world (or the many worlds constructed by other actors in the political system), the policy analyst must also take care to answer the jester's irreverent questions, like "is this perhaps not too neat?" (23).

We can detect here the influence of John Dewey. His thought had a profound impact on the generation of progressive social scientists who laid the foundations of public administration. Dewey defended the idea that the scientific methods should be used to solve social problems (24). But Dewey was not a dogmatist positivist (25), he did not agree that facts and values belong to completely different spheres. On the contrary, he maintained that experience can help us sort out values, that the empirical world is where values can be tested. Democratic procedures are precisely the means to that end. Lasswell had been a student of Charles Merriam, and Merriam had been influenced by Dewey, who had been his colleague at the University of Chicago (Dewey in philosophy, Merriam in political science). As Gerald Caiden explains,

> [Merriam] encouraged his staff to engage in public controversy and reform advocacy. It was from his department that L. D. White produced the first undergraduate textbook, *Introduction to Public Administration* (. . . 1926), which evidenced less enthusiasm for basic principles and scientific management [than authors like Willoughby] and endeavored to take into account the political environment of public administration (26).[5]

To recap, the first steps toward the creation of a new discipline concerned with the study of public administration were taken at the turn of the century by academics who believed strongly that science and technology could improve the efficiency of state institutions. Moreover, they thought a scientific approach to matters of administration would place limits on the irrationality of the political process. However, they were not dogmatic positivists; they did not subscribe to all the tenets of logical positivism as it was then taking shape in philosophy departments (25). Dewey's philosophy is of central importance here. This is because of its significant influence on the thoughts of his contemporaries in academe and beyond, but also insofar as it is symptomatic of the ambiguities—or, complexities—of pragmatism and the Progressive movement. Science and technology were promoted by the reformers in part because of what they represent in terms of analytical rigor and objectivity. Science was valued by many reformers because they also hoped that by making the political process more rational and less subject to partisan influences, the cause of authentic democracy could be further advanced. In other words, the facts/values, politics/administration dichotomy was itself harnessed to a higher end.

It would be a mistake to think that these values and concerns belong to a by-gone age. They reappear in different guises whenever administrative reforms or policy innovations reach the top of the agenda. The next section highlights some of the practical dimensions of these debates.

II. THE PROPER OBJECT OF A POSITIVE SCIENCE OF ADMINISTRATION: MECHANISTIC AND ORGANISMIC METAPHORS

What has been the empirical output of the positivist science of administration? The standard answer to that question can be found in most textbooks.[6] It is the story of the rise and fall of "scientific management." This story contains more than a kernel of truth, however, it also glosses over some perplexing complexities.

It has become very common in the philosophy of science to speak about "paradigms" around which knowledge is structured. A paradigm often evolves from a rather simple picture, usually a metaphorical association between two apparently unrelated domains of experience. Mechanical systems are the sources of powerful metaphors which often have guided scientists in their investigations. Newtonian physics, for example, strongly suggests the image of a universal clockwork—a machine in which all parts normally move and interact through the force of gravity in an unvarying way. It is also commonly assumed that typical bureaucracies "are designed and operated as if they were machines" (31). Gareth Morgan argues that the machine metaphor is still one of the most "ingrained in our conceptions of organizations" (31). It is ironic that today, when reformers articulate bold alternatives to the bureaucratic model, they often speak of "re-engi-neering" government.

Most historical accounts of organization theory and of its relationship to public admin-istration trace the machine metaphor back to the pre-World War II scientific management movement. This school of thought owed a great deal to the pioneering work of Frederick Taylor, although a few decades later (a translation from the French of) Henri Fayol's major work also made a significant contribution (32). Taylor studied industrial organization at the turn of the century, paying particular attention to the rationalization of manual labor (33). But he thought that the principles he had established—principles that Waldo described as "the inauguration of the positivist, the scientific and objective way of regarding human inter-relations" (34)—would be relevant to "management," a concept that was still relatively new then (35). His ideas were in fact carried over into public administration, with special empha-sis on municipal government,[7] by Morris Cooke (36) and, more generally, by the New York Bureau of Municipal Research. One of the most important legacies from this period is the city manager idea. Beyond the local level, scientific management provided the impetus for sus-tained efforts toward the development and implementation of systems of position classifica-tion, notably in the U.S. government (38) and in the Canadian federal government.[8]

Taylor's ideas on scientific management were later recast into a more theoretical and systematic mold by Luther Gulick and Lyndal Urwick, the editors of the seminal *Papers on the Science of Administration* (1937). This text is more concerned with public bureaucracies than Taylor's own work, but its underlying philosophy remains identical. Mariann Jelinek made the point that modern strategic planning systems replicate at the managerial level what Taylor had started at the level of the factory (39). And today the new, and somewhat unfounded belief, in the revolutionary potential inherent in computers and information management systems shows that Taylorism continues to resurface in different forms as circumstances change.

It is generally assumed that Taylor's model was extremely one-sided. According to Hindy Lauer Schachter's detailed analysis of Taylor's life and work, however, scientific management was actually not as mechanistic or authoritarian as commonly thought. It contained utopian prescriptions that did not coincide with the values of the industrial or bureaucratic establishments of the time (41). Certainly, one can find in Taylor's writings examples of mechanistic thinking that seem to reify workers and management alike—af-ter all, the logic of time and motion studies suggests that human beings are the extension of machines. Lauer points out, however, that what he was advocating was the develop-ment of an agreed upon (objective) knowledge basis that would make cooperation among all the members of an organization possible. In the context of his time, the organization of industrial production was very haphazard. While this allowed for some degree of auton-omy on the part of workers and foremen, it also meant that relations of power prevailed in the absence of any shared expectations. Taylor intended to substitute cooperative relations to the arbitrary use of sanctions. If productivity could be increased significantly, both management and the workforce could share the benefits of the technological revolution. Indeed this idea of a mutually beneficial cooperation mattered more to him than merely improving the efficiency of productive activities. Since increased productivity could be achieved only through better training and scientific education, he stressed, with the devel-opment of new skills, workers would find opportunities for personal development. What Schachter very clearly brings out in her analysis of Taylor's work is the idealistic quality of much of what he stood for. Her reading of the reception of Taylor's ideas shows that his contemporaries also perceived that quality in him (42).

The way in which this story unfolds next entails the refutation of the machine metaphor by a series of developments that moved organization theory and public administration in the direction of a behaviorist (and more or less humanistic) paradigm. Mary Parker Follett showed the way in the 1920s (43). But two crucial moments in this evolution were the Hawthorne experiments and the work of Elton Mayo in the 1930s, and, immediately after the war, Herbert Simon's devastating critique of scientific management in his *Administrative Behavior* (44)—a book in which he attempted a synthesis of the economic theory of rational choice and the psychology of decision-making. Simon and authors with whom he collaborated on different projects or who are intellectually close to him (e.g., James March, Richard Cyert (45,46)) do not, properly speaking, belong to the Human Relations school. Their approach is developed by social psychologists (47) and management theorists (48,49,50) in the 1940s, 1950s, and 1960s. What they have in common, however, is a preoccupation with the study of organizational behavior. To describe the behaviorist perspective, Morgan uses the metaphor of the organization as a biological organism (51). This metaphor is not entirely appropriate in the sense that there are ways of conceiving organisms as machines of a special sort, biological machines, as it were.[9] Morgan wishes to underline, that behaviorist theories focus on the individuals who compose organizations, and they treat these individuals as autonomous persons capable of both rational and emotional reactions to their environments. The organismic metaphor is supposed to convey an impression of openness and adaptability. Efficiency and effectiveness remain essential criteria of administrative performance but, for the behaviorist critics of the mechanistic model, these goals can be achieved through relaxed controls and a less authoritarian leadership style.

The displacement of the machine metaphor by the behaviorist approach was a step toward a more sophisticated understanding of organizational dynamics. It was not, however, a radically new departure. Even if this approach proposed a more subtle and realistic account of the psychology of bureaucrats, it was still predicated on the notion that 1. facts relevant to an analysis of organizational behavior can be ascertained by an objective observer; and 2. reliable predictions can be made about the probable effects of specific measure (e.g, changes in the structures of incentives). If anything, the theories that emerged in the 1940s, 1950s, and early 1960s were even more clearly positivist than the classical bureaucratic models of the 1920s and 1930s. As George Frederickson writes,

> Theorists [like Simon, March, or Cyert] enriched their work with a deep understanding of formal and informal patterns of organizational control, the limits of rationality, and the like, but [they] have stayed with the original means-end logic growing out of logical positivism. The close similarities between means-end analysis . . . and the policy-administration dichotomy of the bureaucratic model [i.e, scientific management] are obvious (52).

This approach did not have as noticeable an impact on public administration as scientific management did. In practical terms, the impact has been far more restricted than it was in the corporate sector. Four or five decades ago, most government agencies did not have the flexibility to allow for much more autonomy, let alone risk taking, on the part of their personnel. The clearest example of a direct application of the teachings of the human relations school was the introduction of Organizational Development (OD) techniques in public bureaucracies in the early 1960s (53). (The goal of OD was to use the behavioral sciences as a source of ideas and techniques for improving communications and team management.) OD was not a phenomenal success but it paved the way for more participatory forms of management which are being implemented now and which are arguably less manipulative.

The impact on public administration by the research of Simon and other critics of the scientific management approach who worked from a more or less explicit behaviorist perspective is rather more difficult to assess. The pre-war orthodoxy was seriously shaken by Simon's demonstration that the famed "principles" proposed by Gulick, Urwick, and company were little more than proverbs. They make sense in a given context, but cannot be generalized, in part because they are often contradictory—and "principles" which are not generalizable are not true principles (54). The search for far-reaching principles of that nature was, like putting the cart before the horses. Simon pleaded for the adoption of analytical methods that would a. enable public administration scholars to know what exactly happens within organizations; b. allow them to describe specifically "how (individuals) would behave if they wished their activity to result in the greatest attainment of administrative objectives with scarce means" (55). Then, armed with that knowledge, they could finally attempt a grand synthesis at the level of principles, on the model of what economics has achieved. But that advice has not been very faithfully followed. Today (or not long ago, at any rate) "public administration still lags behind the other social sciences in the application of advanced statistical techniques" (56).

All the authors discussed so far proposed theories and methodologies that are not always compatible. Yet they shared two fundamental assumptions. First, their understanding of the scientific method was consistent with most, of the tenets of positivism. They believed that objectivity is neither impossible nor undesirable when studying human organizations. They tended to favor an inductive, empirical approach to the discovery of causal relationships. Second, their underlying political ideology—for they all had one, regardless of their commitment to objectivity—was, if not statist, at least tolerant of the administrative state and its expanded function in the post New Deal era. The approach discussed in the next section, seemingly perpetuates the positivist tradition. It rests, however, on fundamentally different methodological assumptions since it follows a deductive logic. Moreover, it has been used not as a means to improve the managerial efficiency of the public sector, but as a rhetorical instrument for undermining the legitimacy of the interventionist modern state.

III. PUBLIC CHOICE: POSITIVISM REVISITED?

The belief that *the* scientific method is synonymous with the use of inductive empirical approaches is simply naive. Sophisticated positivists join rank with more radical post-positivists in denouncing this fallacy. The unreflexive and largely a-theoretical methodology of pre-World War II "scientific management" was scientific only in a rhetorical way. Even if was not as empirical and factual as it claimed to be, the strictly empirical approach it advocated was misguided. Karl Popper has convincingly argued that science does merely follow an inductive path to truth (57). From Popper's standpoint, not only are "facts" theory-dependent but theories can never be proven; at best, they can be proven wrong, and even that entails the use of procedures which themselves are grounded in conventionally accepted, but not proven, assumptions (58).

Economics, which is often said to be the most advanced and methodologically rigorous social science, does not adhere to a naive form of empiricism. It is founded upon an impressive theoretical apparatus, and it relies heavily on deductive reasoning. The theoretical foundations of economics are indeed so formidable and the deductions derived from them so elaborate that the question arises of whether its methodology is as "positive" or objective as it is supposed to be by authors like Milton Friedman (59). Economists have taken Popper's lesson to heart but it seems that, in doing so, they have moved rather far away from empirical methods. As a result, they pay far too little attention to the complexities of the actual decisions made by economic agents in constantly changing circumstances. Herbert Simon has done much to expose the empirical limitations of neo-classical micro-economics, and even won a Nobel Prize for his efforts (60). He has been joined by a growing number of psychologists (61,62), philosophers and even a few economists, but their actual impact on economics remains relatively marginal. They have succeeded, however, in establishing the less than entirely "positive" character of economic research.

The degree to which economics is a more positive science than other social science is further complicated by the fundamental axiom according to which economic agents rationally chose among the different alternatives available to them. Although the so-called "Austrian" school of economic theory, which traces its roots back to the works of Carl Menger and Ludwig von Mises, places far more emphasis on subjective choices than mainstream neo-classical economics (63), most economists believe that intentions do matter.

For all these reasons, the current enthusiasm for economic approaches to politics, i.e., public or rational choice models,[10] does not signal a pure and simple return to the positivism of the founders of the discipline. Some critics of rational choice models have intimated that because such models attempt to formulate universal laws of human behavior, beginning with the basic assumptions that humans under normal circumstances act as self-interested utility-maximizers, these models are just as positivistic, and therefore just as flawed, as earlier empirical approaches (64). However, the situation is more complex than these critics pretend. As I have suggested, the (largely Popperian) epistemology of economics diverges somewhat from positivism, as this term is understood in most social sciences.

Moreover, the application of economic reasoning to non-market situations, and to the complex world of public administration in particular, opens up many opportunities for mixing normative assumptions with more strictly empirical observations. For example, advocates of rational choice do not always resist the temptation of drawing an unflattering contrast between the rational behavior of economic agents in competitive markets and the irrational outcomes of political processes like voting. This amounts to an ideologically motivated reduction of rationality to a purely instrumental definition—a definition that ignores the more subtle dimensions of political rationality. Nevertheless, public/rational choice falls closer to the positivist end of the epistemological spectrum than the more explicitly post-positivist approaches I discuss in the next section.

Models used to explain political processes in terms of economic concepts and theories have been used very extensively in political science during the last ten to fifteen years. In fact, Theodore Lowi has described public choice as the "third hegemony" in the discipline, displacing public policy analysis which itself had dethroned behavioralist approaches in the late 1960s (65). The term hegemony is too strong for it leaves far too little room for a variety of other approaches that have also had a noticeable impact on the discipline, notably interpretative and post-positivist/postmodern approaches. Yet rational choice clearly occupies a central place in the constellation of methodologies that define the conceptual universe of political scientists today[11] and students of public policy or public administration. But rational choice has been unevenly applied to the whole spectrum of issues associated with the relationship between the state and its citizens. Public administration and managerial issues in the public sector have received comparatively less attention than voting, electoral competition, interest group behavior, or legislative behavior. To wit, a recent and controversial critique of the applications of rational choice theory in political science does not even mention the study of bureaucratic organizations and their role in policy-making (67). However, two authors have contributed important works on bureaucracy that have been the object of much discussion: Anthony Downs (68) and William Niskanen (69), Niskanen' study being the one that is the most often cited.[12]

Downs' *Inside Bureaucracy* offers a rather broad and somewhat eclectic range of topics. These topics serve to illustrate the explanatory power of Downs' basic premise that bureaucratic officials are motivated by self-interest. They seek to act rationally, although not in the sense of promoting the rationality of the legal democratic order, as in models derived from Weber's work, but in the sense that they act as utility maximizers. This is not a view that all observers of the actual behavior of public servants subscribe to. Steven Kelman, for example, takes exception with the idea—so frequently expressed today—that bureaucratic policy-makers confuse the public interest with their own (72). Admittedly, Downs' open ended definition of the bureaucrat's utility leaves some room for non-myopic and perhaps even altruistic goals. But this commendable attempt to reject simplistic prejudices is both a strength and a weakness. It is a strength because policy-making is a very complex process and there is a risk in trying to reduce a wide range of motivations to a single dimension. It is also a weakness, however, because the theory lacks focus. Downs proposes many interesting hypotheses on management and control, on the life cycles of bureaucratic agencies (or "bureaus"), on internal communications, and so on. So many, in fact, that one tends to loose sight of what his main objective is. It is doubtful that his theory could provide a workable framework for a coherent research program.

To try to validate, or at least falsify, Downs' theory would be a rather daunting project. He himself never attempted to test empirically the hypotheses he proposed. The literature contains very few applications of the model to concrete historical situations. One exception is a paper by Nancy Lind (73). It offers a test of Downs' prediction that the incentives motivating bureaucrats in newly formed agencies differ from those motivating bureaucrats working in older ones. According to Downs, the older agencies are dominated by "conservers" who are more self-interested than the members of newer agencies, which are composed of a larger number of "advocates" and more narrowly committed "zealots," two groups which have more altruistic loyalties. Also, Downs claims that older agencies will be less supportive of innovation than newer ones. On the basis of data collected in six state agencies (two agencies in each one of the following states: Illinois, Oregon, and Tennessee), Lind concludes that "Downs' theory of bureaucratic decision-making is partially supported by state agency data" (74). Specifically, it appears that older agencies are indeed more resistant to change. Lind found, however, that "conservers" are more likely to be found in new agencies than in older ones. The reason why newer agencies are more innovative is that "conservers" are actually less averse to change than the "zealots" whom Downs thinks would be found in newer agencies but are actually more numerous in older ones.

While Downs' study seems to lack focus, Niskanen makes it very clear that his own model rests entirely on one central hypothesis: bureaucrats are budget maximizers. More specifically, Niskanen (69) posits that a. bureaucrats attempt to maximize their budgets; and b. they are usually successful in achieving that goal because the power relations existing between the elected official who control the purse strings and bureaucrats work to the advantage of the latter. The first argument applies to the public sector the fundamental axiom of economic theory that economic agents respond rationally to the incentives facing them. In the case of private firms, profit maximization is the preference that can be reasonably expected. Niskanen argues that budget maximization is the closest equivalent to this objective in the public sector. The second argument reflects Niskanen's belief that politicians normally find it to their advantage to increase the supply of public goods to their constituents. However, the bureaucrats have a monopoly on the policy-relevant information and can thus extract a sort of rent from the politicians. This inexorably lead to bureaucratic expansion, according to Niskanen (75).

Niskanen's model has generated much theoretical discussion (76) and inspired other authors in the formulation of their own formal models of bureaucratic processes (77,78). It has also been subjected to more intense scrutiny than Downs' theory (79–81). These critical evaluations suggest that budget maximization does not always help bureaucrats to maximize their own interests in the political system. For example, Robert Young has come to the conclusion that "there is no strong empirical support for the view that civil servants obtain higher salary increases and faster promotion when they are in bureaucracies that are growing faster than normal." Thus it would seem that "in career terms budget-maximizing behavior simply does not pay" (82). Moreover, now that most governments face severe budgetary constraints and carry a heavy debt load, bureaucrats who would insist on increasing their department's budget would encounter strong opposition from central agencies (e.g., the Office of Management and Budget in the U.S., the Treasury Board Secretariat in Canada), and the political executive. To pursue a budget maximizing strategy under such circumstances would be highly irrational. Niskanen himself has admitted that his original hypothesis needs to be revised. He now claims that rather than seeking to maximize the budget as a whole, bureaucrats attempt to maximize their "discretionary budget" (defined as "the difference between the total budget and the minimum cost to produce the expected output") (83). This was actually a suggestion made some years ago by J.-L. Migué and G. Bélanger (77).

Public choice has brought about more than a methodological challenge to the research methods of public administration. It also compels students of public administration to rethink their a priori and implicit definition of the kind of problems they are (or ought to be) concerned with. Since the reforms introduced in the Progressive era, public administration theorists and practitioners have attempted to find ways of improving the efficiency and effectiveness of government operations. In the post-war years of rapid economic growth and state expansion, they also became interested in the broader question of how to tackle a wide range of socio-economic problems, from poverty to environmental degradation. But the underlying assumption remained that the administrative state—especially at the highest level of policy integration, namely, the federal level—not only had the capacity to achieve its goals, but was the only institution capable of addressing fundamental societal problems. In other words, the consensus was that the common good is best served by the instrument of an efficient and interventionist state. It is precisely this belief that most advocates of public choice question, and Niskanen in particular. (Down's pluralist outlook, however, does not coincide as clearly with the dominant conservative discourse.)

Public choice functions both as an empirical and a normative theory. Vincent Ostrom has dealt with the normative side in a very forthright manner. For Ostrom, the provision of public goods is not the unique responsibility of government. Under certain circumstances, other agencies, from commercial firms to non-profit organizations, or other levels of government, can produce collective goods and contribute to human welfare better than the centralized administrative state and its legions of professional experts (84). Competition between the public and private sectors, and within the public sector between different levels of government, is an idea that public choice theorists tend to favor. Some of them argue that decentralized market arrangements will almost always prove superior to majoritarian political solutions (85,86), prompting equally one-sided criticisms of public choice as a theoretical model and of privatization as a policy options by defenders of the administrative state (87). It is not the intention of this chapter to debate this point, except to note that regardless of the merits of these respective positions, theories do not exist in a vacuum. Contrary to the positivist axiom that facts and values belong to different spheres, and that "ought" statements cannot be derived from factual assertions, talk about self-interested bureaucrats has a tendency to become a self-fulfilling prophecy (65). In any event, there is probably a multitude of defensible positions somewhere between these two extremes. The research program undertaken by Elinor Ostrom, and the network of scholars who gravitate around the Indiana University Workshop on Political Theory, strongly suggests that there are indeed many ways of coordinating the public and private spheres (88–91).

What these controversies serve to illustrate is that the relationships between state and civil society are changing. In the next section, this issue will be considered in a broader political context that is not limited to the opposition between state and markets.

IV.   TOWARD POSTMODERN GOVERNMENT?

Debates and controversies about fundamental concepts used in academic or professional discourses, the emergence of new social movements, the globalization of international markets, and the shift from an industrial to a knowledge-based economy, these are some of the factors suggesting that profound cultural and structural changes are taking place. For the sake of brevity, the term "postmodern" will be used to describe this new era. What the defining parameters of postmodern government and postmodern public administration consist of is an open question. For every generalization about postmodern trends in government, there are significant exceptions (92). The public administration and public sector management literature contain quite a few diverging interpretations of the challenges posed by the new socio-economic, political and cultural contexts. In spite of this diversity, which often reflects not only methodological differences, but also sharp ideological cleavages, there seems to be a fair measure of agreement about the two following points: a. objective analysis by unbiased technical "experts" of the problems facing complex organizations has largely failed (93–96); and b. hierarchical structures and top-down approaches to policy implementation are inadequate management strategies (97–102). Different authors have developed these themes according to their own leanings and with varying degrees of perceptivity. One of the purposes of the next two subsections is precisely to convey a sense of this diversity, while also attempting to discern the elements of an emerging consensus behind the apparent flurry of new ideas and theories.

In the third subsection, the implications of these new theories for the theory and practice of public administration and policy analysis are discussed. The positivist credo was that reality can be faithfully represented—mirrored, as it were[13]—by scientific theories; contemporary epistemology, by contrast, stresses the inevitable role of the observer/knower in constructing a relevant image of the world. The implication of this perspective for public servants is that their expert knowledge of the "facts" offers only one of many possible windows on the complex problems they deal with. Indeed the very definition of what exactly the "problem" is in the political/administrative environment is a contentious issue (104). The implications for public administration research, on the other hand, is that there may be more to gain from the use of interpretive strategies than from trying to apply traditional empirical methods more rigorously.

A.   Toward a More Client-Centered Approach

Over the course of the last two or three decades, many groups have demanded greater public involvement in policy formulation or implementation. In responding to these demands, the public administration community has argued in favor of more client-centered approaches to policy-making and program management (105). This goal has not changed, but the specific arguments used, as well as the groups making these demands, have varied. In the late 1960s and early 1970s, the priority was placed on the need for democratic participation and the importance of giving a voice to the less privileged members of society. To that end, reformers advocated a more active role on the part of civil servants. More recent reappraisals of the structures and goals of the public service, such as The National Performance Review (106) or Canada's Public Service 2000 (107), reflect a greater concern for loss of legitimacy which affects most public institutions today. The political forces behind these reforms are middle class tax payers who have become alarmed by the level of public spending, and who are urging more "business-like" efficiency in government. However, the overall idea remains the same: traditional bureaucratic approaches, or even sophisticated planning systems, no longer offer viable solutions to our problems. In other words, the emblems of reform have changed but the underlying rationale continues to be that there is no store of technocratic expertise vast enough to resolve our pressing social and economic problems. Several forms and degrees of citizens involvement have been proposed as ways out of this impasse. These need to be explored in more detail.

By the late 1960s, public administration was in a state of intellectual disarray. Government had been growing steadily since the war years, but the skilled managers that were recruited in these years had not, for the most part, been trained in public administration; new graduate programs in public affairs and policy analysis were pushing public administration to the side lines of the academic world. What was left of public administration as a discipline, with its heavy emphasis on formal structures and routine processes of resource allocation, was regarded by a new generation of students and scholars as irrelevant to the pressing issues of the day (e.g., the war in Vietnam, poverty, and human rights). The "New Public Administration" emerged a response to this challenge. It originated in the Minnowbrook conference (1968) as a loosely structured group of (mostly) young scholars (108). It is no longer alive as such today, but it was rather central to the discipline for some time, especially during the years when the *Public Administration Review* was under the direction of an editorial team (Dwight Waldo, Frank Marini, and H. George Frederickson (109)) that was committed to the movement's goals.

Not only did the New Public Administration reject the politics-administration dichotomy, but it insisted that administrators make significant policy decisions. If so, then the question of the moral obligations that administrators must consider becomes crucial. The primary goal of the New Public Administration was to make social equity the dominant criterion for policy evaluation and implementation. The most radical message of the movement was that civil servants could—and even should on some occasions—act as advocates of the under-privileged groups in society. This recommendation made sense in the politically charged climate of the time, but it betrayed a certain degree of political naivete. There are obvious limits to the discretionary power of civil servants, not to mention that internal bureaucratic politics often creates obstacles to this kind of pro-active stance. Moreover, as Douglas J. Amy notes (110), administrators are often reluctant to pursue strategies that could threaten their image of neutral technocratic experts, since doing so would clearly be against their interest, both within government and vis-a-vis the public at large.

Social equity, however, can be achieved through other and less radical means. It is also consistent with the pursuit of other values, including bureaucratic responsiveness, citizen choice, and democratic participation. The New Public Administration movement did not stumble across these values by chance. They have always formed an integral part of American political culture. In modern times, John Dewey devoted much of his life to the pursuit of democratic reforms and to the renewal of democratic theory. As I mentioned already, Dewey argued strongly in favor of the adoption of social scientific approaches to public policy analysis and implementation, while also insisting on the need for democratic participation. He sensed that emphasizing the former at the expense of the latter would lead to a serious imbalance, and would be detrimental to the public interest (111). Although, and rather surprisingly, the advocates of the New Public Administration make few references to Dewey's philosophy, it is clear that they were not so much opening new paths as they were rediscovering an underlying current of democratic thought. In more recent years, this current had meandered through a rather different ideological terrain.

The idea of a more client-centered approach to policy development and implementation has not disappeared from the political agenda as the New Public Administration faded away in the 1980s.[14] However, it is no longer presented in the context of a progressive politics, but as an aspect of the current populist wave of anti-bureaucratic sentiments.

One of the four principles identified by the authors of the report of National Performance Review as essential to the reinvention of government is: "Putting Customers First." But in doing so, they were not really breaking new ground. The private sector had been concerned about service quality throughout the 1980s. In fact, North American corporations were responding to the competitive threat posed by Japanese manufactures who, in the previous decade, had invested heavily into quality management, and whose customers reported high levels of satisfaction with the products or services they purchased. The public sector did not turn around until the late 1980s when the industrialized world was confronted with a serious crisis of legitimacy. It is not immediately evident, after all, that government's primary role is to deliver services to is "clients or "customers," nor exactly who these customers might be (e.g., who are the customers of a prison guard?).[15] But movement in that direction began, first, at the state level (e.g., Minnesota) and then spread to the rest of North America, Australia, and the United Kingdom.

The National Performance Review, which was itself the outcome of a wide open consultation process, recommended four steps toward the goal of improving customer service: "giving customers a voice—and a choice"; "making service organizations compete"; "creating market dynamics"; and "using market mechanisms to solve problems" (114).

The report of the Service to the Public Task Force of Public Service 2000 (i.e., the Canadian counterpart to the National Performance Review) did not place quite as much emphasis on competition and the market metaphor. Nevertheless, the approach was similar. That report listed three objectives on the way to the creation of a more client-centered public service: the development of an organizational culture supportive of this idea; more open and frequent consultations with clients and other stakeholders; and a more committed leadership style that would make "public servants feel valued, motivated, informed and challenged to put forth their best efforts" (115).

What emerges from these and other recent blueprints for reform is the realization that public administration is not an end in itself nor a uniquely distinctive institution. Public officials must question their basic assumptions in light of what the public expects of them, and in comparison with what other complex organizations are doing. In other words, they must take a critical look at their own culture and learn to see the world through a multifaceted prism. Problem situations must be defined in partnership with different stakeholders rather than being fitted into rigid patterns reflecting traditional professional standards.

The techniques used to make the public service more client-focused are many and cannot be discussed in detail here. They include public opinion polls and other market research instruments; the use of new informal communication channels like the Internet; task forces and legislative committee hearings; the organization of small workshops, large scale conferences and other means of convening interest group representatives and public officials (e.g., on environmental issues); freedom of information legislation; and the development of new incentives within the public service. Some agencies only implement a few of these measures, other pursue a systematic and comprehensive strategy often known as Total Quality Management (TQM) (116).

B.   Debureaucratization

There is more to the new vision than an awareness that policy-making is a multidimensional process that presupposes on-going consultations, debates, and negotiations. The active search for alternatives to the bureaucratic model constitutes another, albeit related, aspect of the new cultural climate. Managerial hierarchies and rigid control systems are now seen in both the private and the public sectors as outdated structures that need to be redesigned.

According to a classical literature that dates back to Frederick Taylor and even beyond him, the most powerful incentives are monetary rewards. Thus a firm or a public bureaucracy will run smoothly if wages adequately match the amount of effort put into the tasks at hand (e.g., piece-work), and, more generally, if work is distributed in a standardized and predictable manner. As we have seen, this mechanistic paradigm has been challenged on a number of counts and is no longer up to date. Nevertheless, its economic rationale retains some degree of common sensical appeal. The *coup de grâce* to this theory has been delivered recently by Gary Miller. Using social choice theory and game theory, Miller shows that "a narrow neoclassical version of organizational economics self-destructs" (117). What this means, in practical terms, is that organizations that do away with rigid hierarchies, and emphasize innovative leadership and cooperation among employees, are more efficient.

How this transformation can be achieved is a question that has received many answers. Post-bureaucratic theory is still a work in progress. It is clear that the Weberian bureaucratic model is not viable today. When the social and economic environments of policy-making are as rapidly evolving as they are today, and when citizens demand quality services, standardized routines and top-down command style management become largely ineffective. Reformers insist that new, post-bureaucratic organizations are needed. While no organization can do away entirely with command structures, least of all public bureaucracies, the goal should be to design institutions that are flexible and adaptive. But too much flexibility could degenerate into dysfunctional behavior. Thus the new literature strongly emphasizes the importance of leadership (118). The role of the leader of a post-bureaucratic organization is less to issue commands than to inspire a commitment to an integrating and forward looking "vision" and, ultimately, to encourage the development of an organizational culture that promotes cooperation and innovation.

Practitioners and theorists march to the sound of the same drummer on this question: two of the best known books on public management analyze a number of experiments that started more or less independently in a number of separate jurisdictions on several continents, and draw valuable lessons from them (98,99). Perhaps the most original and challenging of such lessons—and one that has a certain postmodern ring to it—is that in adaptive and successful organizations the members have the power to make decisions and to represent the organization in their dealings with people outside of it. Empowerment, which is the opposite of the hierarchical principle, has received considerable attention in the reports and publications of both the National Performance Review in the United States and Public Service 2000 in Canada. (It would be a mistake to think that empowerment has become a trend only at the federal level; as more change has taken place at other levels, especially in local governments). Noting that Ralph Waldo Emerson long ago already had celebrated the potential for genius inherent in every individual, the National Performance Review recommended that decision-making power be delegated to the people who do the work. Central controls must be eased so as to permit prompt and efficient delivery of services. Public servants must become more entrepreneurial, within limits imposed by certain guarantees of fairness and openness. The corollary of this move is that accountability should be rethought; the emphasis must now be placed on responsibility for the results achieved rather than for strict adherence to regulations concerning the use of standardized inputs (119). Hence the title of the report itself: *From Red Tape to Results*. Reflecting upon this evolution, P. De Celles has even suggested that the relationship between bureaucratic and political officials should be reverted in some measure. He argues that empowered managers should have more opportunities for deciding *what* to do, while politicians should be more concerned with *how* to do it, since what citizens want and expect has often more to do with issue of process than with the actual goals of public policy (120).

These ideas have not entirely displace more traditional governance structures. This is partly because of the inertia which exists in all organizations (121). It is also because democratic political processes inevitably create obstacles to the elimination of regulations that may be cumbersome but guarantee openness and transparency in the conduct of public affairs (122). Moreover, the logic of empowerment itself is fraught with intriguing paradoxes. On the one hand, it is predicated on the notion that the politics-administration dichotomy is obsolete and that public servants already do exercise a significant amount of discretionary power, and should be granted more. On the other hand, to fulfill the new mandate that empowered bureaucratic policy-makers are (or would be) given, they must also be able to prove to the public that their new responsibilities leave no room for partisan bias—in other words, they would have to prove that something like the old politics-administration dichotomy still makes sense (123).

These are very important questions but since this chapter is mostly concerned with the epistemological dimension of these transformations, they will not be discussed at any length here. From an epistemological standpoint, the important question is: What kind of knowledge do all these empowered participants in the policy process share, if at all, and how do they communicate their understanding of the problems at hand?

C. From Explanation to Interpretation

All the theoretical concepts and practical developments discussed above cannot be fitted neatly into a single epistemological mold. It would be tendentious to claim that we are witnessing a typical paradigm shift because we are often dealing with approaches that make use of a grab bag of concepts and methods. For example, the development and implementation of TQM schemes may require the same kind of rigorous and empirical study of work habits and service delivery as were required for the introduction of classification systems or other reforms inspired by the administrative science movement in earlier times. Nonetheless, the underlying logic of a move toward more client-focused and decentralized organizations is that there is more than one avenue to efficient management. There are as many potential avenues as there are clients, and/or empowered bureaucrats. Of course, in practice such anarchical diversity is never reached, but the implicit assumption is that there is no such thing as *the* best way of doing things. Strategies and procedures must be negotiated and periodically re-evaluated in light of what a multiplicity of stakeholders think. Knowledge claims grounded in experience now compete with professional expertise or hierarchical status. From a theoretical standpoint, this signifies a relaxation of the implicit positivism that still permeates organization theory since, as Frederick Thayer argues, there is a close relationship of interdependence between the concepts of objectivity and hierarchy—the latter being required to enforce the former (124). From a more practical perspective, it would seem that skepticism about the technocratic experts' superior knowledge of the "facts" cuts across ideological lines. In the 1960s and 1970s, the liberal left used to inveigh against the "technostructures" controlling large corporations and government bureaucracies. The neo-populist mood that now prevails in North America (124) is a reaffirmation of "common sense"[16]in areas like education reform (the return to the three "Rs"), welfare reform, and the administration of justice.

Jay D. White reminds us that "postpositivist philosophers of science have identified three modes of social research—explanatory, interpretive, and critical" (125). Positivist science is interested in causal explanations. But the realization that the kind of "realities" that policy-makers deal with are multidimensional, and in some respects socially constructed, should make the other two strategies more attractive. By definition, democracy places limits on the power of any single individual or group to impose its preferences. Some groups are more influential than others, but no single interest can determine the criteria for selecting the relevant facts or interpreting their meaning. Social realities are never constituted only of brute "facts" about which one can have different preferences. Values and factual events are constantly rearranged into different strategic positions which social actors pursue in trying to influence each other, or simply in making sense of their own situation.

Interpretive research seeks to bring out these relationships. It asks: What meaning do the actors involved in a particular context attach to their own actions and that of others. The interpretive approach, which uses the methodology of hermeneutics, accepts that practically all interpretations deserve equal consideration. The critical approach, by contrast, combines interpretation and evaluation. Inspired by the works of philosophers like J. Habermas, it rests on the assumption that the power structures of capitalist societies systematically constrain certain groups or classes from participating fully into the democratic process. It is precisely because it is constituted as a critique of the obstacles to unrestrained communications that it is known as critical theory or critical research.

Much of the philosophical literature from which the interpretive approach derives its central concepts is rather abstruse. In order to use these approaches, however, policy analysts or managers do not need to use the language of theoretical philosophy. J. D. White aptly suggests that the art of storytelling is an excellent way to put post-positivism into practice: "through storytelling, interpretation and critique enable social change" (128), and many case studies can be read as such. This advice makes plenty of sense considering the very effective way in which the National Performance review has used well chosen anecdotes to illustrate the important points of its message; this was particularly evident in the September 1994 progress report (129).[17] In the same vein, Steven Maynard-Moody and Marisa Kelly have shown that one of the best way to understand how managers create meaning is to examine "a set of stories, or folk tales, collected in several state government organizations" (131). Thus while it is customary to lament the lack of methodological rigor and narrow scope of case studies which the public administration continues to produce in abundance (132), what is really needed are good case studies that combine the critical element inherent in story telling with solid analytical skills and a carefully worked out research design (133).

To what extent has research in public administration been influenced by interpretivist arguments? And to what extent have practitioners become more aware of their own role as creators of meaning? These questions cannot be answered in a clear cut manner. There has certainly been a significant increase in the number of studies that make use of concepts like the construction of meaning and emphasize the role administrators play in interpreting policy relevant information (134–139). However, studies that explicitly incorporate interpretivist elements remain rather exceptional. Much of public administration research continues to be superficially objective and silent about the criteria from which critical comments or policy recommendations are derived almost surreptitiously. It is possible, however, to discern in their implicit methodology an interpretivist logic. What makes a particular situation or problem interesting is, that there is more to it than meets the eye. This often leads the investigator to examine differences in perceptions, values, or judgment. In some instances (e.g., studies on affirmative action, multiculturalism, and the representativeness of bureaucracy more generally, or on the regulation of new technologies, including biomedical research and development) this becomes in fact inevitable. As the problems faced by governments today have become immensely complex, it will become more and more difficult to avoid using interpretive methods for making sense of conflicts over fundamental values, both within government agencies and between government and the citizens.

V. POSTPOSITIVIST SCIENCE AND PUBLIC ADMINISTRATION

Self-consciously postmodernist theorists (e.g., Foucault, Lyotard, Derrida, Rorty) and their followers in the social sciences (140) do not always clearly distinguish between positivist approaches to scientific research and science itself. Their much needed critique of technocracy often leads them to adopt a relativistic understanding of all forms of expression, from science to partisan discourse, as rhetorical weapons in a war of words. The flip side of Michel Foucault's well known pronouncement that all forms of knowledge entail the exercise of power (141) is that power always trumps knowledge. And postmodern critics usually direct their attacks against what they regard as conservative power structures, including science. If this trend was to prevail, public administration, as a discipline, would become limited to the discussions of the politics and questionable ethics of bureaucratic power. As an art, it would become entirely subservient to the logic of political communications and of interest advocacy—indeed some movement in that direction has probably taken place already (93).

The postmodern turn is not limited to the liberal left. There is also a conservative or populist reaction to technocracy and top-down approaches that is less explicitly relativist but is nonetheless rather inimical to scientific inquiry. Moreover, the advocates of the new public sector management paradigm could be faulted for skipping too lightly over the differences between the public and the private sectors. These theorists promote their own brand of relativism, insofar as they pretend not to see, and would like us to ignore, the fundamental difference between the logic inherent in public bureaucracies (i.e., constitutional and political accountability) and the logic of the market (122). This confusion of values could prove to be damaging to the public interest in the long term.

Yet there is no reason to despair about the future potential of a scientific approach to public administration defined as a distinct research domain or as a unique practice. Science itself has moved far way from positivism in this century. Paradigmatic shifts as momentous as quantum physics, which is already an old revolution but one which is still unfolding, and more recent developments like the sciences of complexity (e.g., chaos theory) have opened new perspectives. These theoretical innovations rest on premises that differ very significantly from the positivist dogmas of the last century. Yet they fall squarely within the realm of science. Post-positivist science shares with philosophical postmodernism some important ideas, including the idea that whatever "reality" exists "out there" cannot be known with certainty and effectively controlled, but these two intellectual currents should not be confused.

The social science were slow to acknowledge these transformations. Social scientists have wrongly equated equilibrium models and linear dynamics with the scientific method itself. Equilibrium analysis dominated physics from Newton until it was challenged by quantum mechanics in the 1920s. It no longer defines physics today—in fact, contemporary physics has little to do any more with classical mechanics. The philosophy of science has taken note of this evolution (142) and has engendered an eclectic literature on evolutionary processes in nature and society [143,144]. Linear equilibrium models, however, still remain central to engineering, much of biology, economics, psychology, and the empirically oriented subfields of sociology and political science.

Rather slowly, the new thinking in the physical sciences is gaining acceptance in the other sciences. A suggestive metaphor first proposed by Karl Popper (144) illustrates this: since the Newtonian revolution, science used to see clocks everywhere, now it has discovered clouds. But clouds are puzzling; they are far more complex than clocks. That is, they are made of elements that enter into unstable and largely unpredictable relationships. Precisely, it is around the notion of complexity that the new scientific thinking converges (146,147). In more technical terms; the new tools of scientific inquiry make extensive use of non-linear dynamics (and, to a lesser degree, fuzzy logic[18]), and are applied to the study of non-equilibrium phenomena. Non-linear dynamics describes relationships that are self-referential and such that small inputs can produce unexpectedly large outputs, and dissimilar inputs can have similar effects. Situations far from equilibrium are characterized by considerable uncertainty because they are subject to unpredictable and catastrophic phase changes.[19] Complex systems have a sort of virtual existence; they can acquire, depending on the circumstances, one of several potentially realizable configurations. This is like putting the world of classical mechanics—the world that, as positivists used to reason, science was meant to explain—on its head.

In addition to the displacement of determinism (or, at least, strict determinism), the new scientific vision also introduces another key concept; autonomy. A complex system becomes autonomous from its environment when it acquires the capacity to be self-organizing, that is, when it can maintain its organizational integrity by producing and reproducing its own structures and/or by spontaneously rearranging these structures to produce new ones. Self-organizing systems are not controlled by an external operator or even by an internal and functionally specialized regulator. They operate as integrated but a-centered networks. Slime molds constitute puzzling examples of this dynamics in the living world. They form as a result of the spontaneous cooperation of up to 100,000 amoebae organizing into a quasi-organism which takes a variety of forms through its short life cycle before releasing spores that will start the process all over again (149). In the social world, free markets are often cited as relevant examples of this process of spontaneous self-organization (150,151). Democratic political regimes would be another excellent example (152). But how do these examples relate to organization theory and public administration, considering that bureaucracies are, by definition, centralized and controlled systems? In a sense, it is indeed true that bureaucracies are *not* self-organizing. However, the trends toward a post-bureaucratic public administration alluded to in the previous section suggest that this objection may not be irrefutable. Thus the new sciences of Complexity can assist theorists and reformers interested in the design of post-bureaucratic organizations.

What has been the effect of post-positivist science on public administration research and/or practice? So far, it has been rather limited. But there is already movement in that direction, and the potential for further progress is encouraging. At present, the literature consists of texts that either try to convince scholars and practitioners that these new approaches are relevant to policy analysis or organization theory (153,154), or to articulate and explore metaphorical parallels (155,156), or, closer to the applied end of the spectrum, to illustrate hypothetically how non-linear dynamics could be used to study administrative behavior and organizational change (157,158). What we are still lacking, however, are empirical studies using these new concepts and techniques as means to describe or evaluate the effects of actual programs or institutional arrangements.

Why should the members of the public administration community be impatient to learn about the results of such studies? Because such studies promise to be helpful in assessing the implications of the trends discussed in the previous section without falling into the traps posed by outdated positivist assumptions.

For example, the issue of leadership raises questions that non-linear dynamics could tackle in new ways. Postmodern culture leads to the dismantlement of hierarchical structures that were originally designed to facilitate the communication of standardized instructions, and to the adoption of more flexible leadership styles. We do not really know, however, whether this is a passing fad or an irreversible change. Nor do we know how much more flexible should leadership become. We need a way to find out why traditional bureaucratic organizations are inoperative as such, regardless of how well managed they may be. This would entail a demonstration of the impossibility of mapping data describing discrete and non-linear phenomena onto a continuous and linear space. Using hypothetical data, Douglas Kiel has shown graphically that this appears to be the case. Since organizational behavior is inherently complex, it sometimes results in chaotic variations that cannot be controlled by hierarchical command structures, no matter how efficient and "in control" supervisors appear to be, and even if employees are diligent (159). This is a modest beginning, but certainly a promising avenue of research.

Unfortunately, it may still be too early to carry out this kind of empirical work. To measure realities that are improperly conceptualized sounds like putting the cart before the horse. More qualitative explorations, using a variety of analogies, metaphors, and other imaginative scenarios, will most probably continue to be the preferred strategy of research for the foreseeable future.

VI. CONCLUSION

Pressure groups, editorialists, politicians, ordinary citizens, academics, and administrators themselves have given much thought in recent years to the idea of reinventing government. Public administration has been profoundly affected by these developments. The scholarly (and even not so scholarly) literature abound with new ideas. Administrative reforms have been proposed, discussed, and implemented in capitals around the world, as well as at the local level. Many programs have been reviewed, scaled down, or eliminated.

In the context of profound structural and cultural changes, public administration has become less homogeneously positivist than it was or was believed to be a generation or two ago. Public administration has never completely succeeded in achieving the status of a positive science, as indicated above, nor has it succeeded in becoming a coherent body of professional expertise. Rational/public choice offered the option to public administration of becoming a subfield of economics, a discipline that is presumed to be a positive science by its defenders. However, relatively few scholars agree. (This is not to say, of course, that rational choice is irrelevant to public administration.)

Movement toward the postmodern end of the spectrum has certainly taken place. There is now a sizable literature that discusses the limitations inherent in the experts' "objective" knowledge of policy "facts"; the contradictions involved in trying to control large complex organizations; and the inadequacy of traditional dichotomies like the politics/policy-administration distinction. However, the alternatives are not always carefully thought out. Some of the recent reforms may be, in part, "smoke and mirrors" intended to hide the ruthlessness with which budgetary compressions are carried out. Inversely, some of the new ideas might have been carried out too far, to the point where they blur the constitutionally significant distinction between the rules that apply to public and to private organizations. As these issues are further explored, we should be able to learn to live without the crutch of positivist dogmas and to cope with complexity and multidimensional realities in a sensible manner. The post-positivist sciences of complexity will provide much needed assistance in this regard.

NOTES

1. Jean-François Lyotard [3] establishes a contrast between the modern tendency to frame all meaningful occurrences within what he calls "grand narratives," e.g., either Marxism or market capitalism, and the postmodern condition which he describes as a rejection of grand narratives and a critique of all foundationalist philosophies.

2. Canada adopted the merit system somewhat later. The first Civil Service Act was passed in 1908 and its scope was expanded to include all federal government employees in 1918. Canada, however, went further than the United States in eliminating political patronage. In the U.S. government "political executives" still hold thousands of positions at the top of the hierarchical pyramid, but in regular Canadian government departments all hierarchical levels below the minister, including the position of Deputy Minister (i.e., the Under Secretary in the American system), are staffed by career public servants; the heads of several dozens of non-departmental agencies and public enterprises of the Government of Canada (e.g., National Energy Board) are political appointees, however.

3. Prime Minister Trudeau in the late 1960s and early 1970s attempted to strengthen his own control, and that of his cabinet, on the machinery of government and the policy-making process, but paradoxically ended up creating a more complex bureaucracy (16,18).

4. Originally developed in the Department of Defence under Secretary McNamara, PPBS spread like a brush fire to the rest of the federal government, most of the states, Canada, and several European countries (e.g., France).

5. On White's contribution to public administration, see Storing (27).

6. Hindy Lauer Schachter surveyed 15 textbooks and found that they all propose the same interpretation of the history of ideas in public administration (28). By and Large, the two major Canadian textbooks on public administration tell a similar story (29,30).

7. Not surprisingly, considering that in 1902, nearly 75% of non-military public expenditures in the United States were at the local level (36).

8. In the 1920s, the Canadian Civil Service Commission hired the American consulting firm Arthur Young & Co. for the purpose of classifying approximately 50,000 positions (39).

9. Thomas Hobbes proposed a startling analogy of this kind in the opening pages of his *Leviathan*.

10. "Nonmarket economics" is another label found in the literature.

11. According to Donald Green and Ian Shapiro, the proportion of articles published in the *American Political Science Review* which used the methodology of rational choice jumped from about 20% in the late 1970s to just under 40% in the early 1990s (66).

12. At least two earlier works must be mentioned even though they did not have the same impact as either Downs or Niskanen's seminal texts: Ludwig von Mises' *Bureaucracy* (70), and Gordon Tullock's *The Politics of Bureaucracy* (71).

13. Richard Rorty has attacked the idea that human knowledge, in the form of either science or philosophy, can ever be just a mirror of the truth (103).

14. In 1988 a second Minnowbrook conference was held. It became clear to the participants that although many of the ideals and goals advocated by the New Public Administration movement were still relevant, the movement itself could only be talked about in the past tense (112).

15. According to Michael Barzelay, it is essential to distinguish clearly between real customers and what he calls "compliers" i.e., individuals who are expected to comply with norms or meet certain standards of accountability (113).

16. For at least a decade, the Republicans have appealed to the common sense of American voters in their attacks against the "Washington Establishment." This rhetorical posture is not limited to the United States, however. In September 1995, the Progressive Conservative party won a decisive electoral victory in the province of Ontario; Mr. Michael Harris, the new Premier of Ontario, claims that this victory ushers in "the common sense revolution."

17. Can anyone reading the introduction to that report not be impressed, for example, by the efforts made by the Veterans Administration to treat veterans like Len Davis and thousands others as valued customers and not merely as anonymous cases; or by the extraordianry performance of Dan Beard in turning around the Bureau of Reclamation; the Bureau used to operate as an unresponsive bureaucracy committed to building more and more dams that the public did not really want, but it has been transformed into a lean and competitive organiza-

tion offering professional advice to field agencies in touch with local needs and concerns. The *Report on Progress* of Public Service 2000 also used short case studies but they are more like little vignettes than stories in the fuller sense of the term [130].

18. Fuzzy logic is a multi-valued logic which instead of distinguishing only between true (1) and false (0) statements, posits that there is a potentially infinite number of truth values, just as there is an infinite range of rational numbers (e.g., 0.246) between the natural numbers 0 and 1. This allows for the formalization of ordinary language expressions like "rather big" or "smallish," etc.

19. To illustrate this phenomenon, James Gleick uses the (now famous) example of the "butterfly" effect: a butterfly flapping its wings somewhere deep into the Brazilian jungle can be the remote cause of a tropical storm thousands of miles away . . . (147).

REFERENCES

1. H. G. Frederickson, *New Public Administration*, University of Alabama Press, University, 1980, p. 105.

2. J. Bendor, The Fields of Bureaucracy and Public Administration: Basic and Applied Research, *J. of Pub. Admin. Research and Theory*: 4;27–39, 1994.

3. J.-F. Lyotard, *The Postmodern Condition: A Report on Knowledge*, Manchester University Press, Manchester, U.K., 1984.

4. J. D. White and G. B. Adams, Making sense with diversity: The context of research, theory, and knowledge development in public administration, *Research in Public Administration: Reflections on Theory and Practice*, J. D. White and G. B. Adams (eds.), Sage Publications, Thousand Oaks, 1994, p. 9.

5. J. Hughes, *The Philosophy of Social Research* 2nd ed., Longman, New York, 1990, p. 19.

6. M. Hollis, *The Philosophy of Social Science: An Introduction*, Cambridge University Press, Cambridge, 1994, pp.41–43.

7. D. B. Eaton, *Civil Service in Great Britain*, New York, 1880.

8. W. Wilson, The science of administration, *Political Science Quarterly* 2:200; cited in D. Waldo, *The Administrative State* 2nd ed., Holmes & Meier, New York, 1984, p. 8.

9. N. Henry, *Public Administration and Public Affairs*, Prentice-Hall, Englewood Cliffs, N.J., 1975, p. 192.

10. K. Kernaghan and D. Siegel, *Public Administration in Canada* 3rd edition, Nelson Canada, Toronto, 1995, p. 25.

11. P. P. van Riper, *The Wilson Influence on Public Administration: From Theory to Practice*, American Society for Public Administration, Washington, D.C., 1990.

12. G. B. Adams, Enthralled with modernity: The historical context of knowledge and theory development in public administration, *Research in Public Administration*, White and Adams, (eds.), p. 36.

13. M. Weber, Bureaucracy, *From Max Weber: Essays in Sociology*, H. H. Gertz and C. Wrights Mills, (eds. and trans.), Oxford University Press, New York, 1946.

14. H. Mintzberg, *The Rise and Fall of Strategic Planning*, The Free Press, New York, 1994, chap. 3.

15. A. Wildavsky, *The Politics of the Budgetary Process* 2nd edition, Little, Brown & Co., Boston, 1974, p. 205.

16. L. Dobuzinskis, Rational government: Policy, politics, and political science, *Apex of Power: The Prime Minister and Political Leadership in Canada* 2d ed., T. A. Hockin, (ed.). Prentice-Hall Canada, Scarborough, Ont., 1977.

17. H. Mintzberg, *The Rise and Fall*, p. 32.

18. R. French, *How Ottawa Decides: Planning and Industrial Policy 1968–1980*, Lorimer, Toronto, 1980.

19. G. B. Adams, Enthralled with Modernity, pp. 32–36.

20. D. Lerner and H. D. Lasswell (eds.), *The Policy Sciences*, Stanford University Press, Stanford, 1951.

21. H. D. Lasswell, *A Pre-View of Policy Sciences*, American Elsevier, New York, 1971.

22. H. D. Lasswell, The Policy Orientation, *The Policy Sciences,* Lerner and Lasswell (eds.), p. 4.

23. D. Torgerson, Priest and jester in the policy sciences: Developing the focus of inquiry, *Pol. Sci.*: 25, 228, 1992.

24. C. Frankel, John Dewey's social philosophy, *New Studies in the Philosophy of John Dewey*, S. M. Cahn (ed.), University Press of New England, Hanover, 1977, p. 9.

25. P. Waldo, *The Administrative State* 2nd ed., p. xxxix.

26. G. E. Caiden, *The Dynamics of Public Administration: Guidelines to Current Transformations in Theory and Practice*, Holt, Rhinehart and Winston, New York, 1971, p. 37.

27. H. Storing, Leonard D. White and the Study of Public Administration, *Pub. Admin. Rev.*: 25;38–51, 1965.

28. H. L. Schachter, *Frederick Taylor and the Public Administration Community*, p. 126n1.

29. K. Kernaghan and D. Siegel, *Public Administration in Canada*.

30. R. F. Adie and P. G. Thomas, *Canadian Public Administration*, Prentice-Hall, Scarborough, 1987.

31. G. Morgan, *Images of Organization*, Sage, Newbury Park, 1986, p. 22.

31. G. Morgan, *Images of Organization*, p. 24.

32. H. Fayol, *General and Industrial Management*, Pitman, London, 1949 (originally published in 1930).

33. F. Taylor, *Shop Management*, Harper and Brothers, New York, 1947 (originally published in 1903).

34. D. Waldo, The Administrative State 2nd ed., p. 50.

35. F. Taylor, *The Principles of Scientific Management*, Harper and Brothers, New York, 1947 (originally published in 1911).

36. N. Henry, *Public Administration*, p. 191

37. M. Cooke, *Our Cities Awake*, Doubleday, Page & Co., New York, 1912.

38. N. Henry, *Public Administration*, p. 192.

39. K. Kernaghan and D. Siegel, *Public Administration*, p. 48.

40. H. Mintzberg, *The Rise and Fall*, p. 222.

41. H. L. Schachter, *Frederick Taylor and the Public Administration Community: A Reevaluation*, SUNY Press, Albany, 1989.

42. H. L. Schachter, *Frederick Taylor and the Public Administration Community*, chap. 5.

43. M. P. Follett, *The New State*, Peter Smith, Gloucester, 1965 (first published in 1918).

44. H. A. Simon, *Administrative Behavior: A Study of Decision-Making Processes in Administrative Organizations* 3rd ed., The Free Press, New York, 1976 (first published in 1945).

45. J. G. March and H. A. Simon, *Organizations*, Wiley, New York, 1958.

46. R. M. Cyert et al., The Behavioral Approach with Emphasis on Economics, *Beh. Sci.*: 28, 95–108, 1983.

47. A. Maslow, *Motivation and Personality*, Harper & Row, New York, 1970.

48. C. Barnard, *The Function of the Executive*, Harvard University Press, Cambridge, 1962.

49. D. McGregor, *The Human Side of Enterprise*, McGraw-Hill, New York, 1960.

50. P. Drucker, *The Practice of Management*, Harper & Row, New York, 1954.

51. G. Morgan, *Images of Organization*, chap. 2.

52. H. G. Frederickson, *New Public Administration*, p. 22.

53. N. Henry, *Public Administration*, p. 67.

54. H. A. Simon, *Administrative Behavior*, chap. II.

55. H. A. Simon, *Administrative Behavior*, p. 253.

56. J. Perry and K. L. Kraemer, Research Methodology in *Pub. Admin. Rev*: 1975–1984, *Research in Public Administration* (White and Adams, eds.), p. 107.

57. K. Popper, *Objective Knowledge: An Evolutionary Approach*, Oxford University Press, New York, 1972, chap. 1.
58. K. Popper, *The Logic of Scientific Discovery*, Harper & Row, New York, 1959.
59. M. Friedman, *Essays in Positive Economics*, University of Chicago Press, 1957.
60. H. A. Simon, *Models of Bounded Rationality* 2 vol., MIT Press, 1982–86.
61. A. Tversky and D. Kahneman, Rational choice and the framing of decisions, *J. of Bus.*: 59, S251–78, 1986.
62. R. P. Abelson and A. Levi, Decision Making and Decision Theory, *Handbook of Social Psychology*, G. Lindzey and E. Aronson (eds.), Random House, New York, 1985.
63. K. I. Vaughn, *Austrian Economics in America*, Cambridge University Press, New York, 1994.
64. D. P. Green and I. Shapiro, *Pathologies of Rational Choice: A Critique of Applications of Rational Choice in Political Science*, Yale University Press, New Haven, 1994, pp. 30–32.
65. Lowi and Simon on Political Science, Public Administration, Rationality and Public Choice, *J. of Pub. Admin. Research and Theory*: 2, 107, 1992.
66. D. P. Green and I. Shapiro, *Pathologies of Rational Choice*, p. 3.
67. D. P. Green and I. Shapiro, *Pathologies of Rational Choice*.
68. A. Downs, *Inside Bureaucracy*, Little, Brown, & Co., Boston, 1967.
69. W. A. Niskanen, *Bureaucracy and Representative Government*, Aldine-Atherton, Chicago, 1971; also reprinted in W. A. Niskanen, *Bureaucracy and Public Economics*, Edward Elgar, Brookfield, VT, 1994.
70. L. von Mises, *Bureaucracy*, Yale University Press, New Haven, 1944.
71. G. Tullock, *The Politics of Bureaucracy*, Public Affairs Press, Washington, D.C., 1965.
72. S. Kelman, *Making Public Policy: A Hopeful View of American Government*, Basic Books, New York, 1987.
73. N. S. Lind, An empirical test of Anthony Downs' theory of bureaucratic decision-making, paper presented to the annual meeting of the American Political Science Association, September 1989.
74. N. S. Lind, An Empirical Test of Anthony Downs' Theory, p. 16.
75. W. A. Niskanen, *Bureaucracy and Representative Government*, p. 33.
76. J.-E. Lane (ed.), *Bureaucracy and Public Choice*, Sage, London, 1987.
77. J.-L. Migué and G. Bélanger, Towards a General Theory of Managerial Discretion, *Public Choice*: 17; 1974.
78. A. Briton, *The Logic of Bureaucratic Conduct*, Cambridge University Press, New York, 1982.
79. A. Blais and S. Dion (eds.), *The Budget-Maximizing Bureaucrat: Appraisals and Evidence*, University of Pittsburgh Press, Pittsburgh, 1991.
80. P. Dunleavy, *Democracy, Bureaucracy and Public Choice*, Harvester, New York, 1991.
81. I. MacLean, *Public Choice: An Introduction*, Blackwell, Oxford, 1987, chap. 5.
82. R. Young, Budget Size and Bureaucratic Careers, *The Budget-Maximizing Bureaucrat: Appraisals and Evidence*, p. 52.
83. W. A. Niskanen, *Bureaucracy and Public Economics*.
84. V. Ostrom, *The Intellectual Crisis in American Public Administration*, University of Alabama Press, University, 1973.
85. J. M. Buchanan, *Liberty, Market and State: Political Economy in the 1980s*, Harvester, New York, 1986.
86. C. Wolf, Jr., *Markets or Governments: Choosing Between Imperfect Alternatives*, MIT Press, Cambridge, 1991.
87. P. Self, *Government by the Market: The Politics of Public Choice*, Westview, Boulder, 1993.
88. E. Ostrom, *Governing the Commons: The Evolution of Institutions for Collective Action*, Cambridge University Press, New York, 1990.
89. D. F. Bromley (ed.), *Making the Commons Work: Theory, Practice, and Policy*, Institute for Contemporary Studies Press, San Francisco, 1992.

90. W. Blomquist, *Dividing the Waters: Governing Groundwaters in Southern California*, Institute for Contemporary Studies, San Francisco, 1992.

91. M. Sproule-Jones, *Government at Work: Canadian Parliamentary Federalism and its Public Policy Effects*, University of Toronto Press, Toronto, 1993.

92. E. A. Lindquist, Postmodern politics and policy sciences, *Optimum*: 24-1; 42–50, 1993.

93. R. D. French, Postmodern government, *Optimum* 23-1 (Summer 1992) 43–51.

94. C. E. Lindblom, *Inquiry and Change*, Yale University Press, New Haven, 1990.

95. M. E. Hawkesworth, *Theoretical Issues in Policy Analysis*, SUNY Press, Albany, N.Y, 1988.

96. E. C. Banfield, Policy sciences as metaphysical madness, *Bureaucrats, Policy Analysis, Statesmen: Who Leads?*, R. A. Goldwin, (ed.), American Enterprise Institute for Public Policy Research, Washington, D.C., 1980.

97. D. Osborne and T. Gaebler, *Reinventing Government: How the Entrepreneurial Spirit is Transforming the Public Sector*, Addison-Wesley, Reading, 1992.

98. M. Barzelay, *Breaking Through Bureaucracy*, University of California Press, Berkeley, 1992.

99. R. B. Denhardt, *The Pursuit of Significance: Strategies for Managerial Success in Public Organizations*, Wadsworth Publishing, Belmont, 1993.

100. L. Dobuzinskis, Modernist and postmodernist metaphors of the policy process: Control and stability vs. chaos and reflexive understanding, *Pol. Sci.*: 25, 355–380, 1992.

101. B. G. Peters, New visions of government and the public service, *New Paradigms for Government: Issues for the Changing Public Service*, P. W. Ingraham and B. S. Romzeck, (eds.) Jossey-Bass, San Francisco, 1994.

102. R. B. Denhardt, *The Pursuit of Significance*, chap. 4.

103. R. Rorty, *Philosophy and the Mirror of Nature*, Princeton University Press, Princeton, N.J., 1979.

104. D. Stone, *Policy Paradox and Political Reason*, Harper Collins, New York, 1988.

105. R. B. Denhardt, *The Pursuit of Significance*, chap. 3.

106. National Performance Review, *From Red Tape to Results: Creating a Government that Works Better and Costs Less*, Random House, New York, 1993.

107. Canada (government of), *Public Service 2000, The Renewal of the Public Service of Canada*, Supply and Service, Ottawa, 1989.

108. F. Marini (ed.), *Toward a New Public Administration: The Minnowbrook Conference*, Chandler Publishing Co., San Francisco, 1971.

109. H. G. Frederickson, *New Public Administration*, p. xii.

110. D. J. Amy, Can policy analysis be ethical?, *Confronting Values in Policy Analysis: The Politics of Criteria*, Sage, Newbury Park, 1987, p. 56.

111. R. B. Westbrook, *John Dewey and American Democracy*, Cornell, Ithaca, 1991, chap. 9.

112. F. Marini, Introduction, *Public Management in an Interconnected World*, M. T. Bailey and R. T. Mayer (eds.), Greenwood Press, New York, 1992.

113. M. Barzelay, *Breaking Through Bureaucracy*, p. 107.

114. National Performance Review, *From Red Tape to Results*, chap. 2.

115. Public Service 2000, *Service to the Public Task Force Report*, Ottawa, October 12, 1990, p. 2.

116. S. Cohen and R. Brand, *Total Quality Management in Government*, Jossey-Bass, San Francisco, 1993.

117. G. J. Miller, *Managerial Dilemmas: The Political Economy of Hierarchy*, Cambridge University Press, New York, 1992.

118. P. M. Senge, *The Fifth Discipline: The Art and Practice of the Learning Organization*, Doubleday, New York, 1990.

119. National Performance Review, *From Red Tape to Results*, chap. 3.

120. P. De Celles, Managing change: Going around in circles . . . but in the right direction, *Optimum* 26-1, 32, 1995.

121. K. Kernaghan, Empowerment and public administration: Revolutionary advance or passing Fancy?, *Canadian Public Administration*: 35, 194–214, 1992.

122. D. J. Savoie, What is wrong with the new public management? *Canadian Public Administration:* 38 112–121, 1995.

123. A. Roberts, "Civic discovery" as a rhetorical strategy, *J. of Pol. Anal. and Man.:* 14, 291–307, 1995.

124. C. Thayer, Organization Theory as Epistemology: Transcending Hierarchy and Objectivity, *Organization Theory and the New Public Administration,* C. Bellone (ed.), Allyn and Bacon, Boston, 1980.

125. D. H. Rosenbloom and B. H. Ross, Administrative Theory, Political Power, and Government Reform, *New Paradigms for Government,* Ingraham and Romzeck (eds.), p. 159.

126. J. D. White, On the Growth of Knowledge in Public Administration, *Research in Public Administration,* J. D. White and G. b. Adams (eds.), Sage, Thousand Oaks, 1994, p. 43.

127. R. B. Denhart, Toward a Critical Theory of Public Organization, *Pub. Admin. Rev.:* 41, 628–636, 1981.

128. J. D. White, Knowledge development and use in public administration: View from postpositivism, poststructuralism, and postmodernism, *Public Management in an Interconnected World,* M. T. Bailey and R. T. Mayer (eds.), Greenwood Press, New York, 1992, p. 172.

129. National Performance Review, *Creating a Government that Costs Less and Works Better: Status Report,* U.S. Government Printing Office, Washington, D.C., 1994.

130. Public Service 2000, *A Report on Progress* (by P. M. Tellier), Supply and Services, Ottawa, 1992.

131. S. Maynard-Moody and M. Kelly, Stories public managers tell about elected officials: Making sense of the politics-administration dichotomy, *Public Management: The State of the Art,* B. Bozeman (ed.) Jossey-Bass, San Francisco, 1993, p. 71.

132. Perry and Kraemer, Research Methodology, p. 106.

133. M. T. Bailey, Do physicists use case studies? Thoughts on research in public administration, *Research in Public Administration* White, and Adams (eds.), p. 192.

134. R. P. Hummel, *The Bureacratic Experience* 3rd ed., St. Martins, New York, 1987.

135. R. P. Hummel, Uncovering validity criteria for stories managers hear and tell, *Rev. of Pub. Admin.:* 20, 303–314, 1990.

136. R. P. Hummel, Stories managers tell: Why they are as valid as science, *Pub. Admin. Rev.:* 51, 31–41, 1991.

137. D. Schon, *The Reflective Practioner: How Professionals Think in Action,* Basic Books, New York, 1983.3

138. M. S. Feldman, *Order without Design: Information Production and Policy Making,* Stanford University Press, Stanford, 1989.

139. S. Maynard-Moody and D. S. Stull, The symbolic side of policy analysis: Interpreting policy change in a health department, *Confronting Values in Policy Analysis: The Politics of Criteria,* F. Fisher and F. Forester (eds.), Sage, Newbury Park, 1987.

140. J. Doherty, J. Elspeth, and M. Malek, *Postmodernism and the Social Sciences,* St. Martin's, New York, 1992.

141. M. Foucault, *Power/Knowledge: Selected Interviews and Other Writings,* C. Gordon (ed.), Pantheon, New York, 1980.

142. S. Toulmin, *The Return to Cosmology: Postmodern Science and the Theology of Nature,* University of California Press, Berkeley, 1982.

143   E. Jantsch, *Design for Evolution: Self-Organization and Planning in the Life of Human Systems,* Braziller, New York, 1975.

144   E. Laszlo, *The Age of Bifurcation: Understanding the Changing World,* Gordon and Breach, Philadelphia, 1991.

145. Popper, *Objective Knowledge,* chap. 6.

146. R. Lewin, *Complexity: Life at the Edge of Chaos,* Macmillan, New York, 1992.

147. M. M. Waldrop, *Complexity: The Emerging Science at the Edge of Order and Chaos,* Simon and Schuster, New York, 1992.

148. J. Gleick, *Chaos: Making a New Science*, Penguin Books, New York, 1987.
149   M. Rothschild, *Bionomics: The Inevitability of Capitalism*, Henry Holt, New York, 1990, pp. 255–256.
150   F. A. Hayek, *Rules and Order*, University of Chicago Press, Chicago, 1973.
151   R. Ruthen, Adapting to Complexity, *Scientific American?* 130–140, Jan., 1993.
152   G. diZerega, Democracy as a Spontaneous Order, *Critical Review:* 3, 206–240, 1989.
153. G. A. Daneke, A Science of Public Administration?, *Research in Public Administration*, White and Adams (eds.).
154. W. A. Treadwell, Fuzzy Set Theory Movement in the Social Sciences, *Pub. Admin. Rev.:* 55, 91–98, 1995.
155. L. Dobuzinskis, Modernist and postmodernist metaphors of the policy process.
156   Morgan, *Images of Organizations*, chaps. 4 and 8.
157. L. D. Kiel, The Nonlinear Paradigm: Advancing Paradigmatic Progress in the Policy Sciences, *Systems Research:* 9, 27–42, 1992.
158. L. D. Kiel, *Managing Chaos and Complexity in Government*, Jossey-Bass, San Francisco, 1994.
159. L. D. Kiel, *Managing Chaos and Complexity*, pp. 52–63.

20

ON THE LANGUAGE OF BUREAUCRACY
Postmodernism, Plain English, and Wittgenstein

Robert P. Watson
University of Hawaii at Hilo, Hilo, Hawaii

"As politicians know only too well but social scientists too often forget, public policy is made of language."

> Giandomenico Majone
> From *Evidence, Argument, and Persuasion
> in the Policy Process* (1989)

I. "BUREAUCRATESE," THE LANGUAGE OF GOVERNMENT

"It is a tricky problem to find the particular calibration in timing that would be appropriate to stem the acceleration in risk premiums created by falling incomes without prematurely aborting the decline in the inflation-generated premiums" (1). The previous quote was a statement made by Mr. Alan Greenspan during testimony before the Congress in 1974, years before he would become the Federal Reserve Board Chair. A few years after Greenspan's testimony, President Jimmy Carter proposed new urban policy that was designed "to strengthen linkages among macro-economic sectoral place-oriented economies" (2). The previous quotes, where Mr. Greenspan was discussing economic policy and Mr. Carter was attempting to assist cities, are used as examples of "bureaucratese," or the doublespeak that often passes for language in government.

In official public discourse and public documents taxes have become "revenue enhancements" or "user fees" and dumps are known as "public waste reception centers." The use of such bureaucratic language is thought to be on the rise and is found not only in political speech but has become the language of bureaucracy (3). Such misuse of the English language occurs at all levels of government in the United States and is found in governments throughout the world.

Yet, despite the widespread use of bureaucratese, there has been insufficient research devoted to the study of the language of bureaucracy and little is known about its effect. This chapter examines the phenomenon of bureaucratic doublespeak by analyzing the use and misuse of language in public organizations. Theories on public discourse, language, and the meaning of words as well as a model for understanding bureaucratese are presented. Numerous problems associated with the misuse of language in public organizations including the distortion of meaning and reality, the effect of distancing one from their actions and sense of personal responsibility, and the use of language as a form of deception to misinform and manipulate are discussed.

Many of the problems of public administration are to be traced to, and found in, the language of bureaucracy (4). The language of bureaucracy is not simply a way to articulate the practices of government, but language shapes the thoughts of bureaucrats and frames the nature of public issues. Language shapes our world view and, as such, the language of bureaucracy has guided the practice and study of public administration and has informed the development of theories of public organizations. To explore this dilemma and address the problems associated with the misuse of language, a better understanding of language and discourse is necessary. To conceptualize the nature of bureaucratic language, this chapter draws from the writings on language and meaning of the philosopher Wittgenstein and employs a postmodernist critic of the language of bureaucracy. A new language of public administration, one based in plain English and informed by a postmodern language of thought, is a precondition to moving toward a new practice of public administration.

II. THE USE AND MISUSE OF LANGUAGE IN GOVERNMENT

Public bureaucracy plays an active role in the lives of all Americans. Accordingly, there is perhaps no other institution in America that is placed under more media and public scrutiny than government bureaucracy, the federal bureaucracy in particular. It is not surprising then that there is perhaps no other institution more maligned than public bureaucracy. Whether this reputation is deserved or not can be debated, however, that the perception of inefficient, impersonal, and incompetent public organizations exists is beyond question. There are several reasons for the general public hostility toward, and mistrust of, public bureaucracy. Yet, one of the factors that is often overlooked by scholars of public administration and public bureaucrats interested in the phenomenon of "bureaucracy bashing" is the language of bureaucracy.

The language of bureaucracy known as "bureaucratese" or "bureaucratic doublespeak" has been described by various critics and scholars of bureaucracy as "a strange and somewhat threatening foreign language" (5). "a language which pretends to communicate but really does not" (6), and "the misuse of words by implicit redefinition" (7). Bureaucratic doublespeak has been ridiculed as the art of "talking out of both sides of one's mouth" (8). As such, it "makes the bad seem good, the negative appear positive, and the unpleasant appear attractive or at least tolerable" (9).

Bureaucratese can be defined as the misuse of language in official public discourse and public documents by employees of government. This misuse is not by coincidence or done inadvertently, but rather, it is employed by design and with the purposes of: a. distorting or reversing the meaning of a word or proposition so as to confuse the audience into perceiving, for example, failure as success and bad as good; b. avoiding, minimizing, or shifting responsibility for one's actions to avoid criticism; and c. limiting thought or manipulating the language of thought in a way that frames discussion of the phenomenon favorably for the government or the particular official in question.

Some scholars conceptualize bureaucratese as but one element of public doublespeak, along with other forms of doublespeak like euphemisms, jargon, and inflated language (10). However, bureaucratese, herein, is considered to be the general misuse of language in the public sector and it encompasses related misuses of language such as doublespeak, euphemisms, and jargon. It is a hybrid language of euphemisms, jargon, and abstractions that tends toward the meaningless and pompous. In the popular press various manifestations of bureaucratese have been referred to as "bureauquack," "bureaucratic officialese," "legalese," "Pentagonese," and more commonly "gobbledygook," a term coined by former Texas Congressman Maury Maverick after experiencing bureaucratic terminology that he felt made about as much sense as the gobble of a turkey (11).

Table 1 offers an illustration of bureaucratic doublespeak that is devoid of meaning, can be used to confuse rather than to communicate, and talks without saying anything (12). The four columns in the table are meant to be interchangeable, as one constructs various phrases of bureaucratese.

Bureaucratese has been compared to the "newspeak" used in George Orwell's *1984* as the language of authoritarian manipulation (13). It has also been likened to the speech of the Eighteenth Century figure Mrs. Malaprop from the Richard Sheridan comedy *The Rivals* who misuses and destroys the English language (14). Like Mrs. Malaprop, public administrators and public officials confuse and distort the meaning of words and leave the listener or reader confused. Numerous critical and humorous books and essays have even emerged such as "The Washington Phrasebook" and the "Doublespeak Dictionary" that lampoon bureaucratese and compile lists of words used in public discourse (15).

Bureaucratese is, however, not to be confused with "political correctness" or seen as innocent and overly respectful terminology (16). Whereas bureaucratese is used to intentionally distort meaning or confuse listeners, the use of "physically challenged" in place of "handicapped," for example, is done neither to distort nor to confuse. The same can be said of using the words "deceased" or "passed away" in place of "dead," a substitution that

Table 1 Doublespeak in Public Organizations

Column I	Column II	Column III	Column IV
Ladies and gentlemen,	the realization of the program's goals	leads us to reexamine	existing fiscal and administrative conditions
Equally important,	the complexity and diversity of the committee's areas of concentration	have played a vital role in determining	areas of future development
At the same time,	the constant growth in the quality and scope of our activity	directly affects the development and advancement of	the attitudes of key members regarding their own work
Still, let us not forget that	the infrastructure of the organization	requires the clarification and determination of	a participatory system
Thus,	the new shape of organizational activity	insures the participation of key members in	new proposals

Source: J. R. Killingsworth, Idle talk in modern organizations, *Admin. and Soc.*: 16, 346–384, p. 352, 1984.

Table 2   Language Use Model

Speech In Bureaucracy	Speech In Society
One-dimensional	Reciprocal
Acausal	Causal and contextual
Analogous	Concrete
General	Particular
Referential	Experiential
Reality-imposing	Reality-constructing

Source: R. P. Hummel, *The Bureaucratic Experience: A Critique of Life in the Modern Organization*, New York: St. Martin's Press, 1994.

serves only to comfort and show respect without distorting meaning. Politically correct terms such as "police officer" instead of "policeman" or "biracial" instead of "mulatto" or "half-breed" likewise fall outside of this definition of bureaucratese.

Hummel offers a model of the language of bureaucracy that is useful for understanding the uses and misuses of language in public organizations (17). In Table 2 he contrasts the language of bureaucracy and the language used in society. Hummel sees the use of language in bureaucracy as one-dimensional and, as such, forcing or expecting citizens dealing with government to adjust to what is said to them, as opposed to a more reciprocal, two-way from of communication. Bureaucratese talks *at* you, not *with* you. The function of reasoning in bureaucratese is by analogy, in that what is said is bound by the organization and is internal to that organization. Thinking is by analogy and reasoning is through comparison. Yet, a bureaucrat's reference point is not the people they are serving or even the context or environment in which discourse occurs, in as much as the use of bureaucratese imposes an *ideal* form that emerges over the *actual* environment and context. Normal communication is contextual in that what one says is given meaning by the context in which it is spoken and context is based on the shared experiences of both speaker and listener. However, bureaucratese imposes context and a false order or reality on things.

A.   Typology of Bureaucratese

A typology of bureaucratese is developed so that we can conceptualize the nature of the misuse of language in government. This typology draws on the work of William Lutz, a major voice in the "plain English" movement, who offers what can be considered a model of the forms of doublespeak found in the public sector (18). The typology also borrows from Carl Wayne Hensley, a communications scholar, who cautions against the use of bureaucratese and doublespeak in public speaking and identifies common misuses of language in public discourse (19). The following typology frames bureaucratese as four distinct areas of language misuse.

1.   Euphemisms

Euphemisms are words or phrases that serve to soften or distort harsh realities. A euphemism, when used in place of an unpleasant incident or fact, serves to mislead or deceive. The euphemism downplays the actual meaning or intent of the phenomenon. For example, if "arbitrary deprivation of life" is used in place of "killing," it might minimize the harshness and the effect of the act. It could also confuse the listener or make the act sound as if it is legitimate and acceptable. This can also be seen in the Pentagon's terminology of "incontinent ordinance" or "collateral casualties," used to describe bombings that mistakenly kill civilians.

2.   Jargon and "Technical-speak"

Jargon is specialized language used by members of a profession or those in a select group or organization. While jargon might be necessary for technical communication among members or might be widely understood within the organization, it is possible that it is utterly unknown by nonmembers. It could also function to give a false sense of authority to the speaker. An example comes from the language of security clearances in government. To "run the traps" means to conduct a security clearance which is also known as a "screening," a "check," or "clearing" someone, all forms of bureaucratic gerunds. The bureaucracy, perhaps more than any other institution, ought to be open and accessible to the entire citizenry. When public administrators use jargon that is unfamiliar to the general public it might place public services out of the reach of many people by misrepresenting the availability and nature of such services. It could also function to limit civic participation in government.

Jargon can amount to extremely technical and pseudo-scientific terms. Often such jargon has emerged only recently, borrowed from pop culture or new technologies. The problem is that, without a shared history of the word by the producers and consumers of this technical-speak, meaning cannot exist, especially for those unfamiliar with the technology or cultural reference. Examples include words like "interface," "synergy," "network," "download," and "proactive." Bureaucratic language often adds "isms," "izes," "ations," and "ages" to words that could otherwise be stated in their original form and, in so doing, can confuse or alter the original meaning. For instance, stopping work has become "a work stoppage." Speaking or saying something has become a "verbalization" and bureaucratic improvements "optimize" resources. The excessive misuse of gerunds often accompanies jargon and technical-speak. A gerund is a word that has the characteristics of both noun and verb. An example is using a verb or the verbal form of a word as a noun by ending it in "ing." In bureaucratese, a report is a "finding," using the verb to "find" as a noun. Cliches and acronyms also appear with regularity in bureaucratese. An acronym is a word formed from the first letters of words and is, arguably, one of the most widely used and well known features of bureaucratic language. To the general public, the language of IGR, OSHA, ADA, GAO, ZBB, and CDBGs sounds like alphabet soup.

3.   Complex Syntax

Syntax is the way in which words are used together to form phrases. A common critique of bureaucratic language is the tendency to use confusing syntax (20). Bureaucratese lacks style and precision and appears to go to great lengths to avoid saying something in a plain, simple manner (21). While it may sound impressive, such language usually overwhelms the listener and leaves them uncertain of what was actually being said (22). Examples of complex syntax can be seen in the quotes used in the opening paragraph of this chapter.

4.   Voluminosity and "Bloating"

Voluminosity and bloating refer to the adding of unnecessary or redundant words to communication that could otherwise be said succinctly and in plain English. Using "imports into this country" or "foreign imports" in place of simply "imports" bloats the sentence.

Dorney and Lutz even define bureaucratese as "the voluminous use of words." Such language may overwhelm the audience (23).

Bloating is also when a speaker's use of words is inflated so as to exaggerate the average or make the ordinary seem extraordinary, with the purpose of impressing or confusing the audience. Examples of bloating include referring to janitors or custodial staff as "environmental hygienists" or "sanitation engineers," or calling a routine trip a "fact finding mission," or when diplomatic negotiators from the two sides do not even agree to meet in the same room they are said to still be conducting "proximity talks." Perhaps the best case for depicting the excesses of bureaucratic language can be seen in the federal specifications for a mousetrap that amounted to 700 pages, weighing in at over 3 pounds (24).

Having defined bureaucratese and conceptualized its common forms of usage, there are several problems resulting from the misuse of language in public organizations that need to be addressed.

B.   Distancing Effect of Bureaucratese

A central problem of bureaucratese is that it distances the citizens from their government. The problem of distancing can be seen in four ways: 1. the impersonality of the language, and thus, the very act and exchange become impersonal; 2. removing a sense of personal responsibility for one's actions because of language; 3. public misunderstanding of the meaning and message; and 4. the development of a closed society within the bureaucracy.

1.   Impersonality

Through the use of bureaucratese, the listener is distanced from speaker. Communication exists in third person and is governed by the need for uniformity and sterility. Such bureaucratic language reduces the human element of communication (25). Unfortunately, minus the humaneness, the nature of bureaucratic language is without human values. The rules of the bureaucracy do the talking or communicating for the individual, leaving the speaker as accidental to the message and reducing the margin of flexibility and reciprocity in the message. While it is thought that the messenger shapes the message, in bureaucracy the speaker is detached from the message and from the act. The message becomes an institutional message without a "person" "behind" the message. Official public communication and discourse becomes hierarchical and authoritarian.

2.   Removing Responsibility

When "client" or "case" is substituted for "human" or the individual receiving the public service, the speaker becomes distanced from the responsibility of the act. There exists a psychological proximity to the action that is reduced through the use of impersonal language. The same phenomenon occurs in a larger societal sense when a term like "ordinance" is used for "bombs" and "servicing the target" replaces the reality of the act of "killing."

The institutional message "communicated" from bureaucracy is made sterile so as to be protected from humans and, in turn, public policy actors are "protected" from the reality and responsibility of the act and the message. This is perpetuated when spokespersons are used to communicate messages. In normal communication and language, what is said is not separated from who said it (26). After all, the purpose of language is usually to convey the speaker's intentions. This cannot be said about bureaucratese.

3. Misunderstanding

Perhaps the most obvious problems caused by the use of bureaucratese are that meaning and message are separated and communication is not understood by the public. This may be the intent of the message and the messenger. Even the most rudimentary aspects of communication such as identifying who is saying what to whom and why are unclear. The Reagan Administration's use of "negative economic growth," for instance, to describe the recession the country faced shortly into the President's first term does not clearly describe the economic situation to the general public.

4. Development of a Closed-society

Only insiders understand the jargon and technical-speak of their profession or organization. Excessive use of it alienates outsiders which, for the bureaucracy, includes the general public, and could cause a fortress mentality among users (27). The open or external systems models that the field of public administration strives for are undercut by organizational language that is inherently inward-looking. The elevation of bureaucratese to nearly a secret professional language may also encourage conformity within the organization.

The nature of bureaucracy may be such that it can only respond to well defined needs or demands. If so, the use of bureaucratese may act to further limit bureaucracy's ability to respond to complex needs and demands because the needs will be inadequately and poorly defined.

C.   Deception Effect of Bureaucratese

Another problem associated with the use of bureaucratese is deception. Three areas of language deception are: 1. misinformation; 2. using language to manipulate the audience; and 3. creating a false sense of credibility by using inflated language.

1.   Misinformation

Misinformation occurs all too commonly in politics but it is also found in the bureaucracy. Whether overtly or unintentionally, bureaucratese distorts reality. Selective language makes bad appear good, or at least okay. Misinformation fosters suspicion and cynicism, especially when it is overt manipulation, as the public begins to feel that they should believe nothing that is said by public officials. This could breed a crisis of apathy, alienation, and a feeling of animosity toward bureaucracy. An example of misinformation was the official reference of the American military "excursion" or "incursion" into Grenada in the 1980s as a "Caribbean Peace Keeping Force" that simply performed a "predawn vertical insertion" (28). Not only would the public potentially be misinformed about the nature of the "force" and the activity but there would certainly be less public hostility of this policy than of, say, a military "invasion" of a sovereign state by American forces.

Another example of the use of bureaucratic misinformation pertains to the issue of possible cuts in social security during the 1980s. Some Americans opposed to such a policy suspected President Reagan of favoring cuts. To "clarify" his position and disarm his critics, the President provided the following statement: "I will not stand by and see those of you who are dependent on social security deprived of the benefits you've worked so hard to earn. You will continue to receive your checks in the full amount due to you." While such a statement would appear straight forward and clear, when given a bureaucratese spin, this may not be the case. A Presidential spokesperson offered "clarification" shortly after the statement was issued that was less supportive of social security, by saying that the President's comment meant that he was still trying to determine exactly who was "dependent" on social security, who had indeed "earned" the benefits, and how much the "full amount due" should be (29). There is the very real potential that many Americans were "misinformed" by the original official statement.

2.   Manipulation

It is through language that we understand each other. Yet, if organizations and not humans control language, language can be used as a tool to control and influence at a level larger than that of person to person. Such use of language does not permit feedback or questions and limits two-way communication to one-way manipulation. Information does not flow back up the hierarchy, but only down the ladder, so-to-speak. Bureaucratese also permits management to interpret meaning in several different ways.

Often, such language is not even noticed, as many forms of bureaucratese have found their way into our everyday vocabulary. It has become an accepted part of our culture. For example, public housing has become "sub-standard housing," a term that is both a polite way of describing conditions that often approach a near warehousing of the poor and one that implies society's acceptance of what is an unacceptable condition of housing. The "poor" have become the "disadvantaged," certainly a less problematic condition and one that suggests a handicap needing public attention and assistance.

This language of authority can also be seen in the renaming of the "Department of War" to the "Department of Defense." It is harder, after all, to complain about something when one is not sure what that something is or if the phenomenon appears to be something else. Environmentalists would not be as upset with a forest policy dubbed an "over-mature tree harvest" rather than simply a program of cutting old-growth forests, nor if an administration were to announce its commitment to "intensive forest management," a much more palpable term than "clear cutting" or unmitigated and subsidized timbering, would such a policy of "management" be as readily understood or opposed. Military "peacekeeping" or "rescue" missions are more popular in this day and age of public support than "invasions" and "acts of aggression" that may compromise international human rights agreements or national sovereignty.

3.   Development of Artificial Credibility

The jargon of bureaucratese obscures meaning for the general public and technical sounding terms may serve to legitimize or lend a sense of artificial credibility to something not deserving legitimacy. For example, the prevalence of "straw" polls around election time would seem to those untrained in survey research or political polling to suggest that they are somehow reliable and scientific instruments for gauging public opinion, despite the possible connection of the word "straw" with that which is less than credible. Calling the occupation an "environmental hygienist" and not a "janitor" might lend an inflated sense of importance or credibility to the generally low-paying and unglamourous work.

III.   ON LANGUAGE

A large body of literature exists on the nature of language and discourse. It is too comprehensive to hope to summarize in this chapter but for the purposes of this work an overview of basic theories of language and discourse is presented. Foundational models of linguistics can be used to guide the analysis of the language of bureaucracy.

Table 3 Linguistic Paradigms

Formalist	Functionalist
language as a mental phenomenon	language as s societal phenomenon
language studied as autonomous system	language studied as it relates to social functions
universals of language come from common genetic linguistic aspect of human species	universals of language come from generalities in the uses and structure of language in human society
child's language capability comes from some natural human capacity to learn language	child's language capability comes from their communicative and social needs in society

Source: D. Schriffin, *Approaches to Discourse*, Cambridge, Massachusetts: Blackwell, 1994.

A. Formalist-Functionalist Linguistics Paradigm

Linguistics is the study of the nature and structure of human speech. Conceptually, one can study or summarize the field of linguistics by using the linguistic paradigm shown in Table 3 between the "Formalist" school and the "Functionalist" school of linguistics. The Formalist school (30) is similar to, and at times known as, "Structuralist" linguistics (31) or "a priori grammar," (32) and the Functionalist school (33) is related to "Emergent" linguistics (34) and "Interactive" linguistics (35). These two schools make assumptions about the fundamental objectives of linguistic theory and offer methods for, and approaches to, the study of language and human speech.

The Formalist model recognizes that language has social and cognitive features and functions but considers these as not having a major impact on or altering the organization of language. Whereas, Functionalists argue that society and external features definitely shape the organization of language. Language would then have functions that are apart from the linguistic system itself.

B. Theories of Language and Discourse

In addition to these two primary models of linguistics, several theories exist that forward notions about the use and meaning of language that are applicable to the study of the language of bureaucracy.

1. Speech Act Theory

Developed by the philosophers John Austin and John Searle, Speech Act theory forwards the notion that language is used not merely to describe the world and phenomena, but that it serves many other purposes and actions (36). This is apparent through the actual spoken word or utterance. For example, language can question, request, demand, or promise. Language can perform multiple activities and combinations of the above items simultaneously.

Speech Act theory focusses on the underlying conditions necessary to perform the act of speech. To know the literal meaning of words, one must understand the factors that underlie discourse. There are problems associated with Speech Act theory such as forms of indirect speech, contextual concerns, and the multifunctionality of language.

2. Interactional Sociolinguistics

Associated with John Gumperz, Interactional Sociolinguistics has its roots in anthropology, linguistics, and sociology (37). It asks the question of how people from different cultures share a basic grammatical knowledge of language yet contextualize language in vastly different ways. As such, there are differing messages and meanings. The interactional school looks at the actual words and language used and the social context of discourse. Interactional sociolinguistics theorist Erving Goffman studies how language is used in certain situations in our social lives (38).

The context and structure of language is important to interactional sociolinguists in that people use different words and speak differently depending on to whom one is speaking, the relationship of the speaker to the listener, and the environment in which the discourse takes place. Contextual matters even include how the speaker and listener are standing or whether they are facing one another. The theory forwards the notion that interpretation and interaction are related and based on the relationship of social and linguistic meaning.

3.   Ethnography of Communication

Based in the field anthropology, this school seeks explanations of meaning and behavior. Dell Hymes, for example, looks at "communicative competence," or the cultural, linguistic, social, and psychological knowledge that determines what is considered to be accepted use of language (39). In other words, it studies that which guides the use of everyday language, what constitutes right from wrong usage, and common forms of discourse such as public speaking.

Concepts of communication differ from culture to culture, as concepts of communication depend on cultural values. As such, communication is never completely free of the bounds of culture, values, and beliefs. Other voices in this school argue that grammar reflects culture (40) and that the influence of culture is seen in other forms of communication (41) including even silence (42).

4.   Pragmatic School

This school, which is associated with H. P. Grice, explores the differences in meaning of language and words and identifies distinctions in types of meaning (43). It analyzes the meaning of the speaker's words at the level of the actual utterances. As such, the analysis is at the level of the word and sentence itself, rather than the whole text, the language, or the culture.

5.   Conversation Analysis

Conversation analysis draws from sociology and the philosophical school of phenomenology and is associated with Harold Garfinkle (44). It considers the ways that people in a society develop a sense of social order and maintains that conversation assists in the creation of this order. Language is believed to both create a social order and social context and, in turn, be influenced by the social order. The theory looks to make generalizations about social conduct and social order through analysis of language and communication.

Within conversation itself, there also exists a unique structure and sense of order. There is, in other words, an order by which people talk to one another. Even within telephone conversations, for example, there is a specific order and an established etiquette (45).

6.   Variation Analysis

The variationist school, as affiliated with William Labov, argues that linguistic variation is a product of both social and linguistic factors (46). The school uses the systematic analysis of what is known as "speech communities" to uncover the nature of variation in language. The name of this theory derives from the traditional approach of studying different ways of saying the same thing, known technically as "semantically equivalent variants."

In speech there emerges formal patterns. An interest of this school is how and why this phenomenon occurs and how such patterns are shaped by the narrative or utterance. To determine this, variation analysts separate the text of what is said into sections and each section is then considered to be a part of the structure that has a certain function.

Through these approaches to the study of language, it is evident that language is multifunctional. Language has many uses and forms and not only can one word have a variety of meanings, but there are numerous ways to say the same thing. To know the meaning of words and to assess the language one must examine the culture and context within which communication takes place.

C.   Wittgenstein on Language

I.   Wittgenstein, the Philosopher

Perhaps no philosopher has had such a profound influence on our understanding of language than Ludwig Wittgenstein (47). His work on the meaning and use of language served to refocus the very course of modern philosophic thought in the West away from a theory of knowledge to the study of meaning (48). Wittgenstein held that problems arise in philosophy when the logic behind what is said is misunderstood. He questioned the existing methods of philosophy and thought that his work offered the definitive solution to the problems of philosophy (49). Wittgenstein saw the fundamental problem or illusion that limited our ability to know the truth as one of language. He sought the essence of human language and asked the question: How do sentences and words express what they do? His thoughts and writings on language have found an audience across many disciplines including religion, mathematics, psychology, and linguistics. However, the originality of his work on the essence of language and his ideas have defied attempts to pigeon-hole him into conventional "isms" or schools of thought and there remains disagreement by those interpreting his work (50).

Wittgenstein felt that historically philosophers had approached the discipline and problems of philosophy with preconceived notions about how things should be. This subconscious conception guided their questioning and thus influenced the answers to their questions, yet was often left unexamined. Wittgenstein sought to correct this by looking at the source of philosophic thinking: language. Moreover, he knew that there was a difference between the essence of language and language as we all know and use it.

Wittgenstein, the philosopher, was influenced by Wittgenstein, the man. It has been said that to know Wittgenstein's work, one must attempt to understand the man (51). With a life nearly as controversial and misunderstood as his philosophy, Wittgenstein's eccentric and tormented ways served to perpetuate the mystique and misunderstanding that surrounded his philosophy of language. Often retreating to the solitude of some remote location for long periods of time and hesitant to enter the debate over the concepts forwarded in his seminal work the *Tractatus*, Wittgenstein did little to stem the misinterpretation and controversy that his work generated. Moreover, his writing style and lecture style only added to the intrigue and confusion. His prose was very personal and his concepts were often presented through the use of questions. He was prone to leaving many thoughts unfinished and raising concerns without answering them or asking questions that could not be answered. It would appear that Wittgenstein, at the least, would avoid explaining directly what he wanted to say or, at times, would even try to conceal the very points he was making. He was generally absent and disinterested in the scholarly debate over his philosophy (52). As such, many scholars have supplied the answers to the questions Wittgenstein left unanswered and finished his thoughts for him. This further adds to the misinterpretation of Wittgenstein (53). Wittgenstein scholar J. F. M. Hunter summarizes the problem of understanding Wittgenstein by saying, "Wittgenstein wrote cryptically, and to make sense of his prose is always a challenge" (54). Wittgenstein also did not attempt to do the things that all other philosophers did; namely, offer theories and explanations, or deduce conclusions from data (55).

In the end of the Preface of his posthumous masterpiece *Philosophical Investigations*, Wittgenstein offers his readers a clue as to why he wrote in such a fashion. He states that he did not want his "writing to spare other people the trouble of thinking" and that one of his objectives was to "stimulate someone to thoughts of his own." Not surprisingly, the student of Wittgenstein finds themself functioning as both philosopher and detective when studying his works.

As a lecturer, he permitted only the most serious of students—not "tourists" as he called most students—into his classes and was unconventional in his teaching approach. Rather than present material in an organized fashion, Wittgenstein felt that to repeat the points already made by others was antithetical to the very act of philosophizing (56). He would have nothing to do with such and his lectures at Cambridge amounted to him spontaneously sharing original thoughts as they arose with the approximately twenty students who attended his weekly lecture and weekly discussion (57).

Ludwig Josef Johann Wittgenstein was born on April 26, 1889 in Vienna and was the youngest of nine children. As leaders in the Austrian steel and iron industries, his family possessed great wealth and material comforts. Yet, they would face great sorrow, as three of the five Wittgenstein boys would commit suicide and another would loose an arm in World War I. Ludwig was of Jewish descent, however his grandfather had converted to Protestantism and his mother, a Roman Catholic, baptized him into the Catholic Church. Though never an active churchgoer, Wittgenstein would develop an academic interest in religion.

Wittgenstein was educated at home until the age of 14 whereupon he went to school at Linz for three years and then to Berlin to study engineering for two years. He traveled to England in 1908 to study aeronautics and mathematics at Manchester University. While there he read Russell and Whitehead's *Principia Mathematica* (*Principles of Mathematics*) and developed an interest in the ideas of Bertrand Russell (58). He was also influenced by the famous University of Jena logician Gottlob Frege, whom Wittgenstein visited in 1911. Taking Frege's advise, Wittgenstein enrolled at Trinity College, Cambridge in 1912 to study under Russell. While at Cambridge, Wittgenstein was a student of Russell and G. E. Moore. Russell and Moore recognized Wittgenstein's brilliance and nominated him to the prestigious and secret society of Apostles. Both would later draw inspiration from their former pupil (59).

Wittgenstein's studies were interrupted by World War I. He enlisted in the Austrian Army in 1914, becoming an officer in 1915, and fighting on both the Eastern Front and later the Southern Front, where he was taken prisoner by the Italian Army in 1918. Throughout the War Wittgenstein put his ideas into notebooks titled "Logisch-Philosophische Abhandlung" and mailed them to Russell and Frege. The readers were impressed with their student's treatise. Russell even encouraged Wittgenstein to publish his work. Wittgenstein, however, failed to follow through and even felt that Russell misread the treatise. This would seem to be behavior typical of Wittgenstein, for in not trusting most people and seeing them as intellectually inferior, he would always worry that he would be misread (60). Fortunately, Russell was not deterred and eventually saw Wittgenstein's work published in 1921 under the name *Tractatus Logico-Philosophicus*.

In the *Tractatus* Wittgenstein believed that he offered the definitive solution for philosophy but soon after lost interest in the formal study of philosophy. Pursuing other endeavors, Wittgenstein attended a teacher's training college and taught elementary school students in Austria from 1920 to 1926. Not surprisingly, Wittgenstein did not enjoy a healthy relationship with his employers or the parents of his pupils and would eventually leave, forced out over charges of excessive physical severity against the students. While there, however, he did publish a German glossary for elementary schools, the second and only other book he would publish in his lifetime. As the *Tractatus* was the only work he considered complete enough to be published, his other works were all published posthumously (61).

Wittgenstein also worked as a gardener in a monastery near Vienna and designed a home for one of his sisters. In 1929 he returned to Cambridge, submitting the *Tractatus* for his Ph.D. requirements under Moore and Russell. After completing his Ph.D. he was selected Fellow at Trinity College. He would later hold a professorship in philosophy. Although they would not be published until after his death, while at Cambridge Wittgenstein began work on *Philosophische Grammatik* and *Philosophische Bemerkungen* (*Philosophical Remarks*). He also kept extensive notes from the lectures he gave in 1933–1934 and 1934–1935 which were published posthumously as *The Blue and Brown Books*, respectively, so named for the color of the bound papers.

Another departure from the formal and, what he saw as confining world of academia which he felt infringed on his time to think (62) took Wittgenstein into self-imposed exile to a primitive hut in Norway. While in isolation he worked on *Philosophische Untersuchungen* (*Philosophical Investigations*) which he finished before his death but never published while he was alive. Wittgenstein would periodically return to academic life at Cambridge but spent much of the World War II years working as a medical orderly at a London hospital and later at a clinical research lab in Newcastle. Two years after the conclusion of the second World War, he once again abandoned academic life, traveling to Austria then Ireland, where, for awhile, he returned to living a solitary existence in a remote seaside hut in Galway. His final years were spent between Dublin, Austria, Cambridge, Oxford, and the United States, before moving back to Cambridge, where he died on April 29, 1951.

Ludwig Wittgenstein remains as a giant in modern philosophy and an enigmatic figure. Not to deny him his fame or rightful place in the history of philosophy that he justifiably earned through his intellectual contributions, but part of the allure and mystique of the man would seem to be owed to his eccentricity. Wittgenstein was an impatient individual who could be brutal in his attacks. His personality and intellect made him disliked and feared by many while a few others followed him with such zeal that they have been described as "disciples" and accused of a dogmatic devotion to his work. In return, he held most of his contemporaries in academia and philosophy in low regard and considered most humans to be worthless. Wittgenstein was suicidal, somewhat uncomfortable with his homosexuality, and possessed what could safely be held to be quirky habits (63). He lived much of his life in bad health and without material or financial comfort, for he had given away the inherited fortune his father left him upon his death in 1912. Yet, the man and his work have been described as "genius," "inspired," "passionate," and intense" (64).

2.   The Early Wittgenstein

The controversy and misunderstanding that surrounds the philosophy of Wittgenstein is compounded by the fact that, essentially, there are two Wittgensteins: The early Wittgenstein, as understood in the *Tractatus*, published in 1921; and the later Wittgenstein, as is evident in many of his posthumously published works, most notably *Philosophical Investigations*, published in 1953. Other important works published posthumously include *The Blue and Brown Books, Philosophische Grammatik (Philosophical Grammar)* and *Philosophische Bemerkungen (Philosophical Remarks)*. There are a number of vivid changes evident between the *Tractatus* and later writings. In fact, on some points Wittgenstein moved 180 degrees from his early positions (65). It is even suggested that a reader of the later Wittgenstein might think that the author had never even read the early Wittgenstein (66). Although there is some disagreement as to when and why the change took place, it appears that Wittgenstein started reordering his philosophy sometime after 1929, during his intermediate or transition years 1930 to 1934 (67). His split from the *Tractatus* is also revealed in his lectures at Cambridge in the 1930s. One story on why this transition occurred has a friend and colleague of Wittgenstein's at Cambridge—Piero Sraffa, an Italian economist—raising questions about Wittgenstein's logical form theory and stumping him (68).

The fact that there are two Wittgensteins only adds to the mystique that surrounds the man and his work. As one would expect, Wittgenstein himself did little to clarify the philosophic community's understanding of the nature of this change in thinking or the reasons for the change. To this day there is a school of philosophers who regard the early Wittgenstein's *Tractatus* as his triumph and a school who agree with the later Wittgenstein (69). Because of the later change in Wittgenstein's philosophy and his reluctance to interpret his work, in studying Wittgenstein, one must consider: 1. the *Tractatus*; 2. the various interpretations of the *Tractatus*; 3. his later works such as *Philosophical Investigations*; and 4. the interpretations of these later posthumous publications.

In the *Tractatus* Wittgenstein searches for the meaning of a word and examines the relationship between a word and its meaning and the relationship of language to the world. Words, according to Wittgenstein, stand for things and are used in place of the actual phenomenon. Words also represent expressions or sensations. Words "name" objects and have meaning. The meaning of a word is found in the object for which the word stands. As such, they "picture" facts. To picture something is to reassemble it so that it matches reality. Here, Wittgenstein maintained that there is a relationship between words and aspects of the world; a similarity between the form of what is pictured and that which pictures. That said about words, then sentences would be combinations of words that picture the reality of how objects exist. This reasoning necessitates that the logical form of a sentence and the logical form of a fact must match one another. So, in the Tractarian ontology, language depicts the logical structure of facts. Language must be bound by facts.

Wittgenstein also states that words should be used "commonsensically." To him sentences are either true or false. There should be a corresponding fact to what is said. If a proposition neither denies nor confirms a fact, then it is "nonsensical." A problem with the language of philosophy is that words tend toward nonsense, they are words without meaning. Such words are unintelligible and most philosophical propositions are thus nonsensical. Metaphysical propositions such as those discussing the existence of God and moral judgments were expressions of emotion and therefore did not meet his verification principle. That is not to say that he viewed such statements as unimportant, however, because certain questions could not be addressed through science and fact and were perhaps best suited to aesthetical, ethical, and religious discourse. In the early Wittgenstein, somewhat of a dichotomy emerges between philosophy and common sense and between values and facts, as he attempts to establish boundaries of what can be said or thought intelligibly. In rejecting metaphysics, Wittgenstein refers to the "inexpressible" as things that cannot be expressed through propositions. One can see that Wittgenstein was attempting to place philosophy on firmer ground. Inherently, the questions of philosophy focussed on that which was beyond the factual. So philosophic language and discourse was not based in reality and fact and therein lies the problem of meaning and the dilemma of ever proving or disproving philosophical utterances. Metaphysics, to him, was not a solid instrument of analysis and metaphysical statements were arbitrary and did not possess sense. As such, philosophy should not even try to say what cannot be said.

If a proposition is false, the state of affairs described therein does not exist. Likewise, the realm of fact is devoid of value and focuses on "what is." Values and ethics belong to the other sphere of the nonlogical, focussing on what "ought to be." Wittgenstein's aversion to metaphysics found an audience in many early neopositivists attempting to develop a more scientific philosophy and is believed to have influenced the development of logical positivism and the Vienna Circle (70).

Wittgenstein breaks language down into its basic forms. In section 3 of the *Tractatus* he considers "propositions," which is when a thought finds an expression that can be perceived by the senses. The fundamental or simplest kind of propositions are "elementary propositions," which are presented in section 4. The world consists of facts, referred to by Wittgenstein as "atomic facts" or "states of affairs." Meaningful propositions depict a reality of contingent facts. Each fact is composed of simple objects that can be named. Combining these names and facts produces a simple proposition, or an "elementary proposition." An elementary proposition merely asserts the existence of a state of affairs. As such, it is reflective of reality and cannot be contradicted by another elementary proposition. So, by discovering the logical form of propositions and identifying elementary propositions, one can discover the logical form or truth of states of affairs. It is through analysis of sentences and language to reveal elementary propositions that allows reality to be discovered. Utterances or philosophic discourse that does not meet these factual criteria are "nonsense" and cannot be expressed.

A dominant feature of Wittgenstein's early view of language is reflected in what he refereed to as the "picture theory" (71). This is discussed in section 2 of the *Tractatus*. Wittgenstein uses the illustration of a person picturing facts to themselves. These pictures are logical; in other words, they are what exists in the world or "states of affairs," as he refers to them. A picture is thus a model of reality where objects of the world correspond to pictures. Language is a picture of facts.

To Wittgenstein, language is basically mental. "Pictures" are mental "thoughts" and these "spoken thoughts" are expressed in a way that is perceptible to the senses. Wittgenstein speaks of a "pictorial relationship" when referring to elements of a picture being related to objects in the real world. The way or manner in which things are related to one another is reflected in the "pictorial form." This "form" is connected with reality in that the elements of the picture are related to one another in the same way that things are related in the world. So pictures must be facts.

3. The Later Wittgenstein

The later Wittgenstein repudiates the basic principles put forth in the *Tractatus*. Perhaps the work that best reflects his mature philosophy is *Philosophical Investigations* (72). *Philosophical Investigations* is difficult to read in that it repeatedly refers to other concepts and moves in a non-linear manner but it is held by many Wittgenstein scholars to represent the later Wittgenstein and is important because in it he offers not only a critique of the Tractarian ontology, moving his analysis of language from "thoughts" to "action" and from "meaning" to "sense," but also offers thoughts on new matters. While the early Wittgenstein was based on truth and falsity and strict, simple rules of language, the later work rejects rules and the notion that by following convention, one can arrive at truths or falsehoods.

His later work recognizes that certain pictures are incomplete or distorted. This led him to abandon his earlier views, which he felt led to the distortion and oversimplification of the multiple ways that language is used (73). Language cannot be summed up by the Tractarian method of "naming," which is to say that one cannot simply state that words stand for things and, thus, take their place then simply assign names to things and memorize them. There is not a simple relationship between the name and its bearer. In place, the later Wittgenstein views a word's meaning as related to its "practical use." One cannot know the meaning of words without knowing the environment within which the word is used. He places more emphasis on the study of words as they are used in the everyday sense, where he likened their use to that of a "tool." Tools are purposive and do specific things, as do words. To attempt to do something with the wrong word—or tool— is difficult. One can know the meaning of the word only if one knows how it is used in practice. As such, language must be considered as connected to real activities and the Tractarian notion of an ideal language has been replaced by an emphasis on ordinary language. Wittgenstein also uses the notion or metaphor of "language-games" to show the complex and multiple ways words function. Relatedly, he rejects the Tractarian notion of language consisting only of elementary propositions, something that the later Wittgenstein felt restricted language. The use of such metaphors as tools and games by the later Wittgenstein reveals his interest in the larger activities of language such as how a word is used and what is done with the word (74).

Wittgenstein points out that words have several meanings and that it is not enough to simply know the object that the word pictures, but one must also know the context and meaning by which it is used. A word's use, and thus its meaning, is contingent on the situation in which it is used. It would be wrong to assume then that a word's meaning is constant and fixed. For example, a word or sentence can be used as a question, request, command, prayer, a joke, as a greeting, a way to thank someone, and so on. Moreover, the meaning of a word can change when it is used together with another word. Words are used as more than just names. To really know the language, Wittgenstein says that one must know the various language-games that are played.

Language, in the new Wittgenstein approach, is no longer seen as a picture of the world. Language does not have a single definitive element or property that all words, sentences, and propositions must possess to constitute a language. As such, Wittgenstein says that language cannot be defined. His notion of "language-games" illustrates this, as language-games do not have a sole fundamental property in common, as is also the case with different types of games such as ballgames, boardgames, or cardgames. He does allow for similarities and some common features which he calls "family resemblances."

Unlike the *Tractatus*, the later Wittgenstein forwards the view that facts do not have to have a logical form and the state of affairs in the world does not have to consist solely of objects and elementary propositions. Whereas, in *Tractatus* he conceptualized language very simply, looking for the simple and elementary character of language, the later works view language as more complex. Nor is meaning still tied to an objective truth. For example, if everyone agreed that the Earth is flat, that belief would not necessarily make it the truth. If science "proves" that the Earth is not flat, the meaning of "flat" is still relevant and unchanged. The meaning must be studied prior to discussion of the truth.

Wittgenstein entertained the idea—which he ultimately rejected—that one could have a "private language," a language in which the sense of words would be known only by the user (75). His "private language argument" reasoned that an individual could not express—written or otherwise—her/his inner feelings and experiences in a language that others could understand. Expressions would reflect the individual's experiences and senses, although it is theoretically possible that the individual could infer the senses of others. Though he doubted the possibility of a private language, he speculated that such a language would be driven by the senses, whereas the language shared by everyone would be governed by a set of rules that are taught to all humans (76). Yet, the internal states of language cannot be separated from external influences and there is a public dimension to even the innermost private mental states.

D.   Postmodernism: The Vocabulary of Thought

Many of the problems facing the practice and field of study of public administration are made worse by the narrow thinking that occurs within and about the field. Scholars of public administration, politicians, and bureaucrats themselves routinely bemoan the troubling state of the field. Attention is needed on the language of bureaucracy because not only does language communicate thoughts but it also shapes our thoughts. Language affects the thought process and shapes our world view. It is part of an activity and a form of life.

Since its birth, public administration has embraced the experiment of modernity and, consequently, has been wedded to the existing convention of modernist assumptions. As the dominant paradigm, modernity has had its utility. It helped address the problems of public administration and has occasioned professionalism and reforms in the field. It has also produced a body of "laws," theories, and administrative practices and procedures. As such, a "language" of public administration has emerged, tied to, and embedded in, modernity. This modernist language includes terms like "privatization," "restructuring," "empowerment," and "allocations," but it is also a way of thinking about the roles, scope, and nature of public administration. This way of thinking is defined by conventional forms of power and the merits of growth as well as such concepts as rationality, reason, specialization, impersonality, and faith in formal, general rules. It also has things to say about human nature and behavior. The experiment with modernity has guided training and education in the field and the practices and growth of bureaucracy. Modernist principles have informed the study of public administration and the methodologies and questioning used by public administrationists. It has also guided reforms in the practicing community.

The development of public organization theory and the discipline of public administration have been bound by language. A new language of bureaucracy is necessary for a new approach to governing (77). Deconstructing the old bureaucracy and imagining a new practice and study of public administration requires new questions and a new way of thinking about the very nature of bureaucracy. The language of postmodernism can guide this deconstruction and inform any critical rethinking about bureaucracy (78).

The experiment of modernity is visible in the fundamental beliefs and values of western civilization over the past 300 to 500 years. While identifying just what those core beliefs are is difficult, defining the alternative postmodern paradigm is even more of a monumental task. There exists no single, agreed-upon set of postmodernist doctrine. Perhaps the best way to conceptualize the postmodernist language that could inform a new public administration is to consider what it is not: modernity. Whether a complete deconstruction of modernity or mere reconstruction of the system, the existing bureaucratic order must be rethought.

The old principles of a day and age of "scientific management" and the "proverbs" of public administration, that have long been summarily dismissed by scholars in the field are, if one considers the postmodern critique, alive and well in the form of modernity. The current language of our field reflects biases molded from the forces of scientific management as well as popular culture, capitalism, the mass media, and the political center. One can still see the presence of scientific management and the quest for universal laws or a unifying theory of public administration in the current "facts" or state of the knowledge base in the field. Elements of the post-Gulick and post-Simon era still reflect the language of the heyday of those early voices. This modernist language, for example, still separates facts from moral and value judgments, ala early Wittgenstein, still seeks rational decision making, reasoned action by bureaucrats, the principles of efficiency and economy, and private sector solutions to public problems. One might say that rumors of the demise of the politics-administration dichotomy are, in modernity, greatly exaggerated.

A postmodernist language of bureaucracy would be critical of contemporary thinking in public organization theory that is based in notions of power, excessive rationality, alienation, efficiency, order and narrowly construed concepts of equity, equality, morality, and justness. As such, the tenets of a postmodern language that could be used to guide the field of public administration include: 1. skepticism of applying existing principles of science and rationality to public administration; 2. skepticism of the existing knowledge base—or "facts"—of public administration; 3. skepticism of the ability to develop universal laws or principles to public organizations.

In bureaucratese we witness the possible death of language. Language is communication yet, in bureaucracies, often language does not communicate but only serves to inform. Communication should be considered as a two-way construction of meaning and exchange of thoughts. Information, on the other hand, is one directional and serves to shape another's thoughts. This is especially problematic when the language forwards and legitimizes the existing order and dominant system without the public realizing this or having a chance to participate in the exchange. In playing Wittgenstein's "language-games," for example, the participants—communicators—must agree on the rules of the game prior to communicating. There must be an agreed upon understanding of the fundamentals of language. Wittgenstein felt that this common understanding comes from shared experiences and common expressions of behavior that he called "lebensformen" or "forms of life." Bureaucratese does not draw upon the shared experiences.

Bureaucratese separates the meaning from the message, and in so doing, separates language from meaning by removing the meaning from words (79). It is an attack on formalist theories of language that suggest that words have a determinate meaning. Yet, neither does it fall into the category of deconstructionist linguistics; the notion that a word's meaning varies from reader to reader, person to person. In the language of bureaucracy, it has to be wondered if one can ever even assume that meaning is communicated at all. A new language of bureaucracy is necessary.

E.   Plain English

That bureaucratese is plagued by excessive use of jargon, slang, cliches, and acronyms is obvious. This form of "language" is in danger of becoming institutionalized within public organizations—if it already has not—and an accepted part of popular culture. What is needed as an alternative is the adoption of accurate, plain, simple words and sentences; in short, plain English. To allow for maximal participation by the public in its government and understanding of public discourse and documents by the citizenry, the following criterion or question should be applied: Can the particular public communique in question be stated or written in a more concise, direct, and understandable manner?

Statements need to be shortened and organized as "subject-verb-object" whenever possible. Many basic principles of plain English could be adopted to improve public communication such as avoiding using nouns as modifiers. This is the practice of running several nouns together, as in "the conference program committee recommendations." Another practice that should be limited is the constant use of verbs as nouns when not necessary, such as "to offer some assistance" in place of "to assist," or adding repetitive words to nouns, as in "the color blue" rather than simply saying "blue." Yet another problem with not using plain English is that much of the cliches, jargon, and technical-speak of bureaucracy is based in current or pop culture. Such words or phrases typically have short lifespans of use and their meaning is likewise often short or at least either unstable or not universally agreed upon. As terminology changes so does meaning. Without a common historical or cultural grounding or context, the meaning of words change.

Public agencies are beginning to use plain English in written reports, publications, and public documents in response not only to complaints from the American public and criticism from plain English advocates, but in an effort to improve internal communications (80). Historically, the move toward such public accessibility can be traced to the consumerism movement and open-government reforms of the late 1960s and 1970s. These reforms called for government to operate "in the sunshine" and to make public documents readable and accessible to the general public. (81). From President Richard Nixon's initiative in 1972 to have information in the Federal Register written in "layman's terms" to President Jimmy Carter's 1978 Executive Order mandating that federal regulations and the IRS revise documents so as to make them simpler and easier to understand, there has been the presence of an effort to reduce the use of bureaucratese (82). Likewise, several states have passed legislation requiring that public documents be made shorter, easier to understand, and written in a style of writing that the general public can understand (83).

Numerous organizations have emerged challenging the current language of bureaucracies. The Washington, DC-based Document Design Center, for example, is an advocacy organization that proposes technical writing courses and training for those who draft public documents and for students preparing to enter public service (84). Relatedly, there is a role for educators, especially those teaching English and those in communication and public administration programs, to encourage and train students in the use of plain English. Some universities are emphasizing a return to the basics and requiring writing-intensive curricula. Several states have passed laws specifying a minimum amount of writing in certain college courses. Professional and academic associations, English programs, and English faculty are also active in this issue. NCTE, a professional association of English teachers has, since the 1970s, formally condemned the improper use of language in public discourse and writing public policy (85). The Committee on Public Doublespeak has, likewise, served as a watchdog critical of the use of bureaucratese. The Committee identifies abusers in politics, government, and the military and, since the mid-1970s, has presented awards such as the Orwell Award for outstanding contributions in public discourse and the Doublespeak Award to the worst abusers of bureaucratic-speak. Published by the Committee on Public Doublespeak, the *Quarterly Review of Doublespeak* was started in 1974 and chronicles examples of public doublespeak. There is also a monthly newsletter titled *Simply Stated* dedicated to the use of plain English in writing and other forms of communication.

A viable plain English movement has been working to end the use of bureaucratese, requiring in place of it the use of plain English in official public documents. The academic disciplines of English and communication are in the forefront of this campaign. It is time for the field of public administration and public administrators to commit themselves to plain English reforms.

The benefits of using plain, straight-forward English in public documents and in public communication, both internal and external, are many. There are obvious savings in costs, time, and human resources resulting from less paperwork, repetition, and supervision and lower levels of confusion and mistakes. Research now suggests that people learn better with the use of simple, plain language (86). Whereas bureaucratese is written from the perspective of the organization and is authoritarian in nature, plain English benefits the citizen, the voter, the public employee, and the client or recipient of public services because it uses their words and language.

IV.   TOWARD A NEW LANGUAGE (AND PRACTICE) OF PUBLIC ADMINISTRATION

A new language of public administration, one based in plain English and borrowing conceptually from postmodernism and Wittgenstein's later philosophy of language, would allow public administration scholars and bureaucrats alike to ask the new questions, rethink the old problems, and reorient the very nature of public service in a manner necessary if government is to respond to new challenges facing it and rid itself of the old failures plaguing it.

This "new" paradigm must watch for the subtle and subconscious ways that the present language of public administration still implies a "science" of administration, conceptualizes a separation between politics and administration, and embraces the private-sector notions of economy, efficiency, and a narrowly-construed framework for defining effectiveness and productivity. Postmodern critiques of the dominant mindset in public administration assists in deconstructing the existing "facts" and knowledge base in the field. It permits the field to ask new questions and rethink the dominant paradigm by developing of a new "vocabulary" of thought.

Farmer, for instance, advocates the application of postmodernism to address several needed reforms in the field (87): 1. to move the study and practice of public administration toward deconstructing what are believed to be "truths" and "facts"; 2. broadening existing narrow disciplinary interests that limit the field; 3. replacing the academic preoccupation with scientific methods and a "science" of administration with multiple frames of analysis including ethics, values, and moral philosophy; and 4. expanding the study of public administration beyond the current emphasis on local government and the American experience, which he sees as "particularism," to a global focus. All of this can be aided through the development of a new language or way of thinking about public administration.

Wittgenstein can assist our exploration of the use and misuse of language in public organizations and the examination of its meaning. Although the early Wittgenstein separated metaphysical language from factual language, a new language of bureaucracy would encourage the use of values and ethics in the bureaucratic vocabulary of thought. While Wittgenstein would have referred to such language as "nonsensical," his separation between the metaphysical and the factual is useful in that so much of the present language of bureaucracy is unintelligible and not founded in the factual "state of affairs." Rather than "picture" or mirror reality, the words used in bureaucratese do not correspond to reality but impose a false order of affairs. Wittgenstein's later emphasis on a word's meaning being known through its practical use speaks to the need to base official public discourse and documents on plain English. To know the meaning of a word, one must know the environment and context within which it is spoken. The functions and practices of government must be spoken and written in the words and language of the public it serves.

A "mindset" of bureaucracy emerges through use of a language that is deceptive and distancing, impersonal, and meaningless. The use of a doublespeak vocabulary may produce what could be described as a doublespeak mindset. This is evident in such standard bureaucratic statements as "department policy requires me to . . ." The "governmentality" that is believed to be entrenched in public organizations and is the source of so much of the "bureaucracy bashing" in the press, by politicians, and from the general public may be better understood by an examination of the language of bureaucracy.

The language of bureaucrats does not just depict issues, but it constructs them, frames debate about the issues, and influences the way the public, bureaucrats, and politicians perceive the issues. Public access to, and understanding of, government programs and services are contingent on clear communication. The academic study of the public sector is shaped by the language of analysis and the language of thought. So to are organization policies and practices bound by language. Problem solution, after all, depends on problem construction.

REFERENCES

1. As described in J. M. Dorney, The Plain English movement, *English Journal*: 77, 49–52, 1988.
2. As described in G. Roche, Bureaucracy: Enemy of the people H. M. Levine (ed.), *Public Administration Debated*, Prentice Hall, Englewood Cliffs, NJ, 1988.
3. W. Lutz, Fourteen years of doublespeak, *English Journal*: 77, 40–43, 1988.
4. D. J. Farmer, *The Language of Public Administration: Bureaucracy, Modernity, and Postmodernity*, University of Alabama Press, Tuscaloosa, AL, 1995.
5. G. Roche, 1988, p. 14.
6. W. Lutz, 1988, p. 40.
7. E. S. Herman, *Beyond Hypocrisy: Decoding the News in an Age of Propaganda*, South End Press, boston, 1992, p. 1.
8. D. G. Kehl, The 2 most powerful weapons against doublespeak, *English Journal*: 77, 57–66, 1988.

9. W. Lutz, *Doublespeak: From "Revenue Enhancement" to "Terminal Living," How Government, Business, Advertisers, and Others Use Language to Deceive You*, Harper and Row, New York, 1989, p. 1.

10. W. Lutz, 1989; W. Lutz, Notes toward a description of doublespeak, *Quarterly Review of Doublespeak*: 13, 10–11, 1987.

11. R. F. Dolle, Gobbledygook, or turkey talk, *J. of Environ. Health*: 52; 262, 1990.

12. J. R. Killingsworth, Idle talk in modern organizations, *Admin. and Soc.*: 16; 346–384, 1984.

13. R. F. Dolle, 1990; D. G. Kehl, 1988; W. Lutz, 1989; or see G. Orwell, *1984*, Signet Books, New York, 1949; G. Orwell, Politics and the english language, G. Orwell, *A Collection of Essays*, Harcourt, Brace, Jovanovich, New York, 1946.

14. R. F. Dolle, 1990.

15. L. H. Lapham, Washington Phrasebook, *Harper's Magazine*: 287, 9–12 1993.W.

16. W. Lutz, 1989.

17. R. P. Hummel, *The Bureaucratic Experience: A Critique of Life in the Modern Organization*, St. Martin's Press, New York, 1994.

18. William Lutz is a member of the NCTE Committee on Public Doublespeak, author of books and articles on the issue, and a contributor and instrumental force behind the *Quarterly Review of Doublespeak*.

19. C. W. Hensley, Speak with style and watch the impact, *Vital Speeches of the Day*: 61, 1995.

20. J. M. Dorney, 1988; W. Lutz, 1989, 1988.

21. C. W. Hensley, 1995.

22. W. Lutz, 1989.

23. J. M. Dorney, 1988; W. Lutz, 1989, 1988, 1987.

24. As described in G. Roche, 1988.

25. M. Heidegger, *Being and Time*, Harper and Row, New York, 1962; Hummel, 1994.

26. J. Searle, *Searle on Conversation*, John Benjamins Press, Amsterdam, 1989; see also, J. Searle, *Speech Acts*, Cambridge University Press, Cambridge, 1969.

27. R. F Dolle, 1990.

28. As described in W. Lutz, 1989.

29. As described in W. Lutz, 1989.

30. For information on Formalist linguistics, see N. Chomsky, *Aspects of the Theory of Syntax*, MIT Press, Cambridge, MA, 1965; also, F. Newmeyer, *Grammatical Theory*, University of Chicago Press, Chicago, 1983.

31. For Structuralist linguistics, see D. Hymes, Models of the interaction of language and social life, J. Gumperz and D. Hymes (eds.), *Directions in Sociolinguistics: The Ethnography of Communication*, Holt, Rinehart, and Winston, 35–71, 1972.

32. For a priori grammar, see P. Hopper, Emergent grammar and the a priori grammar postulate D. Tannen (ed.), *Linguistics in Context: Connecting Observation and Understanding*, Ablex Press, Norwood, NJ, 117–134, 1988.

33. For information on Functionalist linguistics, see M. Halliday, *Learning How to Mean: Explorations in the Development of Language*, Edward Arnold, London, 1975; or M. Halliday, *Explorations in the Functions of Language*, Edward Arnold, London, 1973.

34. For Emergent linguistics, see Hopper, 1988.

35. See D. Schriffrin, *Approaches to Discourse*, Blackwell, Cambridge, MA, 1994 for Interactive linguistics and for an overview of the major schools and theories of linguistics.

36. J. Austin, *How to do Things with Words*, Harvard University Press, Cambridge, MA, 1962; or Searle, 1989, 1969.

37. J. Gumperz, *Discourse Strategies*, Cambridge University Press, Cambridge, 1982; J. Gumperz, *Language and Social Identity*, Cambridge University Press, Cambridge, 1982.

38. E. Goffman, *Forms of Talk*, University of Pennsylvania Press, Philadelphia, 1981.

39. D. Hymes, 1972.

40. For an overview of this, see D. Schriffrin, 1994.

41. S. Feld, *Sound and Sentiment: Birds, Weeping, Poetics, and Song in Kaluli Expression*, University of Pennsylvania Press, Philadelphia, 1982.

42. For an over of this, see D. Schriffrin, 1994.

43. H. P. Grice, Utterer's meaning, sentence-meaning, and word-meaning, *Foundations of Language*: 4; 1–18, 1968.

44. H. Garfinkle, *Studies in Ethnomethodology*, Prentice Hall, Englewood Cliffs, NJ, 1967.

45. E. Schegloff, Presequences and indirection: Applying speech action theory to ordinary conversation, *Journal of Pragmatics*: 12, 55–62 (1988); E. Schegloff, Identification and recognition in telephone conversation openings, P. Sathas (ed.), *Everyday, Language: Studies in Ethnomethodology*, Irvington, New York, 1979, pp. 23–78.

46. W. Labov, The overestimation of functionalism, R. Dirven and V. Fried (eds.), *Functionalism in Linguistics*, John Benjamins Press, Philadelphia, 1987, 311–332.

47. H. L. R. Finch, *Wittgenstein-The Later Philosophy: An Exposition of the Philosophical Investigations*, Humanities Press, Atlantic Heights, NJ, 1977; J. Hartnack, *Wittgenstein and Modern Philosophy*, NYU Press, New York, 1965.

48. A. J. Ayer, *Wittgenstein*, University of Chicago Press, Chicago, 1985; H. L. R. Finch, 1977; O. Hanfling, *Wittgenstein's Later Philosophy*, SUNY Press, Albany, NY, 1989.

49. A. J. Ayer, 1985; G. Frongia and B. McGinness, *Wittgenstein: A Bibliographic Guide*, Basil Blackwell, Cambridge, MA, 1990.

50. H. L. R. Finch, 1977; G. Frongia and B. McGinness, 1990; O. Hanfling, 1989.

51. A. J. Ayer, 1985; J. Hartnack, 1965; J. M. F. Hunter, *Understanding Wittgenstein: Studies of Philosophical Investigations*, Edinburgh University Press, Edinburgh, 1985.

52. G. Frongia and McGinness, 1990.

53. O. Hanfling, 1989.

54. J. M. F. Hunter, 1985, p. vii.

55. O. Hanfling, 1989.

56. J. Hartnack, 1965.

57. A. J. Ayer, 1985.

58. G. Frongia and B. McGinness, 1990.

59. A. J. Ayer, 1985; G. Frongia and B. McGinness, 1990.

60. A. J. Ayer, 1985; O. Hanfling, 1989.

61. G. Frongia and B. McGinness, 1990.

62. J. Hartnack, 1965.

63. A. J. Ayer, 1985.

64. A. J. Ayer, 1985.

65. H. L. R. Finch, 1977.

66. O. Hanfling, 1989.

67. G. Frongia and B. McGinness, 1990; J. Hartnack, 1965; J. C. Kelly, Wittgenstein, the self, and ethics, *Rev. of Metaphysics*: 48; 567–590, 1995.

68. J. Hartnack, 1965.

69. G. Bergmann, The Glory and the Misery of Ludwig Wittgenstein, E. D. Klemke, *Essays on Wittgenstein*, University of Illinois Press, Urbana, IL, 1971.

70. A. J. Ayer, 1985; Frongia and McGinness, 1990.

71. R. J. Fogelin, *Wittgenstein*, Routledge and Kegan Paul, Boston, 1976.

72. J. Hartnack, 1965.

73. Fogelin, 1976.

74. H. L. R. Finch, 1977.

75. L. Bermudez, Skepticism and subjectivity: Two critiques of traditional epistemology reconsidered, *Inter Phil. Quar.* 35; 141–158, 1995.

76. C. L Harden, Wittgenstein on private language, *The J. of Phil.*: 56, 517–528, 1959.

77. D. J. Farmer, 1995.

78. D. J. Farmer, 1995.

79. J. Searle, 1989; C. P. Show, *Corridors of Power*, Scribners, New York, 1964.
80. J. M. Dorney, 1988.
81. J. M. Dorney, 1988.
82. W. Lutz, 1989, 1987.
83. G. P. Klare, "Readability" (D. P. Pearson, ed.), *Handbook of Reading Research*, Longman, New York, 1984, 681–684.
84. J. C. Redish and K. Racette, "Teaching College Students how to Write: Training Opportunities for Document Designers." Document Design Project, American Institutes for Research, Washington, DC 1979.
85. W. Lutz, 1988.
86. J. M. Dorney, 1988; M. Graves, "Could textbooks be Better Written, and Would it make a Difference?" Convention on Textbook Reform, The Cooperative Agenda, Washington, DC, June, 1985.
87. D. J, Farmer, 1995.

BIBLIOGRAPHY

Austin J. *How to do Things with Words*, Cambridge, MA: Harvard University Press, 1962.

Ayer A. J. *Wittgenstein*, Chicago: University of Chicago Press, 1985.

Bergmann G. The glory and the misery of ludwig wittgenstein, in E. D. Klemke. *Essays on Wittgenstein*, Urbana, IL: University of Illinois Press, 1971.

Chomsky N. *Aspects of the Theory of Syntax*, Cambridge: MIT Press, MA, 1965.

Dolle R. F. Gobbledygook, or turkey talking, *Journal of Environmental Health*: 52, (1990), p. 262

Dorney J. M. The plain English movement, *English Journal*: 77, (1988), pp. 49–52.

Farmer D. J. *The Language of Public Administration: Bureaucracy, Modernity, and Postmodernity*, Tuscaloosa, AL: University of Alabama Press, 1995.

Feld S. *Sound and Sentiment: Birds, Weeping, Poetics, and Song in Kaluli Expression*, Philadelphia-University of Pennsylvania Press, 1982.

Finch H. L. R. *Wittgenstein-The Later Philosophy: An Exposition of the Philosophical Investigations*, Atlantic Heights, NJ: Humanities Press, 1977.

Fischer F. and Forester J. (eds.). *The Argumentative Turn in Policy Analysis and Planning*, Durham: Duke University Press, 1993.

Frongia G. and McGinness B. *Wittgenstein: A Bibliographic Guide*, Cambridge, MA: Basil Blackwell, 1990.

Fogelin R. J. *Wittgenstein*, Boston: Routledge and Kegan Paul, 1976.

Garfinkle H. *Studies in Ethnomethodology*, Englewood Cliffs, NJ: Prentice Hall, 1967.

Goffman E. *In Forms of Talk*, Philadelphia: University of Pennsylvania Press, 1981.

Graves M. Could textbooks be better written, and would it make a difference?, Convention on Textbook Reform, The Cooperative Agenda, Washington, DC, June 1985.

Grice H. P. Utterer's meaning, sentence-meaning, and word-meaning, *Foundations of Language*: 4, (1968), pp. 1–18.

Gumperz J. *Discourse Strategies*, Cambridge: Cambridge University Press, 1982.

Gumperz J. *Language and Social Identity*, Cambridge: Cambridge University Press, 1982.

Halliday M. *Learning How to Mean: Explorations in the Development of Language*, London: Edward Arnold, 1975.

Halliday M. *Explorations in the Functions of Language*, London: Edward Arnold, 1973.

Hanfling O. *Wittgenstein's Later Philosophy*, Albany: SUNY Press, NY, 1989.

Hården C. L. Wittgenstein on private language, *The Journal of Philosophy*: 56, (1959), pp. 517–528.

Hartnack J. *Wittgenstein and Modern Philosophy*, New York: NYU Press, 1965.

Heidegger M. *Being and Time*, New York: Harper & Row, 1962.

Hensley C. W. Speak with style and watch the impact, *Vital Speeches of the Day*: 61 (1995).

Herman E. S. *Beyond Hypocrisy: Decoding the News in an Age of Propaganda*, Boston: South End Press, 1992.

Hopper P. Emergent grammar and the a priori grammar postulate, in D. Tannen (ed.), *Linguistics in Context: Connecting Observation and Understanding*, NJ: Ablex Press, Norwood, 1988, pp. 117–134.

Hummel R. P. *The Bureaucratic Experience: A Critique of Life in the Modern Organization*, New York: St. Martin's Press, 1994.

Hunter J. F. M. *Understanding Wittgenstein: Studies of Philosophical Investigations*, Edinburgh: Edinburgh University Press, 1985.

Hymes D. Models of the interaction of language and social life, J. Gumperz and D. Hymes (eds.), *Directions in Sociolinguistics: The Ethnography of Communication*, Holt, Rinehart and Winston, 1972 pp. 35–71.

Kehl D.G. The 2 most powerful weapons against doublespeak, *English Journal*: 77, 57–66, 1988.

Kelly J. C. Wittgenstein, the self, and ethics, *Review of Metaphysics*: 48, 567–590, 1995.

Killingsworth J. R. Idle talk in modern organizations, *Admin. and Soc.*: 16, 346–384, 1984.

Kilpatrick J. J. Mrs. Malaprop's mangled prose, *Smithsonian*: 25, 82–87, 1995.

Klare G. P. "Readability" in D. P. Pearson (ed.), *Handbook of Reading Research*, New York: Longman, 1984, pp. 681–684.

Labov W. The overestimation of functionalism, in R. Dirven and V. Fried (eds.), *Functionalism in Linguistics*, Philadelphia: John Benjamins Press, 1987, pp. 311–332.

Labov W. The study of language in its social context, in *Linguistic Patterns*, Philadelphia: University of Pennsylvania Press, 1972, pp. 183–259.

Lapham L. H. Washington Phrasebook, *Harper's Magazine*: 287, 9–12, 1993.

Lutz W. *Doublespeak: From "Revenue Enhancement" to "Terminal Living," How Government, Business, Advertisers, and Others Use Language to Deceive You*, New York: Harper and Row, 1989.

Lutz W. Fourteen years of doublespeak, *English Journal*: 77, 40–43, 1988.

Lutz W. Notes toward a description of doublespeak, *Quarterly Review of Doublespeak*: 13, (1987), pp. 10–11.

MacLeod S. The shifting sands of speech, *Macleans*: 98, 60, 1985.

Newmeyer F. *Grammatical Theory*, Chicago: University of Chicago Press, 1983.

Orwell G. Politics and the English Language, in *A Collection of Essays*, New York: Harcourt, Brace, Jovanovich, 1946.

Orwell G. *1984*, New York: Signet Books, 1949.

Redish J. C., and Racette K. Teaching college students how to write: Training opportunities for document designers, Document Design Project, American Institutes for Research, Washington, DC, 1979.

Roche G. Bureaucracy: Enemy of the people, H. M. Levine (ed.), *Public Administration Debated*, Englewood Cliffs, NJ: Prentice Hall, 6–15, 1988.

Sacks H. Notes on methodology, in J. M. Atkinson and J. Heritage (eds.), *Structures of Social Action*, Cambridge: Cambridge University Press, 1984, pp. 21–27.

Schriffrin D. *Approaches to Discourse*, Cambridge, MA: Blackwell, 1994.

Schegloff E. Presequences and indirection: Applying speech action theory to ordinary conversation, *Journal of Pragmatics*: 12, 55–62, 1988.

Schegloff E. Identification and recognition in telephone conversation openings, in P. Sathas (ed.), *Everyday Language: Studies in Ethnomethodology*, Irvington, New York, 23–78, 1979.

Searle J. *Searle on Conversation*, John Benjamins Press, Amsterdam, 1989.

Searle J. *Speech Acts*, Cambridge: Cambridge University Press, 1969.

Snow C.P. *Corridors of Power*, New York: Scribners, 1964.

Spencer D. Standing up for plain english, *Times Educational Supplement*, 7 (Aug. 31, 1990).

21

Postmodern Philosophy, Postmodernity, and Public Organization Theory

Charles J. Fox
Texas Tech University, Lubbock, Texas

Hugh T. Miller
Florida Atlantic University, Palm Beach Gardens, Florida

This chapter has the difficult task of defining that which, on the basis of principle, resists definition: postmodernism, postmodernity, and the relation of these to public administration and its affairs. Those whose philosophical musings have been labeled postmodern often resist that category. Moreover, there is a confusion between the more inclusive category, postmodernism, and the more local to French intellectual history term, poststructuralism. Although postmodern philosophy contributes in a broad sense to what we distinguish as the postmodern condition, portions of it may also be regarded as simply descriptive. Finally, the effects of the postmodern problematic on public administration/affairs probably lie more in the future than in the present and the past which calls for a more speculative approach than might be appropriate for other contributions to this *Handbook.*

We recommend and instruct those who read this chapter, in light of the unfamiliarity to most public administrators and public administrationists about these matters, particularly the first two sections, with a suspension of disbelief—or better, with sense of intuition activated—in order to grasp concepts that we admit we have difficulty expressing in the already-familiar language of day-to-day conversations.

We will proceed as follows: first, we broadly define what we take to be the main themes of postmodern philosophy; second, with some unavoidable overlap, we will provide sketches of the contributions of the major names generally considered to be postmodern thinkers; third, we define the distinction between postmodernism and postmodernity or what we also call the postmodern condition; finally, we speculate about the effects of these matters on governance.

I. MAJOR THEMES OF POSTMODERN THOUGHT

An elementary grasp of postmodern thought requires understanding of the following interrelated problematics and how a postmodern reacts to them: 1. anti-foundationalism and the "canon"; 2. incommensurability, the "other" and multiculturalism and 3. language, the text and decentered subjectivity.

A.   Anti-Foundationalism

Perhaps the most important and common aspect of postmodern thought is its rejection of what in the history of philosophy has been variously termed universalism, essentialism, ontological realism, and meta-narratives. These various terms connote views which affirm the existence of absolute ahistorical truth; immutable truth good for now and all time past and future. Richard Rorty (1), one of our postmodern philosophers, has usefully depicted such positions as "God's eye" views. In French intellectual circles "totalization," or "totalizing," is similarly employed. They have also been, in epistemological discussions, called "Archimedian standpoints."

Universalism/foundationalism may be fruitfully compared to theological positions. If one embraces one true omnipotent omniscient God who founds the universe, one can simultaneously assume an absolute of sufficient fixity to organize truth and reality claims. One may not be exactly sure of truth and reality in any particular case, but one is sure that there is one to be sought; there is the possibility that one will be found. Particular truths can be deduced or traced back to The Truth of God. Whether the One True word comes to us through revelation, faith, or the exercise of God-given reason can, and has been, vigorously disputed—sometimes with unfortunate life-depriving consequences for those found to be on heretical sides of such arguments. Bottom line: what is, and what is true, is because God decrees it.

Enlightenment and "modern" thought (modern philosophy may be traced back to seventeenth century philosopher Rene Descartes) has a similar form to divine foundationalism except that God is marginalized, removed, or replaced by some other first principle. Chief among these is science and, behind it, the power of human reason. The enlightenment presented the optimistic prospect of the universe as an enormous clockworks operating according to knowable laws. Such was the influence of the work of Galileo, Copernicus, and Newton. The accomplishments of science fueled the optimism (or in retrospect arrogance) of modernity. The French encyclopedists (e.g. Voltaire) believed that the human sciences of governance and political economy would soon achieve the exactitude of Newtonian physics. To be sure, intellectual history is not a lock-step linear progression, but at a high level of abstraction it is possible to identify an overall mood of modernity against which postmodernity can be defined. That mood is one of attempting to identify law like (God's eye) generalizations from which might be deduced explanations of all else. This is why the French postmodernist Lyotard (2) refers to modernity as dominated by meta-narratives and meta-discourse: "I will use the term modern to designate any science that legitimizes itself with reference to a metadiscourse . . . [that makes] explicit appeal to some grand narrative." The (at least vulgar) Marxist view that an inexorable materialist economic dialectic channels all history into predictable concatenations of class struggle is one such meta-narrative. The liberal bourgeois view that all history has been teleologically directed to the present capitalist regime is another. Yet another is the aspiration of positivist and analytical philosophy of science to develop a universal language of scientific explanation—a logic of all logics or a language of all languages.

Now it is true that none of these competing modern aspirants to univeralism (including the theological ones) completely displaced any of the others for even a moment in the hearts and minds of their opponents. So its not so much a matter of some particular all-hegemonic foundationalist point of view prevailing, as it is the attempt to have one at all. What is called by postmodernists "the Western canon" is not a particular substantive dogma but the dogma embodied in the endless permutations of logic and disputation dedicated to finding a fixed dogma. "Canon," of course, denotes unquestionable law-like rules. Implied too is an affective connotation of God-given ecclesiastical laws. In particular the Western canon is thought to be logocentric (having an a priori bias favoring cause and effect deductive logic) by postmodern authors. Jacques Derrida especially is identified with the critique of logocentricism. Privileged status is denied to cool logic, rationalism, the cogito ("I think therefore I am"), and the bourgeois Western males prone to practice them. Given equal legitimacy are other human proclivities and talents that get marginalized by logocentric privileging. This Western canon, then, is "deconstructed" by postmodern thought. Laid bare are its delimiting, truncating, and arrogant visions and its bias toward a hegemonic Western bourgeois class, male gender, and white race versus all thereby marginalized different "others."

Postmodernists, congruently, reject not only specific solutions to the quest for universal meta-narratives; they reject the quest itself as well as the logical, cultural and philosophical imperatives that drive it. Think about it this way: imagine you are a child with a mansion sized sand box and play area. You leisurely explore all the nooks and crannies of this territory perfectly content in the belief that this is the universe of possibility. Suddenly someone comes along and creaks open a gate to reveal whole new universes of possibility that you had not imagined could exist. Having figured and charted all possible permutations of known ground someone comes along and shows the limitations, nay perversity, of ones knowledge of the ground—and more importantly brings into doubt the universality of the ground itself.

The abandonment of foundationalism, universalism, essentialism, meta-narratives, totalizing, Western canon, and more importantly the absolute abandonment of the project to find or establish same, is enormously significant. Foreshadowed by Neitzsche's declaration of the death of God, what follows from this abandonment is relativism and perspectivism in epistemology and philosophy of science. The veracity of contradictory truth claims cannot be adjudicated against some monolithic conception of "The Truth." There is not even an ambiguous Constitution, as in American jurisprudence, to constrain competing interpretations within manageable boundaries. Similarly in ethics, relativism or (some would go so far as to say) nihilism follows from the demise of foundationalism. Without a firm foundation, or even the hope for one, no eternal standard of right behavior can be adduced; ethical judgments lose their ability to claim alignment with eternal verities. At the very worst, ethical assessments become nothing more than matters of taste (3). Murder or chocolate, take your pick.

B.   Incommensurability, the "Other," and Multiculturalism

Another important theme of postmodernism, one following directly from anti-foundationalism, is what might be called incommensurability. Putatively, incommensurability happens in a situation of multiple paradigms, each of which is incommensurable with the others. The term "paradigm" suggests a broad band of definitions. It can mean particular esoteric points of view at one pole, while at the other a more grandiloquent understanding of paradigms as the dominant hegemonic assumptions of an epoch—what Foucault (4) calls an episteme and the Germans a *Weltanschauung* or world view. Centered between these poles is the standard grasp of paradigms as scientific formations as influentially promulgated by Kuhn (5). The thing about paradigms is that they vary and shift; or as Kuhn would have it, they are subject to revolutions whereby one paradigm is completely overthrown by its successor.

One can see that such a view comports with anti-foundationalism because what is counted as truth varies by paradigm, or, understood in the grand sense, the epoch in which a paradigm is hegemonic. In Kuhn's depiction, science advances by way of paradigm revolutions. During periods he calls "normal" science, scientists in like-minded disciplinary clusters clear up contradictions and search out problems which follow from the explanatory laws held dear by a particular paradigm. In the end, the paradigm will be unable to account for anomalies found at its own nether borders. As inexplicable anomalies accumulate, newer generations of scientists will develop alternative paradigms based on entirely different fundamental explanatory principles.

There follows a period of paradigmatic struggle until finally the new paradigm replaces the old—as for example happened in the move from particle physics to quantum physics. Science advances, in other words, not by evolution, but by a series of paradigmatic revolutions. Revolution is necessary because paradigms are incommensurable. Older generations of scientists are, as it were, trapped in the paradigm in which they were trained and are unable to see in terms of the new paradigm, or to recognize the phenomena that it explains. The revolution is consummated when the older generation of scientists dies off to be replaced by the newer generation who inhabit a new paradigm.

The point is that one cannot, as it were, inhabit more than one paradigm, cannot see through the lenses of alternative paradigms. No argument developed in terms of one paradigm can be telling to those who argue in terms of an alternative one. Inhabitants of different paradigms are like ships passing on a moonless night without running lights.

The upshot of all this is that not only do we lack an absolute truth against which competing truth claims might be adjudicated, we also cannot see truths congruent with the explanatory schemes developed by a paradigm inconsistent with our own. We belong, as it were, to disparate paradigmatic tribes. The truths held so fervently by, say, Branch Davidians simply cannot be unpacked by followers of the Dalai Lama. "Others" cannot be converted—short of elimination they can only be let alone. A similar argument is made by the influential contemporary philosopher Alisdair MacIntyre (6). MacIntyre, although a practicing Catholic, affirms Neitsche's point about the death of God in the sense of the demise of a universal set of ethical truths by which people can order their lives. The only hope that MacIntyre holds out is community standards based on more local practices. There can be no assurances that inter-community standards will be compatible.

As foreshadowed above, postmodernism celebrates the "other;" other, that is, than Eurocentric, logocentric, phallocentric, and bourgeois. Others are those whose voices and ways of being have been neglected or even occluded by the Western canon: women, people of color, prisoners, the so-called mentally ill, persons with disabilities, cultures south of the equator and east of the Urals, and people associated with non-majoritarian sexual preferences. Given that a firm foundation of the Western canon becomes increasingly difficult to defend under the assault of postmodern thought, those previously occluded and marginalized voices should now find purchase. This is the theoretical basis of what is now known as multiculturalism, or as voices on the right label it: "political correctness" (7). Thus does an oral history related by a "not conventionally" literate aboriginal South American woman become a relevant part of the curriculum at elite universities. Thus can a student major in "queer studies."

Put another way, multiculturalism is at least a partial reparation for the imbalance in power that is associated with the hegemony of the Western canon. It follows from the main thrust of the work of Michel Foucault. Foucault's tremendously influential work collapsed the previously distinct categories of knowledge and power. If there is no independent fount of truth, then what establishes any particular concatenation of truths is power. Conversely, knowledge is knowledge of the status quo and supports it, making it power. Denial of the truths of the status quo is powerfully and pejoratively rendered as ignorance, to the detriment of "others."

C. Language, the Text, and Decentered Subjectivity

1. Levi-Strauss, Wittgenstein, and the Linguistic Turn

To situate the closely related postmodern themes of language, the text and decentered subjectivity, the works of Claude Levi-Strauss and Ludwig Wittgenstein need to be discussed as exemplars of the philosophical context within which these themes developed. Postmodern thinkers, especially the French (Derrida, Foucault, Lyotard, and Lacan) are often lumped together under the label "poststructuralists." The most direct meaning of that term is that these thinkers, although still influenced by structuralism, have had their major works reach prominence after the 1950s flirtation with structuralism.

But what is structuralism? The most direct answer to this question is that it is the theory of French anthropologist and philosopher Claude Levi-Strauss. Intellectual historians trying to make sense of the Parisian cauldron for American audiences divide postwar French thought into three more or less chronological (although often existing side by side) periods: existential Marxism, structuralism, and poststructuralism (8). Structuralism can be, albeit without nuance, thought of as a reaction to the existential Marxism of Sartre and his colleagues. This was perhaps inevitable as Sartre, driven by the logic of his philosophy of consciousness, took what is now generally regarded to be an extreme voluntaristic stance in regard to individual human freedom. To passively accept one's fate, even in such extreme situations as prison camps, was to Sartre "bad faith." Rather than proclaim pure and passive innocence, one could always choose to project one's thoughts and thereby change one's essential being elsewhere.

Against this radical free will view of individual human agency, Levi-Strauss proposed an equally radical determinism. Particular individual human consciousnesses are naught but articulations of a deeper and all-encompassing structure, a structure thought to control and determine all human variables. This structure manifests itself in primarily linguistic ways. Levi-Strauss' project was to find the expressions of this structure in the myths of diverse cultures. These myths were thought to be synchronic or (to borrow terminology from the similar view of Carl Jung) archtypical: variations on common universal themes (9).

The exact ontological status (where exactly can this structure be found?) of Levi-Strauss' structural order was never established. It was more an *a priori* metaphysical assumption, however, if the evidence proved out and all social variables could be explained by such an assumption, one would be able to claim scientific status at least as justifiable as economics or quark physics. A notable effect of this structural determinism is (in the jargon of structuralism) its synchronic collapse of diachronic historical differentiation. That is to say, myths of aboriginal cultures are not different in kind or content from religions or ideologies of contemporary society. Any belief in historical progress is thereby ruled out. Projects to improve the human condition, such as politics, are chimerical.

This conservative effect of structuralism is largely retained by poststructuralism. There is in all of this what Habermas has called a performative contradiction. If all thought is simply variations and repetitions of primordial sources, what could be the status of structuralism itself? How would it know itself as an independent science of myths if its proponents were as determined by structure as it held all humans to ineluctably be? The difficulties of a determinant structuralism relates to the story being told here because the structuralist meta-narrative is what Jacques Derrida set out to deconstruct.

If Levi-Strauss (10) was influential in turning the minds of what would become known as the poststructuralists to semiotics (the science of signs) or more generally linguistics and philology, his structuralism, and its deterministic excess were not the only contributory to the great river of philosophy with its linguistic turn. Influential everywhere was the Viennese cum Cambridge philosopher Ludwig Wittgenstein. Wittgenstein was a brilliant logician originally pursuing tasks set for him by the logical positivist/atomist context within which he wrote (11).

Now, logic and linguistics can be associated with one another if language contains within itself universal logics or if logics are expressions of linguistic universals. The positivist/atomist project of working out a logic of all logics was at the same time a project of working out a language of all languages or a grammar of all grammars. From a postmodern point of view such optimistic and even arrogant projects are the signature of modernity. Such projects amount to totalizing by thought all which it surveyed.

In his early work Wittgenstein was thought to have filled out, as well as any genius could do, this logical/grammatical project. At the furthest extension of it, he concluded that the project could not be accomplished. Instead of the logic of all logics, Wittgenstein turned to more localized logics: the logics of what he called language games. Turning from meticulous logical analysis of terms, Wittgenstein began to tell stories, relate anecdotes, and put forth aphorisms. To demonstrate what? There can be no logic of logics: there can only be language, signs, significations within the context in which they are being used and, in effect, reciprocally co-determined by the context of that language game. Now rejected by Wittgenstein was any correspondence theory of truth. Signs, words, do not, point by point denote ontologically independent objects or facts. Rather are they part of (possibly incommensurable (see above)) language games.

2.   Text

One should not conclude that Wittgenstein's analysis of language games caused, in some linear geometrical sense, the subsequent postmodern emphasis on text and textuality. But all of the seeds of the textual orientation are there. Language games are an important type of text. In the postmodern lexicon text needs to be understood in its widest possible sense (12). Whole languages can be a text, as can particular writings and particular readings of writings. Regional cultures, like "the South" can be a text as can the myth structure of a Brazilian tribe. The interpretation of texts is of course the main industry of English departments, which in the American scene were the most hospitable to postmodern intellectual tendencies. In the disciplines gathered up by the Modern Language Association, the analysis of a multitude of texts has gained influence over the interpretation of the intentions of famous authors. Authors' own intentions are denied primacy or privilege. The story of, say, a feminist reading of The Great Gatsby is a text of presumably equal status to an autobiography of F. Scott Fitzgerald. (See discussion of the "other" above.)

Similarly, a political culture can be regarded as a text as can, for instance, the commonly held explanatory assumptions that underlie what is called "public administration" (13). The effect of regarding any social formation as a text or narrative is to reduce it to a story. Deconstructed thereby is, among other things, the distinction between fiction and nonfiction. All stories are equally privileged or non-privileged. Accordingly, multicultural-ism is substantiated by the emphasis on textuality and language games.

3.   Decentered Subjectivity

There is a sense in which the Cartesian cogito (I think therefore I am) has dominated modern Western thought. Privileged in such a formulation is individual consciousness. It is the primacy of consciousness which allows the feeling that each person has agency, autonomy, free will, and self-determination. The cogito supports the privileging of au-thorship. Of course, the cogito (and the metaphysics on which it is based) is one of those totalizing universals confuted by anti-foundationalist postmodern philosophy. In its place postmodernism emphasizes signs, significations, linguistic structures, para-digms, and texts. This much of Levi-Strauss' deterministic structuralism remains influ-ential: individual human beings are seen more as particular articulations of a text than authors of it. Individuals must use the languages and signs that precede them. A Serb cannot at the same time express the Chinese text and be a Serb. To put it in a phrase: its not so much that Faulkner writes about the South, it is rather that the South writes Faulkner.

Lost in the scheme of postmodernism is a robust centered self. Less are we unique individuals inventing ourselves, as existentialists would have it. More are we playing out a script among the few that are available to us. X is the script of a white bourgeois male who was expected to go to college and for whom that possibility was vouchsafed. The Y script is about a black male made dysfunctional by lead paint, improper nutrition, and affection deprivation. Script Z is of a Chinese female infant abandoned so that room in the trun-cated family decreed by state policy could be made for a male. The script "I think there-fore I am" seems but a comfortable illusion.

II.   POSTMODERN PHILOSOPHERS

For postmodernists, the self is not subjectively determinant. If it has stability at all, it comes from being embedded in language games not of one's own making. This doubt about the individual's ability to author her own life's script repeats the persistent theme in postmodern thought, the theme of doubt. As Jean Baudrillard put it, "We no longer be-lieve that the truth is true when all its veils have been removed" (13). Neither believing nor believing that we believe are any longer believable. Such mischievous apostasy makes postmodernists mutinous agitators in the eyes of the defenders of the Western canon.

Exactly who deserves the invective/approbation "postmodernist" is not a settled matter. We will include Jacques Lacan, Michel Foucault, Jean-Francois Lyotard, Richard Rorty, Jacques Derrida, and Jean Baudrillard as the portraits in our rogues gallery of post-modernists because we believe that they have important things to say to public adminis-trationists, whether or not they qualify as postmodernists in every commentator's lexicon. Perhaps Jean Baudrillard is the most apocalyptic postmodernist of them all, and we have reserved our discussion of him until last since he has articulated and described with illus-trations the phenomena of hyperreality, simulacra, and the postmodern condition in gen-eral. We will lead with Lacan, the most tenacious in linking the self to language.

A.   Lacan, Poststructuralism, and Discourse

Jacques Lacan is a French poststructuralist whose emphasis on language led to his characterizing the unconscious itself as a discourse. "What can I know? Reply: nothing in any case that doesn't have the structure of language; whence it follows that the distance I can go within this limit is a matter of logic." (15). Lacan argues that language has its own level of determinacy; it produces social effects and is tightly linked to the unconscious. This argument that language has effects is similar in form to structuralist arguments; for example, the argument that class structure is causal. But for Lacan, social structure dissolves when encountered by the preeminent effects of language; what appears as class structure is potently conditioned by language. This is true of social institutions in general.

Social institutions (broadly conceived as social practices) are systems of relations discursively ordered, oriented toward activities such as the production of legal documents, literature, film, or the implementation of public policy. Beyond some institutional structure there is no practice. Lacan has no patience for those (like Foucault below) who would treat institutions as if they were imposed on us for the purpose of our torture, and are not of our own making. After all, institutions provide venues for critique of institutionalized practice (such critique is itself an institutionalized practice). And institutions imply even more: There would be no language and no speech since words themselves are instituted in a culture through repetition. Hence we are more implicated in institutions than we have thought; they are as likely to be manifestations of freedom as restraints against it. Institutions are social spaces in which already-existing antagonisms are played out, where interests are denied or fulfilled, and values are upheld or denigrated (16).

Yet institutions cannot be reduced to outcomes of prior intersubjective struggles, for institutions themselves have determining effects which make them stable as well as malleable. Institutions carry within them the unconscious dimension of the subject. The individual is not an ahistorical subject with fixed preferences and a will to power, but is a subject at odds with itself, possessing among other things a desire not to know. There is no centered, unified self; rather there is a subject that is split between the conscious and the unconscious. An institution's meaning, as well as its complex failures of meaning (its accidents) coincide with the subject's split between conscious and unconscious.

Knowledge exists in the unconscious, Lacan claims, but only a discourse can articulate it. Reality has to reveal itself to us through this discourse. Lacan probes the unconscious not as something underneath discourse, but as an effect of everyday speech or such mental phenomena as works of art or dreams. In his probes, Lacan is fascinated by those instances where expression seems impossible. An encounter with the impossibilities mulling about in the unconscious—where the primal repression of those incongruities occur—is also an encounter with reality. This reality is not an objective, external reality, but a reality within the discourse of the unconscious which results from its impasses. Lacan's real is like Freud's trauma: the hole in discourse. This impasse-reality is the trouble in our lives, the irresolutions that present themselves when the impasses are confronted.

B.   Foucault, Power, and Docile Bodies

For Foucault, this structure of discourse, action, institutions, and belief is a system of knowledge that is interconnected, nay identical, to the system of power. Suspicious of any socialization process, Foucault writes about the regime of power behind all systems of knowledge, and perhaps his most scandalous claim is that knowledge itself is controlled in every society through mechanisms of power. Knowledge and power are linked; they enable each other. This notion cuts against the mainstream sentiment that knowledge is something we all ought to be able to accept; that it is neutral and empowering for everyone who acquires it. Foucault is not only saying that "knowledge is power" but more importantly, that "power is knowledge." This is not news for anyone who is not of the dominant white culture. Women, Native American Indians and African-Americans may well have experienced this aspect of knowledge, aware that knowledge they receive through established institutions reflects the status quo form of power.

Knowledge is comprised of institutional rules (that is, norms that guide recurring human practices) and of discourses that function through rules of exclusion or inclusion that leave some people out of the conversation. The deviants are excluded; criminals are out. Drug users are removed from political and social life. The mad and insane have been marginalized, and so have been the young, the old, the infirm, and the working class in general. Power is expressed in the way that knowledge includes or excludes. Knowledge functions through rules of exclusion; who may speak, about what, for how long, and in what settings and contexts.

Foucault describes the process of exclusion in *Madness and Civilization*. With increasing rationalization of the world, the mad began to be shut away into asylums where conditions were at first brutal, but were eventually "humanized." Foucault has a special disdain for the word humanism since he sees it as a word of exclusion. The Enlightenment reformers, those who would cure madness, created a whole new program for the mad that included observation, drugs, analysis, more analysis, and review. This "social-worker liberalism" formed a new mechanism of control, more totalitarian than before, that amounts to nothing more than therapeutic policing.

Foucault views every social institution as an equally unjustifiable knowledge system that structures domination. There is an inner connection between the domination of nature through knowledge and the domination of man through knowledge. Knowledge is a strategy of power, a discourse of power. He shows in *Discipline and Punish: the Birth of the Prisons* how interlocking systems of knowledge and power function. The book begins by describing, in eighteenth century France prior to the hegemonic rise of a "liberal humanist" episteme, how the body of a condemned man, Damiens the regicide, was drawn and quartered: Flesh was torn from his breasts, arms, thighs, and calves with red-hot pincers, then boiling oil and sulfur poured onto the exposed flesh, then horses were attached to his limbs to pull him apart, and during the ritual the condemned man kissed the crucifix that was held out to him as he asked forgiveness. By the end, the power of the king and the church had totally humiliated and destroyed "the body of the condemned," thereby expressing the king-killer Damiens as a criminal transgressor.

But the whole thing was a circus, "the spectacle of the scaffold." The criminal stole the show and turned out to be the star of the production. (In Damiens' case extra horses had to be brought in to pull his legs off.) As Foucault (17) put it, "the posthumous proclamation of the crimes justified justice, but also glorified the criminal. That was why the reformers of the penal system were soon demanding suppression" of the printed posters that announced the spectacles. Reformers decided that this practice was not healthy, that the wrong people were being celebrated.

So in modern times those defined as criminals undergo "generalized punishment," which includes a depersonalized surveillance that creates docile bodies. The warehousing of prisoners is a hero-less public works program for local economic development. Inmates are re-normalized and discharged back into the social body, rather than celebrated at punishment festivals. Inside the prison, the micro-power of observation is a way of controlling movement of the prisoner, who no longer has to kiss the crucifix; he merely accepts being a docile member of the social body, accepts the rules of the prison. Humanists want normal, docile bodies, Foucault complains, whether by incarceration, lobotomy, or Prozac.

The point Foucault makes is, of course, not only about prisons. He believes that the entire society is composed of docile bodies under surveillance. Women are surveilled with that existential gaze, and not only when walking past construction sights. Behavior is surveilled. Probationary faculty are surveilled. Students are surveilled. Workers are surveilled. Politicians' sex lives are surveilled. Hollywood celebrities are surveilled in tabloid newspapers. Society is its own carceral reformatory.

C.   Lyotard, Postmodernity, and the Condition of Knowledge

Jean-Francois Lyotard has studied the condition of knowledge in highly developed societies, and characterizes that condition as postmodern. Scientific knowledge has become a major force of production but has in the process been reduced to commodity status. He describes and affirms a movement away from scientific knowledge (which sets out conditions of empirical and logical rigor that serve as legitimating devices) and toward narrative knowledge which does not give primacy to its own legitimation, but rather "certifies itself in the pragmatics of its own transmission." Of narrative knowledge, one might simply ask: Does it ring true?

The fact/value dichotomy found in the philosophy of science is one of the first targets of Lyotard's critique. The pursuit of logic and facts corresponds to the aspirations of positivist social science for discovering universal truths. Such an epistemology seeks to find a universal language of all science, a universal logic of scientific explanation. Society is imagined as an objective reality, a unified totality, as it is in structural functionalism. However, when it becomes apparent that society is not an integrated whole—there are haves and have-nots, owners and workers, exploiters and exploited—the second half of the dichotomy is interposed. Critical, reflexive, or hermeneutic approaches are needed to sustain the otherwise one-sided fact-logic realism because, unlike positivistic approaches, these are capable of reflecting on values and aims. Lyotard cannot abide this dichotomizing tendency, with objectivity on one side and subjectivity on the other.

His demur is both astute and multifarious. Part of the problem of scientific knowledge as practiced is that it has become subordinated to the prevailing powers and made into an instrument of them. With Foucault, Lyotard sees knowledge and power as two sides of the same coin. Who decides what knowledge is, and who knows what needs to be decided—these are matters of political struggle.

Lyotard would revoke the licensing of the special procedures of scientific investigation that authorize science, and only science, to make knowledge claims. In the legitimation and proof process, science becomes a force of production, a moment in the circulation of capital. The production of proof is not only about truth; it is also about the best possible input/output equation. It is about "performativity." Indeed, higher education itself is held to performativity criteria as it supplies the economy with its needs. Innovation is under the command of the system and is used to improve its efficiency. Science, like any other hired hand, must perform. Power produces the knowledge that affirms it.

Science is a culture that first isolates its narrators (scientists) to give them a privileged status. Then science asks of the narrator what right he has to recount what he recounts, and the narrator legitimizes his recounting according to the norms of science. The narrator thus relinquishes the authority for his narrative over to the meta-narrative of scientific objectivity. But, protests Lyotard (18), "The narratives themselves have this authority." Lyotard is one of the main sources for affirming an egalitarianism of stories.

Narrative knowledge would be seen by traditional scientists as "savage, primitive, under-developed, backward, alienated, composed of opinions, customs, authority, prejudices, ignorance, ideology" (19). Lyotard, for his part, would prefer to rid the world of metanarratives like "science" (the ideology) and allow legitimacy to reside in first-order narratives.

The narrative approach of Lyotard would not fit the cybernetic, technological models of contemporary science. Instead of dichotomies following from the Cartesian metaphysical bifurcation of spirit and matter (objective/subjective, mind/body, or facts/values), Lyotard emphasizes both agonistic language and social bonds. Agonistic in ancient Greece means "to contend." The adversary may be some other person with a different world view who ascribes a different meaning to a particular speech act. In contrast the adversary may simply be the accepted connotation of a word used differently. Whether the game is highly competitive or one that is not necessarily played to be won, it is a game that cannot be played by the pre-programmed cyborgs of postmodernity. They merely go through the prearranged motions, unable to participate in interactive, agonistic discourse. Nor can cyborgs engage in the social bonding implied in language moves envisioned by Lyotard. Formal bureaucrats and scientistic cyborgs respond to informational cues, rules, and regulations, not to social bonds created in the lifeworld of human experience.

Narratives avoid explicit argumentation. Lyotard has been criticized for this on the grounds that he risks suspending the critical sense. For his part, Lyotard steps back from cultural and political evaluation. He instead accepts a thoroughgoing indeterminacy—utterly beyond ideology, values, and judgment—of cultural products and practices as the distinctive signature of postmodernity. Any standards against which to judge an argument are themselves but narratives. Thus narrative pragmatics advocated by Lyotard are incommensurable with the language game known as legitimacy. Narratives just do what they do.

Of all of our hall of famers, Lyotard is the most doggedly anti-foundationalist. He critiques as "totalizing" even such meta-narratives as "emancipation" even though these meta-narratives would introduce standards against which distinctions between deception and authenticity can be made. He would go so far as to abandon the liberal politics of the Enlightenment to avoid universalistic metanarratives. Not so Richard Rorty.

D. Rorty's Liberal Public Society

Richard Rorty is not as intent on giving up the canons of the Enlightenment as are his European counterparts, but neither does he believe in any foundation or goal—religious, scientistic, or otherwise—shaping society. Compared to poststructuralist European philosophers, Rorty is an upbeat American who hopes good things will become possible when we get out of the "dilapidated house of Being," a rather direct barb aimed toward Heidegger and Heideggerians. It is hard to tell where Rorty would take us with his deconstructive writing, but given his pragmatism and non-revolutionary incrementalism, it would be in a direction a bit different from modernity's, but not radically so.

With knowledge and science biased toward the regime of the status quo, Rorty's philosophy is particularly fitting for those in applied fields such as public administration:

> If we ever have the courage to drop the scientistic model of philosophy without falling back into a desire for holiness (as Heidegger did), then, no matter how dark the time, we shall no longer turn to the philosophers for rescue as our ancestors turned to the priests. We shall turn instead to the poets and the engineers, the people who produce startling new projects for achieving the greatest happiness of the greatest number (20).

Rorty applauds pragmatists such as Dewey who "turn away from the theoretical scientists to the engineers and the social workers—the people who are trying to make people more comfortable and secure, and to use science and philosophy as tools for that purpose" (21). Dewey would subordinate theory to practice, especially that nomothetic, predictive theory that "attempts to have an a priori place prepared for everything that might happen" (22). Positivists and analytical philosophers implicitly claim to have already read the script that we are currently acting out, or at least they aspire to being able to make that claim. Through such criticism, Rorty opposes his colleagues who advocate analytical philosophy, the logic-chopping variety of Anglo-American philosophy that is maternally related to positivism in social science (23). He claims that they are captives of a particular understanding of the mind as a great mirror. Rorty opts instead to tell stories, like Lyotard above, and to construct narratives, which is to put his claims in a context rather than appropriating universal validity for them.

Truth, says Rorty, is but our vocabulary. Truth is what understandings of truth are understandings of. Are there better understanding of truth? To establish criterion to answer that question is to make a power move. Power-truth assertions provoke Rorty's anti-foundationalism and lead also to his critique of the essentialism that drives that sort of truth-trumping inquiry, which, when applied to human affairs and moral/political reflection, has never been fruitful. So instead, Rorty invites us to try something new without actually specifying what the new possibilities would be. Impressed by the distinctive human ability to accomplish feats of social engineering, Rorty envisions a cultural movement away from philosophy and science and toward literature and language, which is one reason that pragmatic philosophy—Rorty's version of it—is useful for such social innovation. Pragmatism has always concerned itself with anti-essentialist interpretations and practice-oriented understanding, along with the utility of language and vocabularies in achieving human desires.

Consistent with the project of the Enlightenment, Rorty himself uses a vocabulary of private self-creation and a vocabulary of public praxis, the latter of which is concerned with the alleviation of oppression: "The point of a liberal society is not to invent or create anything, but simply to make it easy as possible for people to achieve their wildly different private ends without hurting each other" (24).

This vision for philosophy indicates the need for a simple, prosaic moral vocabulary that is intelligible to all (not just philosophers), hence enabling public discussion of issues and possible compromises in an arena of common discourse. A similar ambition underlies the enticement to discourse of Fox and Miller in *Postmodern Public Administration*. This sort of moral identity/vocabulary is called for in the public sphere only. Rorty vigorously defends the liberal distinction between private and public realms in the face of, say, feminists and gay activists who would erase that distinction in order to make their claims and problematics part of the public discourse.

For Rorty, private identities are, or should be, a separate matter. Only those who refuse to divide the public from the private realm, he warns, dream of a "total revolution" for society. Dreams of total revolution inspire counter-dreams of anarchy. By separating the private from the public sphere Rorty affirms the notion of a "limited government" that respects individual rights.

At the same time, Rorty is attentive to public things, and takes care to acknowledge the pubic contributions of trade unions, meritocratic education, the expansion of the franchise, and cheap newspapers. These institutions have allowed him to imagine a "communicative community" where citizens of democracies are willing to say "us" rather than "them" when they speak of political entities beyond their immediate (neo-tribal) associates. This sort of willingness has made religion progressively less important in the self-image of that citizenry. One's sense of relation to a power beyond the community becomes less important as one becomes able to think of oneself as a part of a body of public opinion, capable of making a difference to the public fate. (25)

Given that the Romantic poets and rationalist revolutionaries of the Enlightenment have already conspired to slay God the Father, there remains but a mop-up operation to be completed in that revolution. And once the standards used by the rationalists and Romantics to slay God are themselves unfrocked, the task of modernity will be complete. For Jacques Derrida, that day has arrived.

E. Derrida and Deconstruction

The term deconstruction originates from Heidegger's deconstruction of metaphysics, a project he undertook so he could construct an ontology of "Being." In digging through and underneath the notion of Being, he wanted to uncover its hidden history. In the process he called into question its tie to any stable present. As Heidegger's deconstruction progressed, "Being is _____" remained a difficult blank to fill in. No matter how many times someone offers something with which to fill in the blank, the matter is never settled. Jacques Derrida observes that the blank cannot be filled in. Why not?

Derrida's take on language is that it is full of metaphysical moments. It is the make-up of language that it is *not* constituted by reference (denotation). In a radical reconsideration of words, he is saying that words are necessary only when there is not something there. One might use the word "wedding ring" to refer to a ring on someone's finger. The words stands for something, the actual wedding ring, which itself stands for something, say a husband-wife love-bond; this is the mainstream representational view of words.

But for Derrida, words do something different: They stand *in* for things. Words are anti-representational. The term wedding ring is a matter of convenience; we do not have to present the reader with a wedding ring to write about one. We do not need to have a husband or wife present to communicate about the love-bond. The wedding ring gets its meaning from the absence of the husband or wife, not their presence. The immediate absence of the husband-wife love-bond is what makes the wedding ring, or the usage of any symbols or words, interesting. Absence of the object is one of the constitutive features of symbolic language. The different possibilities for further interpretation are dazzling: Perhaps the wedding ring is there to mask the radical absence of a husband-wife love-bond.

Just as reference to an object cannot account for meanings of words, neither can the intentionality of the speaker. This deconstructs both sides of the objective subjective dichotomy. Meaning is not necessarily what the speaker intends, unsettling as that might be to enthusiasts of the cogito and subjective idealists of all kinds. We are accustomed to the idea that there can be a right answer; multiple choice tests are like that.

But Derrida claims there is no such thing as the correct interpretation. He does not believe that "every reading is a misreading" but he does believe that every text may be interpreted in different ways. Even the speaker of an utterance may not have the "right" interpretation—slips of the tongue, for example, have long been thought of as windows to the unconscious, unintentional but revealing speech acts. Words are never perfectly denotative or representational (i.e., a mirror image of the speaker's intention or the object).

What is represented in the re-presentation is but a presentation. We never can find the word in the dictionary that fits exactly to the object or relationship we are discussing. Words are not that denotative. If they were, a word would have to say the same thing across usages (over time, in different situations, in different places). Words do not retain such constancy; they are but historically and culturally conditioned utterances, the relevance of which is determined by that context. Words as abstractions do not have their own existence, but depend on the possibility of repetition.

Oft-repeated words might especially be mistaken for the thing itself. These oft-repeated words are but human constructions grounded in historically contingent circumstances, though they are often taken (mis-taken) for immutable things. Avoiding such reification, Derrida emphasizes fallibility, contingency, and finitude in his writings. Further, both understanding and mis-understanding are constituent aspects of language. Words can mis-refer as easily as refer. Derrida here applies grand Hegelian dialectics to a kind of micro-dialectics of each sign. Even when we ask the store clerk for "that one" we sometimes have to add, "no, not that one, that one."

The point is that there will be no ultimate, correct interpretation. The attempt to hook words definitively to the external world has failed. This doesn't mean we can't talk about things. But it does leave a meaning vacuum that needs to be filled, a vacuum that gets in the way of being able to reduce meaning into self-evident codes that lie beyond vagueness and ambiguity. There are no unambiguous codes of meaning that are unvarying across all situations and all contexts.

If that is the case, why not teach multiple meaning systems in the universities? If there are no unvarying codes of meaning, why settle only on the meaning codes of dead white European males, analytical philosophers, and positivist social research? This language is as metaphorical as the next (although its poetry may be less aesthetically pleasing). White mythology is okay, but no more okay than women's mythology, Native American Indian mythology, or African-American mythology. This insight of Derrida's opens up the road for many other mythologies to speak with equal right, and has been termed multiculturalism and multi-perspectivalism. This radical ambiguity of meaning is the signature of the postmodern era.

F. Cruising through Hyperreality with Jean Baudrillard

Jean Baudrillard continues this line of thinking and concludes that discourse is no longer simply vague or ambiguous, but indeterminable. Multiple interpretations present themselves, and there is no way to stabilize meaning. He made this point repeatedly in his popular account of the Gulf War, which he believes was more a war against reality than anything else. Baudrillard described it as a technological extravaganza, and proclaimed TV's role in it to be "social control by collective stupefaction." In *The Gulf War Did not Happen*, he wrote "Whom to believe? There is nothing to believe. We must learn to read symptoms as symptoms, and television as the hysterical symptom of a war which has nothing to do with its critical mass. . . ." (26) Media is no longer a "mediating" power between reality at one end and perception at the other; there has been an implosion of the two poles: the medium is the message. CNN is what's happening. For meaning, this is a catastrophe.

The liquidation of meaning understood in power terms may represent the power to manipulate the masses, or, contrarily, it may represent alliance with the masses as they destroy the meaning structure of the status quo. Perhaps media manipulates in all directions at once. Perhaps the strategy of the masses is to reflect meaning without absorbing it. For whatever reason, political participation takes place against a backdrop of spontaneous indifference. Apathy is adaptive in the face of technological simulation.

Sorting out the simulations brought to us by technology is more troublesome than was the search for the essential Being. The business of drawing the line between the real and the hyperreal has become a moment-to-moment lifeworld problem; the essential Being could at least wait until tomorrow. This anxiety is more profound than Cartesian anxiety about relativism; it is a radical doubt about the very ground beneath our feet, like living in a perpetual earthquake.

For Baudrillard the term hyperreality describes this shaky condition. To understand hyperreality, one must also understand simulation and simulacra. The dictionary definition of a simulacrum is image, representation, or an insubstantial form or semblance of something. The definition of simulation is feigning, counterfeiting; a simulation is an imitative representation of the functioning of one system by means of the functioning of the other. A Baudrillardian image might help here:

Suppose, as sometimes still happens to inmates, that a prisoner is handed a representation of Jesus so that he may find solace in religion. Religious redemption is simulated with, say, a plastic Jesus figurine that was made available. Does this Jesus simulacrum really re-present divinity? The straightforward interpretation is yes, it truly does. But then again, maybe not.

Perhaps the truth is that this simulacrum (i.e. the plastic Jesus) effaces God, who is unspeakably glorious. In that case it is best to destroy the images, as the Iconoclasts (who sought true value rather than mere reflections) sought to do with icons. But this possibility brings on the appearance of a third, a destructive, annihilating truth—deep down God never existed, was never anything more than his own simulacrum.

So what to make of this plastic Jesus? Baudrillard (27) offers a four-part all-purpose interpretation:

1. It is, in fact, the reflection of a profound reality.
2. It masks and denatures a profound reality.
3. It masks the absence of a profound reality.
4. It has no relation to any reality whatsoever: it is its own pure simulacrum.

This set of interpretations begins with a straightforward, denotative interpretation. A word or a symbol is a mirror of reality. Then, reinterpreted, we suspect that the word/symbol profanes the actual. How can the glory that is God be represented by a plastic Jesus figure? It doesn't; the plastic Jesus debases God. Thirdly, we can see that the word covers up for the fact that there is no there there. After his visit to Disneyland, Baudrillard pronounced it a simulation of the third order (the one masking the absence of a profound reality): Disneyland hides the fact that it is the "real" America. Disneyland is presented as imaginary in order to make us believe that the rest is real. However, the America that plays in Disneyland is no longer real, but hyperreal, existing in a regime of simulation. By concealing the fact that the real is no longer real, Disneyland saves the reality principle.

Finally, when the reality principle is exposed as fraudulent, we reach hyperreality, the fourth-order interpretation where words and signs displace reality. "The scandal today is no longer in the assault on moral values but in the assault on the reality principle . . . the odium lies in the malversation of the real, the faking of the event" (28).

Hyperreality is a world of simulacra. If a thing cannot be simulated, it's not really real. Hyperreality is more real than real. "Osmos" is virtual reality art that is more real than real, and not only because we saw it on television; put on the headset and you can walk among the flora, go beneath the soil to see root structures, hang a left and go inside a leaf. The map is more real than the territory it represents. The burning house on TV (in some far away city) is more real than the burning house next door, an event not filmed for the 6:00 news. The simulations on the news have become more real than reality itself.

Lost in the process of simulation is the "charm of abstraction" and gained (if hyperreality can be regarded as a gain) is a blurring of the line between reality and image. Reality is that which can be simulated, xeroxed, copied, represented. The real no longer needs to be rational, because there are no reality criteria to measure it against. The real is no longer anything but a technical operation. Hyperreality is produced from a synthesizing, assimilating technology (e.g., VCR tapes, xerox machines, computer files, page scanners, spreadsheet programs, or Warhol's *Campbell's Soup*) and located in a social hyperspace. The "authentic reproduction" is more real than real. Technological reproducibility has become an affirming reality-check.

Still, there remains a curiosity over what a genuine experience would be like if we could have one. Attempts to satisfy this hunger for authenticity have led to further incongruities, however, such as the anthropologists' appeals to the Philippine government in 1971 "to return the few dozen Tasaday who had just been discovered in the depths of the jungle, where they had lived for eight centuries without any contact with the rest of the species, to their primitive state" away from anthropologists, ethnologists, and other manifestations of modernity (29). The anthropologists had already seen indigenous people disintegrate upon contact with outsiders. Science loses valuable assets when the Tasaday are put out of reach, but the object (that is, the Tasaday) will be safe, intact in its "virginity." "It is not a question of sacrifice (science never sacrifices itself, it is always murderous), but of the simulated sacrifice of its object in order to save its reality principle." (30). So instead of a genuine experience, savages are indebted to anthropologists for allowing them to remain savages in a simulacrum of life before anthropology.

If the Inquisition sought an admission of Evil, science seeks from its objects (rats and frogs, but also the Tasaday) an admission of objectivity. Confessions of rationality and objectivity are needed because it is of this very principle that science secretly despairs.

> [N]ever would the humanities or psychoanalysis have existed if it had been miraculously possible to reduce man to his "rational" behaviors. The whole discovery of the psychological, whose complexity can extend ad infinitum, comes from nothing but the impossibility of exploiting to death (the workers), of incarcerating to death (the animals), according to the strict law of equivalencies: so much caloric energy and time = so much work power; such an infraction = such an equivalent punishment; so much food = optimal weight and industrial [turkey factory] death (31).

Fatal Strategies is a book about how people attempt to avoid banality under these postmodern conditions. Consciousness-raising will not help us since there is already an overproduction and regeneration of meaning and speech; this overproduction is the hallmark of the system. Our virtual has definitively overtaken the actual and we must be content with this extreme virtuality which deters any movement toward action. Political nihilism portends the destruction of the era of meaning. This is postmodernity, where we neutrally observe, accept, assume, and analyze. But eventually, even nihilism is impossible because it is still a theory, a world view of catastrophe where meaning still means something.

(W)e will fight obscenity with its own weapons. To the truer than true we will oppose the falser than false. We will not oppose the beautiful to the ugly, but will look for the uglier than ugly: the monstrous. We will not oppose the visible to the hidden, but will look for the more hidden than hidden: the secret . . . We will not distinguish the true from the false, but will look for the falser than false: illusion and appearance (32).

And now, hope for meaning vanishes; the cybernetic system is steadfast. Everything can be poured into indifference. All that remains is fascination for the operation of the system of replication that annihilates us. Baudrillard's dark verdict contains some erudite advice. We need to learn to live with uncertainty and the giddiness of hyperreality, and to be wary of the over-quick reduction of complexity. Rather than be despondent, we should realize that America is the utopia that everyone dreamed of. It may be mournfully trivial, but in spite of this, the end of the world is an opportunity. What is "the world" anyway but a category of domination?

III. POSTMODERNITY AS AN ERA

The previous two sections on themes and players concentrated on postmodernism: essentially philosophical developments occurring within a text whereby a rough agreement exists as to what the important questions are. Writers primarily have each other as their mind's eye audience. We want now to entertain the notion that we are in the process of transition from one era to another, from modernity (understood as an historical period like renaissance, not as a synonym for "contemporary") to postmodernity.

To mark out historical periods is always an assuming and controversial task. This is especially true when those who attempt it, live on the cusp between two of them; standing as it were with one foot in each era. Drawing a line or band of demarcation between eras is especially difficult in relation to modern and postmodern because it requires a distinctly modern god's-eye platform so firmly eschewed by postmodern thinkers. As a final demur, even those who claim to recognize an epochal shift have different names for the newer one: post-industrialism, information age, third wave and high modernism. In what follows in this section we first explore the meanings of "post," and then explicate the aspect of postmodernity most important for public affairs; i.e., the transformation of the mode of production and the accompanying shift to hyperreality.

The "post" in "postmodernity" has two senses: "after" and "over-against." In its "after" aspect postmodernity follows modernity. Modernity, in turn, refers to that period of time corresponding roughly from the Enlightenment (eighteenth century with, in philosophy, the breakout figure being seventeenth century philosopher Rene Descartes). This is the period of the industrial revolution, the triumph of science, the spread of capitalism and the consolidation of nation-states. It may be seen as reaching its high tide in the decade following World War II.

Postmodernity obviously emerges (periods don't happen overnight) after that. In Intellectual history, it may be traced back to Neitzsche and perhaps the American pragmatists. Antinomian to modernity, it corresponds to the post-industrial/information revolution, a sense that science as the conquest of nature may have overreached, the triumph of trans-national or international capital and the advent of the disintegrations of empires and nations.

In the "over against" aspect of the postmodern condition, centrifugal or entropic historical-cultural forces play off modernity's centripetal forces. The following series of oppositions are illustrative.

Problematic	Modern	Postmodern
Mode of production	Mass assembly, factory	Postindustrial, information
Organization	Weberian hierarchy c	Adhocracy, devolution
Sociology	Nuclear family	Fragmented households
Philosophy of science	Logical positivism	Methodological anarchy, narrative, ideography
Philosophy	Search for universals	Anti-foundationalism
Psychology	Integrated authentic self	Decentered self
Ethics	Utilitarian, deontological, syllogistic	Situational, contextual
Media	Print linearity	Video, montage, MTV, channel surfing

Expressed in manner reminiscent of Parsonian pattern variables we get (modernity on the left, postmodernity on the right):

integration versus disintegration
centralization versus decentralization
centripetal versus centrifugal
totalization versus fragmentation
metanarratives versus disparate texts
universalism versus relativism
Newton versus Heisenberg

The most important element of the transformation from modernity to postmodernity for those concerned with public affairs is the economic/production one. It is associated with the widely noted move from an industrial to a post-industrial society; from an economy based primarily on the production of material goods to one based primarily on information technologies, services, marketing, credit, and consumption. To be sure, this transformation, like the earlier move from agricultural production to industrial production, is one of dominant tendencies or ideal-typical profiles. Of course we still produce agricultural and industrial commodities but as the paradigm case of farm labor was replaced by the paradigm case of the assembly line, the paradigm case of work today is an office where symbols (words, numbers, computer icons) are analyzed and manipulated.

This paradigm case increasingly includes declining wages, denial of medical and retirement benefits, and temporariness as opposed to career engagement with the employer. This development has also been heralded as the advent of the information age. Toffler (33) and Newt Gingrich (in his public performances) make a similar point about first (agricultural), second (factory industrial), and third (information) waves.

The main implication of the production metamorphosis to be teased out for an understanding of public affairs is the theory of hyperreality or what we call *self-referential epiphenomenalism*. Analysis of the postmodern condition finds that words, symbols and signs are increasingly divorced from direct lifeworld experience. Part of this results from the switch from a society based primarily on production to one based primarily on consumption and information.

Production requires group activity and communication based on the manipulation and processing of physical objects; there is a rootedness based on the direct interface between humans and material; symbolic meanings are similarly rooted. To the contrary, in the consumptive economic mode of postmodernity symbols float away, and procreate with other symbols leading to what Jameson (34) calls "the free play of signifiers."

As the design of products to which symbols are attached become too complex for the consumers to master, symbols lose their mooring lines. Marketers take advantage of this and manipulate the symbols and attach them to other symbols. Thus do machines become sexy, cleaning fluids repair dysfunctional families and to purchase a particular brand of colored carbonated water is to signify membership in a generation. Some articles of clothing are favored precisely because their manufacturer's name is prominently displayed; wearing, say, "Nike" signifies lean, fit, graceful, sexy, Michael Jordan—much more important than a shirt. The logo or symbol becomes more important than the functional product. Similarly in politics symbols, often purposefully misleading, replace deliberation over policy. Willie Horton becomes a logo for Massachusetts penal policy, "read my lips" a fiscal policy, and "Clinton" as a modifier signifying "big-government-tax-and-spend" when attached to "health plan" or "welfare reform."

As more and more signs detach themselves from lifeworld elements that they were presumably designed to denote, they enter a realm which postmodernists call hyperreality. Once a sign takes up permanent residence in hyperreality any kind of reality which may be called empirical loses influence over it. Better, hyperreality has a life of its own outside and hovering above the experiential reality of day to day life. Celebrities, the O.J. Simpson case, television sports programs, and much of electoral politics exist therein, with only the most tenuous relationship to the phenomenological reality of daily life. Moreover, hyperreality or hyperspace is extremely volatile and thin.

The subjective expression of the same thing is the lament about America's nano-second attention span. It is also the case that exactly what gets paid short attention to is random and arbitrary. Which of hundreds of children's need for an organ transplant becomes publicized depends on whether Bosnia, Somalia, Newt, Bill, or a Congressional vote has hogged hyperspace for that moment. Finally, although there may well be logics to the ascension of symbols to hyperspace (e.g., white Bosnians over black Rwandans) there is no consistent logic which might be unpacked for analysis and correction.

If the postmodern thesis is correct, the result would be the loss of a certain concretized rationality. Rational will-formation becomes increasingly difficult when language loses its ability to communicate the discrete work-a-day reality of public policy implementation and organizational life. Worse, symbols interacting in hyperspace without benefit of mooring in work-a-day reality can only come back around to distort any reform of that reality.

IV. IMPLICATIONS OF POSTMODERNITY AND POSTMODERNISM FOR GOVERNANCE

If it is true that we are on the cusp between eras, the effects on all aspects of life will be incalculably immense. Three problematics for governance emerge from our cloudy "crystal" ball: 1. irrational systems steering; 2. power and domination, and 3. simulacra or virtual bureaucracy.

A. Irrational Systems Steering

To the extent that hyperreality slips underneath work-a-day reality, the steering capacity of government is eroded. When bumper sticker policy analysis based on anecdotal narratives guides policy, policy effectiveness is likely to suffer. At risk, for instance, is sane environmental policy. If, as has been proposed, the Environmental Protection Agency is abolished or slashed based on horror stories of burdensome over-regulation, have we not, even after admitting a certain ham-fistedness at EPA, thrown away a valuable policy tool? Is it rational to render prisons into nursing homes, imposed by the symbolic resonance of "three strikes and you're out," with expenses to be wrung out of education and infrastructure? Is the unproven neologism that "welfare causes dependency" a good guide to child sustenance systems?

There are in public administration already a plethora of impossible jobs in case work, regulatory work, and financial management work. Until some way is found to tether wildly fluctuating affective signs, one can only look forward to the jobs becoming more impossible.

B.   Panopticon

Another possible implication of postmodernism/postmodernity relates to the internal dynamics of organizations. If postmodernists (especially Foucault) encounter domination in all social institutions, bureaucratic hierarchical authority is the epitome of the theme. Organizational structure is not only a structure of discourse/action/institutions/belief; it is also a system of power. Institutional norms, which guide recurring human practices and their related discourses, function through rules of exclusion or inclusion that leave some people out of the conversation. Power is expressed in the way that institutional practices include or exclude: who may speak, about what, for how long, and in what settings or contexts. Every social institution, it would follow, structures domination. Organizational actors are themselves implicated in the daily re-creation of bureaucratic institutions, which, for all the complaints about domination, also enable the sorts of discursive associations that the expression of professional competence requires. Bureaucratic institutions are social spaces in which antagonisms are played out, factional interests are denied or fulfilled, values and aspirations of coalitions of players are upheld or disparaged and a discourse of power and domination happens.

In public administration, for example, knowledge institutions (especially MPA programs) explicitly endorse the system of hierarchical domination, most obviously by socializing (for example) city managers who sit at the apex of systems of domination. Institutions are cages, social spaces where conduct is disciplined, where individuals are under surveillance, and where institutional practices favor the regime of the status quo. It is not anticipated that even the autocratic, bullying city manager will be displaced by revolution among the city employees.

Unlike the emancipatory doctrines of modernity, revolutionary movement away from status quo practices is not anticipated by postmodernist thinkers. Continued surveillance and repetition are more likely than revolution, and neutral indifference is the best attitudinal response available to the inmates.

C.   Simulacra

Analysts, bureaucrats, and managers surveil their charges as they count their variables: Name? Social security number? Phone number? Have you ever been on AFDC? What is your monthly take-home pay? We need a urine sample. But, surveillance is not personal, it is aggregate. It's not John Doe qua John Doe that interests the for-hire data analysts, it's his credit rating, the statistical profile within which he fits, a series of binary ciphers in cyberspace.

Institutions themselves are also under epiphenomenal surveillance. Actual performance is no longer the criterion against which institutions are evaluated; they must produce simulacra of performance, paperwork that indicates performance has occurred. Simulacra of performance have displaced performance as the criteria against which institutions are evaluated. The proof is in the computer records, and available in hard copy or on disk. Is the indicator replicable, countable, verifiable? Do graduates of the school score well on standardized tests? What is the bed ratio at the local hospital? What is the clearance rate of the police department? What is the bacteria count at the restaurant that may be shut down by the Public Health Department? Should students learn, or should course evaluations scores be high? Should clients be assisted, or should cases be processed? Should public order be maintained, or should convictions of those arrested be attained?

Even the Alabama chain gangs are only simulating real chain gangs. There is no industrial need for smashed-by-hand rocks when big machines can accomplish the same task far more efficiently. Sufficient staffing with bull-whip shotgun-toting uniformed officers is too expensive to enforce "hard labor." Chain gangs in postmodernity are for media consumption, the TV-authenticated simulacra of the newest and latest "get tough on criminals" motif.

Yet even in the face of postmodern hyperreality, there is the possibility of optimism (35). Organized public action indicates the need for a common, principled vocabulary that is intelligible to all, hence enabling public discussion of issues as well as the development of possible rapprochement in an arena of common discourse. This ambition to discourse calls for a common identity and vocabulary among society's many sub-groups—sub-groups that may have quite separate languages for their private lives. A common ground is needed if the public conversation is to be a shared temporal one.

Our depiction of postmodernity leads to this fork in the road: With Baudrillard, we might forge an armor of neutral indifference as a sensible strategy for fending off degenerated hyperreality in which words and signs have become estranged from meaning; or, with Rorty, we might, in the face of this same hyperreality, commit to communal development of a democratic discourse of action—"what should we do next?"

NOTES

1. R. Rorty, *Philosophy and the Mirror of Nature*, Princeton, New Jersey: Princeton University Press, 1979.

2. J. F. Lyotard, *The Postmodern Condition: A Report on Knowledge*, (G. Bennington and B. Massumi, trans.), Minneapolis: University of Minnesota Press, 1984, p. xxiii.

3. We do not think that anti-foundationalism necessarily leads to nihilism. Actually, in our view, only disappointed or nostalgic foundationalists make such claims against postmodern views. If postmodernists, including on this issue phenomenologists, pragmatists, nominalists and so on are correct about the questionable ontological status of absolutes, then absolutes have never really anchored judgments in the ways that those who embrace absolutes suppose. Thus to now claim that the kid who recognized that the emperor has no clothes is at fault for the disrobement seems to us fatuous. See C. J. Fox and H. T. Miller. *Postmodern Public Administration: Toward Discourse*, Thousand Oaks, California: Sage Publications, 1995, ch. 4.

4. M. Foucault, *The Order of Things*, New York: Pantheon.

5. T. Kuhn, *The Structure of Scientific Revolutions*, (2nd. ed.), Chicago: University of Chicago Press, 1970.

6. A. MacIntyre, *After Virtue*, 2nd ed., Notre Dame, Indiana: Notre Dame University Press, 1984.

7. C. J. Fox and H. T. Miller, Public administration: A short treatise on self-referential epiphenomena," *Administrative Theory & Praxis*: 15, 1–17, 1993.

8. M. Poster, *Critical Theory and Poststructuralism: In Search of a Context*, New York: Cornell University Press, 1989.

9. We are troubled here by the dilemma of over-simplification versus explication tangential to this forum. The problem of deep structure was willed to philosophy by the Kantian distinction between phenomena (that which human minds grasp) and noumena (things-in-themselves). Kant and any philosophical stance that can be called neo-Kantian holds that only phenomena can be apprehended. But what, so to speak, unites the phenomena of human minds? Kant argued that it is the universal (to human minds) categories of time, space and causation which allow for intersubjective validation of, say, scientific truths. It is but a short step from this to neo-Kantian theories which attempt to moderate or improve on Kant's categories. We are concentrating on the French versions of these but the work of Noam Chomsky on deep structures of grammar, pre-programmed (or wired, as it were) in human minds is an allied tendency. Similarly derivative of this Kantian problematic are such metaphysical constructions as (to give the main French referent) Durkheim's collective unconscious. Depth psychology, Jungianism, psychoanalysis and even some of the more idealistic variants of phenomenology (e. g. Schutz's interpretation of Husserl) posit similar loci for unifying human minds. An accessible overview of Kant and how his Continental successors dealt with his legacy is W. T. Jones, *A History of Western Philosophy, Vol. IV, Kant to Wittgenstein and Sartre*, 2nd. ed., New York: Harcourt Brace & World, 1969.

10. For a more complete program of players see E. Kurzweil, *The Age of Structuralism: Levi-Strauss to Foucault*, New York: Columbia University Press, 1980. To those who want the whole story please note the enormous influence of Saussere and his followers in the French context and such pragmatic (pragmaticist) thinkers on the American scene as Charles Peirce.

11. Again, to those who want to pursue a more fulsome story it is necessary to understand the projects of the Vienna Circle and the problematics of Moore and Russell's *Principia Mathematica*. See, for an overview, C. J. Fox and H. T. Miller, Positivism, J. Schafritz (ed.) *International Encyclopedia of Public Administration*, Denver: Westview (forthcoming 1997)

12. D. J. Farmer, *The Language of Public Administration: Bureaucracy, Modernity, and Postmodernity*, Tuscaloosa: University of Alabama Press, 1995.

13. D. J. Farmer, *The Language of Public Administration: Bureaucracy, Modernity, and Postmodernity*, Tuscaloosa: University of Alabama Press, 1995.

14. J. Baudrillard, *Simulacra and Simulation*, (Sheila Faria Glaser trans.), Ann Arbor: University of Michigan Press, 1994, p. 77.

15. J. Lacan, *Television*, (D. Hollier, R. Krauss, A. Michelson, and J. Mehlman trans.) (J. Copjec, ed.) New York: W. W. Norton & Company, 1990, p. 36.

16. J. Copjec, "Dossier on the Institutional Debate: An Introduction," in Lacan, *Television*, 1990, pp. 49–52.

17. M. Foucault, *Discipline & Punish: The Birth of the Prison*, (Alan Sheridan trans.) New York: Vintage Books, 1979, p. 68.

18. J.-F. Lyotard, *The Postmodern Condition: A Report on Knowledge*, Translated by Geoff Bennington and Brian Massumi. Minneapolis: University of Minnesota Press, 1984, p. 22.

19. J.-F. Lyotard, *The Postmodern Condition: A Report on Knowledge*, (Geoff Bennington and Brian Massumi trans.) Minneapolis: University of Minnesota Press, 1984, p. 27.

20. R. Rorty, *Essays on Heidegger and Others: Philosophical Papers*, Vol. 2, New York: Cambridge University Press, 1991, p. 26.

21. R. Rorty, *Essays on Heidegger and Others: Philosophical Papers*, Vol. 2, New York: Cambridge University Press, 1991, p. 9.

22. R. Rorty, *Essays on Heidegger and Others: Philosophical Papers*, Vol. 2, New York: Cambridge University Press, 1991, p. 11.

23. C. J. Fox and H. T. Miller, *Postmodern Public Administration*, 1995.

24. R. Rorty, *Essays on Heidegger and Others: Philosophical Papers*, Vol. 2, New York: Cambridge University Press, 1991, p. 196.

25. R. Rorty, *Essays on Heidegger and Others: Philosophical Papers*, Vol. 2, New York: Cambridge University Press, 1991, p. 171.

26. J. Baudrillard, *The Gulf War Did Not Take Place*, (Paul Patton trans.), Bloomington: Indiana University Press, 1995, pp. 41–42.

27. J. Baudrillard, *Simulacra and Simulation*, (Sheila Faria Glaser Trans.) Ann Arbor: University of Michigan Press, 1994, p. 6.

28. J. Baudrillard, *The Gulf War did not take place*, (Paul Patton trans.), Bloomington: Indiana University Press, 1995, p. 76.

29. J. Baudrillard, *Simulacra and Simulation*, (Sheila Faria Glaser trans.), Ann Arbor: University of Michigan Press, 1994, p. 7.

30. J. Baudrillard, *Simulacra and Simulation*, (Sheila Faria Glaser trans.), Ann Arbor: University of Michigan Press, 1994, p. 7.

31. J. Baudrillard, *Simulacra and Simulation*, (Sheila Faria Glaser trans.), Ann Arbor: University of Michigan Press, 1994.

32. J. Baudrillard, *Fatal Strategies*, (Philip Beitchman and W. G. J. Niesluchowski trans.), Jim Fleming (ed.), Semiotext(e): New York, 1990, p. 7.

33. A. Toffler, *The Third Wave*, New York: Bantam Books, 1981.

34. F. Jameson, *Postmodernism or the Cultural Logic of Late Capitalism*, Durham, North Carolina: Duke University Press, 1991.

35. C. J. Fox and H. T. Miller, *Postmodern Public Administration*, 1995.

Part VII
Postmodern Alternative

PUBLIC ENTREPRENEURISM

We must turn bureaucratic institutions into entrepreneurial institutions, ready to kill off obsolete initiatives, willing to do more with less, eager to absorb new ideas (David Osborne and Ted Gaebler, *Reinventing Government*, 1992).

TWENTY-FIRST CENTURY PHILOSOPHY AND PUBLIC ADMINISTRATION

The rational, male, technocrat, quantitative, goal-dominated, cost-benefit driven, hierarchical, short-term, pragmatic, materialistic model must give way to a new kind of leadership based on different assumptions and values (Charles Garafalo, *Leadership, Ethics, and Change*, 1995).

22

Public Entrepreneurism

A New Paradigm for Public Administration?

Alan C. Melchior

Towson University, Towson, Maryland

"We must turn bureaucratic institutions into entrepreneurial institutions, ready to kill off obsolete initiatives, willing to do more with less, eager to absorb new ideas."

David Osborne and Ted Gaebler

From *Reinventing Government*

I. INTRODUCTION

Scholars in the field of public administration have long struggled to define a theme that unites them. The search has led public administration from the initial focus on neutral competence first articulated by Woodrow Wilson in *The Study of Administration* to criticisms of neutral competence based in a concern for the political aspects of public administration. The latest episode in the quest to establish a paradigm for public administration is the emergence of the public entrepreneurism movement.

Like its theoretical predecessors, the public entrepreneurism movement has enriched the debate over appropriate principles for public administration in the U.S. Proponents of public entrepreneurism, such as Osborne and Gaebler, aspire to usher in a new paradigm of public administration scholarship and practice. Entrepreneurial theories of public administration promise to resolve value conflicts arising around issues of institutional design and public administration practice that earlier theories could not resolve.

The analysis presented in this chapter argues that entrepreneurial theory provides an inadequate basis for a new paradigm of public administration. Entrepreneurial theory does, however, make an important contribution to public administration theory and practice by rendering a previously overlooked perspective on the reality of public organizations. In particular, it highlights the importance of competitiveness as a value for public administrators that rivals more familiar values such as responsiveness and technical competence.

This chapter explores the role of entrepreneurial theory in the development of a paradigm for public administration theory, reform, and practice in the U.S. In discussing this subject, four topics are explored. First, the historical context of public entrepreneurism is examined. The public entrepreneurism movement traces its origins to the development and intersection of two theoretical traditions: entrepreneurial theory and public administration theory. An investigation of evolving themes in public administration literature and trends in governmental reform demonstrates how the principles of entrepreneurial theory satisfied expectations of government that were not satisfied by the principles supporting earlier theories.

Second, the content of the theory and practice of public entrepreneurism is examined. A key aspect of entrepreneurial initiatives in the public sector is the application of the principles of entrepreneurial management, as presented in the works of Peter Drucker as well as in Osborne and Gaebler's *Reinventing Government*. The tenets of entrepreneurial management and efforts to get government agencies to adopt them are explored here.

Third, the rhetoric of public entrepreneurism is evaluated on two fronts. An exploration of the meaning of the key concept, "entrepreneurial management," shows how nebulous this term is. As a result, it is difficult to identify public entrepreneurism as a clear set of principles or practices for public administrators. Even if one can identify who a public entrepreneur is and what he or she does, it is unclear what the utility of public entrepreneurism is.

Public entrepreneurism promises an increased capacity for productivity and a shift in who controls public organizations. In assessing the utility of public entrepreneurism, one must ask "how much capacity for whom?" and not simply "how much capacity?" This assessment explores the opportunities and problems that entrepreneurial theory presents for technically-oriented public administrators known as public professionals. While trying to enhance an organization's capacity to serve all of its constituents creates conflicts for all public administrators, such conflicts are particularly acute for public professionals.

Fourth, the contribution of entrepreneurial theory to public administration theory is reconsidered. If the marriage of these two theoretical traditions does not lead us to a new paradigm of "the entrepreneurial state," then what has it led us to? The answer is that entrepreneurial theory provides us with one more piece in the puzzle known as normative public administration theory.

Each of the prior attempts to establish a normative theory of public administration rests on a particular principle, which reflects the interests of some constituencies over others. The nineteenth century emphasis on loyalty and partisanship favored control of government capacity being in the hands of political parties and elected officials. The subsequent movement towards technocracy and "neutral competence" reflected the public administration community's value for deference to scientific claims of knowledge.

Proponents of public entrepreneurism place a value on competitiveness in a changing environment. Political responsiveness, professional competence, and competitiveness are all desirable qualities for public agencies in a democratic system. A question remains, however, about whether these values can be achieved concurrently. If not, public administration theorists and practitioners are left to complete the puzzle of how to reconcile the divergent norms of public administration theory.

II. HISTORICAL DEVELOPMENT OF PUBLIC ENTREPRENEURISM

The story of the development of public entrepreneurism as a theoretical and practical concern is an account of the meeting of two theoretical traditions. The first is a tradition of normative public administration theory, which has sought to prescribe an appropriate set of values to guide the evolution of the bureaucratic state. The second is a tradition of entrepreneurial theory, which aims to identify and describe the factors that make markets dynamic.

The marriage of these two traditions reflects a pair of acknowledgments. Scholars of public administration and entrepreneurism alike have recognized that the public sector, like the private sector, is a dynamic and competitive environment. Thus, these scholars spotted an opportunity to apply principles of economic theory to the empirical study of political institutions. Both groups also recognized a void in normative theories regarding political institutions. Specifically, political actors and organizations must understand how to negotiate their changing environments in order to attain goals and govern effectively, yet there had been no focused discussion in the public administration community regarding the value of entrepreneurism as an administrative value.

In order to understand how these two theoretical streams converged, one must trace the discussions regarding public administration norms and entrepreneurism up to the point of their intersection. An examination of the values inherent in public administration and entrepreneurial theories prior to the public entrepreneurism movement illuminates the void in each that needed to be filled. This examination also demonstrates how the public entrepreneurism movement has attempted to fill these voids.

A.   Normative Theories of Public Administration

Early American scholars' conceptions about the role of public administrators stem from the works of Max Weber. Public bureaucracies, according to Weber (1), grew in reaction to the complex changes taking place in modern society, such as the development of money-based, capitalist economies, the expansion of public-sector activity, and the transition from agrarian to industrial society. These changes led to increases in political and economic power for many who previously could not make demands on the state. The state responded to new demands by turning over much of the task of governance to bureaucrats. Because bureaucracies are staffed by technically-trained specialists and structured hierarchically so as to make them accountable to politicians, the state was able to harness the power of the latest technological advances for its own uses. Weber argued that the primary end of government is to maintain power, and toward that end bureaucracies help governments to address the various demands of constituents.

The Weberian model of bureaucracy as scientific, impartial, and obedient to popular will was attractive to the proponents of the Progressive Reform movement of the late nineteenth century and early twentieth century. Progressives were troubled by the prospect that the U.S. may not be immune to the problems associated with industrialized European countries (2). They attributed a declining U.S. economy and morality to the growth of populism in general and to the governance of cities by political machines in particular. Progressives promoted bureaucratic organization as a means for improving a system of government that was becoming increasingly incompetent and corrupt. By applying science to the process of administration, experts with "proper" training would be entrusted with the responsibility of resolving factual disputes and introducing "morals" back into the political process.

Reformers were generally concerned with promoting rationality and morality in all aspects of society (3). They assumed that individuals could perfect themselves through knowledge. In a society of knowledgeable individuals, factions dissipate and a public interest can be identified. In *The Study of Administration*, Woodrow Wilson proposed that an administrative science was needed in order to help public bureaucrats pursue the public interest (4).

Wilson defined the role of bureaucrats according to their relationship with elected officials. He recommended a separation of labor between elected and administrative officials along the fault lines of a "politics-administration dichotomy." According to Wilson, elected officials represent the popular will by making policies that reflect the values of their constituents. Once values were incorporated into policy, questions remained regarding how to implement policy as to best reflect the values of their electorate. Wilson saw this task as a factual proposition, and he prescribed that administrators were to act as legitimate arbiters of factual controversies.

In performing this function, public administrators have to be responsive to both their hierarchical superiors as well as to the communities served by their agencies (5). While Wilson was not the only Progressive Reformer to make this distinction between political and administrative officials, he is credited with being the first scholar to propose a separate discipline devoted to the study of public administration (6).

During the early years of public administration's development as an area of scholarship, leaders in the field, such as Louis Brownlow, Leonard White, and Luther Gulick, built an academic community based on the natural science model. By marketing their research as "impartial and objective," public administration scholars could investigate controversial policy issues without opening themselves up to criticisms of political bias (7). Early public administration organizations, such as the Public Administration Clearing House and the Social Science Research Council's Advisory Committee on Public Administration, were vulnerable to such claims, largely because of their ties to the philanthropy of the Rockefeller family. The emphasis on scientific research meant that public administrators were expected to be accountable to scientists as well as elected officials and communities.

As the idea of the politics-administration dichotomy gained acceptance among scholars and practitioners, another idea took hold: adherence to scientific principles and the professional norms they generate enhances the capacity of public organizations. This idea was legitimized by the report of the President's Committee on Administrative Management (8), also known as the "Brownlow Commission." In particular, the Commission argued that administrative executives could rely on scientific expertise to free themselves from the ill effects of political control. The theme of professionalism as a capacity-building force was echoed twelve years later by the First Hoover Commission, which recommended an increase in professional management.

As the number of governmental agencies grew in response to the perceived need to respond to changing conditions and citizen demands, an already well-established fear of bureaucracy began to grow (9). The report of the First Hoover Commission reflected the changing mood. Recommendations revealed an attempt to reconcile increased capacity with increased political control through lines of command that linked public agencies with the President through cabinet-level officials (10). Though few of its recommendations were accepted, the Second Hoover Commission went even farther in its attempts to constrain the public bureaucracy (11).

Both the "neutral competence" and "political responsiveness" models of public administration rested on arguments about what kind of government official is best equipped to represent the will of the public regarding administrative matters. By the late 1960s, many scholars of public administration began to question whether government officials, either elected or appointed, had lost touch with the public. These scholars, united by their advocacy for more democratic public administration, referred to themselves as the "New Public Administration" movement.

Proponents of the New Public Administration refocused the discussion of public administration theory away from the question of who should act on behalf of the public to how bureaucratic organizations could increase public involvement in civic life. The New Public Administration movement's normative emphasis was on *"the reduction of economic, social, and psychic suffering and the enhancement of life opportunities for those inside and outside the organization"* (12, italics in original). Rather than being beholden to the dictates of elected officials or professionals, "new" public administrators would play a distinct role in advocating for the interests of minorities who are not adequately represented by elected officials (13).

The social and economic problems that fueled the urgency of the New Public Administration message ultimately led to the movement's demise. Key scholars in the movement offered a new role for public administrators in the lives of ordinary citizens, calling for organizations that address "relevant" issues and build an awareness of their interactions with clients (14). However, growing impatience with the seemingly intractable problems of poverty and urban violence led to a decrease in confidence in the political system. A series of "national disgraces" during the 1970s contributed to the mood: protracted U.S. military involvement in Southeast Asia, the Watergate scandal, the oil crises of 1973 and 1979, the taking of American hostages in Iran. Whereas trust in political executives was once the plug that help in the dike of a growing agenda and expanding policy commitments, without widespread trust in the system, politicians were left without a defense against the public's disappointment in government's insufficient capacity to handle its commitments.

In this climate of decreasing expectations of government competence and increasing public discontent, the focus of public administration theorists swung from the issue of control to the issue of capacity. Politicians, and public administrators themselves, needed a new rhetoric to convince the public that it still needed government. However, the new rhetoric could not call upon the public to trust or give responsibility to government. Entrepreneurial theory was able to provide politicians and the public administration community with the foundation for an attractive new rhetoric.

B. Entrepreneurial Theory

Though public entrepreneurism did not gain wide popularity until the 1980s, its theoretical basis goes back to the early 1800s. J. B. Say defined an entrepreneur as someone who combines the agents of production, namely land, capital, and labor, into an organized venture (15,16). The concept of "entrepreneurism" was first incorporated into a systematic theory of economics by the Austrian School economists, such as F. A. Hayek and Ludwig von Mises. According to the Austrian perspective, the key features of an economic system are the mechanisms which bring about disequilibrium.

Economists define equilibrium as the state that occurs when all parties involved in a transaction receive the highest possible net benefit, and thus, have no incentive to execute the transaction with another party. The Austrians' focus on the disruption of equilibrium was developed in response to the Anglo-American theoretical tradition, and the works of Adam Smith and David Ricardo in particular, which emphasized the development of a theory of equilibrium states (17,18). The importance of the shift in emphasis is that the Austrian economists were the first to suggest that *changes* in prices were the central activity in market institutions.

Prices change, and thus disequilibrium occurs, when either the buyer or seller receives new information about a good. For example, if a seller discovers resources that make the production of a particular good less expensive, then he or she may lower the price in order to become more competitive in the marketplace. If buyers and sellers do not receive new information about goods, then market exchange becomes a mechanistic exercise in which goods are exchanged routinely by the same people for the same price. The Austrian economists made economic theory more realistic by introducing a key individual: one who organizes new market activity by obtaining, sharing, and acting upon new information. This key individual is the entrepreneur.

Joseph Schumpeter further analyzed the role that entrepreneurs play in making markets dynamic. Schumpeter's analysis highlighted the features of the entrepreneur that were distinct from those of other participants in the market. As a prerequisite for organizing various agents of production in new ways, entrepreneurs must be able to spot opportunities for innovation. They must also be bold enough to take advantage of the opportunities when they are present and have the charisma necessary to convince others to invest their resources in the innovation. Entrepreneurs also invest their own resources, namely their vision of innovation and expertise in organization (19).

Schumpeter indicates that entrepreneurial resources are distinct from the resources of those he or she organizes. In particular, Schumpeter makes a distinction between the entrepreneurial and capitalist roles in the market. The entrepreneur identifies and seizes an opportunity for an innovation that would provide an enterprise with a competitive advantage. The capitalist's role is to provide capital for the venture, and therefore, assume the risk of failure. While entrepreneurs can play other roles in market transactions (either simultaneously or in succession), the other roles cannot be characterized as entrepreneurial. Schumpeter argues,

> If providing the capital is not the essential or defining function of the entrepreneur, then risk bearing should not be described as an essential or defining function either, for it is obviously the capitalist who bears the risk and who loses his money in case of failure. If the entrepreneur borrows at a fixed rate of interest and undertakes to guarantee the capitalist against loss whatever the results of the enterprise, he can do so only if he owns other assets with which to satisfy the creditor capitalist when things go wrong. But, in this case, he is able to satisfy his creditor because he is a capitalist himself and the risk he bears he bears in this capacity and not in his capacity of entrepreneur (20).

Schumpeter also made a distinction between entrepreneurs and managers. When entrepreneurs successfully organize innovative enterprises, they engage in acts of "creative destruction." Uncompetitive forms of organization become outmoded and perish in the market as they are succeeded by new, more competitive forms. Entrepreneurs are responsible for the introduction of innovative organizations into the marketplace, but have no interest in ensuring their survival, at least in the form in which they were created. Like entrepreneurs, managers are entrusted with coordinating various elements of production. However, managers are responsible for the maintenance of organizational stability, and therefore, have an interest in protecting the status quo.

Israel Kirzner developed a revised definition of the entrepreneur, in which the entrepreneur's roles are distinct from those of other market participants, but also entail the assumption of risk (21). Kirzner depicts entrepreneurs as individuals who affect the choices of others by obtaining and sharing overlooked information regarding resources (e.g., the prices associated with production technology) and goals (e.g., the inherent worth of consuming the good).

Whereas Schumpeter claimed that the entrepreneurial role requires special skills, Kirzner argues that anyone can be an entrepreneur. All that is required is the fate of being privy to an opportunity. Since anyone can be an entrepreneur, the competition to reap the profits of entrepreneurial activity is more fierce than for any other type of market activity. As Kirzner writes, "whereas the market participation of asset owners is always to *some* extent protected (by the peculiar qualities of the asset possessed), the market activity of the entrepreneur is *never* protected in any way." (22, italics in original) Since entrepreneurs are especially exposed to competition, they risk the security they would be more likely to have if they were asset holders.

C.   Theories of Public Entrepreneurism

Political scientists have borrowed the concept of entrepreneurism from economists in order to describe and explain the dynamic nature of political transactions. Just as private entrepreneurs affect the choices of individuals in the marketplace, public entrepreneurs can shift the preferences of policy actors by providing new information regarding political ends and means. Also like their private-sector counterparts, public entrepreneurs organize resources in new ways and produce and distribute new products (23). In the public sector, the entrepreneurial function creates profits for a variety of actors in the political system (e.g., new service delivery systems), as well as for the entrepreneur (e.g., enhanced power base, desired policy outputs or outcomes) (24).

Political scientists have varying views as to whether entrepreneurs have special attributes. Many analyses of public entrepreneurism, particularly those based on case studies, depict the entrepreneur as a heroic figure who forges an organization in his or her image by force of charisma and intelligence (25–27). Other political scientists hold the Schumpeterian view that entrepreneurs are otherwise ordinary people endowed with special skills that allow them to identify and seize opportunities for innovation (28–31). In *Public Entrepreneurs*, Schneider, Teske, and Mintrom share Kirzner's view that anyone can be entrepreneurial (32).

Scholars of public entrepreneurism also disagree about whether entrepreneurism is risky (33). Nancy Roberts sides with Schumpeter in arguing that risk-taking is strictly a function of the capitalist (34). In Roberts' model of the policy process, the equivalent of a capitalist is a "policy champion." Roberts describes "policy champions" as being "involved in both the design and implementation phases . . . of the innovation process. In the case of legislated innovation, they could be governors, administrators, and or legislators who participate in the various design steps either to initiate a proposal, set the agenda, or to carry the bill through enactment" (35). In doing so, champions use their own resources in order to put the idea into operation.

A number of other scholars argue that entrepreneurism is inherently risky (36–38). Entrepreneurs face the threat of failure, and even when they succeed, they are confronted by competitors looking to emulate their success. Competition has the effect of cutting into entrepreneurial profits by "turning the entrepreneur's unique insights into routine products or commodities" (39). Schneider, Teske, and Mintrom argue that entrepreneurs often invest ample resources into promoting a new idea, but that the level of personal profit rarely makes the investment worthwhile. However, they do not specify what alternative role the entrepreneur could play that is less risky.

Political scientists have also described and defined the activities that entrepreneurs perform in the political arena. Rational choice theory depicts the public entrepreneur as someone who organizes and maintains interest groups for the purpose of ensuring the provision of public goods. Public entrepreneurs secure participation in the group, and thus, contributions to the public good, through several organizational activities: communication, administration of selective incentives (40), administration of collective goods, structuring member interactions, and cultivation of external resources (41). Each of these activities shapes individuals' perceptions about the benefits and costs of group membership (42).

This model of public entrepreneurism suggests that there is consensus regarding the desired ends of policy: the resulting allocation of goods or services should yield the greatest utility for each individual involved in the transaction. The role of the entrepreneur is to discover new resources, technologies, or ideas that will maximize utility when public goods are allocated and consumed. Because this conception of entrepreneurism focuses on transactions, it has been termed a "transactional" model of entrepreneurial leadership (43,44).

Whereas the transactional entrepreneur relies on appeals to individuals' economic welfare, the heresthetic entrepreneur's appeal is emotional. A heresthetician promotes an issue by associating it with another. By linking issues together, entrepreneurs can broaden the appeal of supporting them. The risk involved with linking issues is that some individuals will be repelled by the association. The heresthetician's goal is to find a linkage that attracts a coalition powerful enough to sustain any political challenge.

Like the "transactional" leader of rational choice theory, heresthetic entrepreneurs can organize and maintain groups on the basis of a cost-benefit calculus. However, they also use symbols which evoke alternative conceptions regarding the ends of policy, as well as alternative conceptions about how to best achieve a given end (45). Herestheticians can be "transformers" as well as "transactors."

Both the transactional and heresthetic conceptions of entrepreneurism are based on an economic model of politics, which focuses on the efficient aggregation of individual choices. Other analyses of public entrepreneurism have emphasized the relationship between entrepreneurs and institutions.

Entrepreneurial behavior can entail shaping institutional structures by imbuing them with new purposes (46), or creating new institutions by coordinating the efforts of various political actors (47,48). In these instances, entrepreneurs act as transformational leaders, because they promote ideas regarding the meaning of the institution and its role in the policy process, rather than ideas that are solely about policies themselves. Public entrepreneurism can also involve avoiding constraints imposed by institutional value systems (49). In playing this role, entrepreneurs behave as strategists who identify institutional settings that are hospitable settings for reform.

The activities of market entrepreneurs were characterized by Schumpeter as "creatively destructive." Public entrepreneurs also create innovations that contribute to the destruction of old policies, service delivery systems, missions, and organizations. The political science literature is largely silent regarding the question of the respective roles of managers and entrepreneurs in the policy process. Nancy Roberts includes a place for entrepreneurial administrators and executives in her theoretical framework, but she does not indicate whether they fulfill the entrepreneurial or managerial function when they act on behalf of their agencies' long-term interests (50).

Political theories of entrepreneurism have given us insight as to how the principles of entrepreneurial theory apply to the making of public policy. Yet these theories have had little influence on the theory or practice of public entrepreneurism in the public administration community. The public entrepreneurism movement in public administration is mostly influenced by management theory. This body of literature applies the themes artic- ulated by economists, such as Say, von Mises, Hayek, and Schumpeter, to a theory of management that applies primarily to private firms. The following section outlines the themes of the management literature and the entrepreneurial movement in public admin- istration and describes the connections between them. The subsequent section explores the deficiencies of a public entrepreneurism movement that is not informed by a specifi- cally political theory of entrepreneurism.

III. BRINGING ENTREPRENEURISM INTO PUBLIC ADMINISTRATION

The most influential figure in the public entrepreneurism movement is someone who has written about private sector management for decades: Peter Drucker. It is Drucker who provides a bridge between economic theory (and, specifically, the work of Schumpeter) and messengers of the public entrepreneurism movement, such as David Osborne and Ted Gaebler. The popularity of so-called "management gurus" like Drucker, W. Edwards Deming, Tom Peters, and Robert Waterman, Jr. in the early 1980s spilled over from the business world into the public sector. Since then, the concept of entrepreneurism has gradually become a part of the discourse in public administration.

How did a scholar of management, such as Drucker, become influential in an entre- preneurism movement? After all, Schumpeter made a distinction between the entrepre- neurial and managerial functions of the market. The entrepreneur organizes elements of production in new ways, and the manager maintains the organization. Entrepreneurism is characterized by creative destruction; management is distinguished by preservation.

Drucker combined these two elements of Schumpeterian theory into a phenome- non he calls "entrepreneurial management" (51). An entrepreneurial manager uses inno- vation as a tool for exploiting change to the advantage of his or her organization. Like Schumpeter's entrepreneur, Drucker's entrepreneurial manager combines elements of pro- ductions in new ways in order to create either a different type of product or a new mode of production. Entrepreneurial managers also perform specific market functions, such as identifying opportunities for innovation, understanding the needs and values of con- sumers, and successfully exploiting change as an opportunity to improve productivity. Unlike Schumpeter's entrepreneur, however, the entrepreneurial manager is not endowed with exceptional talents or skills; almost anyone can perform these functions. An even more significant departure from Schumpeter for Drucker's entrepreneurs is that they per- form their functions to further the interests of a particular organization.

During the 1980s, Drucker was only one of a number of management scholars to encourage service organizations to become more innovative. Aside from Drucker, Pe- ters and Waterman's work on "excellent companies" and Deming's total quality ap- proach were notable in their popularity and impact on management practices (52,53). The management literature on entrepreneurship was aimed primarily at managers of private corporations; however, Drucker stated explicitly that the principles of entre- preneurial management applied to any service organization, private or public. What set Drucker apart from other proponents of "entrepreneurial management" was his at- tempt to base his theory on concepts introduced by economists, such as Say and Schumpeter.

In *Innovation and Entrepreneurship*, Drucker declared that entrepreneurial management was an important development in corporate America, leading to changes in the way that companies are organized and run. Seven years later, David Osborne and Ted Gaebler made a similar statement about government organizations: There is a new model of government emerging in the U.S. and it is *entrepreneurial* government (54). Citing Drucker as a major influence, Osborne and Gaebler outlined a management theory for public administrators based on examples of agencies that coped with change through innovative programs. Each entrepreneur they describe "uses resources in new ways to maximize productivity and effectiveness" in a public-sector organization (55). As with Drucker's entrepreneurial manager, creative destruction is encouraged for the purpose of preserving the organization.

Both Osborne and Gaebler's argument and the examples they use to illustrate it echo two themes often heard in the complaints of bureaucracy-bashers. First, public bureaucracy is rigid and, thus, ill-equipped to cope with the rapid pace of change affecting most U.S. communities; second, the public sector cannot provide goods and services in an efficient manner. These themes illuminate two of the larger concerns of many Americans during the 1980s and into the 1990s: our capacity for solving problems cannot keep up with the onset of new problems, and the United States' status in the world community is diminished because of decay in our political, economic, and social systems. Both concerns represent a pessimistic view of the future of the U.S. The former implies that the reasons for our demise are out of our control, whereas the latter implies that our national character is at fault. Osborne and Gaebler provide a set of principles that addresses both concerns.

Reinventing Government (now commonly known as *ReGo*) lays out its program in ten principles. Osborne and Gaebler acknowledge that their principles are consistent with those presented by prior champions of entrepreneurism, Deming being mentioned specifically (56). However, they argue that they are going beyond Deming's Total Quality Management to construct a set of principles that integrates entrepreneurial values with concerns (e.g., promoting community ownership) that are not addressed by entrepreneurial theory. Osborne and Gaebler do not argue for government that is entrepreneurial at the expense of all other qualities, but rather government that is more adaptable and efficient.

Still, *ReGo* does not address the issue of the compatibility of entrepreneurial values with other values, such as political responsiveness and neutral competence. When Osborne and Gaebler acknowledge the importance of nonentrepreneurial values, they cite anecdotes to demonstrate how entrepreneurial and non-entrepreneurial values intersect. For example, they believe an entrepreneurial health care reform could achieve greater competitiveness and social equity.

> An entrepreneurial government . . . would encourage enterprising behavior by health care institutions, making them survive in a competitive (although carefully structured) marketplace. And it would structure that marketplace to meet social needs. Simply by requiring that insurers and prepaid plans take all comers, for example, it could end the current practice of competing for the business of low-risk patients and dumping the rest on the public sector (57).

What the authors do not address is how an entrepreneurial government can "structure the marketplace" to achieve these dual aims without "structuring out" political responsiveness. Recent attempts at health reform at national and state levels have failed to require insurers to provide universal coverage. Is this a failure of policy makers to be more entrepreneurial or is it a failure of entrepreneurial theory to account for the limited capacity of elected representatives to legislate all desirable structural reforms? Osborne and Gaebler sidestep these questions.

What *ReGo* does contribute is a framework for enabling public administrators to implement entrepreneurial principles. Though the authors claim to be promoting a program that goes beyond entrepreneurism, *ReGo* does not provide public administrators with guidance on how to promote democratic, organizational, or professional values or how to balance these with entrepreneurial values. In fact, all non-entrepreneurial values are condensed into a single category: bureaucratic values. Implicit in Osborne and Gaebler's emphasis on entrepreneurism is an assumption that public administrators do not need any further guidance in promoting "bureaucratic" values; these are already too ingrained in most public organizations.

The absence of a discussion of potential value conflict in *ReGo* makes entrepreneurial theory an even more attractive guide for reform. As it is presented in *ReGo*, entrepreneurial management is a means for achieving more efficient service delivery and more flexible organizations. The riddle of how to improve government capacity for problem-solving without making government bigger is solved. Because no competing values are presented, the benefits of entrepreneurism are apparent, while its costs are not discussed.

Osborne and Gaebler also omit one other important element from their discussion of entrepreneurial management: a description of the entrepreneurial manager. They outline entrepreneurial principles and describe innovative programs and agencies, but do not characterize the public entrepreneurs themselves. Levin and Sanger add to Osborne and Gaebler's theory of public-sector entrepreneurial management by analyzing how public executives and managers perform the entrepreneurial function for their organizations (58).

Levin and Sanger derive their definition of entrepreneurial management inductively, by learning from their observations of managers in innovative organizations. Nonetheless, the characteristics they identify are consistent with some of those delineated by Say and Schumpeter, such as the capacity to organize and find opportunities. Other facets of Levin and Sanger's definition of entrepreneurism appear to be borrowed from Kirzner, such as risk-taking and the absence of special entrepreneurial skills or talents.

Entrepreneurial activities took place in the public sector long before *Reinventing Government* was published, and as a movement, public entrepreneurism was picking up steam before Osborne and Gaebler reported on it. However, *ReGo* presented proponents and scholars of public entrepreneurism with a common frame of reference; it defined the phenomenon for a larger public.

At the national level, both the Clinton Administration and Congress have spawned their own reinvention efforts. Vice President Gore is overseeing the execution of the National Performance Review (NPR), a federal initiative that identifies inefficiencies in the federal bureaucracy. The NPR report recommendations included substantial reductions in the number of staff positions, abolition of the *Federal Personnel Manual,* new performance measures, and the establishment of laboratories of innovation ("Reinvention Labs"). Most significantly, the NPR report called for a redefinition of the role of government from service provider to coordinator of public and private service organizations (59,60). On the opening day of the 104th Congress, led by Speaker Newt Gingrich, the House of Representatives passed a series of rule changes that weakened its powers and decentralized decision-making activity (61).

State and local governments also followed the reinvention trend. In 1993, the National Commission on State and Local Public Service published its First Report. Though the Commission makes no specific references to entrepreneurism or reinvention, the Report's language is influenced by the entrepreneurial management literature.

Recommendations include creating a "skills package" for public administrators consisting, in part, of "1. the ability to shape a persuasive message for a particular audience and 2. the ability to understand what the audience thinks and wants" (62). The former is a prerequisite for organizing productive resources. The latter is analogous to the ability to understand the meaning of value to a customer, an ability which Drucker identifies as an important entrepreneurial competency. The Report also recommends that public managers "champion" the innovative ideas of employees. Peters and Waterman use the term "champion" to describe individuals who volunteer to play the entrepreneurial role in an organization (63).

Entrepreneurial theory has influenced public administration literature and practice because it provides an explanation of how to increase organizational capacity for productivity without building up the organization itself. In translating the meaning of entrepreneurism from the market context to the public administration context, some of the concept's clarity has been lost. Is there such a thing as an "entrepreneurial manager," as Osborne and Gaebler discuss, or was Schumpeter right to claim that managers kill the entrepreneurial spirit? Is entrepreneurism as desirable in public administration as it is in the market or are there instances in which other organizational values should be privileged? In assessing the contribution of entrepreneurial theory to a normative theory of public administration, it is necessary to clarify the meaning of entrepreneurism in a public administration setting and determine the appropriate scope of entrepreneurial behavior in public organizations.

IV. ASSESSING PUBLIC ENTREPRENEURISM

At the center of the entrepreneurism movement (both public and private) is a desire to cope with change in a way that makes society better off. Other positive organizational traits, though not central to any theory of entrepreneurism, are also associated with entrepreneurism, such as "empowerment," "holistic thinking," and "learning organizations." Though it is less often discussed, entrepreneurism also has a darker, tougher side. The rhetoric of the entrepreneurial movement promises "leaner, meaner" organizations, which do not tolerate waste and promote a culture of competition. Although the aspects of entrepreneurial theory that emphasize quality of the work environment are central to the theory's appeal, the focus on increased efficiency and capacity is at the core of the entrepreneurial approach. Efficiency and capacity are values that were critical to early entrepreneurial theory and are essential to the appeal of public entrepreneurism as an antidote to the modern ills of government.

The privileged position of efficiency and capacity among the many entrepreneurial values mirrors the preoccupation of the American media and public with the economic decline of the U.S. An important part of the American myth is that the U.S. is a country of unlimited economic potential. This is a myth fueled by the postwar stretch of economic growth the duration of which is unprecedented in recorded history (64). An important test of whether the public entrepreneurism movement is moving the U.S. into a new paradigm of public administration is whether it can change the public's assumptions regarding the purpose of government. Since entrepreneurial themes have been used to evoke a new faith in government's ability to get better results with fewer resources, the test for entrepreneurial theory requires entrepreneurism to deliver on its promise to increase public sector capacity for productivity and efficiency.

In addressing this issue, two questions persist. First, how do we know entrepreneurism when we see it in public organizations? Political scientists have documented entrepreneurial behavior in the political arena, but have paid little attention to the special case of administrative entrepreneurism. The political science literature makes no distinction between bureaucratic entrepreneurs and non-bureaucratic entrepreneurs, but the distinction is important because of the mutual exclusivity of the managerial and entrepreneurial functions in Schumpeter's model. Second, even if public administrators can reconcile the managerial and entrepreneurial functions, does public administration need a new paradigm to account for the lessons of entrepreneurial theory? Do entrepreneurial values transcend all other norms?

A. Reconciling the Managerial and Entrepreneurial Functions

Public administrators commonly understand entrepreneurship as it has been described by Drucker, as a particular type of management. According to Schumpeter, management is an organizational function that is incompatible with entrepreneurism. Entrepreneurism requires boldness, independence, and energy, whereas management requires a conservative, thoughtful approach. Schumpeter even blamed the growing stature of managers for the decline in entrepreneurism he observed in his lifetime (65).

Much of *Reinventing Government* was based on Drucker's theory of entrepreneurial management, yet Osborne and Gaebler have more to say about entrepreneurial governments than entrepreneurial managers. Because their focus was on organizational behavior and structure rather than leadership, they were able to skirt the issue of the entrepreneurial manager paradox. None of the entrepreneurial theorists, including Schumpeter, argued that entrepreneurs could not also be managers, but that managerial and entrepreneurial functions rest on different principles. Over the long run, every organization must confront change, and change may require that the organization radically change its mission or cease to exist. At this point, the entrepreneurial manager must choose one role over the other.

Public health agencies provide a good example of this phenomenon. Rapid change in the structure of health service delivery systems, largely driven by fierce competition, is forcing many public-sector health agencies to enter into partnerships with private and not-for-profit organizations. Specifically, public-sector health agencies are competing for a share of the growing managed care market, in which various providers form a partnership and sell their services as a package with one price. Historically, the mission of public-sector agencies has been to provide preventive, population-based services to the public, with a special focus on providing services to the medically indigent.

These agencies are now forming partnerships with other providers, some of which place an emphasis on providing individual-based, curative medical services. Because administrators rather than health professionals make and enforce policies in managed care organizations, monetary profits and not medical criteria are often the criteria for organizational decisions. Thus, when directors of public-sector health agencies enter into managed care partnerships, they often must compromise their organization's mission to do so.

If public administrators are looking toward entrepreneurial theory to provide them guidance for coping with a rapidly changing world, then they need a theory stronger than that provided by Drucker, Osborne, and Gaebler, and Levin and Sanger. In the economics and political science literature, entrepreneurism refers to a distinct role that is critical to market and political transactions. In the management literature, the fact that the entrepreneur exists in the context of a transaction is ignored. Since this context is removed, the role of the entrepreneur is not defined in terms of his or her relationship to other participants in a transaction. Thus, the management literature embraces nearly any human agent of change as an entrepreneur. Ultimately, any theory of entrepreneurism based on such a loose definition is misleading, because non-entrepreneurial functions, such as management, are characterized and promoted as being entrepreneurial.

Schneider, Teske, and Mintrom's discussion of entrepreneurial city managers provides a basis for a stronger theory of administrative entrepreneurism. In this model, the incentives for entrepreneurial behavior lie, not in the administrator's own agency, but in the rewards that are independent of the organization. Schneider, Teske, and Mintrom cite the opportunity to find "a higher salary, more resources to control, more autonomy, and greater prestige within the profession" in another agency as a set of incentives that induce administrators to become entrepreneurs (66).

They also note that "managers are also motivated by the desire to achieve specific policy goals, by the desire to solve problems, and by the desire to serve the public" (67). These bureaucratic entrepreneurs use a combination of hierarchical controls and leadership skills to build support and cooperation for proposed initiatives and to discourage shirking or free-riding. They coordinate actors in the political marketplace for the purpose of implementing an innovative idea and yield political capital for those willing to invest. In performing these functions, the bureaucratic entrepreneur acts on his or her own behalf rather than as a manager of an agency or as an advocate with political capital.

A theory of administrative entrepreneurism that is explicit and tied to theoretical concepts provides a better guide to public administrators trying to cope with change. This does not imply, however, that such a theory would provide a desirable set of guidelines for organizational behavior. The concerns of entrepreneurial administrators (e.g., career advancement, promotion of specific policy initiatives) need to be balanced against the concerns of the organization, the concerns of the community being served by the organization, the concerns of the professions who supply the organization's work force, and the concerns of the elected officials who oversee the organization. If public administration is heading towards a new paradigm, it must be a paradigm that accounts for the values that undergird the concerns of each of these groups.

B.   Reconciling Entrepreneurism with Other Norms

Assessing the impact of entrepreneurism on administrative capacity is complicated, because there are numerous criteria for assessing organizational capacity in the public sector. The discussion of organizational capacity in the public administration literature evokes an image of a pie to be distributed among various constituents. However, the various constituencies of a given agency expect to receive different "pies" rather than different slices of the same pie. The rhetoric of public entrepreneurism promises a more productive government but does not ask *what kinds* of marginal benefits are produced and whom different kinds of increases in productivity benefit. Entrepreneurial theory, as it has been applied to public administration, ignores the political implications of productivity. When public agencies are viewed as venues for political conflict, the question regarding the impact of public entrepreneurism becomes "For whom is productive capacity used?" rather than "How much productive capacity is there to use?"

1.   Expanding Capacity Versus Different Capacities

The national political agenda of the last fifteen years has been dominated by concerns about American productivity and affluence. Elected officials' attempts to enhance the productive capacity of the public bureaucracy has been part of a strategy to allay concerns about declining affluence. The rhetoric of public entrepreneurism rests on the claim that government agencies forced to compete for revenues will be more efficient and responsive to taxpayer preferences, thus producing "more bang for the buck."

However, the entrepreneurial approach to public-sector reform should not be framed as a return to an emphasis on developing capacity-building structures. While entrepreneurial reforms do privilege capacity-building over political control, ultimately agency executives, such as those described by Osborne and Gaebler, adopt entrepreneurial initiatives not for the purpose of enhancing capacity, but rather to enhance organizational stability over the long term. Entrepreneurial reforms produce incentives for agencies to provide goods and services that are responsive to market demand, regardless of whether the array of goods and services provided enhance productivity over time or address salient policy problems. Public entrepreneurs choose between different types of capacities, which coincide with serving the preferences of different constituencies. The choice of a particular type of capacity to be built is largely driven by the probability of organizational survival being enhanced.

Because public administrators serve multiple constituencies with divergent interests, any decision that responds to the values of one constituency will eventually neglect the values of other constituencies. The nature of this tension varies for different kinds of public administrators. The following analysis focuses on public administrators with specialized, professional training. These public administrators, who will be referred to as "public professionals," have obligations to a number of different constituencies, including the members of their own professions (68). A focus on public professionals is warranted due to their plentiful numbers among the ranks of public administrators and their special obligation to their professions.

2.   Capacity-Building Choices for Public Professionals

Normative theories of public administration have prescribed different roles for public administrators over the years. Since the Jacksonian era, there has been some expectation that public administrators will be held accountable to the electorate through elected officials. Progressive-era reforms advanced scientific expertise and neutral competence as desirable values for public administrators. The entrepreneurial movement renders a model of the public administrator as a competitor in the marketplace. Public professionals are expected to emulate each of these models. As government employees, they are expected to answer to elected officials; as professionals, they are expected to be accountable to the norms of their professions; as public officials, they are expected to be responsive to citizens; and as providers of goods and services, they are expected to respond to the market and be competitive.

Because each successive model of the public administrator does not supplant its predecessors, public professionals are expected to balance the values inherent in their roles as government employees, professionals, public officials, and providers of goods and services. These roles correspond with the partisan, technocratic, stewardship, and entrepreneurial models of public administration, respectively (69). Balancing the values inherent in these models entails trying to respond to four different sets of constituencies. In attending to each of these constituencies, public professionals are attempting to integrate the components of an idealized system. Elected officials provide the values. The professions provide the expertise on how to convert the values into an implemented policy. Citizens comprise the community served by the organization, thus providing the mission. Market competition puts the organization in a better position to survive over the long term (even if the entrepreneur is not part of the organization's long-term plans), thus protecting its capacity for pursuing its mission.

If each of the four types of constituencies can be satisfied simultaneously, then one can determine whether entrepreneurism allows public professionals to expand their capacity to serve all of their constituents. However, each set of constituencies requires a different type of relationship with the public agency. Public professionals have assimilated each of the four normative role models, but the relationships they have with each type of constituency are based on a singular principle. Certainly, elected officials may espouse that public professionals should play an entrepreneurial role or public professionals can themselves acknowledge their responsibility to the community or their profession. However, when the principle undergirding one of the relationships comes into conflict with another principle, constituent groups will expect that the principle supporting *their* relationship with public professionals will have primacy.

What are the principles that support each of the normative models for public administrators? Each model rests on a vision of what constitutes responsible behavior. Both the partisan and stewardship models rest on a conception of responsibility that values commitments to favored individuals or projects. The concept of neutral competence is supported by the principle of responsible action being guided by human rationality. The entrepreneurial model stresses the fundamental importance of productivity, or alternatively, the maximization of individual net profit. These three principles are consistent with three types of moral claims (partiality, deontology, and consequentialism, respectively) that have been staked out by political philosophers for centuries (70).

In some instances, public professionals can successfully integrate the principles that underlie each of the models. The needs of particular individuals or projects (e.g., voters in the community) may coincide with the dictates of rationality (e.g., vaccinating children in order to prevent disease) and promote the maximization of welfare according to some criteria (e.g., Pareto optimality). More often, however, these principles are in conflict. The consequentialist principle, which underlies the entrepreneurial model of public administration, can resolve conflicts regarding the allocation of goods and services as long as there is consensus over which individuals or projects should be favored and which policies represent a rational approach to serving the needs of those favored. Only in rare instances are both of these conditions met (71,72).

The problem with viewing entrepreneurial theory as the foundation for building the capacity of public organizations is that in most cases, there is uncertainty as to whom capacity is supposed to benefit. Even in cases where the "public interest" might be identified, the entrepreneurial approach to serving it is often not the same as the scientific approach. Under the neutral competence model, if there is consensus over values, dialogue tends to be restricted to the realm of resources or means. In this context, a public administrator has an incentive to think and behave like a technocrat, because claims of factual knowledge are not likely to be challenged (73). However, entrepreneurs focus on how to modify ends and means as a way to hone their competitive edge. The entrepreneurial approach to serving the public places a higher premium on knowing and responding to public preferences, rather than referring to professional norms to decide what is best for the public.

The rhetoric of entrepreneurial theory equates responsiveness to stated public preferences with capacity for serving the public. What this rhetoric ignores is the possibility of serving the public interest through attention to issues that the public itself does not put on the political agenda. Osborne and Gaebler's forementioned example of health care reform provides an example. An entrepreneurial public administrator's main concern regarding this issue is that his or her agency finds a niche in a rapidly changing industry. The entrepreneur's key strategy is to package a product attractively for the public (e.g., through new pricing mechanisms or the integration of previously decentralized goods and services). Whereas, the technocrat considers alternative means for improving community health status (e.g., preventive versus curative strategies). The public, or segments of the public, is more likely to contribute to the debate over how they want to pay for services than to decide what types of services would best promote community health status. Nonetheless, the latter approach to agenda setting and problem-solving does consider the public's interest.

V.   RECONCEPTUALIZING PUBLIC ENTREPRENEURISM

Entrepreneurial theory is insufficient as a foundation for a definitive set of normative values for public administrators. This is not due to any relative deficiency of entrepreneurial theory as compared to any other normative theory of public administration. The entire quest for a single normative theory of public administration is misguided. The "public" nature of public administration requires that many different constituencies need to be served. The "professional" nature of many administrative positions further complicates the demands on public bureaucracy. In addition to sorting out the competing demands that citizens and elected officials pose, public administrators need to satisfy professional standards and safeguard the future of their own organizations.

Whereas the public entrepreneurism movement has been framed as an attempt to expand the capacity of the public sector, it is really the latest argument in a debate over which principles should guide administrative behavior. Reforms that gave elected officials greater control over public agencies were justified by the partiality principle. The deontological principle helped to justify reforms that loosened political control of the bureaucracy in the name of neutral competence. The introduction of public entrepreneurism as an alternative role model simply brings the consequentialist perspective into the debate. Specifically, the public entrepreneurism movement has produced an integration of utilitarian theory, which has long been recognized as a critical value in democratic theory, with the existing body of public administration theory.

If entrepreneurial theory, like other theories, represents a single thread in an eclectic normative public administration theory rather than a guiding principle, then what role does normative theory play? Normative theories can play two important roles in public administration theory. First, theories with competing principles collectively provide public administrators with an ideal for which they can strive, though rarely hope to attain. Though instances are rare where the values of elected officials, professionals, citizens, and organizations can be served simultaneously, it is desirable to satisfy each of these interests if it is at all possible.

Second, and more importantly, normative theory provides public administrators with insight into their empirical world. Each model proposed in the public administration literature implies a set of undesirable consequences that will occur if the model is not adopted. The "spoils system" warned against elitism; the Progressives cautioned us against the perils of incompetence; New Public Administration raised awareness of the prevalence of irrelevant and unjust solutions to social problems; and the public entrepreneurs alerted public administrators to the dangers of being uncompetitive. Normative theories are very useful for informing both practitioners and scholars of the empirical realities of public administration. Far from providing an overarching paradigm, each theory presents a different, yet equally valid, perspective.

Thus, the main contribution of entrepreneurial theory to public administration theory is that it provides one more perspective on the realities that public administrators face. In an ideal state, public administrators are aware of the importance of competition in addition to being technically and politically competent and having a moral vision. Public administration theory does not address the question of how administrators integrate these perspectives into a coherent system. If there can possibly be a comprehensive normative theory of public administration, it would need to explain this.

There are already the beginnings of a debate over this question. One recent trend in management literature and practice has been strategic management (74–77). Like much of the written work on entrepreneurism, the strategic management literature advises organizational leaders on how to position their agencies to be competitive in the long run. Strategic management theory is distinguished by its holistic approach and futurist orientation: preparing for the future by determining the direction in which managers want their organizations to move, "scanning" environments, and taking in and assimilating as much information as possible. Issues are identified according to their impact (as a threat or an opportunity) on their organization's ability to meet its objectives; these are called "strategic issues." The aim of environmental scanning and strategic issue analysis is to gain control over a dynamic ecology by identifying "stakeholders," determining the impact of strategic issues on them, and reconciling differences when conflict over strategic issues arises. The impact of the political process is, at best, seen as a strategic issue to be manipulated, and at worst, completely ignored.

Robert Behn provides an alternative to strategic management. He suggests that managers experiment with different ways of achieving objectives to see what works and what doesn't rather than set a course based on a "master plan." Behn terms this managerial approach "Management By Groping Along" (MBGA) (78). The "groping" analogy may be useful in helping public administrators to understand how to integrate numerous pieces of information about their empirical environment without setting up unrealistic expectations about their own performance. Public administrators can try out different models in different situations and observe how well they work in pursuing various objectives.

VI. CONCLUSION

The public entrepreneurism movement has made an important contribution to normative public administration theory. It has alerted the public administration community to a set of concerns and interests that can no longer be ignored. By raising awareness of the importance of entrepreneurship as a core value of public administration, the public entrepreneurism movement has already made the noteworthy accomplishment of shifting discussion away from the tired theme of the politics-administration dichotomy.

However, the public entrepreneurism literature has perpetuated the debate over capacity and control as competing values for administrative reform. If entrepreneurial theory is to have a lasting place in the public administration literature, it needs to be understood as a framework for enhancing a particular kind of capacity. Adoption of the entrepreneurial perspective does not settle the capacity-control debate. It merely establishes a norm stating that having the capacity to compete is a necessary but insufficient condition for successful public administration.

Entrepreneurial theory does not provide us with a new paradigm for understanding the American administrative state. However, it brings our old ways of understanding the administrative state into question. As communications networks become faster and more widespread, technologies change more frequently, and the diversity and severity of demands on the public sector increase, we can no longer afford to view institutional reform as a matter of tweaking. Marginal modifications to enhance control or capacity are unlikely to be effective means for coping with rapid change.

At this stage of world history, the ability of government to cope with rapid change has to be considered a critical value for public administrators in any regime. At this stage of U.S. history, the American public administration community must grapple with the importance of entrepreneurism as a public administration value. These values compete with concerns for a government that is responsive to majority and minority interests and effective in program implementation. A new vision of public administration is needed, yet it is needed at a time when there are so many different visions of what constitutes good public administration. The current challenge requires public administrators to grope their way through this unfamiliar territory until they have mastered the delicate balancing act of managing a public organization.

ACKNOWLEDGMENTS

The author wishes to thank Vincent Marando, Mary Beth Melchior, Thomas Oliver, Ulf Zimmermann, Michael Gusmano, and J. P. Singh for their contributions towards many of the ideas presented in this article.

REFERENCES

1. H. H. Gerth, and C. W. Mills, *From Max Weber: Essays in Sociology*, Oxford University Press, New York, 1946.
2. R. Hofstadter, *The Age of Reform*, Alfred A. Knopf, New York, 1972, p. 166.
3. J. A. Uveges, Jr., and L. F. Keller, The first one hundred years of American public administration: the study and practice of public management in American life, *Handbook of Public Administration* (J. Rabin, W. B. Hildreth, and G. J. Miller, eds.), Marcel Dekker, Inc, New York, 1989, pp. 2–4.
4. W. Wilson, The study of administration, *Political Science Quarterly*; 197–222 (1887).
5. D. Wright, *Understanding Intergovernmental Relations*, 3rd ed., Brooks/Cole Publishing Company, Pacific Grove, CA, 1987, p. 226.
6. L. D. White, *The Republican Era: A Study in Administrative History, 1869–1901*, Free Press, New York, 1958, p. 396.
7. A. Roberts, Demonstrating neutrality: the Rockefeller philanthropies and the evolution of public administration, 1927–1936, *Public Administration Review*; 225 (1994).
8. President's Committee on Administrative Management, *Report*, 1937.
9. U. Zimmermann, Democracy and bureaucracy in the U.S., *Perspectives on American and Texas*

Politics, 3rd ed. (K. L. Tedin, D. F. Lutz, and E. P. Fuchs, eds.), Kendall/Hunt, Dubuque, IA, 1992.

10. G. Garvey, False promises: the NPR in historical perspective, *Inside the Reinvention Machine: Appraising Governmental Reform* (D. F. Kettl and J. J. DiIulio, Jr., eds.), Brookings Institution, Washington, DC, 1995, p. 95.

11. J. A. Uveges, Jr., and L. F. Keller, The first one hundred years of American public administration: the study and practice of public management in American life, *Handbook of Public Administration* (J. Rabin, W. B. Hildreth, and G. J. Miller, eds.), Marcel Dekker, Inc. New York, 1989, p. 16.

12. T. LaPorte, The recovery of relevance in the study of public organization, *Toward a New Public Administration: The Minnowbrook Perspective* (F. Marini, ed.), Chandler, Scranton, PA, 1971, p. 32.

13. H. G. Frederickson, *The New Public Administration*, University of Alabama Press, Tuscaloosa, AL, 1980.

14. F. Marini, The Minnowbrook perspective and the future of public administration education, *Toward a New Public Administration: The Minnowbrook Perspective* (F. Marini, ed.), Chandler, Scranton, PA, 1971.

15. J. B. Say, *A Treatise on Political Economy or The Production, Distribution & Consumption of Wealth*, Augustus M. Kelley, New York, 1964 [1821], p. 315.

16. As discussed in J. A. Schumpeter, Economic theory and entrepreneurial history, *Essays on Entrepreneurs, Innovations, Business Cycles, and the Evolution of Capitalism* (R. V. Clemence, ed.), Transaction, New Brunswick, NJ, 1989 [1949], p. 254.

17. J. A. Schumpeter, Economic theory and entrepreneurial history, *Essays on Entrepreneurs, Innovations, Business Cycles, and the Evolution of Capitalism* (R. V. Clemence, ed.), Transaction, New Brunswick, NJ, 1989 [1949], pp. 254–255.

18. V. Ostrom, Some developments in the study of market choice, public choice, and institutional choice, *Handbook of Public Administration* (J. Rabin, W. B. Hildreth, and G. J. Miller, eds.), Marcel Dekker, Inc, New York, 1989, p. 864.

19. J. A. Schumpeter, Economic theory and entrepreneurial history, *Essays on Entrepreneurs, Innovations, Business Cycles, and the Evolution of Capitalism* (R. V. Clemence, ed.), Transaction, New Brunswick, NJ, 1989 [1949].

20. J. A. Schumpeter, Economic theory and entrepreneurial history, *Essays on Entrepreneurs, Innovations, Business Cycles, and the Evolution of Capitalism* (R. V. Clemence, ed.), Transaction, New Brunswick, NJ, 1989 [1949], p. 256.

21. I. M. Kirzner, *Competition and Entrepreneurship*, University of Chicago Press, Chicago, 1973.

22. I. M. Kirzner, *Competition and Entrepreneurship*, University of Chicago Press, Chicago, 1973, p. 16.

23. T. Oliver, Ideas, entrepreneurship, and the politics of health care reform, *Stanford Law & Policy Review*: 169 (Fall 1991).

24. M. Schneider, and P. Teske, with M. Mintrom, *Public Entrepreneurs: Agents for Change in American Government*, Princeton University Press, Princeton, NJ, 1995, p. 10.

25. E. Lewis, *Public Entrepreneurship: Toward a Theory of Bureaucratic Power*, Indiana University Press, Bloomington, IN, 1980. '

26. R. Caro, *The Power Broker: Robert Moses and the Fall of New York*, Random House, New York, 1974.

27. J. Doig, and E. Hargrove, eds., *Leadership and Innovation: A Biographic Perspective on Entrepreneurs in Government*, Johns Hopkins University Press, Baltimore, 1987.

28. W. H. Riker, *Liberalism Against Populism*, Waveland Press, Prospect Heights, IL, 1982.

29. J. W. Kingdon, *Agendas, Alternatives, and Public Policies*, Little, Brown, Boston, 1984.

30. N. Polsby, *Political Innovation in America*, Yale University Press, New Haven, CT, 1984.

31. T. Oliver, Ideas, entrepreneurship, and the politics of health care reform, *Stanford Law & Policy Review*; 160–180 (1991).

32. M. Schneider, and P. Teske, with M. Mintrom, *Public Entrepreneurs: Agents for Change in American Government*, Princeton University Press, Princeton, NJ, 1995.

33. For a more detailed discussion of this controversy, see R. A. Peterson, Entrepreneurship and organization, *Handbook of Organizational Design*, vol. 1 (P. C. Nystrom and W. H. Starbuck, eds.), Oxford University Press, Oxford, 1981.

34. N. C. Roberts, Public entrepreneurship and innovation, *Policy Studies Review*; 57 (1992).

35. N. C. Roberts, Public entrepreneurship and innovation, *Policy Studies Review*: 61 (1992).

36. J. W. Kingdon, *Agendas, Alternatives, and Public Policies*, Little, Brown, Boston, 1984.

37. S. Cohen, *The Effective Public Manager*, Jossey-Bass, San Francisco, 1988.

38. M. Schneider, and P. Teske, with M. Mintrom, *Public Entrepreneurs: Agents for Change in American Government*, Princeton University Press, Princeton, NJ, 1995.

39. M. Schneider, and P. Teske, with M. Mintrom, *Public Entrepreneurs: Agents for Change in American Government*, Princeton University Press, Princeton, NJ, 1995, p. 7.

40. M. Olson, *The Logic of Collective Action*, Harvard University Press, Cambridge, MA, 1965.

41. T. M. Moe, *The Organization of Interests*, University of Chicago Press, Chicago, 1980, pp. 38–64.

42. T. M. Moe, *The Organization of Interests*, University of Chicago Press, Chicago, 1980, pp. 168–200.

43. J. M. Burns, *Leadership*, Harper & Row, New York, 1978.

44. E. C. Hargrove, Two conceptions of institutional leadership, *Leadership and Politics* (B. D. Jones, ed.), University Press of Kansas, Lawrence, KS, 1989.

45. W. H. Riker, *Liberalism Against Populism*, Waveland Press, Prospect Heights, IL, 1982, pp. 213–219.

46. J. March, and J. Olsen, The new institutionalism: organizational factors in political life, *American Political Science Review*; 734–749 (1984).

47. J. W. Kingdon, *Agendas, Alternatives, and Public Policies*, Little, Brown, Boston, 1984.

48. T. Oliver, Ideas, entrepreneurship, and the politics of health care reform, *Stanford Law & Policy Review*: 160–180 (1991).

49. F. R. Baumgartner, and B. D. Jones, *Agendas and Instability in American Politics*, University of Chicago Press, Chicago, 1993.

50. N. C. Roberts, Public entrepreneurship and innovation, *Policy Studies Review*: 62–63 (Spring 1992).

51. P. F. Drucker, *Innovation and Entrepreneurship: Practice and Principles*, Harper and Row, New York, 1985.

52. T. J. Peters and R. W. Waterman, *In Search of Excellence*, Harper and Row, New York, 1982.

53. W. E. Deming, *Out of the Crisis*, MIT Press, Cambridge, MA, 1982.

54. D. Osborne and T. Gaebler, *Reinventing Government: How the Entrepreneurial Spirit is Transforming the Public Sector*, Addison Wesley, Reading, MA, 1992, p. xix.

55. D. Osborne and T. Gaebler, *Reinventing Government: How the Entrepreneurial Spirit is Transforming the Public Sector*, Addison Wesley, Reading, MA, 1992, p. xix.

56. D. Osborne and T. Gaebler, *Reinventing Government: How the Entrepreneurial Spirit is Transforming the Public Sector*, Addison Wesley, Reading, MA, 1992, pp. 21–22.

57. D. Osborne and T. Gaebler, *Reinventing Government: How the Entrepreneurial Spirit is Transforming the Public Sector*, Addison Wesley, Reading, MA, 1992, p. 313.

58. M. A. Levin and M. B. Sanger, *Making Government Work: How Entrepreneurial Executives Turn Bright Ideas into Real Results*, Jossey-Bass, San Francisco, 1994.

59. D. Kettl, Building lasting reform: enduring questions, missing answers, *Inside the Reinvention Machine: Appraising Governmental Reform* (D. F. Kettl and J. J. DiIulio, Jr., eds.), Brookings Institution, Washington, DC, 1995.

60. M. Kelly, Rip it up, *The New Yorker*; 32–39 (Jan 23, 1995).

61. M. Kelly, Rip it up, *The New Yorker*; 35 (Jan 23, 1995).

62. National Commission on the State and Local Public Service, *Hard Truths/Tough Choices: An*

Agenda for State and Local Reform, Nelson A. Rockefeller Institute of Government, Albany, NY, 1993.

63. T. J. Peters and R. W. Waterman, *In Search of Excellence*, Harper and Row, New York, 1982.

64. J. Madrick, The end of affluence, *New York Review of Books*: 13 (Sep 21 1995).

65. R. L. Heilbroner, *The Worldly Philosophers*, Simon and Schuster, 1953, p. 304.

66. M. Schneider, and P. Teske, with M. Mintrom, *Public Entrepreneurs: Agents for Change in American Government*, Princeton University Press, Princeton, NJ, 1995, p. 149.

67. M. Schneider, and P. Teske, with M. Mintrom, *Public Entrepreneurs: Agents for Change in American Government*, Princeton University Press, Princeton, NJ, 1995, p. 150.

68. C. Stivers, The politics of public health: the dilemma of a public profession, *Health Politics and Policy*, 2d ed. (T. J. Litman, and L. S. Robins, eds.), Delmar, Albany, NY, 1991, p. 361.

69. C. J. Bellone, and G. F. Goerl, Reconciling public entrepreneurship and democracy, *Public Administration Review*; 131 (1992).

70. S. Lukes, Making sense of moral conflict, *Liberalism and the Moral Life* (N. L. Rosenblum, ed.), Harvard University Press, Cambridge, MA, 1989, pp. 131–132.

71. A. Wildavsky, and E. Tennenbaum, The Politics of Mistrust, Sage, Beverly Hills, CA, 1981.

72. A. Mazur, The *Dynamics of Technical Controversy*, Communications Press, Washington, DC, 1981.

73. A. Wildavsky, and E. Tennenbaum, *The Politics of Mistrust*, Sage, Beverly Hills, CA, 1981, p. 11.

74. W. R. King, Using strategic issue analysis, *Long Range Planning*; 45–49 (August 1982).

75. J. E. Dutton, L. Fahey, V. K. Narayanan, Toward understanding strategic issue diagnosis, *Strategic Management Journal*; 307–323 (1983).

76. J. E. Dutton, and R. B. Duncan, The creation of momentum for change through the process of strategic issue diagnosis, *Strategic Management Journal*; 279–295 (1987).

77. C. R. Schwenk, Linking cognitive, organizational and political factors in explaining strategic change, *Journal of Management Studies*; 177–187 (1989).

78. R. D. Behn, *Leadership Counts: Lessons for Public Managers from the Massachusetts Welfare, Training and Employment Program*, Harvard University Press, Cambridge, MA, 1991.

23

Twenty-First Century Philosophy and Public Administration

Thomas D. Lynch
Public Administration Institute, E. J. Ourso College of Business Administration, Louisiana State University, Baton Rouge, Louisiana

Cynthia E. Lynch
Scott Balsdon, Inc., Baton Rouge, Louisiana

I. INTRODUCTION

This chapter argues that public administration uses philosophy as a lens of understanding and the current lenses that are available to us are inadequate for the twenty-first century. Perhaps the metaphor of eyeglasses is the best means to explain the argument in this chapter. When we are young, we may be lucky enough not to need glasses but many of us soon have to get them to bring our eyesight up to a standard that permits us to function in our environment. As we grow older, our prescription often needs to be adjusted. This chapter argues that humankind has also grown older; and as that aging process occurred, humankind needed to and did change its prescription to adapt to its current circumstances. The twenty-first century is an extension of that evolution process of humankind and the various prescriptions, called philosophy, are again inadequate especially in the area of ethics and morality. We need an enhanced or improved prescription to help us live our lives in the twenty-first century.

In 1991 Joseph Rost in *Leadership for the Twenty-First Century* argues that the world is experiencing a radical transformation which futurists claim is changing the basic values of the present industrial era. Professor Garafalo predicts that the "rational, male, technocrat, quantitative, goal-dominated, cost-benefit driven, hierarchical, short-term, pragmatic, materialistic model must give way to a new kind of leadership based on different assumptions and values" (1). A pervasive sense exists that our fundamental perspectives on life are changing radically and any new values or perspectives built on the industrial paradigm are not adequate for the next century. "We are becoming rootless, a culture of the crowd, not the community. Our civilization is unbalanced, with our material culture far ahead of our ethical, moral independence and personal liberty and ignore the need for cooperation" (1).

This chapter makes the case for a fundamental change in perspective or "lens change" in the vocabulary of the metaphor. This chapter also explains the basics of that desired change. The first section after this brief introduction explains why we need to rethink philosophy and especially its role in our lives. It also critiques modernist and post modernist philosophy and makes the case for not using the fundamental assumptions that underlie those philosophies. The next major section describes the changing circumstances at the beginning of the twenty-first century and asserts that these changes cannot be resisted; change is part of a cycle of history. An illustration of that cycle is presented as are the implications of that change on human activities such a public administration. The last major section before the conclusion argues we need to rethink philosophy. A new lens prescription is especially needed in the area of ethics. Public administration and all aspects of humankind need to create a global ethic with a new prescription. The conclusion explains the imperative and summarizes the chapter.

II. RETHINKING PHILOSOPHY

A. Role of Philosophy

In thinking about the role of philosophy in our lives, some consider philosophy as a means to explain phenomena and answer larger questions such as the nature of understanding, the basis to judge good and evil, or the proper role of government in society. In this chapter, philosophy is viewed as a conceptual lens through which we understand the thoughts and phenomena about us.

In this chapter, philosophy is a dependent variable shaped by society that, in turn, is shaped by technology. Philosophy is a product of linear influence, or more properly, in many cases a synergistic minor influencer and major influencee with society. That point is illustrated by the various chapters in this book. They explain society's influence on key philosophers who are products of their society and reflect the influence of the leading key changes in each of their times. Because of the lag time of certain cultural influences, the views of some philosophers did not become significant until later periods.

The importance of technology upon society was dramatically presented in Alvin Tofler's *Future Shock*. In that book, the driving force changing society was not philosophy but rather technology. For example, the invention and eventual use of gun powder revolutionized the art of war by ending the importance of the defensive castle that was key to the decentralized power relationships of the baron to the king in feudalism. Gunpowder strengthened the role of the crown and greatly strengthened the power of what eventually became the nation state. Another example was the invention of the precise clock that allowed accurate navigation by longitude to become possible. In turn, this meant that an economic philosophy built on mercantilism was not only possible but superior to war for increasing the wealth of emerging nation states such as England.

A major thesis of this chapter is that certain key technologies in various eras drive and shape society that eventually needs to be reinvented using new philosophies. New technologies advantage certain people in society that think and act in a manner more compatible with the changing society. They often comprehend their advantages and adapt their lens of understanding accordingly. As a result in the evolved society, they tend to be more successful than others in terms of wealth, power, or both. Others may be slower to recognize the changing opportunities, but eventually they learn by experience and demonstrated successes of those that adapted earlier. As their success becomes more obvious, others follow the example of success. In the past two hundred year period, the two defining technologies can be labeled industrialization and information. In their respective eras, each had broad and remarkable impact on almost every aspect of society.

As society changes, intellectuals cast about for new lenses to use to understand the conditions that are changing their lives. New philosophies are born as the older lenses become inadequate at explaining the shifting paradigm brought on by technological change.

For example, industrialization resulted in the concentration of wealth and political power in the hands of a few economic barons. This situation meant that government could take over or control those limited power centers with an administrative state. The lenses to accomplish that end were socialism and progressivism that both accepted and championed the primary role of the state in society.

Philosophy acts as a mental filter for the more intellectual among humankind and it also biases humankind to act and judge in ways defined by the philosophy. Because philosophy has influence, it advantages and disadvantages various groups in society. Over time, the advantaged groups prosper and gain increasing power. Commonly, even the disadvantaged groups begin to adopt the philosophy of the successful groups if they are permitted to do so by the ruling elite. A good example is the invention of modernism. In western Europe, modernism fit their new industrial society particularly well because the so-called objective empirical inquiry using the so-called scientific method tended to create functional knowledge for advantaged elite groups. Those industrial and government groups tended to prosper and other societies around the world saw the remarkable successes and began to emulate and use modernism.

Modernism, as developed and used by John Locke and Jeremy Bentham, biases human thinking toward left brain analysis and away from religious right brain thinking that dominated the very being of human behavior in the centuries prior to the arrival of modernism. With modernism, religious thinking became marginalized and even dysfunctional. With modernism, gifted analytical left brain thinkers were advantaged and had greater success in society. Right brain thinking did not disappear but those who thought in that manner became less central to power and economic success. Among the world's intellectuals, power became secularized and religious thought became decreasingly important, even in such matters as values and ethics.

Philosophy does influence the way humans see, understand, and judge. Philosophy does not advantage all humans in exactly the same way because other factors such as heritage and social conditions are also important. Nevertheless, philosophy is a remarkable powerful influence on humankind in general and some people in particular.

B.   Critique of Modernist and Postmodernist Philosophy

Certainly, humankind is at its zenith and modernist philosophy can take some of the credit. Today, modernism leads humankind to believe that it can eventually know everything and with knowledge there are no limits. Postmodernism is an active minority voice of realism that questions the optimism of the modernist and takes some of the authority out of what could be an intellectual tyranny. Because of modernism, humankind has concentrated on developing left brain analytical capabilities. In contrast, postmodernism reminds humankind the left brain is insufficient. Thus the two contesting yin and yang positions present humankind with a balance that is inconsistent but also dynamic and functional. Nevertheless, this chapter argues both are inadequate for the twenty-first century.

Modernism and postmodernism place belief in an ultimate truth or Absolute as either beside the point or simply not relevant. The role of doubt in philosophy need not be debated again but the issue of the Absolute's existence shall be discussed as it is central to this chapter. Postmodernism adopts a relativist perspective that only accepts judgments of truth within the confines of a paradigm. Modernists adopt a temporary version of truth that is subject to continual revision. Neither accepts a fundamental universal permanent truth especially on the existence of an Absolute. In different ways, both say truth is relative and ultimate values, including ethics, are as well.

What are the consequences of relative values and ethics? Looking at past conflicts that could be resolved by addressing logic that exposes foolish reasoning and the evolutionary nature of human limited understanding, relative values and ethics are a certain formula for human conflict. With modernism and postmodernism, such conflict can only be resolved by consensus or when some key groups voluntarily do not assert their claims by aggression or capitulation. With modernism and postmodernism, there is no ultimate means to settle a dispute by appealing to ethics or morality. With those lenses of understanding, people can be fools but they can never be correct as no such condition exists. Such a reasoning process leads to openness but it also creates a cynicism in the value of consensus and the character of what the other groups claim to know.

Is there an escape from this philosophic cul de sac? In Chapter 1, the altruistic/materialistic, rational, and government capability dimensions were said to constitute three sets of two choices each. For example, some argue like Thomas Hobbes that mankind is essentially materialistic and in need of a sovereign header to address the needs of us all. Some argue like Jean-Jacques Rousseau that mankind over time is essentially concerned with the needs of all. Some argue like Bentham that humankind can reason through its general welfare by using rational thought including analysis. Others argue like Edmund Burke that such large matters are beyond rational human inquiry and that such decisions need to rest on appeals to historical traditions. Twentieth-century liberals and nineteenth-century conservatives argue that government can be a positive instrument to direct society. Still others, like twentieth-century conservatives and nineteenth-century liberals, argue that government cannot be a positive instrument for society.

C.   Thinking Outside the Box

Chapter 1 noted that the three dimensions constituted a box but that need not limit the choices of philosophers. They could reconceptionalize the box in a more sophisticated way or even think outside the box. Staying within and reconceptionalizing the box was done by James Madison. He decided each dimension was not a matter of one or the other but really a mix of both. This primary author of the U. S. Constitution assumed that humankind was both altruistic and materialistic, and the goal of the government process was to maximize the likelihood of the altruistic choice. Madison did not choose between rational or incremental decision making but assumed either could exist and most likely would exist in combination. In a similar manner, he assumed that government was not necessarily the agent to solve society's problems but could be if it acted accordingly.

Another option is to transcend the box entirely. For example, instead of assuming that people are either altruistically or materialistically ego driven or even a mix of the two, we can assume that individual free choice allows people to move from being materialistic ego driven to the higher plane of altruistic motivation. Under this assumption, free choice is critical: humankind need not be bound to any motivation but can transcend to a higher plane or even fall back to a lower plain. With such an assumption, the role of philosophy is not to interfere with free choice but rather help those who wish to transcend to the higher plane of altruistic choice. Those that make this assumption are similar to James Madison in that they also recognize that many and possibly most will still select the materialistic ego driven choice in spite of their freedom to select the higher plane.

Another assumption that transcends the box looks at the rational dimension differently. It agrees with the nineteenth century conservatives that complete rationality is impossible but then argues that with God's help humankind can transcend to a higher thinking capability that somehow combines left and right brain thinking. For example, humankind is not capable of reaching a viable global ethic with mere rational thought. However, if that rational thought is combined with the feelings of the heart associated with the Absolute, then a global ethic is possible. Such a decision making process can establish a universal ethic and encourage decision making using the full range of human capability.

The last assumption to transcend the box concerns the dimension of the appropriate role of government in society. The assumption can be simply that this decision is not really important or salient to the real purpose of life. Frankly, in the larger scheme of things, the role of government in society is not really all that significant and not one of the appropriate questions for philosophy to address. What is salient is the care one takes in others and nature. That care can be manifested in government or private action or in some combination of the two. The key is human caring and not the instrument used to manifest that caring.

Philosophy is a lens of understanding that helps people realize that the fundamental solution for society's problems is primarily a matter of getting people to think of themselves as an interconnected being. When that is done, government is sometimes the solution depending on contextual situations that change with times and places. The answer to the government dimension is not a constant "yes" or "no" but rather "it depends." That answer transcends the box.

Is a philosophy that transcends the box possible? The answer is "yes" and it has existed since the beginning of recorded history. The common spiritual wisdom literature (e.g., those found in the holy scriptures of the Hindu, Jewish, Buddhist, Christian, and Islamic traditions) provides that philosophy. Humankind need only understand and apply it as a lens of understanding. For example, the *Koran* uses the metaphor "blind" and says, "Momentous signs have come to you from your Lord. He that sees them shall have much to gain, but he who is blind to them shall lose much indeed" (Koran 6:104). In other words, we are continually given signs and messages from God and unless we learn them with our hearts we will remain blind and will be unable to change our lens by which we understand life. The scriptures of all traditions teach us that government is not the answer to society's problems but rather the answer is individually and collectively within each of us.

Moving from the abstract to the practical application is always the most difficult aspect of philosophy. What would such a philosophy mean to public administration? To the maximum extent possible, society would need to minimize judgmental behavior and maximize positive supportive altruistic behavior. Certainly materialistic and ego driven behavior would exist, but it would be accepted. However when such behavior caused harm to other individuals and nature, it would either be discouraged, or when necessary, curbed to protect the society and nature. Social goals would be set to minimize divisiveness among groups and maximize supportive behavior of individuals and groups that supported the whole of society.

Making decisions using this philosophy would be significantly different. Individuals would be encouraged to use their total mental capabilities including their intuitive sense of righteousness. Under this philosophy, improving the total mind becomes important. The following will hopefully clarify the importance of the total mind: "Everything has mind in the lead, has mind in the forefront, is made of mind. If one speaks or acts with a corrupt mind, misery will follow, as the wheel of a cart follows the foot of the ox. Everything has mind in the lead, has mind in the forefront, is made by mind. If one speaks or acts with a pure mind, happiness will follow, like a shadow that never leaves" (Dhammapada 1:1–2). Following this philosophy, part of professional training and education is the subject of ethics and values applied to the work context so that administrators are well equipped to exercise their professional judgments through their responsibilities.

Under this philosophy, government is merely an instrument that is ultimately of secondary importance. Policy makers and public managers would need to consider themselves in their governmental roles as radically less significant than their roles as human beings. Their primary purpose in life is their own spiritual development and their service to their fellow humankind. This philosophy does not stress status or power of the administrator but rather the central role of their total growth as a person and their service to others. With such thinking, corruption does not make any sense and decisions that are meant to benefit the whole rather than one group, makes all the sense in the world.

Applying philosophy in this manner is not a call for a theocracy but merely a call to look and apply the spiritual wisdom that informs all of our religions. The scriptures of all traditions warn us that religious leaders are not immune to materialistic ego driven decisions. Often their claims to being religious enables them to easily abuse their special regard afforded them by others. This philosophy is not a call to select leaders by religious tests but rather a call to realize that inner worth of the individual is important. This worth is defined not in terms of religious zeal but rather accumulated daily actions that reflect a person's continuing concern for the interests of the whole over the causes of one or any given group in society.

Although the previous discussion does argue in favor of a universal philosophy grounded in the accumulated spiritual wisdom of all major faiths, care must nevertheless be taken to recognize the significance of context especially influenced by shifting technology. The next section of this chapter briefly explains how technology changes society and has induced the critical need for a shift in philosophy itself that reinvents society. That section argues there is a need for a constant universal philosophy but it nevertheless also needs to be adaptive to changing times and circumstances.

III. CYCLE OF HISTORY

A. Changing Tide

Change in society is occurring and cannot be successfully resisted. The tide is a useful metaphor to explain the nature and strength of the change. The tide comes in and the tide goes out. It happens. Now, one can stand on the shore like the fabled king and command the tide to stop, or one can channel the course of the tide using a great deal of imagination and effort in order to meet the challenges of the day. Centralizing and decentralizing power shifts happen in society. This section argues it happens in predictable patterns and the current portion of the pattern is moving toward decentralization of power. The decentralization is running from the public sector to the private sector, from the executive to the legislative, from the national level of government to lower levels of government, and from the top level executive to lower level managers. Given the larger pattern, arguing over the merits or demerits of decentralization is mostly a fruitless task. One is wiser to deal with change with imagination and work designed to mitigate the negative and promote the positive aspects as much as possible.

With the decentralization of power, the role in government in society is affected. Public administrators can channel the decentralizing change but the change itself will happen regardless of whether those in the profession are for or against the change. Centralization/decentralization of power acts in a specific cycle like the tide. One phase of the cycle is an increasing centralizing political and economic power. In this phase, the central government gets stronger, the executive in government increases power, and the government increases its scope of influence over the private sector. In the alternative phase of the cycle, there is a decreasing centralizing political and economic power. The central government gets weaker, the sub-units gain in strength, and the private sector gains in political and economic strength compared to the government. In the decreasing phase, the executive grows weaker especially related to the legislative or judicial branches of government.

The cycles of changing power relationships recur in a pattern. In other words, history "repeats itself" in continuous circles or more accurately cycles of ebbs and flows. According to Eastern thought, history progresses through circles or cycles of *yin* and *yang*. In Western economic thought, cycles are used to discuss the ups and downs in business activity over a period of years. Here history is described as moving through time in cycles of increasing government centralization and then government decentralization. The ebb and flow seem to be caused by landmark technological innovations that have a radical impact on the economies, social structure, and even how work is done in the major societies in the world.

The ebb and flow shifts also influence the conduct of public administration. At the beginning of the twenty first century, civilization is at one of its major turning points in history. Those of us interested in public administration need to recognize the changing of the tide and adapt themselves to the new environment. About every two hundred years, a new cycle of centralization and decentralization occurs. For about one hundred years, there is either increasing reform bringing strong central political control in the major nations of the world or a trend toward greater decentralization in those same nations. In about the fiftieth year of the century, a significant emerging influential technology is discovered and slowly it influences basic institutions and relationships in society. Eventually, the transformation is reflected in some major historical political circumstances. The current phase shift became politically noticeable prior to the beginning of the twenty-first century (e.g., 1970s).

B. An Illustration

Possibly the best way to explain the cycle is to focus on the United States and its short two hundred year history. Both the centralizing and decentralizing of power are reflected in both a. the role of the national government and state governments and b. the relative power relationship between the executive and legislative branches of government. In both situations, the budget as a process reflects the shifting power relationship. Budget power has altered over the last two centuries and budget reforms describe how the actual power relationships change in the various time periods (2). The American public administration reform history reflects the larger ebbing and flowing of power to and from central authorities such as between the executive and legislative branches of government. Prior to the American revolutionary war, the colonies, part of the British Empire, experienced strong mercantilistic policy in which the power was concentrated in the central government. The "mother country" created colonies to establish strong trading relationships between the colonies and the mother country. The colonies were expected to supply raw materials to the mother country and then purchase the finished products back from the mother country. In the 1770s, England used a strong central government authority to advance its economic well being but it was politically resisted by a successful rebellion in its American colonies.

Right on schedule in 1776, two landmark events occurred: the American *Declaration of Independence* and the publishing of Adam Smith's *Wealth of Nations*. Both heralded a reversal toward a decentralized economic and political authority in the new nation. In 1789, a counter trend established a potentially strong national government and executive branch within government. The counter trend lasted about a decade. Again, on schedule at the beginning of the ninetieth century, the spirit of 1776 reasserted itself with the election of Thomas Jefferson. The early and middle 1800s were a period of minimal and decentralized government except during periods of war. By the middle 1800s, the technological innovations of mechanization, such as the cotton gin and other manufacturing innovations, began to influence the society. In time, they led to the undoing of the decentralized policy, but before that occurred those policies greatly benefited the economic interests of the emerging industrial barons of the middle and late 1800s.

As those changes influenced the society, the majority of the work force shifted from agricultural to manufacturing employment and the nation shifted from a rural to an urban society. A strong need for raw materials such as coal, steel, and other materials essential to supply the industrial revolution became important. Urban living conditions grew worse and included poor housing, inadequate roads, inhumane working conditions, unsanitary conditions for food processing, and so on. Those very changes created wealth at a remarkable rate, but it was disproportionately distributed to the new economic elite of the nation.

Not surprisingly, political movements arose in reaction to the new conditions. Political reform groups advocated transformation to a centralized and stronger government to confront the economic barons who were then the decentralized power sources. In the United States, the progressive reform movement was successful. In Europe, the socialists and communists were successful. Starting in the 1880s, reforms moved toward strong centralized role for government using strong executive leadership to address the national problems. In the United States, an early landmark reform was the adoption of the civil service. In America, the political centralizing reform movement existed in both major political parties. It was first championed within the Republican party by Theodore Roosevelt; later, the reform movement gained success within the Democratic Party due to Woodrow Wilson and Franklin D. Roosevelt.

C.   Tide Shift

According to authors like Alvin Toffler, John Naisbitt, Robert Reich, and Peter Drucker, at the end of the twentieth century another fundamental transformation is taking place. Power is again shifting right on schedule. The engine of the power shift is technology with the computer being the current device. From the middle 1900s, the computer began the process of converting society in fundamental way; revising organizational patterns from pyramid designs to largely web and often virtual associations that employ a much more decentralized approach to work. With this shift, most new jobs are no longer in manufacturing but rather in service/information activities. By the 1980s, the political mood of the people also started to move away from wanting strong national government policies toward favoring the new information elites in society who are decentralized from the traditional power centers in society. At the close of our century, the mood in America no longer supports strong national government actions that characterized the middle twentieth century and its political reform agenda.

In this yin and yang cycle of history, a change occurs swinging the power structure in society from its previous orientation. In the twentieth century, the political reform orientation began as an increasing centralization of power. Starting in mid-century, a major technological innovation, the computer, started to change the very nature of society. At the three quarters mark in the century, a landmark political milestone occurred—President Nixon's resignation and ensuing fallout including several laws in the mid-1970s—that denoted a fundamental political alteration started bringing society to the decentralization reform of the state. Notice the dominate political reform movement started the twentieth century by continuing the nineteenth century's centralizing of power. By the mid-century, however, power slowly began shifting to a decentralized political pattern giving important advantages to a new decentralized economic elite. In this yin and yang cycle, political reform of a centralizing nature dominates for about one hundred years then the political reform movement switches to a decentralizing nature for about one hundred years. The primary causal factors of transformation emerges in mid-century and becomes apparent on the political scene about the three quarter mark of the century.

Given the repetitive nature of the cycle's pattern, there will be major disagreements on the role of government in society with a nation's political parties playing a leadership role in the redefinition. In the events currently unfolding in the cycle, not surprisingly the fundamental reforms are being advocated by both political parties with the initial successful reforms coming from the majority party of the last portion of the last century (i.e., the Democratic Party in the United States). If the pattern prevails, the party associated with the previous century's dominant reform themes will have political successes at the end of this century but that it will last only a few elections.

Eventually, the forces for lesser government will succeed in the twenty-first century. They will dominate the policy agenda for the next seventy-five years. However, halfway into the century, a major new technology will appear that will start transposing society again toward a centralization of power and in about seventy-fifth year the leadership in the nation will clearly see the need to shift back to a strong national government with strong executive leadership. Wars and environmental emergencies are likely to interrupt this trend but the overall trend will remain dominate until it starts to ebb seriously in the seventy-fifth year of the century.

During the decentralizing phase of the cycle, income distributions will move significantly away from the lower and middle income peoples to the upper economic elite. If the cycle maintains its pattern, concerns that are important to the whole population such as environment will be addressed minimally unless those conditions negatively affect the well being of the economic elite. Some sets of people will be particularly disadvantaged in this period with the most likely set being those who have few skills and cannot benefit significantly from education. By the fortieth through sixtieth year of the century, conditions will occur to accelerate the decentralization policy trend. By the sixtieth through the seventieth year, the negative aspects of these policies will prompt political unrest.

Of course all of this is speculation is based on the assumption that a yin and yang cycle exists. However, if it is true, the very nature of society and government will be significantly altered in the next few decades. In fact, those changes are already occurring. At the beginning of the twenty-first century, the success or failure of both private and public sectors are interconnected (1). Both have to operate efficiently but more significantly both have to complement each other. For example, public entities need to reform their budget and financial practices to increase not only their efficiency but also to help the private sector increase its efficiency. Government must lead the competitive market with rapid change based on improving information technology and the knowledge explosion from the information highway. Government can not be immune from the fundamental paradigm shift that is occurring in the world today (3,4).

Government reform takes place when society is not pleased with the results of government. That displeasure occurs when society is undergoing rapid change and government's processes are not capable of adapting quickly enough. Under those conditions, reform is recognized as essential. Consider the new information age where transformation is occurring the most quickly. If government slows up the reaction time to information change and the advantages that occur from an ability to process data quickly, then those government processes are the most likely target for reform. Government is itself information intensive. Today, the call for reform is not the old routine academic response to the death of one reform or another due to a shift in presidential leadership (5). Today, the call for reform is much more fundamental.

IV. RETHINKING PHILOSOPHY

A. Lens Prescription

To be consistent with the information age society, the elements of a useful philosophy are apparent. Increasingly, society is going to be decentralized with nation states seeing their power shift to both lower levels of government and to virtual supernational governments in other situations. For example, key services such as welfare are increasingly becoming a state activity and "peace keeping" are being done by virtual supernational groups established for a limited time bound purposes. Increasingly, society needs to enable and even foster greater empowerment of its creative technical talent so that the quality of life in society can be significantly advanced. Such talent is both rare and easily frustrated by conventional road blocks common in twentieth century society. In the twenty first century the challenge will be to foster, protect, and encourage talented people while maintaining the necessary other values critical to making a society work in a peaceful well working world.

In the information age, networks and web communication and organization arrangements will become more common (6). Such ideal working arrangements require 1. an overall agreement on the common mission for each such arrangement, 2. relatively equal knowledge and expertise among the partners so that no one partner is likely to take advantage of the relationship, 3. transparency meaning honest and fully shared information especially on group members performance, and 4. a comparable ability to negotiate group arrangements among all parties. The philosophy of the information age should encourage these conditions to exist and be followed.

Partnerships or any arrangements, especially in the information age where shared talent is critical, must be based on mutual trust and shared purpose. In the information age, group members are highly dependent on other parties to perform their agreed upon duties. If one group or even one person begins to feel that another partner is not pulling their weight or is cheating, then the distrust can lead to frustration, anger, and even retaliation that will eventually destroy the fragile nature of the agreement. Each partner must feel their expertise and actual work is acceptable and they must be reasonably satisfied with their partners' work effort. Such trust commonly must be earned overtime based on earlier more limited relationships that worked well. It is like deposits in a bank account that accumulate interest over time. If the human trust balance is kept high, a mistaken can be forgiven (7). In establishing such virtual partnerships, care must be taken to think through expectations, to create honest and useful information monitoring system, and to establish mechanisms that will be used when the partnership is ended.

In the twenty-first century, there is likely to be greater use of public and private partnerships. In such situations, each partner needs to approach the relationship with equal expertise in terms of establishing and following through on the arrangement. If one partner can bargain better and establishes an inequitable agreement, then dysfunctional attitudes are created that will hurt the whole effort over time. For example, if an information technology contract between a developing country's government and a first world contractor gives good profits to the company but gives a worthless machines to the government, then the people of the developing country are hurt and the trust necessary for future relationships with the first world would be seriously harmed.

B.   Needed: A New World Ethic

The information and industrial ages have raised the possibility of humankind "suicide." With its emphasis on the machine, the industrial age radically multiplied the muscle power of humankind. A person need only look at agriculture practices in many developing societies to see the small production resulting from huge human muscle power that does not multiple itself with machines and contrast that to first world farming practices with their high farm mechanization and high per farmer yield. The industrial age taught humankind that machines can radically enhance our muscle power. With its emphasis on the computer, the information age radically has and is multiplying the left brain mental power of humankind. A person need only look at the formidable task of inventory control before the use of computers with bar code technology. The information age is teaching humankind that computers can radically enhance certain mental powers. The result of this remarkable enhanced humankind is our potential collective suicide.

Prior to being enhanced by the two ages, humankind was able to eliminate huge segments of itself and its environment by such practices as war and foolish environmental policies. Since the two ages, humankind is still able to accomplish the same ends but at a much grander scale. Three examples illustrate the challenge: First, military armament can cause much greater harm to more people than ever before. Secondly, in spite of the fact that we can easily feed the world, more people are dying of hunger in our times. Thirdly, our environmental policies today cause vast deforestation and loss of wet lands that in turn push more and more species of plants and wild life into extinction.

Look into the mirror and see the problem. For almost all of us, the person who will do us the most harm personally in our lives is ourself. Our enemy is ourselves both individually and collectively. Because we ignore our own responsibilities, we are literally killing ourselves much like the cigarette smokers with cancer who refuse to quit smoking. We are in denial and we cannot face up to our own responsibility for our fate. Our so called progress has led to "inhuman" consequences we label with such words as "side effects" of scientific progress and "external effects" of economic success. Although we are one people living on one planet, we refuse to think holistically and instead continue our lemming like march toward "progress" with all its side and external effects. Not only is a new covenant between humankind and God's nature urgently needed, but the old covenant is being marginalized and considered foolish.

Mankind is in denial. The world today is a polycentric constellation of interrelated regions (e.g., North America, a changing former Soviet Empire, the European union community, and the Pacific rim) but our vision remains riveted on key rival nation states (e.g., England, France, Germany, Japan, Russia, China, and the U.S.). Foreign policy is a matter of cooperative internationalism but our vision remains imperialist and post-colonial. Economic policy is eco-social market but our vision is capitalism and post-capitalist. Social policy is post-capitalist and post-socialist but our vision remains capitalist and socialist. Sexual equity is more than a male female partnership but our vision remains either patriarchal or a simple post-patriarchal society. Culturally, we are moving toward an overall plurality but our vision remains diversity. Religiously, we are moving toward an ecumenical inter-religious world but our vision remains our religion against the others (8).

Modernism and post modernism produced a marginalized, relative, or absence of ethics and faith. Given the human condition, this is inadequate. Humans have an innate conscience; and as Kant noted, we must realize ourselves and shape our world (8). To accommodate an enhanced humankind, we need to enhance our faith and our ethics as an ethic free or even relative ethical society will not create an ethically responsible society. Modernism and post modernism cannot provide a reason for the absoluteness and universality of ethical obligation (8). Without absoluteness and universality, the denial will continue and the grounds for resolution do not exist. Mankind needs to move from a technology which dominates people to a technology which serves the humanity. Humankind needs to move from industries that destroy the environment to having industries which further the holistic interests and needs of men and women including being in harmony with nature. Humankind needs to move from a legalistically bound democracy to having a freedom and justice that is reconciled (8).

Humankind needs a world ethic so we can survive ourselves. Humankind needs an enhanced faith and ethic to match the enhanced humankind that resulted from the previous industrial and information ages. We need a common ethical system grounded in a philosophical and theological theory of values and norms that directs our decisions and actions. But why? Why be moral? Why not, as Nietzsche tells us, accept that human beings are beyond good and evil? Why not lie, deceive, rob, or otherwise do what we wish if we have either no fear of discovery or can escape punishment? Why shouldn't politicians be corrupt as long as their agree with the briber and the briber's discretion is without question? Why should any business person place a limit on their profit given the capitalist system? Why should a scientist curb research that can hurt someone if no one can make that determination? Why shouldn't any people, race, religion, or group not hate, harass, exile, or liquidate who ever they wish if they can get away with it? (8).

Being ethical is not only not being evil, it is also being good. Why should people be friendly, compassionate, and even ready to help others? Why should a person in business behave with absolute correctness even when there are no controls or sanctions? Why shouldn't lawyers lie for their clients and present arguments they know to be false? Why shouldn't a person or set of persons show tolerance for another even if they have no such tolerance? Why should a religion tolerate another religion when they believe the other religion is wrong? Why should leaders commit themselves to peace and always avoid war or conflict? (8).

There are two answers: One is consequences or karma. When we are evil or refrain from being good, there are individual and collective consequences that we often do not comprehend until the consequences become real to us. Given the enhanced nature of humankind, consequences are also often enhanced. If those consequences do not hurt us individually but hurt others, we are often ignorant or chose to be ignorant of them. Nevertheless, we cannot divorce ourselves from the reality that we are all interconnected and our demise is a joint undertaking. The second answer is relevant only to those of faith. The golden rule exists in various forms in all faiths and such action is linked directly to a belief in God. You should be ethical precisely because you believe in God. For many, this is the reason for their ethical behavior.

V.   TOWARD A GLOBAL ETHIC AND FAITH

The 1993 Parliament of the World Religions issued an initial declaration and the words of the last two paragraphs are as follows:

> In conclusion, we appeal to all the inhabitants of this planet. Earth cannot be changed for the better unless the consciousness of individuals is changed. We pledge to work for such transformation in individual and collective consciousness, for the awakening of our spiritual powers through reflection, meditation, prayer, or positive thinking, for a conversion of the heart. Together we can move mountains! Without a willingness to take risks and a readiness to sacrifice there can be no fundamental change in our situation! Therefore, we commit ourselves to a common global ethic, to better mutual understanding, as well as to socially beneficial, peace-fostering, and Earth-friendly ways of life.
>
> We invite all men and women, whether religious or not, to do the same (9).

A common global ethic will be difficult to achieve but it is more unlikely to be achieved outside the context of religion. Modernist and post modernist do not provide a reason for absoluteness and universality of ethical obligation (8). Neither of them have lenses of understanding that permits them to follow unconditional norms that run contrary to their interests. However, what is an ethic worth if it is not observed by everyone? What is an ethic worth if it is not unconditional and categorical? Modernism and post modernism cannot place an unconditional inner obligation on anyone for anything including human existence. Under modernism and post modernism, ethics depends on consequences but those consequences can be misunderstood, misperceived, or not perceived at all. Without consequences, modernism and post modernism cannot say why anyone should be against killing hostages in be in favor of some good. Nietzsche's glorification of "beyond good and evil" removes the categorical imperative. The categorical quality of ethical demand cannot be grounded in modernism or post modernism. It must be grounded in an Absolute which provides an over-arching meaning which embraces, permeates, and includes the whole of human society and indeed everything (8).

Only the one unconditional in all that is conditional can provide a basis for the absoluteness and universality of ethical demand critical for the survival of enhanced humankind. The relative ethic can deteriorate into human arbitrariness such as the Nazi experience. Only the bond to an infinite offers humankind the ultimate freedom in a world bound by the finite. This is not arguing that religious leaders and doctrines are not commonly dominated by human ego, quick to judge others, but remarkably forgiving of themselves but not others. There is too much history that demonstrates that the religious commit evil, but there is also too much history that demonstrates that the secularized also commit evil. Clearly, religions do distort that which purports to be sacred. Nevertheless, belief in God is critical to establishing a global ethic that can guide our enhanced humankind (8).

Believers speak with absolute authority. They can and do shape the whole human existence for all peoples including intellectual elites and the population. Believers can create an all embracing horizon of meaning even in the face of suffering, injustice, guilt, and apparent meaninglessness. Belief can speak to supreme values, unconditional norms, deepest motivations, ideals, and define responsibility. Belief can create feelings of home, trust, faith, certainty, self, security, and hope regardless of one's circumstances. Belief can provide the justification for protest and even resistance against unrighteousness in spite of impossible conditions (8).

Unfortunately, religions tend to focus on their particular version of belief rather than look toward what defines the substance of all believers. Religions know all too well where each of them in practice have differences but not how each of them share the same common spiritual wisdom. Religions focus on themselves and not on the wholeness of the Absolute that constitutes and defines the believer. Religions all share a concern for human well being and they all provide the basis for a unconditional global ethic and faith. In positive ways, religions can give unconditional meaning to human dignity, human freedom, and human rights that should always be non-negotiable standards based on an unconditional Absolute (8).

This is arguing that ethics is neither dogma or tactics as neither legalistic ethics nor the situation should dominate the other. Ethical norms without a situation are empty and the situation without norms is ignorance. There is a synergistic relationship that requires human introspection and continual learning. Ethical norms should also help us illuminate the situation and we should always use situations to help us reconsider and interpret our ethical norms. Each of us must live our situation and go down our own unique spiritual path, but we can and we will be faced by decisions that will be for us unconditional if we are believers and have ethics that arrive out of our beliefs. For us, we are always situational defined but certain situations leave the believer with categorical moral choices without any ifs or buts. For believers, there are universal normative constants that occur in the context of particular variables that can and are conditioned by situations (8). In other words, we need always to apply the golden rule but the context in which we apply it is always conditioned by our situation (8).

By looking to the greatest thoughts on spiritual wisdom through out all recorded history, we can define a common spiritual wisdom that in time permits us to define a new world ethic. The key is looking for the common rather than the differences. For example, what do all faiths share in common? An answer flows out of the proceedings of the Kyoto conference on religion and peace. That conference noted we share:

- A conviction of the fundamental unity of the human family, of the equality and dignity of all human beings;
- A sense of the sacredness of the individual person and his conscience;
- A sense of the value of the human community;
- A recognition that might is not right, that human power is not self-sufficient and absolute;
- A belief that love, compassion, unselfishness and the force of inner truthfulness and of the spirit have ultimately greater power than hate, enmity and self-interest;

- A sense of obligation to stand on the side of the poor and the oppressed as against the rich and the oppressors; and
- A profound hope that good will finally prevail (Kung, 63) (8).

VI. CONCLUSION

For the twenty-first century, this book argues that philosophy is relevant to public administration and this chapter argues that philosophy needs to adopt a lens of understanding that is universal and unconditional rather than relativistic in character. This is true especially for matters of ethics if public administration is to be part of the process of establishing a global ethic. According to Sergiovanni, the values now considered legitimate in society are biased toward rationality, objectivity, self-interest, individuality, detachment. As a result, emotions, the importance of group membership, sense and meaning, morality, self-sacrifice, duty, and obligation are neglected. Today, public administrators at all levels are asking for ethical models and ethical guidance (1). This chapter argues a philosophy is needed that builds upon the spiritual wisdom of all recorded knowledge in such books as the *Upanishads*, *Bible*, *Dhammapada*, and the *Koran*.

Due to page limitations, a book of this character does not cover all the philosophers that could be included. One such philosopher is Immanuel Kant who lived from 1724 to 1804. In some respects, he illustrates how spiritual wisdom can be included in the development of a philosophy. For example, Kant uses the new testament spiritual wisdom phrase "Be wise as serpents and innocent as doves" to point out the conflict of politics and morals but also to point out that this conflict causes humankind no real difficulty. Any conflict between politics and morality is to be resolved by the subordination of politics to morality, but there is much practical room for action as any government official knows before such a conflict must be resolved by subordination (10).

For purposes of public administration, philosophy should be viewed as a lens of understanding that is both universal and contextual. It should be universal in using the infinite and constant of the Absolute especially in developing a global ethic. It should be contextual in adapting to the changes in time and space. Humankind is constant but the industrial and information ages have enhanced humankind with the very real potential of our mutual suicide unless we learn to act as one people on one planet. This is the context of the twenty-first century.

Again we can turn to Immanuel Kant for clarity. Humankind needs to apply Kant's "categorical imperative" that is based on the golden rule at the point of action in order to decide if that action is "ethical." To illustrate, let us say a person can borrow money but he knows that he will not repay the loan. The ethical question is "Should he promise to do so nonetheless?" Kant says the man should use the categorical imperative and ask: "If everyone borrowing money acted in the same way, what would be the result?" Because his false promise would be dysfunctional to society, the man now knows that he should not make such a false promise. His concept is captured in the words: "Act so that the maxim of your action might be elevated by your will to be a universal law of nature" (10).

Another example from Kant illustrates his use of spiritual wisdom. The concept of karma exists in both Eastern and Western spiritual wisdom and Kant uses that notion in his kingdom of ends. Kant argues for a kingdom of ends in which the duty of the individual is not addressed to the ruler but rather to each member of the kingdom in the same degree. Duty is the practical necessity of acting according to the principle of reciprocity that defines the logic of the equality of human beings in dignity. In this kingdom, Kant argues passion must be subordinated to reason. With this logic, Kant asserts first, to respect the right of humanity in oneself by refusing to allow others to treat one as a mere means and by demanding to be treated as an end; second, to harm no one; third, for the sake of the foregoing, to enter into a society in which the property of each can be guaranteed against the others. To Kant, the love of humanity is conditional, but respect for its rights are a sacred and absolute duty. To Kant, moral duty means that one must respect everyone's morally neutral rights, even if it is the right to immorality (10).

We use lenses of understanding as we move through our lives and philosophy can help us appreciate the impact of those lenses on our vision. The current modernist and post modernist philosophies are not the correct prescriptions for the twenty first century with its enhanced humankind that can easily commit suicide without a firm global ethic. Fortunately, there is an alternative that builds on the spiritual wisdom found through out recorded history. Philosophy can use spiritual wisdom as Kant did and the result can be a prescription that enhances our ethical being to match the challenges of the next millennia.

REFERENCES

1. C. Garafalo, Leadership, ethics and change, American Society for Public Administration's 1995 National Conference in San Antonio, Texas, 1995.
2. J. L. McCaffery, The development of public budgeting in the United States, R. C. Chandler, ed.), *A Centennial History of the American State*, The Free Press, New York, 1987, pp. 345–377.
3. D. Tapscott, and A. Caston, *Paradigm Shift*, McGraw Hill, New York, 1993.
4. D. Tapscott, *The Digital Economy*, McGraw Hill, New York, 1996.
5. J. D. Straussman, A topology of budgetary environments: Notes on the prospects for reform, R. T. Golembiewski and J. Rabin, (eds.), *Public Budgeting and Finance: Behavioral, Theoretical, and Technical Perspectives*. Marcel Dekker, Inc., New York, 1983, pp. 83–90.
6. R. Reich, *The Work of Nations*. Vintage Books, New York, 1992.
7. S. R. Covey. *The 7 Habbits of Highly Effective People*. Simon and Schuster Inc. New York, 1987.
8. M. Küng, Global Responsibility—In Search of a New World Ethic continuum, New York, 1990.
9. N. Hodes & M. Hays (eds.), The United Nations and the World's Religions Prospects For A Global Ethic, Boston Research for the 21st Century. Cambrigdge Ma., 1995, pp. 135.
10. P. Hassner, "Immanuel Kant," (L. Strauss and J. Cropsey eds.), *History of Political Philosophy*, University of Chicago Press, Chicago, 1987, pp. 581–621.

BIBLIOGRAPHY

Drucker P. F. *New Realities*, Harper and Row, New York, 1989.
Drucker P. F. *Managing For The Future: 1990s and Beyond*, Talley/Plume, New York, 1993.
Naisbitt J. *Megatrends*, Warner Books, New York, 1982, 1984.
Naisbitt J. *Global Paradox*. Avon Books, New York, 1994.
Reich R. *The Next American Frontier*. New York: Penguin.
Rost J. C. *Leadership for the Twenty-First Century*, Praeger, New York, 1991.
Sergiovanni T. H. *Moral Leadership: Getting to the Heart of School Improvement*, San Francisco Jossey Bass Publishers, 1992.

INDEX